Sociology

Sociology

Beth B. Hess

COUNTY COLLEGE OF MORRIS

Elizabeth W. Markson

BOSTON UNIVERSITY

Peter J. Stein

WILLIAM PATERSON COLLEGE

MACMILLAN PUBLISHING CO., INC.
NEW YORK

Collier Macmillan Publishers
London

Macmillan Publishing Co., Inc.
866 Third Avenue, New York, New York 10022

Collier Macmillan Canada, Inc.

Library of Congress Cataloging in Publication Data

Hess, Beth B.,
    Sociology.

    Includes bibliographies and index.
    1. Sociology. I. Markson, Elizabeth Warren.
II. Stein, Peter, J. III. Title.
HM51.H46   301   81-13636
ISBN 0-02-354120-2   AACR2

Printing: 3 4 5 6 7 8   Year: 3 4 5 6 7 8 9

ISBN   0-02-354120-2

Preface

*I*n our years of teaching introductory sociology, we have found that what our students want, above all, is to discover a distinctly *sociological* perspective, and then to apply these insights to everyday life. They want a clear framework without being locked into one doctrinaire scheme. They wish to be neither mystified nor patronized. And they want to deal with material that is current, in a format that is readable. From an instructor's point of view, an introductory text should be comprehensive, accurate, shaped by some guiding vision, yet adaptable to individual teaching styles. We have accommodated these varied but essentially compatible goals by writing a text that is accessible to students and stimulating to instructors. *Sociology* accomplishes this in a clear, readable style using nonsexist and nonracist language.

We have avoided the narrow focus of many textbooks by weaving together three major strands of modern sociological thought—functionalist, conflict, and interactionist—into one unified model. While remaining close to the classic concerns of sociology, we have brought a modern, critical consciousness to bear on traditional subject matter. Ours is a new way of looking at the basic features of social life, and one that conveys a particularly sociological viewpoint to students while allowing instructors to emphasize the approach they find most congenial.

ORGANIZATION

The text is divided into five Parts, each of which develops a major sociological theme. Part I, The Study of Society, introduces The Sociological Perspective and discusses the methods of research in The Sociological Enterprise. Part II, Self in Society, applies the concept of the self to four social contexts: The Culture Context, Social Structure and Social Groups, The Social Self, and Conformity and Deviance. Part III, Social Differences and Inequality, emphasizes stratification and inequality as a crucial aspect of social structure. Chapters include Social Stratification, Social Inequality, Gender and Age Stratification, and Racial, Ethnic, and Religious Minorities. Part IV, Institutional Spheres, examines the various institutions within which Sociology enfolds: Marriage and the Family, Economic Systems, Politics and Power, Education, and Belief Systems. Part V, Contemporary Issues, is concerned with the consequences of broad trends and social change: these chapters include Population and Health, Crime and Punishment, Urban and Suburban Life, Collective Behavior and Social Movements, and Modernization and Social Change.

FEATURES

Many in-text aids are provided to clarify concepts and highlight additional information. *Marginal Comments* appear throughout the text and reinforce concepts as they are presented; these comments provide an excellent study tool for chapter review. *Boxes* appear throughout the text and complement in-chapter material short readings. *Illustrations* and *photographs* visually reinforce text material, and *charts, graphs,* and *tables* illustrate sociological data. Every chapter ends with a *Summary* that reviews major topics. *Suggested Readings* are also found at the end of every chapter to encourage additional research. A comprehensive *Glossary* is found at the end of the text and includes major concepts, and definitions.

SUPPLEMENTS

The Study Guide, prepared by Robert P. Lamm, contains Learning Objectives, Chapter Highlights, Glossary Terms for completion, True-False Questions, Multiple choice Questions, Fill-In Questions, Glossary Definitions, and Answers to all the questions.

The text is also accompanied by an Instructor's Manual, prepared by Mary Kay Cordill, and containing lecture, discussion and in class exercises, take-home assignments, questions, and sources for audio-visual materials as well as additional source readings. All of these have been classroom-tested by Professor Cordill and her colleagues. The Test Item File contains additional teaching material as well as nearly 1,000 multiple choice questions and 100 essay questions drawn from the text materials.

ACKNOWLEDGEMENTS

We are grateful to our colleagues who offered many useful insights and suggestions. The reviewers who contributed so much to this endeavor are:

Kenneth Benson—University of Missouri
Leo Carroll—University of Rhode Island
Michael Chernoff—Georgia State University
Jerry Clavner—Cuyahoga Community College
Jay J. Coakley—University of Colorado, Colorado Springs
Harold D. Eastman—Northeast Missouri State University
William Feigelman—Nassau Community College
Thomas Hood—University of Tennessee
David E. Kaufman—Central Weshington University
Bebe F. Lavin—Kent State University
Sharon McPherron—St. Louis Community College
James D. Orcutt—Florida State University
Fred Pampel—University of Iowa
Ellen Rosengarten—Sinclair Community College
Rita P. Sakitt—Suffolk Community College
Stephen Schada—Oakton Community College
Charles Selengut—County College of Morris
David Snow—Arizona State University
Kendrick Thompson—Northern Michigan University
Eric A. Wagner—Ohio University
Jules J. Wanderer—University of Colorado
Robert A. Weyer—County College of Morris

We also owe a special debt to our colleagues whose assistance and critical suggestions were crucial in the preparation of the first draft: Gretchen Batra, Patrick Biesty, Henry Etzkowitz, Natalie Hannon, Elizabeth Higginbotham, Rosanne Martorella, Victor Marshall, Carol Mueller, Charles Selengut, and Robert Weyer. In addition, at various stages, we have benefited from the comments of Beverly Amsel, Rhoda Blumberg, Lucile Duberman, Ronald Glassman, Lynda Glennon, Cathy Greenblat, Vincent Parrillo, Fred Pincus, Janet Pollak, Natalie Sokoloff, David Sternberg, and Joan Waring. Christine Spellman, Liz Greene, Christopher Carriou, and Paula Walzer provided valuable research assistance. The manuscript was typed by Miriam Martin Del Campo, Susan Kirby, Elaine Marchese, and Ellen Kane, without whom we could never have met our deadlines.

Our most immediate debt is to the editorial staff of Macmillan: Kenneth J. Scott, Kate Moran, Ellen Rope, Wendy McDermott, and Linda Berman whose advice and support was invaluable in preparing the final version. Our institutions—Boston University, County College of Morris, and William Paterson College of New Jersey—provided generous support during the several years of manuscript preparation.

To all these, as well as other friends, colleagues, and students, we express our appreciation and hopes that this volume meets their high standards of approval.

This book is dedicated to our spouses and partners—Richard, Ralph, and Michele—and to our children—Laurence Hess, Emily Hess Robinson, and Alison Markson—all of whom were encouraging, supportive, and very, very patient as we wrote and rewrote. Peter Stein would also like to give special thanks to his parents, Helen Kvetonova Stein and Victor J. Stein, who in their lifetimes lived under seven different political systems in four different countries.

Contents

Part II: Self in Society

6 Conformity and Deviance   134

Part III: Social Differences and Inequality

7 Social Stratification   162

8 Social Inequality   180

9 Gender and Age Stratification 210

10 Racial, Ethnic, and Religious Minorities 240

Part IV: Institutional Spheres

17 Crime and Punishment 468

18 Urban and Suburban Life 502

(Source: *Stock, Boston.*)

Part I

The Study of Society

We begin by defining sociology as a scientific discipline and differentiating it from other social sciences. Chapter 1 provides an historical background and introduces some of sociology's founders while summarizing their major theoretical contributions. We also introduce terms and concepts that will serve as basic tools throughout the text. Chapter 2 moves from the question of *what* sociologists study to *how* they conduct and evaluate their research. Sources of information are identified as well as numerous ways in which to gather sociologically-pertinent data. With a grasp of the sociological perspective and enterprise, we can begin to examine our social selves.

1

The Study of Self and Society

What Sociologists Study

DEFINING SOCIOLOGY

Power and poolrooms, suicides and singles' dances, religion and race relations—what academic discipline studies these topics and almost every other aspect of our lives? Sociology.

Sociology is the systematic study of human behavior, of the groups to which one belongs, and of the societies that human beings create and within which their lives unfold. It is not unique to humans to live in some kind of patterned relationship to others; birds, bees, and great apes also do. But humans have the particular ability to imagine a great variety of responses to the problem of survival, to construct rules that govern behavior, and to build increasingly complex forms of group life.

Once in place, these rules and structures take on an existence of their own; they become the social environment in which we live. Like the fish in a bowl of water, we cannot conceive of any other way of life. But humans are also curious, and so some adventurous persons have always wondered about the human fishbowl. This is sociology.

As the subject matter of sociology is our everyday world, much that we study may seem self-evident. For most of us, most of the time, the way in which we and those around us live is accepted without question. Or, when a pattern of behavior is questioned, one is told, "Dad sits at the head of the table because fathers always sit there." But the sociologist will take this explanation and ask the simple question, "Why?" Why do fathers sit at heads of tables? The answer tells us about the relative power of men and women in a society. In this fashion, the examination of everyday life can add to your understanding of the underlying rules of behavior.

SOCIOLOGY AND THE OTHER SOCIAL SCIENCES

Sociologists are not the only ones to study human behavior. Historians, economists, political scientists, and psychologists also observe everyday life and attempt to understand why humans act as they do. Sociology differs from these other *social sciences* by its particular emphasis on people in groups and on group structure. Sociology shares this perspective with *anthropology*, which is primarily the study of prehistoric, or preliterate, societies.

While *historians* focus on broad trends through time, on wars and leaders, the sociologist is more concerned with the underlying patterns of relations between individuals and groups in the society. The interests of *political scientists* in governments, politics, and power cover only one aspect of social structure that sociologists place in context with other specialized areas of social action (such as the religious, educational, economic, and family spheres). By the same token, *economists* also study only one area of social life—the production, distribution, and consumption of goods and services—which, however important to

Sociology is the study of human behavior, of group life, and of the societies created by human beings.

Anthropology is primarily the study of prehistoric or preliterate societies.

History is the study of broad societal trends over time.

Political Science is the study of governments, politics, and power. **Economics** is the study of the production, distribution, and consumption of goods and services.

all members of the society, cannot be fully understood in a vacuum. In contrast, the sociologist or the anthropologist focuses on the *entire* range of social behavior rather than on one aspect.

The distinction between sociology and psychology is, however, more difficult to describe to introductory students. Part of living in the contemporary North American fishbowl is believing that human action flows from needs or motivations of the individual. This is the psychological perspective: Behavior is determined by an individual's mental and emotional states. A sociologist, however, will begin by examining the *context* within which the individual is acting. This is the sociological perspective: Behavior is largely influenced by social forces impinging upon the person. Let us look at an example illustrating the difference between the psychological and sociological perspectives.

A noted psychiatrist recently wrote an essay on the link between psychological depression and unemployment among black males (Morowitz, 1978). He called for an extensive mental health effort to relieve the depressive symptoms so that these men could seek out and maintain steady employment. He assumed their mental health was the cause of poverty.

A sociologist would suggest the contrary: Depressive states result from unemployment. Men who are unable to function as breadwinners, which is a crucial basis of masculine identity in our society, will experience unemployment as a loss of self-worth and will display depressive symptoms (as well as anger). The cure is not more mental health clinics but more jobs targeted to minority males. Similar responses to unemployment were recorded for white males during the Great Depression (reviewed in Riley, Foner, Hess, and Toby, 1968), and

X

The **psychological perspective** emphasizes the importance of an individual's mental and emotional states in determining behavior.

X

The **sociological perspective** emphasizes the importance of environmental factors in determining an individual's internal state and subsequent behavior.

Why do fathers sit at the head of the table? The sociological perspective can add to your understanding of the underlying rules of everyday life. (Source: Magnum.)

Depression and anger often result when one's social identity is brought into question by a crisis such as the loss of a job, as the faces of these people on an unemployment line reveal. (Source: Magnum.)

are evident today whenever the unemployment rate rises. Note, for example, the increase in divorce, alcoholism, child abuse, and mental breakdown among unemployed auto workers in Detroit in 1980.

To treat these problems as personal failures is to blame the victim and to overlook the social origins of individual troubles. The sociological perspective begins with the societal setting and then turns to the consequences for individuals. The psychological perspective begins with the mental states of individuals and then looks at the outcomes for self and others.

Sociology differs from psychology also in its emphasis on *group* influences over behavior rather than on individual urges or motives. A person acts as a member of a social network composed of other people who expect certain behaviors and react accordingly. These group influences are the subject matter of this book.

The Sociological Imagination. The American sociologist C. Wright Mills (1916–1962) spoke of "the sociological imagination" in trying to identify this societal perspective. Central to Mills's work (1959) is the distinction between "personal troubles" and "public issues." *Troubles* are private matters, limited to aspects of everyday life of which the person is directly aware. By contrast, *issues* are generated by forces outside the control of most individuals—business cycles, political decisions, or religious traditions—that ultimately affect daily life.

Using our example of unemployment again, to be out of work is to experience personal trouble, but when large numbers of people are unemployed, the situa-

C. Wright Mills defined "personal troubles" as private problems experienced directly by individuals, whereas "public issues" refers to crises in the larger system.

5

tion may be defined as a public issue. When the unemployment rate reaches an unacceptable level, political and economic policies will be modified in order to relieve the private problem. It is this process whereby private troubles become transformed into public issues that fascinated Mills. How do individuals come to define their personal condition as a consequence of impersonal forces operating throughout the society? As long as individuals are unaware of others like themselves, they will perceive their troubles as of their own making. Once in contact with others who share that trouble, people realize that they are not alone. They can then redefine their common problem and reduce feelings of personal inadequacy.

COMPONENTS OF THE SOCIOLOGICAL PERSPECTIVE

In discussing the differences between sociology and other social sciences, we identified several characteristics of the *sociological perspective:*

The **sociological perspective** is characterized by concern for the **totality** of social life, the **context** of social action, and the individual as a part of a social **group.**

A concern with the *totality* of social life; for example, not simply economic behavior but the links between the economy and other areas of social life.

An emphasis on the *context* of social action, that is, the social forces that shape and channel individual choices.

A focus on the *group* rather than on individuals. We are interested in the individual as a member of a group.

Sociology is based upon the assumption that group phenomena are different from the individuals who make up the group. This means that the group has characteristics, such as a division of labor, that cannot be found in its constituent parts. It also means that being a part of a group has specific effects on its members. A ball club, for example, is composed of specialized players who together form a team that has a won-lost record, defensive and offensive capabilities, and a character that does not reside in any single individual player, but only in the total unit.

In all these aspects, sociologists seek *patterned regularities* in human behavior; for example, that fathers do not sit at the head of the table in some societies, or that men without jobs tend to become clinically depressed. When patterned regularities are found at the level of the society as a whole, we speak of *societal* characteristics, such as male dominance or the value of work.

Social facts are patterned regularities in human behavior.

Social Facts. Patterned regularities are the *social facts* that form the special subject matter of sociology. A social fact typically refers to the group. When individual actions are summed, the result constitutes a group reality. Although *individuals* are unemployed, the unemployment *rate* is a social fact. It is also a social fact that the unemployment rate is higher for nonwhites than for whites, for women than for men, and for teenagers than for adults. These patterned differences strongly suggest that discrimination by race, gender, and age are widespread.

Social characteristics, such as gender, religion, age, country of origin, income, educational level, and place of residence, have all been shown to be related to individual outcomes such as life satisfaction, occupational success, probability of divorce, life expectancy, and the likelihood of commiting suicide. That's what this book is all about.

The decision to have children, for example, is typically made by a couple in the privacy of the home. This decision is not made in a social vacuum but is influenced by the age, income, and religion of the couple as well as by broader forces such as the state of the economy, war or peace, availability of contraceptives, and the tax structure. Added together, these decisions result in a *birth rate* that is a characteristic not of individuals but of their society. So, too, with death. Although individuals rarely decide when or how to die, each society has a characteristic *death rate* depending upon public health factors, diet, the condition of the economy, and so forth. In other words, birth and death are *social facts*, with rates that vary from one society to another and among subgroups in that society. In the United States, for instance, birth rates for Catholics are higher than for Protestants or Jews, and those of the poor are higher than those of the nonpoor. Therefore, being of a certain religion or income group is related to the decision to have children. Moreover, in the United States, year after year, more children are born in late August and early September than at any other time of year. Can you guess why?

Emile Durkheim on Social Facts. In defining sociology, authors typically begin with the work of Emile Durkheim (1858–1917) on suicide. When Durkheim demonstrated how *suicide rates* varied consistently from one country to another, and among subgroups within a country, he sought to explain these social facts by other social facts rather than by personality factors. The question posed by Durkheim's collection of suicide data was this: How can we explain the lower suicide rates of Catholic compared to Protestant countries, of the married compared to the nonmarried, and of parents compared to those without living children?

Durkheim showed that theories related to climate, or to religious teachings about suicide, or to biological differences, could not explain such regularities. He then proposed that the underlying element was *social integration,* by which he meant the extent to which a person is part of a larger group or community of believers whose members support and watch out for one another. Marriage, parenthood, and the communal emphasis of Catholicism (in contrast to Protestantism's individualism) are all ties that bind the individual to others. Recent studies have verified Durkheim's findings on the importance of marriage and parenthood (Danigelis and Pope, 1979).

Therefore, to predict the likelihood of suicide, information about psychological states may be less helpful than knowledge of a person's enduring social relationships. Even if, for example, every suicide left a note saying, "I'm too depressed to go on living," we would still have to explain why mental depression is more prevalent among the nonmarried, the unchurched, and those without children. The goal of sociologists is to determine the *probability* of certain events. Unlike psychologists, we do not try to predict what any given individual will do, only that a given proportion of particular types of individuals is likely to behave in a certain way. We are concerned not with which persons will jump off the bridge, but with what proportion of those jumping is likely to be female or elderly or to do so in January rather than June.

In this section we have described social facts, using birth and death rates to illustrate the concept. Because entering and leaving life are typically thought of as uniquely personal events, these examples also demonstrate the overlooked importance of *social forces* on individual decisions.

Birth rates and **death rates** are social facts that are characteristic of a group.

Durkheim claimed that suicide rates reflect the degree of **social integration** of members of a society.

Sociologists predict the **probability** that a proportion of individuals will behave in a certain way.

Reification is the fallacy in logic of making a thing of an abstract concept.

Social Facts and Reification. While acknowledging social facts, one must be careful *not* to personify "society" as if "it" were one big social actor. All too often one reads, even in sociological articles, that "society does this" or "says that." This is the logical fallacy of *reification* (from the Latin *res* meaning "thing"), making a thing of an abstract concept. Societies are composed of people engaged in patterned behaviors, and we must always take care to specify just who and what are being referred to when speaking of society.

Social Facts and Subjective Reality. Thus far we have discussed social facts as group characteristics composed of many individual acts. Another type of social fact is the meaning that social actors give to their shared experiences. Aspects of the world do not come neatly labeled.

Individuals make sense of their experience by **defining the situation** in conversations with others.

People often need to define human experience in conversation with others. *Reality is socially constructed.* How often have you asked a friend, "This is a great party, isn't it?" or "What's so awful about that?" You are engaging in the process of making sense out of your experience, of *defining the situation* so that you can respond appropriately.

The ideas and feelings and values that we carry in our heads and consider our *subjective reality* are developed through social interaction. In other words, the way we think and feel are products of social life, and the shared thoughts and feelings of members of a group are a type of social fact. If the party is defined as a "bummer," few will enjoy it; if the same participants consider it a "gas," what fun!

Sociological Theory

THE IMPORTANCE OF THEORY

The study of society begins with some general idea of how social life is organized and how groups affect human behavior. The terms *theoretical perspective, conceptual model,* and *paradigm* refer to these organized schemes for the analysis of social facts. A *theory* is a set of logically related statements that attempt to explain an entire class of events. For example, the findings of relatively higher unemployment among nonwhites, women, and teenagers in the United States and Canada suggests a statement concerning the distribution of power in any society. Can you make such a statement?

A **theory** is a set of logically related statements that attempt to explain an entire class of events.

This chapter would be easier to write—and shorter—if a single theoretical framework existed into which all sociology could fit, or that all sociologists could accept. Such is not the case. Competing theories and world views are the rule in sociology, and there are several different conceptual models capable of explaining any given set of social facts. Each theory embodies a special way of viewing the world and will, therefore, direct attention to different aspects of society and yield different insights. This situation might tempt you to reword George Bernard Shaw's comment on economists: If sociological theories were laid end to end, they could not reach a conclusion. Nonetheless, theory is important as a guide to research and as a means of organizing a vast number of social facts. Without theory, we would be left with meaningless bits and pieces of haphazard observation.

In the remainder of this chapter we shall discuss the emergence of sociology as a field of study, examine the ideas of sociology's founders, and describe the dominant models in contemporary sociology.

THE ROOTS OF SOCIOLOGY

Sociology—the scientific study of group life—has its roots in late eighteenth-century Europe, the Age of the Enlightenment. The collapse of the medieval order of Europe was followed by a century of great ferment and change in all areas of social life. The power of the Catholic Church had been successfully challenged by Protestantism and the rise of nation states. New forms of economic organization replaced village and farm production. The French and American revolutions proclaimed the rights of citizens against their rulers. Science was extolled above faith as the only valid source of knowledge required for this new age of human creativity. The old order had collapsed. A new model of the world was emerging.

The intellectual movement known as the Enlightenment was characterized by its emphasis on the ideas of progress, order, political and economic liberalism, the scientific method, skepticism, and a profound belief in the ability of human beings to solve human problems.

The scientific study of social life was a logical extension of these liberating currents. If all else could be subjected to systematic, rational analysis, why not society and social behavior? In other words, sociology itself is a social product, emerging from a need for certain types of information at a specific moment in European history. The study of how the production of knowledge is shaped by the social context of thinkers is called the *sociology of knowledge*. The theorists described in this chapter and their particular perspectives are all products of their time and place.

> The **sociology of knowledge** is the study of how the production of knowledge is shaped by the social context of thinkers.

Enter Sociology—Auguste Comte (1798–1857).   The honor of being called the "founder of sociology" is usually bestowed on Auguste Comte who coined the word *sociology*. *Socio* is the Latin for "companion," stressing the fact that the *social* takes place in relations with others. *Logy* is Greek for "word" or "reason," which has come to mean "the study of." As befits a person of the Enlightenment, Comte saw sociology as the queen of the sciences, the ultimate source of all knowledge because it involved understanding the most complex phenomena.

> **August Comte** defined **sociology** as the systematic study of group life.

Comte distinguished this new field by (1) its separate subject matter—the study of *society* as something other than the sum of the experience of individuals; and (2) its *methods*—observation, measurement, and comparison. To the great question of the Enlightenment—"What shall be put in the place of the traditional order?"—Comte answered, "The scientific study of society and group life through time."

Karl Marx (1818–1883).   Comte and other early students of sociology emphasized the coherence, unity, and consensus of the social order. Their aim, after all, was to explain the persistence of social life and its underlying laws. Karl Marx had a very different agenda: to explain the logic of history in terms of the struggle to end human oppression.

Whereas other European intellectuals expressed a belief in progress as the

> **Karl Marx** explained history in terms of conflict and the struggle for an end to oppression.

supreme law of the universe and marveled at modern civilization, Karl Marx saw only exploitation, misery, and injustice. British workers and miners, including children and women harnessed to carts in mines, were treated no better than animals (perhaps worse, given the English love of animals). Marx was struck by the great inequality in power and wealth between those who controlled the land, factories, educational system, and political offices (the "means of producing goods and services") and those who had only their labor to sell on a market crowded with other potential workers.

Marx's view of history, then, was *not* that of the continual perfection of humankind, but of a continual struggle for equality and justice that will end only when there is no longer a distinction between owners and workers; that is, when the workers themselves own the means of production.

Marx's most important contributions to sociological theory, however, came from his analysis of how societies are organized rather than from his interpretation of history. Among Marx's major insights, two deserve special mention here:

The Primacy of the Economic Sector.   Whereas Comte and other early theorists likened society to an organism such as the body, with each part especially designed to perform a specific function, Marx had a much more complex perception of how the various parts fit together to form the whole society: Because it is the economic base of the group that creates the distinction between owners and workers, this sector actually determines the character of the entire society at any historical moment—its family structure, political organization, religious beliefs, and educational systems. Marx called these the superstructure or culture that served to support and justify the crucial division of people into owners and laborers.

Control over Beliefs.   Control over the beliefs of others follows from ownership of the means of production; that is, ideas themselves are social products. In Marx's own famous phrase, "the ideas of the ruling class are in every age the ruling ideas" (Marx, 1864/1964). *A Marxist analysis of contemporary North America*, for example, would stress that the flow of information is controlled by the small circle of wealthy people who own and operate newspapers, magazines, and television and radio stations, and who can present audiences with only one version of truth. In the absence of any other knowledge, individuals develop a *false consciousness* of the world and themselves. Part of the false consciousness of blue-collar workers, according to many Marxists, is their belief that hard work will lead to success or that their children will have the same life chances as the offspring of wealthier families.

Max Weber (1864–1920).   Weber (pronounced Vey-bear) lived and worked during the great age of German intellectualism before World War I, which was also a period of great flux and change in Western civilization. The new, modern age of technology was about to begin. The social upheavals brought about by the industrialization of Europe weighed heavily upon Weber.

Rationality, science, and all the other qualities of the Enlightenment once viewed as the salvation of humankind were, for Weber, tinged with ambiguity. When science demystifies nature, some of the wonder of life is lost. Weber spoke of the "disenchantment of the world" and of society as an "iron cage." Far from liberating the human spirit, modern technology and modes of organization can

Marx viewed economic relationships as primary and other aspects of the society as secondary and supportive of the structure of economic inequality.

In the absence of other knowledge, individuals develop a **false consciousness** of the world and themselves.

Max Weber lived in the great age of German intellectualism prior to the First World War.

Weber felt that science "demystifies" nature and leads to a "disenchantment of the world."

become a new type of prison, without any of the magic that helped people survive in the past. A strain of pessimism runs through Weber's work, in contrast to the angry optimism of Marx or Comte's blind faith in the future.

Weber departed from the theorists who preceded him in his analysis of the social system as well as in his view of history. Sharing Marx's interest in the links between economic power and dominant beliefs, Weber turned Marx's thesis around by proposing that ideas can have an independent effect on the other sectors of social life. We will discuss Weber's theories of social order and social change in later chapters.

Weber was also concerned about the place of value judgments in sociological analysis. If sociology is to fulfill its claim to scientific stature, scholars must make every effort to be objective observers. At the same time, sociologists must understand social reality as it is experienced by the actual participants. Sociology is the study of both (1) social forces that shape a society and affect the lives of individuals, and (2) the processes through which people make sense of what happens to them. The former can be studied through the ordinary methods of science; the latter require the ability to imagine the world as others might experience it—for which Weber used the German word, *Verstehen*.

Verstehen is the ability to imagine the world as others might experience it.

Emile Durkheim (1855–1917). Although Durkheim's lifespan was almost the same as Weber's, his intellectual world was very different, as were his interests and approach to the study of society. Durkheim was concerned with establishing sociology as a separate and distinct academic field. Following Comte, Durkheim saw society as having a reality in its own right. Individual members of a society are born, live, and die, but a certain structure to their activities remains. The arrangements that govern family life, for example, or politics and economic activity, exist above and beyond the efforts of particular people: this is *social structure*, the subject matter of sociology.

Emile Durkheim sought to establish sociology as a separate academic field by emphasizing **social structure.**

Social phenomena, claimed Durkheim, must be explained by other social facts; they cannot be reduced to individual behavior or to psychology. We have seen how Durkheim attempted to explain suicide rates by variations in social integration as measured by religion, marital status, and parenthood. Ideas and beliefs also express a *social reality*, shared by members of a society, and are as much a part of social structure as the rules that govern behavior. To discover these *social facts* Durkheim proposed methods of social research that use carefully gathered statistics from official records.

Georg Simmel (1858–1916). Georg Simmel was fascinated by a set of interests very different from those motivating the other founders of sociology. To the question, "How is society possible?" Simmel proposed that the sociologist examine individuals in relationships rather than the broad course of human history. Society, for Simmel, was individuals whose interaction formed groups. Thus, relations among group members is the proper subject matter of sociology.

Georg Simmel suggested that sociology should be the study of social relationships examined in natural settings.

Simmel began with the elements of everyday life—playing games, flirting, secrecy, friendship, domination, being a stranger, and so on—and arrived at insights about the quality of relationships. This is both subject matter and method quite different from that of Durkheim or even Weber. Each of Simmel's essays is a gem of illumination, but they do not add up to the grand synthesis attempted by the other founders. Yet Simmel was as insistent as they that the social must be understood on its own terms and not by reducing social behavior to personality or historical principles or divine faith. Rather, said Simmel, the reality *is* the relation among individuals and the unity created through that interaction.

Charles Darwin (1809–1882) and Sigmund Freud (1856–1939). There are two other towering figures of the late nineteenth century who also left their impact on sociology, although neither was a sociologist: Charles Darwin and Sigmund Freud. The two represent almost opposite poles in the study of human behavior. Darwin's theory of the origins of human beings traced their evolution from the earliest fossil record through the same stages of variation and survival experienced by all other living things. What emerged from this process covering millions of years was a creature able to speak, to think about itself, and to adapt to any type of environment. This is Homo sapiens (thinking person), our species.

Charles Darwin traced the evolution of Homo sapiens.

If Darwin takes us back to the origins of life on this planet, Freud leads us to the very depths of the human mind, to the *unconscious* forces that often lead people to behave in ways that are not governed by reason. This may seem to contradict the rational, orderly modern mentality proposed by theorists of the Enlightenment; but by founding the science of psychoanalytic psychology, Freud applied rational modes of analysis to the nonrational.

Sigmund Freud studied the **unconscious** forces that influence human behavior.

Consideration of the origins of the species, on the one hand, and of the organization of mental life on the other, establishes the boundaries of the study of human behavior. Between these two poles comes the great bulk of individual experience, played out in relationships with others in some patterned manner, within the confines of an established social order. It is the enduring legacy of sociology's founders that they defined this vast expanse of social life as a field of study in its own right.

Let us now turn to contemporary sociological theories. We will examine three of these: the structural-functionalist approach, the conflict model, and symbolic interactionism. Although adherents of each school of thought tend to think of their model as capable of replacing all the others, all three are useful to a full understanding of social life. Some theories explain certain social facts better than others, but each model is important for understanding some aspects of social reality. In actuality, most researchers typically use a combination of theoretical approaches in their studies. This chapter will end with our own conceptual model embracing all these approaches.

Modern Social Theory

THE STRUCTURAL-FUNCTIONAL MODEL

Very briefly, the structural-functional model has two focuses. The first emphasizes the ways in which the interactions of individuals and groups maintain the society as a whole. The relationship between parts and the whole is central.

What do the parts contribute to the maintenance of the society, and how does the particular structure of the society affect the workings of its constituent elements (groups and individuals)? The criterion of success is survival over time.

Once the social scientist has identified the components of structure, one society can be compared to another. In each, for example, there will be some means of providing essential goods and services, rules to regulate sexuality and to maintain social order, techniques for training children, and a set of rituals and beliefs that unify the group. The specific content of these patterns will vary from society to society, but each task must be accomplished if the group is to persist as an identifiable unit.

This consideration leads to the second focus of structural–functionalism: the concept of social function. The functional question is "What does this element of structure or this behavior pattern contribute to the ability of a social system to adapt and survive?" This is the *function* of that component.

Talcott Parsons (1902–1979). The American sociologist Talcott Parsons is the best-known proponent of the structural-functionalist perspective. Over four decades of theoretical writing, Parsons has developed an extremely complex and sophisticated conceptual model. We will not try to fully describe Parsons' theory, but note that he begins with the concept of *social systems* of interrelated parts (which are the major sectors of social life, such as economics, politics, religion, education, and family) that can be analyzed in terms of the tasks performed (*functions*) for the society as a whole and for the other parts.

As an example of functional relationships between system parts, the links between religion and family could be examined. Most religions are highly supportive of the family. Couples are urged to have religious weddings and to remain married. Children in religious school are taught to obey their parents. In return, most families observe religious customs, and raise their children in the same tradition. A similar analysis can be made of other exchanges among system parts or of relations among groups and individuals.

The whole—a group or a society—is kept together not only by the functional relationships between the various parts, but also by *value consensus* among members of the group. Value consensus refers to an underlying unity or agreement regarding the goals of the system and the appropriate means for achieving these ends.

Criticism of the Structural-Functional Model. Finding flaws in this conceptual model, and in Talcott Parsons' version especially, has been a minor industry in academic sociology for decades. Attempts to explain everything usually explain little at the level of everyday life; the concepts are just too general, and real life never seems to fit neatly into the theoretician's boxes. In other words, according to most critics, the theory is too abstract.

A second target of criticism is the conservative bias of functional theory. If the parts fit together so smoothly, then it follows that the system is working well. The tendency to treat conflict as if it were an illness in an otherwise healthy system follows from this emphasis on the essential orderliness of social structure and a balance or *equilibrium* between the parts and the whole.

Functional theorists have also been faulted for being ahistorical, that is, for failing to trace the development of social systems over time, and for overlooking

Structural-Functional theory examines the relationship between the parts and the whole of society.

Talcott Parsons examined **social systems** in terms of interrelated areas of activities and their **functions** for the whole.

Value consensus refers to a general agreement among group members regarding goals and the means of achieving them.

Critics of structural-functionalism claim that the theory is too abstract, too conservative, and ahistorical.

the historical context in which a given system operates. Yet social theory itself is historically grounded, and it is easy to see why American theorists working in the period between 1947 and 1960 would have such a positive view of social order. The social upheavals of the 1960s came as a shock to many North Americans precisely because of their implicit belief in value consensus and the stability of social structure.

Robert Merton is concerned with the predictable impact of social structure on individuals.

Robert Merton (1910–   ) and the Refinement of Functional Theory. Abandoning the search for "a total system of sociological theory," Merton, a student of Parsons, has consistently sought to illuminate social behavior through "theories of the middle range," that is, theories of limited application. Merton was concerned with demonstrating the *predictable impact* of social *structure* on individuals: If this is how the larger system is constructed, then these are the logical alternatives that will shape behavior.

For example, if immigrants need assistance in dealing with various government agencies where no one speaks their language or seems to care what happens to them, the situation is ripe for the emergence of political operators who will intervene on behalf of the powerless in return for their votes. Here is a social structural explanation of the rise of the political machine in big cities in the late nineteenth and early twentieth centuries, an explanation that does not depend on examining the psychological characteristics of city bosses (such as greed or a lust for power). The political machine was therefore functional in terms of the needs of the urban poor whereas the votes of these individuals were functional to the maintenance of machine power in the larger political system.

In the essay "Manifest and Latent Functions" (1968), Merton makes several important distinctions that will be used throughout this textbook. Not all behavior patterns or elements of social structure will be functional, that is, will contribute to the maintenance of a system. Some patterns will lessen the adaptability of the system and may thus be considered *dysfunctional.* In evaluating elements of social structure, the question must be this: What are the consequences of such a pattern? Does it aid or impede the operation of a social system? Are goals of individuals and groups achieved?

Functions must be specified for what or for whom.

Not all goals can be achieved, and one group's success may involve another's failure. Therefore, the sociologist must specify *functional for whom or for what.* Clearly, a war may be functional for a society (defeating an enemy, gaining resources, or reducing threat) but highly dysfunctional for most soldiers and civilians. The war, then, has different consequences for various kinds of persons and for different sectors of the larger society (defense industries gain, consumer industries lose).

Manifest functions are open, stated, or intended consequences. **Latent functions** are unanticipated or unintended consequences.

Another crucial distinction, according to Merton, is that between *manifest* (open, stated, intended) and *latent* (unanticipated, unintended) functions, or consequences, of behavior and structure. No human action or social arrangement has only one consequence, but many unforeseen outcomes as well. That unintended consequences can undermine the manifest functions of public policy is especially obvious in the case of programs for the poor, as when urban renewal projects destroy natural communities and compound the problems of inner-city residents, or when welfare regulations encourage the breakup of families by denying benefits when there is a man in the house.

Merton has also developed the widely-used concept of *functional alternatives*. We must not assume that only one structure can fulfill a given function. There is a range of possible variation so that "... just as the same item may have multiple functions, so may the same function be diversely fulfilled by alternative means" (Merton, 1968, p. 878). For example, the physical care of children and their training and protection are primary responsibilities of the immediate family. But these tasks today are shared with schools, peer groups, and the mass media. The notion of functional and structural alternatives has been widely used in writings about such contemporary family forms as communes and single-parent families.

Functional alternatives refer to different patterns for achieving the same goal.

THE CONFLICT MODEL

In contrast to the orderly view of social structure of the functionalists, proponents of *conflict theory* focus on dissension, friction, and strife among individuals and groups in society. Such theorists claim that it is conflict and value *dissensus* (lack of agreement) that are normal, and social order that is highly problematic. Social structure is a temporary and often fragile combination of competing social forces. Individuals and groups are constantly struggling for a share of scarce resources, and these conflicts will be intensified when resources are especially scarce. Periods of economic recession or slow growth are more strife-ridden than periods of economic prosperity. It should not be surprising, then, that in social theory as well as other areas of social life, the conservative functional model of the 1950s was replaced by the conflict framework, appealing to a new generation of sociologists in the late 1960s.

Conflict theory owes much to Karl Marx:

Conflict theorists examine **dissensus** and **friction** in society.

> The history of all hitherto existing society is the history of class struggles. Freeman and slave, patrician and plebian, lord and serf, guildmaster and journeyman, in a word, oppressor and oppressed stood in constant opposition to one another ...   [Marx & Engels, 1847; in Feuer, 1959, p.7]

This emphasis on class struggle characterizes the work of many contemporary conflict theorists. Dahrendorf (1959) claims that the structure of industrial society breeds conflict in every area of social life. Some individuals will exercise dominance over others in every type of relationship, and some groups will dominate others. Conflict not only characterizes the internal aspects of any society but relations among societies. Thus it is conflict rather than consensus that is the normal condition of social systems. The social scientist should, therefore, concentrate on sources of tension and techniques of conflict resolution in order to understand how social life is possible. For example, a functionalist view of the use of police violence would emphasize the need to restore order; a conflict perspective would direct attention to the ways in which police violence protects the interest of the powerful.

Conflict theorists claim that industrial society breeds conflict among economic groups and between societies.

In a similar vein, conflict sociology, as described by Collins (1975, 1979), is the study of how people in power, who are largely representatives of inherited privilege, maintain and enlarge their sphere of influence over every aspect of social structure, including values and beliefs. The belief that modern social arrangements are rational and therefore inevitable, for example, is considered a myth manufactured by the ruling elite to enhance its monopoly of power and

Those with power influence every aspect of social structure, including values and beliefs.

wealth. Therefore, the social order at any given historical moment reflects the outcome of struggles among groups of unequal power and resources, and not the blind forces of technology or any other impersonal factor.

Conflict within a society is most visibly expressed through public protests which serve as a sign that the social system is not functioning smoothly, that some members of the society are hurting, and that the hurt should become a social issue. Clashes between strikers and police (when they themselves are not the strikers), or between whites and nonwhites over housing, or between French- and English-speaking Canadians over jobs are symptoms of social instability. Whereas functionalists might perceive these issues as signs of some temporary system malfunction that can be handled by legislation or special programs, members of the conflict school would claim that the very structure of the system requires radical (root) changes.

The conflict and functional perspectives are similar, however, in their focus on the society as a whole. This larger view is called a *macrosystem* orientation in contrast to the study of face-to-face interaction, or the *microsystem*. As macrosystem analysis will be relatively abstract, that is, less tied to visible behavior than are microsystem theories, theoretical statements are often very difficult to prove. It is easier to observe daily life than to demonstrate the existence of a ruling elite or the functions of religion.

SYMBOLIC INTERACTION

More a diversity of approaches than a fully developed theory, *symbolic interaction* refers to the study of the "peculiar and distinctive character of interaction as it takes place between human beings" (Blumer, 1969). In reaction to the abstractness and societal-level focus of most social theory, the symbolic interactionist studies the microsystem: the ways in which social actors make sense of their world, act upon one another, and define who they are and what they are doing. External forces do not play on passive creatures. To the contrary, humans interpret their condition and they organize responses to their environment. Neither clever theory nor careful statistics can substitute for asking the participants what they think they are doing (Blumer, 1951).

The term "symbolic interaction" incorporates two essential features of social life: that human beings are able to deal in symbols (to imagine what does not exist and to create meaning) and that humans must live in social groups. Both of these facts will be elaborated throughout this book. The more basic point is that there is no reality other than that existing in the minds of human actors. What is real is what members of the group agree is real, *including their own identities.*

Social organization, in this perspective, is an uncertain and temporary form of order arrived at by bargaining (*negotiation*) or force, and held together because it exists in people's minds. Therefore, it is the interaction itself that must provide the material of sociological analysis: the words and gestures, what is said and not said, making contact or breaking off. This is not pure subjectivity because each individual arrives at some understanding only through conversations with others. Thus, while social structure is subordinated to the actual interaction, there is something distinctly sociological in this perspective: Human beings create their worlds and their selves.

[margin notes:]

Social protests are a sign of malfunction in the social system, as well as personal discontent.

Macrosystem analysis focuses on entire systems. **Microsystem** analysis focuses on face-to-face interaction.

Symbolic interaction focuses on the microsystem, and how individuals make sense of their worlds and themselves.

In the symbolic interaction perspective, social organization is achieved through **negotiation** and is always somewhat uncertain and temporary.

Other Microlevel Approaches. Locating sociology in the minute details of everyday life is also the concern of Erving Goffman (1959, 1961A, and 1971, among other works) and Harold Garfinkel (1967).

Goffman's studies are described as dramaturgical because interaction is seen in terms of ritual dramas in which actors present images of themselves, protect their identity, and develop rules for their encounters. It is these rules that are the essence of social structure, providing the framework of daily activity. Goffman's world is neatly summarized by the title of his best-known work, *The Presentation of Self in Everyday Life* (1959).

Garfinkel's approach is called *ethnomethodology* and involves the meanings that social actors give to their words and behaviors as the first step in sociological analysis. Because most behavior is produced without conscious awareness, the observer must probe beneath a "taken-for-granted" world to discover the rules guiding social action. This is done not by imposing abstractions from outside but by getting inside the heads of individuals by questioning participants and accepting their explanations. For example, one Garfinkel experiment has students attempt to behave as if they were boarders in their parents' home. Try it and see how quickly you discover all the hidden, assumed rules governing the relationship between parents and adult offspring.

SUMMARY OF THE THREE PERSPECTIVES

The three modern perspectives all attempt to organize facts and to provide an answer to the same question faced by classical theorists: How is society possible? Functional theorists follow Durkheim in focusing on macrosystem features such as interdependence and consensus, whereas conflict theorists expand on Marx's concept of class conflict. At the microsystem level of everyday life, symbolic interaction studies, building upon Simmel's analysis of pure sociability, explore the flexibility and uncertainty of social behavior and the active creative capacities of social actors.

Combining insights from all these models, we can say that society is possible because human beings construct a world of reality, including rules of cooperation that most members perceive to be in their best interests, so that social order is maintained, even though some groups will profit more than others.

Each model provides some insights into the workings of social life. Taking the example of unemployment, functional analysis would focus on the fit between the economic system's need for workers and the supply of people with particular skills. Conflict theorists note that the unemployed are the relatively powerless and suggest that their joblessness serves the interests of those who have the jobs and the power to explain unemployment as a consequence of lesser ability.

In contrast, microlevel analysis would consider the meaning of unemployment to the individual, how he or she develops the identity of a jobless person, and presents this "self" to others. Imagine yourself as an unemployed worker; how would this affect your feelings about yourself and your dealings with others? What little dramas will you experience in trying to maintain self-esteem?

As different as these perspectives are, they are all sociological.

Erving Goffman perceives interaction in terms of the drama of everyday life.

Harold Garfinkle defines **ethnomethodology** as the study of the meanings that people give to their words and behaviors.

REFLECTIONS ON SOCIAL THEORY

What makes any theory sociological is its focus on *interaction*: among individuals, between groups, or across the major areas of activity in a society. Although no one set of propositions so dominates the field that we can speak of *a* theory of society, we can describe a sociological perspective, imagination, or focus. Sociology is really a way of looking at how humans behave because they live in groups. Sociologists acknowledge that human behavior may have many causes, and that a single cause has many outcomes, and that the cause-effect relationships will vary from one situation to another. Specifying these changing relationships is the heart of sociology, and the function of theory is to provide a framework upon which to drape our findings.

Reductionism refers to the attempt to reduce social behavior to individual psychology or biology.

Reductionism. At times, social scientists must struggle to preserve their vision of social life against powerful *reductionist* trends. Throughout this book we will have many occasions to criticize attempts to reduce social behavior to individual psychology. Another type of reductionism comes from students of animal behavior, who claim that humans are simply more developed apes than those found in game preserves. The differences between animal and human behavior will be discussed in Chapters 3 and 5.

It is appropriate, though, to discuss *theories of biological determinism* in this introductory chapter. Theories of biological determinism seek to demonstrate that biological differences are responsible for differing abilities between races, or sexes, or ethnic groups.

Theories of **biological determinism** claim that biological factors predetermine group differences in abilities and performance.

Sociobiology is the study of the evolution of social behaviors.

Sociobiology. The most recent, and most sophisticated, theory of the inheritance of genetically-determined behaviors is sociobiology. (Wilson, 1975; Barash, 1977). As Darwin traced the evolution of physical traits, sociobiologists attempt to do the same for social behaviors. Briefly, what this means is that some behaviors that characterize primates (the family of monkeys, apes, and humans) proved to have survival value, that is, were *adaptive*, in the long course of evolution, and have therefore become part of our biological endowment. Lionel Tiger (1969) claims, for example, that the several million years of human evolution have firmly established traits linked to the hunt—quickness, motor skills, male bonding, and a sense of control and dominance—in men, and traits linked to child care—nurturance, emotionality, sociability—in women. But no one has yet isolated any of these genes in humans.

For example, since every society requires that members mate and have children in order for the group to survive, sociobiologists would suggest that there is a strong genetic tendency for humans to want to pair off and produce offspring (stronger in females than males because they must bear and care for the infants), and that if this were not so, the species might have disappeared along with the woolly mammoth. A sociologist would be more likely to attribute the universality of marriage to a general *social need*. This is what is required for a group to endure over time, and those that do not figure out some way of meeting this need will not survive. It is the *variation* in the expression of a trait that fascinates the social scientist—the changes from society to society. Some form of marriage is found in every society. It is the many different arrangements humans have devised for pairing group members that is of interest.

We do not deny that biology, and psychology, and even body chemistry affects human behavior. Many people believe the same to be true of tides, the full moon, and the devil. But whatever the direct effect of any of these factors (the devil not excluded), each human being is in some relationship to others, and each group exists in a context that shapes and modifies the expression of any trait. *All human behavior is mediated* by social systems. If, for example, mating genes really influenced human behavior, we would still want to know about variations by age, social class, religion, and nationality groups. The answers do not lie in the genes, the brain, or the moon, but in the structure of social relationships in a given society at a certain historical moment.

A Working Model for the Study of Self in Society

In the pages that follow, we shall outline a working model for the study of self in society, taking from each theoretical approach elements that could combine to allow you to apply the sociological perspective to the events of your own lives in this society.

REQUIREMENTS FOR GROUP SURVIVAL

Every group, from a family to a university to an entire society, must accomplish certain tasks if it is to survive over time. These tasks are called *functional requisites* because they are necessary for continued existence of the group. There are five of these needs that must be met if the group is not to collapse or disintegrate. The essential question is this: What does the pattern contribute to group survival?

Functional requisites are tasks necessary for individual and group survival over time.

1. Adapting to the Environment.   Each group must find within its geographic location the inputs required for physical survival. Members of a society need food and shelter; a university requires land, buildings, and financial support; and a family must have a place in which to live and a means of getting food and other necessities.

Adapting to the environment refers to physical survival in a given geographic location.

2. Maintaining Order and Providing Defense.   Every group must evolve some methods for settling disputes, enforcing rules, and defending the group. Some members will be assigned the task of rule-making, or ensuring compliance, or defense of the group. In a society, these positions are often labeled "lawmaker," "police officer," or "warrior." The university has an administration, processes for resolving grievances, and a security force. A family has its rule-givers, its enforcers, and its defenders.

Maintaining order is another necessity of group life.

3. Reproduction or Recruitment of New Members.   Any group is limited to the lifespan of its current members and will disappear if no replacements are produced. Therefore, each group must find some mechanism for the *orderly replacement* of members. Societies have rules of courtship and marriage; universities recruit students; and families are specifically designed for producing new members.

Replacement of group members ensures the group's continuance through time.

4. Training of New Members.   Recruitment and reproduction provide new blood, but these individuals must be taught to behave in that environment. There are elaborate techniques for training entrants into a society: universities have orientations; and families are preoccupied with the raising of infants.

New members must be **trained** in the ways of the group.

Belief systems serve to explain the origin, purpose, and destiny of a human group.

5. Constructing a Set of Beliefs. The last task, that of constructing a set of beliefs, is ideological; that is, it is concerned with things of the mind and spirit rather than the body or social interaction. It would appear that no group can sustain itself over time without a belief system: a set of ideas about the origin of the group, rules for conduct in this world, and some conception of destiny—the meaning of it all. These beliefs serve to allay anxiety about existence ("Why am I, are we, here?"), and also act as a social glue ("We are those who share these beliefs").

Societies have histories, often mythical, which are stories about how the group originated and why things are as they are. Universities also have histories, real or imagined: tales of the past, of famous professors, great classes, wild parties, and a sense of mission reinforced by rituals such as Class Night, Spring Festival, Homecoming, and Commencement. Families have their myths, a belief in their essential goodness and place in the world, their rituals and sacred occasions.

INSTITUTIONAL SPHERES

Institutional spheres are patterns of rules and behaviors developed to meet these functional requisites.

These five problems of survival that each group must solve are the origin of *institutions*. Institutions, or *institutional spheres*, as shown in Table 1-1 are patterns of rules and behaviors developed by a group to meet a crucial need. Each society is different from every other because the trial-and-error attempts to solve the functional problems will be historically unique. So, also, are groups within a society somewhat different from one another because of their peculiar solutions to the tasks of survival.

This scheme of functional requisites allows comparison of social groups, societies, and cultures. Although the content of the institutional spheres will vary, the institutional spheres are *universals*.

STABILITY AND CONFLICT IN SOCIAL SYSTEMS

It cannot be assumed that social order is automatic once the functional requisites have been met. To the extent that any society's resources are limited, not

Table 1-1. Functional Requisites and Institutional Spheres

Universal needs	Group response
Adaptation to the environment; sustenance, shelter	Economic activity: production and distribution of goods and services
Maintenance of order; rule enforcement; dispute settlement; protection and defense	Political behavior; lawgiving, policing; defending; judging
Orderly reproduction and recruitment of new members	Marriage and family rules
Training new members to the ways of the group	Socialization and education
Constructing beliefs that relieve anxiety and make members feel responsible for one another	Belief systems

all individuals or groups can achieve their goals or share fully in the wealth of the society. This being the case, conflict is built into every social system. Individuals and groups are, to a greater or lesser degree, in continual competition for the means of meeting their needs and securing their goals. The crucial sociological questions for any social arrangement are these: Who gets what? And whose interests are being served?

Once we see that certain social systems are structured to benefit certain individuals or groups over the claims of others, we can then ask how did the arrangement develop, how is it maintained, and what are the probabilities of open conflict in that system or in the society as a whole? What passes for social stability at any given moment represents a balance of opposing forces and the ability of dominant groups to appease or convince others that the distribution of valued resources is fair and/or necessary.

In other words, we conceive of social systems as *dynamic*, always in the process of change through the interplay of competing interests. If functional theory helps us grasp the concept of a social system, the conflict model is essential to analyzing who gets what and who constructs the dominant ideology that justifies this particular distribution.

UNDERSTANDING EVERYDAY LIFE

Ultimately, social action revolves around what people think they are doing, and for this knowledge, one must go directly to the field of action—to daily life and its dramas, its moments of triumph, defeat, and struggle as social actors strive to preserve their identity.

Sociology, then, covers a field that encompasses everything from an abstract macrosystem (society) to the most fragile microsystem (self and others). It is not enough to take the world at face value, for underneath all social life are other patterns and meanings. To reveal them is the task of sociology. How we go about doing this—finding the patterns and meanings beneath the event—is the subject of the next chapter.

Summary

Sociology is the systematic study of human behavior, of groups to which one belongs, and of the societies formed by human beings. Other social sciences also study everyday life and try to understand human behavior, but sociology is particularly interested in groups and group structure.

C.W. Mills distinguishes between "personal troubles," which are private matters experienced directly by individuals and "public issues," which are a result of forces outside of the immediate control of most people that nevertheless affect their daily lives. Accumulated troubles can be translated into public issues, so that the personal becomes political. The interplay between social and personal level phenomena is an important object of sociological analysis.

The sociological perspective is also characterized by concern for the totality and interconnection of social life, the context of social action and the person as a part of a social group. Sociologists do not predict what any given individual will do, but only the probability of certain behaviors among different types of persons. Sociologists study social facts; patterned regularities such as the unemployment level or birth rates, which typically refer to the group rather than individual action. Social facts also include the meanings that people give to their common experiences. Thus, reality itself is socially constructed.

Sociology as a special subject area emerged in late eighteenth century Europe. Among the most influential early theorists were Auguste Comte, Karl Marx, Max Weber, Emile Durkheim and Georg Simmel, each emphasizing a different aspect of social order and change. Charles Darwin and Sigmund Freud also had a strong impact on the development of the sociological perspective.

Each of the following major contemporary sociological models is important for understanding some aspect of social reality: 1) structural-functionalism, emphasizing the interrelationship between the various parts of a society and the society as a whole; 2) conflict, focusing on the tensions created by structured inequality among subgroups and by uneven social change; and 3) symbolic-interaction, analyzing the processes of everyday life, particularly the ways in which individuals interact with others and come to define themselves.

The lack of one exclusive theory in sociology indicates that social behavior may have many causes, that any one cause has many outcomes, and that cause-effect relationships will vary from one situation to another. The authors conceive of social systems as dynamic, continually changing through the interplay of competing interests. The task of sociology is to reveal the underlying patterns and meanings of all varieties of social structure, from the abstract macrosystems of society to the fragile microsystems of self and others.

Suggested Readings

BART, PAULINE, and LINDA FRANKEL. *The Student Sociologist's Handbook* (Third Edition). Chicago, Ill.: Scott, Foresman, 1981. A witty and useful student survival kit for introductory sociology: where to find information, the mechanics of research, and how to write a term paper.

BERGER, PETER L. *An Invitation to Sociology*. New York: Doubleday, 1963. An extended essay on sociology as a humanistic pursuit.

CAMERON, WILLIAM. *Informal Sociology*. Philadelphia, Pa.: Philadelphia Book, 1963. Provides illuminating answers to the question of how to apply sociological concepts to an understanding of everyday life.

COLLINS, RANDALL, and MICHAEL MAKOWSKY. *The Discovery of Society* (Second Edition). New York: Random House, 1978. An articulate account of the development of sociological theory from eighteenth-century France to the contemporary United States, including analyses of the major contributions of Marx, Weber, Durkheim, Cooley, Mead, and Parsons.

MELTZER, BERNARD, JOHN W. PETRAS, and LARRY T. REYNOLDS. *Symbolic Interaction: Genesis, Varieties, and Criticism*. Boston: Routledge and Kegan Paul, 1975. A thorough and balanced presentation of the many types of symbolic interactionist theory and research styles.

MILLS, C. WRIGHT. *The Sociological Imagination.* New York: Oxford, 1959. The classic statement of the conflict perspective in sociology. Mills criticizes both the abstract theorists and those who are preoccupied with statistical methods, and locates sociology in the intersection of history, society, and individual experience.

REISMAN, DAVID. *The Lonely Crowd: A Study of the Changing American Character.* New Haven: Yale, 1950. Another classic of American sociology, analyzing the link between social structure and personality.

2 *The Sociological Enterprise*

*I*n this chapter we examine the ways in which sociologists test their theories of social life. We first consider several general issues: the need for research, the scientific nature of research, and the research process. These are the whys and whats of the sociological enterprise. The remaining sections will consider the various hows of research—the *methods* employed to gather information, the types of facts (data) derived from these methods, and the statistics used to analyze and describe the data.

Why Research?

It is often said that sociology is the study of the commonplace, and simply repeats what everyone knows through his or her own observation or just plain common sense. Because sociologists do deal with everyday life, with situations and events that we all experience, it would seem that one person's interpretation of reality should be as valid as another's. But it is precisely our ideas about what is natural or self-evident that need to be examined. A great deal of what we think is common-sense knowledge turns out to be neither common nor accurate. In later chapters, for instance, you will find that many taken-for-granted assumptions are not correct, such as the following:

> There was a time when most Americans grew up in three-generation households where large numbers of relatives lived in harmonious cooperation.
>
> Welfare supports large numbers of able-bodied males too lazy to work.
>
> Members of different races have different intellectual capacities.
>
> Agressive instincts lead men to fight.

Such statements assume connections that are actually *problematic;* that is, they must be researched rather than accepted as given. It is often more important for sociologists to understand why such beliefs, if they are not based on fact, are generally thought to be correct. Why do we want to believe certain things and not others?

Moreover, regardless of the truth value of a belief, those who believe will behave as if it were true. This is the important sociological concept of the *definition of the situation:* What people believe to be real is real in its consequences. If, for example, most Americans believe that poor women have children in order to increase their welfare benefits, few citizens will favor expanding the Aid to Families of Dependent Children Program. Thus, the belief has real consequences for poor women and their children. In actuality, evidence exists that women on welfare are *less* likely to have additional children than are equally-impoverished women outside the welfare system because they come into contact with social workers and family planning information and facilities. (Placek & Hendershot, 1974)

What we think is common sense often turns out to be neither common nor accurate.

Definition of the situation means that what people believe to be real is real in its consequences.

The systematic investigation of the relationship between *social facts* is, therefore, essential if we are to understand the world around us and to make wise policy choices. But how do sociologists go about investigating the relationships among social facts?

WAYS OF KNOWING

Human beings arrive at knowledge by a variety of routes. Some things are a matter of *faith* ("parents know what's best for their children"), others appear to be *common-sense* observations of the world around us ("young people don't pay attention to authority anymore"), and still other pieces of knowledge are matters of *intuition* ("I know just how that must feel") based on empathy or gut reactions. These are examples of *subjective modes* of knowing. Max Weber used the term *verstehen* to refer to the basic insights and understandings that come from sharing the view of the world of other people. Yet these shared perceptions, and the application of *verstehen*, however accurate, tell very little about the larger systems in which an interaction is embedded, or about the broader processes of social change taking place in the society.

Moreover, actions taken in accordance with a shared definition of the situation compose a social reality that—to be studied—must be analyzed with methods more objective than intuition. So most sociological research today—at both the level of micro- and macrosystems—attempts to approximate the exactness of the scientific model of explanation.

THE SCIENTIFIC METHOD

Ideally, the scientific researcher follows a series of procedures to insure honesty and accuracy throughout the research process. The *scientific method,* in contrast to intuition, common sense, or faith, involves (1) *objective observation*, (2) *precise measurements*, and (3) *full disclosure* of the research techniques and results.

1. Objectivity. Scientists must, in so far as possible, be conscious of their own attitudes, values, and expectations that might affect their research, and then they must work in such a manner as to minimize the influence of these factors. But there is no method that can totally eliminate researcher bias. Even under carefully controlled laboratory conditions the researcher's own expectations can influence the outcome of an experiment, as was the case with two sets of rats carefully bred for sameness. When student experimenters were told that some rats were brighter than others, those rats whose human managers expected them to do well did, indeed, run the maze better than did identical rats whose managers expected them to be a bit slow (Rosenthal and Jacobson, 1968).

How much more difficult it is, then, to measure people and their ever changing relationships. For example simply asking a question of a respondent will subtly influence that person's answer to the same question at a later date. If a researcher asks what you think about a candidate or a breakfast cereal or United States foreign policy, you must stop and think about it. The next time your opinion is sought, it will have been affected by your thinking about it the first time. There are many ways in which you are not precisely the same person from one moment to another. Observer bias and the changeability of human subjects mean that no measurement in sociology can ever be as accurate as, for example, the temperature of boiling water that remains the same from one observation to another.

Subjective modes of knowing are based on an individual's own perception of society.

The **scientific method** is based upon **objective observation, precise measurements**, and **full disclosure**.

Objectivity is the ability to view the world from outside one's own immediate experience.

2. Precise Measurement. The goal of objectivity is supported by the construction of measurement devices that leave as little as possible to the discretion of the observer. One way to avoid the trap of subjectivity is to develop research *instruments* (questionnaires, checklists, interview schedules, ways to map positions of interacting individuals, and the like) that different observers can use to obtain comparable information. In this way, research findings can be compared or combined to arrive at statements that cover more than one observation at one time.

Deciding just what to measure is the first problem a researcher faces. Not everything that a sociologist is interested in can be measured directly, especially such abstract concepts as, for example, religiosity, marital satisfaction, or student activism. Something that can be counted must be selected to stand for the abstraction. The things that are measured and counted are called *empirical referents*, meaning observable acts used as evidence of the abstract concept. For example, the abstraction "religiosity" has been measured by a number of empirical referents, including attendance at services (an objective referent) or feelings about one's beliefs (a subjective referent). The following diagram shows these relationships at a glance.

Abstraction: ——————————→ Religiosity
        ↓   ↓
Empirical Referents: ——→ Going to religious services
          Answer to question "How important
          is religion to you?"

There are two major problems in the measurement of empirical referents. One is the question of *reliability:* Does the instrument measure something consistently? The other is the issue of *validity:* Does the instrument measure what the researcher claims it does? (Stouffer, 1962) Reliability is tested by the similarity in results from different researchers using the same or a similar instrument in various settings and at different times. If, for example, the question about attending religious services was asked in a number of separate studies in which approximately equal proportions answered weekly, daily, or sometimes, the question appears reliable. But does it measure religiosity? This can be discovered if there are additional measures of religious behavior that demonstrate the same response pattern; if so, the question is assumed to have validity.

Reliability and validity are never assured, but are goals to which the researcher aspires. How close one has come to achieving precision and accuracy is a matter for other researchers to decide.

3. Full Disclosure. It is a scientific duty to make research methods and evidence available to colleagues. Every published research report must contain information on the subjects used, what was measured, and a description of the techniques employed as well as the findings. Even after the report is published, the researcher should be willing to provide additional information to colleagues who have some doubts about the presentation of the data. Such disclosure will aid others in repeating the research if the methods used were reliable.

The Science in Social Science. Researchers have followed the scientific method in their explorations of social life with varying success. Every study is somewhat flawed for the reasons already mentioned—the essential changeability of humans, problems of reliability and validity in measurement, and the

---

Precise measurement is necessary for objective research and results that are valid and reliable.

Reliability is tested by the similarity in results from different researchers using similar instruments.

Validity is tested by more than one type of measurement of the same behavior with similar results.

Full disclosure is the scientific duty to make one's results available to colleagues.

impossibility of total objectivity. Yet sociology is often called a social science (along with psychology, political science, and economics). How valid is this claim to scientific rigor?

The basic difficulty in social science is that when humans set out to make sense of other humans, the likelihood of error or misinterpretation exists on *both* sides—in the researcher's bias, and the possibility that the subject is responding to cues not understood by the observer. For this reason, many sociologists insist that sociology is not scientific, can never be, and ought not try to be; that, in fact, it is fraudulent to claim an exactness that cannot be substantiated. Nonetheless, the major sociological journals continue to report highly sophisticated research designs with complex statistical analyses and all the features of the scientific method.

Sociologists prefer to be thought of as social scientists for many reasons. North Americans have traditionally placed great faith in the scientific, the practical, and the rational application of knowledge. Prepared to perceive truth in what can be counted, they tend to find numbers more compelling than an idea (though the data may be no more accurate). Advertisers have long recognized the instant authority of a figure in a white coat reading statistics from a clipboard, even though the authority is an actor who has just walked in off the street. The scientific impression is what counts and leads a buyer to choose one toothpaste over another.

However, as we shall see on the following pages, a great deal of the scientific does exist in sociology. The standards of objectivity, precision, and disclosure that govern the sociological enterprise will become clearer as we follow the research process from its origins in theory to ultimate presentation to colleagues.

Scientific and Nonscientific Factors in The Research Process		Scientific Factors	Nonscientific Factors
	Step 1 Select the Research question	Based on theory of general interest	Based on values of the researcher or considerations of time and money or as requested by funding source
	Step 2 Choose appropriate method	Based strictly on requirements of hypothesis testing	Convenience and expense considerations
	Step 3 Gather information	Pretested instrument and scientific sample selection	Interviewer bias and respondents' self-selection
	Step 4 Analyze the data	Objective measurements	Researcher bias
	Step 5 Report findings	Full disclosure	Withholding data

The Research Process

Four major steps comprise the research process:

1. Selecting the research question.
2. Choosing the appropriate method for gathering information.
3. Analyzing the data.
4. Reporting the findings.

The **research process** involves four major steps.

Each step involves choices, sometimes dictated by the conceptual model or theory the researcher holds about the nature of social life, and sometimes by practical considerations such as availability of subjects, funding, and the time factor. In other words, selectivity and compromises characterize most research so that nonscientific elements enter the process at the very beginning.

1. SELECTING THE RESEARCH QUESTION

Deciding what to study may be the most nonscientific step of all, because researchers are likely to be influenced by their own values and attitudes in selecting just what question to examine. What we think is important, what we want to know more about, and what subject matter appeals to us are as much personal as professional matters. The choice of research goals today, however, is greatly complicated by the problem of funding. The broader, deeper, or more complex the research design, the more financial support is required for observers and interviewers, printing and support services, and computer time. As few universities or colleges can afford such assistance, the major funding sources today are foundations, private research organizations, and departments of government, all with their own agendas and priorities in the pursuit of knowledge. Even so, North American scholars enjoy relative political freedom in selecting research topics. In many countries, this is not the case. Sociology was one of the first disciplines to fall under political control in Nazi Germany and in the Soviet Union during the Stalin Era.

As a mental exercise, ask yourself what you would like to research, what question you would want answered. Notice that such a question will follow from your view of the world and the conceptual model you have about how it works. Because it is the connection between one social fact and another (or others) that most researchers seek to discover, think of two social phenomena that you suspect are related, as for example the previously mentioned link between being on welfare and bearing children. In that example the two social facts to be examined are (a) whether or not a woman receives welfare, and (b) her subsequent fertility history. These are called *variables*—factors that display differences among individuals or change from one measurement to another—as opposed to *constants*, which are characteristics that do not vary from one person to another or from one time to another, such as the fact that humans have heads or must eat to stay alive (though what they eat and how often are variables).

1a. Variables and Their Relationship. Most research attempts to find out how change in one variable is related to change in another—that is, the *correlation* between variables. This type of information often permits prediction of

Correlation refers to the effect of one variable upon the other.

change in one variable from knowledge of the other. To know, for example, that early marriage is directly related to the likelihood of divorce suggests the proposition that as the average age of first marriage rises, the divorce rate should level off (all other factors remaining the same).

Independent variables are considered to have greater influence and to be relatively unchangeable.

In defining the research question, a scientist typically has some idea, *derived from theory*, about what variables are more powerful than others in causing change. *Independent variables* are those thought to come first, to be most important, or to be relatively unchangeable such as race, sex, and age (at a given moment). As the word suggests, the independent variable stands alone.

Dependent variables are influenced by changes in the independent variable.

Dependent variables, in contrast, are those assumed to be influenced by (dependent upon) changes in the independent variable. In our earlier example, being on welfare was treated as the independent variable and fertility became the dependent variable.

In most cases it is easy to identify the independent and dependent variables. If one studies black and white high school students' college plans, it becomes quite clear that planning to attend college cannot affect one's race, but that race is strongly associated with college plans. However, there are instances in which it is unclear what variable is the independent and what one is the dependent; the correlation, remember, tells us only that the two are related.

Independent Variable ——————————→ *Dependent Variable*

Example: 1. woman receives welfare ——→ subsequent fertility history
2. age at first marriage ——→ probability of divorce

Having been guided to a topic by one or more nonscientific factors, and having defined the research objective in terms of key variables, the careful sociologist will then conduct the actual research project in as scientific a fashion as possible. An extensive review of the existing research literature is a necessary first step in familiarizing oneself with what is already known about it.

Hypotheses are specific propositions derived from a general theory about the relationships among variables.

1b. Theory and the Formation of Hypotheses. The next step involves applying one's theoretical model to the research question: "If social life proceeds as my theory suggests, then how would the variables of interest be linked?" This question leads from general theory to specific propositions, or *hypotheses* (hypothesis, in the singular), about the relationship between variables.

The statement, "If variable Y changes in a given direction, variable X will change in a specified manner", is a hypothesis that can be tested with data from scientific observations; it is subject to *empirical* verification through carefully gathered evidence.

But what evidence?

Operationalizing the variables translates the abstract into something observable.

1c. Operationalizing the Variables. What will the researcher measure? As noted in our discussion of validity, the variables must be translated into something observable. This is called *operationalizing* the variables. For example, variables such as family violence or unemployment, that seem so simple to measure, are not at all clear-cut. When does disciplining a child become abusive behavior? How many weeks, or months, or years of nonwork constitute "unemployment?"

Often, grave questions about *validity* remain. This is especially so when dealing with variables such as happiness or prejudice. How would you measure happiness, or father–son relations, or bigotry? Each researcher must make a choice of what *empirical referents* will represent the concepts in the theoretical proposition. The next step is to select a method for obtaining the data necessary to test the hypothesis.

2. CHOOSING THE APPROPRIATE METHOD FOR GATHERING INFORMATION

In general, the research objective dictates the particular method to be used. Much depends on whether information must be gathered from a large number of respondents or from a particular type; whether the information is intimate or not; and whether the data refer to one point in time or require follow-up studies to measure change. With respect to this latter consideration, the first methodological choice is one of time frame.

Cross-section studies take place at one time only and can be thought of as slices into ongoing social life. At a given moment, this is how different kinds of people behaved or answered certain questions. The cross-section study is like a snapshot, capturing events of a moment. For information on process and change—a moving picture, so to speak—we need a number of cross-section studies conducted at different times.

Panel or longitudinal studies are those that follow one group of respondents over time. It is not always easy to keep track of people for long periods, and those who remain in the study may be quite different from those who drop out, reducing the value and accuracy of the findings. With these considerations in mind, let us turn to descriptions of the major research methods of contemporary sociology.

2a. Surveys. The large scale social survey is typically designed to yield data from a *representative sample* of respondents. Because it is usually impossible to

Time frames are determined by whether or not the research question requires follow-up studies to measure change.

Cross-section studies take place at one time and are slices into ongoing social life.

Longitudinal studies follow one group of people over periods of time.

A common method of data gathering is through large-scale social surveys. (Source: *Magnum.*)

Surveys question a **sample** that represents a larger population.

question each member of the population of interest to the researcher—all voters, for instance, or parents, or hospital employees, and so forth—some selection of respondents is necessary. This smaller group is called a *sample,* and can be considered representative of the larger population when selected through techniques of probability sampling.

Random sampling occurs when all possible respondents have an equal chance of being selected.

Random sampling occurs when all possible respondents have an equal chance of being selected. A scientifically-selected subgroup drawn from this population is a sample that, within certain statistical limits, accurately reflects the distribution of characteristics in the population. Common *random selection* techniques include pulling names from a rotating drum (as is done in many state lotteries), or picking every hundredth (or fifth or tenth) name from a directory. Contrary to its popular usage, randomness in sociology refers to a scientifically-rigorous procedure of sample selection.

Contacting the sample can be done by mail, phone, or personal visit.

The researcher prepares a pretested set of questions designed to tap the relevant variables, and then administers the questionnaire to the sample. This can be done by mail, telephone, or personal visits, each of which has advantages and disadvantages in terms of cost, time, and response rate. In any survey, the amount and quality of information gathered depends on the respondents' willingness to answer. These limitations, however, are balanced by the method's advantages in scale and representativeness; a large amount of data can be gathered from a large number of people in a short time. And if the sample is scientifically selected, findings can be generalized to the larger population.

"And don't waste your time canvassing the whole building, young man. We all think alike." (Drawing by Stevenson, © 1980 *The New Yorker* Magazine, Inc.)

To evaluate the findings of survey data, however, it is also necessary to look closely at the wording of questions. The way a question is framed can influence responses in a certain direction. In an analysis of public opinion poll data on equal rights for women, for example, one team of researchers (Hesse, Burstein, & Atkins, 1979) discovered that the questions being asked were not as neutral as the polling organizations claimed. The actual question used by the 1976 Gallup Poll was this: "Do you approve of a married woman earning money in business or industry if she has a husband capable of supporting her?" This is not the same as asking if respondents approve of women in the labor force, and the question itself is worded in a way to elicit negative responses. Consider the difference if the question read this way: Do you approve of a woman's right to pursue gainful employment?

Progress in Polling.   In the decades since *The Literary Digest* poll of 1936, political polling has become a fine art. In the 1976 presidential election, the three major polling organizations—Roper, Gallup, and Louis Harris—each using a base of approximately *1,500* respondents, were able to predict within a few percentage points the actual popular and electoral vote. In 1980, however, predictions of a close race were rendered inaccurate by last-minute decisions on the part of many voters. Polls by the candidates' own organizations, though, did pick up these shifts, so that the outcome was clear to the major participants even before the voting booths opened on November 4.

2b. Intensive Interviews. Sometimes a large representative sample is not necessary when conducting exploratory (*pilot*) research before designing a larger study or when seeking information of great intimacy (sexual behavior, for example). In these circumstances, a small sample of key respondents will suffice. In some types of research—such as studies of influence—only key respondents need be used (Merton, 1949). Often one or two carefully selected cases can provide information on processes that are not easily visible to an observer but are thought to have universal application. Such *case histories* are more common in psychology, especially in psychiatry, than in sociology, although case history material can be used to add the flavor of real life to survey

The way a question is worded can influence responses.

Personal **interviews** are very useful for pilot research or intimate questioning.

Case histories provide in-depth information from examination of a few cases.

data. For some researchers, particularly those using the ethnomethodological approach, intensive examination of one or a few cases is the only valid method for penetrating the taken-for-granted world.

Observation is a most effective way to study actual behavior.

2c. Observational Techniques. Survey and interview data can only tell us what people *say* they do. But how can we study what people actually do? Observation is time-consuming and limiting in regard to the number of individuals and occasions that can be studied. Nor is it possible for an observer, however carefully trained, to see everything; each of us perceives selectively, tending to recognize what we expect to be there and overlooking the unexpected. Because the observer must also be careful not to disrupt the ongoing activity being researched, observations are confined to settings in which a researcher will be unnoticed or taken for granted. Otherwise, people might act as they wish to be seen rather than as they would without such self-consciousness.

Many of these observational barriers are reduced when the researcher can become part of the interaction under study, but *participant observation* has its

To be most effective, observation of behavior should take place in a setting in which the observer is careful not to disrupt the ongoing activities. (Source: Magnum.)

Through a combination of observation and nonjudgmental questioning, Whyte was able to find patterns of social relations that were not evident to outsiders (or even to insiders, who were basically acting out of custom and habit). Far from being the disorganized slum that social theory had assumed, Cornerville, like any other community, was organized into social systems in which individuals had particular positions and were expected to behave accordingly. There were patterns of action and rules of conduct, and a hierarchy of personal relationships based on favors and obligations. Thus, Whyte's patient, sustained exploration of everyday life unearthed information that ultimately changed the way in which slum life was perceived and studied. Whyte's methods have set the standard for subsequent exercises in participant observation.

A detailed account of Whyte's study appears in William Foote Whyte, *Street Corner Society: The Social Structure of an Italian Slum.* Chicago: University of Chicago Press, 1943.

Participant observation occurs when the researcher becomes a part of the interaction under study.

hazards. It may take a long time before the participant observer is fully accepted and the other people behave naturally. There is also the ethical question of using material gained from those whom you have asked to trust you in order to further one's own career. Researchers who have used this method typically explain themselves and their presence at the beginning of their participation. Again, at the end of the study, many researchers ask their subjects to read and comment upon the material gathered. There is, however, no way to measure the extent to which the participant observer has subtly changed the group and its interactions.

Nonetheless, participant observation yields the richest type of data: authentic behavior, the self-explanations accompanying these, unconscious gestures, and the little details that speak volumes. The drawbacks of this method are the amount of time devoted to just one group, and the near impossibility of generalizing from a sample of one.

Secondary analysis involves the use of data collected by others.

2d. Secondary Analysis. Surveys, interviews, and observations are methods for generating *original data*. Yet libraries are stocked with material already gathered. Secondary analysis involves the use of data collected by others.

Official Data. The United States Government alone produces volumes of information daily. So also does the government of Canada. In fact the United States Government Printing Office is the world's largest publishing house.

Nonofficial but often useful information is provided by business and trade associations, special-interest groups, and profit-making research establishments. Very little in North America has not been counted by someone at some time.

Of special value are the periodic official censuses in the United States and Canada. Although the count is taken only once a decade, census publications

Although the census is taken only once a decade, census data are used continually by government agencies and social scientists. (Source: Woodfin Camp and Associates.)

are issued over many years as the data are worked and reworked to provide supplementary information. In addition, both countries conduct a continual series of special studies on selected populations, and current vital and health statistics are continually published by the appropriate departments.

Historical Records. Another type of secondary analysis uses the past as a basis for comparison. Which relationships among variables are relatively constant and which are modified as a social system changes over time? The answers lie in letters, archives, and other historical papers. Among the classic works of sociology is the enormous study, *The Polish Peasant in Europe and America* (1918/1958), by W. I. Thomas and Florian Znaniecki, using as primary material the letters exchanged among family members who remained in Poland and those who emigrated to America.

Books, newspapers, and magazines are often used as source material for *content analysis,* which is a careful counting of the number of times particular images, words, or ideas appear. From the content analysis, the researcher can test hypotheses about values or social change; for example, trends in sexual behavior between 1940 and 1980, or in the portrayal of women and blacks in the media.

Comparative Studies. A powerful method using secondary analysis for testing the universality of hypothesized relationships among variables is to compare a variety of societies. Information on other cultures, especially preindus-

Historical records reveal the patterns among variables over time.

Content analysis counts the number of references to certain items in a sample of publications.

Cross-cultural comparisons study relationships among variables in different societies.

Cross-Cultural Analysis of Gender Roles

A perennial topic for cross-cultural comparisons is the generality of sex-linked behaviors. Some researchers, finding a fairly similar division of labor across large numbers of societies, have concluded that basic biological and personality differences between men and women account for these social patterns and for the universality of male dominance. More recently, feminist scholars have examined the comparative literature for information specifying the conditions under which women have more or less power compared to men. By looking at degrees of difference, attention shifts from inflexible characteristics such as gender to those social situations that have undergone historical change.

Thus, Morris Zelditch in the early 1950s examined data on 56 societies and concluded that husband and wife units tend to display a common division of labor, with men assuming positions of leadership and task achievement, while women perform emotionally supportive tasks. In contrast, Peggy Sanday (1974) focused on a society's economic base, defense requirements, population density, and natural environment as these correlate with variations in women's power in the public sphere. In general, Sanday found that when women are producers of economically-important goods, and where men are absent owing to warfare, the power of the women in shaping personal and societal decisions is increased.

Zelditch's study, "Role Differentiation in the Nuclear Family: A comparative study," may be found in Talcott Parsons and Robert F. Bales, *Family, Socialization and Interaction Process.* Glencoe: Free Press, 1955.
Peggy T. Sanday's essay, "Female Status in the Public Domain" is printed in Michelle Zimbalist Rosaldo and Louise Lamphere (eds.), *Women, Culture, and Society.* Stanford: Stanford University Press, 1974.

trial and preliterate societies, is contained in *The Ethnographic Atlas* and *Human Relations Area Files* at selected universities, but available to all scholars. These sources provide ready access to anthropological material, coded and indexed for *cross-cultural comparisons*.

Limitations of Secondary Analysis. Using available data, although often a great saver of time and money, has certain disadvantages. As the information was originally collected for other purposes, data are sometimes incomplete, or biased by the original researcher, or in a form inappropriate for use by the secondary analyst.

Experiments are closest to the scientific ideal in their **control over the variables.**

2e. Experiments. Of all the methods described in this section, experiments are closest to the scientific ideal. The essence of the experimental design is *control over the variables*, a requirement that also makes it the least appropriate method for sociologists. In everyday life, such control over the situation or people is impossible because behavior stems from the interpretations that people bring to the situation and then modify during the interaction. Yet experimental research, however artificial, *can* clarify relationships that are not easily identified in everyday observation. See Figure 2-1 for an example of a classic experimental design.

The Logic of the Experimental Design. As described by Riley (1963), "the controlled experiment is a powerful design for testing hypotheses of causal relationships among variables. Ideally . . . the investigator throws into sharp relief the explanatory variables . . . [while] controlling or manipulating the independent variable (X), observing its effect on the dependent variable (Y), and minimizing the effects of the extraneous variables". *Extraneous variables* are those outside the hypothesis, but which, since they can affect the findings, must be minimized or controlled through sample selection.

1. The classic experiment begins with subjects assigned to groups that are as similar as possible in all factors likely to affect the results. This is done by matching subjects (by age, sex, or some other variable of possible importance) and then using a technique of random selection to assign them to one group or another.
2. Once the two samples are drawn as alike as possible or with differences randomized, members of both groups are measured on the dependent variable, an attitude or behavior that the researcher thinks will be influenced by introducing the independent variable.

Figure 2-1.
A classic experimental design.

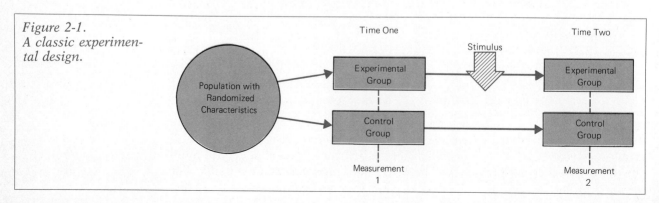

In a series of experiments on the topic of obesity and eating, Stanley Schachter and his colleagues found much support for the symbolic interactionist perspective on behavior (Schachter, 1975). Intrigued by the consistent failure of medical treatment of overweight people by diet and drugs, and the equally unsuccessful results of psychological therapies, the researchers sought to explore the *meanings* attached to eating for the obese and for those of normal weight.

In one of a series of experiments, the researchers manipulated the variables of food deprivation and fear. At Time One, obese and normal subjects were assigned to one of four conditions: All subjects came to the laboratory without having eaten the meal preceding their appointment; some were left without food and some were told to eat as many roast beef sandwiches provided by the experimenters as they wished. Some of each group of eaters or noneaters were also told that very mild electrical shocks would be administered as part of the experiment, and others were warned that the shocks might be quite intense ("Do you have a heart condition?"). Subjects were then asked to sample freely from bowls of crackers while filling out a questionnaire on taste: Are the crackers salty, cheesy, spicy, and so forth?

The dependent variable measured at Time Two was simply the number of crackers eaten by each subject. Consistent with other findings from previous studies, the results indicated that normal-weight people were strongly influenced by the experimental conditions; their consumption of crackers dropped off under situations of high fear and full stomachs. But the manipulation of these independent variables did not affect the appetites of the obese; if anything, consumption of crackers slightly increased under conditions of fear and full stomachs!

The conclusion arrived at by Schachter and colleagues was that fat people respond to different cues than do the nonfat. Quite clearly, actual hunger as measured by time since last meal had little effect on fat people; regardless of the state of their stomachs, they ate when they thought it was appropriate to do so. They responded to *external* rather than internal stimuli. The meaning of food and eating was different for the two groups, and various changes in the experimental situation affected the two types differently.

These experiments were reported by Stanley Schachter, in *"Obesity and Eating,"* in Darrell J. Steffensmeier and Robert M. Terry (eds.), *Examining Deviance Experimentally*. Port Washington, N.Y.: Alfred, 1975, pp. 137–153.

Who Wants a Cracker? and When?

3. The independent variable, or *causal factor*, is introduced to *one sample only*. This sample becomes the *experimental group* (E) while the sample from which the factor is withheld becomes the *control group* (C).
4. Members of the experimental and control groups are measured on the dependent variable at a later date. Changes in both groups between Time 1 and Time 2 are compared. Any group differences on the dependent variable can then be attributed to the manipulation of the independent variable.

Such a design is most easily carried out where the researcher can control all extraneous elements, as in a social-science laboratory. Experiments are more difficult to conduct in the everyday world, but *field experiments* are possible. For example, social psychologists have devised numerous field experiments to test

Field experiments are conducted in the everyday world.

helping behavior, that is, under what circumstances people return lost wallets or help someone in distress. In these studies, the causal factor is varied—as when a "victim" thought to be bleeding (red liquid) was helped less often, less quickly and less directly than one whose collapse was bloodless (Piliavin & Piliavin, 1972). Assuming a basic similarity in subjects, a control group is not necessary because what is crucial is the manipulation of the experimental situation.

Natural experiments measure subjects before and after a natural phenomenon.

There are also *natural experiments* in which the same population is measured before and after an event that changes their situation, such as a natural disaster or the introduction of new laws. Studies of the effect of capital punishment on criminal acts often compare murder rates in a state before and after the passage of death penalty legislation. In these cases, the general population is its own control, assumed to be the same before and after with only the independent variable changing.

3. ANALYZING THE DATA

Statistics are numerical techniques for the **classification** and **analysis of data.**

Numbers alone rarely permit adequate testing of hypotheses. The many pieces of data must be arranged in such a way as to allow comparison between groups or among variables. Sociologists today are trained in the use of *statistics*, numerical techniques for the classification and analysis of data. If you were to look through current issues of the two major sociological publications, *The American Sociological Review* and the *American Journal of Sociology*, you might think you had picked up the journal of the American Statistical Society.

As introductory students, you are not expected to learn most of these procedures. But as a citizen of a society that venerates numbers, you should be able to interpret some very basic statistics: percentages, rates, ratios, and measures of central tendency.

A **percentage** indicates how many in every one hundred.

Percentages. The simplest and most important statistic is the percentage, or how many in every one hundred, often referred to as the *proportion*. Percentages allow researchers to compare groups of different size. How easily can you tell which is the larger proportion—25 out of 300 cases or 30 out of 400? The use of percentages simplifies such a comparison: 8.3 per cent vs. 7.5 per cent—the larger number, 30, actually represents a smaller part of its total.

Rates and Ratios. There are two other frequently used statistics that an introductory student should readily recognize.

Rates indicate the number of times a given event occurs in a specified population.

Rates. Rates, like percentages, are the number of times a given event occurs in a specified population. For example, we have already spoken of birth and death rates. The birth rate can be computed on the basis of the whole population: in 1975, in the United States, the birth rate was 14.8 per 1,000 population. But since that population includes males, children, and the very old, a more informative statistic would be based on the population of females age 15–44. In 1975 the rate for this subpopulation was 66.7 per 1,000 women of childbearing ages (down from a high of 118.3 in 1955). It is important, therefore, to take careful note of the base upon which a rate is computed.

A **ratio** compares one subpopulation to another.

Ratio. A ratio compares one subpopulation to another, such as males to females, or suicides to homicides, or legitimate to illegitimate births. For example, the ratio of males to females is a statistic that varies over time and with age. In 1978, in the United States, among persons under age 14, there were 104.3 males for every 100 females, but by ages 25–44 there were only 96.7 men for each 100 women, and among those age 65+, the ratio is 68.5 men to every 100 women. By the year 2000, there may be fewer than fifty men age 65+ for every 100 older women.

Measures of Central Tendency. Three of the most common statistics you will encounter in this book, or deal with as an informed citizen, are single numbers that summarize an entire set of data: *measures of central tendency*. These three important summary statistics are the *mean*, the *median*, and the *mode*. Most of you will have heard others speak of the "mean test score," the "median income," or "modal family patterns," without knowing precisely what the terms mean. The three measures are very different, as the following example illustrates:

A group of 100 respondents has taken an "altruism" test to measure willingness to help another person. The highest score is ten and the lowest is zero. The one hundred scores were distributed in this manner:

Score	Number of respondents with that score
10	6
9	8
8	12
7	14
6	20
5	10
4	9
3	8
2	7
1	3
0	3
	N = 100

Total scores: 573

Mean. The mean is an arithmetic average; in this case 100 respondents had a total score of 573, for a *group mean* of 5.73 (the total scores divided by the number of respondents).

Median. The median is the *mid-point* of a distribution of cases, with fifty per cent of the cases above and fifty per cent below that number. In the preceding example, the mid-point, or fiftieth case, comes somewhere between scores 6 and 7.

Mode. The mode is the single most common category of cases; in this example, the largest number of respondents (20) had scores of 6. Therefore, 6 is the mode for this group.

To compare this set of respondents with any other group, only one of these measures of central tendency is needed, rather than the hundred individual scores.

Measures of central tendency are single numbers that summarize an entire set of data.

4. REPORTING THE FINDINGS

The Decision to Publish.   We have already mentioned the importance of full disclosure of the research techniques, instruments, and findings. But suppose that you, the researcher, have generated data that you do not want to disclose, that you think might be used against groups with which you are in sympathy. Some researchers will elect not to publish, and others will attempt to minimize negative outcomes by interpreting the findings as narrowly as possible.

There are several recent cases in which sociologists have published very controversial reports—Daniel Patrick Moynihan on the black family, and James Coleman on school desegregation. The Moynihan study was widely interpreted as attributing the educational and economic failures of many urban black males to the likelihood of being raised in female-centered families. Coleman's report claimed that court-enforced school desegregation, especially when involving crosstown busing, was responsible for "white flight" to the suburbs. Both studies have been refuted by other sociologists, who have also raised what they consider the ethical issue of a more general responsibility of social scientists *not* to increase the level of racism in our society.

Presentation of Findings.   Sociologists communicate with one another through publication in professional journals, by reading papers at professional meetings, and by circulating copies of research papers among friends and colleagues. A crucial, if not the most important, part of a research report is the presentation of data in tables, charts, graphs, or diagrams.

Reading Tables.   A table consists of columns and rows of figures, arranged in a way that clarifies relationships among variables. A glance at the table should, in most cases, convey information more readily than descriptive prose. It would take several sentences to tell you in words what you should be able to read at a glance from a table such as Table 2-1 below.

There are certain steps that should be followed to help you interpret a table, beginning with a careful reading of the title, the headings, and the footnotes. Only then will you understand the numbers in the body of the table (often called *cells*). In Table 2-1, for example, the title tells you that the cell numbers are per cents of people aged 65 and over who were either single, married, widowed, or divorced in 1978 in the United States. The footnote in this case gives

> Sociologists communicate through journal publications, reading papers at meetings, and circulating research reports.
>
> **Tables** present information more concisely than descriptive prose.

Table 2-1. Marital Status and Sex of Persons 65 Years Old and Over in the United States, 1978 (in percents):

	Male	Female
Single	5.4	6.2
Married	77.5	38.6
Widowed	14.2	52.0
Divorced	2.9	3.2
Total	100.0	100.0

Source: *Statistical Abstract of the United States*, 1979, p. 32.

the source as the *Statistical Abstract of the United States,* 1979, which indicates official Bureau of the Census data.

The cells illustrate the extreme difference between older men and women in the likelihood of being married rather than widowed. Over half of all elderly women are widowed whereas over three-fourths of older men have a living spouse. Once the cell data have been described, the researcher has the exciting task of exploring its meanings. What processes account for these differences by sex? One clue is contained in the data on sex ratios given on p. 40, which reflect the higher death rates of males compared to females at all ages. The fact that women typically marry men older than themselves is another causal variable. What differences do you think being married or widowed makes in terms of satisfaction or standard of living in old age?

Charts and Graphs.   Tables are only one way to present data. Throughout this book, we shall also use other techniques for displaying information. For example, the data in Table 2.1 could be expressed either in *bar graphs* or in pie-shaped diagrams, as shown in Figure 2-2.

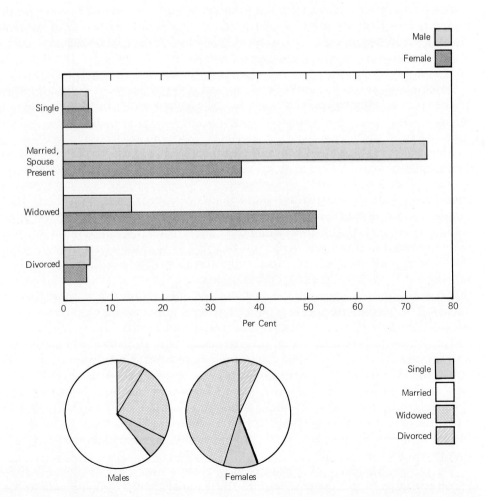

Sociology for What and Whom? Ethical Considerations in Social Science Research

Research ethics are involved in decisions to use human subjects to accomplish goals of researchers or funding agencies.

Experimental Designs. Social scientists often manipulate human subjects through the use of experimental designs that place them in a contrived situation or expose some but not others to a stimulus condition. In certain cases, such as juvenile delinquency research, a treatment that is intended to reduce harmful behavior may be applied to certain youngsters and withheld from similarly needy youth. By what criterion can this selection be justified? For the most part, random selection is used as a justification in that each research subject had an equal chance of being selected for the experimental group. A more serious question is that of giving any treatment at all to those who have not specifically requested it. Yet if all experimental subjects were self-selected, the findings might be biased. An additional dilemma centers on the degree of consent required from experimental subjects and the amount of knowledge they must be given in order to secure their "informed consent." If the subjects are told in advance about the research goals and precisely what awaits them, they will no longer be naïve, spontaneous reactors to stimuli. For these reasons, laboratory-type experiments are often conducted with "captive audiences," inmates of institutions and college students being the most common. Other studies rely on volunteers who agree to serve as experimental subjects for payment.

Observations. Conducting research through observations can also present moral dilemmas. In one controversial study, Laud Humphreys (1975) observed impersonal homosexual encounters in public restrooms ("tearooms"). In serving as a lookout to warn the participants of approaching policemen, Humphreys aided and abetted illegal behavior. As a participant-observer, he did not tell the other men that he was also engaging in research (although a few were later informed and interviewed). Additionally, Humphreys was able to record the license plate numbers of men leaving the area. One year later, as part of a larger health survey, he changed his appearance and interviewed fifty of the tearoom traders, whose addresses he had obtained from a state motor vehicle agency. The health interviews produced general information on the men's nonhomosexual activities—their work, marriage, and family life.

The important finding from this research was the utter normality and ordinariness of their lives. For most, their homosexual acts were an episodic and isolated part of otherwise unremarkable existences. This might explain why they preferred the impersonality of the restroom encounters—no conversation, no emotions, no involvement other than sexual. It is probably true, as Humphreys claims, that no other technique could have produced such fascinating information on the very small population of homosexuals who engage in tearoom trade.

The ethical problems of the study are many: taking part in illegal activity, warning others of the approach of the law, following innocent subjects to their homes, conducting interviews under less than fully honest circumstances, and publishing the findings without the consent of the observed. The objections are not to the subject matter—homosexuality—but to Humphreys' methods of inquiry. The argument over this one study continues to rage wherever the question of professional ethics is debated. Indeed, Humphreys himself (1975) has acknowledged these criticisms and now believes he should have identified himself as a researcher even though some information would have been lost.

Questionnaires. It could be argued that every request for information represents an invasion of another's privacy, and there are many potential respondents who refuse to take part in surveys for that very reason. Provided that the participant has this right of refusal, are further safeguards needed? Most universities today have Human Subjects Review Committees that must approve all research using respondents. Some interview schedules might be considered misleading or too intimate, particularly if there is no assurance of respondent anonymity.

The Uses and Abuses of Information. As research today is often expensive and done under grants from funding sources, a new element has been added to the ethical equation. Does the one who pays the piper call the tune? To what extent are those who fund research entitled to shape the questions and decide what to do with the findings? The United States Army has supported research by political scientists in order to help military dictatorships in South America prevent civil unrest (Horowitz, 1965).

Reflections on the Sociological Enterprise

Although most current research is shaped by the scientific method, both the choice of research topic and the decision to report one's findings are essentially determined by nonscientific considerations. It is in the process of conducting the research that one can most closely approximate the objectivity and precision of science. But the peculiarly human characteristics of interpretation and construction of reality make generalizations difficult, if not impossible.

The choice of research topic is often **nonscientific** whereas ideally the research methods used are **scientific.**

Each piece of research will be somewhat flawed; it is impossible to attain total accuracy, to control for all possible variables, or to be without bias. The scientific researcher is, at the very least, aware of these pitfalls and tries to take them into account when designing the study and reporting the findings.

Another way in which social science departs from the ideals of the scientific method is in its failure thus far to be *cumulative*, that is, to build upon previous research. This failure has led many critics to compare social science to the humanities rather than to the sciences. Some types of research—participant observations, case studies, and explorations of everyday behavior—do resemble works of art in their attention to detail and nuances of conversation, and in their focus on character. At the other extreme, some sociological research is presented with such complex statistics that few others can understand either the data or their implications. Clearly, any field that encompasses research on cocktail lounges and on modernization in developing nations will not be characterized by one set of basic theoretical propositions and fixed canons of research. This shapelessness can be both an irritant and a liberating factor.

More troublesome to deal with is the claim of *value neutrality* on the part of the social scientist. However scientifically research is carried out, can studies sponsored by funding organizations, which are increasingly departments of government, or research organizations ("think tanks") supported by business or labor interests, be value-free in choice of topics? And to what uses will the data be put? If information gathered by respected investigators is then applied to maintaining repressive institutions or to stifling dissent, for example, have the social scientists "sold out to the establishment"? An often-debated case in point is research into worker motivation that is then used by management to increase output. Thus, the claim of value neutrality can itself be taken as a value-laden position *not* to care about the consequences of one's research or the uses to which others might put the data.

Either way, the social scientist is not an entirely objective or neutral observer. Every piece of research, however carefully constructed and scientifically pursued, has an implicit or explicit value orientation.

Summary

Sociologists test their theories of social life through research. This chapter examines the importance of research, the scientific and nonscientific factors involved in the research process, the methods used, the type of information derived, and ways in which data are described and analyzed.

Much of what we think is common-sense knowledge is neither common nor accurate. The systematic examination of relationships among social facts is crucial for our understanding of the world and for making sound social policy decisions. Knowledge is gained in different ways. Whereas subjective understanding is based on the individual's own perception of the world, or intuition, the scientific method involves objective observation, precise measurement, and full disclosure of research methods and results.

The research process involves four major steps: (1) selecting the research question, (2) choosing the most appropriate method for collecting the necessary information, (3) analyzing the data gathered, and (4) reporting the findings. Deciding what to study may involve nonscientific factors, such as the researcher's values and attitudes, or considerations of time and funding. Framing the research question involves the selection of variables, and formulating hypotheses regarding the relationship among variables. The translation of these hypotheses and abstract variables into observable items is called "operationalizing the variables."

Selecting the most appropriate research method depends on the respondents sought, the nature of the information, and the type of data required. Methods chosen may involve cross-section studies, panel or longitudinal studies, large-scale social surveys, intensive interviews, observational techniques, secondary analysis of available official, historical, and comparative data, and/or an experimental design.

The collected information must be arranged so that groups of respondents and variables can be compared. Statistics such as percentages, ratios, and measures of central tendency are used to describe the data.

When completed, research findings are published or reported to colleagues at professional meetings. The reporting of findings enables others to evaluate the research and to judge those seeking to influence social policy. Although the research process is guided by the scientific method, the choice of research topics and the decision to report findings are influenced by nonscientific considerations. These considerations involve ethical issues such as the uses to which the data can be put, and the extent to which funding agencies shape and control the findings. Sociologists cannot be entirely value neutral, although they can conduct their research in as scientific a manner as possible.

Value neutrality refers to the ideal of objectivity in all aspects of the research project. (Drawing by Fraden, © 1980 *The New Yorker* Magazine, Inc.)

Suggested Readings

BECKER, HOWARD S., BLANCHE GEER, EVERETT C. HUGHES, and ANSELM STRAUSS. *Boys in White: Student Culture in Medical School.* Chicago, Ill.: University of Chicago Press, 1961. The link between theory and observation is well illustrated in this influential longitudinal study of medical students as they are transformed from idealists into professional physicians.

COLE, STEPHEN. *The Sociological Method* (Third Edition). Chicago, Ill.: Rand McNally, 1980. A very clear and concise introduction to the methods and logic of sociological research.

HOROWITZ, IRVING LOUIS. *The Rise and Fall of Project Camelot.* Cambridge, Mass.: M.I.T., 1967. A case study of what happens when the needs of government determine the nature of academic research.

LOFLAND, JOHN. *Analyzing Social Settings.* Belmont, Calif.: Wadsworth, 1971. A useful guide to the collection and interpretation of nonstatistical or qualitative data.

MILLMAN, MARCIA. *The Unkindest Cut.* New York: Morrow, 1977. A two-year observational study of American medicine—the operating and emergency rooms, the mortality review committees, the hospital staff meetings, and the patterns of thought and action that allow medical personnel to cope with stress, mistakes, and failure.

SHOSTAK, ARTHUR. *Our Sociological Eye: Personal Essays on Society and Culture.* Sherman Oaks, Calif.: Alfred, 1977. Vivid firsthand accounts of the personal and professional problems and satisfactions of being a sociologist.

(Source: *Stock, Boston*.)

Part II

Self in Society

In the following four chapters you will learn about the many ways human beings create a world of meaning and patterns of conduct that allow groups to survive over long periods of time. In Chapter 3, *culture* is described as an enveloping context of values, rules, behaviors, and products created by a particular social group. Chapter 4 examines social structure: those regularities of thought and action that make group life predictable. The process whereby infants learn the culture and its structured expectations is *socialization* and is described in Chapter 5. The goal of socialization is conformity on the part of group members, but no human can be so fully socialized that variations in thought and behavior do not occur. Indeed, the active mind is by definition capable of thinking about the unknown, the forbidden, and the unthinkable. Thus, conformity and deviance, which is behavior outside the accepted rules for that group, are both possible outcomes of social interaction. They are examined in Chapter 6.

3

The Culture Context

*I*n 1966 a native Indian trapper in the Philippines discovered a group of about two dozen individuals living in the depth of a rain forest. These people, who called themselves Tasaday, had evolved their own astonishingly simple way of life in almost total isolation from other groups of Philippine natives. They had no clothing other than an orchid leaf or two; they had bamboo blades and chipped stone hammers for tools, monkey skulls for toys, wooden drills for making fire, and caves for homes. The Tasaday had a Stone Age *culture*—a fully developed way of life perfectly suited to their environment.

Culture is the design for living of a group whose members share a given location, feel responsible for one another, and call themselves by the same name. The culture of such a group (or society) consists of (1) solutions to the problems of survival, (2) the ideals and values that shape rules of conduct, and (3) tools and other human-made objects (*artifacts* or material culture).

Culture is the design for living of a group whose members share a consciousness of kind.

Tasaday Culture

In terms of our model of cultural components, the Tasaday way of life can be described in this way.

Adaptation to the Environment. Living in the jungle, near fresh-water streams, the Tasaday catch frogs, tadpoles, and crabs by hand. Roots, berries, fruits, and grubs can be gathered in a few hours each day. The only tools required are digging sticks for roots, fire for cooking the frogs and crabs, scrapers to sharpen bamboo, and a stone axe for cutting stalks. Their caves offer protection from weather and animals.

Order-Keeping and Defense. A group of two dozen individuals isolated from other societies needs very little in the way of either formal organization or weapons. Decisions are made by the adults together. Division of labor is minimal, with both men and women gathering food and tending the children. Since there is nothing from which to be defended, the Tasaday have no words for *war* or *fight*. Nor are their tools defined as being usable for fighting. The stone axe is for cutting vines; it has not occurred to the Tasaday to use it to harm people.

Orderly Reproduction. The primary survival problem for the Tasaday is orderly reproduction. The group has very few females, either adult or child, and the Tasaday have lost contact with the two small groups with which marriage partners had been exchanged in the past. The four female children cannot be expected eventually to replenish the group, especially since one or two may die during childbirth. If the unmarried males do not soon find brides, the Tasaday will disappear (as have thousands of such small bands before them).

The Tasaday evolved a Stone Age culture perfectly suited to their environment. (Source: Magnum.)

Socialization. With so minimal a culture there is little to be learned that cannot be directly transmitted from parent to children. The children are treated very gently, and the youngest are invariably cuddled or held by both the men and women of the group.

Belief System. As in most societies, an elaborate set of beliefs about life, death, dangers, dreams, and a Great Provider characterize the Tasaday. Told to remain in their caves by remote ancestors, the Tasaday believe that illness will destroy them if they move, and that a Bringer of Good Fortune will ultimately arrive.

THE LESSONS OF THE TASADAY

What can we learn from such a small group whose ways are so very different from our own?

Many anthropologists believe that the culture of the Tasaday is similar to that developed by the earliest groups of human beings. In observing the Tasaday, then, we may catch a glimpse of the past. Perhaps this is how most people lived 100,000 years ago in what are called the Stone Ages.

If so, at least some of our ancestors were gentle, unaggressive, child-centered, and generous. Far from being engaged in a vicious struggle for existence, they

Many anthropologists believe that Tasaday culture is similar to that of the earliest human groups.

could provide subsistence with a few hours' effort each day. Neither aggressiveness nor acquisitiveness (the desire to accumulate goods) is any more natural than caring and sharing. When metal tools were distributed among the Tasaday, one axe was left over, but no one claimed it because "no one needed another." Nor was any Tasaday concerned with acquiring control over the others. It is when resources are scarce that within-group and between-group conflicts emerge. Human nature embraces capacities for a range of behaviors—cooperative and competitive—that are selectively called forth by the demands of the situation.

Note also that the Tasaday had developed clear rules about who can marry whom. Bachelors without wives could *not* share those of the married men (that would disrupt social order), and they remained sexually unfulfilled because that was the way of the group. It is culture and not biological drives alone that shape human behavior; and this may nowhere be more true than among the earliest human groups whose survival must have depended on firm control of impulses and desire.

More importantly, it must *not* be thought that the Tasaday people are any less developed than contemporary North Americans. All living groups of human beings are fully evolved members of the same species—Homo sapiens. What distinguishes one group from the other is not a different type of body or mind, but differences in culture. The Tasaday have a Stone Age culture in terms of tools and social organization just as we have a culture and social structure based on industrialization. We may appear to be more intelligent but this is because we "stand on the shoulders of giants" in the sense that we have the whole of Western history and culture to build upon. Surely, the great affection which the Tasaday display toward one another and especially toward their children could be considered superior to the feelings and customs of many other societies.

From Simple to Complex

You may often have heard the Tasaday and similar groups described as *uncultured* or *primitive* or *uncivilized*. Such terms are inaccurate as well as value-laden. As we have just demonstrated, the Tasaday have a culture, but one that is considerably less complex than ours.

Cultures (and social systems) may be arranged along a continuum from the most simple to the most complex.

Cultures can be roughly arranged along a continuum of complexity.

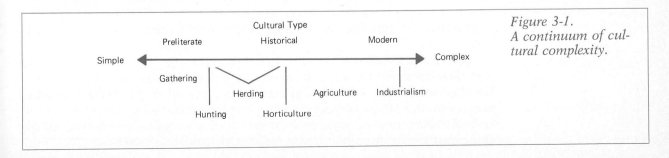

Figure 3-1.
A continuum of cultural complexity.

In today's world, cultures vary from the most simple to extremely complex.
(Sources: Photo Researchers, Inc. and the Museum of Natural History.)

The Tasaday culture is the most simple we know today, whereas that of North American and Western European societies are the most complex. Complexity is typically measured by the number of different characteristics and artifacts, or by the level of technology. If we were to use religion or family relationships as criteria of complexity, the placement of cultures would be reversed, with technologically simple societies having the most elaborate belief systems and kinship arrangements. The scheme we have chosen, therefore, represents a value judgment and one that is rooted in our culture—that economic variables and behaviors are dominant. We make this choice because the productive base of a society has the most extensive effects on all other aspects of social life, especially through its consequences on the size and density of populations. In general, cultural complexity can be classified by the *mode of subsistence*, that is, how the group adapts to the environment.

Mode of subsistence refers to how a group adapts to its particular environment.

MODE OF SUBSISTENCE

With each shift to a wider economic base, a larger population can be supported. An increase in population creates problems of order, division of labor, and coordination of activities. The more specialized the tasks of group members, the more training is required for each type of worker. No longer are people somewhat interchangeable; rather, groups of specialists emerge.

For example, when *hunting* is added to a gathering economy, some individuals (young males, typically) become exclusive hunters, whereas others (women) are primarily gatherers. Hunting requires new tools—spears, clubs, bows and arrows—and the technology for preparing and using them effectively. Skins must be scraped, meat cooked (perhaps even stored); hides, bones, and sinews used to make other tools. All these new traits increase the pool of knowledge and collective talent of the group.

Herding adds such specialties as the care and breeding of animals, and *horticulture* (simple farming) involves elementary knowledge of plants, harvesting, and preparing land. Each of these economic systems is more complex than the preceding mode. Settlements are larger and more permanent; the number and variety of tools and activities increase; new traits are invented or borrowed from other societies—basketry, weaving, pottery.

The discovery of *agriculture* marks a great turning point in social and cultural development. Agriculture differs from horticulture by being more systematic. Rather than letting seeds fall where they may, furrows are plowed, seeds planted and crops harvested at set times, and a surplus is created in good seasons. This surplus leads to a variety of new group characteristics and adaptations. For example, trading with other groups becomes possible, leading to travel and culture contacts. Means of transportation and methods of bookkeeping are required. For the surplus remaining with the growers, storage facilities—warehouses, pots, or baskets—must be created, and some means of record-keeping devised. This is the origin of number systems and writing, as ways of keeping track of who owns what.

A very late but equally revolutionary shift in the mode of subsistence was introduced with the *industrial revolution* of the past 150 years. The construction of factories for the production of goods has radically changed the culture base and social structure of most societies throughout the world.

TYPES OF SOCIETIES

The terms we shall use in place of value-laden words such as *primitive* or *uncivilized* are *simple* or *preliterate*. *Preliterate* means without a written language and correctly describes most preagricultural societies. Agricultural societies are considered *historical* because some written record has been left, although preliterate people have fully developed languages and a vital tradition of oral history. *Modern* societies are those that have entered the industrial mode. All three types of society are contemporary in the sense that examples of each exist today. In North America, for example, within the two major industrial societies there are also Inuit herders and Amish agriculturists, among others.

Hunting is a more specialized mode of subsistence than gathering and requires a new technology.

Herding is based on the care of domesticated animals.

Horticulture involves knowledge of plants and land preparation.

Agriculture is more systematic than horticulture and its discovery was a major turning point in cultural development.

The **industrial revolution** based on the factory system marked another dramatic shift in the mode of subsistence.

Preliterate societies are those that do not have a written language.

Historical societies have left some form of written records.

Modern societies are characterized by industrial production.

The Importance of Culture

Culture refers to whatever is learned and created by members of human groups. At least 3 million years ago, an almost-upright creature roamed central Africa. When it achieved an upright posture, many other changes took place, including the development of larger brains and voice boxes, and a narrowing of the pelvic

Culture replaces physical evolution as the means whereby humans adapt to their environment.

Culture is based on the capacity for language, and on the relative helplessness of human infants.

canal. These changes were crucial for the emergence of culture as the prime means of adapting to the environment.

Humans have the great gift of language as a result of their larger and more complex brains combined with flexible voice apparatus. The fact that human infants, with their larger brains, must be born at a relatively early stage in development in order to pass through the narrowed birth canal, means that they are born in a more helpless, unfinished state than other animal young, and must depend upon others to care for them during their formative years. Here is the key to social life: the requirement that human beings live in groups able to care for their dependent infants. Here, too, is the key to culture: the ability to use language to share experiences and to communicate knowledge so that each generation need not reinvent the wheel.

Relative to body size, the human brain is larger than that of other animals. The human brain is also more complex, with a larger number of pathways, connections, and specialized parts than is that of the chimpanzee, our closest relative in terms of shape and behavior. What this human brain does is to *mediate*—come between—the impulses inherited as part of our primate past and our ability as Homo Sapiens to use this thinking capacity to select courses of action.

In other words, *human behavior is guided by the human mind.* Thus, human evolution and the emergence of culture can also be described as a progressive weakening of instinctive behavior in favor of behavior mediated by thought. Very little, if any, human activity can be considered dominated by instinct if instinct is defined as an automatic response to some urging from within the body, as illustrated in the classical model of instinctual behavior of Figure 3-2:

Instinct refers to drive arousal and subsequent action as one unbroken chain of behavior.

$$\text{Drive arousal} \longrightarrow \text{Action}$$

In this model, a drive or deep impulse of the organism is aroused, typically through the absence of some activity essential to survival (eating, sleeping, eliminating, sexual release). The aroused need then leads to some tension-relieving action, *all as one unbroken chain of behavior.*

With human behavior the continuous sequence of drive arousal and tension-relieving action is monitored by the thinking, choosing and interpreting capacities of homo sapiens. Our complex brains allow us to control our behavior rather than be driven by automatic responses. Human beings can reflect on the state of their bodies—define what is arousing and when—and can select from a range of approved behaviors those that will reduce discomfort. A model of human behavior is illustrated by Figure 3-3:

$$\text{Drive arousal} \xleftarrow{\hspace{1cm}} \overset{\text{Reflective mind}}{/\ /} \xrightarrow{\hspace{1cm}} \text{Action}$$

Human behavior is mediated by the reflective mind.

The reflective mind is one that permits us to see ourselves as both the subject and object of action, and this capacity distinguishes humans from other animals. Note that the mind affects both sides of the model: how the state of one's body is interpreted and what one does in response.

Hunger pangs, for example, are a universal bodily reaction to an empty stomach. But how an individual's brain records and interprets these signals depends on the eating schedules of the group and the meanings attached to eating. If three meals a day is the custom, a person is likely to recognize hunger three times a day; if one meal, then only once. Religious fasters may interpret their stomach rumbles as a sign of virtue; dieters will try to ignore them. What the individual does about hunger, once its existence is recognized, is similarly varied from one society to another, or from one situation to another within a society. North Americans do not, as a rule, growl or grab whatever edible is in sight, but rather, select from a range of appropriate responses. We may wait until the next scheduled meal, beg food from others, buy a snack, or whatever else is in keeping with our definition of the situation and our ideas about ourselves.

It is those active, creative, selecting capacities made possible by the human brain that account for our humanness. Of all creatures on Earth, we are the least driven by uncontrollable impulses. In fact, it is precisely this *flexibility* or lack of a single set response that has been selected for in the millions of years of human evolution. We alone can create rules for our own behavior, agree together on what can and cannot be done in our group, *and* change these rules when conditions require it. It is this flexibility which gives humans their evolutionary advantage. Our minds allow us to transcend (overcome) the limitations of the body and its drives. We devise rules for living and extend the possibilities of our bodies by creating culture.

> The human evolutionary advantage is the ability to transcend instinct and select from a variety of learned behaviors.

In one of the first systematic explorations of the link between culture and society, Clyde Kluckhohn, an anthropologist, and Henry Murray, a psychologist, presented a scheme we can paraphrase as:

In some respects, all humans are alike.

In other respects, they are like some others.

And in still other ways, no person is like any other.

(Adapted from Kluckhohn and Murray, 1948)

In other words:

1. Our common humanity makes us alike in certain needs and capacities. Every society must deal with basic human drives, and there are limits to what is humanly possible. These human needs give rise to the broad patterns of behavior found in all societies—the institutional spheres.
2. But since each society evolves in a different fashion from any other, members will share certain characteristics as a result of common experiences, while each society differs from any other. This accounts for similarities among members of the same society, and the great differences in customs and personality types between societies.
3. Yet within the same society, even within the same subgroup or family, no one person has precisely the same experiences as another. Therefore, each individual is unique because she or he is responding to a unique set of life events.

> Human beings share many basic traits, but there are also cultural variations that make each group different, and individual experiences that make each person unique.

The end result of growing up in a particular society and family is an individual who can adapt to that society's requirements but who remains a distinct personality. Diversity exists within limits necessary for human and social survival.

Studying Culture

Anthropologists typically study preliterate cultures whereas sociologists study modern societies.

Field work is the method by which anthropologists study the culture and social organization of human groups.

Culture is an abstraction that is inferred from what people do and say.

In general, anthropologists study simple or preliterate cultures and sociologists study modern societies and cultures. Both use similar perspectives but differ primarily in method. Anthropologists conduct *field work* with the group under study, much like participant observation. The modern anthropologist must know the language of the group and must be trained to observe all behaviors. Native informants are a frequent source of information, but above all, the contemporary anthropologist lives with the people being studied, and becomes immersed in their way of life.

Sociologists use the various methods described in Chapter 2 to gather data on relatively complex societies or particular groups within a society. From this data, statements can be made about patterned behaviors, values, and beliefs. But describing culture is not an easy task because culture is an abstraction. Most of its elements cannot be touched or tasted, but must be inferred from what people do and say about what they do.

Kluckhohn and Kroeber (1952) have compared describing culture to constructing a map:

> A map is not a concrete piece of land but, rather, an abstract representation of a particular area. If a map is accurate and one can read it, one does not get lost. If a culture is correctly portrayed, one will realize the existence of the distinctive features of a way of life and their interrelationships (p. 50).

The major points to keep in mind are these:

Culture develops over time according to the specific history of the group.

Culture is learned and transmitted from one generation to another.

Culture is understood and shared by members of a particular society.

Various **culture traits** (single characteristics) usually form **patterns** (sets of traits).

The culture of any one group is composed of many elements that form a relatively unified whole. That is, there is a tendency for various *culture traits* (single items) and *patterns* (sets of traits) to be consistent with one another. This is called *cultural integration.*

A distinction must be made between *ideal* and *real* elements of culture. Few individuals are perfect embodiments of ideal traits, and societies are rarely as smooth-running as they "should" be.

Culture may be experienced and enacted differently by different members of the group. Not all are expected to behave the same way or to participate similarly in the life of the group, as for example, adults and children, or men and women in most societies.

In most respects, culture is the water in the fishbowl—the beliefs, values, and knowledge in our heads, the rules that guide behavior, and the language through which all these are expressed. This chapter is titled the "Culture Context" precisely to convey the sense of culture as encompassing all social action. The phrase "web of culture" also suggests the image of an intricate framework of many strands that fit together to compose an integrated whole: the way of life of any human group.

Culture can be described in terms of both the structural elements common to all and the particular selection of traits that compose any given pattern of culture.

CULTURAL UNIVERSALS AND CULTURAL VARIABILITY

To what degree are all cultures somewhat similar? And to what extent are they unique? Broadly put, because every culture is created by human beings with basic needs and capacities, and because every society must solve the same problems of group survival, there are certain elements found in all cultures. These are *cultural universals*.

Cultural universals are elements found in all cultures.

Social institutions are universals because groups failing to develop effective patterns for adapting to the environment, maintaining order, reproducing new members, training new members, and developing belief systems, cease to exist. Thus in every society there exists a set of rules and behaviors that can be identified as economic, political, familial, educational, and religious. In addition, anthropologists have found dozens of items that appear in all known cultures: body adornment, funeral rites, food taboos, medicine, magic, and tool making, to mention only a few (Murdock, 1945).

Yet each society will differ from all others in the unique content of its culture: its precise economic system or courtship rituals, and so on. Because of history, the geographic location of the group, and unpatterned trial-and-error attempts to stay alive and stick together, each group evolves its own selection of cultural items, rules, and behaviors. This process accounts for *cultural variability* and the astonishing variety of customs, beliefs, and artifacts that characterize Homo sapiens. Within the limits of human imagination and human abilities, people have devised any number of solutions to the tasks of survival. For example, since no group can endure over time without arranging for the orderly reproduction of infants, there are rules of courtship and marriage in all known societies, but these range from a communal ceremony among individuals who may never live together, to child marriages, to two North American couples on a double date.

Cultural variability refers to the diversity in any one culture's specific set of traits.

The Basis of Culture: Symbols and Language

One crucial consequence of the evolution of the human brain is the capacity to use *symbols*. The Greek word *symbola* refers to the two halves of an object that are kept by individuals to remind them that they have entered a contract with one another. The symbola stand for the contract as a whole. The meaning of a symbol is determined by people who agree, for example, that the Star of David will stand for Judaism, the Cross will symbolize Christianity, and a Crescent and Star will signify Islam. Neither the star nor the cross nor any other object is self-evident; its meaning is conferred by human beings in communication with each other. *Language* is the means whereby symbols are created and transmitted.

Symbols are items to which meaning is attached by members of a group.

Language is the means by which symbols are created and transmitted.

Animals can be taught the meaning of certain gestures; a raised hand, for instance, can mean "stay"; and pets soon learn to recognize the sound of their own names. Some chimpanzees have even been taught Standard American Sign Language. There has been controversy over whether or not one or two highly trained chimpanzees have been able to create a few new (untaught) gestures. Such an ability, however, seems very limited when compared to the human child's capacity for handling hundreds of symbols, generating new meanings, and producing a steady flow of untaught concepts.

It is this human capacity for symbol creation and transmission that is both the basis of culture and its product. The same evolutionary developments that produced the reflective mind—the reduction of jawbone muscles, the placement of the head on a spinal column, the hand–eye interaction required by standing upright—also freed areas in the throat and brain for the equipment that makes controlled speech possible. The voice box, tongue, and special sectors of the brain for the production and deciphering of sounds, all evolve in a reinforcing spiral along with the other physiological changes that make human beings peculiarly dependent upon one another. The combination of a complex brain and the capacity for speech lead to the emergence of language as the critical factor in the development of culture. "Human social systems are all mediated by language; perhaps this is why there are no forms of behavior among nonhuman primates that correspond to religion, politics, or even economics" (Washburn, 1978, p. 208).

Nonverbal Communication.   Not all communication is through speech. Gestures, facial expressions, and body movements are all means of transmitting a message without words. The study of nonverbal communication is called *kinesics* (Birdwhistle, 1970), and, as is the case for spoken communication, requires knowledge of the culture for correct interpretation. Some gestures in different societies can have very different meanings, whereas other gestures are more universal—a smile, for example, conveys much the same message in any culture.

> **Kinesics** is the study of nonverbal communication.

Within one society the same gesture can have different meanings depending upon the context: saluting an officer on a military base is a sign of respect; saluting one's parents is a gesture of defiance. Gestures that are appropriate in one circumstance may not be so highly regarded in another—the raised fist of black athletes at the 1968 Olympic Games was widely interpreted as a Black Power statement thought to be out of place on the winners' platform. The athletes felt that their gesture was an appropriate symbol of discontent with race relations in the United States.

Edward Hall, in *The Silent Language* (1959), has noted the characteristic distance maintained between individuals speaking to one another in various cultures: head-to-head in some societies, several feet away in others. These distances signify general ideas about privacy and the "bubble of personal space" to which one is entitled. More recent studies have focused on the hidden messages concerning power and social worth that are conveyed by body gestures. For example, the relative power of individuals is expressed in the greater tendency for men to touch women and for adults to violate the private space of children (Thorne & Henley, 1975). In the United States, whites have traditionally been the initiators of conversations with blacks. When the situation is re-

Cultural ideas of privacy and personal space are conveyed by the distance maintained by interacting individuals. (Sources: Stock, Boston and Photo Researchers, Inc.)

versed, whites become anxious ("they're so pushy") because their power to control the interaction is challenged.

LANGUAGE AND PERCEPTION

Not only do language and nonverbal communication reflect the values, norms, and relationships of a culture, but they also *structure perception*. That is, a member of a given society sees, interprets, and understands the world through the screen of culture as embodied in language.

This thesis—that language shapes the form and content of a person's thoughts—was most forcefully argued by the linguists Edward Sapir and Benjamin Whorf, and is known as the "Sapir-Whorf Hypothesis":

> Human beings do not live in an objective world alone . . but are very much at the mercy of the particular language which has become a medium of expression for their society.
> The 'real world' is to a large extent unconsciously built up on the language habits of the group. No two languages are ever sufficiently similar to be considered as representing the same social reality. The worlds in which different societies live are distinct worlds, not merely the same world with different labels attached. [Sapir, 1949]

Sapir and Whorf arrived at their hypothesis from studies of the way members of various societies perceived such fundamental aspects of the world as time, space, and color. For example, Whorf reported that the Hopi Indians of the Southwest United States had no words to convey past, present, or future time because the Hopi way is timeless. Therefore, the Hopi sense of time is very different from that of the linear, clock-obsessed North American. This type of distinction is familiar to watchers of cowboy movies, who may remember that some Native Americans measure distance in terms of time: "How far to the nearest town, Tonto?" "Two moons, Master."

Language and nonverbal communication reflect values, norms, and relationships, and **structure perception.**

61

Vocabulary provides a clue to understanding aspects of the environment important for group survival.

Language is also useful for understanding aspects of the environment that are important for group survival. The Eskimo have over a dozen words to describe snow because it is essential to know whether or not the snowfall will be wet or dry, from a certain direction, likely to be long or of short duration, and so on. North American teenagers know the year, style, and make of scores of automobiles because it is a matter of reputation among males to be aware of these subtle differences. In another, less complex society, one word would embrace all "vehicles with four wheels" just as we have one word for "snow" with a few descriptive terms.

Words also have an evaluative dimension; some will connote "good" things and others the "bad." The use of words to evoke emotion and to structure thought is most obvious in the political arena. Anticommunists in the United States are fond of referring to the Soviet Union as "atheistic," and the Communists of the People's Republic of China used to speak of "capitalist running dogs" when alluding to the United States.

Because members of any society learn a particular version of reality through the lens of language, cross-cultural understanding is problematic. This is why an anthropological field worker must learn the language of the group under study and come to see the world as a speaker of that tongue. Otherwise false meanings will be attributed to the actions of others, as was common among nineteenth-century social scientists and is still common among naïve observers today.

Manipulation of the Symbolic Significance of Words

The current struggle between feminist and antifeminist forces in North America is characterized by a war of words. Very cleverly, antifeminists have defused the negative thrust of their "anti" stance by referring to themselves as "pro-family," a double plus. *Pro* means "for" and *family* arouses positive sentiments. By claiming that they are pro-family, these groups place the feminists on the defensive as "anti-family." Similarly, groups opposed to abortion call themselves pro-life. Those who support a woman's ability to terminate a pregnancy therefore become "anti-life." In an attempt to counteract the extremely negative connotation of anti-life, or even pro-abortion, leaders of the Women's Movement speak of "reproductive freedom" and a "woman's right to choose." *Freedom* and *rights* evoke positive values, whereas the opposition becomes *anti-choice*.

Another facet of feminist concern with language revolves around the use of the word *man* to mean humans in general. If language channels perception and structures thought, some feminists contend that women are rendered invisible by the use of the term *man* for all humans. A study of students' reactions to sociology textbooks (Schneider & Hacker, 1973) found that students interpreted the universal *man* to mean actual male figures; but when sex-neutral terms were used, students were able to visualize females in important social positions.

Attempts to desex the language in order to broaden perception are often subjected to ridicule. The question of what to call manhole covers usually reduces the issue to absurdity. Words *can* kill. Yet how would a man react to the continual receipt of letters addressed to "Dear Madam"?

ETHNOCENTRISM AND CULTURAL RELATIVISM

In making cross-cultural comparisons, we tend to evaluate the customs of others in the light of our own beliefs and values. After all, one universal characteristic of culture is the assumption that one's own design for living is the best and only correct way. Often, the name chosen for the group means "the people," with the understanding that those not sharing the culture are not "people" but "them," outsiders, who are often identified by words that consciously dehumanize (for example, "pig," "gook," and other terms used to designate members of religious, racial, or ethnic minorities).

The belief that one's own culture represents the only true and good way and the subsequent tendency to judge other cultures by those standards is called *ethnocentrism* (from *ethno* = race, group, people; *centric* = revolving around, tending toward). Ethnocentrism serves several important functions for individuals and groups: A conviction of the righteousness of one's beliefs and behaviors reinforces the tendency to conform and to defend one's society. Ethnocentrism may be essential for social solidarity, the glue that holds the group together.

Ethnocentrism is the belief that one's own culture represents the only true and good way.

Ethnocentrism becomes dysfunctional (reduces the adaptability of a social system) when beliefs in one's superiority lead to hostility, misunderstandings that provoke conflict, and a refusal to find value in other peoples' ways of life. Tensions between groups and nations are often heightened by ethnocentrism. If other people are judged less than human, it becomes possible to treat them differently from those defined as "like us." In North American history, each new ethnic, religious, or racial group was thought to be inferior to white, Anglo-Saxon Protestants, and therefore deserving of less than humane treatment.

The social scientist strives to rise above ethnocentric limitations and adopt the stance of objective observer of all cultures. Aspects of culture should be judged in terms of the meanings attached to them in a given society and not by standards derived from another culture. This attitude of objectivity is called *cultural relativism* and involves the attempt to understand the world as seen by members of other societies. Value judgments based on one's own culture are replaced, as far as possible, by an appreciation of the values embodied in other cultures. The social scientist does not ask if cultural elements are good or bad according to some absolute yardstick but, rather, why does the element exist, how is it sustained, and what purpose does it serve in that culture? "Does it work for that group?" is the standard for evaluating culture items. The basic assumption—itself a value judgment—in cultural relativism is that each group's solutions to the tasks of survival are as valid as any other's, however unappealing these patterns may seem to someone from another society. Cultural adaptations, therefore, can be compared in terms of the degree to which they appear to enhance the survival of the group, but not by other criteria imposed from outside. In practice, however, all definitions of what works are bound up in culture-specific values. Perhaps the best one can do is to try to remain aware of the biases brought to any value judgment.

An attitude of objectivity assumed by social scientists towards other cultures is called **cultural relativism.**

Ideal and Real Culture. Within any society, the observer distinguishes cultural *ideals* from the actual content being transmitted among members. In the United States, for example, a cultural ideal, enshrined in law, is tolerance of diverse religious beliefs. Nonetheless, children are taught to abhor atheists, and adults regularly attempt to introduce prayer periods into the public schools.

Cultural ideals reflect the highest virtues and ideal standards of a society, whereas **real culture** refers to actual behavior.

There are many such examples in every culture. Few members of any society can consistently maintain ideal standards of conduct. Thus, the *real culture* often consists of explanations for behavior that falls short of the highest virtue. The rationalizations used to deny equality to members of racial minorities in North America demonstrate the strength of the real culture when in conflict with the ideal.

Elements of Culture

TRAITS, COMPLEXES, AND THEMES

The simplest unit of culture that can be isolated for analysis is the **trait.**

A **culture complex** is comprised of a network of patterns encompassing individual traits.

The simplest unit of culture for cross-cultural comparison is the *trait*, a single item that can be isolated for analysis: a tool, a form of greeting, a technique, a belief, and so forth. Each culture trait, however, is actually embedded in a set of patterns called a *culture complex*. As one example, the manner in which a son addresses his father is a culture trait that varies widely among societies, from great formality (My master) to relative informality (Dad). Yet to understand these differences, it is important to place the father–son relationship in the broader complex of traits that compose that society's kinship system.

Similarly an ice hockey game is composed of many elements that combine to create the reality of ice hockey in North America: skates and skaters; techniques and skills; arenas and rinks; fans and bettors; attitudes about bravery, grace, and violence; local pride and nationalistic fervor; even drinking beer and brawling in the stands. All together, these traits, each of which could be found in another context, form the culture complex of contemporary ice hockey.

Culture complexes reflect general **themes** or core values and assumptions that shape beliefs and behaviors.

To understand fully the meaning of ice hockey, or any other aspect of culture, one must also realize that this set of activities is a subunit of a larger cultural pattern or *theme;* in this case, the place of sports in our society. Sports in North America are woven into a set of values and beliefs about masculinity and achievement, just as the buffalo hunt symbolized individual courage and tribal solidarity among the Plains Indians, or as the tea ceremony reflects the themes of courtesy and elegance among Japanese.

NORMS AND VALUES

X **Social norms** are rules regarding behavior that are both **prescriptions**—details of acceptable acts, and **proscriptions**—lists of actions that are not acceptable.

Part of the learned tradition of any group are rules of conduct and the broader values from which the rules are derived. Rules regarding behavior are called *social norms*. These are both *prescriptions*—the details that make up an appropriate act (just as a physician's prescription specifies the chemicals to prepare a medication)—and *proscriptions*—lists of actions that are not acceptable (*taboos*).

Some norms are more important than others. For example, rules that involve behavior essential to group well-being ("thou shalt not steal") are typically of greater weight than rules of personal hygiene ("brush your teeth"). Many norms are simply a matter of taste and others allow little leeway. Yet behaviors thought essential in one society may not be in another. Putting color on one's face is relatively optional in North America, but is an essential element of culture in Hindu societies where social position is symbolized by such markings.

Body scars that would lead to revulsion in our society are requirements for becoming an adult among many African tribes, and prior to World War I, German military officers intentionally rubbed salt into a facial wound to produce a scar that testified to their courage and nobility. In other words, the meaning and strength of a norm must be found within that culture and in relation to ultimate values held by its members at any given time.

How can the observer evaluate the strength of a norm? Usually members of the society will be able to indicate which rules are more important than others, but the confusion between ideal and real culture may render such testimony questionable. If you were asked to describe the norms of your society in rank order from most powerful to least, could you do so easily? Would you list ideal norms such as playing the game well or real norms such as playing to win at all costs?

Classifying Norms.   One common scheme for classifying norms distinguishes *folkways*, *mores*, and *laws*.

Folkways.   Quite literally, folkways are the way of the people; that is, customs and habits that are passed from generation to generation as "the way we do it." Eating with a knife and fork in contrast to chopsticks or one's fingers is an example of a folkway. Generally, folkways govern behavior relatively unimportant from the standpoint of group survival. Our society will not be threatened if all infants refuse to use their spoons, although parental authority might suffer. Quaint folkways such as opening a door for a woman, once defined as a sign of respect is now often perceived as an act of condescension.

However trivial these examples may appear, some societal values are involved: standards of hygiene in the case of eating utensils, an assumption of female fragility in the case of chivalry. Yet the folkways are not considered crucial enough to be strongly enforced. No officer of the courts will punish the little girl who eats with her fingers or the man who refuses to tip his hat to a woman. The parent who seeks to teach proper eating habits will perhaps strike the child's hand, take away the plate of food, ask the child to leave the room, or convey disapproval in some direct but nonviolent fashion. These reactions to nonnormative behavior are called *informal* because they are handled in face-to-face interaction. Such attempts to shape the behavior of others are called *sanctions*. Sanctions are responses from others that convey the information that a person is either performing within normative limits or has violated their expectations. Folkways, then, are enforced by *informal sanctions* administered by others in the interaction. Negative sanctions warn the individual to observe the folkways more closely; positive sanctions give assurance that one's behavior is approved.

Mores.   Always spoken of in the plural (*mos* is the singular), mores are customs and rules of conduct that have acquired a sense of necessity. No longer is this behavior pattern simply "the way we do it" but, now, "the way it *must* be done." It is this added dimension of command that distinguishes mores from folkways; a touch of sacredness has been attached. Mores are considered to have a moral component that reflects their greater importance to the group. Respect for authority, observance of civic and religious ritual, restraints on sexuality, and helping friends are all behaviors that add to the well-being and adaptive potential of human groups.

Folkways are customs and habits passed on from generation to generation.

Sanctions refer to reactions that convey approval or disapproval of one's behavior.

Folkways are usually enforced through **informal sanctions.**

Mores are customs and rules of conduct that have acquired a sense of necessity and sacredness.

Those who violate the mores are, therefore, subject to stronger sanctions than are those who transgress folkways. Whereas the folkways depend upon people's willingness to adhere to custom, mores are almost obligatory standards. Group reactions such as scorn, withdrawal, and ostracism replace the more personal reactions to violators of folkways. These sanctions are still informal, but increasingly powerful because the full force of the community is brought to bear on the offender. Thus, adulteresses in New England once wore red *A*s to set them apart from moral members of the society; unwed mothers were shunned; town drunks avoided; sinners expelled from religious bodies; and disloyal individuals placed outside the protection of the group.

Yet however firmly the mores are enforced, individuals may choose to violate expectations if they are willing to accept the consequent loss of interpersonal support. Folkways are recommended behavior; mores are strongly encouraged. But the most powerful norms are those that apply to all members of a given group and are considered crucial standards of conduct: these are termed laws.

Laws.   Laws are *universal rules* that set clear limits on the behavior of all members of a given group. The laws are enforced by *formal sanctions*, that is, by designated individuals outside the circle of family and friends whose specific duties are to respond to violations of the norms.

Laws do not necessarily have to be written. It is from the force of the sanctions that an observer can differentiate laws from folkways and mores. And the force of sanctions is derived from the assumed importance of the behavior to the survival of the society. Laws, therefore, are rules that govern essential aspects of everyday life: honesty in business dealings, sanctity of family relationships, protection of public peace and similar aspects of orderliness in human affairs. The *Ten Commandments* can be considered the prime example of laws in this sense: they are the minimal set of rules that make social life possible.

> ✗ **Laws** are **universal rules** that set limits on the behavior of all members of the group, and that are enforced by **formal sanctions.**

The Ten Commandments

Thou shalt have no other Gods before me.
Thou shalt not make unto thee any graven image.
Thou shalt not take the name of the Lord thy God in vain.
Thou shalt observe the Sabbath and keep it holy.
Thou shalt honor thy father and thy mother.
Thou shalt not murder.
Thou shalt not commit adultery.
Thou shalt not steal.
Thou shalt not bear false witness against thy neighbor.
Thou shalt not covet thy neighbor's wife nor anything
    that is thy neighbor's possession.

—Deuteronomy: 5:7–18

These few simple laws can be seen to embrace all the elements of social order: obedience to a higher principle; respect for family elders; prohibitions against taking things from another, including life; honesty in testimony; and a reduction of jealousy. To have these rules actually written down may add to their effectiveness, but the laws of nonliterate groups were similarly thought to have divine origin. It is not the clay tablets but the significance of the behavior that creates laws.

Why are certain rules of conduct selected and not others? In general, the norms of any group are derived from some broader ideas about good and bad, right and wrong. These overarching concepts are called *values*.

Values. Ideas about what is worthwhile—the central beliefs of any society—form a standard against which the norms can be evaluated. Specific norms such as "thou shalt not murder" reflect a belief in the sanctity of human life and also the need of the group to avoid the internal feuds that might follow the murder of a family member. There are, however, exceptions even to universal values. Murder is condoned when done to the enemy during a war (indeed, honors are bestowed on those who kill the most), and death is the penalty imposed for breaking certain norms in many societies.

Each society is characterized by certain concepts of ultimate good, virtue, beauty, rightness, justice, and other abstract qualities. The norms reflect these values. If certain norms—those folkways, mores, and laws, for example, that in the past governed white–black relationships in the United States—are actually in conflict with values such as equality and justice, citizens are faced with a moral value conflict. The genius of the civil rights leadership of the 1960s was to appeal to the "higher" set of values of tolerance, brotherhood, and fairness that could no longer be easily ignored, and to use these values as the basis of social change.

The more complex the society and the more heterogeneous its population, the more likely it is to experience value conflicts. Different values in the same society can lead to norms and behaviors that encourage conflict, or individuals may find themselves forced to choose between opposite courses of conduct based on the same values. An example of the latter is the dilemma of olympic-class athletes in North America. Many were torn between patriotic motives to withdraw from the 1980 Olympiad in Moscow in order to protest the Soviet Union's armed intervention in Afghanistan and equally strong patriotic motives to participate in the games and excel for their country.

Ritual. *Rituals* are culturally patterned ways of dealing with drive-based behaviors and other anxiety-producing life events. For example, most societies have highly ritualized courtship and mating patterns, not genetically programmed as in the case of animals, but taught to each incoming generation of marriage partners. Similarly, birth, death, and the transition from childhood to adulthood are moments in the life course of individuals typically marked by elaborate ritual.

Public ceremonies that mark some important change in an individual's position in the society are known as *rites of passage* (Van Gennep, 1908/1960). Initiation ceremonies at puberty are among the most common. The precise ceremony varies from culture to culture: Plains Indian males are left on mountainsides to experience a vision; Jewish boys at age 13 recite from the Holy Scriptures during a Bar Mitzvah; Christians celebrate Confirmation; and in the Andaman Islands, a dance is held in honor of the boy who is soon to become a man, while his back and chest are specially scarred. Comparable ceremonies for females are very rare; the onset of the menstrual cycle is typically ignored or dealt with by avoidance, and in some societies an unmarried female must leave the village altogether during her menstrual period. But there are signs of change in modern societies. Among some Jewish congregations, for example, girls are also permitted to celebrate their passage to adulthood by reading from the scriptures.

Values are the central principles of a culture that provide a standard for the evaluation of rules of conduct.

Every society can be identified by ideas of ultimate good, virtue, beauty, rightness, justice and other abstract qualities.

Rituals are culturally patterned ways of dealing with biological drives and anxiety-producing life events.

Rites of passage are ceremonies that mark an important change in an individual's position in the group.

Varying from culture to culture, rites of passage mark some change in an individual's status in society. Here, a 13-year-old Jewish boy is initiated into manhood during his Bar Mitzvah. (Source: Photo Researchers, Inc.)

In every society, certain life changes are recognized as potentially dangerous for the individual and the group—a cultural universal. In each society, the ritual and its symbolism are different—cultural variation. The function of ritual, everywhere, is to relieve anxiety about the unknown and to bring human drives and emotions under the control of the group through the enactment of time-honored ceremonies.

These, then, are the essential elements of culture: traits, complexes, themes, norms, values, and rituals. Beliefs and behaviors, attitudes and artifacts compose the unique adaptation of any human group to its environment.

Cultural Integration.   Societies will vary in the degree to which the elements of culture are internally consistent. *Cultural integration* refers to the fit among culture complexes and themes and institutional arrangements. Professional sports could not be important in a society where competition is not considered a prime virtue, nor can marriages be arranged in a society where romantic love is thought to be the appropriate basis for mate selection. Human rights and

Cultural integration refers to the consistency among cultural complexes, themes, and institutional arrangements.

Among the strongest drives of humans are those aroused through hunger and thirst. Yet seldom does a person eat or drink the first things at hand. Unless under the most extreme circumstances, for example, North Americans would not drink urine or eat the flesh of another person, although both behaviors have been documented.

Eating, a simple and universal human activity, is everywhere surrounded by rules, rituals, values, symbols, and taboos. The individual act is transformed into a social event. There are typical foodstuffs for each society— Americans are great consumers of sugar, the French of wine, Italians of pasta, the Tasaday of tadpoles, the Eskimo of blubber, and so forth. A set of values and beliefs develops around these foods; special utensils and behaviors are required; the food has a "meaning" conferred by the group. One need think only of the Thanksgiving turkey in the United States to realize that we are not speaking of quaint customs of preliterate tribes: the nation's earliest settlers are evoked, the traditional/ideal family is sentimentalized, people are expected to give thanks to God. In sum, the value system of the United States is reinforced in this version of the world-wide custom of celebrating the harvest. In many societies the end of the growing season is an occasion for excesses—overeating and drinking, and sexual license not otherwise permitted. These releases of energy serve to reward past abstinence and to prepare members of the society for the relatively quiet months ahead.

Within a society, some individuals are distinguished from others by what they can eat and how much of it. Often, men and women have different food taboos, children have different diets from adults, the well-off from the poor, and strangers from natives. For example, in most cultures males are fed first and given choice pieces of food. Women and children are frequently forbidden to eat with adult males. Some insights into the relative power and prestige of members of your own family can be gained from observing who gets which portion and in what order.

civil liberties are foreign concepts in societies where the needs of the group are considered more important than those of individuals.

There is, in other words, a strain toward consistency among the various elements of culture. The more complex the society, the less likely the integration of its culture, simply because of the multiplicity of traits to be accommodated and the probability of rapid social change. Conversely, simple societies often have highly integrated cultures that may be more vulnerable to disruption and eventual disintegration when any one part undergoes change. The culture of a tribe called Yir Yorant collapsed when missionaries distributed steel axes to all members of the group, thus upsetting an authority structure based on the exclusive possession of stone axes by certain males and tribal elders (Sharp, 1952). In contrast, the introduction of new beliefs or techniques into North American societies can be absorbed without necessarily causing immediate adjustments in other areas of culture.

SUBCULTURES

We have defined culture as a group's response to the conditions of existence, that is, the adaptive, coping solutions to the problems of survival and the effects of history. If subgroups within a society have different experiences and if needs and opportunities vary from group to group, then we should expect diversity in

X Subgroups within a society that display differences in values, beliefs, norms, and behaviors are called **subcultures**.

lifestyle among these subgroups. Such differences in values, beliefs, norms, and behaviors are called *subcultural adaptations* or *subcultures*.

Subcultures are likely to appear wherever access to the general culture is not the same for all members of a society. As all but the most simple societies are characterized by division of labor, specialization, and differences in power and prestige, subgroups can be identified in almost every society. The more complex the culture and social system, and the more heterogeneous the population, the greater the probability that a society contains a number of subcultures.

Subcultures are variations on the general cultural themes that permit the subgroup to survive under different conditions than those that face the dominant group(s). In North America, racial, ethnic, and religious minorities have constructed subcultural adaptations to their situation. In many cases, retaining some of the Old World customs and language permitted the first generation of immigrants to survive their abrupt change. In the case of French-speaking Canadians, Puerto Rican citizens of the United States, and blacks throughout North America, their language, skin color, or cultural distinctiveness still elicit discrimination. As long as this is so, the need for subcultural adaptations and supports will remain strong.

Jargon is the special language adapted by members of a subculture to protect themselves from outsiders.

Boundary Maintenance.   Members of subgroups can protect themselves from outsiders by creating and reinforcing group boundaries. This is the function of special languages or *jargons*. Just as physicians and attorneys talk to one another in a specialized vocabulary that serves to identify group members while mystifying and confusing patients and clients, so also do members of gangs or racial and religious minorities have secret handshakes, special items of clothing and other signs of recognition, and a jargon that is incomprehensible to nonmembers. Such boundary-keeping devices reinforce solidarity among the in-group and protect against invasion by the out-group. In some respects, any group of individuals who regularly perform some task sufficiently different from other individuals will tend to construct boundary-maintenance devices. Athletes, musicians, military personnel, fire and police officers are among most thoroughly researched subgroups.

X **Counterculture** refers to an alternative lifestyle for those who do not conform to the dominant norms. **Contraculture** goals involve the overthrow and replacement of existing cultural patterns and values.

Counterculture and Contraculture.   Some subcultures reflect not only protective variations on general cultural themes, but contain elements of clear opposition to the values and beliefs of the larger society. The distinction between *counter* (contrasting) and *contra* (against) is often one of degree. A *counterculture* may be thought of as providing an alternative lifestyle for those who cannot or do not wish to conform to the dominant norms, as, for example, the beatniks of the 1950s, flower children of the 1960s, members of the 1970s drug subculture, and various other cultural dropouts. Similarly, those who live in communes or religious communities cut off from the larger society exemplify a way of life very different from the mainstream (Roszak, 1969).

Contracultural groups, in contrast, have as their goal the overthrow and replacement of existing cultural values and patterns. The Weather Underground, the Symbionese Liberation Army, and similar "revolutionary units" growing out of the social movements of the past two decades, are contracultural manifestations.

Both countercultures and contracultures are distinguished from subcultures by their opposition to the existing social patterns. Subcultural adaptations are attempts to integrate members into the dominant culture while retaining the uniqueness of racial, religious, occupational, or ethnic-group identifications. In contrast, individuals who cannot or will not conform to accepted codes of conduct tend to seek out others who share their views and who will reinforce their opposition to mainstream values and behaviors. This is how contra- and countercultural movements originate.

The Value System of the United States

What can one say of a society whose most successful daytime television program is a game show in which a man's secretary and wife vie to see who can tell the most intimate details about him? Indeed, what about a society in which the man, his wife, and his secretary are willing—actually, eager—to appear on this program? And where, in 1980, a "Hitlerfest" rally and cross burning were held in rural North Carolina? Yet this is the same society in which hundreds of thousands marched in support of civil rights for blacks; to which others throughout the world look for refuge; and that is generally considered the bulwark of personal freedom. Paradoxically, it is a society in which North American Nazis and the Klu Klux Klan can hold their "Hitlerfest."

Possibly no country containing dozens of religious, racial, and ethnic minorities, could be characterized by a standard culture, one clear set of values and approved behaviors. Heterogeneity is a prescription for subcultural development in North America. But there are some overarching values and beliefs that are shared by most members of the society. *Nationalism* and *patriotism* as the natural outgrowth of ethnocentrism are powerful factors in all societies as a form of social cement that can unite otherwise different segments of the population. This is the function of national anthems, colorful ceremonies for inaugurating leaders, and national holidays commemorating important military victories.

Core Values. Robin Williams, Jr. (1951, 1960, 1970) has spent several decades identifying a set of core values underlying the beliefs and behaviors of North Americans. These fifteen value orientations represent a conception of the good life and the goals of social action, what might be called *the American ethos:*

1. *Achievement and Success* are the major goals of individuals.
2. *Activity and Work* are favored above leisure and laziness.
3. *Moral Orientation,* that is, absolute judgments of good/bad, right/wrong.
4. *Humanitarian Motives* as demonstrated in philanthropy and crisis aid.
5. *Efficiency and Practicality* expresses a preference for the quickest and shortest way to achieve a goal at the least cost.

The value systems of Canada and the United States are characterized by **heterogeneity** owing to the many religious, racial, and ethnic subgroups within the society.

Nationalism and **patriotism** are powerful forces that can unite different segments of the population.

The **American ethos** is a set of core values that inform the beliefs and behaviors of North Americans.

6. *Process and Progress:* represent a belief that technology can solve all problems, and that the future will be an improvement over the past.
7. *Material Comfort* as the American Dream.
8. *Equality* as an abstract ideal.
9. *Freedom* as an individual right against the state.
10. *External Conformity* refers to the ideal of going along, joining, and not rocking the boat.
11. *Science and Rationality* as the means of mastering the environment and securing a better life in terms of material comforts.
12. *Nationalism* is the belief that American values and institutions represent the very best on Earth.
13. *Democracy* based on equality and freedom of individuals.
14. *Individualism* means that emphasis is placed on personal rights and responsibilities.
15. *Racism and Group-superiority Themes* that periodically lead to prejudice and discrimination against those who are racially, religiously, and culturally different from the white, Northern European stock that first settled the continent.

This is a bewildering list, combining political, economic, and personal traits, some of which actually conflict with others, as the history of both the United States and Canada attests. Equality is an uneasy partner of racial superiority beliefs, whereas nationalism often restrains the exercise of freedom. The coexistence of such contradictory values accounts for a certain vitality as well as divisions within the society.

The course of history will bring changes over time in the composition and importance of any set of value orientations. In contrast to the Williams list, here are the values of one of the founding fathers of the United States.

1. *Temperance.*—Eat not to dullness; drink not to elevation.
2. *Silence.*—Speak not but what may benefit others or yourself; avoid trifling conversation.
3. *Order.*—Let all your things have their places; let each part of your business have its time.
4. *Resolution.*—Resolve to perform what you ought; perform without fail what you resolve.
5. *Frugality.*—Make no expense but to do good to others or yourself; that is, waste nothing.
6. *Industry.*—Lose no time; be always employed in something useful; cut off all unnecessary actions.
7. *Sincerity.*—Use no hurtful deceit; think innocently and justly; and, if you speak, speak accordingly.
8. *Justice.*—Wrong none by doing injuries, or omitting the benefits that are your duty.
9. *Moderation.*—Avoid extremes; forbear resenting injuries so much as you think they deserve.
10. *Cleanliness.*—Tolerate no uncleanliness in body, clothes, or habitation.
11. *Tranquillity.*—Be not disturbed at trifles, or at accidents common or unavoidable.
12. *Chastity.* . . . . .
13. *Humility.*—Imitate Jesus and Socrates.

—Benjamin Franklin, 1784/1970.

The Roots of the American Value System.   The continuities between Ben Franklin's moral virtues and the contemporary themes listed by Williams demonstrate the enduring strength of concepts described by Max Weber (1904/1958) as forming the core of a Protestant ethic in the sixteenth century, or what is now often referred to as the *work ethic*. The work ethic allowed the emerging merchant class to accumulate capital, retain their profits from both Church and State, claim a wide area of personal freedom, and generally lay the foundation of modern capitalism.

The moral virtues of Franklin, the ideals described by Weber, and the value orientations listed by Williams all form the core of the **work ethic.**

Central to this ethic are the following values.

Work as a "Calling."   A calling is sacred task. In most societies throughout history, work has been something people did to survive. To consider physical labor of whatever type as a divine duty is a powerful motive for producing more than what is required simply for survival.

Success as a Sign of Grace.   If work is a sacred task, there must be some way of distinguishing those who perform well from the sluggards. Success in one's chosen occupation seemed a clear and simple sign of divine favor.

The Individual as Monitor of Her or His State of Grace.   What this means is that, according to Protestant theology in its inception, there should be no intervening group of priests between the human being and the Lord. Martin Luther's revolt against the Church of Rome was primarily an attempt to do away with the layers of churchly authority that interferred with direct communion with God. The individual, alone, is responsible for his or her own fate. The Protestant symbol is the lonely pilgrim, negotiating the terrors and temptations of earthly life, ever anxious about his or her own fate, and never certain that God's will is being done. The inner fears of eternal damnation serve to regulate social behavior.

Originally, also, the early teachers of Protestantism stressed *simplicity in lifestyle*. One should live in this world with few belongings and needs and no great displays of wealth. That is, one should practice, "worldly asceticism." This made demonstrations of success somewhat difficult, and over the past three hundred years, worldly asceticism has given way to its precise opposite behavior, what Thorstein Veblen (1899) has called *conspicuous consumption*. Wealth, today, is openly and wastefully displayed; in fact, the extent to which people can throw away their money signifies success.

Early Protestantism stressed **simplicity in life style,** with few belongings and no great displays of wealth.

Conspicuous consumption refers to the open and wasteful display of wealth.

These few concepts are the roots of our North American emphasis on individualism, on work and achievement, on progress, on a sense of morality for oneself and personal philanthropy for the less fortunate, and, as a consequence of these, a sense of righteousness tempered with doubts that must never be openly shown lest one lose certainty in salvation.

CHANGING VALUES?

But surely, you are probably protesting, there are other ideals and goals that motivate our behavior. What about caring, tolerance, openness, cooperation, and community? Did not the 1960s bring this other set of value orientations into prominence, at least for the young?

There is evidence that the strength of the work ethic has diminished in recent years. Daniel Yankelovitch (1981) speaks of a *New Breed ethic* characterizing younger people whose devotion to work is tempered by considerations of self-fulfillment, family involvement, and enjoying the good life as portrayed in the

In recent years the work ethic has been challenged by the **New Breed ethic** stressing self-fulfillment and enjoying the good life.

media and advertisements. Data on retirement suggest that older people, also, are less tied to work than previously thought. Leisure, once thought to be the breeding ground for sin, is now as valued as work for most adults.

The 1960s did leave a legacy of tolerance, involvement, openness to experience, concern for the environment and its preservation, increased support for the civil rights of blacks, women, and homosexuals, and a strengthened desire for peace. For some, the more traditional values of patriotism, competition, personal achievement, and hard work appear to be less compelling now.

Traditional values are very much alive, though. One of the sociologically fascinating phenomena of the past few years has been the fierce backlash against the New Breed values in the United States. Public opinion polls in 1980 showed strong support for the military and for expensive weapons systems, and increasing opposition to the Equal Rights Amendment and homosexual rights, while a well-financed campaign has begun for the return of prayers and the elimination of sex education in the schools. It is too early to tell whether these backlash movements represent the dying gasp of the old ethic or its bed-rock strength. What we can say at this moment is that there are two competing value constellations in North American societies. The dynamic tension between the two sets of values is a theme that runs throughout this book.

Traditional	*New Breed*
Individualism	Involvement
Competition	Cooperation
Achievement	Equality
Patriotism	Tolerance
Work	"Good Life"

Summary

Culture is the design for living of a group whose members share a given location, feel responsible for one another, and call themselves by the same name. The culture of a society includes (1) solutions to the problem of survival, (2) the ideals and values that shape rules of conduct, and (3) tools and other human-made objects. Cultures range from the simplicity of the Tasaday to the complexity of contemporary industrial societies such as the United States and Canada.

The culture of any society is composed of many elements that form a relatively unified whole. Cultural universals are elements found in all cultures: families, economic patterns, political structures and belief systems. Cultural variability refers to the unique way in which these elements have developed in any one culture. The capacity to create and transmit symbols is both the basis and the product of culture. Language is the most important symbol system, permitting individuals to create meaning and to convey the culture to new members. Languages—verbal and nonverbal—shape and reflect the values, norms, and relationships of a society, and also structure people's perceptions of the world around them.

In evaluating other cultures, people tend to be ethnocentric, looking through the lens of their own culture rather than from the perspective of cultural relativism, whereby items of culture are judged in context.

Social norms are prescriptions and proscriptions derived from the central values of a society that guide behavior in all situations. Societies vary in the extent to which elements of culture are internally consistent or integrated. Subgroups whose history and experiences are different from those of the dominant group develop subcultural variations on the general cultural themes.

The chapter concludes with a discussion of the core values and historical roots of the dominant North American culture. The traditional values of individualism, competition, achievement, patriotism, and the work ethic are in competition with a New Breed Value constellation emphasizing involvement, cooperation, equality, tolerance, and the 'good life.'

Suggested Readings

BENEDICT, RUTH. *Patterns of Culture*. Boston: Houghton Mifflin, 1934. An early and still unsurpassed statement of the need to view culture as an integrated whole, reflected in all aspects of social structure and personality. The portraits of Zuni, Dobuan, and Kwakiutl cultures are unforgettable.

HALL, EDWARD. *The Silent Language*. Garden City, N. Y.: Doubleday, 1959. An anthropologist describes how nonverbal communication conveys cultural values, and how these shape characteristic behaviors of members of different societies: why, for example, North Americans maintain greater distance in conversation than do South Americans.

HARRIS, MARVIN. *Cannibals and Kings: The Origins of Culture*. New York: Random House, 1977. An irreverent view of contemporary anthropology by a contemporary anthropologist.

SERVICE, ELMAN R. *Profiles in Ethnology*. New York: Harper & Row, 1963. Fascinating profiles of twenty-one preliterate societies at various stages of cultural development.

SLATER, PHILIP. *The Pursuit of Loneliness* (Second Edition). Boston: Beacon, 1976. A penetrating examination of the problematic and pathological effects of American culture in the 1970s.

WOLFE, ALAN. *The Seamy Side of Democracy* (Second Edition). New York: Longman, 1978. As the title indicates, a critical analysis of the value system of the United States and its consequences.

YANKELOVICH, DANIEL. *New Rules*. New York: Random House, 1981. Basing his findings on a number of national surveys and interviews, the author examines the "new rules" in American life which include an increasing search for self-fulfillment, greater diversity in personal and social values and an increasing acceptance of cultural pluralism.

4 Social Structure and Groups

On February 26, 1972, a makeshift dam holding 132 million gallons of dirty water used in the mining process, gave way after several days of rainy weather. Buffalo Creek, West Virginia, a mountain hollow where some 5,000 people lived, was flooded. Within a few hours, 4,000 of the hollow's residents were homeless. One hundred twenty-five people lay dead in the mud that had once been a relatively secure, cohesive, mining community. The survivors of the flood were so deeply shocked by these events that they withdrew into themselves emotionally, feeling alone and helpless. Moreover, the very fabric of social life that had held them together was damaged. The flood not only destroyed property, life, and individual sense of well-being, but it disrupted the social bonds and relationships that had provided a sense of community. In other words, the *social structure*, as well as the physical environment, of Buffalo Creek had been destroyed (Erikson, 1976).

What do we mean by *social structure?* Social structure is the ordering of everyday behavior and social relationships in a relatively predictable fashion. A key concept in sociology, social structure contains several basic elements, including system, norms, status, role, interaction, and groups. These elements and their interplay are the subject of this chapter.

Social structure is the ordering of behavior and social relationships in a predictable way.

The term *structure* should immediately alert you to the fact that sociologists assume that social behavior is to a large extent both orderly and predictable. Societies exist and persist because there are underlying patterns that allow members of the group to know what they should be doing and to anticipate the behavior of others with some reliability. Otherwise we could not live with one another. If we each had to rethink every response every moment, we would be forever paralyzed with indecision. Humans are able to live together because they have the ability to construct rules of conduct, *norms*, that define acceptable behavior in given situations. What happened in Buffalo Creek, for example, disrupted these usual responses and ways of acting so that a kind of "collective trauma" occurred. As Erikson described this process, "while both 'I and you' continued to exist physically, 'we' no longer exist as a connected pair or as linked cells in a communal body" (Erikson, 1976, p. 154). This chapter deals with the emergence and the consequences of behavioral norms that pattern social relations.

Norms are rules of conduct that define acceptable behavior in given situations.

The Importance of Social Structure

The concept of social structure is somewhat difficult for North Americans to grasp. As part of our cultural inheritance, we tend to think in terms of the individual and to look for the causes of behavior *within* the person. There is, for example, much information showing that women are likely to have lower job

The small proportion of women in executive positions is attributed mistakenly to a lack of ambition inherent in the female temperament rather than to cultural biases. (Source: *Photo Researchers, Inc.*)

aspirations than men. Most Americans have interpreted this finding as evidence that something in the feminine temperament makes women less determined to succeed. Traits cited are an innate nurturance that is out of place in the hard-hearted world of business, or a fear of success because they would appear to be unfeminine, or an absence of certain hormones thought to be associated with aggressiveness. But is this actually the explanation? It is possible that individuals behave as they do because they are placed in different social positions precisely *because of* their different color or sex or culture.

From a conflict-theory perspective, the most essential aspect of any society is the way in which modes of economic production are organized. The majority of the population in any society is engaged in production, with a small minority controlling their labor and the things they produce. These social arrangements of production, whereby some control the labor of others, provide the basis for social structure, as shown in Figure 4-1. In other words, social structure is a codification of the social relationships of production, as in employer–employee, or boss–worker. The view that the economic base of a society creates social structure, which in turn gives rise to particular forms of behavior, is a far cry from the explanations of behavior based on individual motives and characteristics! The placement of men and women in the hierarchy of mode of production is seen to influence their behavior in the organization. You may want to apply this view to the analysis of other work situations known to you.

Figure 4-1.
A conflict theory perspective on social analysis. (Source: *Sherman and Wood, 1979, p. 207.*)

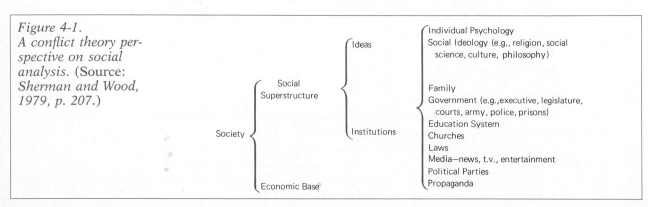

Research conducted by Rosabeth Moss Kanter is important not only for what it tells us about the effects of social structure, but for the evidence it provides of the tendency to personalize behavior. Focusing on the behavior of men and women in corporate settings, Kanter found that both men and women act in what is thought to be a feminine manner when they are placed in jobs that offer little opportunity for promotion. It is the *job* and its potentials rather than being male or female that evoke certain attitudes and preferences. Writes Kanter,

> . . . some women do have low job aspirations, but so do men who are in positions of blocked opportunity. Some women managers are too interfering and coercive, but so are men who have limited power and responsibility in their organizations.

Gender differences turned out to be less important than characteristics of the organizations in which the worker was situated, namely, the opportunity for advancement, the power associated with the job, and whether or not the individual was a token (the only member of that sex in the work group). The facts of working life are that women are more likely than men to be in dead-end positions, to have limited power, and to be given only token advancement when promoted. In this fashion the behaviors become sex-linked.

Of equal interest, however, is the original title—"Why Bosses Turn Bitchy"—given the article by the editors of *Psychology Today* without the author's knowledge. In a subsequent issue, Kanter wrote a strong letter of condemnation, noting that use of the term *bitchy* not only reinforced sexist stereotypes but contradicted the whole thesis of the article: that personality traits are not necessarily expressions of gender differences but are produced by positions in social systems.

Kanter's research is reported in "The Job Makes the Person," by Rosabeth Moss Kanter, *Psychology Today*, May 1976, pp. 56ff.

Components of Social Structure

Although conflict theories emphasize the importance of the mode of production in determining all other relationships, the structural-functional approach has been more concerned with analysis of the *components* of social structure (see, for example, Parsons, 1951 and Levy, 1952). Because these are not only basic and useful concepts in understanding the structural-functional views of society but also shed light on other schools of thought in sociology, we shall focus on these components in some detail.

SOCIAL SYSTEMS

The concept of social systems allows us to perceive one way in which social behavior is patterned. A *system* is an entity with mutually-dependent parts joined in some patterned manner; change or movement in one part will affect the other elements. Structural analysis consists of identifying the system, its parts, and the way in which the parts are connected. The whole and its parts can be the society and its institutional spheres, a subsystem such as the family

A **system** is an entity with mutually-dependent parts joined in a patterned way so that change in one part will affect the other parts.

An analysis of the social behavior of this dating couple would first identify the social system of which they are a part and then study their interaction as a component of this larger system. (Source: Woodfin Camp and Associates.)

and its members, or any group in which individuals interact over time and establish habitual ways of acting toward one another.

Common to all systems is the notion of interdependent parts that compose a totality distinct from a simple sum of the parts. Can we, for example, characterize a dating couple in terms of each one's unique personal characteristics? Probably not. Any couple is more than the two individuals who comprise it. Thus the couple will be distinguished by how power is distributed among the two, a division of labor such as arranging dates, paying, driving, and so forth, and by a way of presenting themselves as a couple. These do not reside in the individual but *only* in their interaction with each other. In other words, each social system has properties that refer only to it and cannot be reduced to its components. Conversely, being a part of the whole affects the nature of each part, and subunit, that cannot be fully understood without reference to the larger entity. Interconnections between various components of the system are illustrated in Figure 4-2.

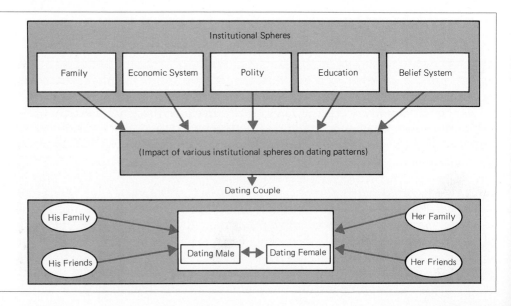

Figure 4-2. Components of the social system. Arrows indicate pathways of exchange of influence and sociability.

MICRO AND MACROSYSTEMS

In some respects, social life is similar to a series of Chinese boxes, each nesting within another. Sociologists speak of microlevel or *microsystem* when referring to very simple and elementary forms of social interaction, primarily the immediate behavior of people in a situation, such as a couple, a group of friends, or workers in an office. Macrolevel or *macrosystem* refers to a social system at a higher level of abstraction, such as the economic system rather than the assembly line at General Motors, or the criminal justice system as contrasted to interaction in the courtroom. Each higher level encompasses the lower.

The **microsystem** refers to very simple and elementary forms of social interaction.

The **macrosystem** refers to a social system at a higher level of abstraction.

STATUS

The term *status* is used in sociology to mean *position in a social system*. Statuses are always linked. Any particular status implies at least one other to which it is related. The classroom, for example, is composed of two status categories: teacher and student. Without reference to any particular person, we can speak of teacher and student as abstract types. We have, in other words, mental maps of status systems that remain to be populated by particular individuals. You yourself fill the status of student in a variety of classrooms, with different teachers, but in each case there are patterned regularities: teacher in front, students together, big desk or table for the teacher, little chair flaps for students, freedom of speech for the teacher, permission required for students, and so on. This structuring of classroom behavior will endure as an arrangement of statuses long after you and others leave the school.

A **status** is a position in a social system.

We can now elaborate upon the concept of *social system* as a set of linked statuses composing the whole. For example we can speak of the family system of any society. A family is a recognized unit of *status incumbents*, that is, individuals who occupy certain positions at a given time. The number and type of statuses comprising the family will vary from society to society and from one time to another. In some societies, a family is composed of all those related by blood. In the United States and Canada, it is most often the married couple and

Status incumbents are individuals who occupy certain positions in a social system at a given time.

A classroom illustrates the reciprocal relationship between statuses: the patterned regularites of this classroom help both student and teacher respond appropriately to each other. (Source: Woodfin Camp and Associates.)

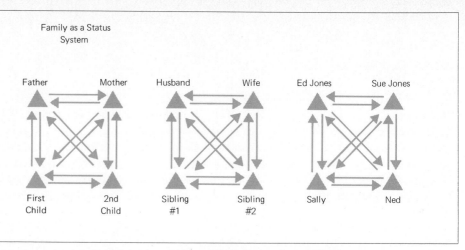

Figure 4-3.
The family as an abstract unit of status incumbents, and a specific family, the Jones family. Note that in the family each person occupies dual statuses, e.g., father/husband, child/ sibling, that can be a source of role conflict and strain. Arrows indicate patterns of interaction.

Family as a Status System

Father   Mother   Husband   Wife   Ed Jones   Sue Jones

First Child   2nd Child   Sibling #1   Sibling #2   Sally   Ned

their dependent children. "The family" is an abstraction. The Jones family, however, is not an idea but an active group of status incumbents whose behavior may or may not approximate the cultural standard. This distinction is illustrated in Figure 4-3.

Ascribed and Achieved Status. Some social positions are based on characteristics that are relatively unchangeable or over which the individual has no control. Age, sex, and race, for instance, are not easily changed (although some individuals may attempt to appear otherwise). These are *ascribed* attributes, often associated with positions that are occupied regardless of effort or desire. To be a certain age is to be able to do some things and not others. To be born the son of a monarch is to be a prince. In some societies, the social position of one's parents determines the course of one's life, whether prince or pauper.

In contrast, *achieved statuses* are positions occupied by choice, merit, or effort. Becoming a husband or wife today in our society is an achieved status. We choose to marry. So, increasingly, is parenthood a matter of choice. One is able to make many decisions about the kind of work or level of schooling to be gained. Still other statuses are filled through election or appointment. Generally, the more complex the society, the more likely are statuses to be occupied through achievement rather than ascription. This range of choice, considered the hallmark of modernism, can lead to great anxiety, but this is the price we pay for the opportunity to decide for ourselves.

To know a person's status in a system, whether ascribed or achieved, is also to have some expectations regarding that person's behavior. For each status, there is a code of conduct defining how the incumbent should relate to others. This is what we call *role*.

ROLE

A central concept in sociology, *role* refers to the ways in which the status incumbent is expected to act. A role is a prescribed pattern of behavior defined as appropriate for the occupant of a particular status. For example, the status of father prescribes a range of behaviors very different from the range prescribed for son. Each status has its own set of rights, duties, and obligations, and this is the role. Think how surprised we would be if the individual in the status of father caught the schoolbus or played on the Little League team. We would be equally surprised if the 10-year-old son went to the office each morning or coached in the Little League. Both would be violating the norms for permissible

Ascribed characteristics are those over which the individual has no control, like age, sex, and race.

Achieved statuses are positions occupied as a result of choice, merit, or effort.

Role is the expected behavior of those who occupy a given status.

82

and desirable behaviors, or *role prescriptions*, for their particular status in both the age and the family systems.

Role Performance. Role performance refers to behavior that more or less approximates the prescribed ideal. Role performance is an ongoing process in which the individual in a given role attempts to live up to the obligations of the role and also insists that others meet her or his claims. Thus, roles are behaviors performed with others—*role partners*—who convey expectations, approve or disapprove, and thus mutually influence each other's performances.

Role Taking. An important aspect of role behavior is *role taking*, in which the individual projects his or herself into the position or perspective of another. Role taking is different from role performance, for role performance is basically the organization of behavior according to group norms. Role taking, however, is a more reflexive process, in which one tries to imagine how she or he looks from the viewpoint of another (Shibutani, 1961). Put differently, one pretends momentarily to be somebody else. For example, a student asking for an extension on a term paper tries to imagine how this request is likely to sound to the professor and acts apologetic or demanding according to inferences made about which behavior is more likely to influence the professor. Role taking thus is an attempt to anticipate the appropriate response or action according to the expectation of others. It is a process based both on one's own experiences within the culture, and one's understanding of the norms and reactions of others. The ability to take the role of the other, however, is limited by our background and experience. As Shibutani (1961) points out, "A person who has never been beaten to the point of losing consciousness can hardly be expected to understand the fear that haunts many boys who grow up in slum areas. The fortunate individual who has always been treated with affection . . . has great difficulty in comprehending the hatred some people have for their parents . . . (and) feels this is a violation of group norms of [family respect]" (p. 507). It is when group members are not able to anticipate others' actions with some reliability that successful role performance breaks down.

Role Creating. The general orderliness of everyday life means that all of us perform a series of roles without thinking much about them; they seem natural. Although role performance is never static, as individuals are constantly interpreting and defining one another's behavior, there are certain boundaries, or *parameters*, within which we enact our conventional roles without a great deal of thought. In new situations, status incumbents must create new roles. The college freshman or army recruit enters a new status and must learn the range of expectations for behavior in that setting, and fashion an appropriate role. This process is called *role creating* (Shibutani, 1961). The kind of role one creates for one's self within a given system will be influenced not only by the norms but also by prior experience and ability for role taking. Cues are sought from others about the norms for behavior, and a role with which one is reasonably comfortable is created to go with a particular status.

Role and Status Sets. As every status has a particular set of possible role behaviors associated with it, it is not surprising that statuses and roles occur in organized *sets*, where they complement each other. For example, as Williams

---

Role prescriptions are norms for permissible and desirable behaviors.

Role performance refers to enactment of the role.

Role partners convey expectations and judgments concerning role performance.

Role taking is a reflexive process by which the individual projects himself or herself into the role of another person.

Role creating occurs in new and ambiguous situations where the status incumbents must develop new roles.

Status and roles occur in organized **sets** complementing each other.

(1970) pointed out, everyone is either male or female and of a certain age, and thus every other status is influenced by age and gender statuses. The flexibility one may have in playing any given role is limited by one's multiple statuses. For example, the role behavior as a father of an 18-year-old high school student will differ appreciably from that of a 35-year-old business executive. Their multiple statuses affect the options for behavior available to them. In general, middle-aged adults occupy more statuses than the very young or very old, and therefore are more embedded in complex role sets. The multiple roles of parent, spouse, employee, son or daughter, member of civic and religious associations influence performance in any one status.

Role conflict is the result of contradictory or incompatible demands in two or more roles.

Role Conflict. Sometimes people have different, even contradictory, expectations for role performance. This leads to one type of *role conflict*. Another type of role conflict occurs when different roles require incompatible behaviors from the same person. In either case an individual experiences inner conflict because one can meet only one set of demands at one time.

The first type of role conflict, contradictory demands, is common in occupations that straddle labor and management, such as foreman or noncommissioned officer. In these cases, status incumbents are usually drawn from the ranks of workers but given the task of securing management goals. The individual is caught in a bind, where lower-level workers expect sympathetic consideration from one of their own, but the employer expects loyalty to the organization. The second type of conflict, between incompatible demands in two or more roles, is clearly illustrated in a dilemma common to students who are also parents of young children: to come to class or to stay home with a sick child.

Role strain occurs when an individual must perform more roles than can adequately be fulfilled.

Role Strain. Just as competing expectations produce role conflict, so do many roles produce *role strain*. Role strain, as analyzed by William Goode (1963), occurs when the sheer number of roles that an individual must perform demand more than she or he can adequately fulfill. One simply does not have the energy or resourcefulness to change roles that often. For example, role strain is evident in the young man struggling to establish himself in an occupation, and whose wife has left the labor force to care for small children. Bosses, co-workers, wife, and children expect undivided attention at some time or another—often at the same time! Another increasingly common example is the woman who returns to the labor force when her children are still young. She must often juggle child care, her husband's needs, and perhaps the care of an aging parent with the requirements of the work role.

Are there any solutions to role strain? Alas, there is no magic answer. One way to reduce role strain is to reinterpret or redefine some of one's roles. Thus the young man might define his family obligations in terms of earning ability so that devotion to work is interpreted as devotion to family (although family members may not accept this definition). Another solution is to delegate part of the role to another person in the role system as when the young man's parents offer to help with child care. The success of either of these strategies will depend on one's ability to convince others that their needs are being adequately met within the role system.

Another type of role strain occurs when the norms governing the performance, and hence the expectations of role partners, are unclear or in the process of revision. Such is the case today with male and female roles in the family, at work, and in society. Although the issue has usually been formed in terms of changing female roles, there are also many men who feel confused about their own roles (Komarovsky, 1976; Pleck & Pleck, 1980).

The Context of Social Interaction

EMERGENT NORMS

Most of our daily activity takes place in established systems with recognized rules, statuses, and roles. Even when strangers meet, there is a certain pattern to their interaction, although that pattern may vary among cultures. No society leaves such potentially troublesome encounters to chance, but what of a situation that has never before occurred? How can participants know what is normal?

Most daily activities occur in social systems with recognized rules, statuses, and roles.

Anomie. *Anomie* is a French word that literally means "without meaning." Emile Durkheim (1897/1966) coined it to refer to situations in which norms are absent, unclear, or confusing; that is, where no clear normative guidance is offered to role players. Yet we have described humans as rule-making and rule-following creatures. How, then, can humans tolerate anomie? We cannot, and therefore individuals attempt to impose meaning and order on anomic situations.

Anomie refers to situations in which norms are absent, unclear, or confusing.

In England in the early days of World War II, for example, when people first streamed into air-raid shelters, no clear norms existed; after all, no one had ever before needed to spend night after night sleeping and living underground. But soon codes of appropriate conduct were developed, and typical divisions of labor emerged. Families occupied the same places each night; leaders, jokesters, comforters, and other role players were acknowledged. Within days, a social system of the air-raid shelter had been constructed, and anomie was replaced by order. Similar order-creating behaviors have been reported among members of a jury, a random group of individuals who gradually construct a workable status system (Strodbeck, James and Hawkins, 1958).

DEFINITION OF THE SITUATION

To a large extent, one's behavior is determined not only by the status occupied, but by definition of the situation. A concept introduced by W. I. Thomas, *definition of the situation*, refers to the fact that behavior in a role is not simply a response to the environment but an active effort to define and interpret the context in which we find ourselves, assess our interests, and then select appropriate attitudes and behaviors. To paraphrase: What people believe to be real, is real in its consequences. When others agree with our definition of a situation, we have consensus and can share common understandings and expectations that facilitate interaction. As situations do not define themselves, but have meaning conferred on them by the participants, social actors are always engaged in defining their situations.

Definition of the situation refers to the process whereby individuals interpret and evaluate a set of circumstances in order to select appropriate responses and attitudes.

If behavior is a response to the situation as perceived by participants, then situations defined as different are likely to produce variation in behavior. This point is particularly well illustrated by the work of the social psychologist, Stanley Milgram (1965), in a series of experiments in which unknowing subjects were told they were taking part in a study of learning. As part of the study, these naïve subjects were informed that they would be required to administer electric

Modesty in a Nudist Camp

Martin S. Weinberg, from his participant observations of nudist camps, has written a number of essays on the ways in which members of nonconforming groups define and redefine the social situation so that order can be maintained. That is, even when engaging in behavior that others consider improper or crazy, participants create definitions that rationalize their actions, and rules that allow them to live together harmoniously.

The case of a nudist camp is particularly interesting. In the larger society, modesty is usually defined as keeping one's clothes on and acting in a manner designed to minimize sexual excitement. If modesty also serves to control the potentially disruptive expression of sexuality in the group, how can nudist camps enforce standards of sexual privacy?

In Weinberg's words,

The ideology of the nudist camp provides a new definition of the situation regarding nudity, which in effect maintains that:

1. Nudism and sexuality are unrelated.
2. There is nothing shameful about exposing the human body.
3. The abandonment of clothes can lead to a feeling of freedom and natural pleasure.
4. Nude activities, especially full bodily exposure to the sun, leads to a feeling of physical, mental and spiritual well-being.

These definitions are sustained by nudists to a remarkable degree, illustrating the extent to which adult socialization can function in changing long-maintained meanings; in this case regarding the exposure of one's nude body in heterosexual situations.

How are the norms maintained? Weinberg points to several aspects of the social organization of the nudist camp: (1) screening applicants for admission to eliminate single people, especially young men; (2) strict rules of interpersonal behavior (no staring, no sex talk, and body contact); (3) forbidding alcoholic beverages; and (4) restricting use of cameras.

Under these definitions and rules, Weinberg concludes, "sexual interests are very adequately controlled in nudist camps; in fact, those who have visited nudist camps agree that sexual interests are controlled to a much greater extent than they are on the outside." It is on the outside that clothes are used in a suggestive fashion to arouse sexual interest, as, for example, in television programs featuring young women in tight T-shirts.

Weinberg, Martin S., "Sexual Modesty and The Nudist Camp: The Social Construction of Norms," *in* Earl Rubington and Martin S. Weinberg, (eds.) *Deviance: The Interactionist Perspective*, N.Y.: Macmillan, 1968, pp. 271–9.

shocks to those who gave incorrect answers. The experimental situation was manipulated in a number of ways: whether the subject saw the "learner" (actually a paid assistant) going into the learning room, or could hear the learner's presumed reaction to the electric shock, or whether the experimenter stood over the subject or gave orders via headphones or a public-address system. What affected the subjects' willingness to inflict pain was neither background characteristics of the individuals nor psychological traits but the *experimental situation* itself. That is, when the instructor stood over the subject, it was difficult not to obey; when the authority figure was not present, subjects were less likely to administer shocks. The key point here is that individuals are most strongly influenced by the situations in which they find themselves and by the interpretations they give to that situation. The tendency to obey, therefore, is not a fixed attribute of individuals but a variable response to a specific social setting as interpreted by participants.

Groups

Thus far, we have focused primarily upon elements in the social structure such as status and role, and upon the context for social interaction. Yet, a society is not a mere aggregate of interacting individuals but of individuals connected to one another in some patterned fashion, that is, who live in *groups*. Throughout our lives, we belong to a variety of groups, each of which can influence our actions and our very concepts of self. To be human is to live in groups, although the relationship between individual and group takes a number of forms.

Group refers to any collection of people bound together by a distinctive set of shared social relationships.

Group refers to any collection of people bound together by a distinctive set of social relationships. Groups are highly varied, ranging from members of a family to workers in an automotive factory, from patient–doctor to children attending a summer camp. Their membership may be stable or fluid, but groups share two common elements: (1) *mutual awareness* of other members of the group; and (2) *responsiveness to members* so that actions are shaped in the context of the group as a whole.

The term *group* is deceptively simple, for it is used in everyday conversation to refer to a variety of things. In sociology, however, the word has a very specific meaning. *Groups*, whether small or large, are patterned by shared social relationships. Not every collection of individuals is a group in the sociological sense. A group, in the sociological sense, has the following characteristics: (1) a distinctive set of social relationships among members; (2) interdependence among various individuals; (3) a feeling that the behavior of each member is relevant to other members; and (4) a sense of membership or "we" feeling.

GROUP CHARACTERISTICS

Primary Groups. A basic distinction in sociology is made between small and intimate groups, on the one hand, and large, impersonal groups, on the other. Charles Horton Cooley (1864–1929) introduced the term *primary group* to describe situations in which members have warm, intimate, personal ties with

Primary groups are small groups in which members have warm, intimate, personal ties with one another.

one another. Calling the primary group "the nursery of human nature," Cooley saw it as the source of the individual's earliest and most nearly complete sense of social unity. The family is our first primary group. Primary groups involve an identity of goals among members who share a similar world view and strive for shared goals. Because of their close ties, each person in the primary group is concerned with the welfare of all the others. (Cooley, 1902, 1909)

Belonging to a primary group is thus an end in itself; relationships among members are valued in their own right rather than as means to another goal. Behaviors that are engaged in for their own sake alone are called "expressive". Because contacts are enjoyable, primary groups are relatively permanent. Face-to-face association, spontaneous interaction, involvement with the whole of oneself rather than just a part, and intensity of relationships are hallmarks of the primary group. Cooley stressed the point that human nature is not something that exists separately in each individual but rather is developed in simple, face-to-face groups.

Secondary Groups. Unlike primary groups, secondary groups are characterized by few emotional ties among members, limited interaction involving only

Categories and Aggregates— Not Groups

An important distinction is that between a group and a social category. *Social categories* are classifications of individuals who share one or more common characteristic but are *not* interacting. Undergraduate students majoring in sociology, single parents, Canadians, children under the age of six, and overweight men are all social categories. But simple possession of an attribute or occupancy of a status does not make one member of a sociological group. Nor does awareness of similarity alone produce group membership. The aged are most often spoken of as a group when they are actually a social category, sharing an ascribed status—age—with one another, but otherwise diverse and representing many different perspectives. In some cases, however, sharing common statuses can lead to group formation. The Gray Panthers are an example of an organization formed because of shared concerns about the elderly in the United States. But without mutual awareness and interaction of others with like characteristics, a social category will not be a group.

The term *aggregate* should also be distinguished from *group* and *organization*. Aggregates are collections of individuals in one place, such as an elevator or a movie theater. Such a collection of people in a common place does not constitute a group because there is no notion of interdependence among various individuals, or sense that the behavior of each person has some relevance to others.

Imagine the audience of a movie theater. The people attending have chosen that film at that time for a variety of reasons and have little or no interest in interacting with the rest of the audience. If social interaction does occur, it will be limited, perhaps to expressions of annoyance if someone spills popcorn on the lap of another. The individuals are together but do not form a social unit. If, however, the movie audience were to be locked in together overnight, group characteristics would soon emerge.

"Now, should you decide to join our organization you will be surrendering certain liberties." (Drawing by Chas. Adams, © 1980 The New Yorker Magazine, Inc.)

Table 4-1. Comparison of Primary and Secondary Groups

Structural characteristics	Processes	Sample relations	Sample groups
PRIMARY GROUPS:			
Physical proximity	Whole person relationships	Husband–wife	Family
Small number of members	Spontaneity	Close friends	Neighborhood
Long duration	Informal social control	Close work group	Work team
Shared norms and values	Expressive behavior	Parents–children	"Gang"
Shared goals			
SECONDARY GROUPS:			
Large number of members	Segmented role relationships	Student–teacher	College freshmen
Limited sharing of norms and values	Formality	Officer–subordinate	Army
Limited shared goals	More formal social control	Boss–worker	Corporation
No physical proximity necessary	Instrumental behavior		Alumni Association
Contacts of limited duration			

✗ **Secondary groups** are characterized by few emotional ties among members, and limited interaction involving only a part of each person.

a part of the person. Furthermore, the goals of participants in the secondary group may vary. Formal relationships replace the informal spontaneity of the primary group. Examples of secondary groups include students in a lecture hall, large work settings, and organizations such as the University Alumnae Association. All members share one common interest, but otherwise their goals diverge, their contacts with one another are relatively temporary and their roles highly structured. Indeed, interaction is viewed as a means to a more distant goal: diplomas, wages, the good of the group, and so forth. Behavior that is directed toward a more distant goal is called "instrumental," literally, a means to achieving some other end.

Primary groups are often formed within secondary settings, in which the friendship of peers can have important effects on the larger social system. For example, a variety of studies of the behavior of combat soldiers during the Second World War showed that the average American soldier was driven neither by patriotism nor hatred of the enemy when under fire but rather by loyalty to his outfit, particulary his buddies (Stouffer et al., 1949; Shils, 1950). The primary group has a dual function in combat settings. First, it establishes group norms for behavior and defines roles; second, it supports and maintains soldiers in stressful situations.

Gemeinschaft is Toënnies' term for small, traditional communities, characterized by primary group relationships and intergenerational stability.

Gesellschaft is Toënnies' term for societies characterized by contractual relatioinships, where social bonds are voluntary and based on rational self-interest.

Gemeinschaft and Gesellschaft. Akin to the distinction between primary and secondary groups is that made by German sociologist Ferdinand Toënnies (1853–1936), who used the terms *Gemeinschaft* (literally, community) and *Gesellschaft* (society) to describe two types of relationship (1957). *Gemeinschaft* exists in communities characterized by many primary group relationships, in which people have known one another for generations and associate in informal ways. Groups are united by common ancestry or geographic closeness. Membership is usually ascribed, and a traditional outlook prevails. Roles seem natural because they are products of ascribed status. Leadership, when present, follows habitual patterns.

In the *Gesellschaft*, relationships are more businesslike and contractual. Major social bonds are voluntary and based on rational self-interest to achieve a particular goal or set of goals. These concepts are closely related to primary and secondary group relationships.

In general, the development of modern societies can be seen as a progressive replacement of *Gemeinschaft* by the impersonal, fragmented, goal-directed relationships of *Gesellschaft* settings. Although Toënnies and others have lamented this shift in contemporary society from a reliance on primary groups to increasing involvement in secondary groups, the intense, personal nature of emotionally-charged relationships in the *Gemeinschaft* has costs to the individual that are often overlooked. *Gemeinschaft* ties, although a source of personal gratification and socialization, are also restrictive. They may inhibit individuality, spontaneity, and creativity. Personal freedom is cramped in a society where primary group membership is the only type of affiliation available. When given the opportunity, young people have typically fled such communities in order to achieve independence. Only recently have sizable numbers of youth sought the restrictive embrace of primary-based religious communities or communes.

A Special Case: the Pseudo-primary Group. Because modern society is complex, and most roles and statuses are characterized by relative impermanence, individuals generally belong to a relatively small number of primary groups. Indeed, the emotional intensity of a primary group places constraints on membership in many such relationships. To fill the void between primary groups and secondary groups, many of us belong to *pseudo-primary* groups, which, like primary groups, have a small number of members, are informal, involve the whole person, but are of limited duration and may or may not have shared norms, values, and goals. The neighborhood bar, the encounter group, and the senior citizens center are examples of such groups. The social function of these is to protect the individual against the impersonality of the larger society without demanding deep emotional involvement.

An example is the Oasis, a family tavern, the location of a year-long participant study by LeMasters, 1975. It is *not* a neighborhood tavern. Patrons come by car but are of similar backgrounds, mostly blue collar workers. Not only men but entire families come to the tavern. There is very little transient trade. The Oasis is a center of social life for its regulars who share interests in bowling, shuffleboard, pool, card games, boating, horseshoes, and gambling. The regulars are also a source of support in times of trouble; funerals are attended, hospitals are visited, and funds collected for families in need. Yet the Oasis customers do not form a primary group. Rather, regular attendance at the Oasis fulfills some of the needs these men and women have for a place to congregate, share experiences, and accept one another before returning to the routines of their daily lives.

In-groups and Out-groups. In his study of the Oasis tavern, LeMasters noted that only some people participated fully in the many social activities of the tavern, and thus formed an *in-group*, with which each member feels a strong identity. Strangers who entered the tavern were treated as outsiders.

The terms *in-group* and *out-group* were coined by William Graham Sumner (1840–1910) and are defined much as they sound. In-groups are ones to which we belong; out-groups are ones to which we do not belong. Sumner noted that the amount of hostility directed toward out-groups is related to the degree of in-group solidarity. Such antagonism is closely aligned to *ethnocentrism*, or the belief that one's own group is best, providing the standard against which all other groups should be measured. After all, if one's own way of doing things is the correct one, other ways must be wrong! (Sumner, 1940)

Strong in-group/out-group feelings reinforce competition. This may be clearly seen at any athletic event, where the fans for each team root fiercely, sometimes insulting the other side or even destroying property. Members of the in-group are more likely to perceive any defeat of their team as due to *external* factors, such as referee bias or poor sportsmanship by the other team rather than as a result of poor playing by their own side (Mann, 1973). The strong "we" feeling of the in-group permits members to rationalize events and to interpret social reality in a way that supports their existing beliefs and justifies continued allegiance. This cohesion is not without costs. The ethnocentrism dominating "we" sentiments may serve as a justification for violent and destructive acts. By using words that dehumanize members of an out-group, people are freed from the restraints on behavior toward others like one's self.

Pseudo-primary groups are similar to primary groups in size, informality and involvement, but are of limited duration and may not be characterized by shared norms, values, and goals.

In-groups are primary or secondary groups we belong to; **out-groups** are ones to which we do not belong.

Reference groups are those exerting a strong influence on one's identity, norms, and values, whether or not one actually belongs to that group.

Reference Groups.   Thus far, we have discussed groups to which individuals belong. There is, however, one specific type of group to which one need not belong, but is nonetheless a strong influence on identity and placement of the self—as well as upon norms and values. This is the *reference group*. First described by Herbert Hyman in 1942, reference group denotes a *checkpoint* or *standard* against which one may assess one's own status and role performance, whether or not the individual is a member of that group. A second dimension of the reference group, allied to the first, is that it denotes a group to which an individual *aspires to gain or maintain acceptance*. The athlete on a Little League team may have the Boston Red Sox as a reference group, modeling his or her playing style and behavior after these unmet heros.

A third aspect of reference group is that it provides a *frame of reference*, or perspective, and thus a way of organizing one's own experience. As Shibutani (1955) has pointed out, this usage of the term does not necessarily mean that the individual aspires to belong to the group or models his or her behavior after it, but merely that she or he is able to assume the perspective attributed to members of that group. Put another way, we all take part in a variety of social worlds simultaneously. Most of you participate in the world of your parents, the world of your college or university, the world of summer jobs or travel, the world of your religious group, your ethnic group, and so on. Not all of these group mem-

Attitude Development

Theodore Newcomb, a social psychologist, measured political orientations of Bennington College students over several years in order to investigate how attitudes change with the college experience. He found a general tendency for students to move from conservative political attitudes toward more liberal ideologies during their college careers. Whereas all participants belonged to the total membership group at the woman's college, those students who shifted from conservative to liberal political views were particularly likely to take campus leaders as role models. Thus, students who acquired the more liberal attitudes were attracted to specific, identifiable people and groups. Those who remained strongly conservative, on the other hand, continued to use their home and community as reference groups and to be relatively isolated from student leaders. For attitude change to occur, students had to be both aware of their own political orientations and to want to acquire the new, more highly valued, attitudes espoused by campus leaders.

How do students maintain their attitudes over time? Newcomb followed up his original group of students approximately 25 years later and found that the liberal Bennington women tended to remain relatively liberal thereafter. Moreover, most had chosen a spouse who was similarly politically oriented. Conservative women who had experienced no attitude change at Bennington tended to remain conservative, again by choosing a spouse or set of friends who supported this perspective.

The results of Newcomb's study are reported in "Attitude Development as a Function of Reference Group: The Bennington Study," by Theodore Newcomb in Eleanor Maccoby, Theodore Newcomb, and Eugene L. Hartley (eds.) *Readings in Social Psychology*, New York: Holt, 1958, pp. 265–275.

berships are compatible, and you may need to segment your life accordingly. But the concept of reference group enables you to understand the world of your parents versus the world of your college and, depending on your own identity with each, to reconcile differences and to make choices. The reference group thus provides a way of experiencing different social categories and integrating this knowledge.

Group Structure and Processes

Social groups are the building blocks of social structure. Differing widely in size, purpose, and membership, groups nonetheless share several common structural elements and processes that affect their functioning.

GROUP STRUCTURE

Group Formation and Membership. Homans (1950) pointed out that group membership is a circular process. The more often people associate with one another, the more they come to share common norms and values, and the more they tend to like one another. The net result of this process is that group ties are strengthened by similarity of activities, mutual friendships, and shared norms and values. This is not an accidental process, for we gravitate toward groups that reinforce our values and our beliefs that our behavior is correct. Newcomb (1943) has called this a *need for consensus* that reduces conflict over correct behavior. When individuals are caught in a value difference among groups to which they belong, they generally resolve their discomfort by selecting the group that offers the most immediate rewards, namely affection, approval, companionship, and participation. In high school and college, many students are caught between competing groups such as the family and the peer group. To reconcile the differences in norms and values between one's family and peers, some may rebel against their family and align more closely with peers with whom there is more daily contact. That is, they resolve the conflict by accepting the peer group's definition of families as "old fashioned" or somehow detrimental to the growth of the individual. These shared meanings then draw peers closer together.

The **need for consensus** makes people gravitate toward groups that reinforce their own values and validate their behavior.

Group Size. The size of a group is an important structural property that dominates interaction within the group and the statuses and roles available. You will recall that one distinction often made between primary and secondary groups is size; primary groups are always relatively small.

The sociologist Georg Simmel was particularly interested in the effect of the number of people in a group. The most simple form of the group described by Simmel is the *dyad*, or two-person group, such as a dating couple. The dyad is characterized by (1) intimacy, in which there is high tension and emotion; (2) a tendency to avoid disagreement; (3) high exchange of information; (4) high potential for deadlock and instability; and (5) joint responsibility. The dyad is always threatened by termination, for one or the other person can destroy it by leaving or by withdrawing affection or needed resources (Simmel, 1950).

Interaction   In the highly charged emotional context of the dyadic group, how are role relationships maintained? Pamela Fishman studied 52 hours of taped conversations by three different male/female dyads in their homes. Although the couples were free to turn the tape recorder on or off, or to delete portions of the tape, most of their everyday conversation was recorded.

Fishman found an unequal division of labor in making and maintaining conversation between men and women. Women put more effort into sustaining interaction than do men; they also fail to succeed more often. Men put little effort in trying to keep the conversational ball rolling or to make the other comfortable. They did, however, decide what was important to talk about. Thus, in the couple relationship, the role of men was to shape the social reality while that of women was to supply routine support.

These findings are particularly interesting, for they emphasize the emergence of one role partner in the dyad as the power figure, the other as worker. That this division of labor was associated with gender role is all the more intriguing since two of the three women were avowed feminists and the other participants claimed to be sensitive to the goals of the women's movement.

Fishman's studies are reported in "Interaction: The Work Women Do," Pamela Fishman, *Social Problems* 25, April 1978, pp. 397–406.

The *triad*, or three-person group, is typically more stable than the dyad. Although the triad usually has less affection and intimacy than the two-person group, it is typified by greater division of labor and interdependence among the three members. Two members can unite against one member, but the coalitions generally shift so that unity is maintained; no one person dominates the triad.

Size is also related to interaction in groups other than the dyad or triad. Long ago the British politician Disraeli commented that the proper number of guests for a dinner party is "more than the Graces(3) and fewer than the Muses(9)," and results from research on small groups indicate that, indeed, the optimal size for an informal group lies between five and seven people. (Berelson & Steiner, 1964) Formality within a group tends to increase rapidly beyond seven, as do the number of subgroups.

INTERACTION PROCESSES

Interaction processes refer to the manner in which role partners agree on the goals of the interaction, negotiate behaviors, and distribute resources.

Perhaps because we spend so much time in groups, we tend to regard their processes as spontaneous. Yet even in the most relaxed and unstructured groups, established interaction patterns evolve. Interaction processes refer to the manner in which role partners agree on the goals of the interaction, negotiate the behaviors required to achieve the goal, and distribute resources. Although each interaction has elements of uniqueness, there are a limited number of ways in which role players can interact. These processes can be placed on a continuum, ranging from very willing and positive exchanges of goods, services, or feelings to coerced responses. As long as two or more role partners are involved, their potentially conflicting needs and resources must be taken into account.

Figure 4-4 presents one commonly used set of categories in observation and analysis of the interaction process within a small group. As you can see, most behavior falls within a very limited set of categories.

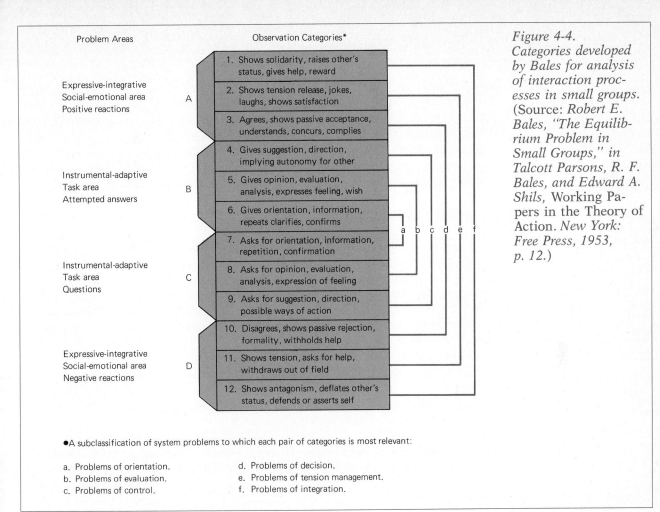

Figure 4-4. Categories developed by Bales for analysis of interaction processes in small groups. (Source: Robert E. Bales, "The Equilibrium Problem in Small Groups," in Talcott Parsons, R. F. Bales, and Edward A. Shils, *Working Papers in the Theory of Action*. New York: Free Press, 1953, p. 12.)

Problem Areas

Expressive-integrative Social-emotional area Positive reactions — A

Instrumental-adaptive Task area Attempted answers — B

Instrumental-adaptive Task area Questions — C

Expressive-integrative Social-emotional area Negative reactions — D

Observation Categories*

1. Shows solidarity, raises other's status, gives help, reward
2. Shows tension release, jokes, laughs, shows satisfaction
3. Agrees, shows passive acceptance, understands, concurs, complies
4. Gives suggestion, direction, implying autonomy for other
5. Gives opinion, evaluation, analysis, expresses feeling, wish
6. Gives orientation, information, repeats clarifies, confirms
7. Asks for orientation, information, repetition, confirmation
8. Asks for opinion, evaluation, analysis, expression of feeling
9. Asks for suggestion, direction, possible ways of action
10. Disagrees, shows passive rejection, formality, withholds help
11. Shows tension, asks for help, withdraws out of field
12. Shows antagonism, deflates other's status, defends or asserts self

● A subclassification of system problems to which each pair of categories is most relevant:

a. Problems of orientation.
b. Problems of evaluation.
c. Problems of control.
d. Problems of decision.
e. Problems of tension management.
f. Problems of integration.

PRINCIPLES OF EXCHANGE

When individuals interact, elements of exchange characterize the relationship. Each exchange is a trade-off between what one has to give up in order to secure what one desires to receive. In the ideal case, *A* has a surplus (goods, energy, affection, approval) that he or she is willing to exchange for some desired object (love, money, attention) that only another can provide. Just what is considered a fair exchange depends on each individual's own history, needs, resources, and alternative sources of supply (Homans, 1961: Blau, 1964).

Exchange principles, when applied to small groups, predict who is likely to interact with whom, under what circumstances, for how long, and with what sentiments.

Person A   Person B

Has *X* ——————— Has *Y*

Needs *Y* ←———→ Needs *X*

Group relationships emerge from the process whereby participants bargain for advantage, and the system will persist only as long as participants perceive that the exchanges are beneficial. But some participants have greater power than others to define the terms of the exchange. For example, those with monopolies on something desirable have more power. Teachers have a monopoly over grades, parents over rewards for the child's activities, and bosses over jobs. College students can change schools, and workers can change jobs, but children are rarely able to select another set of parents. Moreover, students can attend

95

only schools that will accept them, and workers can accept only jobs offered to them. Power, in other words, varies with the number of possible alternatives available to an individual. Where there are no alternatives, people will remain in relationships that often appear intolerable to an outsider.

Short of the extreme case of *coercion* (the unchecked use of force to induce compliance), interaction processes are typified by some degree of willing agreement to interact according to certain rules. Cooperation, competition, and compromise are all modes of exchange, with the rules of the game agreed upon for the particular interaction.

Coercion is the unchecked use of force to induce compliance.

Competition.   When individuals or groups interpret the situation as one in which scarce rewards will go to some and not to others, *competition* results. Usually the competition is framed as a test of some virtue or quality that is unevenly distributed among persons and groups: talent, skill, intelligence, strength, or courage. *Meritocracy* is a term that means rule of the talented, and it is assumed to be the outcome of a situation in which all are free to compete so that the best person wins.

When individuals or groups interpret the situation as one in which scarce resources will go to some and not to others, **competition** results.

Competition is basically social in that the participants agree to the rules of the game. There is a shared belief that the competition is either necessary, fair, or both. Only thus can the losers accept their failure. The belief serves, in the vocabulary of the confidence game, to "cool out" losers (Goffman, 1962). To *cool out* means to reduce anger over failure, and the belief that only the fittest survive a competition helps to sidetrack losers so that the rules of the competition are believed to be fair even where participants have unequal opportunities. The costs of competition are often personal strain and tension (Stein and Hoffman, 1980).

Cooperation.   *Cooperation* occurs when people agree to pool their resources to achieve a common goal. Cooperation involves taking others into consideration. The welfare of the group supersedes that of each member, although the individuals must perceive that their needs are being adequately met. From an exchange perspective, cooperation is the basis of social order and the most social mode of interaction.

Cooperation refers to the sharing of resources in order to achieve a common goal.

Compromise.   One can describe *compromise* as a cooperative effort to minimize the all-or-nothing aspects of competition. Here again, there is a basic agreement among group members on principles and shared meanings of fairness. Individuals (or groups) mutually forego extreme demands and expectations in order to achieve some more limited goal. The essence of compromise is that all parties appear to receive important benefits.

Compromise represents a cooperative effort to minimize the all-or-nothing implications of competition.

CONFLICT

Conflict occurs when parties cannot agree on rules for the distribution of scarce resources and attempt to meet their needs by destroying or disabling opponents. Unlike the other modes of interaction, conflict does not assume an underlying allegience to the social order. Conflict occurs precisely because such support has been withdrawn, so that the existing order is defined as oppressive or unfair. The goal of conflict is to defeat and replace those who make and enforce the rules.

Conflict occur when groups or individuals fail to agree on rules for the distribution of resources.

Cooperation and Competition

The study of interaction process cuts across psychology and sociology and has been undertaken by social psychologists who measure the ways in which attitudes, perception, feelings, and behavior are influenced by the groups in which individuals are placed. One of the most important studies of cooperation and competition was an experiment conducted over three decades ago by Morton Deutsch.

Deutsch divided a class of fifty male students into ten groups of five each (recall that between five and seven is the optimal size of a small group). Because he had given all the men psychological tests at the beginning of the semester, he was able to match the groups on personality and capacity variables. All ten groups were given a human-relations problem to solve; each group was graded on how well it performed this task. On the basis of this information, Deutsch redivided the groups into two sets of five each, with matching sets of high- and low-scoring groups. In other words, the two sets of groups were as alike as possible in terms of the individual members and of the group's abilities.

Each new set of groups was assigned to one of two experimental conditions. One set was told that the *group as a whole* would be rated and that each person in the group would get the score achieved by the group in comparison with the other task groups. The other set was told that group members would be rated on their *individual* performances in solving logical puzzles and problems in human relations, the same tasks given to all groups. Thus, one set was placed in the condition of cooperation, the other in a condition of individual competition.

Trained observers sat in on each group's deliberations, three hours a week for six weeks. Groups were rated on their productivity, the quality of interaction, and the members' behavior toward one another.

Deutsch's major finding was that the cooperative groups were more productive. That is, problems were solved more quickly because members helped one another. The cooperators also rewarded one another with approval more frequently than did the competitors, and their groups were characterized by friendliness, member satisfaction, and easier communication. In the competitive groups, hostility was high and courtesy low.

In this type of experiment, at least, cooperation produced better results in task accomplishment and in personal satisfaction. This is not, of course, to say that competition is always less effective than cooperation; much depends upon the nature of the task and the overall value system of the society.

The results of Deutsch's experiments are reported in "An Experimental Study of the Effects of Cooperation and Competition upon Group Process," Morton Deutsch, *Human Relations*, 2, 1949, pp. 199–232.

From a structural-functionalist perspective, conflict is a symptom of disequilibrium within the social structure. From the conflict theory approach, conflict is seen as stemming from the economic relationships in a society as manifest throughout the social structure. No interaction is without some element of conflict because social relationships are influenced by the struggle for scarce resources (Sherman and Wood, 1979; Anderson and Gibson, 1978).

In many cases, conflict has redeeming social value; long-smoldering issues such as racism or sexism become defined and brought to public attention through confrontation and conflict. Over the last two decades, groups in opposition to official policy have used conflict effectively, due to the presence of television cameras and the media's need to present exciting images on the home screen each evening. The antiwar, gay rights, civil rights, Gray Panthers, and women's movements have all used the media to force viewers to face issues and to take sides. Viewers, though, have not always sided with the activists. In fact, to the degree that opposition is sharpened by such images, counterforces emerge. In the United States, gay rights activism gave rise to Anita Bryant's crusade for decency; the women's movement produced Stop ERA; the antiwar movement brought out swinging hard-hats, and the civil rights movement has given new life to the Ku Klux Klan. In sum, conflict presentation, whether in the small group or on a national level, tends to polarize opinion, leading to greater conflict and overt violence but often, also, to major change in the social system.

Conflict Reduction.   Each side in a conflict assumes that its goals are correct. This sense of rightness permits members to engage in behavior that might not be acceptable in other situations. Because the societal and personal consequences of conflict are potentially disruptive of social bonds, a number of conflict-reducing mechanisms can be activated. They include (1) *cooptation;* (2) *mediation;* and (3) *ritualized release of hostility.*

Cooptation involves the absorption of dissidents into the dominant group or the absorption of their ideas into the mainstream.

Cooptation occurs when the members of the dissenting group are absorbed by the dominant group, thus giving them a stake in the peaceful settlement of the conflict, or when the ideas of the opposition filter into the mainstream so that there is no longer a need for confrontation. An example of the first would be to appoint Ralph Nader to the Federal Trade Commission. The latter was exemplified by extending the vote to women.

Mediation involves the use of a third party to resolve conflict.

Mediation, or the use of a third party to resolve the conflict through various means, frequently occurs in labor-management conflicts, and in the small group. (This is why, incidentally, the triad is more stable than the dyad; the dyad, having no third party, has no possibility of mediation between the two when conflict arises.)

Ritualized releases of hostility are ceremonial occasions developed for the contained expression of conflict.

Ritualized release of hostility is a mechanism developed in some societies and groups to express conflict in a contained fashion. Anthropologists have reported many instances of ritualized warfare between groups within a society or between members of adjacent societies. The hostility is real, but its expression is conducted in a manner to preserve both lives and reputations. Among the Tahitians of Polynesia, Service (1963) reported "a sort of moral equivalent of war . . . in the practice of competitive athletics" (p. 263). In such cases, conflicts that have built up between factions are permitted symbolic expression, in which a few warriors or athletes represent the whole unit. Nor is ritual conflict found only in traditional societies. Regional conflicts in North America are often displaced onto athletic teams: North-South football games, for example, become an occasion for waving the Confederate flag.

We have talked at some length about processes that occur in social systems ranging from the dyad and small group to whole societies. Similar processes characterize formal organizations, the final aspect of social structure that we shall discuss in this chapter.

Formal Organizations

Formal organizations are an important part of the social system because we all spend so much time in them; only preschool children and adults not working outside the home or engaged in volunteer work are exempt from being "organization people." Formal organizations, (sometimes called complex organizations), are characterized by

Formal organizations are characterized by impersonal rules, hierarchy, large size, relative complexity, and duration longer than the members comprising it.

Formality.

Ranked positions.

Large size.

Relative complexity.

Duration longer than that of the members comprising it.

Examples of complex or formal organizations include such diverse phenomena as local school systems, colleges, universities, hospitals, businesses, the Red Cross, the State Employment Office, the American Nursing Association, and the administrative staff of the White House.

Formal organizations are larger and more structured than are smaller groups. They also involve greater differentiation of tasks. Statuses are prescribed, with a clearcut division of labor following an organizational blueprint. Role behavior stems primarily from one's status in the organization, and thus may be less fluid than in informal groups.

The formal organization is an effective and efficient way of getting a large job or number of tasks accomplished. In any group, as the complexity of tasks increases and as more and more specialization is required, the level of organization and the size of the group also increase. For example, the one-room schoolhouse of the late nineteenth and early twentieth centuries had many of the characteristics of a small, relatively informal group. The contemporary elementary school is a formal organization in which various teachers specialize in diverse fields, students move from one classroom to another, and both students and faculty are accountable to the principal, who in turn is accountable to a still different level of centralized authority, the superintendent.

The *Gemeinschaft* society, based on kinship and occupational or traditional ties of one kind or another, has few formal organizations; complex modern societies, on the other hand, tend to have large numbers of social relationships organized into formal patterns.

Bureaucracy

One particular type of formal organization that is prevalent in modern societies is the *bureaucracy*. Initially described by Max Weber (1922), a bureaucracy has the following distinguishing features:

The AMA as a Professional Organization

Professional associations are one kind of formal organization. Freidson (1970) has observed that the term *profession* usually has a dual meaning: It refers to an occupation of a specific type, such as doctor, lawyer, or clergy; and it also refers to a commitment or promise. Medicine is particularly interesting to view as a profession, for it is both an occupation with its own special skills and a promise to the layperson—improved health. It also has an extensive system of self-regulation, typical of professional associations.

Generally, professions are distinguished from occupations by several attributes: (1) a specified body of theory, generally attained through education; (2) a notion of authority or special knowledge not shared by the layperson; (3) authority, power, and privileges (monopoly) given it by the community in general; (4) ethical code or rules for appropriate professional conduct; and, lastly, (5) its own culture, including values, norms, and symbols (history, folklore, jargon, and heroes [Greenwood, 1957]). How does one such organization—the American Medical Association—reinforce and maintain these characteristics of a profession?

1. Specified Body of Theory. Although some sort of treatment for illness has existed in almost all cultures (the witch doctor was one of the first specialists in history), the development of modern medicine is usually dated from the Greek, Hippocrites, who lived around 400 B.C., but there was no practitioner with a special title of "doctor of medicine" until very recently. With the founding of the American Medical Association in 1847, medical *men* began to assert their claim to exclusive treatment of illness, as opposed to herbalists, midwives, and other female practitioners. By the early twentieth century, medical licensing and uniform standards had evolved.

2. Authority or Special Knowledge. During the nineteenth century, anyone with the necessary money could obtain a medical degree and practice medicine in the United States. In 1904, however, the AMA established a council to

---

Bureaucracy is one type of formal organization, characterized by rules and regulations, rationality, efficiency, merit, hierarchy, and a precise division of labor.

1. Defined rights and duties are written into rules and regulations.
2. Appointment and promotion of personnel are based on merit and contract rather than on hereditary status or favoritism.
3. Technical skills are a prerequisite for employment and promotion; one stays in the job (has tenure) unless proven technically unfit for the task.
4. Statuses are arranged in a *hierarchical* position, where each lower position is under the supervision of a higher one. (See Figure 4-5.)
5. Division of labor makes each employee responsible only for specified types of work.
6. Power, rights, and duties belong to the office (*bureau*) and *not* to the officeholder. The individual occupying the office acts as a representative of the organization.
7. Fixed, predictable salaries are paid in accordance with the place of the office in the hierarchy.
8. Managerial activity is viewed as a full-time occupation rather than as a by-product of other work.
9. Records must be kept of every transaction (red tape).
10. Impersonal treatment within the bureaucracy and between bureaucrats and clients prevails. This assumes equal treatment of all individuals at the same level, reducing irrational factors such as prejudice or the whim of the bureaucrat. [Gerth and Mills, 1958]

suggest ways in which medical education could be improved. Thereafter, specific standards for medical-school entrance and curriculum were set, and medicine as a distinct discipline became recognized.

3. Authority, Power, and Privileges (Monopoly). The American Medical Association has continued to set minimum educational standards, license individual physicians, and approve medical schools and hospitals. To date the AMA is the most powerful influence in monitoring and regulating medical care in the United States. Hierarchial and conservative, this professional association, unlike many others, has been successful in molding public opinion while at the same time, protecting its own occupational self-interests. It has been devoted to maintaining the individual autonomy of physicians, and particular methods of care, free of oversight from nonphysicians.

4. Ethical Code. Not only does the medical profession have its own ethical code, but the AMA has the authority to set its own qualifications for membership. Official AMA policy dictates that all reputable, ethical licensed M.D.'s are eligible for membership, but ascribed status such as race, sex, or ethnicity, or a refusal to conform to individual fee-for-service practice, have been used as screening criteria. Threat of expulsion or denial of membership are instruments of control invoked to punish physicians who work at fees inconsistent with those reached by consensus of local medical societies.

5. Own Culture, Norms and Values, Folklore, Heroes. Medicine not only has its own language but also its own norms, values, folklore, and history. Various means have been used to teach these to new members; the medical school experience provides a first entry. Membership in the local medical societies that comprise the AMA reinforces consciousness of kind, and the *Journal of the American Medical Association*, published by the AMA, not only transmits the latest medical techniques but also enhances allegiance to the medical profession.

Basic to the concept of the bureaucracy is that it is a rational mode of organization, oriented to efficiency, with positions filled according to technical competence. Statuses are achieved rather than ascribed. Discipline, too, is a hallmark of the bureaucracy. Adherence to general and specific norms for conduct and work performance is expected and maintained by both informal social

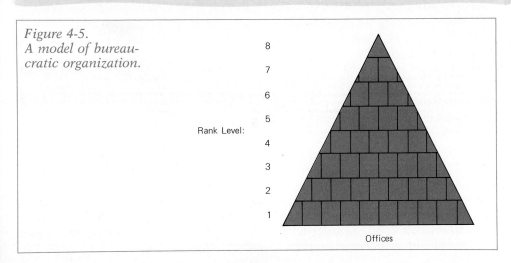

Figure 4-5.
A model of bureaucratic organization.

Rank Level:

8
7
6
5
4
3
2
1

Offices

pressure and formal actions (reprimand, demotion, firing). Job security is designed to insulate the office holder from political or outside pressures.

The growth of the bureaucratic system is linked to the development of a money economy and the modern state. The bureaucracy, with its relative impersonality and high degree of specialzation of tasks, has proved very useful in the administration of large-scale organizations in the business, military, government, and education sectors of modern societies.

Weber's description of the bureaucracy was designed as an "ideal type" or extreme case that may never exist in its pure form. The definition, however, highlights the essential features of real-world bureaucracies, each of which possesses the elements described by Weber in varying degrees. What any particular bureaucracy will look like depends not only on the function of the organization but the society in which it emerges. Virtually all modern nations have extensive bureaucracies, but they differ in a number of ways owing to their unique histories, current tasks, available technology, and value systems.

The Bureaucracy at Work: Positive Features.   Positive aspects of bureaucracy include a division of labor according to a rational plan of specialization, and an appropriate delegation of responsibilities to meet the needs of the organization. In a complex society such as the United States or Canada, the simplicity of *Gemeinschaft* organization is inappropriately geared to production of motor cars, breakfast cereals, large crops of wheat, ranching, or treatment of a heart attack victim. Tasks and knowledge are too complex and technology too intricate for each person to master all aspects of even a single specialty such as farming, production, or hospital administration.

What about the relative security of position within the bureaucracy—is this boon or boondoggle? The view of the bureaucrat as concerned only with strict adherence to the rules and to pay raises, is a popular one. Yet the security of position provided within the complex organization may be a hidden strength. Kohn (1971), comparing people in high-ranking positions in bureaucratic organizations with those in smaller, nonbureaucratic systems, found that the bureaucrats were *more* creative and had *more* diverse interests. Perhaps this is because the large corporations that he studied had the "pick of the crop" of college graduates. Another explanation is that the relative security freed the bureaucrats to explore new ways of doing things without immediate fear of reprisal.

Inefficient channels of communication, red tape, and overly complex regulations are some of the **negative features** of bureaucracy.

The Bureaucracy at Work: Negative Features.   The gap between the ideal bureaucracy and the real world is often considerable. Inefficient channels of communication, red tape, and incomprehensible and unnecessarily complex regulations have been roundly criticized. A case in point is the following passage from a Federal regulation.

No person shall prune, cut, carry away, pull up, dig, fell, fore, chop, saw, chip, move, sever, climb, molest, take, break, deface, destroy, set fire to, burn, scorch, carve, paint, mark, or in any manner interfere with, tamper, mutilate, misuse, disturb, or damage any tree, shrub, plant, grass, flower or part thereof, nor shall any person permit any chemical, whether solid, fluid, or gaseous, to seep, drip, drain, or be emptied, sprayed, dusted on, injected upon, about, or into any tree, shrub, plant, grass, flower . . . (*New York Times*, May 10, 1977)

In plain language, "Don't damage plants, trees, or flowers!" Tax forms have been similarly criticized; only in 1980 were United States income tax instructions issued that for the first time are almost understandable to the lay reader. The reasons for such complexity and wordiness are related to the nature of bureaucratic organization. Because a bureaucracy has written rules that specify appropriate behavior, there is a tendency to make these rules cover all possible events. This is one of the by-products of "doing things by the book" in the bureaucracy.

Professor Lawrence Peter, co-author of the book, *The Peter Principle*, (1969), has, with tongue firmly planted in cheek, developed a new science—hierarchiology, or the study of hierarchies. Hierarchiology is the analysis of how individuals rise to their level of incompetence within any bureaucracy. This is the Peter Principle:

> "Early in life, I faced the problem of occupational incompetence. As a young schoolteacher, I was shocked, baffled, to see so many knot-heads as principals, inspectors, and superintendents. I questioned older teachers. All I could find was that the knot-heads . . . had been capable (once) and that was why they had been promoted. Eventually, I realized the same occurs in all trades and professions . . . a competent employee is eligible for promotion, but incompetence is a bar to promotion. So an employee's final position must be one for which he is incompetent!

The Peter Principle described above and Parkinson's Law (1957) ("Work expands to fill the number of hours alloted to do it") are pointed to by critics of bureaucratic inefficiency. That "officials beget officials" has also been noted. One of the authors of this text worked in a department of state government that had 39 assistant commissioners—a fact that caused much merriment until the

(Drawing by Handelsman, © 1976 *The New Yorker* Magazine, Inc.)

NEITHER LETHARGY, INDIFFERENCE, NOR THE GENERAL COLLAPSE OF STANDARDS WILL PREVENT THESE COURIERS FROM EVENTUALLY DELIVERING SOME OF YOUR MAIL

fortieth Assistant Commissioner was appointed in the same week that lower-level employees were laid off owing to legislative budget cuts.

The impersonality of the bureaucracy, has also been criticized. Not only may members of the public feel frustrated by the impersonality of an organization such as the Employment Office, but the absence of flexibile and personalized authority has proved to be a straitjacket for many workers. They feel locked into a structure that they are powerless to alter. Yet few would prefer being judged and treated on the basis of personal qualities such as skin color or religion. And in the case of bureaucracies dealing with clients, impersonality is a guarantee of equal treatment. That is, although bureaucrats are impersonal toward clients, at least they give each client the same treatment.

Mediating Groups within the Bureaucracy.   Because the ideals of rationality and discipline are never really fulfilled in a complex organization, informal social structures develop to fill gaps. The formal structure is, as we have emphasized, impersonal. Changes in rules, communication patterns, and official leadership lag behind daily events. Furthermore, no matter how complex the wording, rules must be general enough to allow for new situations or contingencies. The impersonal pattern of relationships within the bureaucracy gives rise to the creation of informal, primary-group relationships among members of

Banana Time

Within a number of work situations, especially where the work is repetitive or boring, informal work groups violate officially instituted work rules in order to relieve boredom and to maintain social solidarity. Restriction of output, wasting time on the job, intentional absenteeism, and illicit work breaks are some of the more common tactics used by informal work groups to express their distaste with the work situation.

Donald Roy studied a small group of factory workers who used unofficial workbreaks to counteract the tedium of their jobs and to enhance primary group relationships. These illegal work breaks were known as "times" because they were generally occasions in which pauses from the day's work were taken to eat specific types of food. Thus, they had "coffee time," "banana time," "fish time," "coke time," as well as the customary "lunch time."

To control the work expectations imposed by superiors in the factory, workers used two kinds of output restriction: "quota reduction," used to limit the amount of work expended on easy jobs so as not to "ratebust," and "goldbricking," or failure to put extra effort out when the job was difficult. These informally agreed-upon techniques of manipulation were engaged in collectively by the workers. In addition to enhancing the social cohesion of the small work group, these ploys were also means of rebelling against the impersonality of the hierarchy of the factory. Unable to assert their individuality by other means, such techniques as the illegal work break (banana time) strengthened worker morale.

Roy's study, "Banana Time: Job Satisfaction and Informal Interaction," appears in *Human Organization*, Vol. 18, Winter, 1959, pp. 158–168.

Table 4-2. Typical Patterns of Group Membership Throughout the Life Course

Stage in life course	Primary group membership	Secondary group membership
Infancy	Family	None
Preschool	Family Playmates	Distant relatives Neighborhood Church
School	Family Close friends/peers	Pupil-teacher Classroom/school Distant relatives Neighborhood Church Hobby groups/sports
Adolescence	Family Close friends Mediating work groups	School, plus part-time/summer work groups
Young adult	Family of origin Close friends Lover/spouse Family through marriage and parenthood Mediating work groups (Pseudo-primary groups)	Formal work organization Professional/union group Church Neighborhood Hobby/sports/special-interest groups
Middle-aged adult	Family of origin Close friends Lover/spouse Family of procreation Mediating work groups (Pseudo-primary groups)	Formal work organization Church Neighborhood Civic groups Hobby/sports/etc. Parent groups
Old age	Lover/spouse Children Close friends (Pseudo-primary groups)	Church Neighborhood Civic groups Special-interest groups
Old, old age	(Lover/spouse) (Close friends) (Children) (Pseudo-primary group)	(Church) (Neighborhood) (Civic groups) (Special-interest groups)

work teams. This kind of informal structure may either reinforce the purposes of the organization (as does the primary group in the military) or subvert its goals (as when workers set informal production goals and punish "rate-busters").

Informal groups within the formal organization have several functions: (1) to provide personal satisfaction; (2) to break down barriers in communication that otherwise exist within the formal structure; (3) to create an informal source of discipline within the group, and (4) to create personal attachments that bind the individual to the organization because of loyalty to fellow group members (Blau and Scott, 1962).

In Table 4-2 those groups that one is most likely to belong to at different points in the life course are listed. In parentheses are groups to which one may or not belong, but which are open to at least some people at a given stage in their lives. For example, in old-old age, one may continue to enjoy many of the same primary group relationships as in old age although many possibilities are likely to have been foreclosed through illness and death of role partners.

Informal social structures are nonofficial groups that develop as workers interact in bureaucratic settings.

105

Summary

This chapter began with a description of the flood at Buffalo Creek and the observation that more than homes and property had been demolished. The unexpected disaster also destroyed the web of relationships that bound members of the community together in a network of mutual duties and obligations. When habitual ways of interacting are disturbed, individuals lose their certainty that the world is an orderly and predictable place. As a result many will experience emotional as well as physical stress.

Social structure is the actual working out of cultural ideals and expectations in the patterned behaviors of individuals who are linked to one another in some fashion (as kin, neighbors, coworkers, citizens). The key concepts in the study of social structure are systems, statuses, and roles. The smallest unit of social structure is the role—a set of behaviors expected of a person in a given status. A status is a position in a social system, linked to other statuses by rules or guidelines for behavior (the norms). Together, these patterned statuses form a system, a totality composed of interdependent parts. In other words, members of a status or role system are bound together by predictable actions.

Statuses can be given at birth—ascribed—or gained by one's own effort—achieved. One feature of modern societies is the increasing importance of achievement as compared to ascription in the assigning of social positions. The roles attached to statuses give shape to human behavior. Most of our daily activity is channeled by the demands and possibilities of the roles we perform. Often, the sheer number of roles causes strain; then, too, diverse expectations of role partners can lead to conflict both within an individual or between role partners.

But without the guidelines of role expectations we would not know how to behave. The anxiety of normlessness—anomie—is relieved when individuals define their situation and develop appropriate rules of behavior. Order is restored in human affairs.

At the level of face-to-face interaction, status/role systems form human groups whose members are aware of or sensitive to the actions of others. Groups are generally described as either primary or secondary, depending upon the degree of closeness, informality, intimacy, and totality of the relationships. Industrial societies are characterized by a proliferation of secondary group settings.

Membership groups provide individuals with the information and emotional support required for appropriate role performances. Reference groups— whether or not one is a member—provide the standards against which an individual measures role behavior. Throughout our lives, the various groups in which we are embedded or to which we look for guidance are essential for constructing definitions of reality, shaping attitudes, and governing behavior.

Groups have characteristics of their own, such as size, division of labor, and degrees of formality, all of which affect their functioning. Interaction within a group involves elements of exchange, cooperation, competition, and even conflict; and each group will vary in its unique mix of these interaction processes. Moreover, groups interact with other units of the society, and these intergroup relationships involve exchange, cooperation, competition, and conflict. Frequently, in-group solidarity is enhanced by directing hostility toward out-groups.

Groups are also the building blocks of larger systems called organizations, in which a number of smaller units are coordinated in order to achieve some specific goal such as educating children, defending a society, or dispensing justice. The sum of organizations in any one sector of a society form institutions, or institutional spheres that are the interdependent parts of the society as a whole—its economic system, for example, or its family system.

Social structure, then, encompasses the patterned, normative interaction of systems as small as the dyad and as large as the entire society. In modern societies, small face-to-face groups are often overshadowed by large formal organizations, particularly the type known as bureaucracy, with its rational specialization of tasks, hierarchical structure, and merit/tenure system of promotions. Bureaucracies have many positive as well as negative features, and are also the setting for primary-group relationships among the workers.

The concepts presented in this chapter—structure, system, status and role, groups, complex organizations, and bureaucracy—are important basic tools of sociological analysis. Social structure is the other side of the coin from culture, the enactment of those ideals that form the essence of human societies. In the next chapter we will discuss the link betwen culture and social structure—the process whereby human beings learn the ways of their culture and the specific groups in which they are embedded.

Suggested Readings

ERIKSON, KAI. *Everything in Its Path*. New York: Simon & Schuster, 1976. What happened when the dam burst at Buffalo Creek, destroying life, property, and the social fabric of an entire community. A very readable, sensitive account of this tragedy and its aftermath.

GUBRIUM, JABER F. *Living and Dying at Murray Manor*. New York: St. Martin's, 1975. An ethnographic account of one total institution, in which group structure and relationships determine life or death.

KANTER, ROSABETH MOSS. *Men and Women of the Corporation*. New York: Basic, 1977. How the corporation's own structure, chain of command, and promotion system affects the behavior of employees. It is the job, not gender, that produces different styles of working.

MILGRAM, STANLEY. *Obedience to Authority*. New York: Harper & Row, 1973. Milgram's controversial account of experimental studies that demonstrate the crucial importance of the definition of the situation in affecting behavior.

PORTER, JOHN. *The Vertical Mosaic*. Toronto: U. of Toronto, 1965. A landmark report on Canadian social structure, its cross-cutting groups, and the distribution of influence.

WHYTE, WILLIAM H. *The Organization Man*. New York: Simon & Schuster, 1956. Another sociological classic. Whyte describes the pervasive influence of the corporation on the lives of its management personnel, including lifestyles and the behavior of their children and spouses.

5

The Social Self

A recurring figure in folklore and popular literature throughout the world is the *wild child*, an infant lost or abandoned in a forest and raised by animals. From the wolf child of Hesse in 1344 to this day, such reports have periodically fascinated the general public and intrigued scientists. In no case has the existence of such a *feral* (wild or untamed) child been proved. Human infants cannot be raised to normal adulthood by apes or wolves, Tarzan the Ape Man and Mowgli the Jungle Boy notwithstanding.

Were such an abandoned child to be discovered tomorrow, the entire debate would be revived, and in time it would be found, once again, that it is impossible to become a human being without interacting with other humans. Human physical and social development does not unfold automatically, and animals cannot do the job of human caretakers.

In a phrase, *human behavior is primarily learned.* The process through which one learns to behave as a human being is called *socialization*, and involves the transmission, through language and gestures, of the culture into which the child is born. At the same time the newborn (*neonate*) is also learning about itself as it begins to develop a sense of self.

The first part of this chapter examines the nature and processes of socialization—learning the culture. The second part will present a sociological perspective on personality formation and the emergence of the "self."

Socialization is the process whereby one learns how to behave in a given society, and develops a sense of self.

Socialization

EFFECTS OF EXTREME ISOLATION

Some forty years ago an article by Kingsley Davis (1940) appeared in which he described a case of extreme isolation. Since that time there have been no discoveries that would lead sociologists to change their view of the necessity of human interaction in the growth and development of infants. Davis related the case of Anna, a child of about eight years old when found by authorities. For the first six years of her life, Anna had been deprived of all but minimal contact with others. Anna was a sickly, illegitimate child at birth, was shunted around for the first several months of her life, and was finally hidden by her mother in a small dark room where she received food and very little else. When discovered, she was emaciated and unable to walk or talk or "do anything that showed intelligence."

Two years after she was found and removed from her mother's home, she was able to feed herself, walk, and follow simple orders, but she still could not talk. In another few years she was beginning to speak at the level of a two-year-old, and doing other tasks that one would expect of a child of that age. Unfortunately, Anna died shortly thereafter, making any firm conclusion about her basic abilities impossible. Davis remarks that the data seem to bear out a diagnosis of mental retardation (her mother was mentally deficient), but one cannot tell whether this was so at birth or caused by isolation and neglect during her earliest years.

In comparison, Davis was able to report on another female child, Isabelle, born at about the same time as Anna and experiencing similar seclusion for about six years. In this case, Isabelle's mother was a deaf-mute. When discovered, Isabelle, like Anna, was unable to walk or talk, and appeared to be feeble-minded. Unlike Anna, Isabelle was assisted by a team of professionals who organized an intensive effort to stimulate her capacity for language. Eventually, Isabelle not only learned to speak but went through the entire course of child development in a very short time, reaching the normal level for her age in two years. In just a year and a half her IQ was raised three times its initially-tested level.

THE BIOLOGICAL BASES

Humans are distinguished from all other animals by their ability to learn rather than being instinctively programmed for action. We have already described the crucial characteristics of the reflective mind and, with it, the capacity for speech. This means that humans have both the mental and vocal *capacities* required for learning. Evolution has also operated to produce a creature who *must* learn *in order to survive*. Standing upright narrows the pelvic area and the birth canal through which human infants must pass. Therefore, the human infant is born at a *less developed* stage than other animal young, before its nervous system is fully linked and before it can care for itself. This is the biological basis for the extraordinary helplessness of the human neonate.

Physical Helplessness.   You may have observed newborn kittens or puppies which, within weeks, are able to get around on their own and even to be parted from their mother. Those animals closest to us on the evolutionary scale, the great apes, have neonates somewhat similar to humans: typically one at a time, spaced several years apart, and relatively helpless—clinging to the mother. And for a year or so, there are many parallels between the infant ape and the human child.

Infant and Ape Behavior.   Observations of apes and of human infants have found many similarities in behavior patterns during the first two years of life. Both progress in the same order and timing through basic stages of motor and intellectual development during the first 24 months: from grasping to self-exploration, followed by reaching out and experimentation, to the sophisticated stage of problem solving. The crucial difference is that apes do not follow the human course of vocalization. Apes cry and grunt and make other sounds indicating emotion. Human infants proceed to babble, coo, combine sounds, and ultimately to use words and combine these into phrases.

Dr. Suzanne Chevalier-Skolnikoff, in an interview in the *New York Times* (July 3, 1979), interpreted these findings as "emphasizing our close relationship with the apes. . . . One more example that animals and man are not as different as generally believed." We would suggest precisely the contrary; that in spite of many visible parallels between human and ape behavior, a fundamental distinction exists. The capacity to vocalize and eventually to construct worlds of meaning through speech is more than a slight difference or simply a matter of

The biological bases of human socialization are the mental **capacity** *for reflective thought, and the ability to create language.*

degree. It is an advantage that allows humans to conduct experiments on apes, publish their findings and to discuss these with reporters.

The human mind that both requires and permits social life, is, at birth, a bundle of *potentials*. Unguided by instinct, prepared to learn the language and culture of its society, the neonate is dependent upon its human environment. In the setting of the family, the infant's mind matures as it is nurtured. Although we have used the word *helpless* many times in this discussion, it should be understood as a physical helplessness. The infant's *mind* is actively coping with a multitude of sensations, processing information about itself and the world around it, and organizing this experience. The brain itself is developing during these early years as various nervous system circuits are completed. In fact, never will the brain grow more rapidly than in the first years of life.

> The human mind is a bundle of **potentials,** capable of learning the language and culture of any society.

Dependency. The physical dependence upon caretakers induced by helplessness is an essential precondition to learning. Because the brain and nervous system are developing at the same time that an infant is being fed and cared for, a basic sensitivity to the nurturers' expectations is built into our earliest experience. This dependence on others never leaves us, although the objects may shift—from parents to friends to lovers and even to one's own children. But throughout life, humans need other people to provide them with the affection first experienced in dependent infancy.

> **Dependency** induced by physical helplessness is a precondition of learning.

The mind that reflects on itself, it seems, is never altogether certain: Who am I? What am I? Am I loved? Am I good? These are the questions that haunt human beings. One is not born with such knowledge, but must seek the answers from others—beginning, of course, with those who attend one's earliest needs.

Each society has evolved some relatively stable unit to accomplish the tasks of caring for helpless young. This is typically a group centered on the mother (which is also true of other primates). Having carried the infant and given it birth, the mother is the obvious person to care for it. She is also restricted in her mobility, somewhat weakened by childbirth and often limited by the requirements of breast feeding. There is no maternal instinct, but there are many reasons why women behave maternally: the sheer helplessness of the neonate being one, and her own emotional and physical investment in the product of her body being another.

Within the nurturant setting, the neonate becomes especially sensitive to cues from its caretakers. Over time, the infant will discover that it, too, contributes to the interaction: a wail will bring attention, vocalizations will thrill an audience, and whining can bring harsh words. An *interdependence* develops between infants and caretakers, although overwhelming power resides in the adults, who can provide or withhold what the infant requires for survival.

Human Needs. Nurturance for physical survival is only one need of the infant. We propose three other responses from others that are essential for well-being throughout the life course: affection, approval, and some assurance that one is who one claims to be (*validation of the self*). The people who are in a position to give these responses are precisely those whose failure to do so would hurt most, so that throughout life there will be others who matter very much and whose reactions are especially important.

> Four basic **human needs** are **nurturance, affection, approval,** and **validation of the self.**

In infancy this need for others is physically based. In later years, the ties are

Affection, approval, and self-validation are social responses necessary for well-being throughout the life course. (Source: *Photo Researchers, Inc.*)

almost purely emotional—but built on the model of the earliest dependency. The cases of Anna and Isabelle are eloquent testimony to the need for human contact in order to *become* a human being. Continued interaction is required in order to *remain* a stable person, and, in many cases, to remain alive and healthy. There is increasing evidence of a link between health and having family and friends as a support network (Cobb, 1979; Lynch, 1977). For example, a longitudinal study of residents of one county in California found that people without social and community ties were more likely to die in the nine-year follow-up period than were those with extensive contacts (Berkman & Syme, 1979).

Individual differences. Although all neonates are alike in having undeveloped potential, they are not, of course, identical. Some will learn faster than others, be musical, be tall or fat, placid or fidgety, and so on throughout a lengthy list of attributes that have some *genetic component*. That is, there may be inherited tendencies toward certain types of behavior or appearance. Each infant is a unique combination of such traits, with the possible exception of identical twins, who share the same genetic material.

But—and this is crucial—*genetic tendencies* do not automatically produce behavior. A tendency is just that, the likelihood that one response will occur rather than another. Tendencies develop within social structure, and can be stifled or encouraged.

Genetic tendencies refer to the likelihood that one or another response will occur; they do **not** automatically produce behavior.

Bearing in mind that each person is a unique combination of innate and learned traits, we turn now to the process by which the individual learns the rules of the culture and the particular roles she or he is expected to play throughout life.

The Socialization Process

The neonate is born with the ability to learn any culture, to speak any language, and to organize experience in different ways as it matures. Infants will not learn to walk or talk until stimulated to do so, even though they have the necessary physical equipment.

The function of primary (early) socialization is to present "one world of meaning as the only possible world" (Berger and Luckman, 1966). The definitions of reality developed within one's culture become the water in the fishbowl as infants are taught a particular language and way of life. At the microlevel, this information is conveyed through specific training for social roles.

LEARNING ONE'S PLACE ✗

As individuals assume certain statuses, they must learn both the appropriate *role* and the *rules* governing interaction with role partners. Role learning involves a number of elements: information, opportunities to rehearse, the reactions of others, and social supports.

Although the physical ability is present, infants will not walk or talk until they are socialized to do so. (Source: *Bohdan Hrynewych, Stock, Boston.*)

X Information. At some point the learner must receive enough information about the role to give shape to the performance. The military recruit will receive detailed descriptions from a Drill Instructor; mothers-to-be frequently attend child-care classes; and children are told to be a good girl or boy.

Roles and *rules* are learned through direct *training, rehearsal*, and *anticipatory socialization.*

Rehearsal. Most performances benefit from the chance to practice in the role. Opportunities for trial-and-error learning under fairly tolerant conditions are usually granted to people just entering a role—the honeymoon period for newlyweds, political newcomers, and college freshmen.

Another form of role rehearsal is called *anticipatory socialization*, wherein a person practices in advance of occupying a status. Thus, little girls play house, and older boys play soldier; high-school seniors begin to wear their college colors; employees expecting a promotion dress more carefully; and older adults take up hobbies and interests that they hope to follow in retirement.

In role modeling one assumes the characteristics of those admired and respected persons one wishes to resemble.

Somewhat related to anticipatory socialization is the phenomenon of *role modeling*, assuming the characteristics of admired and respected persons one wishes to resemble. Parents, movie stars, and other famous people are common role models. One of the reasons often cited for the small numbers of women in certain occupations is that there have been so few role models for young females to use as examples.

Positive sanctions convey the message that the role performance is being well received; *negative sanctions* withhold approval of the performance.

Reactions of Others. Role performances take place before an audience composed of role partners with the power to judge and to *sanction. Positive sanctions* are those reactions that convey the message that the role is being well played, and *negative sanctions* are either the withholding of approval or the transmission of information that criticizes the performance.

Depending on the importance of the sanctioner, an individual will change his or her behavior in order to receive positive sanctions. Clearly, some sanctioners will be more important than others. There are many people whose opinions will have no effect, but there are also those whose judgments are crucial.

Social supports refer to networks of relatives, friends, or teachers that assist and sanction successful role enactment.

Social Supports. Frequently, success in a role depends upon the assistance of people who are willing to train and equip the role learner, and to tolerate role rehearsals. A supportive social network is often the difference between success and failure in learning a new role or relinquishing a valued one. Women with many friends, for example, cope with widowhood more successfully than do those who isolate themselves within their homes (Lopata, 1973).

X LEARNING SEXUALITY

Most North Americans assume that there is a powerful sex drive determining the expression of sexuality. Yet, as natural as sexual activity may appear, there is strong evidence that this, too, is learned behavior, perhaps the first human impulse to be brought under control of the group. The socialization of sexuality is a requirement of orderly social life even today, though perhaps less so than in the past.

Paradoxically, because the sex drive is so thoroughly socialized, it seems that we are "doing what comes naturally." Yet if you think about your own experience, you will recognize that your entire life to date has been spent in *learning* the what, who, when, where, and how of appropriate sexual conduct. What humans learn, say John Gagnon and William Simon (1973) are *sexual scripts,* or ✗ ways of interpreting events so that certain responses are either called forth or repressed. The script and its role requirements permit the individual to organize impressions and experiences into a coherent whole, as, for instance, defining some male-female relationships as sexual and others as not.

If there is no fixed sexual outcome determined by either biology or early childhood experience, then sexuality is actually a rather flexible set of behaviors, liable to change throughout the life course as different realities are socially constructed. There are also many subcultural variations on the general norms governing sexual behavior. Both the definitions of what is sexually arousing and the choice of ways to reduce the tension of the sex drive will vary from one subgroup to another—by religion, race, income, education, ethnicity, and age, to name the most common variables associated with differences in sexual practices among North Americans.

Cross-culturally, also, there is a great range of differences in sexual rules and roles. What is sexually arousing to a teenage youth in our culture may appear hopelessly ugly to a Balinese, and vice versa. Extremely fat people, for example, are sexually arousing in some societies whereas thin figures are admired in others.

Subcultural Differences

Sexuality is only one of many areas of role learning in which young people receive different norms and values according to the parents' income, education, or occupational placement. Weinberg and Williams (1980) note that children of working-class and middle-class parents still behave differently with regard to age of first sexual experience, number of partners, and the frequency of adolescent sexual activities. Working-class youth begin sexual activity earlier, with more partners, and with greater frequency than do offspring of the middle-class.

These findings illustrate the importance of parental occupation in value formation and transmission. A general discussion of *social class* appears in Part III of this book. In terms of socialization, however, some mention must be made here of the work of Melvin Kohn (1977) on the link between occupation and socialization. Most middle-class occupations entail the ability to deal with people, to solve problems, and to manipulate symbols. Therefore a degree of intellectual curiosity, imagination, and creativity are encouraged by parents. Most working-class jobs, on the other hand, call for being on time, following orders, and dealing with machines. For these tasks, parents attempt to instill punctuality, obedience to authority, and technical skills.

Another class difference in child rearing that has been reported is the tendency for working-class parents to respond specifically to the child's act and its consequences, whereas middle-class parents are more likely to respond to the child's intent. For example, if the youngster breaks a window, the working-class parent might punish the child for destroying property, and worry about replacing the window. The middle-class parent, however, would want to know "why

Parental occupational values influence the content and method of socialization.

Table 5-1. Two Patterns of Child-Rearing

"Traditional" or status-centered	"Modern" or person-centered
1 Each member's place in family is a function of age and sex status.	Emphasis is on selfhood and individuality of each member.
2 Father is defined as boss and more important as agent of discipline; he receives "respect" and deference from mother and children.	Father more affectionate, less authoritative; mother becomes more important as agent of discipline.
3 Emphasis on overt acts—*what* child does rather than *why*.	Emphasis on motives and feelings—*why* child does what he or she does.
4 Valued qualities in child are obedience, cleanliness.	Valued qualities in child are happiness, achievement, consideration, curiosity, self-control.
5 Emphasis on "direct" discipline: physical punishment, scolding, threats.	Discipline based on reasoning, isolation, guilt, threat of loss of love.
6 Social consensus and solidarity in communication; emphasis on "we."	Communication used to express individual experience and perspectives; emphasis on "I."
7 Emphasis on communication from parent to child.	Emphasis on two-way communication between parent and child; parent open to persuasion.
8 Parent feels little need to justify demands to child; commands are to be followed "because I say so."	Parent gives reasons for demands—e.g., not "Shut up" but "Please keep quiet or go into the other room; I'm trying to talk on the telephone."
9 Emphasis on conforming to rules, respecting authority, maintaining conventional social order.	Emphasis on reasons for rules; particular rules can be criticized in the name of higher rational or ethical principles.
10 Child may attain a strong sense of social identity at the cost of individuality, poor academic performance.	Child may attain strong sense of selfhood, but may have identity problems, guilt, alienation.

Source: Arlene Skolnick, 1978, p. 357.

did you do that?" in an effort to have the child recognize the motivation for the behavior.

These differences can also be thought of as "traditional" vs. "modern," as summarized in the Table 5-1 from Skolnick (1978).

Agents of Socialization

Agents of socialization are individuals and organizations responsible for the transmission of culture.

If culture is learned, there must be channels of transmission. This is the task of *agents of socialization*—people and organizations charged with conveying the rules. Chief among these are parents, peers, teachers, the media, and religious authorities.

The child's first understanding of the surrounding culture is mediated through nurturing adults.

Parents. The first and most important agents of socialization are the people who care for infants. In the earliest months, messages from nurturers constitute the child's basic understanding of the world around it. This is the infant's first introduction to the *language* that shapes perception and elicits emotions. What the child learns is the culture as mediated through others. A desire for continued interaction with the nurturers, combined with a fear of losing these sources of pleasure, motivates the infant to become sensitive to the cues of those entrusted with its care.

Many of these cues are *preverbal*, matters of mood and feeling expressed in the way a caretaker holds, touches, plays with, and responds to the child. These communications are crucial for establishing trust between the child and its socializers. The *quality* of interactions is as important as the *quantity and content*, especially the ability to empathize, to put oneself in the place of the other. Parents who empathize with their offspring are also teaching the child to imagine the feelings of others.

Preverbal communications such as mood and feeling are important for establishing trust.

Nurturers can also send out contradictory messages (Ruesch and Bateson, 1951) such as the scream "Shut up!" or the slap to stop a child from hitting. In these double-bind situations in which a child does not know which message to heed or which cue to answer, communication breaks down, leading in some extreme cases to mental illness. The term *mystification* (Laing, 1977) has been used to describe similar barriers to parent-child understanding, especially where a parent says one thing but may mean another: "Stay out as late as you want; don't mind me." Often, parents mystify by attributing their own feelings to the child: "Don't you feel hungry?", thereby destroying the authenticity of the child's own feelings.

Mystification occurs when contradictory messages are conveyed.

Thus it is that parents have enormous power over their young. The culture is *internalized* (brought into the mind of the infant) through parental expectations. These earliest learnings are the foundation of later development, and the guilt caused by failure to live up to parental expectations can affect the human being throughout life. However, most parents, if not all, attempt to teach their children what they believe is required for success in that culture, namely, how to be a capable adult. When parents say, "this is for your own good," they believe that what they are teaching will be important, then and later.

Culture is internalized in the mind of the infant through parental expectations.

In a simple society, parents can probably teach the growing child all that will be necessary to function as an adult. But in societies characterized by rapid rates of social change, and where the knowledge of one generation is rendered obsolete even during their lifetime, additional agents are required to teach the child, and later the adult, all that is necessary for appropriate role performances. The modern parent, then, is only one of many socialization sources, the primary one, to be sure, but limited in effect on the offspring. Perhaps the most that parents today can hope to achieve is to lay down a groundwork of motivation to learn, some basic values that guide future conduct, and a bundle of interpersonal skills.

Peers.   Another powerful source of information and socialization is the friendship group of *age peers*. Peers are equals, whereas parents are superiors in relation to the child. The greater power of parents makes some kinds of learning difficult. A distance and formality must be observed even in the most indulgent homes. Peers, on the other hand, are those one can deal with on the same level as oneself: tease, insult, let imagination loose upon, share dreadful mistakes with, and so on, but without the heavy emotional overlay of family relationships.

Peers are equals, and age peers are important sources of information and socialization.

In childhood, friends are needed to learn many things about being a child, such as how to take turns, share, fight fairly, deal with adults, and prepare for

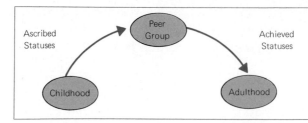

Figure 5-1.
The peer group as a medium for the transition from childhood to adult statuses.

the next stage of growth. At school age, the peer group provides vast stores of important knowledge about how to handle authority, manipulate the system, act in and out of school, and approach members of the opposite sex. Even in adulthood, peer groups are important agents of socialization—to marriage, parenthood, retirement, and widowhood. But the adolescent peer group has received the greatest popular and scientific attention.

Adolescent Peer Group.   For several decades North American parents and other adults have looked with dismay and often anxiety at the friendship groups of young people between age 13 and 18. Parents fear the power of the group as a challenge to family values and as a rival for the teenager's loyalty.

It would appear, however, that the adolescent peer group provides a necessary function for young people in their journey from dependence to independence, from childhood to adulthood. The peer group becomes a supportive environment for anticipatory socialization to adult roles (Eisenstadt, 1956; Erikson, 1963), where adolescents tolerate one another's attempts to construct an identity.

The process whereby the peer group operates as an agent of socialization is similar to that described for infant socialization. Members become emotionally dependent upon one another for affection, approval, and validation. The adolescent still needs support from parents, though, and most research indicates continued and sustained bonds of affection between parent and child (Bengtson and Troll, 1978).

"Mother, I get enough pressure from my peer group without getting it from you." (Drawing by Weber; © 1980 *The New Yorker* Magazine, Inc.)

Studies of the relative importance of parents and peers as agents of socialization typically conclude that parents are important in setting long-term goals and basic values, whereas peers have greatest influence over more immediate lifestyle choices such as appearance, sexual behavior, and leisure activities (Kandel and Lesser, 1972; Troll and Bengtson, 1979). Of course, this can lead to the tyranny of the peer group, but where else can an adolescent turn? The major task of adolescence in most industralized societies, after all, is precisely to be able to leave one's home and parents. The strength of the adolescent peer group may simply reflect the difficulty of this task in modern society. As a consequence, a subculture of adolescent roles and attitudes develops, in which the young person can outgrow childhood and prepare for adulthood.

Teachers. Much formal socialization is placed in the hands of professionals. Teachers from kindergarten on are specifically designated agents of socialization, and are paid for the task. Ideally, a teacher is one who has both knowledge and the skills to present it. During the course of teaching their subjects, classroom instructors provide role models and attempt to convey the excitement of learning itself.

Teachers are professional agents of socialization who convey knowledge and skills to their students.

During their high school and college years, some young people form especially close relationships with particular teachers, who become their *mentors* (guides and sponsors). A mentor can influence career decisions and open the necessary doors for advanced training (Levinson, 1978).

Marijuana Use

Where the power of the peer group is most evident—and most upsetting to parents—is in support for nonconforming and/or illegal behavior. Denise Kandel obtained anonymous questionnaire data from over 8,000 New York State high school students in 1971–72, from which she was also able to identify the best school friend of each respondent. An additional questionnaire was sent to either the father or mother of each student (to be unsigned, although it was possible to match with particular students). In all, Kandel had over 1,000 cases for which a triad of student, the best friend, and one parent could be accurately identified.

The questionnaire covered the use of drugs, alcohol, and cigarette smoking by each respondent, the perception of such use by other triad members, involvement in student peer groups, sources of information on drugs, and closeness to friend and parent. Kandel found that the most significant correlate of marijuana use by adolescents is involvement with drug-using peers. Parental use of drugs does not determine the offspring's behavior as much as modify the influence of peers; that is, youngsters are less likely to follow the lead of drug-using friends when their parents do not use drugs than when the parents drink, smoke, or take pills. "Peer behavior is the crucial determining factor in adolescent drug use; parental behavior becomes important when such behavior exists in the peer group," either reinforcing or slightly inhibiting the offspring's involvement in drugs.

Report of the Kandel findings was presented in "Inter- and Intragenerational Influences on Marijuana Use," Denise Kandel, *Journal of Social Issues*, Vol. 30, No. 2, 1974, pp. 107–136.

The **media,** especially radio, television, and movies, are powerful agents of socialization in modern societies.

The Media. In an earlier time, parents, friends, and teachers would comprise the list of primary childhood socializers. Children's books, comics, and magazines might also have been mentioned as sources of information on norms and role models. Today one must add three powerful indirect (nonpersonal) socialization agents: radio, movies, and television. Many people learn about politics, form a vision of the good life, and develop attitudes toward others from what they see on the screen and hear through loudspeakers.

Most research has centered on the importance of television in the life of the young person who typically spends as much if not more time in front of the set as in school—over 50 hours a week. The effect of television violence on the child has been most studied. Some argue that watching violence reduces the viewer's aggressive impulses by allowing a cathartic outlet. Others claim that children can tell the difference between reality and make-believe. Those opposed to television violence cite studies of children's modeling of brutal behavior (Bandura, 1973), and the fact that physical disciplining of children, ultimately raises rather than lowers the level of aggression in the family system (Straus, Gelles and Steinmetz, 1979).

Personality Formation

Transmission of the culture is only one aspect of socialization. While individuals sort out information about the culture and role expectations, they also learn about their *self*. The self is an organization of perceptions about who and what kind of person one is. Humans are not born with such knowledge. It comes gradually through precisely the same socialization experiences by which the culture is learned.

Self is a learned organization of perceptions about one's identity.

As self-concept is the central component of personality, the study of socialization is also the study of personality formation.

120

COOLEY, MEAD, AND THE SOCIAL SELF

Only gradually does the infant come to distinguish itself from its nurturer. It is, of course, impossible to question the neonate (or even the young child) about its feelings and perceptions. Social scientists can only imagine how it must feel to be an infant, which may not be an accurate account since it is filtered through adult recollections and experience. In the absence of more certain knowledge, then, social scientists have devised this plausible scenario:

> The neonate is totally absorbed in the nurturer-infant system. But the human mind is reflective, and at some point the infant begins to perceive itself in contrast to the overwhelming other. As the caretaker coos and murmurs addressing a "you," the infant will dimly begin to differentiate (separate) itself, to see itself as being that "you." This is what is meant when the sociologist speaks of the human mind taking itself as an object; the infant can reflect on the "you" which is itself.

But what is this "you?" It is what others lead you to believe it is. As they talk to you, handle you, and discuss you with others, you learn who you are.

The Social Self. The concept of a "social self" was introduced to American social science by the psychologist William James (1842–1910), who stated that a person has as many social selves as there are individuals who recognize that person and carry an image of him or her in their minds. The self, therefore, is not some abstract essence, but is rooted in social interaction. Individuals are linked to society through their very self-concept: I am the one who acts and believes and feels in a manner guided by the norms established in a given society at a particular historical moment.

The **social self**, a concept introduced by William James, states that there are as many selves as there are others who carry an image of her or him.

The Looking-glass Self. Building upon James' concept of the social self, Charles Horton Cooley (1864–1929) proposed that the self is composed of a basic, instinctive self-feeling that is then shaped and given specific content through interactions with important others.

Charles Horton Cooley's concept of the "looking-glass self" proposed that our self-image is reflected in the reactions of others. (Source: Leonard Freed, Magnum Photos, Inc.)

The **Looking-glass self**, described by Cooley, suggests that we derive a self-concept from the reflected impressions of others.

Cooley is best known today for his image of the "looking-glass self." Just as a mirror reflects a reverse image, our perception of self is never direct. Rather, we see ourselves reflected back in the reactions of others. According to Cooley, the ideas that we have of our self come from (1) our imagining how we appear to other people, (2) how we think they judge our appearance, and (3) how we feel about all this. In other words, our sense of self is more like a process than a fixed object; it is always developing as we interact with others whose opinions of us are ever-shifting.

Cooley's looking-glass imagery, however, should not be taken as implying that the child—or adult—is a passive recipient of impressions. To the contrary, Cooley's social being is a person actively engaged in manipulating the reactions of others, in selecting which cues to heed, and in judging the relative importance of role partners. Not all reflected images will influence the self-process. In general, we tend to accept perceptions that reinforce a basic identity, while resisting those that do not. Cooley's suggestion that individuals vary in the degree of empathetic response to specific others, with some having greater effect than others, is elaborated in the work of George Herbert Mead.

Mead's theory of the development of self is based on the capacity to see ourselves from the perspective of others.

Taking the Role of the Other.   If, as Cooley proposes, we learn about ourselves from imagining how other people judge our appearance, then the reflective mind not only sees itself as an object, but is capable of seeing into the minds of others! For Cooley's colleague, George Herbert Mead (1863–1931), this imaginative leap into the minds of others, and the capacity to take the role of the other toward oneself, is central to the development of a self.

Crucial to the theories of both Cooley and Mead is the fact that our first socialization experiences take place in primary groups. The unity of the primary group, and the dependencies built up among its members, lead to shared meanings. We can guess what others are thinking because we share language, symbols, gestures, and meanings. With similar sets of expectations, each knows how the other should behave and can judge performances by the same standards.

Gestures are verbal and nonverbal symbols shared by actors in the process of role performance.

The child learns by precept (being told how to behave) and practice (trial and error, and feedback). The medium for this learning is language, both verbal and nonverbal. Mead uses the word *gesture* to refer to a symbol that is shared by group members and made part of a role performance. Simply put, we internalize the culture and social structure by taking on the role of others, and society thus becomes part of our self.

✗ The **significant other** is a specific person in the individual's environment whose approval and affection are especially desired.

✗ **Significant Other.**   Particularly important to the formation of self are those specific persons in the individual's environment whose approval and affection are especially desired. Parents at first, then peers, role models, and other authorities, can all become significant others, with special power to shape one's perceptions.

✗ The **generalized other** is Mead's term for generally-held expectations of any person in a given status.

✗ **Generalized Other.**   For Mead the phrase "generalized other" describes the generally-held expectations for any person in a given status. This is the community's standard of performance. In other words, we must learn both *particular standards* of conduct (from significant others) and *universal norms* (from the generalized other).

Through game play-ing, children learn the complexity and diversity of roles and role partners and the rules governing their interaction. (Source: Charles Harbutt, Magnum Photos, Inc.)

Stages of Role-Taking. Role-taking, the central concept in Mead's theory, develops by stages. At first, the child *imitates* or mimics others in its immediate environment, primarily family members. This type of activity is relatively disorganized and spontaneous, but paradoxically allows the child (up to age three) to differentiate itself from others through becoming another for a moment or two. Even the imaginary playmate that some children persist in talking to, much to their parent's dismay, serves an important socializing function in extending the child's role-taking experience. At ages three and four, the child begins to play-act certain roles—firefighter, doctor, and the like, in addition to family-based roles—with greater intensity and skill than in infancy. This *play* is actually very serious business, because the child is learning to take the role of others toward itself, and to build a collection of "role others."

Later, upon entry into kindergarten and a society of peers, *games* become the means whereby children learn a more sophisticated and complex form of role-taking. Games, in contrast to play, are organized. They have rules and structure and they involve a specific set of role partners. The child must learn the whole system of roles.

For example, playing catcher in a game of baseball requires the child to take the perspective of the whole team toward her or him as a player occupying a specific position. To think of oneself as a catcher involves having knowledge of everyone else on the field (the team, officials, opponents), the object of the game, and the specific relationship of the catcher's position to the entire cluster of activities that constitute the baseball game. Not just the one specific game, but the abstraction called baseball as a set of rules and statuses.

The Emergence of Self. These consequences of role-taking are only one aspect of what Mead considered the *process of self.* If internalization were all that

Stages of role taking are **imitation, play,** and **games.**

123

was required for the formation of self there would be little spontaneity or novelty in individual experience. Mead distinguished the "I" and the "me." The "I" is a creative, acting aspect of self that reflects upon and responds to the "me" composed of internalized attitudes of others. The self is thus a process, in which the "I" interacts with the "me" in a constant conversation running through one's mind. This dialogue produces an *organization of perceptions* that form the self-concept and that guide behavior at any one time. Thus society is possible, according to Mead, only because we can take on the attitudes of others and share a world of meaning. Mind is possible only because the human being can reflect upon itself and become both the subject and object of thinking.

The **emergence of self** involves both self-reflection and interaction with others.

OTHER VIEWS OF THE SOCIAL SELF

Cooley and Mead have had great impact on American sociology. Their emphasis on role performance and the reactions of others are integral to the sociological conception of personality. Although the idea that the self is a social product is generally accepted by most social scientists, there is considerable difference of opinion over the relative input of innate and learned factors in the development of personality and subsequent behavior.

On the one hand, some *symbolic interactionists* such as Goffman see personality as a presentation of self and, therefore, as constantly in need of validation, with each encounter a contest in which the self is at stake. All this makes for very dramatic and richly descriptive studies.

Symbolic interactionists see personality as a presentation of the self that is in constant need of validation.

On the other hand, psychologically oriented social scientists view personality as a relatively fixed pattern of responses, shaped largely by intrinsic factors such as temperament, intelligence, genetic threshholds, and so forth. In this perspective, personalities are core identities that can only be more or less influenced by the social environment. Two decades ago, in a classic essay, Dennis Wrong (1961) criticized the "oversocialized conception of man." He suggests that sociologists have gone too far into areas that impinge on biology and psychology, overlooking the emotional and physiological foundations for behavior. Some individuals have less impulse control than others; some personality traits are inborn, and others will be set at early ages regardless of the changing social scene. Socialization, claims Wrong, cannot fully explain impulsive acts and *affective* (emotional) behavior. Another set of traits often neglected by sociologists are those having to do with *cognition*, which is the mental capacity for processing information, that is, the process of *knowing*. Although the study of affective and cognitive factors in socialization has been largely left to psychologists, certain basic ideas and theories deserve brief mention here.

The "oversocialized" conception of human beings underestimates the emotional and physiological bases of behavior.

Cognition is the mental process of **knowing.**

FREUD, ERIKSON, AND STAGES OF DEVELOPMENT

Sigmund Freud, the founder of psychoanalysis, has had an enormous impact on American thought. Today Freud is viewed as a nineteenth century culture-bound theorist whose concepts have never been subjected to rigorous empirical testing. Nonetheless, for many decades Freudianism was extremely influential among those who created the intellectual climate of our society. Moreover, as an example of theories of conflict between the individual and society, Freud's formulation in *Civilization and Its Discontents* (1930/1962) is unexcelled.

Freud, the founder of psychoanalysis, has had an enormous impact on the intellectual climate of our society.

Society and the Individual.   The basic theme of *Civilization and Its Discontents* is the dynamic tension between the individual striving to satisfy instinctual needs, and the social order that requires members to renounce such instant gratification. Humans are born as bundles of desires, but if each was to seek to satisfy all desires, social life would be impossible. Society—or, as Freud preferred, *civilization*—is built upon the repression of desire. Socialization is learning to renounce pleasure. This renunciation is made possible through the manipulation of guilt feelings by the socializers, typically parents. The infant and then the child is dependent upon the mother for nurturance, so that fear of her withholding such pleasures becomes a basic anxiety that can subsequently be manipulated to secure the child's conformity to expectations.

The Freudian theory is really not all that different from other theories we have discussed. But unlike the child in theories of the social self, Freud's child does not then achieve harmony with the group. Rather, a residue of anger, anxiety, and guilt must be dealt with through *repression*, that is, placing unpleasant emotional traces in the subconscious, where they remain below the level of consciousness, but are capable of being brought to mind whenever similar situations recur in later life. Civilization, according to Freud, is thus built upon repressed desires.

> **Repression** places anger, anxiety, and guilt below the level of consciousness.

The Freudian Self.   For Freud, as for Mead, the mind, or psyche, of the socialized individual is a process. In Freud's formulation, this process is a dynamic interplay among (1) the instinctual desires (*id*), (2) the socialized self (*superego*) composed primarily of prohibitions that control the id, and (3) the mediating, directing aspect of the self (*ego*) that links the psyche to reality. There is, of course, no way at all that this scheme can be proved, even though the terms *id*, *superego*, and *ego* have become part of everyday speech. That there are such human attributes as desires, internalized standards of conduct, and a sense of location in the real world cannot be denied. So whether called id, superego and ego or some other names, Freud did identify aspects of mental life that have some influence on behavior.

> The **id** consists of instinctual desires, drives, and urges; the **superego** is the socialized self composed of prohibitions controlling the **id**; the **ego** is the conscious part of the self that links the psyche to reality.

Stages of Development.   One final contribution of Freud deserves mention: the idea that there are well-defined phases or stages in psychological and social development that form a sequence which a child must go through on the journey to adulthood. Even though Freud's specific scheme of *developmental stages* is little used by sociologists, the concept has been extremely important in psychology.

ERIKSON AND EGO THEORY

In the decades since Freud's death, the idea of *psychosocial development* has been taken up by other psychologists. Most of these depart from Freud in two major respects. First, Freud's emphasis on the preadolescent years has proved too restrictive; much personal growth is accomplished throughout life. Secondly, the Freudian emphasis on the instinctual desires of the id has also been questioned. The newer theories are more concerned with the *ego*, the rational, directing, reality-oriented aspect of self. The most influential of these post-Freudian theories of life stages and ego development is that of the contemporary psychologist Erik Erikson.

Erikson extends the stages of personality growth and change to encompass the entire life span. His emphasis is on the organization of perceptions about the self called *ego*. By proposing that the life course is composed of a series of challenges that require reorganization of the ego, Erikson opens up the possibility for continual restructuring of the self. But not all is in flux, because each new element is added to the existing structure. However, the potential for personality change and for undoing previous failures makes Erikson's scheme more flexible and liberating than that of Freud.

Erikson identifies eight stages in the life course, each of which is linked to transition points and status changes.

Erikson (1964) describes eight stages that are tied to social system changes in the lives of individuals, typically transition points where important statuses are assumed or relinquished, and where a new type of role playing is required. Each stage involves a developmental task with the possibility of a positive or negative outcome in terms of the individual's ability to adapt to life changes.

Stage 1. From experiences with nurturers, the infant develops either a sense of *basic trust* or *mistrust*.

Stage 2. In the first three years of life, the child learns and practices all kinds of new skills, emerging with either a feeling of *autonomy* (self-regulation) or *doubt and shame* over its abilities.

Stage 3. Success in exploring the environment and dealing with peers by the 4–5 year old can lead to a sense of *initiative* and self-confidence; failure can produce feelings of *guilt*.

Stage 4. Between ages 6 and 13, the child's focus shifts from family to school, and can develop either the self-concept of *industriousness* or of *inferiority*.

Stage 5. In adolescence, the developmental task is *identity* formation, while failure to create a firm sense of self leads to *confusion* about one's self.

Stage 6. The great challenge of young adulthood is the establishment of stable love relationships, and the outcomes are *intimacy* as opposed to *isolation* and loneliness.

Stage 7. Citizenship, work, and family formation are the primary tasks of mature adulthood, leading to *generativity*, in contrast to the *self-absorption* and stagnation of people who do not contributre to the well-being of others.

Stage 8. Even the end of life poses a developmental challenge: finding continuity and meaning in one's life— *integrity*—or, being unable to break out of isolation and self-absorption, giving way to *despair*.

Critique of Stage Theories. Erikson's descriptions of these stages are *ideal types:* few individuals go through life experiencing precisely these emotions. Most people meet life's challenges with only partial success—a little guilt, some self-confidence, general satisfaction and gnawing doubts. Erikson's model is probably most useful as a broad outline of development across the life course. Erikson's accomplishments are to see all stages of life as offering opportunities for ego development and personal growth.

There are many contemporary versions of life-span developmental psychology, that, following Erikson, are ego-centered and focused on transition points in the life course (see Sheehy, 1976, for a journalistic review). These models are psychological in that they are basically concerned with changes within the psyche, but many are also sociological in their emphasis on the *social role changes* that trigger the need to adjust the ego.

Stage theories based on the relatively normal transitions of adulthood have been criticized by sociologists (Clausen, 1972; Bates and Brim, 1980), who generally prefer the term "life course" with its implication of flow and continuity (Stein and Etzkowitz, 1978). The concept of stages has great appeal to the modern mind, as a rational and orderly way to organize masses of information, but it is also a confining and arbitrary way of looking at adult development.

COGNITIVE DEVELOPMENT—JEAN PIAGET

The psychological literature on personality development reviewed thus far has been largely concerned with the emotional or self-concept aspects of ego growth. But there is another dimension to the mind, one that also changes as the organism matures: cognitive capacities. *Cognition* refers to how the person perceives and thinks. The major figure in this field was Jean Piaget (1896–1980), a Swiss psychologist. Piaget began with basic observations. He watched youngsters playing marbles, and asked them to teach him the game. Over and over, he watched, asked, and observed children at all ages. From his observations, Piaget concluded that children at different ages were also at different stages of cognitive development; that is, they had very different understandings of what they were doing.

Piaget observed that children at different ages are also at different stages of cognitive development.

Along with age-related shifts in cognitive complexity, Piaget also found changes in *moral reasoning*. As the mind is able to deal with increasingly sophisticated perceptions, so also can the child handle other types of abstractions— ideas of justice, fairness, and the like. In the marble games, for example, very young children took the rules as unquestioned givens, allowing no modifications. Slightly older children were more flexible, changing the rules to meet unexpected situations. And at a more advanced age, youngsters realized that a game is composed of rules agreed upon by participants who can change the rules and invent new games.

Moral reasoning is the complex cognitive capacity to handle abstract ideas such as justice and fairness.

Thus do children gradually learn that absent people have not disappeared, that effects have causes, that the same quantity can take different shapes (for example, that a long string of clay can contain as much material as a ball of clay), and so forth. So, although cognitive development is age-related, the child's mind will not automatically develop without real-life experiences. As the cases of Anna and Isabelle remind us, environmental stimulation, trial-and-error attempts to understand and master, and feedback from others, are all essential to cognitive maturation.

B. F. SKINNER AND OPERANT CONDITIONING

Behaviorists, as the name implies, concentrate on *behavior*, with minimal attention to such subjective factors as emotions and ego functions. Behavior is the observable act that can be measured with precision. The behaviorist who influenced sociologists most is B. F. Skinner (1904–   ), who has applied his observations of pigeons and other laboratory animals to condition human behavior.

Skinner applied his observations of laboratory animals to human behavior.

Conditioning shapes behavior through the manipulation of rewards.

Operant conditioning refers to the shaping of behavior through the manipulation of rewards. When an act is rewarded, it is likely to be repeated. When rewards are withheld the act is less likely to recur. *Positive reinforcers* are reactions from others or the environment that encourage repeat performances. *Negative reinforcers* are responses that do not encourage repetition of certain behaviors. Some actions thus become associated with pleasurable outcomes. To the degree that the reward is desired by the organism, appropriate behavior is elicited.

Positive reinforcement encourages repeat behavior; **negative reinforcement** discourages repeat behavior.

Skinner Boxes.   Skinner achieved some notoriety many decades ago by tending an infant daughter for part of the day in a completely controlled environment that became known as the *Skinner Box.* The child, incidentally, not only survived but thrived, contrary to the expectations of many. The concept of the environment as a box has important sociological applications. Although humans, unlike pigeons, construct their own environments, they, like pigeons, have their behaviors positively or negatively reinforced and base subsequent actions on the knowledge of these sanctions. The social system can be thought of as one big Skinner Box in which people act within a system of rewards and punishments.

The **Skinner Box** is a completely controlled environment.

Behavior Modification.   The principles of operant conditioning have been applied as therapy in cases in which extreme behavior change is desired by authorities. Prisons and mental hospitals, because they are environments that can be thoroughly controlled twenty-four hours a day (*total institutions*), have been prime sites for experiments in *behavior modification*. All rewards are withheld from the inmate until he or she performs actions desired by custodians. Over time, regardless of the internal state of the organism (drives, motives), behavioral change will take place.

Behavior modification involves the withholding of rewards in exchange for desired behavior.

Many contemporary behaviorists, however, do take into account a step between presentation of a stimulus and the response of the actor:

The inclusion of an interpretive element brings behavioralism closer to the symbolic-interaction approach.

A SOCIOLOGICAL PERSPECTIVE ON PERSONALITY

Many sociologists view personality as a reflection of the *cluster of roles* being enacted by an individual at any point in the life course. You are what you do; or, as Kenneth Burke puts it: "Doing is Being" (Goffman, 1963B). Although there may be some core identity laid down in childhood, personalities are unique and ever-changing accumulations of experience. Childhood measurements of psychological functioning do not predict adult mental health because so many intervening experiences and relationships shape and channel the development of self (Skolnick, 1978).

Sociologists often use the term *self* rather than *personality* to focus on the more social, active, role-involved aspects of the individual's inner being. The self is something that one can reflect upon and then share with others. Goffman in *The Presentation of Self in Everyday Life* (1959) suggested the extent to which a self is a social construct, carefully prepared and presented as "the real me" in order to influence others. There is, says Goffman (1961B), a "virtual self" that awaits every role player—the societal ideal for that role. This ideal offers an opportunity to become a certain kind of person, regardless of the personality traits of a specific individual.

Self-in-the-role is the identity available to a person in a given role.

The Mind as a Jailor. In an experiment that has received much publicity, Philip Zimbardo and his colleagues (1973) found that the line between self and self-in-role can be readily erased under some circumstances. Answering an ad in local and campus newspapers for "a study of prison life," at $15 per day for two weeks, twenty-one average, middle-class, college-age males (twenty white, one oriental), carefully screened for physical health, emotional maturity, and law-abiding orientations, were accepted. The experimenters randomly assigned the subjects to the status of either prisoner or guard in a "mock prison" constructed in the basement of an unused college building. Every conceivable step was taken to make the prison as authentic as possible.

Both prisoners and guards were *deindividualized* through typical prison processes of removing civilian identities. The prisoners wore smocklike uniforms and had to ask the guards for permission for most normal activities. The guards also had their uniforms: khaki, with night sticks, handcuffs, whistles, and reflector sunglasses.

Neither group was given much formal instruction in how to play their roles, yet within days each individual had *disappeared into the appropriate role*. The guards quickly learned to enjoy arbitrary power over the prisoners, and the latter began to "behave in ways that actually helped to justify their dehumanizing treatment at the hands of the guards." The researchers were amazed at the speed and ease with which the assigned roles and definition of the situation controlled the behavior of psychologically-sound individuals.

One prisoner was released after a day and a half "because of extreme depression, disorganized thinking, and uncontrollable crying." On each of the next three days, one additional prisoner developed similar symptoms, and was released. A fifth man broke out in a psychosomatic rash. By the end of six days the entire experiment was called off, so transformed had these "normal, healthy, educated young men" become. What caused the transformation? Obviously nothing in the subjects' personality, for all had been carefully screened and randomly assigned. As the experimenters conclude,

Rather, the subjects' abnormal social and personal reactions are best seen as a product of their transaction with an environment that supported the behavior that would be pathological in other settings, but was "appropriate" in this prison. Had we observed comparable reactions in a real prison, the psychiatrist undoubtedly would have been able to attribute any prisoner's behavior to character defects or personality maladjustment, while critics of the prison system would have been quick to label the guards as "psychopathic." This tendency to locate the source of behavior disorders inside a particular person or group underestimates the power of situational forces. (Zimbardo et al, 1973)

Role distance is the space that a role incumbent can place between the self and the self-in-the-role.

Role Distance.   When there are no alternatives, individuals may indeed disappear into roles that are not intrinsically appealing, as did Zimbardo's "prisoners." But Goffman suggests that the relationship between self and self-in-the-role can take several forms. Role enactment can be thought of as a continuum from total involvement to denial, or from *embracement* to *rejection* of the self-in-the-role that awaits the status incumbent. *Role distance* refers to the space that a role player can place between self and self-in-the-role.

There are a number of distancing devices that people use to warn others not to take them as the virtual self implied in the role. Those of you who have had temporary jobs—busboy, waitress, cashier, stock clerk—that place you in a position you consider inferior to your true status have probably acted in such a way as to let others know that you are really a college student or on your way to better things. Perhaps you brought an impressive textbook to work, where others could see it, or did your job in such a slapdash manner that no one could possibly take you for someone who would be serious about such a role. Role distance is a way of protecting the self, offering leeway for the expression of personal style.

Even in roles that one embraces, there is a tendency to create space for individuality in the performance. Goffman uses the term "petty truancies" to describe the minor deviations whereby an actor can express individuality. These are the little rebellions against norms that remind us and others of our uniqueness.

Socialization and Culture

As described in Chapter 3, each culture is a selection of traits from the range of human possibilities. So, also, in each culture certain personality traits are approved and desired. In some societies, fearlessness and courage are exalted; in others, wisdom and prudence; in still others, skill at making baskets, pottery, or money. Typically, too, one set of traits is desired for females and another for males (Bernard, 1981). And in many cultures, the personality characteristics of children are very different from those expected in adults (Benedict, 1938). In other words, there is immense cross-cultural variation in character traits and temperament, as well as age and sex differences in personality within each culture.

There are important differences among cultures in values, skills, and traits that are emphasized in socialization.

This variety is possible because the processes of socialization tend to produce the type of person rewarded and encouraged by agents of socialization. What is normal in one society can be pathological in another. For example, Ruth Benedict (1934) describes the inhabitants of the Island of Dobu as being deeply mistrustful of one another but most especially of close family members. The Zuni Indians of the Southwest United States are socialized to an entirely different personality style of noncompetitiveness, a trait that makes possible the kind of cooperative living that is the Zuni way. Different socialization practices and experiences produce different types of people.

TWO WORLDS OF CHILDHOOD

Professor Urie Bronfenbrenner (1970), an authority on childhood socialization, spent many years observing how children are raised and trained in the United States and in the Soviet Union. Comparing the behaviors and personalities of American and Soviet youngsters, Bronfenbrenner found differences great enough to speak of "two worlds" of childhood. How are these differences produced? Through very different socialization experiences.

Both American and Soviet children are socialized by parents at first, then by teachers and peers, but with almost opposite outcomes. The Soviet child is trained to become a cooperative and conscientious member of a group; the American child is encouraged to be individualistic.

In the Soviet schoolroom, for example, the teacher is an unquestioned authority, but the peer group enforces the norms and sanctions members. The teacher rewards students on the basis of *group performance* rather than individual abilities. The group therefore has a stake in each member's performance, and every child becomes sensitive to the needs of the peer group. Older grades "adopt" and guide younger ones. In this fashion, the good of all becomes the goal of each. These are obviously individuals who will fit well into a collectivist society. Socialization systems, after all, are designed to prepare youngsters for successful adulthood in a given type of social system.

The American child, working to get better marks than peers in each grade, is being socialized to competitive behaviors throughout life. This is what many believe to be *the* important lesson for success in our society: that the good of each is the good of all. Thus, two modes of socialization produce two very different types of young person, each presumably equipped to function appropriately as an adult—Two Worlds, indeed.

Socialization appears, then, to account for most of the uniformity in personality found within a culture. Can socialization also account for personality changes in a given society, especially those that distinguish the young from the old?

SOCIALIZATION THROUGH THE LIFE COURSE

It is obvious that socialization in childhood cannot prepare a person for the many different roles of adulthood in a modern industrial society. Just think of the major role changes of early adulthood: graduation from college, entry into an occupation, marriage, parenthood, community and civic involvements. These changes require *desocialization* (learning to relinquish a role), *resocialization* (learning new ways to deal with old role partners), as well as *socialization* (learning the new role). And each major role change carries with it the potential for reorganization of the self.

How many times have you said of someone, "How he's changed since he has been married," or "That job certainly made a new person of her," or "My father's been impossible now that he's retired." These are not new persons, of course, but the same people undergoing important role transitions. Their way

Desocialization is learning to give up a role; **resocialization** is learning new ways to deal with role partners.

It is important to realize the extent to which we follow predictable lines of development as well as the degree of flexibility and change possible in personality.

of life has been altered and so, accordingly, has their view of themselves and their way of dealing with others.

If the self were as fixed as some wish to believe, there would be no point in going to a therapist or joining an encounter group, or attempting to turn over a new leaf, or engaging in any of the self-improvement schemes that so characterize this society. Paradoxically, Americans believe in the ability to change oneself, while still clinging to the illusion of stable personality traits. This latter view may be necessary to generate a sense of self-continuity although, in fact, a great deal is always changing.

Summary

An infant cannot become a human being without interacting with other humans. Humans differ from all other animals in their capacity to learn rather than being instinctively programmed for action. Human behavior is primarily learned through the process of socialization, which involves the transmission, through language and gestures, of the culture of the groups into which the child is born.

Socialization occurs as individuals assume statuses and learn the appropriate roles and the rules guiding interaction with others. Roles are learned by acquiring the necessary information shaped through the reaction of others to one's role performance, and reinforced by social supports for role enactment.

In North America the major agents of socialization are parents, peers, teachers, and the media. Socialization practices vary within a society among different occupational groups and subcultures.

Socialization also involves the development of self. Cooley proposed that the self is shaped and developed through a "looking glass" process reflecting the reaction of important others. Mead stressed the capacity to "take the role of the other" toward oneself as crucial to the development of a self.

Cooley and Mead emphasized the reinforcing interests of self and society, but Freud focused on the fundamental conflict between personal desires and social restraints. The Freudian self is characterized by a dynamic interplay among the innate desires and urges of the id, the controls of the superego, and the ego. Erikson, placing greater emphasis on ego development, proposed that the life course is composed of a series of challenges requiring the reorganization of the ego, opening up the possibility of personality change and development throughout one's life.

Other psychologists have studied the development of thought and perception in children. From his observations of children, Piaget concluded that children of different ages were at different stages of cognitive development, with older children able to handle more complex concepts than were younger children.

Other social scientists minimize such subjective factors as emotions and ego development and concentrate on behavior. B. F. Skinner has demonstrated how behavior is conditioned by the manipulation of rewards, that is, by positive and negative reinforcement.

From the sociological viewpoint personality is conceptualized as the cluster of roles being enacted at any point in the life course. The relationship between self-concept and self-in-role has been described by Goffman in terms of role distance and embracement.

Cross-cultural studies demonstrate great variety in the content of socialization, as in Bronfenbrenner's report of childrearing in the Soviet Union and the United States, producing two different worlds of childhood.

Major role changes carry the potential for reorganization of the self. Socialization, the process of learning one's culture and forming one's personality, produces certain regularities in behavior, but personality change can occur throughout the life course, and each person develops unique ways to express individuality—within limits.

Suggested Readings

BRONFENBRENNER, URIE. *Two Worlds of Childhood*. New York: Russell Sage, 1970. Observational study of child rearing comparing the United States and the Soviet Union.

FROMM, ERICH. *Escape from Freedom*. New York: Holt, 1947. An analysis of the interplay between individual needs, personality, and the social structure. Fromm suggests that the burdens of personal choice drive many people into obedience to authority.

GAGNON, JOHN, and WILLIAM SIMON. *Sexual Conduct: The Social Sources of Human Sexuality*. Chicago: Aldine, 1973. The authors develop a social learning theory of sexual behavior. Individuals learn a complex social script that guides their sexual conduct in situations defined as appropriate for that behavior.

GOFFMAN, ERVING. *The Presentation of Self in Everyday Life*. Garden City, N. Y.: Doubleday, 1959. Ordinary social interaction as high drama. We are all actors presenting a version of ourself to an audience of others, on various stages, in different roles, every day.

HEWITT, JOHN P. *Self and Society*. Boston: Allyn, 1976. The concepts of symbolic interaction clarified. How the self develops through social interaction and how social order is created.

ROSE, PETER I. (Ed.) *Socialization and the Life Cycle*. New York: St. Martin's, 1979. An excellent anthology dealing with various aspects of the life cycle.

SIDEL, RUTH. *Women and Child Care in China: A First-Hand Report*. Baltimore: Penguin, 1972. Sensitive observations of the effects of collective child-rearing on women, children, and the nature of the family in the People's Republic of China.

6

Conformity and Deviance

ocial order depends on most individuals doing what is expected of them by others. Yet, we are generally fascinated by tales of those who break the rules. *Deviants* are people who violate group norms, and we tend most often to think of criminals or the mentally ill. But deviance can also describe acts that are more industrious, more ambitious, more heroic, or more honest than that generally found or expected within the social system. For example, war heroes, self-made millionnaires, and Nobel prize winners are as deviant in terms of non-normative behavior as are skid row alchoholics or bank robbers.

The sociological study of deviant behavior, however, has been almost exclusively concerned with socially *disapproved* deviation from the norms of a society or group. Where there are rules of conduct, there are also definitions of deviance. To define *A* (acceptable behavior) is automatically to create another class of events, non-*A* (unacceptable behavior). Deviance and conformity thus are two sides of a coin; one cannot exist without the other.

By studying *disapproved* behaviors, we may learn what is valued in a society or subgroup, or at least what those who make the rules find threatening. Many theorists have proposed that people who violate norms must suffer from some sort of personal pathology; that is, they are immoral or sick. Yet, as we shall see in this chapter, deviant behavior differs in content, but not in essential nature, from what we call conformity. Indeed, the process whereby both deviant and nondeviant roles are constructed and performed is quite similar, flowing from group experiences and sanctions.

This chapter examines the types of norms members of groups and subgroups are expected to observe and how these are internalized, the social functions of deviance, the kinds of people and situations that are likely to be called deviant, and how norms are enforced and deviants punished.

Deviants are people who violate group norms.

Deviance refers to variations from the rules for usual, approved behavior.

The sociological study of deviance has focused primarily upon socially **disapproved** deviation.

By studying **disapproved** behavior, we also learn what is socially valued.

Structuring Conformity

Whereas deviants were once thought to be possessed by devils, the deviant of today is viewed as in need of psychiatric help or punishment (or both). In either case, the deviant has disrupted ongoing relationships within a system by behaving in an unpredictable manner. But how is deviance possible given the powerful forces toward conformity?

EMERGENCE OF NORMS

Norms are arrived at through social interaction and represent a kind of negotiated consensus, dominating individual perceptions and behaviors in diverse situations. Even in situations where no norms have been established, their emergence can be predicted.

In 1935 Muzafer Sherif, a social psychologist, performed a now-classic exper-

Deviant behavior shares many characteristics with conforming behavior; both occur within a social context. (Source: Stock, Boston.)

iment that illustrates how norm formation occurs among individuals in new and ambiguous situations. The laboratory experiment used an optical illusion, the so-called autokinetic effect, where, if a small fixed point of light is briefly exposed in a dark room it appears to the viewer to move erratically in all directions. Not surprisingly, people differ in their estimates of how it moves. Sherif asked a series of individuals, one at a time and alone, to estimate how far the spot moved. Although there was no objective basis for knowing, each person developed a unique standard or norm of movement. Sherif then organized groups composed of the original subjects divided in such a way that individuals who had established very different standards in their solitary sessions were placed together. Interestingly, convergence toward a common norm or standard occurred within the groups, although the majority of people were unaware of the fact that they were being influenced by others. Nor were they aware of their convergence toward a common norm. In fact, just the contrary was reported by the participants, who indicated that their individual judgments were made *before* the others spoke and, furthermore, that they had not been influenced by one another (Sherif, 1935).

In the experiment just cited, as in other laboratory studies, three factors appear to be significant determinants of conformity. First, in an unstructured situation, there is some distortion of perception that takes place to relieve uncertainty. The individual believes that he or she sees an object or event as others do and is unaware of the role of group pressure. Secondly, group pressure may distort one's own judgment, so that one doubts one's own sensory perceptions in the face of contradictory information from a larger group. And lastly, one may decide to "yea say" or agree, even if unconvinced that one's own feelings or perceptions are incorrect. After all, who wishes to appear stupid?

But life is not lived in a laboratory, and, despite these pressures toward conformity, complete compliance with all norms is unlikely, and each of us has deviated from one norm or another at some point in our lives, probably even today. Conformity and deviance may be thought of as the opposite ends of a continuum, recognizing that any individual's position on the continuum will vary from one norm to another.

High   Norm compliance   Low
<—————————————————————————————>
Absolute   Absolute
conformity   nonconformity

DIFFERENTIAL STRENGTH OF NORMS

Because a norm is a general standard for conduct, any individual or group behavior may—and indeed probably will—differ from the norm unless some control, such as a sanction, is imposed to bring about conformity. In the experiment performed by Sherif, the sanction was an informal one, that of *group pressure*, leading to the establishment of a group norm. Generally, the more important the norm, as a reflection of social values, the greater will be the sanctions imposed for its violation. There are several broad categories of norms, as Table 6.1 illustrates.

Group pressure leads to the establishment of a group norm.

Within contemporary industrialized society, *moral* and *institutional norms* are considered more important for conformity than are aesthetic, cognitive, or conventional norms. For example, deviance from the norm of having only one husband or wife at one time may be prosecuted by law. The bigamist is not only the butt of jokes, but could also serve a prison term. The man or woman who wears a purple suit, orange shirt, and white socks to a formal dance or who paints a house with scarlet polka dots—both examples of deviations from current aesthetic norms—may be considered eccentric and avoided or teased, but will not be subject to more severe sanctions. Similarly, people who refuse to acknowledge introductions or do not say "thank you" upon receiving presents have also violated a set of norms—conventional rules for behavior—and are considered boors, but not public menaces deserving punishment.

Moral and **institutional norms** are considered more important for conformity than aesthetic, cognitive, or conventional norms.

Not only do norms evoke more or less harsh sanctions depending on their importance to the group, but they may be either *proscriptive* ("thou shalt not") or *prescriptive* ("thou shalt"). Sociologists have observed that deviations from

Norms can be **prescriptive** (what should be done) or **proscriptive** (what should not be done).

Table 6-1. *Varieties of Norms Within a Society*

Types of norms	Purpose	Example
Technical or cognitive	'How to' standards guiding knowledge and task performance	Cookbooks Textbooks Safety codes
Conventional	Standards for polite/ socially-appropriate behavior	Etiquette Manners
Aesthetic	Standards of taste and beauty	'Good taste' Art appreciation
Moral	Standards of right and wrong	The 10 Commandments; prohibition of murder, rape, theft
Institutional	Standards essential to survival of complex social patterns	One marriage at a time U.S. President must be native born citizen Wage-earners must pay income tax

proscriptive norms are more likely than violations of prescriptive norms to activate extreme forms of reaction and sanctions.

Yet, norms are essentially arbitrary. Indeed, there is no one, eternal universal standard of behavior. We are constantly surrounded by rules internalized through the process of socialization, so that as sociologist William Graham Sumner suggested almost a century ago, they appear to be only "the right and proper way of doing things." Yet what is defined as normative, and therefore what is defined as deviance, changes over time and varies from society to society. At one time or another, all of the following activities, currently considered normal or at least not particularly deviant, were defined as criminal deviant acts: printing a book; professing the belief that the earth is round; claiming that the earth is not the center of the universe; performing an autopsy upon a dead human body; not attending church; and boxing or prize fighting. Indeed, some of these "deviant behaviors" were punishable by death. Even minor deviations might be dealt with harshly; only a hundred fifty years ago, stealing linen was grounds for being hanged.

HOW CONFORMISTS SEE DEVIANTS

What is deviant behavior? Simmons (1969) administered a questionnaire to 280 respondents, selected for diversity on such characteristics as age, sex, race, education, and region of the country. He was particularly interested in the degree of intolerance toward various kinds of behavior. To measure this, he constructed a scale of social distance (the extent to which one would be willing to accept various categories of unconventional people as a close relative, friend, neighbor, community member, resident of the country, or not accept them at all). He then computed the average social distances accorded the different types:

Groups (Listed from least tolerated to most.)	Mean social distance (High score means high rejection.)
Homosexuals	5.3
Lesbians	5.2
Prostitutes	5.0
Marijuana smokers	4.9
Political radicals	4.3
Adulterers	4.1
Alcoholics	4.0
Beatniks	3.9
Gamblers	3.6
Ex-convicts	3.5

Source: Abridged from J. L. Simmons, *Deviants*. Berkeley, Calif.: Glendessary Press, 1969, p. 33.

What an odd assortment, and what curious patterns of rejection, with homosexuals so much more feared than ex-convicts. Nor would all these behaviors necessarily be considered deviant today. A recent repeat of this exercise with two classes of undergraduates found that political extremism, homosexuality, and marijuana use were no longer viewed as deviant by college-aged respondents. Instead, gambling, and several new categories (elicited from the students themselves) were listed: rapists, child abusers, plane highjackers, and wife beaters. Neither beatniks nor their 1960s counterparts, hippies, were even mentioned in 1979.

What may one conclude about deviant behavior? Its common denominator obviously rests not in the particular behavior itself but upon the definitions by some social group, such as college students, middle-aged parents, or legislators. Deviance is signified by the *societal reaction* to an act or lifestyle that violates currently popular institutional or moral norms.

> Deviance is signified by **societal reactions** to acts or lifestyles that do not conform to current norms.

SOME SOCIAL FUNCTIONS OF DEVIANCE

The insight that deviance does not reside in the act itself but rather in how the act is interpreted by others was noted by Emile Durkheim (1893/1960) who further proposed that deviance, than being totally destructive or evil is necessary to societal well-being. To hope to eradicate all sin and waywardness is to neglect the very real functions that deviance plays in maintaining social order. Behavior that seems abnormal from a psychological or psychiatric viewpoint is not necessarily pathological from the perspective of the sociologist. Durkheim, for example, pointed out that crime is a necessary part of all societies. Paradoxical as this may sound, crime fulfills an important service to the extent that it generates *social cohesion* in opposition to such behavior. As members of a community or society come together to express outrage and to ventilate their anger about "criminal" acts, they develop closer ties to one another than previously existed. This coming together in shared moral indignation creates what Durkheim termed the "public temper," that is, a feeling shared by members of the group and belonging to no one individual in particular. Through creation of the public temper or, in more current terminology, group consensus, social organization is strengthened. This process is well illustrated by the public temper created in the United States by reports of mistreatment

> Deviant behavior, such as crime, generates **social cohesion** in opposition to such behavior.

upon the release of the fifty-two persons held hostage in Iran for fourteen months in 1979–81. A wave of shared moral indignation swept the country, generating a sense of solidarity, and defining the Iranians as barbarians and outlaws with whom promises need not be kept. When deviants are identified and punished, members of the society are united in a common morality that strengthens their own belief system. Thus deviance has a dual function: *unification of the group* and *boundary setting*.

Boundary setting is the process by which norms and values are established, setting limits on acceptable behavior.

What do we mean by *boundary setting*? It is a process by which shared norms and values are established within a social collective such as the family, the school, the workplace, a professional group, one's hometown, or the entire society. Within these social collectives, boundaries are placed at the outer limits of acceptable and permissible behavior so that people's actions are limited in range, and made relatively stable and predictable. In other words, conduct is confined to legitimized forms; behavior outside the boundaries is clearly identified as unacceptable. Kai Erikson (1966) suggests that people learn boundaries through the process of *confrontation*. That is, the limits of acceptable behavior are constantly being tested to ascertain the boundary lines. Often, the nature of this confrontation is public, as are the demonstrations in support of gay rights or in the current controversy about hand-gun control.

People learn where boundaries are set through the process of **confrontation.**

SOCIAL CONTROL

Social control refers to processes by which normative behavior is enforced.

Social control refers to planned or unplanned social processes by which people are taught, persuaded, or forced to conform to norms. It is the complement of deviance, for without deviant behavior there would be no need for social control and without social control there would be no way of recognizing the boundary between the acceptable and the unacceptable. In every society, some punishments or negative sanctions are established for deviant behavior, and the weight of the community is brought to bear on the deviant.

Social control may be **formal** or **informal.**

Social control may be either *formal* or *informal. Informal mechanisms* include expressions of disapproval by significant others, shunning, and witholding of positive rewards for the disapproved behavior. As discussed in Chapter 5, most people internalize norms in the course of socialization. This is any group's most powerful protection against deviance, in that the individual's own conscience operates as an agent of social control.

Informal mechanisms of social control include disapproval by significant others and withholding of positive rewards.

When informal sanctions fail, *formal agents* of social control may be called upon. In contemporary society, such formal agents and agencies include psychiatry and other mental health professions; mental hospitals; police and the courts; prisons; and social welfare agencies. All these formal agents function to limit, correct, and control violation of norms. Conflict theorists would also point out that social control agents and systems tend, in any society, to serve the interests of powerful groups and to enforce the norms most beneficial to those who make the rules and who, therefore, define unacceptable behavior.

Formal agents of social control include mental hospitals, police, courts, and prisons.

Social control, whether formal or informal, has a dual function. First, it punishes the wrongdoer and reaffirms the boundaries of acceptable behavior. Second, and less recognized, it regulates the flow and manner in which deviants are treated. Currie (1968) has suggested that there are two types of formal control systems: *repressive* and *restrained*. A *repressive* control system is characterized by unrestrained power to suppress deviance and by a high level of interest in ensuring conformity. The secret police force of the former Shah of Iran,

Repressive control systems are characterized by unrestrained power to suppress deviance.

for example, was a repressive social control system, as were the Islamic courts that followed.

In comparison, *restrained* formal social control systems are distinguished by a greater level of public accountability, a lack of extraordinary powers to restrain and detect deviance, and a lower degree of interest in apprehending norm violators. Canadian and United States courts and police units are operated in a relatively restrained fashion, although excesses have occurred.

Restrained control systems are relatively more accountable and less powerful in suppressing deviance.

DEVIANCE AS A SAFETY VALVE

A certain amount of deviance, however, is permitted in most societies as a *safety valve*, that is, as a means of ventilating frustration and anger. One illustration is the current attitude toward prostitution in the United States. Illegal in every state, prostitution continues to flourish with only occasional raids and arrests by police and exposés by the media. Why? Many sociologists would argue that prostitution continues to exist and to be more or less tolerated, albeit stigmatized, because it fulfills a variety of functions within the society. One

Some deviance is permitted in most societies as a way of ventilating frustration and anger, a **safety valve** function.

Despite opposition, one reason prostitution continues to flourish is that it is a multi-million dollar industry. (Source: Marvin E. Newman, Woodfin Camp & Associates.)

function is a conservative one; since historically, Americans have distinguished between two types of women—"good" women, whom one married, and "bad" women, with whom one had sexual relations but did not marry—prostitution reinforced the double standard of morality. Sexual latitude was permitted for men without threatening either family relationships or mythologies about female sexuality, and at the same time the anonymity and business nature of prostitution allowed men to explore new, sometimes unconventional, sexual avenues without affectional commitment or involvement. The business nature of prostitution also exemplifies the basic values of materialism in our culture. Moreover, the young, the isolated, and the unattractive male, who is afraid or unable to make a conventional approach to a woman, can have sexual intercourse in a manner in which he, as temporary employer, maintains control.

There are many in the society who see no redeeming social value in prostitution. Conservative religious groups and others view it as both criminal and immoral. Feminists object to the assumption that "*men* need their sex, not . . . people. So they get it by exploiting women . . ." (Mercer, 1977, p. 289). Those on the political left regard prostitution as a consequence of the authoritarian family structure of capitalistic society. It is a multimillion dollar industry involving pimps, employers, lawyers, law-enforcement personnel, and a cast of thousands. In short, the prostitute's need for referrals, services, and protection produces jobs for others. Her very existence also provides employment for those charged with the maintenance and enforcement of legislation prohibiting prostitution (for example, the vice squad of a police force). In general, deviance of all types creates employment and promotion opportunities for agents of social control. It is in this sense that police are dependent upon crime, and psychiatrists have a vested interest in mental illness.

Employers, Exploiters, and Prosecuters of Prostitutes

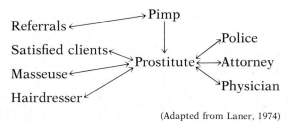

(Adapted from Laner, 1974)

EXPRESSING DISCONTENT AND PROMOTING SOCIAL CHANGE

Boundaries, however, are not immutably fixed but are constantly shifting owing to a variety of factors, including changes within the society and its leadership. In some cases, deviance is consciously intended to express discontent with the *status quo*. The "youth revolt" of the 1960s, for example, involved primarily middle-class young people who openly rejected the values of success and conformity popular in the 1950s. As products of a relatively affluent society engaged in a war that seemed meaningless to many, the students who demonstrated on campuses, adopted casual dress styles, and rejected conventional modes of behavior were not only testing boundaries but searching for something beyond the boundaries. Note, also, the closing of ranks among other seg-

Deviance may be a way of expressing discontent with the **status quo.**

ments of the society in opposition to the young: hardhats and college administrators, large numbers of parents, and Vice-President Spiro Agnew created a public temper of shared moral indignation at such ungrateful youth.

Violation of norms may signal defects in the organization of the social structure itself. For example, the Civil Rights Marchers of the 1960s violated many local norms of conventional behavior as well as testing the law itself with their nonviolent attempts to gain equal access to seats on buses and at lunch counters. Similarly, a 1979 demonstration at a large New England university was staged by faculty and other employees to protest administrative actions regarding salary provisions, tenure, and fringe benefits. University professors are an unlikely group to strike, but in this instance they did so, although such action violated conventional norms for appropriate faculty behavior and disrupted the campus instructional routine.

In many instances, continued boundary testing can promote social change as definitions of deviance are liberalized. For example, persistent and open challenges to the norms have led to increased tolerance toward pot smoking and homosexuality. But when severe boundary crises occur, members of the community begin to censure activities that had been ignored before the crisis. Kai Erikson's analysis of *Wayward Puritans* (1966) demonstrates that "crime waves" in Puritan New England came at moments when the colony was under stress from outside forces or faced with pressure for internal change. Searching for criminals within allowed the colonists to reaffirm their shared identity and goals. Only when such diligence in destroying evil influences threatened the stability of the entire group, as when the Governor's wife was accused of witchcraft, did the persecution of deviants subside.

> Boundary testing is a challenge to accepted norms.

The example of colonial New England also emphasizes the point that what is defined as deviant behavior depends upon both the sociopolitical context of the society and upon the needs of those in power. We can learn much about a group's values by observing who are labeled deviant. As Erikson noted, those people who most fear witches are most likely to find them in their midst.

Theories of Deviance

There are a number of theories that attempt to explain why people deviate from the expected. Each theory represents not only a series of propositions about the nature and origins of deviant behavior but also embodies a philosophic perspective with distinct consequences for the way in which deviance may be controlled.

> Theories of deviance that attempt to explain behavior also represent particular ideological orientations.

NONSOCIOLOGICAL EXPLANATIONS OF CRIMINALITY AND MENTAL ILLNESS

Biological Theories. The notion that there is something inherently wrong with the deviant person is an old one, for which biologists, physiologists, and other scientists have sought evidence for many years. A variety of biologically-based predispositions to deviant behavior have been proposed since the nineteenth century, many of which were initially linked to both the evolutionary

Eugenics refers to the belief that humans can be improved through selective breeding.

work of Charles Darwin and the *eugenics* movement that followed. *Eugenics* means to enhance human improvement through selective breeding (from *Eu* = "good"; *genes* = "inherited traits").

Body Types. In the nineteenth century, investigations of crime were influenced by phrenology (the study of character and mental capacity from the general configuration of the human skull). Caesar Lombroso, an Italian army physician, whose studies of the anatomy of various criminals were published in 1876, thought that the deviant was a genetic throwback to earlier forms of human evolution, observable in the individual's physical appearance. Lombroso identified two types: the "insane" and the "criminaloid." The insane were physically different (unusual skulls, deformities, or facial disfiguration) whereas the criminaloid had *innate* tendencies toward crime—a sort of "bad seed" theory.

The idea of body type as associated with particular forms of criminality or mental disorder remained popular until very recently. One relatively sophisticated analysis was proposed by Sheldon (1949), who classified each individual according to body types called endomorphy, ectomorphy, or mesomorphy. These three types are illustrated in Figure 6-1 and the characteristics of each type are shown in Table 6-2. This typology, incidentally, was used in studies of physical appearance and delinquency that were highly influential in the 1950s, for example, the work on delinquent boys by Sheldon and Eleanor Glueck (1952).

Although the idea of body type has been intuitively appealing to researchers for many generations, it has several major flaws, not the least of which is the contradictory nature of the findings of different studies. For example, Hooton (1939) reported that the genetically inferior were usually "runty", whereas Sheldon (1949) found that husky, athletic types were more often defective. Furthermore, no evidence has ever been presented to demonstrate how a person's physique can cause crime or any other deviant behavior. Most of the studies based their findings on the small proportion of people who have been caught or sought treatment. This is a sampling bias that distorts the findings. Those who

*Figure 6-1.
Body types. Three idealized figures are shown at the top right. Can you identify the three types from Shelton's description of the endomorph, ectomorph, and mesomorph?*

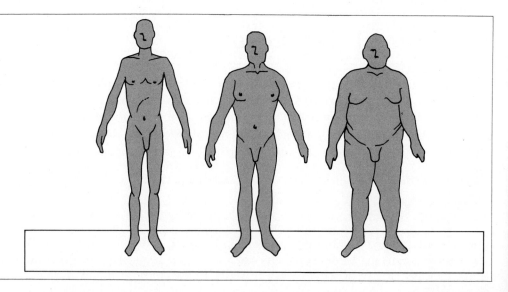

Table 6-2. *Classification of Body Types Proposed by Sheldon and Their Relationship to Deviant Behavior*

Body type	Appearance	Type of deviance likely
Endomorph	Soft, fat	Manic depression, alcoholism
Ectomorph	Thin, small-boned	Schizophrenia
Mesomorph	Muscular, big-boned	Delinquency, alcoholism, manic depression

Source: Based on Sheldon, 1949, and Wittman, Sheldon, and Katz, 1948.

are already under treatment for mental illness, for drug addiction, for alcoholism, or who have been apprehended as criminals represent the unsuccessful deviant. They tell us nothing about the successful ones! Besides, if there are three basic body types and each has a predisposition to one or another kind of deviance, what of the millions of individuals who fit into each type but are not deviant?

Chromosomal Theories. Although work on body type and deviance has generally fallen into disrepute, the search for the link between biological characteristics and deviance has continued. Most influential, currently, is the hypothesis that abnormal chromosomal patterns may be linked to deviant and antisocial behavior. A number of studies have suggested that there is a greater than expected frequency of men with XYY chromosomal patterns in prisons and in mental institutions. Normally, males have an XY chromosomal pattern. However, investigations have not presented any clear evidence that there is an

Criminality and Chromosomes

A 1976 study by Herman A. Witkin and his associates was undertaken in Denmark, a country with excellent social records on the general population, to determine whether (1) XYY men have an elevated crime rate, and (2) if so, what are the factors that intervene between the extra Y chromosome and increased antisocial behavior? They examined the records for three groups of men; those with the normal XY chromosome pattern, those with an XYY pattern, and those with an XXY pattern. Their findings indicate that people with an "XYY syndrome" are more likely to have a criminal record than are members of the other two groups. However, both the XYYs and XXYs were more likely to have significantly lower IQ test scores, to have less education, and to be taller than were the XY men.

Having established that men with abnormal chromosomal patterns differ from those with normal patterns, the researchers analyzed the types of crimes committed by members of the three categories. XYY males were no more violent or aggressive than men in the other two groups. Rather, their low intelligence, low level of education, and greater height increased the probability that they would be detected and imprisoned.

This study was reported in "Criminality in XYY and XXY Men," Herman A. Witkin et al., *Science,* August 13, 1976, pp. 547–555.

"XYY syndrome" of which antisocial behavior is an element. Nor is the true prevalence of XYY in the general population known. Put differently, no one can tell how many XYY men are *not* criminal or mentally ill but, rather, are model members of the community.

Psychological Theories.   The belief that deviant behavior results from some kind of moral flaw or mental abberation in the individual remains as popular today as during biblical times. By the nineteenth century, physicians and reformers had begun to identify certain types of people as morally insane, that is, they demonstrated unusual behavior although their reason and intellect were intact. "Moral imbecility" was another term applied to the norm-breaker. With the growth of the mental health movement during the nineteenth century, however, such terminology was considered too unscientific, and a new set of categories, including psychopath, sociopath, and antisocial personality took their place. The diagosis of *sociopathy* has often been used by mental health professionals to describe those who violate moral or institutional norms.

The concept of sociopath is convenient, for it bridges biological and psychological theory. Investigators have suggested that sociopathy is related to a generalized brain disorder, to an XYY chromosomal pattern, and to the hyperactive child syndrome (Arthurs and Cahoon, 1964; Hook, 1973; Satterfield, Cantwell, and Satterfield, 1974). The sociopath is indeed a bad seed from this perspective.

The concept of **sociopathy,** or the antisocial personality, bridges biological and psychological theories.

Another approach to sociopathy is that it results from faulty childhood socialization, so that ability to form relationships or to feel guilt or anxiety is impaired. This is a relatively old idea. In 1829, officials at one prison in the United States began collecting life histories of convicts to discover why they were criminal. Of 173 cases examined, 99 were seen as directly due to parental failure (Rothman, 1971). Deviants were thought to be "depraved on account of they were deprived," to paraphrase a song from the musical, *West Side Story.*

Despite the attractiveness of sociopathy as the cause of deviance, it too has come under serious criticism. Sociopathy is diagnosed by rule breaking, yet rule breaking is caused by sociopathy. This essentially says that a sociopath is a deviant because he or she deviates, somewhat akin to saying that one has measles because one has a rash and one has a rash because of having measles. No new information is gained because the explanation contains circular logic.

Sociopathy, however, is not the only mental condition believed to cause deviant behavior. A number of mental health professionals, heavily influenced by the work of Sigmund Freud and his followers, feel that deviance is indicative of underlying psychic disturbance. In the Freudian model, the deviant is a person whose psychological development was stunted in early childhood, and who, for one reason or another, wants to be caught for nonconformity. Intriguing as such arguments may be, a review of the literature on the predictive validity of such judgments shows little agreement (Norris, 1959; Steadman and Cocozza, 1978). Nor, despite the prevalence of headlines such as "Ex-Mental Patient Commits Crime" is there evidence that former mental patients are more likely than anyone else to commit a criminal act. Indeed, for a number of years, a lower arrest rate for former psychiatric inpatients than for the general population has most often been observed (Ashley, 1922; Cohen and Freeman, 1945).

In general, psychological perspectives have failed to predict or explain deviant behavior.

Such individualistic theories of deviance deflect attention from societal factors such as inequality in resources and the power to define appropriate behavior thereby creating the category of deviant conduct.

SOCIOLOGICAL PERSPECTIVES ON DEVIANCE

Although sociologists are aware of what psychologists, psychiatrists, and biologists say about the origins of deviant behavior, it is the *social* act that is our major concern. Social explanations of deviance must be analyzed both within the context of the society in which the behavior occurs and within the framework of social interaction. Psychologists, psychiatrists, and biologists cannot accurately predict deviance from their knowledge of the mind and the body precisely because both the deviant and those who seek to control or limit deviant behavior are acting within a *social context*. The social fabric in which individuals are embedded may or may not encourage expression of particular types of behavior and may or may not invite its condemnation.

A variety of sociological approaches to the study of deviant behavior have been proposed, most of which are complementary and shed light upon (1) the reasons why deviance exists within every known human society, (2) the processes by which people become deviant, and (3) the mechanisms for social control used to contain and punish flagrant violations of socially significant norms.

*The sociological perspective on deviance is concerned with the actual **social behavior** rather than with its remote causes.*

*Deviance occurs in a **social context** that includes those who react to the behavior.*

The Functionalist Approach. Functional theory directs attention to the ways in which elements of social structure and behavior maintain the stability or relative equilibrium of societies or groups. Deviance, therefore, is not viewed by the functionalist as random but as purposeful behavior within a social context. Thus much of the conduct that we label as deviant actually reflects the cultural values of the society in which it occurs—even if only by offending agreed-upon standards of behavior. As Erikson (1966) states, "the thief and his victim share a common respect for the value of property; the heretic and inquisitor speak much the same language and are keyed to the same religious mysteries; the traitor and the patriot act in reference to the same political institutions." Rather than being a symptom of disorganization, deviance is thus interpreted as a means of enhancing group solidarity by reinforcing the authority of the norms.

Erikson also proposed that the volume of deviants is likely to stay relatively constant over time. In his studies of Puritan New England, Erikson observed that, although the number of convictions fluctuated from year to year, the offender *rate* was fairly constant. This constancy reflects definitions of deviance that are roughly equivalent to the capacity of the social control apparatus of the community. When the resources to control deviance are overtaxed by an unusually large number of norm violators, social change is likely to occur and boundaries to be redefined. Otherwise, the social control apparatus itself must be modified.

The functionalist perspective sees deviance as goal-directed behavior within a given context.

*Functionalists contend that individuals or acts are labeled as deviant to insure **survival** of particular social systems.*

Labeling Theory. Labeling theory complements the functionalist approach and deals with two fundamental questions: First, how is deviance socially produced? Second, what is the effect of labeling on the individuals subsequent conduct? It is the emphasis on the *process* of defining a person's behavior that has given this approach its name. In this view, deviance is not perceived as a

*Labeling theory emphasizes the **process** whereby behavior is defined as deviant.*

Labeling theory focuses on the **interaction** between the person acting and those who respond.

quality that lies in behavior itself but in the *interaction* between the person who commits the act and those who respond to it (Becker, 1963). *Deviant behavior is behavior that people label deviant.*

Likewise enforcement of a rule will depend on a number of factors, including *who* violates the rule, *who* perceives this violation, whether or not the perceiver feels that the rule breaking is harmful to himself or herself and other members of the community, and the social *context* in which the rule breaking occurs.

Two women are shopping in the major department store of your hometown and each picks up merchandise that she immediately stuffs in her handbag. One is from the finest residential section in town, the other from the poorest section. If both are apprehended by the store detective, do you think they will be defined similarly or that the consequences will be the same for both? It is likely that one will be labeled *kleptomaniac* and sent to a psychiatrist, and the other will be booked as a *thief* and processed through the courts. Same act, different social types, and, therefore, different definitions. Such definitions of normality are likely to reflect the interests of powerful groups. As the French author Anatole France has written: "The law in its majestic equality forbids both rich and poor alike to beg in the streets, steal bread, or sleep under bridges."

It appears that there is no social act that is in and of itself wrong or evil regardless of context. Murder becomes heroism when performed by soldiers; hitting another person is automatically assault unless it is your child or spouse; people who hear voices are crazy, however, those who hear God are saints.

Deviant Careers

Becoming deviant involves a process of **social learning.**

Becoming a deviant is not only a matter of labeling but of *social learning* by the rule breaker. First, the rule breaker is caught and publicly labeled. One may catch oneself—for example, recognize that one is dependent upon alcohol and decide voluntarily to join Alcoholics Anonymous—or others may brand one as alcoholic. Once tagged, the individual's new label is treated as a *master status trait* (Goffman, 1963); his or her other identities and roles (student, athlete, friend, dog trainer) are virtually ignored, and the rule breaker is treated not as John the A student but as John the deviant alcoholic.

Possession of this one deviant trait may also be generalized, so that people

Figure 6-2.
How John Smith be-
came labeled and in-
ternalized the identity
of an alcoholic.

automatically assume that its bearer posseses other undesirable traits. A *stigma*, or "sign of moral blemish," attaches to a characteristic that differs from the normal or normative in a society. Individuals possessing such an attribute are treated as if they bear a mark of disgrace. Thus, the individual is *stigmatized* as others withdraw their acceptance and distort the person's identity to fit the stereotypical expectations (Goffman, 1963). In turn, the response of the stigmatized person is to internalize part or all of the views of the labelers concerning the stigma, altering his or her self-concept in the process. Stages in a deviant's career are shown in Figure 6-2.

The possession of a deviant trait leads to that person being **stigmatized.**

The Jazz Musician

Writing about jazz musicians in the 1960s, Howard S. Becker observed that their subculture was essentially a deviant one. Although jazz musicians as described by Becker are no longer dominant in the music world, the same observations apply to current rock musicians. According to Becker, the world of the musician has its own particular belief system, including the notion that the player is an artist who "either has it or not." As an artist, the musician feels that he or she is different from and better than other kinds of people and thus should be exempt from the control of outsiders in any branch of life. Sexual prowess, unconventional behavior, and freedom both musically and socially are valued among musicians, with few peer group controls over behavior. The audiences who attend musicians' performances or buy their records are seen as basically ignorant and insensitive people, incapable of understanding the world of the artist, but also as somewhat of a threat to one's artistic identity.

How does the musician maintain the deviant lifestyle just detailed when her or his very livelihood is dependent upon the majority culture? Essentially self-segregation is practiced; musicians isolate themselves physically and socially from nonmusicians. Even in performances, the spatial isolation of the stage and avoidance of eye contact with the audience permit musicians to maintain an essentially deviant lifestyle, unstigmatized by people who might otherwise condemn their behavior.

Both jazz musicians and marijuana smokers are discussed in Howard S. Becker, *The Outsiders: Studies in the Sociology of Deviance.* New York: Free Press, 1963.

At point *A*, John is on his way to the Sunnyside Bar to have a few drinks. At point *B*, John has finished drinking and is on his way home, perhaps somewhat drunk but not viewed as deviant. At point *C*, however, a different course of events, the process of labeling John as an alcoholic, begins. He is perceived by others as an abuser of alcohol, and is labeled as an alcoholic. At point *D*, he internalizes this label of himself and at point *E* slinks into the bar to enact the deviant role assigned to him. Alcoholism has become his master status trait. Were he to try to remain sober, others would not believe his motivation, would assume he was joking, and would urge him to be the "good old John" they know and can deal with, namely John the alcoholic.

The last step involves seeking out others who share the stigma. Since interaction with nondeviants is so painful, the deviant avoids their presence. With others who are similarly stigmatized, the deviant at last finds a supportive peer group. Not only is one socially accepted in this group, but a particular world view that rationalizes the stigmatized behavior is created and maintained: We're the smart ones, and all those nondrinkers are the poor stiffs. . . This supportive network is called a *deviant subculture*, and represents the last stage in the deviant career.

Stigma is reduced through membership in a supportive **deviant subculture.**

ANOMIE

Anomie refers to the disorganization that exists in individuals or society when norms are conflicting, weak, or absent. When one has been socialized to the *norms* and *goals* that govern behavior within a particular culture but is denied access to the *means* of expressing that commitment, anomie may result. Assuming that the goal in North American societies is to be rich or successful, obviously certain people, by virtue of birth or ability, are denied the opportunity to achieve this goal by legitimate means. While the commonly accepted folk myth is that success may be achieved by hard work, members of minority groups—blacks, Hispanics, Orientals, Native Americans, French-speaking Canadians, and women—are aware that there is a gap between myth and reality.

X **Anomie** refers to disorganization within individuals or a society.

When the opportunity to achieve wealth and success is unequally distributed among subgroups in most societies, how may the individual who has been socialized to believe that these are desirable goals react? Robert Merton (1957) proposes five ways in which the individual may adapt to the means and goals of his or her culture.

As Table 6-3 shows, people may adapt by a variety of mechanisms, all but one of which is deviant, that is, does not conform to both the culturally-determined goals and the legitimate means of achieving these goals. The *innovator* will seek new and probably illegitimate means of acquiring wealth and success—for example, racketeering. The *ritualist* resigns herself or himself to fate, recognizing that fame and fortune are out of reach, and tends to over conform to the rules for good conduct. The white-collar bureaucrat more concerned with keeping a job than with upward mobility or achievement, is a type of ritualist. The *retreatist*, however, rejects both the means and the goals of the society and drops out—into drug use, mental illness, alcoholism, or hoboism. Finally, the *rebellious* reject both means and goals while seeking social change. Political radicals, members of new religious cults such as the Moonies, and followers of the alternative lifestyles so popular in the late 1960s all rejected conformity and adopted new goals and means.

The **innovator** will seek new and perhaps illegitimate means of acquiring desired goals.

The **ritualist** recognizes that fame and fortune are out of reach and tends to overconform to rules of good conduct.

The **retreatist** rejects both the legitimate means and the valued goals of society.

The **rebellious** will seek social change, replacing both existing goals and means.

Table 6-3. *Merton's Typology of Individual Modes of Adaptation to Cultural Means and Goals*

Individual mode of adaptation		Accepts cultural goals	Accepts institutionalized means of attainment
	Conformity	Yes	Yes
	Innovation	Yes	No
Deviant	Ritualism	No	Yes
Behaviors	Retreatism	No	No
	Rebellion	No/but seeks to replace with other goals	No/but seeks to restructure means of attainment

Source: Adapted from Merton, 1957, p. 140.

Those who are denied access to or repudiate the legitimate means and goals of their society also tend to reject former peer and reference groups in order to seek out new ones that accept and reward their nonconforming behavior. Hence, subcultures arise for homosexuals, rock musicians, drug users, political terrorists, hustlers, and safe-crackers, among many, many others.

ECCENTRIC BEHAVIOR

Although the person who has been labeled as deviant often becomes locked into a deviant career, there are certain situations in which difference is *tolerated* and the nonconformist is not rejected or isolated from normal social interaction. The concept of social distance is pertinent here. Some types of deviant behavior do not evoke extreme stigmatization. The individual may be simply considered an "oddball" or *eccentric*. Eccentrics, like deviants, are recognized rule breakers, and are observed and defined by others as unusual. When the behavior is labeled eccentric, however, the rule breaking is not interpreted as either disruptive or threatening to the social order. Eccentricities may be tolerated for several reasons. 1. They are viewed as inconsequential oddities. or 2. They are members of an in-group that protects them. or 3. They are famous and protected by their high social position, wealth, or superior knowledge.

Eccentric behavior is rule-breaking that is not judged as disruptive to the social structure.

Fame and fortune may protect one from stigma and from being locked into a deviant career even when public labeling has occurred. In 1974 Richard Nixon was forced to resign as President of the United States—the first president ever to do so—because of a series of events generally labeled Watergate. Much of his staff, including the Attorney General of the United States, had already resigned. Several had been charged and convicted of serious crimes. Yet their convictions and imprisonment did not ruin their lives, nor were they tracked into criminal careers. Many turned to lecturing and writing, with several of them earning hundreds of thousands of dollars.

PETTY AND INSTITUTIONALIZED EVASIONS OF THE NORMS

Petty violations of the norms often are ignored until they become so widespread and open that they pose a threat to social order. Charging personal expenses to a business account, failing to report all sources of income on tax

Petty evasions of norms and institutionalized deviance are often ignored.

returns, appropriation of office supplies such as pencils and paper for personal use, parking illegally, and using another student's notes to study for classes are petty violations that pervade daily life.

Although aware that such rule breaking carries the risk of negative sanctions, the petty norm-breaker is generally not concerned with the consequences. The rule itself may seem stupid, or it may be inconvenient. The acts may not be detected, but if they are, the effects are typically not frightening. The breaking of these rules may even be justified as fair compensation for a fancied or real loss. ("It's OK to cheat on your taxes because the government takes too much anyway.")

Institutionalized evasion of norms often occurs within an organization as a permanent, unofficial part of the system. These evasions may be tolerated because they actually help to achieve the goals of the organization, as the Bensman and Gerver study of illegal work practices illustrates. Joseph Bensman and Israel Gerver (1963) focused their attention on how a particular type of illegal work practice—use of a tap—develops and persists in an aircraft factory. The tap is a tool whose ends are slotted to cut away waste material from the wing plate of an airplane, and it is employed when a nut does not fit easily into its assembly. Rather than hold up the entire production line, a worker will reshape the groove with a tap, but because this procedure reduces the strength of an aircraft's wings, it is the most serious violation of workmanship in the factory. A worker can be fired simply for possessing a tap. Yet, in the aircraft factory studied, at least half of the workers owned this tool. Use of the tap is learned within the work group of the factory. The new worker is instructed in the practice by more experienced colleagues. The foreman, too, may instruct the new worker but also warns *never* to get caught.

Inspection is lax. Government inspectors are few, and their visits are well-announced through the factory grapevine. Although everyone in the organization knows that taps are used, the practice is tolerated and encouraged as long as no one is caught because by not stopping the production line in order to do the job correctly (1) costs are reduced for the company and profits increased; (2) the government gets its planes sooner; (3) the work group's productivity earns raises and promotions for the foreman; and (4) the inspector can become "one of the guys" while meeting the inspection quotas.

In this illustration, institutional deviance as represented by the workers' private, illegal norms allows the company to fulfill its public, socially-valued purpose—the production of airplanes. The specific workers, who are guilty of improper performance of their job duties are playing roles tacitly legitimated within the factory system. In this fashion, the deviant act on the assembly line is conforming in terms of the goal of the larger system.

PRINCIPLED CHALLENGES TO THE NORMS

Principled challenges are moral protests to norms.

Principled challenges differ from other kinds of rule-breaking because they are deliberate attempts by an individual or group to force a confrontation with the norm-setters. The challenge is seen as having a moral component and is most often an attempt to reform or modify a specific aspect of the society without changing the basic social or normative structure. These moral protests frequently occur when conventional, legitimate means of bringing pressure have either failed or have moved too slowly to satisfy the interests of those seeking change.

For example, within the past few years there have been dozens of protests against the building and use of nuclear power plants. In the 1960s and early 1970s, opposition to nuclear power centered in established groups that used normal channels of publicity and lawsuits (Barkan, 1979). The course of these law suits has been slow and costly, and also uncertain, leading some individuals to mount their own principled challenge to nuclear power. In May 1977, 14,000 people illegally occupied the construction area at Seabrook, New Hampshire and were arrested. Suddenly national publicity was directed toward the movement and its goals. The impact of principled challenges rests on too many external variables to be predictable. At the very least, however, a previously neglected source of discontent is placed on the public agenda.

Principled challenges are deliberate attempts to force confrontation with authority in order to create a social consensus on an issue seen to have a moral component. (Source: Barbara Alper, Stock, Boston.)

Mental Illness as Deviant Behavior

Whereas psychologists focus on the classification, causes, and treatment of mental disorders, sociologists have been interested in (1) the social factors associated with their occurrence, and (2) the process by which people are defined as mentally ill. To the sociologists, mental illness is *residual deviance*, that is, it defies easy inclusion with more obvious types of norm violation such as theft, murder, treason, and bigamy.

To sociologists, mental illness is a **residual deviance**, less identifiable than more obvious norm violations.

Diagnoses of mental illness tend to reflect the norms of the times. For example, in the eighteenth century, Benjamin Rush discovered a new form of madness, *revolutiona*, the distinguishing characteristic being opposed to the American revolution. In the nineteenth century, escaping slaves were diagnosed as suffering from a psychosis that led them to run away! Also in the nineteenth century, both masturbation and homosexuality were condemned by physicians as symptoms of mental pathology. Today, neither is considered a mental disorder.

Diagnoses of mental illness reflect the norms of the historical period in which the behavior occurs.

It is interesting to note that, when the American Psychiatric Association voted to drop homosexuality from its list of mental illnesses, a new illness was added—habitual tobacco use. Jerome H. Jaffee, a vocal advocate of labeling smoking as a mental disorder, has proposed that the habitual teenaged smoker is probably one who derives so little esteem from school performance that he or she adopts precocious behavior such as alcohol use, heterosexual activity, and smoking. Control of negative sanctions; desire for a stimulant from nicotine; reduction of tension, irritability, and boredom; and the alleviation of hunger have been noted as motivations for smoking among adults (Jaffee, 1975).

That habitual smoking has emerged as a mental disorder at a time when there is heightened awareness that smoking is harmful to one's health emphasizes the importance of contemporary norms in determining exactly what kind of behavior will be labeled as indicative of mental illness. Mental illness, like other forms of social deviance, is defined within a social context.

Another question of great interest to social scientists concerns the distribution of mental illnesses within a population. Are members of certain subgroups groups more likely than others to be diagnosed as mentally ill, and if so, what can this tell us about the social factors involved in mental disorder?

An early sociological explanation of mental illness focused on **social disorganization**.

One of the early sociological hypotheses about mental illness was that it was caused by *social disorganization*. Followers of the social disorganization model found that almost *all* types of psychosis were localized in the most deteriorated areas of the city. However, the hypothesis that slums breed mental illness has been challenged by more recent data, indicating the importance of characteristics such as sex, race, ethnicity and social class in the diagnosis of mental disorder. For example, elderly blacks are more likely than whites of the same age and degree of impairment to be committed to state mental hospitals rather than nursing homes (Kart and Beckham, 1976). Other studies demonstrate that when samples of psychiatrists are asked to read case history data—the same reports with only the occupation of the subject changed—a diagnosis of mental illness is more likely for blue-collar in contrast to white-collar workers.

MENTAL ILLNESS AS A SOCIAL PROCESS

How does residual deviance, regardless of its causes, become labeled as mental illness? Thomas Scheff (1966) has proposed that residual rule-breaking stems from a number of different sources. Obviously there are many reasons why people may see, hear, or experience the unusual: genetic, family, and stress factors; psychoactive drugs; infection, starvation, or fatigue; deliberate attempts to achieve altered states of consciousness.

Furthermore, most residual rule-breaking is denied or ignored by others until it can no longer be avoided. Members of a family or other close-knit group are reluctant to shift definitions of a person's behavior from "normal" to "sick." Thus, relative to the rate of *treated* residual deviance, the rate of *untreated* rule-breaking is quite high.

Tracking the Patient's Career. Erving Goffman has been particularly interested in how changes in the individual's belief system occur as she or he moves from the status of normal to that of mental patient (Goffman, 1961, a). According to Goffman, the process of becoming a mental patient is only recognized after the fact by the person experiencing it. Career contingencies play a large role in determining who will actually become a mental patient. Career contingencies include the occupation and income of the rule breaker, the visibility of the rule-breaking, the proximity of a psychiatric institution, the community regard for this facility, and the type of norms that were broken. Individuals who are placed in mental hospitals are usually put there because their behavior, albeit usually not illegal, disturbs others who can no longer tolerate it. Thus, a *circuit of agents* is needed to finalize the definition of someone as a mental patient. Circuits include both *informal social control* agents such as family members, friends, and neighbors, and *formal agents*, representing the community, such as the police, clergy, social agencies, and physicians. These formal agents are sometimes known as *gatekeepers* because they act as security guards, regulating the entry of people into a variety of community treatment agencies.

Career contingencies are a complex of social factors that determine outcomes for individuals by opening up or closing off certain options.

Circuits of agents define a person as a mental patient and include both **informal** and **formal social control agents.**

Gatekeepers are formal agents who regulate entry into treatment agencies.

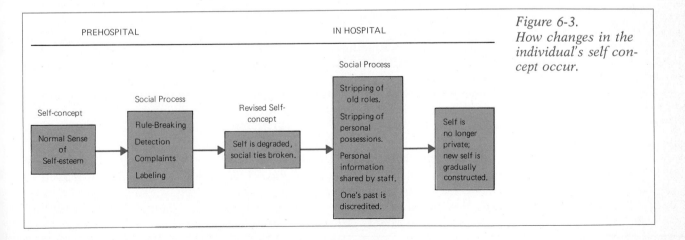

Figure 6-3.
How changes in the individual's self concept occur.

PREHOSPITAL   IN HOSPITAL

Self-concept

Normal Sense
of
Self-esteem

Social Process

Rule-Breaking
Detection
Complaints
Labeling

Revised Self-
concept

Self is degraded,
social ties broken.

Social Process

Stripping of
old roles.

Stripping of
personal
possessions.

Personal
information
shared by staff.

One's past is
discredited.

Self is
no longer
private;
new self is
gradually
constructed.

Once in the hospital, other social processes ensure further changes in the self-concept. Stripped of outside roles and everyday possessions such as clothing, razor, pens, paper, the patient also finds that all the personal information acquired about her or him both prior to and during hospitalization is recorded and shared by the staff. Any attempts made by the patient to maintain a positive, private, respectable self-concept are discredited by the staff. Instead, one is asked to face up to one's illness. Patients respond in a variety of ways to these processes, but the net result for the self is that it is no longer private. A new self, adapting to the situation, is gradually reconstructed but unlike the old self, "is not a fortress but a small open city" (Goffman, 1961, a).

After Treatment, What? Throwing off the label of mental patient is not easy. Most of us have stereotypical pictures of particular kinds of deviants, including mental patients. These stereotypes are reinforced and continually reaffirmed through ordinary social interaction. Terms referring to mental disorder are used in everyday conversation in a variety of ways. "You must be some kind of a nut" indicates social disapproval. In advertising, such slogans as "we may be crazy but we've slashed prices to below cost" are common. In the media, the former mental patient who commits an offense is immediately identified as a *mental* patient, although she or he occupies other statuses and roles. The common denominator of stereotypes about mental illness is that people who have ever been treated are likely to be irrational, unpredictable, unpleasant, and perhaps violent. These stereotypes have an obvious effect on those who have been labeled as mentally ill. Like other stigmatized people, they risk being locked into a deviant role unless they conceal their stigma.

TREATING MENTAL ILLNESS

Regardless of the symptoms, not all people seek and receive treatment for mental illness. Whether or not treatment is sought will depend on the individual's degree of discomfort, the responses of role partners, and the person's social position. For example, people who view the self as an object to be developed and explored and are familiar with the psychological literature are far more likely to seek treatment from a mental health professional than are members of conservative religious groups who, when experiencing problems in living, will look for other treatments such as prayer or repentance.

Nor is treatment readily accessible to everyone. For example, Hollingshead and Redlich (1958) found that people with low incomes were more often treated by hospital residents and interns rather than by psychiatrists. People of greater wealth and education, however, were more likely to be accepted for treatment, to be seen by experienced clinicians, and to be treated for a longer period of time than were those with fewer resources. The poor and disadvantaged were, when treated, more likely than the relatively advantaged to receive shock therapy, brain surgery, and drugs rather than psychotherapy or psychoanalysis.

At one time, those diagnosed as mentally ill were placed in prisons. In the nineteenth century, a prevalent treatment was a stay in an *asylum* designed to provide a respite from the immediate cares of everyday living. Recently, however, the asylum concept has been challenged as antitherapeutic, as mounting evidence indicates that the traditional setting of an institution may do more harm than good. Some patients tend to assume the sick role and act out the expectations of their caretakers; others find the asylum so comfortable that they maintain the behavior that keeps them safe from the difficulties of everyday life on the outside. In general, it is difficult, if not impossible, to be socialized for return to the outside world while conforming to the norms of a total institution.

Accordingly, increased attention has been placed on ways in which the environment of those diagnosed as severely mentally ill might be used to treat them more positively and economically. In the traditional asylum or mental hospital, the social system was knit together essentially by the similarity of patients. Durkheim has termed this form of social organization *mechanical solidarity*, in which people were bound together by ties of their alikeness on a variety of characteristics. In the *therapeutic community* concept, however, each person in the social system is seen as contributing something different to the social process and each has a necessary and complementary social role in the system. This, in Durkheim's terms, is *organic solidarity*, the unity of interdependent parts.

In a **therapeutic community** patients are encouraged to take more responsibility for their daily lives.

The concept of therapeutic community was first introduced in mental hospitals where patients were encouraged to participate in self-government and to take more responsibility for their daily lives than was permitted in the typical asylum. Within the past decade or so, the dominant trend in treating mental illness has been *deinstitutionalization*, which involves treating the severely mentally ill within their own community. An outgrowth not only of the therapeutic community concept but also of increasing costs of psychiatric hospitalization, the *community mental health movement* emphasizes treatment of the person within a social context as opposed to the social isolation of an inpatient facility. The major difficulty has been the failure of communities to provide these essential outpatient services with the result that released mental patients have no support systems.

Some Reflections on Deviance and Conformity

In all societies there are rules that govern behavior. Obviously, there are cultural differences among societies regarding rules and there are also changes that take place over time within a society. Variations in norms for behavior exist among subgroups within modern societies reflecting the value priorities of each group or subgroup. In nations as complex as the United States or Canada, a number of values compete. For example, abortion rights are strongly supported by those who value sexual equality and female autonomy and just as vehemently opposed by others who value adherence to certain religious doctrines. People concerned with the preservation of various species of wildlife are far more likely to sponsor a "save the whale campaign" than are those who make their living from the whaling industry.

The more powerful groups within a society are more likely to establish norms and therefore also define conformity and deviance.

Given the extreme diversity of norms within a complex society, how do some norms assume more importance than others? Quite simply, the relative power of competing interest groups determines which norms will be defined as paramount. The more powerful the group, the more likely are its values to become the standards of right and wrong. In other words, the content of norms is a less important variable than the relative power of their believers.

Issues of deviance and conformity become defined as "social problems" when there are unresolved conflicts among competing groups about the norms or the ways in which norms should be enforced. For example, although it is currently illegal to use or possess the mood-altering drug LSD, its usage became a social problem in the late 1960s precisely because of differences of opinion about the effects of the drug and ways in which its consumption could be controlled. When first discovered, LSD was the subject of experimentation by many reputable scientists. Others used it for recreational or political purposes. For a variety of reasons, agreement on proper use of the drug could not be reached. Some interest groups proposed legalization of the drug, others sought to control its use for laboratory experimentation, and some opposed it entirely. Those with the most moral zeal—the opponents of the drug for any purpose— were successful in defining its possession or manufacture illegal, and its consumers deviant. The study of deviant behavior is replete with such illustrations, in which the interests of one group have prevailed within a society to make all groups recognize—if not accept—a particular practice as deviant. More generally, ideas and behaviors do not exist in vacuums but are embedded in group processes. Their fate is determined by the relative strength of those who adopt the norms to shape and define cultural products.

Summary

In every human group some behaviors become defined as appropriate standards of role performance. Once these *norms* are developed, conformity is encouraged and enforced through agents of social control. Norms set boundaries for acceptable behavior, and simultaneously define nonnormative behavior that is beyond the boundary. *Deviance* refers to activities that violate the expectations of others and the rules of appropriateness. A *deviant* is one who others define as requiring attention by agents or agencies of social control.

In general, deviant behavior can be seen as a functional necessity in any society. Deviance *mobilizes the community* in support of its values and norms; it *clarifies the boundaries* between the accepted and the unacceptable; it *provides channels for the release of antisocial feelings;* and it can become the *cutting edge of long-term changes* that enhance the group's adaptability.

In the past, a great deal of research has focused on the individual causes of deviance. Theories based on *biological differences* have been particularly popular. Yet none of this research has demonstrated a direct link between a particular biological characteristic and a specific form of deviant behavior. Similarly, *psychological theories* have failed to establish any clear relationship between early childhood experience or mental states and a given act of nonconformity.

Sociological theories of deviance, by contrast, focus on the deviant act in its full *social context:* who does what, when, and where, and how do others respond. It is not the action that is central, but rather the response or effect the action has on others and society that defines the act. *Labeling* occurs when the behavior is judged to be outside normative boundaries, and when the individual is held responsible for that behavior.

Once labeled, the deviant individual experiences varying degrees of stigmatization. When the label is internalized as one's definition of self, a deviant career is launched. The labeled person may seek to avoid negative sanctions by joining a deviant subculture that supports the stigmatized behavior and restores self-esteem.

Another sociological perspective seeks the source of deviance in the *social structure* rather than in the individual. When commitment to socially approved goals and/or access to legitimate means of achieving these goals are blocked, individuals may choose nonnormative actions, rejecting either goals or means, or seeking to replace these with new ones. In some cases, the refusal to conform is a consciously chosen *principled challenge* to the norms in the name of some higher social good.

Mental illness can be seen as *residual deviance*, that is, behavior that can be variously defined by different people under different circumstances. Mental illness is a social process involving labeling, stigmatization, internalization, career stages, and treatment.

Suggested Readings

BECKER, HOWARD S. *The Outsiders: Studies in the Sociology of Deviance*. New York: Free Press, 1963. The labeling perspective is applied to the study of jazz musicians and marijuana smokers.

ERIKSON, KAI. *Wayward Puritans*. New York: Wiley, 1966. Another classic in the labeling tradition, this time a historical analysis of the ways in which deviant behavior was created and dealt with in Puritan New England.

GOFFMAN, ERVING. *Stigma: Notes on the Management of a Spoiled Identity*. Englewood Cliffs, N.J.: Prentice-Hall, 1963. Goffman's title is self-explanatory. This essay deals with reactions to labeling; the ways in which a stigmatized individual protects the self-image and learns to negotiate social interaction.

MERCER, JANE. *Labelling the Mentally Retarded*. Berkeley: Univ. of California, 1973. A careful, well-documented study of children defined as mentally retarded in the California public school system. The disproportionate number of minority children in this group led Mercer to devise more appropriate measures of intelligence, with the result that large numbers were found capable of normal functioning.

ROTHMAN, DAVID. *The Discovery of the Asylum*. Boston: Little, Brown, 1971. This is an historical overview of the ways in which deviance has been treated in the United States. The creation of special, isolated environments for those called mad or criminal is only one technique explored and exploited in our history.

SZASZ, THOMAS. *The Myth of Mental Illness: Foundations of a Theory of Personal Conduct*. New York: Harper and Row, 1961. In this controversial book, Szasz argues that the label "mentally ill" has been used to control individuals who present problems to others but who are not ill in any medically-acceptable way. With the exception of those very few people who suffer organic brain disorders, most of what is called mental illness reflects difficulties in interpersonal relations.

(Source: *The Bettman Archive*.)

Part III
Social Differences and Inequality

The four chapters that follow describe the process by which members of a society are grouped into categories on the basis of characteristics such as gender, age, skill, strength, skin color, intelligence, or any other human attribute, and how these categories are arranged in a ranked order by virtue of the different value placed upon that characteristic in that society.

Assuming that in each social system there is a limited supply of valued resources—both material goods and intangibles such as honor and affection—the sociological question becomes: how are scarce resources distributed within the stratification system? That is, what is the link between social differences and social inequality? And what are the mechanisms used to acquire or command the major types of social desirables: *power, prestige,* and *property?*

In Chapter 7 we discuss the stratification process and the distribution of scarce resources among individuals and groups. The outcome of stratification is social inequality on the basis of access to, or possession of, power, prestige, and property. Chapter 8 deals with the consequences of inequality in contemporary North America, and with the movement of individuals and groups from one stratum to another.

Both *ascribed* and *achieved* characteristics are used to place persons in the stratification system. In Chapter 9 we examine the importance of gender and age in the division of labor and the stratification hierarchy. Chapter 10 focuses on the attributes of race, religion, and ethnicity, as these serve to classify individuals and groups, and to determine their social standing.

7 Social Stratification

In 1954 the British author George Orwell captured the essence of stratification systems in one phrase from his book *Animal Farm*: ". . . all the animals are equal here, but some are more equal than others."

Is this always the case? Are some individuals inevitably more equal than others? These seemingly simple questions form the center of unending debate in philosophy and the social sciences. Such questions address fundamental conceptions of the nature of humans and of social structure. In essence, is the good society one that recognizes the similarities among people—their common needs and capacities—or their differences in skills and talents? Can both be done? The next four chapters examine the phenomenon of *social differences* and *social inequality,* or the ways in which members of a society vary, and decide who are more equal than others.

In all societies there are three types of socially-valued resources:(1) *power*—the ability to realize one's own goals even against the will of others; (2) *prestige*—the respect of others; and (3) *property*—wealth, whether measured in dollars, oil, land, wampum, or yams. And in all societies these are unequally distributed among individuals and groups. Systems of *social stratification* develop when distinctions among individuals or groups become the basis for claims on scarce resources. As a result social hierarchies are formed. A hierarchy is a ranked set of stratification units (*strata* in the plural; *stratum* for the singular), with a narrow apex and broad base, as seen in Figure 7-1.

Principles of Stratification

Although one may imagine a society in which all members are equally valued, the human experience appears to be that some form of stratification exists in all but the most simple bands of gatherers. At the very least, age and sex differences in the division of labor are almost universal, and when members of a group perform different tasks they are likely to be rewarded differently. Thus, in all societies, some individuals and groups have more of whatever is considered a desirable in that society than do others. In general, the more specialization in the society, the greater the differentiation between subgroups because members will be engaged in varied activities. So a member has more in common with those who do similar things than with people who do other things. Yet differentiation of tasks is a necessary *but not sufficient* cause for a stratification system. Rather, the different tasks must be differentially *evaluated;* that is, some jobs will be considered important and other jobs less so.

Stratification systems, therefore, depend upon a division of labor in which some people and groups perform roles considered more worthwhile than those performed by others. How does this come about? Sociological theorists differ in their analysis of the principles of stratification.

Some form of stratification exists in almost all societies.

Stratification systems depend on a division of labor in which some people and groups perform tasks considered more important than others.

THE FUNCTIONAL THEORY OF STRATIFICATION

The functional perspective explains social stratification in terms of the consequences of a given social arrangement for the overall society.

The *functional perspective*, remember, attempts to explain social structure in terms of the consequences of a given arrangement: "What happens because?" What are the consequences of stratification that might explain its almost universal existence? The functional argument was best presented several decades ago by Kingsley Davis and Wilbert E. Moore in a famous essay, "Some Principles of Stratification" (1945). Their argument is essentially as follows: Quite simply, not all individuals have the same abilities. Some will have more of the qualities needed and valued by members of a society at a given historical moment: strength, hunting ability, wisdom, interpersonal skills, ambition, and so forth. The other side of the stratification equation is that a desirable reward is always limited in quantity (if everyone has it, it loses its value).

Greater rewards are thought necessary to motivate those able to perform rare and valued services.

Thus, if skills are unevenly distributed among members of a society, it is in the interest of all that those few with the required abilities perform their rare and valued services for the well-being of the society. For these performances, often involving risk, the individual deserves a greater reward than that given to those who do not play such important roles. The assumption is that it may be impossible to elicit the rare and necessary service without the promise of a differential reward; that is, people will not take risks or use their skills for others unless they perceive a return worth the effort. This being the case, the distribution of desirables reflects a socially-beneficial situation. A recent examination of the correlation between levels of income and prestige and occupations requiring talent and training finds support for the Davis–Moore position, although not all differences in income and prestige between occupations could be accounted for (Cullen and Novick, 1979).

A meritocracy is a ranked order of talent produced by the educational system.

One contemporary context for the functionalist thesis is the controversy over educational equality. The functionalist believes that the educational system produces a hierarchy of intelligence, which is a ranked order of talent often called a *meritocracy* which serves as the criterion for rewards and success. Clearly, then, full professors represent an intellectual elite, as do attorneys and physicians. That these status incumbents happen to be almost exclusively white males is assumed by many to reflect the actual distribution of talent and rewards by race and sex. The implications of the functional model, therefore, are that stratification is inevitable, beneficial to a complex society, and a powerful motivator of individual performance.

Almost a decade after the Davis and Moore article, an extended critique by Melvin Tumin (1953) was published. Among Tumin's major points were these: (1) the possibility that stratification can be dysfunctional because of the many social problems created when status aspirations are blocked; (2) extreme differences between the top and bottom segments of a hierarchy will breed resentment; (3) scarcity of top spots rather than differential abilities might account for the distribution of individuals; and (4) many top positions are inherited rather than earned.

CONFLICT THEORY

Conflict theory interprets stratification as the result of competition for scarce rewards.

Conflict theory, as described in Chapter 1, interprets social structure as the outcome of competition for scarce rewards. Individuals and groups struggle to claim high status, and, once that status is gained, will fight to maintain their position in the social hierarchy.

The struggle between those who control the economy and those who must sell their labor was central to the work of Karl Marx, as was the claim that the dominant ideas of a society represent the world view of its dominant strata. Contemporary conflict theorists have expanded this thesis, borrowing the concept of *ideological hegemony* from the twentieth-century Italian theorist Antonio Gramsci. Hegemony means control, and ideological hegemony refers to control over cultural objects and symbols. In other words, not only are those at the top of the power and property hierarchies able to pass their high statuses on to offspring, but, through their control of educational and religious institutions and the mass media, their view of the world comes to be accepted as truth. The ideology of those in power will, of course, rationalize their positions: We are here, at the top, because we deserve to be, and others are at the bottom because they lack certain qualities of mind or temperament.

Gramsci's original goal was to explain how European workers could embrace antilabor fascist governments. Contemporary conflict theorists in North America are similarly intrigued over the failure of a socialist movement to emerge in the United States. One answer is that workers also subscribe to the ideology of the dominant groups, which is consistently reinforced, as Gitlin (1979) notes, even in the structure and content of television programming.

Support for the conflict model of stratification is also reported by Squires (1977), who finds that expansion of the education system in North America has not reduced economic inequality, but, rather, has served to reinforce cultural hegemony. Similarly, the conflict view received empirical support in a study of the use of police power in the various states of the United States. Jacobs and Britt (1979) found that homicides by police officers were most frequent in states with the greatest income inequality and largest percentage of blacks. The authors conclude that force or its threat is essential for preserving order in societies characterized by extreme inequality.

A UNIFIED VIEW

The functional and conflict perspectives need not be considered mutually exclusive. Gerhard Lenski (1966) has pointed out that the functional model could account for an original stratification hierarchy, but that conflict factors are important in the maintenance of inequality long after the basic needs of the group have been met. In other words, people with unusual talents can claim or amass disproportionate power or wealth at certain historical periods. However, once established, they seek to pass along these advantages to their children, whether or not the offspring have any special talent. Transmission of social status is possible because members of each generation do not all start out as equals in social position. The analogy is often made to a foot race in which some individuals will be naturally more swift than others, but some runners will also have better equipment and training provided by their parents, and still others will be disadvantaged by poor diet, lack of training, and inadequate equipment. More importantly, the runners do not begin at the same starting line (as will become clearer in Chapter 8).

Explaining the existence of social hierarchies is one task. Defining and measuring the dimensions of stratification is quite another, and one that has preoccupied sociologists for the past century. In the remainder of this chapter we

Ideological hegemony refers to the control of cultural objects and symbols by those in power.

The functional and conflict perspectives can complement each other.

shall explore the distribution of power, prestige, and property in contemporary North America.

Dimensions of Social Stratification

Social stratification will be defined as the ranking of statuses in a social system in terms of the differential distribution of power, prestige, and property. The first questions to be raised are whether or not the three attributes are distributed in the same way. Is one more important for social standing than the others? And how are the three related?

The historical view of Karl Marx, remember, was of a dynamic struggle between the few who own the means of production (from bows to plows to land to factories) and those who do not. In every age, therefore, some individuals will

Social stratification refers to the differential distribution of power, prestige, and property. While the Shah of Iran had a vast amount of wealth, most of those he ruled were impoverished. (Source: Marilyn Silverstone, Magnum Photos, Inc.)

have greater control than others: parents over children, husbands over wives, landlords over tenants, employers over employees, and so forth. A central assumption of Marx was the fundamental unity of dimensions of stratification. Wealth *is* power, and can command deference and respect (*prestige*). Underlying all three aspects is the importance of control of the means of production.

In contrast to a Marxist emphasis on the convergence of status dimensions, Weber distinguishes several facets of stratification: (1) *Class* refers to groups of people at the same economic level, who can become aware of their common interests. (2) *Status groups* are communities distinguished by a common lifestyle and based upon the degree of *honor* or esteem with which an individual or group is held in the society. Status honor is not necessarily determined by class position; there are cultures in which the renunciation of goods is considered most honorable. If classes are economic divisions, and status groups are essentially social divisions, (3) *parties* are political expressions of different interests. Parties are politically-oriented, competing for domination in the society, and may or may not reflect class interest.

The concept of social class is particularly difficult to define, measure, and discuss in the North American context. There is something vaguely subversive about stressing social divisions in societies founded upon principles of equality. Yet we all recognize great differences in the distribution of property, prestige, and power in society. What transforms these differences into social classes? And what are the consequences of stratification for individuals, groups, and whole societies? Before continuing this chapter, you might take a moment to consider your understanding of social status. Do you recognize class distinctions? By what clues? Where do you place yourself? Why? What kind of comparisons do you make about the power or prestige of individuals? And how do you evaluate members of the different categories?

One interesting clue to your understanding of status differences is the use of *terms of address*. That is, whom do you call Mr. or Mrs. So-and-So? Whom do you call by his or her first name? Or by a nickname? Or just "hey you"? When you select one or another of these terms of address you are also making a judgment about social status—who is superior, inferior, or on the same level as yourself. Such judgments of social status are ultimately based on your perception of the social divisions within society.

THE DISTRIBUTION OF PROPERTY

Every culture contains some cherished items that constitute wealth. These may be piles of yams (in Dobu), or marriageable children (daughters in a society with bride price, sons where a dowry is required), or land (almost everywhere), or, in the case of modern industrial societies, gold, currency, and stock certificates.

Most members of society take it for granted that some people or groups will be wealthier than others. The unequal distribution is usually supported by other values of the culture and reinforced by the belief system. Movements to change the stratification system occur when the unequal distribution is perceived as *inequitable* (unfair) by large numbers of citizens. Such movements will be discussed in Chapter 19.

Marx assumed a basic unity of dimensions of stratification wherein wealth commands prestige and power.

Weber distinguished between the three major aspects of stratification: class, status group, and political party.

Class refers to those at a common economic level who can become aware of their common interests.

Status groups are communities based on similar degrees of honor or esteem.

Parties are political groups with particular concerns that may or may not reflect class interest.

When substantial numbers of citizens perceive the distribution of wealth as **inequitable**, movements to change the stratification system occur.

Table 7-1. *Distribution of Wealth in the United States: 1962*

Per cent of population by wealth level	Per cent of total wealth controlled
99.8–100%	17%
99.0–99.8	16
95–99	20
80–95	24
60–80	16
40–60	5
20–40	3
Bottom 20	−1 (in debt)

Source: Rose, 1979, p. 28.

The distribution of wealth in the United States has not appreciably changed in this century.

The top .002 per cent of the population controls 17 per cent of all personal wealth in the U.S., but the bottom 60 per-cent control less than 10 per cent of all personal wealth.

According to these data the top 2/10 of one per cent of the population control 17 per cent of the nation's personal wealth. In contrast, the bottom 60 per cent of the population control *less* than 10 per cent of personal wealth (see Table 7-1). This information comes from a survey of wealth-holdings made by the United States government in the early 1960s, but there is no reason to believe that the distributions are any less skewed today. Rose (1979) suggests that we have no more recent data on wealth, although everything else has been counted every year, because no one in power is especially interested in having this information gathered (see also Turner and Starnes, 1976). Another factor is the great difficulty in discovering who owns what stocks, bonds, bank boxes, foreign accounts, or other forms of wealth.

Figures on yearly incomes are used as a rough measure of the distribution of wealth (see Figure 7-1), but it is very likely that income grossly underestimates

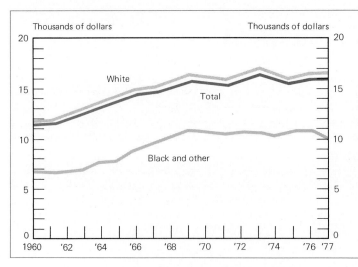

Figure 7-1. Median annual money income of families, by race, in constant 1977 dollars, 1960–1977. (Source: Statistical Abstract of the U.S., 1979, p. 436. U.S. Bureau of the Census.)

Table 7-2. Distribution of Individual Earned Income in the
United States: 1978

Income	Per cent of population
Under $6600 per year	Slightly less than 15
6,600–10,999	Slightly over 15
11,000–17,999	25
18,000–27,000	30
27,000+	15

Source: Rose, 1979, p. 9.

the actual distribution of property of all types. For the very rich, salaries represent only part of their yearly income. Ownership of property, stocks, and bonds provides additional income in the form of rents and interest. These are sources of wealth that can be transferred within the family from one generation to another. Most millionaires have inherited the assets that make them extremely wealthy. Very few have made fortunes on their own (Lundberg, 1968).

Rose (1979) estimates that less than 1% of the population is wealthy, defined as yearly income in excess of $75,000. Fifteen per cent are in the high budget stratum with incomes of $27,000 or more. Thirty per cent fall between the high- and medium-budget levels of $18,000. Slightly over 25 per cent of the population have incomes between $17,999 and the low-budget line of $11,000. An additional 15 per cent have incomes below low budget but above the poverty level (about $8,400 a year for a nonfarm family of four in 1980). The remaining 15 per cent are below the poverty line. The differential between the top and bottom income-earners in the United Stated today is roughly 600 per cent (see Table 7-2).

Household Income. Unlike personal income, household income includes the wages of as many members of the household as are in the labor force. Considering that at this time over half of all married women in the United States are employed, many households will have two full-time workers. The statistic commonly used to describe household income is the *median* or midpoint. In 1978 the median household income was about $16,000, with half of all American households higher, and half lower. Husband/wife couples had a median income of $18,562 whereas all other types (including one person households of elderly widows and young people just beginning their work life) had a median of $7,578, ranging from $5,192 for single women to $16,667 for a male head of household (Rose, 1979).

There is some indication that although the distribution of individual earnings has not changed much in the past thirty-five years, household income has become more equally distributed. This change is due to increases in monies transferred to the aged and poor (through Social Security and welfare programs) as well as to the probability of multiple wage-earners in low-income families.

Household income includes the wages of all household members in the labor force.

Table 7-3. *Distribution of Families by Income Group in Canada and the United States, 1975*

Income group	Canada Per cent of families	U.S. Per cent of families
Under $3,000	2.8	4.7
$3,000– 4,999	5.6	7.5
5,000– 6,999	7.6	8.3
7,000– 8,999 } 9,000– 11,999 }	19.3	21.7
12,000– 14,999	14.5	13.4
15,000– 24,999	35.2	30.4
25,000 and over	15.0	14.1
Totals	100.0	100.0

Source: *Canada Yearbook*, 1978–79, and Statistical Abstract of the United States, 1979, p. 450.

Family income is the income of a household with at least two related individuals.

Family Income. Family income is the income of a household containing at least two related individuals (see Table 7-3). In 1978 the median family income in the United States was $17,640 (compared to about $18,000 in Canada). The median for husband-wife families where the wife was in the labor force was about $22,000, compared to approximately $16,000 when the wife was not in paid employment. The median for white families was $18,370; for blacks, $10,880; and for Spanish-speaking families, $12,570 (U.S. Dept. of Commerce, June 1980).

The distribution of family income in Canada is roughly similar to that in the United States but the distributions of wealth and income in other societies varies widely. In many countries of South America, for example, close to 90 per cent of the wealth is controlled by a mere 5 per cent of families. At the other extreme, conscious efforts to reduce inequality in some European countries have been largely successful. Sweden, for example, has the smallest spread between high- and low-income recipients.

Unequal Distribution of Property and Social Order. However unequally wealth is distributed, this does not necessarily lead to social instability. The crucial factor is the perception of inequity. As long as many South Americans, for example, feel that their military dictatorships are providing order and stability, and even bringing glory to their country through its displays of wealth and military might, there will be little active rebellion.

In the United States, unequal distribution is legitimated by the belief that everyone has a chance to succeed and that people must be differentially rewarded in order to spur initiative. Wealthy families are honored, admired, and have great public power. Most Americans believe that with a bit of luck and hard work, it could be they who succeed.

At some point, where the distribution of incomes and wealth are extremely skewed, and where those without resources can no longer be convinced that it is their fate to be poor, the society will be weakened by the withdrawal of commitment on the part of the have-nots. When that withdrawal becomes open defiance, civil unrest follows. The great strength of communist and insurgent movements in the Third World (undeveloped and developing nations) today comes precisely from the Marxist ideology of equal distribution and its obvious appeal to lower-income strata of most societies.

POWER

Power, the ability to impose the will of an individual or group on others, is unequally distributed in almost every relationship, group, and society. Some individuals and groups will have greater decision-making force than others. Our interest here is in power as a social resource. It is important to distinguish between individual power and that which stems from control over decision making by a particular group of people.

Authority refers to legitimated power, that is, power granted by members of the society to the few who make and enforce the rules. Power accompanies a social position such as President or Prime Minister. Legislators and administrators are likely to come from the upper strata of the economic hierarchy, and those entrusted with highest office are often persons of great wealth, and with very few exceptions are white and male. In many ways, then, positions on one hierarchy can be exchanged for position on the other—wealth for power, and power for wealth. Few people have left public office poorer than when they entered. And very few poor people have run for office or have been appointed to high positions (Domhoff, 1980).

But not all power is legitimate. Illigitimate power is taken by force or other means outside the law. Organized crime, for instance, is a powerful economic and political force operating with few constraints from the legal system.

Even power in everyday life tends to reflect other statuses: husbands often control their wives and children; employers usually command employees; students usually defer to teachers. That is, power relationships tend to reflect the differential statuses found in the larger social order. The ultimate test of power is in decision making; the person who decides for the other has power. And people who make decisions are often those with attributes of superior status.

PRESTIGE

Unlike property and power, prestige (or *status honor*) is less a characteristic of the individual than the result of action by others. An individual has prestige only when others decide to hold that person in high esteem.

Prestige is a matter of cultural evaluation of personal qualities (Goode, 1977). In some societies the holy or wise are honored; in others, the strong and warlike. In North America, it is the successful who are honored, and especially those whose high incomes are the result of long training, that is, *professionals*. Scientists, lawyers and judges, professors and physicians rank high on any measure of prestige. The table below presents data of "Prestige Rankings of Occupations" for two years, 1963 and 1977. With very few exceptions, the top rankings are reserved for those with graduate school educations. Even though the studies used different scoring techniques, the relative positions of certain occupations are strikingly similar at the two time periods as shown in Table 7-4.

Rankings of occupational prestige also display remarkable cross-national consistency. An extensive review of 85 studies of occupational prestige in 60 countries found that similar prestige judgments are made by respondents in

Power is the ability to impose one's will upon others.

Authority is legitimated power granted by members of the society to those making and enforcing the rules.

Some power is not legitimate, but taken by force or applied outside the law.

Prestige is a result of cultural evaluation of personal qualities.

Table 7-4. Prestige Rankings, 1963 and 1977

Occupation	1963 (Hodges) Score	1977 (NORC) Score	Occupation	1963 (Hodges) Score	1977 (NORC) Score
Physicians	93	83	Sales representative	66	40
College teachers	90	78	Carpenters, plumbers	65	40
Lawyers	89	76	Factory workers	63	40
Physicists	92	74	Gas station attendants	51	22
Dentists	88	74	Taxi drivers	49	22
Bank officers	85	72	Garbage collectors	39	17
Airplane pilots	86	70	Janitors	48	16
Sociologists	83	66	Food counter and fountain workers	44	15
Elementary school teachers	81	60	Bootblacks	34	9
Musicians and composers	78	46			
Mail carriers, post office	66	42			

each country, at all social-class levels, and regardless of the specific questionnaire used (Treiman, 1977). The explanation offered by Treiman for this seemingly universal hierarchy of prestige is based upon structural-functional theory. All complex societies are characterized by a division of labor that creates occupational roles involving different levels of control over resources such as skills, authority, information, and wealth. Therefore, similar stratification systems develop, and prestige is distributed accordingly.

In most cases, high prestige is also associated with wealth, as with physi-

Americans accord high prestige to professionals in the belief that their success and high income is justified by their long training. (Source: Sherry Suns, Photo Researchers, Inc.)

cians, dentists, bank officers, and lawyers. But not always, as in the case of college professors. Low-prestige rankings are more perfectly associated with low income. In general, then, the prestige hierarchy reflects skills, training, and income.

Since prestige is indicated through the *deference* that others show, the symbolic-interaction perspective is especially helpful in analyzing how actors manage the impressions they create, and manipulate the responses of others. There are many such "status cues": dress, speech, and deportment being the most obvious. Individuals spend a great deal of time determining the relative status of self and others. This information is an important guide to conduct. Who speaks first, forms of address, who touches whom, and who has the power to end an interaction are all related to placement on the status hierarchy.

Deference shown by others is an indication of prestige.

SOCIOECONOMIC STATUS

As a simplified measure of general social standing, many sociologists speak of *socioeconomic status* (SES). The concept of SES suggests the overlap but not complete unity of power, prestige, and property. Researchers typically construct an index that combines *education, occupation* (as an indicator of prestige), and *income* to arrive at a single measure of SES.

Education, occupation, and income are considered *achieved characteristics* although we discuss in the next chapter the degree to which a young person's probability of achievement is greatly influenced by family SES, along with *ascribed characteristics* such as race, ethnicity, sex, age, and religion.

Socioeconomic status (SES) is an index that combines education, occupation, and income.

Education, occupation, and income are considered **achieved characteristics.**

Discussing nonverbal communication and gender roles, Laurel Richardson Walum notes the importance of *space* as a symbol of social position. Professors stand over students, separated by a platform or lectern; ministers are set above their flock; executives have different-sized desks and offices according to their rank in the firm; and the wealthy are allowed more personal space than are the less affluent. So, too, with gender.

"The principle of the higher the status, the greater the space, when applied to males and females, suggests that even in the nonconscious use of interpersonal distance, females have lower status than males." Over a period of years, Walum's students recorded their experimental findings on sitting and standing distances. The conclusions reached from over 800 observations were that women were more likely than men to tolerate invasion of personal space by both men and women; that when women got close to men, the latter retreated; and that when men got close to other men, the latter accused the experimenter of being pushy or homosexual.

What these data indicate is the link between gender and differential status. Similar findings have been reported for a range of nonverbal behaviors. Women are more likely than men to be interrupted, touched, addressed by their first name or an endearment ("honey," "sweetie") by strangers, and to be recipients of "playful aggression."

The Use of Space

Laurel Richardson Walum's observations on the use of space are to be found in *The Dynamics of Sex and Gender*, Skokie, Ill.: Rand McNally, 1977.

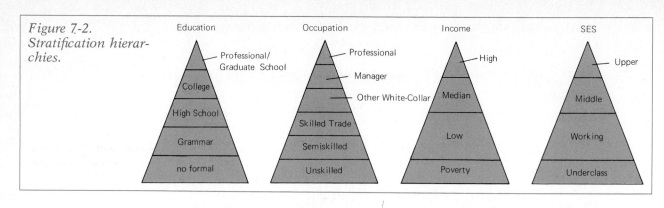

Figure 7-2. Stratification hierarchies.

Figure 7-2 provides a graphic representation of the dimensions of stratification of education, occupation, income and socio-economic status.

Social Classes in North America

The Myth of Classlessness. It has long been thought that while North Americans acknowledge the existence of an upper and a lower class they do not typically perceive their society as fully structured into distinct classes. When North Americans are asked to describe themselves, social class appears to be less important than its component aspects such as occupation, ethnicity, religion, or education. But this does not mean that North Americans are unaware of social status. There is an important distinction between *class awareness* and *class consciousness*. An individual can be aware of differences based on income and occupation, or prestige and power, yet not have this awareness be central to his or her life. Thus, while granting that class awareness may exist, most social scientists claim that North Americans, especially in the working class, do not demonstrate class consciousness.

The reasons most often given for a lack of class consciousness in North America are these: (1) The absence of a feudal past with its hereditary aristocracy and entrenched privilege; (2) the essential egalitarianism of early Protestantism and the ideals of equality and freedom enshrined in documents such as the United States Constitution; (3) our history of immigration which cut traditional ties, and provided the experience of starting anew; (4) the failure of the labor movement to generate a sense of working-class solidarity in opposition to the managers and owners as a class; (5) the expectation and reality of social mobility generated by geographic and economic expansion over the past three centuries; (6) the existence of many cross-cutting loyalties, such as race, religion, ethnicity. In other words, the very heterogeneity of North American societies works against the emergence of uniquely class-based identities.

However, it is not accurate to speak of North American societies as classless. And in fact there are both subjective and objective differences among the various strata sufficient to allow sociologists to describe a system of social classes in both Canada and the United States.

A six-part division into social hierarchies is shown in Figure 7-3.

Class awareness is the recognition of differences based on income, occupation, prestige, and power, whereas class consciousness makes such awareness central to self-definition and to social action.

Measuring Social Class. Determining social classes in general and the placement of individuals and families within a class is not a simple task. However, it is possible to divide the class structure into six traditional categories, as shown in Figure 7-3.

For ultimately, while many researchers use *occupation* as a simple indicator of class, individuals with the same occupation could be in very different settings that affect one's esteem, identity, and feeling of control over the conditions of work. For example, a doctor in private practice has a very different relationship to her or his work than does the physician in a Public Health Department.

Education, as an index of class, is even less precise. Individuals with the same level of education can be dispersed throughout the SES hierarchy. There are millionaires with little formal education (though not many), and Ph.D. holders with incomes below the median (very common). In general, though, college-educated individuals are assigned middle-class status compared with those whose education ended with high school.

Income might seem a very clear and appealing criterion, and it is often used to stratify individuals and families. The United States Government, for example, in setting low-, medium-, and high-budget levels, also provides descriptions of lifestyles for each level. A "high budget" family ($27,000–$75,000) owns its home and has a new automobile as well as a "complete line of household appliances" in contrast to the "low budget" ($11,000–$17,000) family that rents housing without air conditioning, uses public recreation, eats less meat and more potatoes, and drinks more beer and less wine than those with higher budgets (Rose, 1979, pp. 7–8). However, as a person's exact income is rarely

Occupation is often used as an indicator of class.

Education is also an imprecise index of class.

Income is a precise and often used measure of stratification.

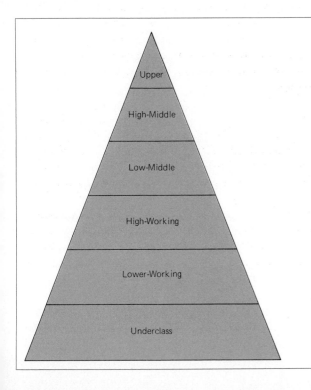

Upper stratum. Family incomes or net assets in excess of $100,000. Typically college graduates. Includes those of very high occupational status.

High-Middle. College-educated managers and owners, with incomes between $50,000 and $90,000.

Low-Middle. Other white-collar employees, with salaries between $30,000 and $50,000; or college teachers and other low-paid, high-prestige job-holders.

High Working. Skilled blue-collar workers (electrician, plumber, and so on); storekeepers; clerical and factory workers earning between $15,000 and $30,000 per year.

Lower Working. Semi- and unskilled workers, in low-status occupations, earning between $8,000 and $15,000.

Underclass. Underemployed and unemployed, low-skill workers, with incomes below the poverty level ($8,400 for a family of four).

Figure 7-3. Six-part division of the social structure into hierarchies.

Many researchers use occupation as an indication of prestige. Blue-collar workers usually are manual laborers whose work involves considerable physical effort. (Source: *Abigail Heyman, Magnum Photos, Inc.*)

known to others, judgments about social standing are usually made on the basis of *lifestyle*, that is, how one lives.

Richard Coleman and Lee Rainwater (1978) have attempted to ascertain how individuals arrive at evaluations of social standing, and the relative weight of the various ingredients that go into that judgment. Their conclusion is that income is the primary factor—increases in income enhance social status to a much greater degree than either increments of education or occupational prestige. Income or wealth is displayed in both the qualitative and quantitative dimensions of standard of living (cars, homes, appliances, generosity, and community service). The Coleman and Rainwater research is an important attempt to integrate the various components of social standing, including *subjective* (how people rank others) as well as *objective* measurements (how much money one earns, and how one earns it).

The importance of occupation and education has been documented by Nock and Rossi (1979), who asked respondents to evaluate the social standing of families described in a series of vignettes. In this study, occupation was the key variable, followed by education. And although the husband's occupation was the single most important factor influencing the assignment of social standing, respondents also took into account the occupation and education of the wife and adult children. In other words, Nock and Rossi found that a number of characteristics are combined when evaluating the social rank of families. The sociologist who selects but one simple objective criterion may be missing a very complex social process whereby individuals evaluate one another.

IDEOLOGICAL SUPPORTS FOR THE AMERICAN CLASS SYSTEM

Research indicates great inequality in the distribution of desirables and individuals and groups located at different levels of the SES hierarchy do not have equal probabilities of achieving high status. There is a class system in North American societies, recognized by people and usually accepted by them.

That this has not led to heightened class consciousness is probably due to a widely-held and strong belief that ours is an open class society; that is, that someone with talent and drive can move upward in the status hierarchies.

When inequality is not perceived as inequity (unfairness), we must look to ideological factors to explain how individuals interpret their experience. Recalling the discussion of *ideological hegemony* earlier in this chapter, it seems logical to propose that those who control the production of ideas and symbols will have constructed a set of beliefs that rationalize and sustain the existing distribution of desirables. There are at least four major premises that reinforce the North American class system by identifying *individual characteristics* as the basis of stratification.

> The class system in America is reinforced by identifying **individual characteristics** as the basis of stratification.

1. The Promise of Equal Opportunity. The belief that any person can rise "from rags to riches" is one of the most enduring myths of the dominant North American culture. A beacon for generations of immigrants, this belief was long supported by the expanding geographic and economic frontiers of the New World.

2. The Work Ethic. The Puritan work ethic emphasized the concept of *individual responsibility* and hence one's success or failure at a "calling." Personal qualities account for both success and failure. Those who are graced have the attributes of hard work, punctuality, and perseverance. By the same token, people who do not succeed are characterized by personality traits such as laziness or lack of ambition. Therefore, some moral flaw in the individual accounts for an inability to hold jobs and save money. The work ethic diverts attention from such *structural* causes of occupational failure as discrimination, dead-end jobs, and an industrial economy's dependence on a pool of temporary labor. Actually, many of the poor work longer and harder than those with higher incomes.

> The **work ethic** emphasizes **individual responsibility** for successes and failures.

3. Individualism. North Americans have also been attracted to a belief in individualism that stresses psychological traits and internal states such as motivation, intelligence, attitudes, and impulse control. This line of thought is very compatible with the Puritan stress on personal responsibility, and with a wish to believe in free will and self-determination.

> **Individualism** stresses an individual's psychological traits and internal states as explanations for success or failure. ✓

4. Theories of Biological Determinism. Theories of *biological determinism* focus upon the uncontrollable aspects of behavior, and can be used to rationalize social outcomes as being biologically inevitable—"the beast within," "natural submissiveness," and so on. Such theories support the view of the world as a jungle where only the most fit survive, and, by extension, where the survivors are perceived to have superior qualities. All these aspects of ideology condition North Americans to perceive inequality as a reflection of a natural order based on inborn differences among individuals.

> **Biological determinism** rationalizes social outcomes as being inevitable because of innate differences between types of people. ✓

In a study of school children in grades three, six, nine, and twelve, Cummings and Taebel found that in each successive grade the children's answers to open-ended questions were increasingly likely to explain poverty in terms of "character flaws and motivational deficiencies", such as: "Rich people are usually the more intelligent; they just worked real hard; and they just climbed the ladder from the bottom". And: "People are poor . . . because they are ignorant, uneducated; a lot of them just don't care; they just don't want the money; they're happy the way they are . . . if you really want to have money, you can have it no matter how poor you have been" (Cummings and Taebel, 1978). The authors conclude that schools support this view of the world wherein the rich are superior and the poor are inferior, providing ideological support for the maintenance and reproduction of inequality.

Summary

Social stratification refers to the existence of differences within social groups based on ascribed and achieved characteristics. Some form of stratification exists in virtually every society. Stratification systems stem from a division of labor in which some roles are considered more worthwhile than others, and typically leads to an unequal distribution of scarce resources—power, prestige, and property.

Functional theories explain stratification in terms of its consequences for society and its members. Differential rewards for different tasks are necessary in order to motivate people to train and develop their talents so that important roles in the society are filled. Conflict theory interprets stratification as the outcome of competition for scarce rewards. Those who control scarce resources will seek to maintain their advantage in various spheres of the social system. Functional and conflict perspectives can be used to complement each other in the study of the causes and consequences of social stratification.

What are the shape and content of stratification hierarchies in contemporary North America? Data on the distribution of total wealth and annual income indicate substantial differences between the top and bottom of the hierarchy. Power, the ability of imposing one's own will or the will of one's group upon others, is also unequally distributed. The authority to make decisions and enforce the rules is largely exercised by those who have greater wealth and economic power. Prestige, unlike property and power, is less a characteristic of the individual than a result of cultural evaluation of personal qualities. Prestige tends to reflect the skills, training, and income of various occupational groups.

Socioeconomic status (SES) is used by sociologists as a general measure of social standing. Socioeconomic status refers to an index that combines educational attainment, occupational prestige, and income.

Although a general awareness of social-class position exists among North Americans, there is disagreement among sociologists as to the existence and extent of class consciousness. Although most North Americans do not perceive their political orientations as based on class interests, neither the U.S. nor Canada is a classless society. Studies of social class in North America indicate great variation in the distribution of desirables, with different probabilities of achieving high status for individuals and groups at different levels of the SES hierarchy. That this inequality has not been perceived as inequity by many is attributed to the strong belief that ours is an open class society in which persons who have talent, ambition, motivation, and who are willing to work hard, will succeed and make it to the top. There are strong ideological supports for this view that explain success or failure as due to characteristics of individuals.

Suggested Readings

BRAVERMAN, HARRY. *Labor and Monopoly Capital: The Degradation of Work in the Twentieth Century*. New York: Monthly Review Press, 1974. The development of class structure in the United States and the prevalence of alienation in many occupations is thoroughly analyzed.

CLEMENT, WALLACE. *The Canadian Corporate Elite: An Analysis of Economic Power*. Toronto, Canada: McClelland and Stewart, 1975. A powerful recent analysis of the role of Canadian economic elites in shaping and controlling the structure and processes of Canadian society.

PORTER, JOHN. *The Vertical Mosaic*. Toronto, Canada: Toronto Press, 1965. The classic study of stratification in Canada, the composition of the Canadian class structure, and an examination of Canadian elite groups.

ROSE, STEPHEN J. *Social Stratification in the United States*. Baltimore, Md.: Social Graphics, 1979. The most recent empirical information regarding the nature and distribution of inequality in the United States.

SENNETT, RICHARD, and JONATHAN COBB. *The Hidden Injuries of Class*. New York: Random House, 1973 (Vintage Books). A sensitive discussion of the subjective experience of social class.

TURNER, JONATHAN, and CHARLES E. STARNES. *Inequality: Privilege and Poverty in America*. Santa Monica, Calif.: Goodyear, 1976. An analysis of the patterning and persistence of inequality particularly through the policies of wealthfare and welfare.

8

Social Inequality

Introduction

Whether or not members of a society recognize the crucial importance of social class placement, sociologists are obsessed by the variable because it is a powerful predictor of behavior, of lifestyle, and of life chances. If a researcher could have only one item of information in order to predict individual outcomes, social class location is more valuable than any measurement of personality, intelligence, or skill. For this reason, much effort has gone into the study of the consequences as well as the causes of social stratification.

Social class is of critical importance to sociologists in predicting life chances, lifestyles, attitudes, and behavior.

SOCIAL CLASS AND LIFE CHANCE VARIABLES

Life Expectancy. The higher the class position, the longer one lives. Death rates are highest among the very poor and decline steadily as income and education rise. This is probably due to a combination of better prenatal care, diet, medical treatment, less stressful lives, and safer neighborhoods. Although there are genetic determinants of life expectancy, such environmental factors exert a powerful effect on length of life.

Life expectancy and family events are directly related to class position.

Family Events. The lower the class position, the more likely a person is to marry before age 20; to have more than three children; to be divorced, separated, or deserted; and to experience violence in one's family life. The higher the class position, the more likely a person is to marry relatively late, have a small family, remain in the first marriage, and to experience greater satisfaction in that marriage. There is simply less strain on family members when there is enough money to go around.

Institutionalization. Individuals with fewer resources are more likely to be placed in mental institutions than are those with greater material and interpersonal resources (Dohrenwend and Dohrenwend, 1974). It is not altogether clear whether strains such as an inadequate income, unemployment, low self-esteem, and feelings of powerlessness lead to mental illness, or whether the poor are more often committed to public mental hospitals whereas the more affluent receive treatment within a private setting.

Emotional health and the probability of institutionalization are also linked to social class.

Similar processes may also account for the higher representation of poor persons in prisons. Although there is conflicting evidence regarding class differences in the tendency to commit crimes (Hindelang, Hirschi, and Weis, 1979; Tittle, Villemez, and Smith, 1978), there are great differences in the subsequent fate of lower- and higher-status criminals, as will be described in Chapter 17.

Emotional Well-Being. One of the most consistent findings in the behavioral sciences is a relationship between social class and psychological health. The higher their class position, the less likely people are to have symptoms of emotional disorder. To some extent, this reflects class-based probabilities of stress-ful events occurring to an individual. Recent research, however, suggests that the crucial variable accounting for different mental health outcomes by social class is *coping styles*—how one interprets the event and reacts to it (Kessler and Cleary, 1980). The same stressful event—death in the family, job loss, chronic illness, for example—will have a greater impact on those with the least per-sonal and social resources. People with low incomes and limited educational attainment are simply more vulnerable than those who can purchase the goods and services that make life comfortable even in the face of personal disasters.

SOCIAL CLASS AND LIFESTYLE VARIABLES

Lifestyle is often used as a measure of social class.

There are also social class differences in *lifestyle*, or the way in which people spend their time and money. People who own rather than rent are typically of higher status, as are those who vacation in Europe compared to those who take the family in a camper to a National Park. Diet, especially to the extent that good nutrition is related to education and income, varies by social class. Other areas of class differences in lifestyles are these:

Attitudes, values, and beliefs vary with social class.

Attitudes, Values, and Beliefs.   In general, working-class people are con-servative on matters such as sexuality, women's rights, and patriotism, but relatively liberal on political and economic issues such as unemployment com-pensation and health insurance. In contrast, members of the upper and high middle class tend to be liberal with regard to lifestyle but conservative on polit-ical and economic grounds. Yet middle-class intellectuals have provided ideo-

---

How the Donald Trumps Live

Donald Trump is a young real estate tycoon whose holdings are estimated by *Fortune* Magazine at roughly $400 million. This is not "old wealth" nor are the Trumps in the *Social Register,* but they live very well. In August 1979, the "Living Section" of the *New York Times* featured an article on the Trumps' new Manhattan apartment, one of their three residences—the oth-ers are in Colorado for skiing, and on Long Island for the summers.

On a typical day, Donald Trump is up at 6 A.M. to spend an hour and a half with their infant son before going to work in his chaffeur-driven car. Mr. Trump's days are spent "in one big negotiation" as he arranges real-estate deals.

Mrs. Trump leaves the house at 10:00 o'clock in order to oversee the pur-chase of furnishings for a Trump project, or to attend an exercise class three times a week, or to keep a hairdresser's appointment twice a week. Then she returns to the apartment around four P.M. for her daily appointment with a masseuse.

"I have to look pretty and fresh . . . because we have to entertain people so much." When the Trumps are in Manhattan, most nights are spent at restau-rants, night clubs, Broadway plays, or sports events.

"And then we have big social parties which we have to go to," Mrs. Trump adds, "and a lot of dinners with lawyers and bankers. We are very busy."

(Lynden, 1979).

Harry Martin: The Dreams of a Six-Year-Old

logical leadership in the civil rights agitation of the 1960s, the antiwar movement of the 1970s, and the women's movement.

Self-esteem. Class status also affects self-esteem among adults, though not necessarily among children (Rosenberg and Pearlin, 1978). Apparently, youngsters judge themselves in relation to those who are very similar to themselves, since residential areas and neighborhood schools tend to be class-homogeneous. But adults are judged by more general standards in settings where class distinctions become obvious. Moreover, the adult has had an opportunity to achieve a social status, whereas the child has not yet built upon the ascribed status.

Leisure. The use of nonwork time and the consumption of leisure products vary greatly by social status. For example, upper-strata members are likely to play tennis and golf, visit museums, attend concerts and the theater, and read "serious" books. In contrast, working-class members are likely to play softball, go bowling, watch television, and read "light" entertainment. These examples should indicate the extent to which class placement is correlated with every aspect of social life. Moreover, not only are individual outcomes greatly influenced by stratification processes, but the stability of the entire social system can be affected. For these reasons, it is important to take a closer look at the issue of poverty in the land of plenty.

Poverty in America

The Other America. Few single sociological studies have had the enormous impact of Michael Harrington's *The Other America* (1962). The complacency and faith in continual progress that marked postwar America (1945–60) was shattered by Harrington's account of national neglect. The poor had remained invisible because the great exodus from the cities to the suburbs had removed the poor from sight. Nowhere were affluent citizens forced to confront the fact that in 1960 over 39 million persons—22.3 per cent of the population—had incomes below the official poverty level of $3,000 for a nonfarm family of four. An additional 10 per cent had incomes only slightly over this level. In other words, almost *one-third* of the nation lived in poverty while a majority of Americans were experiencing unprecedented prosperity. This was three decades *after* the Great Depression, when President Franklin Delano Roosevelt spoke so movingly of "one-third of the nation ill-housed, ill-clad, and ill-nourished."

The "War on Poverty" and Poverty Today. Under the leadership of President Lyndon Johnson, in the mid 1960s, Congress passed major legislation designed to assist the poor with housing, food stamps, job training, and health services. These efforts suffered from a lack of sufficient planning and study. The war on poverty also fell victim to the war in Southeast Asia, which siphoned off the money, energy, and commitment that had previously been directed to domestic matters. As the Vietnam war grew more intense, less and less attention was paid to America's poor. Moreover, by the late 1960s many Americans were bored with the subject, tired of civil rights activism, and made fearful by the riots in Cleveland, Detroit, and Los Angeles. But most importantly for sociological analysis, most poverty programs were designed to change *people* and not the larger systems in which they were located.

Ironically, it is the accepted wisdom today among many Americans that "the war on poverty failed." The Reagan administration's first budget-cutting targets were precisely the programs listed at the beginning of this section: housing, food stamps, job training, and health care for the poor. The reasoning, again, is that poverty is an individually-determined outcome about which little can be done through legislation or "throwing money at the problem."

Yet there is much evidence that the percentage of people in poverty in the United States has decreased in the past twenty years, as shown in Table 8-1.

This 11.6 per cent below the poverty level represents about 25.2 million individuals. In 1980 the poverty threshold was defined as $8,400 per year for a nonfarm family of four. Some sociologists and many politicians claim that cutting the poverty percentage in half in two decades demonstrates success in raising the "deserving" (willing to work) poor above the poverty level, leaving only "hard core" cases that it would be all but impossible to improve (Kristol, 1978). Others (Rose, 1979) note that *changing definitions* of poverty artificially reduce the proportion below the threshold and that much of this reduction has come through public assistance programs: food stamps, rent subsidies, and other transfers of money or goods, so that some individuals and families are raised above the poverty level while still remaining without adequate earnings or suitable job skills. For example, 27 per cent of all families in 1977 had in-

Table 8-1. Percentage of Population Below Poverty Level

1959	22.4
1966	14.7
1969	12.1
1976	11.8
1979	11.6

Sources: *Statistical Abstract*, 1979, p. 462; *CPR*, Series P-60, No. 124, July 1980, p. 2, and No. 125, October 1980.

comes below the poverty level before receiving cash transfers such as Social Security, unemployment insurance, various government pensions, or Supplemental Security Income (SSI, a program that replaced public assistance in 1974). These transfers reduced the poverty percentage to 13.8. When the value of food stamps, Medicaid, and child-nutrition assistance are added in, the figure below the poverty threshold can be statistically reduced to less than ten per cent. Nonetheless, depending on who is doing the counting—the government or its critics—there are between 25 and 35 million citizens of the United States who exist in poverty or close to it, most with yearly incomes of under $3,000 per person.

Changing definitions of poverty can artificially reduce the proportion of the poor within the population.

In Canada in 1977, 11.3 per cent of all families and 36.6 per cent of all unattached individuals were classified as "low-income," defined as approximately an $8,000 per year income for a family of four (the level varied greatly by urban or rural residence). Over half of this yearly income came from government transfer payments such as medical, education, housing, and income-maintenance benefits (*Perspectives Canada* III, p. 105–6). A Canadian National Council of Welfare report issued in 1979 noted that 16 per cent of adult females and 11 per cent of adult males fell below the official poverty level.

WHO ARE THE POOR?

Race. In the United States, of the 24.5 million individuals classified below the poverty level in 1978, 16.3 million were white, 7.6 million were black, and 2.6 million were of Spanish origin. But since whites compose 80 per cent of the total population, only about 9 per cent of all whites live in poverty. Conversely, slightly over 30 per cent of blacks and 21.6 per cent of Hispanics are in the poverty population. In other words, nonwhites are three times more likely than whites to be very poor. Race and ethnic factors appear to be less important than regional differences in the distribution of poverty in Canada as seen in Table 8-2.

Table 8-2. Proportion of Canadian Families and Unattached Individuals Classified as Low-income in Each Province and Specified Areas of Residence, 1977

	Families	Unattached individuals
Newfoundland	15.8 *per cent*	53.7 *per cent*
Prince Edward Island	11.2	44.5
Nova Scotia	12.4	44.0
New Brunswick	13.8	43.0
Québec	12.7	40.6
Ontario	9.8	34.1
Manitoba	13.8	44.8
Saskatchewan	12.1	36.5
Alberta	9.8	28.9
British Columbia	10.4	33.9
Canada	11.2	36.6

Source: *Perspectives Canada* III, table 6-7, p. 105.

The probability of poverty varies by **race, family status, gender, age,** and **place of residence.**

Family Status. People who are "unrelated individuals," that is, not living in families, are over twice as likely as those in families to be among the poor in both Canada and the United States (22 per cent of Canadians to 9 per cent in the U.S.). But as most North Americans live in families, the majority of the poor are family members, especially women who are heads of household and their children. In both countries, almost one-third of women who are family heads have incomes below the poverty line.

Gender and Age. Women are more likely than men to be living in poverty, and children are more often affected than adults. Persons over 65 are also disproportionately among the poor. In the United States in 1979, 15 per cent of the elderly were below the poverty level, although persons 65+ represented only about 11 per cent of the population as a whole. This is, however, only half the percentage of old people who were classified as poor in 1959, before the passage of Medicare legislation and increases in Social Security. The 1977 figure for black aged was 36.3 per cent below the poverty level compared with 62.5 per cent in 1959. Thus, elderly blacks are 2½ times more likely to live in poverty than elderly whites. To be old, female, black, and not living in a family is to be among the most deprived of Americans. Similarly in Canada, higher proportions of persons 65+ are in the low-income category than is the case of other age groups, and among unattached individuals, over half those 65+ are so classified.

Places of Residence. The poor in the United States are primarily located in the inner cities and in the rural areas of the South. In 1978, for example, about 8

In the United States many of the poor are located within the inner cities. (Source: Bruce Davidson, Magnum Photos, Inc.)

per cent of whites living in metropolitan areas were below the poverty line, compared to almost 30 per cent of blacks. In rural areas, the proportions of poor were approximately 11 per cent for whites and 39 per cent for blacks. The South has twice as many poor as any other region of the country—many being elderly blacks.

In contrast, rural/urban differences are less marked in Canada, with rural areas containing a slightly higher percentage of poor families and small towns (under 12,000 population) having the highest proportions of individuals living in poverty.

CAUSES OF POVERTY

A number of theories have been advanced to explain why some people are poor and others are not. These explanations fall into four broad categories: (1) reasons that locate the causes of poverty in the individual's personality and behavior, or (2) in the socialization environment and experience; (3) reasons that evoke the element of chance—fate, bad luck, or forces beyond one's control, and (4) reasons that emphasize the effects of social structure—particularly the job market, educational system, and discriminatory practices.

Individualistic Explanations. Ten years after Harrington's *The Other America,* Joe R. Feagin conducted a national probability sample survey to discover the public's beliefs about the causes of poverty. The results of his findings are shown in Table 8-3.

Clearly, most respondents believe that personal characteristics determine success and failure: "lack of thrift," "lack of effort," and "loose morals and drunkenness" were three of the four first-ranked explanations. The other leading cause, "lack of ability and talent," is also an individual characteristic, but one that could be thought of as a matter of fate beyond the person's control. That the Puritan ethic is alive and well in contemporary North America is sug-

> Individualistic theories of poverty locate causes in an individual's personality and behavior.

Table 8-3. *Reasons for Poverty Selected by Americans in National Survey*

	Very important, per cent	Somewhat important, per cent	Not important, per cent
1 Lack of thrift and proper money management by poor people.	58	30	11
2 Lack of effort by the poor themselves.	55	33	9
3 Lack of ability and talent among poor people.	52	33	12
4 Loose morals and drunkenness.	48	31	17
5 Sickness and physical handicaps.	46	39	14
6 Low wages in some businesses and industries.	42	35	20
7 Failure of society to provide good schools for many Americans.	36	25	34
8 Prejudice and discrimination against Negroes.	33	37	26
9 Failure of private industry to provide enough jobs.	27	36	31
10 Being taken advantage of by rich people.	18	30	45
11 Just bad luck.	8	27	60

Source: Joe R. Feagin, *Psychology Today*, November, 1972, p. 104.

gested by the title of one of Feagin's essays, "We Still Believe That God Helps Those Who Help Themselves" (1972). Similar findings are reported from a recent study conducted by Michael Lewis (1978).

The Culture of Poverty Explanations. Another approach to explaining poverty in terms of the characteristics of the poor has focused on subcultural factors: family relationships, values, attitudes, and norms of conduct in everyday life.

The most influential work on this theme is that of the anthropologist Oscar Lewis (1959), who has published life histories of Mexican poor in the inner city. Lewis developed the concept of a *culture of poverty:* a set of beliefs and behaviors for coping with poverty that are transmitted from parent to child, thus ensuring that the cycle of poverty is continually reinforced.

Lewis accounts for the persistence of poverty by referring to socialization experiences. The child learns poverty-related values and behaviors from the parents and recreates these in his or her own life. Whereas the personality-factor approach has limited policy implications, the culture of poverty perspective suggests that deliberate changes in socialization experiences will have a positive effect. This belief has guided most federal programs in the United States over the past two decades. Changing people through early intervention (preschool centers) and adult re-education (various training programs) has proven to be a long and difficult task, but not without some limited successes— Head Start and the Job Corps, for example (Levitan and Johnson, 1976). Yet the resocialization of some individuals has not greatly affected the poverty status of the millions of poor locked into the central cities because nothing affecting their life has changed for the better.

Fatalistic Explanations. In some ways, the personality and culture of poverty explanations could be thought of as fateful; having the bad luck of being born in the underclass dooms the child. Others believe that some people are just prone to ill luck or fail to take advantage of opportunities—characteristics that are also individual attributes.

There is also a fatalism associated with beliefs in divine powers that determine the life course of mere mortals. As it would be foolish and futile to question life's outcomes, the best thing to do is to accept quietly one's fate. And many of the poor themselves subscribe to just such a belief and await a better life in the next world. Religious commitment is often stronger among the disadvantaged than among the successful. Certainly it is easier in many ways to blame fate rather than one's own flaws or a system over which one feels so little control.

Structural Explanations. In contrast to these other approaches, that many define as *blaming the victim* (Ryan, 1972), most sociologists focus on aspects of the social structure to explain poverty (and affluence). The three major focuses of structural analysis are economic factors, the educational system, and discrimination.

Economic factors. The structural approach explains poverty as a consequence of an economic system that no longer needs the labor of the unskilled except in the most menial servant-type tasks, and that cannot absorb all possi-

When David Caplovitz did his research on poverty many years ago (1963), he was struck by the large number of appliance and furniture stores in low-income areas of New York City. Under what circumstances, he wondered, would it be profitable for a merchant to locate in such neighborhoods? The answer, of course, was that the poor had consumer demands similar to those of the more affluent, but their lesser capacity to purchase outright made it likely that they would *buy on credit*, which, in the long run, costs the buyer considerably more than the purchase price.

Today, after the inner-city riots of the late 1960s, and given the high levels of street crime in those areas, many merchants have left. This change in the availability of goods and services increases the likelihood of prices being raised even further in the few stores that remain.

People who live in poverty neighborhoods cannot do comparison shopping; they cannot travel great distances for bargains; and they often do not have enough ready cash to buy food at supermarkets in their neighborhood, but must use the corner shops where they can buy on credit—and at an even higher price per item than in the chain stores. Far from the cost of living being cheaper, it is actually higher in low-income areas than elsewhere.

---

ble workers. For example, the introduction of farm machinery reduced the demand for sharecroppers, tenant farmers, and migrant labor. Because the machines can efficiently work large areas of land, agribusiness (large landholdings owned by national corporations) has replaced the small farm throughout most of the United States and increasingly in Canada.

The city worker is not much better off, especially since many manufacturing firms and light industry have moved from the cities to the suburbs, where taxes are lower and commuting easier for the managers (see Ch. 18). But the unemployed cannot move to the suburbs. There is no low-cost housing in most suburban communities, no possibility of getting a mortgage without some income and assets, and it is quite likely that one's family would not be welcomed, particularly if dark-skinned.

As for the skilled trades, entry into these occupations has been rigidly controlled by unions through their apprentice programs, with entrants traditionally drawn from the families of those in the unions and rarely from other racial or ethnic groups unless forced to by law.

Most of the very poor are women and children, for whom there is often no place in the economy. United States welfare payments are pegged at subsistence levels, and job training for the female head of household is not a national priority. Legislators might state that mothers should be at home caring for their children, but offer few supports for poor women in this task. Legislation establishing child-care centers was vetoed in 1973 by President Nixon as being destructive of the American family, yet, child care for the poor is supported as necessary for "getting those women off welfare." Too often this has meant encouraging them to find unskilled jobs or to engage in "workfare," that is, cleaning public buildings in return for welfare payments. Few women will escape poverty by this route.

The population of poor and near poor in both Canada and the United States contains large numbers of intact families with at least one adult who holds a full-time job. These full-time jobs are in service occupations—janitors, cleaning

Factory workers are frequently victims of economic fluctuations and corporate decisions to lay off workers or close plants. (Source: *Burk Uzzle, Magnum Photos, Inc.*)

women, kitchen help, porters, washroom attendants, laundry workers—where wages are inadequate for raising a family. Such workers have little job security, receive few benefits such as medical insurance, and are rarely covered by collective bargaining contracts. Even where husband and wife both work at these types of jobs or where the husband moonlights on a second job, total family income cannot support an urban family of four. In the United States a person earning the minimum wage for a 40-hour work week, fifty weeks a year, still has an income below the poverty threshold for a family of four.

Educational factors. School systems, particularly in urban areas, often fail to provide students with the skills necessary to escape poverty. Large numbers of students drop out or find the whole enterprise meaningless. As many as one-third of the school children in some areas of New York City were not in regular attendance in 1978. Lack of preparation and motivation, overcrowded conditions, difficulties in finding rest and quiet in order to do homework, and an absence of realizable goals have all been cited as contributing to this very high rate of educational failure.

In the case of many young black men and women today, the educational factor may be less direct in its effect on employment and earnings. In 1976, the unemployment rate of black youth with some college education was three times higher than that for whites of similar age and education, and two and one-half times higher for white youngsters with only a high school education. In fact, a white high school drop-out is significantly more likely to be employed today than is a black who completed high school (Hill, 1975). Thus, even when black youths remain in the school system and earn a diploma, their return on this investment of time and effort is considerably lower than that for whites.

Discrimination factors. Since poverty is more widespread among blacks than whites in the United States, discrimination factors must be examined. Racial feelings are far more intense than ethnic or religious prejudices, and they have served to block the path of most blacks even after civil rights legislation of the 1960s. Much of the poverty of blacks, and, increasingly today, Hispanics, is built into the social structure.

Consequences of Structured Poverty. In structural explanations, personality traits are viewed as *responses* to the conditions of poverty rather than its cause. If there is a culture of poverty, it is an adaptation to the realities of existence. Under conditions of blocked mobility, dropping out, lowering aspirations, and living for the moment are very logical adaptations to reality. When each successive generation of poor meets the same barriers to employment and acceptance, the same set of behavioral responses will emerge, giving the impression that a culture of poverty has been transmitted from parent to child (Rainwater, 1966; Liebow, 1967; Coward, Feagin and Williams, 1974). As long as structural restraints persist, so will a culture of poverty—but as a *consequence*, not the cause, of poverty.

The behavioral patterns of the poor can be seen as a direct **response** to **structural conditions**, rather than as a cause of poverty.

Living in poverty is a troubled existence. The poor often commit suicide, undergo psychological traumas, get sent to prison, fail in marriages, and suffer from malnutrition and a number of debilitating diseases. The consequences of poverty are deep and extensive; no phase of life is left untouched. Even life itself is shortened and often filled with violence. Nor can the poor easily turn to local officials for assistance. For many reasons—including mistrust and communication difficulties on both sides—impoverished clients present almost insoluble dilemmas to the social welfare personnel with whom they must deal (Sheehan, 1976).

The Persistence of Poverty

How can we explain the persistence of poverty in the richest nation on earth? Conflict theorists feel that the poor are too weak to challenge the power of the affluent, who control the distribution of goods and services, access to high positions, and the ideological justifications for inequality. Symbolic interactionists say definitions of the situation reinforce and verify identities based on lack of mainstream success, by extolling other virtues—loyalty, sexual exploits, toughness, and so forth.

But what of functional analysis? How can poverty be considered adaptive for a society? In an article that has stirred a great deal of controversy, Gans (1972) combines conflict and functional analysis to compose a list of the "Positive Functions of Poverty." Whereas poverty is clearly dysfunctional for the poor, Gans claims that the nonpoor benefit from it in ways that can be considered adaptive for the society as a whole. Among Gans's 15 positive functions of poverty are the following:

Gans suggests that poverty persists because of benefits realized from it by the nonpoor.

1. The poor provide a pool of applicants for low-paid, irregular, and menial jobs, ensuring that "dirty work" (in all senses of the term) gets done.

2. Low income to the poor means that more money is available for the wealthy to invest.

3. Domestic workers free the wealthy from many chores of daily life.

4. Poverty creates many jobs for the nonpoor: law-enforcement personnel, social workers, pawn-shop owners, numbers game runners, drug sellers, liquor-store owners, faith healers, and so forth.

5. The poor can be condemned and punished for their misdeeds, giving the impression that law and order are being maintained. It is much easier to condemn "welfare cheats" than stock market manipulators or presidents who commit illegal acts, although there are probably proportionately fewer cheaters among welfare recipients than there are income-tax violators in the middle class or bribe-takers in elective office.

6. The poor can also be used as an example of what not to become, against which others can compare themselves favorably. Poor people also provide objects for altruism and charity.

7. But above all, poverty removes large numbers of individuals from the struggle for success, and in so doing improves the chances of other groups, particularly those who make a living providing goods and services to the poor.

Gans concludes by pointing out that functional theory itself leads to the conclusion that poverty will persist as long as its benefits outweigh costs to the nonpoor. The solutions to poverty are (1) to make it dysfunctional for the affluent (through public disorder or the threat of violence, or through increased taxes), or (2) to develop *functional alternatives* that will be seen as less costly to all groups. However, all the alternatives that Gans suggests will be more costly to the affluent than the continuation of the *status quo*. The *status quo* reflects a set of programs designed less to reduce poverty than to minimize its impact on certain groups of the poor—the elderly, women, and children. These programs are often lumped together in the public mind under the word *welfare*.

WELFARE

Welfare covers a number of government programs designed to assist people in need.

The term *welfare* covers a number of separate programs funded and administered at the federal, state or province, and local levels. These are programs that have been put in place by law and are designed to assist people who are in need of housing, food, money, and medical care. In Canada, family allowances, pensions and a national health service are available to all, while special programs assist the blind and disabled. In 1980–1, health and welfare costs accounted for one-third of federal spending.

In the United States, the four largest *federally* financed welfare programs are these:

1. *Medicaid.* Pays hospital bills and other medical benefits to all Americans with incomes below the poverty line.

2. *Supplemental Security Income (SSI).* Replacing many scattered public assistance programs, SSI pays benefits to the blind, disabled, and aged who have no other source of income or whose Social Security benefits are still below poverty level. In 1978 the average monthly payment was $100 for the aged and $155 for disabled persons.

3. *Food Stamps.* A subsidized food program for people with no income or below poverty level. In 1979, over 17 million individuals received stamps

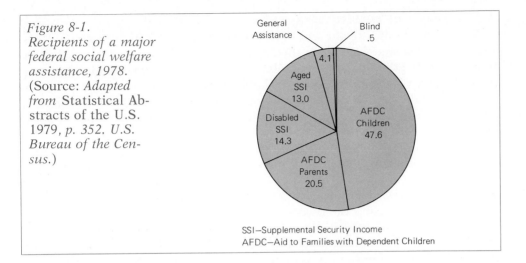

Figure 8-1.
Recipients of a major
federal social welfare
assistance, 1978.
(Source: *Adapted*
from Statistical Ab-
stracts of the U.S.
1979, *p. 352. U.S.*
Bureau of the Cen-
sus.)

General Assistance
Blind .5
4.1
Aged SSI 13.0
AFDC Children 47.6
Disabled SSI 14.3
AFDC Parents 20.5

SSI—Supplemental Security Income
AFDC—Aid to Families with Dependent Children

worth an average of $30.00 toward monthly food purchases, or about $1.00 a day.

4. *Aid to Families with Dependent Children (AFDC).* These are unemployed or underemployed single parents (almost totally mothers) and their dependent children (under 18). In 1978, over 3 million families received AFDC payments, including 7.5 million children, two-thirds of whom were under eleven years old. The average monthly payment in 1978 was $86 per person, or $254 per family (ranging from a low of $61 in Mississippi to $375 in New York).

From this list, it is quite simple to see that very few able-bodied males receive federal welfare payments, and many who do are single-parent fathers engaged in raising small children. No more than 2 per cent of welfare recipients are men who could be considered mentally and physically capable of full-time employment. The major exception is the food stamp program, in which many men are enrolled primarily because of lack of employment. The overwhelming majority of federal welfare recipients are children, their mothers, the blind and disabled, and those over 65.

A larger number of unemployed men and women without primary child care responsibilities are receiving *state* and *local* welfare payments than are in the federal programs. However, most state and local welfare offices provide only temporary aid to people ineligible for unemployment benefits or who cannot work full time. The payments are quite low, averaging about $160 a month, although there are wide variations by region and state.

Contrary to other widely held assumptions, few families remain on the welfare rolls for long periods or pass welfare status from one generation to another. Despite the many drawbacks imposed by poverty, most families drift in and out of the welfare system. Divorce or separation can plunge many women and children into poverty, whereas remarriage, reconciliation, and employment pull the family back over the threshold (Morgan, 1974). In 1977, for example, only about 5 per cent of AFDC families had been receiving payments for ten years or more. (*Statistical Abstract*, 1979, p. 357).

Of all who receive federal welfare payments, less than 2 per cent are males capable of full-time employment.

THE REDISTRIBUTION OF WEALTH

Welfare payments are one way of transferring money from the nonpoor to the poor. But because the amounts involved are barely adequate for survival, the placement of individuals and families in the United States social-economic status hierarchy remains unchanged. Although the proportion of below the poverty level in the United States has steadily decreased since 1960, the share of personal wealth held by the top one per cent of income earners has changed only slightly since 1945 (*Statistical Abstract*, 1979, p. 470). In Canada, the various transfer programs, especially health and education benefits, appear to have had a more equalizing effect on the distribution of income (*Perspectives Canada III*, p. 100).

Income redistribution is designed to reduce both extreme poverty and the concentration of great wealth.

However, the primary means of redistributing income in a modern society is through taxation, using the revenue received from high-income earners to set an income floor under the impoverished. Although tax rates have not inhibited the amassing of large fortunes in the United States, middle-income earners are feeling the effects of both increased tax rates and inflation. Taxes in Canada are slightly higher than those in the United States, but Canadians receive many more health, education and family benefits from the government. The tax burden falling on individuals is almost identical, as shown in Table 8-4.

Another source of perceived tax burdens is the fact that state and local taxes have risen dramatically since the 1950s, as state and local governments have taken increasing responsibility for the health, safety, and welfare of their citizens. But increased taxes would not be sufficient to produce a taxpayers' rebellion if citizens felt that they were getting their money's worth. In the late 1970s in the United States the situation was quite the reverse; most citizens thought that governments were wasteful, inefficient, and unconcerned about taxpayers' needs (Yankelovich and Kaagan, 1979). There was also a pervasive belief that government has favored blacks over whites (New York *Times*, Aug. 5, 1979), and that the middle class had been penalized.

Yet there is no public sentiment in favor of additional taxes levied against the wealthy. In 1978, the majority of respondents in a United States national survey indicated that they supported legislation that would *lower* the tax rate on profits from investments, a change that would clearly favor the wealthy much more than the middle classes (Yankelovich and Kaagan, 1979). Tax changes currently proposed by the United States government are in the direction of greater tax relief for the wealthy. Why do the great majority of voters, who are not wealthy fail to insist on higher taxes for higher incomes? The answer to this

Table 8-4. Personal Taxes as a Percentage of Personal Income, 1977

	Canada	United States
Personal Income Tax	13.55	12.14
Social Security Taxes	1.53	3.27
Estate and Gift Taxes	4.09	0.53

Source: *Perspective Canada III*, p. 305.

Tax laws are written by legislators who are themselves in the top 3% of income earners in the United States. They are also influenced by special-interest lobbyists and by potential campaign contributors, who rarely represent low-wage earners. Tax loopholes are special provisions that benefit a particular group of taxpayers. Loopholes are legal ways to minimize one's tax liabilities, but they eventually add to the relative burden of all other taxpayers.

As reported by *Dollars and Sense*, three such loopholes accounted for a loss of over $40,000,000,000 in 1979, which was almost exactly the size of the entire budget deficit (for which the government had to borrow money from banks and now pays interest—an inflationary procedure that disproportionately reduces the spending power of the nonwealthy).

not on TEST

1. Mortgage Interest and Property Tax Deduction

This regulation allows deductions on money used to pay property taxes and interest on mortgage payments, but has the practical effect of a regressive tax, subsidizing owners of expensive homes and vacation houses, while offering nothing to renters:

Per cent of all taxpayers	Per cent of all taxes avoided	Average avoidance per taxpayer
Top 3%	25%	$1,906
Second 9%	35%	785
Third 30%	35%	230
Bottom 59%	5%	18

2. Charitable Gift Deduction

Donations to nonprofit organizations are deductable, but people with higher incomes benefit more from the same size donation than do those with low income. All taxpayers subsidize the charitable choices of the wealthy:

Per cent of all taxpayers	Per cent of all taxes avoided	Average avoidance per taxpayer
Top 3%	47%	$1,325
Second 9%	25%	219
Third 30%	24%	60
Bottom 59%	4%	5

3. Capital Gains Tax Exclusion

Only 40% of profits from the sale of real estate and investments held over one year are considered taxable income in comparison with 100% of wages:

Per cent of all taxpayers	Per cent of all taxes avoided	Average avoidance per taxpayer
Top 3%	82%	$5,186
Second 9%	10%	185
Third 30%	7%	39
Bottom 59%	2%	5

Source: *Dollars and Sense*, May-June 1980, pp. 14–15.

question, as Yankelovich and Kaagan conclude from their survey, is that many feel that, with just a bit of luck, they too could be wealthy:

> The American concept of fairness does not involve leveling, which is interpreted as taking away from the successful the fruits of what they have earned.
>
> The national psychology holds that those who play the game according to the rules (and the rules include such things as luck, chance, hard work, and "good connections") are entitled to their success. . . . [p. 20]

Similar views are expressed by Canadians (Marsden and Harvey, 1979, p.145). We shall now explore these chances for upward movement in the stratification system.

Social Mobility

Social mobility refers to the movement of individuals and groups within the stratification system.

Social mobility refers to the movement of individuals and groups within the stratification system. The distinction between *caste* and *class* societies is the degree to which status boundaries can be crossed.

CASTE SYSTEMS

In caste societies, most movement is within a narrow range, typically through a marriage that slightly raises the social standing of one of the families. Caste systems depend primarily upon *ascription*, so that family status at birth

In caste systems, an individual's status is determined at birth by his or her family's caste. In India, members of the lower castes, such as these laborers in Bombay, usually perform menial tasks. (Source: J. P. Laffont, Sygma.)

determines the usual life course for an individual, with the exception of a few especially talented or lucky persons. Caste barriers are maintained through control of marriage, education, and employment. Caste is usually associated with preliterate societies, but it would be a mistake to consider such phenomena a holdover from an unenlightened past. Caste controls are still very common, even in modern societies. *Apartheid*—separation of the races—in South Africa is based on a caste system, as is the denial of civil rights to Native Indians in many parts of North and South America. In the United States, marriages between blacks and whites were prohibited in a number of states until 1965. Fittingly, the case that ended this practice was brought against the State of Virginia by a couple named Loving.

There are many ways in which the United States has elements of a caste society: (1) residential patterns that clearly separate the races; (2) educational settings in which blacks and Hispanics are almost totally absent, regardless of ability; and (3) an occupational structure with certain minority groups concentrated on the lowest strata. So it is possible to have elements of both open and closed systems in the same society. No society is entirely open or entirely closed, but there can be immense variation in the probability of movement up or down status hierarchies.

CLASS SYSTEMS

Class systems are based on achieved as well as ascribed characteristics; that is, talent, skill, and luck allow individuals to reach statuses higher or lower than those of their parents and kinfolk, or to move through the stratification system during one's lifetime. The former type of movement is called *intergenerational* mobility because it compares one generation with another. A comparison of status changes occurring *within* an individual's life are called *intragenerational* mobility.

Upward Mobility. The prototype of an upwardly mobile individual is Abraham Lincoln, whose progress from log cabin to the White House is often used to illustrate the belief that hard work and talent will ultimately be recognized through the achievement of higher status. In the late 1800s an immensely popular series of books for juveniles written by Horatio Alger, with titles such as *Luck and Pluck, Ragged Dick,* and *Tattered Tom,* were designed to instill the Puritan work ethic in their young readers. It was the application of capitalist virtues—punctuality, thrift, hard work, clean living, and self-discipline—that permitted a young man to rise from rags to riches. As we have seen, such beliefs are still strongly held by many adult Americans who feel that it is only a matter of luck that their hard work has not made them millionaires—but that it could happen to their children.

Downward Mobility. There are few shining examples of downward mobility, and no folklore or juvenile literature of the stature of Alger's work. There are, however, *cautionary tales* about shiftless and lazy individuals who do not maintain their positions, much less rise in the status system: bums, hoboes, derelicts, and other pitiful creatures. Whole ethnic groups have been thought indolent or untrustworthy, and young people were warned to have no dealings with such poor examples of American virtues.

Caste systems depend upon *ascription* so that family status at birth determines what follows for the individual.

The practice of *apartheid*—separation of the races—is a means of maintaining a caste system.

Class systems are based on the evaluation of achieved as well as ascribed characteristics.

✔ *Intergenerational* mobility refers to status change from one generation to another; *intragenerational* mobility refers to status change within the individual's life.

✔ Mobility may be upward, downward, or horizontal.

Horizontal Mobility. Many people today, perhaps a majority of Americans, will change jobs during their careers. Not only will career ladders be less consistent than in the past, but individuals and families move around the country, so that at the same income level, the style of living can vary greatly. Most of these changes involve small increments of gain or loss of social standing. Unless the shift is dramatic enough, for example, to move one out of a working class city neighborhood into middle-class suburbia, most status changes are of the horizontal variety: slightly up or down within the same stratum.

A woman's mobility is measured by comparing the social status of her father with that of her husband. Marriage or divorce could therefore, have instant mobility effects on women. Today, however, more women than not are in the labor force, contributing to the family's standard of living and attaining occupational prestige in their right. They are also reaching educational levels comparable to men. In the future it seems likely that the wife's characteristics must be included in measures of family status.

SOCIAL MOBILITY IN THE UNITED STATES

In general, a high degree of social mobility is characteristic of industrial societies with democratic political institutions, low birth rates, and an ideology of equal opportunity. Individuals and groups are able to change status because many positions are not hereditary, because new occupations are created, and because established elites cannot fill all the top slots in an expanding economy.

The considerable upward mobility found in many industrial societies can be attributed to the structure of the economy rather than to the achievements of the individual.

Most sociologists agree that there is considerable upward mobility in the United States, and that this pattern characterizes most industrial societies (Lipset and Bendix, 1959). The United States and Canada are not unique in the proportions of workers moving from blue-collar to white-collar (nonmanual) employment in the past several decades. Gerhard Lenski's (1966) massive study of stratification indicates that whereas about one-third of males were upwardly mobile in the postwar period (1945–65) in the United States, so were 32 per cent of Swedish men, 31 per cent in Britain, and 30 per cent in Denmark and Norway. In most of these studies, the comparisons have been between occupational status of father and that of son at the time of measurement. Intragenerational mobility, as measured by the difference between first jobs and final destination, appears to be of lesser magnitude than the intergenerational rates.

The consistency of upward mobility patterns across modern societies, and the higher intergenerational than intragenerational rates, indicate that it is the *structure* of modern industrial economies that encourages upward mobility rather than being solely a manifestation of individual achievement motivation and golden opportunity. Most movement in the stratification system can be accounted for by societal rather than personal factors. Such societal factors (*demand mobility*), include changes in the economic structure and birth rates of different generations that affect the *rates* of intergenerational and intragenerational mobility, that is, the probabilities that members of particular subgroups will move up or remain at the same status level. Personal factors such as talent, motivation, and luck are probably important in explaining *who* is socially mobile or not (*pure mobility*), but most research on mobility attributes the greater influence to structural forces.

Structural mobility refers to changes in the economic system that affect the distribution of occupational openings.

Structural mobility refers to changes in the economic system that open up employment in the white collar area while decreasing the proportion of manual

Table 8-5. Major Occupational Groups in the Civilian Labor Force, 1900–1977

Year	Occupational groups as per cent of labor force					
	Professional and technical	Managers, officials, and proprietors	Clerical and sales	Craftsmen and foremen	Manual and service	Farm
1977	15.3	10.5	24.5	13.1	33.7	3.0
1970	14.6	8.3	25.0	13.8	35.2	3.1
1960	11.4	8.5	22.3	14.3	37.1	6.3
1950	8.6	8.7	19.3	14.2	37.4	11.8
1940	7.5	7.3	16.3	12.0	39.5	17.4
1930	6.8	7.4	15.2	12.8	36.6	21.2
1920	5.4	6.6	12.9	13.0	35.1	27.0
1910	4.7	6.6	10.0	11.6	36.2	30.9
1900	4.3	5.8	7.5	10.6	34.3	37.5

Source: U.S. Bureau of the Census. *Historical Statistics* and *Statistical Abstract of the United States, 1977*. Figures for 1977 are not strictly comparable with prior years because of reclassification of census occupational categories.
  Reprinted in Szymanski and Goertzel, 1978, p. 132.

jobs. Modern industrial societies are characterized by the following structural changes:

1. *Mechanization of agriculture.* Mechanization dramatically lessens the need for farm labor. Younger sons, tenant farmers, and sharecroppers are all pushed off the farm, and must seek employment elsewhere. Sharecroppers and tenant farmers typically are without education or other skills, and become manual laborers and low-paid service workers. The sons of *farm owners,* however, are quite likely to move into white-collar employment.
2. *Expansion of managerial and other nonmanual positions.* Such expansion takes place as large national corporations replace smaller firms and self-owned businesses. Clerical and sales jobs have tripled since 1900.
3. *Enormous growth of the public service sector*—government, education, health care, and social services. Between 1950 and 1978, the number of all city government employees in the United States has doubled whereas urban population remained stable or declined (*Statistical Abstract*, 1979, p. 318). The same dramatic growth characterized the fields of health care and education.

As Table 8-5 clearly illustrates, the long-term shift is away from farm labor and toward white-collar employment, a trend that accelerated dramatically after World War II.

A number of factors explain the high rates of upward mobility among young adults in the late 1940s and throughout the 1950s. First of all, these young people were from the very small birth cohorts of the Great Depression when birth rates were at an historic low, especially among the nonpoor. Secondly, the economy expanded at a very rapid rate following the end of the war. Thus, white-collar jobs were opening up at a faster rate than children of the middle class could fill them, offering an unprecedented opportunity for working-class youth to become upwardly mobile. In addition, the G.I. Bill and comparable measures in Canada, providing educational benefits to returning veterans in

199

Sports and Upward Mobility

Sports and other entertainments have been a successful route out of poverty for a few selected individuals in both the United States and Canada. An analysis of the ethnic, religious, and racial background of singers, comedians, and sports figures in the United States would find Irish names predominating in the early decades of this century, followed in the 1930s and 1940s by Jews and Italians (many of whom shortened and anglicized their names), then large numbers of blacks in the 1960s and 1970s, and now, increasingly, Hispanics. The extremely high salaries and visible popularity of superstars give the impression that major changes are also occurring in the distribution of power, prestige, and wealth in the society. Not so.

We suggest that access to fame and wealth through entertainment is possible precisely because the major status hierarchies are *not* disturbed. Playing outfield for the Yankees is not a position of great power in the economic sector, and a Las Vegas stage is a far cry from Wall Street.

Moreover, entertainers are just that, people who entertain those who can pay for their services. The essential social relationship of master and servant is maintained, although the financial status of the two may be reversed. While a rough equality of opportunity for individual players has been achieved in North American sports, this development has had minimal impact on the distribution of power either within the world of sports or in the larger social system.

In fact, the success of blacks and Hispanics in sports in the United States has not even been translated into real power within that institution. Owners, managers, front office personnel, coaches, athletic directors, and broadcasters are overwhelmingly white males, often quite wealthy ones. (Edwards, 1973)

In Canada, similarly, sports and entertainment have provided opportunities for instant fame and wealth to a talented few. The most visible ethnic minority, Francophones, remained virtually unrepresented in Canadian international team sports up until the past decade (Landry et al., 1972; Gruneau, 1972; Roy, 1974). Even in the sport for which French-speaking Canadians are best known—ice hockey—there have been only a few coaches or general managers of French-Canadian background in the National Hockey League.

the 1940s, financed the college education required for these jobs. Sons of farmers, of immigrants, and of small town tradespeople moved into the suburbs of industrial cities and became part of the new middle class.

Although these young men and women surpassed their parents in terms of education and occupation, as well as income in most cases, much of this mobility is structural. That is, it is due to the changing structure of occupations. Their mobility, therefore, results in an *absolute* increase in status compared to social class origins, but may not have changed the relative rankings of parent and child, as Figure 8-2 suggests. If the father, for example, was a skilled worker and his son an insurance salesman, the latter has a job that places him in the middle class, but in comparison with all the others in the status hierarchy he may be at relatively the same location as the father was. In other words, the hierarchy itself was upgraded between 1920 and 1960.

Statistics on intergenerational mobility are often misleading if *all* the off-

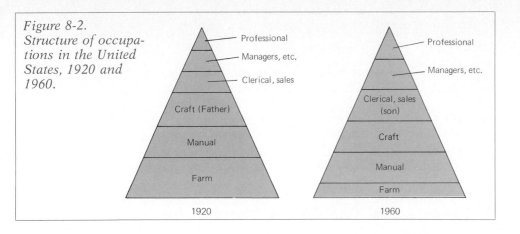

Figure 8-2.
Structure of occupations in the United States, 1920 and 1960.

1920

1960

spring are not considered. Sons and daughters who stay at the parental level or who move down are often not mentioned during research interviews. Families tend to remember and remark on their successful members, although there is probably at least one downwardly mobile person in every family, and several members who remain at the status level of the parents (Rubin, 1975). One effect of the American Dream is to direct attention to those who fullfill its promise.

Nonetheless, the net mobility rate in North America is upward, so that the Dream is fulfilled frequently enough to give it reality. Compared with other societies, moreover, although overall mobility rates are similar, there is more opportunity for someone from the lowest stratum to make it to the middle class in North America than in other industrial societies (Blau and Duncan, 1967) in which young people from the lower middle class move to the upper ranges of that class but rarely beyond.

INDIVIDUAL CHARACTERISTICS OF THE UPWARDLY MOBILE

Beyond the structural factor in mobility, are there any individual attributes associated with success in the stratification system? Research in both Canada and the United States suggests that it is best to be white, male, an only or first child, and to be raised by middle-class norms of *deferred gratification* (the putting off of immediate pleasures for a future goal).

Otto and Haller (1979) reviewed four major studies and proposed a process through which parental *aspirations* are transmitted to sons (daughters were not included in any of the studies examined by these authors) via socialization within the family. Since achievement-oriented interactions are more characteristic of middle-class than of working-class homes, parental aspirations are passed on to the sons through continually supportive feedback that results in motivating the sons to fulfill parental expectations. However, other studies have found only limited class or racial differences in the transmission of values and behaviors supporting mobility. For example, in a study of middle class and working class black college women, Higginbotham (1981) found uniform parental support for the daughter's aspirations.

Also it is difficult to separate family interaction variables from the other advantages of middle-class homes: providing tutoring, ensuring appropriate curriculum placement, and being able to afford a college education for offspring. Ambition and achievement motivation may simply reflect the social location of the child—its gender, race, and family status.

It should be obvious that not all members of the society start out together nor

Deferred gratification is a middle-class norm that encourages one to put off immediate pleasure in return for future success.

end up together. What is less clear is the process or paths whereby certain individuals get from one position in the stratification hierarchy to another.

STATUS ATTAINMENT STUDIES

Status attainment refers to the social position achieved by the individual in her or his own lifetime.

In a major study of social mobility—often called *status attainment*—Peter Blau and Otis Dudley Duncan (1967) found that father's occupational status and the individual's own education and first job were the best predictors of respondents' eventual occupational status. However, it is highly likely that the parents' social standing affects both the kind and length of education received by offspring, and this, in turn, has an influence on that very important first job as shown below:

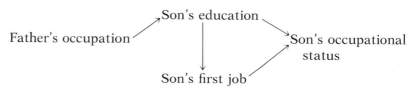

An update of the Blau and Duncan study has recently been published by Featherman and Hauser (1978) using 1972 data to compare with the original 1962 study. Although the initial conclusions remains valid, the effect of parental status has lessened over the decade, leading to greater intergenerational mobility (more upward than down), especially for black males. Status attainment for individuals, then, appears to be an increasingly open process, less tied than in the past to ascriptive statuses such as race, sex, or parental socioeconomic status (Hauser and Featherman, 1977).

However, analyzing data from eleven national surveys (again using only male respondents), Jencks and his associates (1979) found that although luck still plays some part in determining a man's earnings, family background factors are the single most powerful influence on both occupational status attainment and upon earnings. It is best, in the struggle to get ahead, to be white, of northern-European background, Jewish or Protestant, from a small family, with parents who have college educations and whose income is relatively high. Test scores do have a strong independent effect on occupational status, not so much as a sign of great ability but because of the encouragement given students who appear to be bright. Years of schooling completed are an important factor primarily if the individual completed college. The college degree, regardless of grades or curriculum, is a credential that opens doors in the occupational hierarchy. Further, what Jencks et al. call "teenage personality characteristics"—sociability and leadership—are related to later earnings within an occupational level, but are not strongly associated with occupational status attainment. It would be better to finish college than to be a well-liked leader in high school.

This may be more true of the United States than of Canada where the economic elite remains almost exclusively WASP and male (Clement, 1975; Porter, 1965). Elite status is transmitted from father to son through a private school system in which entry is carefully controlled. These ties are reinforced by a hierarchy of men's clubs, much as in England, where social standing is determined and valuable contacts are made. Women, Jews, and French-speaking

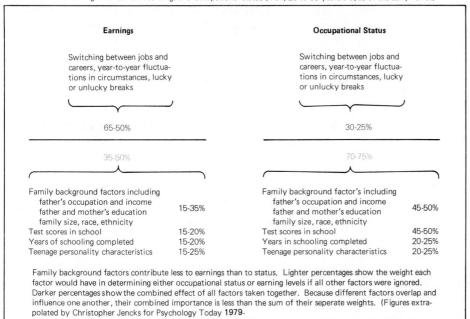

INFLUENCES ON SUCCESS

Factors affecting differences in earnings and occupational status (men, 25 to 65 years old, as of the early 1970s)

Earnings	Occupational Status
Switching between jobs and careers, year-to-year fluctuations in circumstances, lucky or unlucky breaks	Switching between jobs and careers, year-to-year fluctuations in circumstances, lucky or unlucky breaks
65-50%	30-25%
35-50%	70-75%

Earnings		Occupational Status	
Family background factors including father's occupation and income father and mother's education family size, race, ethnicity	15-35%	Family background factor's including father's occupation and income father and mother's education family size, race, ethnicity	45-50%
Test scores in school	15-20%	Test scores in school	45-50%
Years of schooling completed	15-20%	Years in schooling completed	20-25%
Teenage personality characteristics	15-25%	Teenage personality characteristics	20-25%

Family background factors contribute less to earnings than to status. Lighter percentages show the weight each factor would have in determining either occupational status or earning levels if all other factors were ignored. Darker percentages show the combined effect of all factors taken together. Because different factors overlap and influence one another, their combined importance is less than the sum of their seperate weights. (Figures extrapolated by Christopher Jencks for Psychology Today **1979**.

Canadians are almost totally excluded from entry into the elite through these channels, regardless of their talent, wealth, or educational attainment.

Critique of Status Attainment Studies.   Most status-attainment studies derive from a functionalist perspective. The argument, essentially, is that individuals with certain characteristics—education, motivation, luck—are worth more than others. This is a *human capital* approach to stratification, whereby the value of a person to the economic system is translated into occupational status, income, and prestige. In other words, the qualities that an individual brings to the economic system determine that person's social placement, and cases where qualifications do not bring fair rewards are seen as "market imperfections in an otherwise orderly system."

From a conflict perspective such inequities are not chance irregularities but are part of the economic system. Women, blacks, and working-class youth are channeled into sectors of the economy where they seldom experience upward mobility (Beck et al., 1980). Although there may be more individual mobility than in the past, the relative position of subgroups has not changed. Despite the more frequent successes of individual blacks and women, the overall status of women and blacks in the hierarchies of occupations and earnings has remained stable over the last few decades. There is some evidence that average earnings of black males, for example, have slightly declined as a proportion of white earnings, and employed women still, on the average, earn 59 cents for every dollar received by a male worker.

It should be noted that most of the work on status attainment has taken white males as subjects (Burawoy, 1977). Recent studies of blacks and women

The **human capital** approach to stratification indicates that an individual's personal characteristics determine his or her economic value.

indicate that status attainment may be very different for them than for white males. For example, blacks and women typically receive smaller status returns for their investments in education. That is, college degrees lead to less important and lower-paying first jobs for women and blacks compared to white males.

Controversies over the measurement and meaning of social mobility data are far from over. Sociologists will continue to debate the relative weight of intelligence, education, and family background in determining status attainment. However, the key variable for most is the family into which the child is born and such class placement is more important than are personality profiles or IQ scores in predicting occupational success.

Social Status and Everyday Life

Impression management is the way in which individuals manipulate information about themselves to protect their self-esteem.

In the give-and-take of everyday encounters, individuals continually transmit and receive information about themselves. Goffman (1959) uses the term *impression management* to describe these attempts to manipulate the image we present to others. The goal of impression management is to maintain "face," to have one's definition of self accepted by others.

Because people behave differently to those they perceive as socially superior, inferior, or as social equals, being able to place others is an important guide to conduct. Whether or not to show deference, to speak or be silent, to stay or walk away, to pat on the back or keep one's distance, all depend on status cues exchanged.

Status symbols are the outward signs of social rank.

Status symbols are the outward signs of social rank by which impressions are managed. "Keeping up with the Joneses" describes the behavior of people who attempt to equal the status displays of neighbors lest they lose status. It is the great accomplishment of advertising that status cravings and jealousies have been successfully stimulated in order to increase consumer demand. The home in the suburbs, two cars, a swimming pool—these are all symbols of the "good life."

Status cues are signals of social rank conveyed through clothing, speech, friends, and other attributes.

Identifying Status Cues.   We are all rather skilled in judging social status and making relative comparisons. Although most of you might claim to be totally unaware of doing so, it is likely that you immediately place others in terms of age, sex, and race. Religion and ethnicity are less visible but often readily discovered. A person's clothing, speech, friends, and neighborhood are primary clues to socioeconomic position. In many high schools, for example, a distinct status hierarchy can be constructed on the basis of who wears what, drives which type of car, joins which clubs, and dates whom. Members of specific subgroups—jocks, grinds, rah-rahs—are also easily identifiable by a set of *status cues* (Larkin, 1979). Among adults, the person in the three-piece suit is obviously someone who wishes to be thought important, compared to the man or woman in jeans and a T-shirt. The messages on T-shirts convey further information such as whether or not the wearer is to be taken seriously. As people

Status symbols, such as expensive clothes and large suburban homes, are outward signs of social rank. (Source: Arthur Tress, Magnum Photos, Inc.)

Status messages can be conveyed in a number of ways including printed messages on sweatshirts. (Source: Anestis Diakopoulos, Photo Researchers, Inc.)

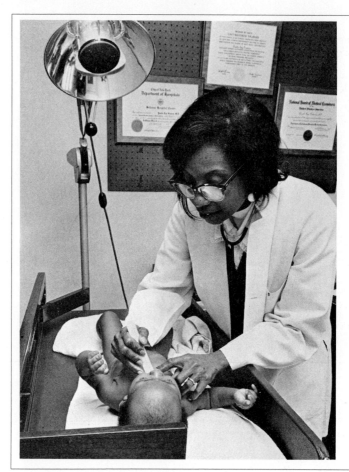

Status inconsistency may present difficulties for black, female physicians. (Source: Abigail Heyman, Magnum Photos, Inc.)

send and receive these status cues, they adjust to one another and select appropriate responses, maintaining the interaction while protecting their self-images.

STATUS CONSISTENCY AND INCONSISTENCY

Status consistency refers to the uniform placement of an individual on status hierarchies. A male executive will rank high in power, wealth and prestige. Similarly a minority cleaning woman occupies consistent positions at the base of the same hierarchies. Status consistency will be greater at the extremes of a stratification system than in the middle area, and more characteristic of a caste rather than a class society (Hartman, 1974).

Industrial societies display relatively high levels of class mobility, and multiple bases of stratification are possible. Therefore, a high probability of *status inconsistency* is characteristic of modern societies. For example, the head of a crime syndicate may have substantial wealth and considerable power but low prestige. A professional athlete may have considerable wealth and prestige but little political power.

Status inconsistency has important consequences at the interpersonal level.

Status consistency is the extent to which rank in a given hierarchy is associated with a similar position in other hierarchies.

Status inconsistency is the extent to which an individual occupies different statuses in different hierarchies.

Because each individual occupies positions on a number of status hierarchies, status messages are often ambiguous. The female attorney or the black physician, for instance, presents inconsistent cues—a combination of low-ascribed and high-achieved statuses. Some people respond by assuming that the black or woman is really less qualified than a white male. From the point of view of the status-inconsistent individual, the problem is one of wanting to be accepted in one's higher status (doctor, lawyer), while partners may be responding to the lower status (Lenski, 1966).

College students often experience such status inconsistency. Some may be the first in the family to be educated beyond high school and may find themselves higher on the prestige hierarchy but remain low on wealth and may have difficulty retaining friendships with age peers who went directly from high school into the labor force.

Reflections on Social Inequality

In no known society are power, prestige, and property equally distributed. At the very least, age and sex are universal bases for division of labor, and different types of labor are rewarded differently. Much of the stratification literature is in the form of debate. For example, do men have higher prestige than women because they perform more valued social tasks, or is men's work more valued because it is men that do it?

The functional view is that skills and talents that are scarce or that require long periods of training must be highly rewarded to assure their use for the good of the society. Critics of this view point out that the rewards accrue largely to those who are allowed to receive the special training, whereas other members of the society are excluded, and that most talents are rather evenly distributed throughout a population. Conflict theorists note that the range of difference between the top and bottom of most stratification systems is considerably greater than required for ensuring needed performances. Perhaps the most telling argument against the meritocratic and functional view is that members of the same families tend to control the distribution of rewards over several generations. Robert Merton (1973) has described this type of distribution as "The Matthew Effect," from the New Testament: "For unto everyone that hath, shall be given in abundance, but from him that hath not, shall be taken away even that which he hath."

> The functional view states that skills and talents that are scarce or require training must be highly rewarded.

> The conflict view states that differential rewards reflect the outcome of power struggles within the society.

This phenomenon raises another point of debate: Do members of certain families and social strata consistently reach the top of status hierarchies because they have inherited, genetically or through socialization, the qualities that make for success? Some argue that the persistence of elites is a natural outcome of the inheritance of intelligence and its link to achievement, but other social scientists point to elite monopoly over the means of achievement: education, professional training, corporate jobs, bank loans (Ratcliff, 1980). In both the United States and Canada, only when the upper strata fail to reproduce sufficient numbers of offspring, or when the economic system undergoes major expansion, do other groups experience upward mobility.

Summary

The chapter focuses on the causes and consequences of social inequality: the unequal distribution of power, prestige, and privilege and the consequences of this inequality for people's life chances and lifestyles. Knowing an individual's social-class location provides the sociologist with many clues about that person's way of life, attitudes, and values, and the probability of encountering certain life experiences. For example, the higher one's class position, the longer one's life expectancy, the greater the likelihood of a satisfactory marriage, the lower the probability of being institutionalized, and the better one's emotional well-being. People with higher incomes and educational attainment have greater personal and social resources to cope with stressful events; people with lower incomes and limited education are more vulnerable. Social class differences also lead to lifestyle differences in attitudes, values, and beliefs, child-rearing practices, leisure-time activities, self-esteem, and even friendship patterns.

Michael Harrington's *The Other America* identified the 39 million Americans who lived in poverty in 1960 (then about one-third of the population). The War on Poverty sought to assist the poor, but was cut short by expenditures on the war in Southeast Asia, shifts in political priorities, and a lessening of public concern.

United States statistics indicate a reduction in the proportion of the population living in poverty between 1960 and 1980, even though some of this decline reflects changes in the official definitions of poverty. As of 1979, between 25 and 35 million individuals in the United States had per person incomes of under $3,000—poverty or very near it. Among the poor are disproportionate numbers of nonwhites, women, children, the aged and residents of inner cities. Poverty in Canada affects a similar proportion of citizens, primarily women and rural residents.

Major explanations for the persistence of poverty are reviewed: poverty is caused by the individual's personality, behavior, or cultural environment; it is a result of bad luck or forces beyond one's control; poverty is the result of social-structure factors such as employment opportunities, access to educational facilities, and residential patterns. The consequences of poverty are deep and extensive, influencing every aspect of life. Caplovitz reports that the poor are even likely to pay more than the nonpoor for such necessities as food and clothing. Poverty persists amidst the affluence of our society, due, in part, to the "positive functions" poverty performs for the nonpoor and the powerful.

The welfare system consists of a number of federal, state, and local programs, designed to aid people in need of food, housing, medical care, and money. Inequality may also be reduced through various methods designed to redistribute wealth. Taxation is the major method used in our society, though the wealthiest continue to be the major beneficiaries of various tax shelters and tax-relief bills.

Social mobility involves the movement of individuals and groups; caste societies are typified by limited mobility whereas class societies, stressing achieved as well as ascribed characteristics, allow greater intergenerational and intragenerational mobility. The considerable upward mobility in industrial societies is largely a consequence of structural changes in the economy that affect the types of jobs available. Although some recent studies indicate an increased openness in status attainment, parental social class standing continues to influence the status attainment of offspring. Though chance, luck, and contacts are important, Jencks found that family background factors continue to be the most powerful influence on occupational status attainment and earnings.

Status symbols are signs of social rank that are used to manage the impressions that individuals convey to one another. Statuses occupied in various hierarchies may be consistent, facilitating impression management, or inconsistent, thus hindering interaction among people.

No society distributes power, prestige, and property equally. Sociologists vary in their explanations of this condition and the continuing causes and persistence of inequality in a land of affluence.

Suggested Readings

BLAUNER, ROBERT. *Alienation and Freedom: The Factory Worker and His Industry*. Chicago: Univ. of Chicago Press, 1964. A major analysis of the processes of worker alienation under modern methods of production that influenced much subsequent research and theory.

BLUMBERG, RAE LESSER. *Stratification: Socioeconomic and Sexual Inequality*. Dubuque, Iowa: Brown, 1978. The author integrates the concepts of sexual and socioeconomic stratification in an historical and comparative analysis of inequality.

HARP, JOHN and JOHN HOSLEY (Eds.). *Structured Inequality in Canada*. Scarborough, Ontario: Prentice-Hall of Canada, Ltd., 1980. The many facets of inequality among Canadians are examined by contributors to this recent collection. Regional, class, and gender differences, income distribution, poverty, and the political economy of status groups are discussed.

HARRINGTON, MICHAEL. *The Other America*. New York: Macmillan, 1962. A classic study in which Harrington helped "re-discover" the prevalence of poverty among one-third of the population at the same time that the majority of U.S. families enjoyed unprecedented prosperity.

HAUSER, ROBERT and DAVID FEATHERMAN. *The Process of Stratification: Trends and Analysis*. New York: Academic, 1977. In a 1972 update of the original Blau and Duncan study of the U.S. occupational structure (1962), the authors conclude that the chances of upward mobility have increased over time as the effect of parental status has lessened.

JENCKS, CHRISTOPHER et al. *Who Gets Ahead?* New York, Basic, 1979. This extensive reanalysis of eleven major studies of status attainment identifies the primary variables in upward mobility for U.S. males and provides estimates of their relative importance in this process.

SEIFER, NANCY. *Nobody Speaks For Me! Self-Portraits of American Working-Class Women*. New York: Simon & Schuster, 1976. A sensitive portrait of ten working-class women and their struggles with work, their family lives, community involvements, and political activism.

9

Gender and Age Stratification

by males takes up a great deal [...]
the total food supply of the gro[...]
warfare, and conducting long-d[...]
clusively, masculine activities. [...]
mies are thus crucial to family [...]

Yet, despite the relative flexi[...]
tions of women to the economy [...]
men's work is valued more tha[...]
stratification: the higher evaluat[...]
sequently higher position on all [...]
ence of gender stratification has [...]
who, in a study of feminine rol[...]
shaped less by official ideology [...]
spite the emphasis placed by M[...]
women are still socialized to ex[...]
paid, unskilled work roles.

BIOLOGICAL BASES OF GENDE[...]

Greater body strength and a[...]
sources of masculine power. H[...]
apes closest to humans, indicate[...]
to protect one's "turf"), and fe[...]
among them than among other[...]
males are not greatly different i[...]
are relatively noncompetitive. F[...]
behavior and social structure. I[...]
humans are the *least* likely to [...]
based explanations of gender st[...]

The somewhat crude naked a[...]
ences between the sexes that hav[...]
Tiger and Fox, 1978) have given [...]
basic thesis, however, remains w[...]
bearing have produced very diff[...]
male capacities are more condu[...]
biological position is that survi[...]
gramming, in which women are [...]
and rearing of the young, while [...]
children. However such popula[...]
stratification are not really usefu[...]
ior and social structure, for they[...]
ences. Thus we must look for v[...]
ences in the degree of inequalit[...]
another.

THE MEANING OF GENDER-BA[...]

Any system of stratification [...]
those on the top of the hierarc[...]
success not only possible but nec[...]
lower rungs of the hierarchy lac[...]

hile we tend to take gender and age for granted, not thinking about their importance in influencing one's position in the stratification hierarchy, both are powerful factors in determining social status. What, for example, is the importance of masculine versus feminine characteristics in assigning and evaluating adult roles? Are males more likely to have higher prestige, more power, and more control over wealth and property than females? What are some of the reasons for these differences? Similarly, how does age influence access to societal resources? Are power, wealth, and property unequally distributed among age groups? Does one's social status change throughout the life course? In what ways?

These are topics that we shall discuss in this chapter, the first half of which addresses gender stratification, and the other half age stratification.

Gender Stratification

Female and male are biological categories. Feminine and masculine are social constructs. Once this distinction is clear, we can describe maleness and femaleness as *ascribed statuses* (sex status) and masculinity and femininity as *achieved characteristics* (gender roles), that is, the culturally-defined attitudes, behaviors, and social positions of persons of each sex. Definitions of masculinity and femininity thus vary from one society to another and undergo changes over time within any given society.

Not only are definitions of gender role differences culturally variable, but the degree to which masculine and feminine characteristics vary is culturally patterned. Newborn infants are assigned to a sex category (ascribed status) at birth on the basis of anatomy. In some societies, these ascribed statuses have little relevance for the development of gender roles; both sexes have essentially similar temperaments and perform similar tasks. Data on the wide range of gender differences have been highlighted by anthropological studies, which make it very clear that, in some societies, males and females are expected to be basically similar in temperament. In other societies, they are expected to be very different kinds of people. Both the great range of personality traits displayed cross-culturally by both sexes and the variability of gender differences within a single society lead to the conclusion that socialization (training for gender role performances) and social structure, especially economic and family spheres, are far more powerful than biological factors in determining sex-typed temperament and behavior.

Yet there are limits to cultural variation. In the great majority of societies, for example, females are entrusted with child care and other tasks centered around the hearth and home. They are socialized accordingly so that feminine personality traits supportive of this type of role performance are encouraged. Males are most often assigned roles that involve sustained travel and physically

Male and female are **ascribed statuses** whereas masculinity and femininity are **achieved characteristics.**

Gender role refers to culturally-defined attitudes and behaviors.

Gender role differences are culturally patterned and culturally variable.

In most societies women are assigned roles involving child care and tasks centered around the home whereas men are assigned roles involving travel, physical risks, and defense of the group.

It is not enough to cite male-female differences in size or aggressiveness. For these comparisons to have any explanatory power, they must be linked with *abilities* to exercise leadership or to make wise decisions. That men are more likely to rule, or that they are somewhat larger than women, has often been interpreted as a cause-and-effect link; that is, that they rule *because* they are larger. Yet size or aggressiveness are rarely correlated with wisdom, restraint, or cooperation, and it seems highly unlikely that combativeness could provide a basis for male superiority. You will recall that the evolutionary success of humans depended upon their ability to control self-centered drives.

A parallel line of reasoning is that women are less rational than men because they represent the forces of nature: birth, the earth, the mysterious, and the unpredictable in human life. Men, freed of the tasks of bearing and nursing infants, are able to pursue things of the spirit and to renounce narrow interests in pursuit of higher goals. Such beliefs are found today in several religious traditions as well as some contemporary psychological theories. There are social scientists who believe that men can command respect by virtue of hormone-based qualities of leadership, and that males are innately more rational and farsighted than women (Tiger, 1969; Goldberg, 1973). By the same theory, women, preoccupied with the details of daily life (diapers, dirty laundry, spotty silverware, and so forth), obsessed with the need to remain attractive to men, and rendered untrustworthy by the menstrual cycle, are thus considered too unstable to fill leadership statuses.

The central question becomes this: Despite the impact of culture and social structure, are there any important distinctions between females and males that will *always* lead to gender differentiation of power and prestige? Through the centuries, many explanations have been proposed, including Aristotle's (350 B.C.), claiming that brain weight accounted for the superior talents of males, a view not substantiated by subsequent research. In an extensive evaluation of current studies, Maccoby and Jacklin (1974) concluded that there are few demonstrable differences that are biologically based. Furthermore, many of the most widely held beliefs about male-female differences are folk myths. Thus, for example, there is no factual basis for the beliefs that girls are more social, or more suggestible than boys; nor is it true that boys are more analytic or better at tasks that require higher-level reasoning (Maccoby and Jacklin, 1974). And to the question, "Is the female more passive than the male?" the evidence suggests that the answer is "No" (Gagnon and Greenblat, 1978).

Until recently few differences between the sexes have been measured scientifically with proper controls. Moreover, our very belief systems influence what is studied and how we think about it. For example, the psychological trait of field independence, or the ability to pick out a detail embedded in other details, has received a great deal of attention in recent years. Individuals who find it difficult to abstract one detail among many are said to be field dependent; those who can do so fairly rapidly are called field independent. While there is considerable overlap of male and female scores, males in contemporary western societies are likely to score higher in field independence than females. But as Grady (1979) points out, the very choice of the words "independent" and "dependent" are value-laden, the implication being that "dependence" is a negative trait. This, incidentally, is true of most words used to describe females in psychological literature. For example, in one well-known study (Broverman et al., 1979) when mental health professionals were asked to describe mentally healthy males and mentally healthy females, the sets of descriptive terms were polar opposites, such as independence for men and dependence for women. When the same subjects were asked to describe a mentally healthy adult, sex unspecified, they listed the traits typically ascribed to males. The only logical conclusion is that a mentally healthy female is a mentally unbalanced human being! If, as Grady (1979) suggests, "field dependence" was called sensitivity instead, how would gender differences then be described and evaluated?

There is also extensive research on the importance of early socialization in encouraging field independence. For example, a high level of interaction between mother and child fosters the child's verbal ability, but inhibits freedom to experiment, and to develop field independence (Bing, 1963). Such socialization is more common for female than male infants. However, when children of either sex are given leeway to experiment and test the world on their own, they tend to develop field independence (Freeman, 1976).

Reviews of research in the social sciences have isolated very few consistently reported gender differences. Those that have been reported with some regularity include the following: (1) higher levels of physical activity among infant males as well as a higher incidence of birth defects and brain damage; (2) higher scores on tests of verbal abilities for females but lower scores in tests of mathematical skills; (3) more frequent displays of overt aggression among males of all ages; (4) a longer life span for females, and (5) slight differences in height, weight, and forms of athletic achievement between populations of males and females. It should be kept in mind that many of these traits are variable. Size differences, for example, are minimal among the Balinese, and exaggerated among the Masai of Africa.

Nor is it clear which traits are advantageous. Most research findings are often ambiguous, and findings of no gender differences are frequently unreported or unpublished because interest has centered on sex-linked differences rather than similarities (Parlee, 1979). In response to the question "What are the biological differences between the sexes?" the answer would seem to be that anatomy is not destiny. Rather, depending on the nature of the particular society, the ascribed status of sex will provide a basis for socialization to gender roles, which are, in turn, used as a justification for gender stratification.

THE NATURE OF DIFFERENCES BETWEEN THE SEXES

For most sex-linked differences it must be kept in mind that the data reported are for *group differences*. That is, when a number of males and females are tested, their measurements will vary *on the average* for that group. For example, if a researcher is studying acts of nurturance among boys and girls, it is very likely that the total score for girls will be higher than that for boys. Let us say that 100 girls produced 600 acts of nurturance in the period under study, whereas 100 boys produced 400. This does not mean that every girl produced two more nurturant acts than each boy. Rather, when each child's score is arranged along a continuum, the pattern illustrated in Figure 9-1 emerges.

Notice that some boys will outscore the average girl, and some girls will score below the average boy. The great majority of both sexes will have scores clustering around 5. Moreover, the difference between the highest and lowest

Most reports of sex-linked differences are based on **group differences.**

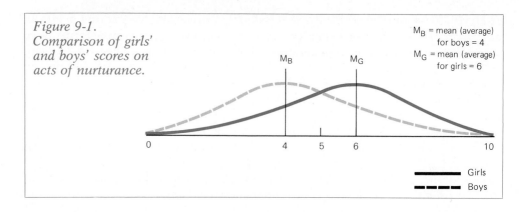

Figure 9-1.
Comparison of girls'
and boys' scores on
acts of nurturance.

M_B = mean (average) for boys = 4
M_G = mean (average) for girls = 6

—— Girls
- - - - Boys

scoring girls or boys (0–10) is greater than the difference between the group averages (2). This means that there is more variation *within* each gender group than between the two sexes. If an observer were to guess which children were more nurturant than others on the basis of sex status only, he or she would be correct in six out of ten guesses. By chance alone, an observer would be correct five out of ten times. The added advantage of the sex-linked guess is often only slightly greater than the accuracy to be obtained by picking names from a hat.

There is more variation **within** each gender group than between the two sexes.

A similar diagram would describe almost every other male-female difference that has been systematically studied, as well as black-white differences in scores on various tests of intellectual functions. In other words, group differences that are often assumed to be absolute are really matters of degree. The ascribed characteristics of sex and race, and in some respects age, do not have as much direct effect on behavior or abilities as we commonly think. Rather, any effects are largely due to the ways in which these ascribed characteristics are viewed by others and used to control access to opportunities and the allocation of scarce societal rewards.

SOCIALIZATION TO GENDER ROLES

Learning one's gender role involves the same processes of socialization as learning any other role.

Whatever innate differences there may be between males and females, the unquestionably greater influence on gender behavior is sociocultural. Learning one's gender role is like learning any other role through the same processes of socialization and from the same agents—parents, peers, teachers, and mass media. *Becoming* feminine or masculine is thus very different from *being* male or female. Sex is ascribed at birth, but it takes several decades of learning to produce a functioning adult woman or man. No society leaves this process to chance or to the natural development of inborn tendencies. Rather, constant pressures are exerted on the growing child, more severely in some societies than others depending upon how much gender differentiation is considered appropriate in that culture.

In fact, gender stereotyping begins with expectations for the infant *before* its actual birth. These expectations become the social reality upon which parents act when they respond to the baby's appearance and first gestures. From birth on, individuals receive gender-typed messages concerning appropriate behavior, and they are rewarded for conformity and punished for deviation.

The research team led by Jeffrey Rubin interviewed parents of first-born sons and daughters—fifteen of each sex—as soon as possible following birth. The fathers had been able to view the infant through windows in the hospital nursery; the mothers had held and fed the child. Parents were asked to "describe your baby as you would to a close friend or relative" and also to fill out a short questionnaire containing descriptive terms along which to rate their infant; for example, firm–soft, fussy–easy going, hardy–delicate, cuddly–not cuddly, and the like.

Parents of sons were more likely than parents of daughters to rate the infant as firm, large-featured, well-coordinated, alert, strong, and hardy. Parents of female infants tended to describe their daughters as small, cute, delicate, and cuddly. In most sets of parents, the father gave *more extreme* ratings to their children than did the mother.

These findings are especially significant in view of the fact that the infants themselves *did not differ significantly* by sex on measures of weight, length, skin color, muscle tone, reflexes, heart beat, or respiratory rate. In other words, parents saw in their newborns the characteristics associated with adults of the same sex as the baby. Knowing whether or not the infant was male or female allowed parents to organize a host of perceptions around that piece of information, regardless of objective data.

Source: The research here discussed was reported in Jeffrey Rubin, Frank Provenzano, and Zella Luria, "The Eye of the Beholder," in Juanita Williams (ed.) *Psychology of Women*. N.Y.: Norton, 1979.

Children learn gender roles in the same way that they learn other roles: through the process of socialization. (Sources: Left—Bill Strode of Woodfin Camp and Associates; Right—George Bellrose of Stock, Boston.)

The primary benefits of being male are access to positions of power and prestige, whereas the advantages of being female are less clear and less direct.

CONSEQUENCES OF GENDER STRATIFICATION

What is the effect of gender stratification upon one's position in the opportunity structure? The major advantages of being male in most societies are access to positions of power and prestige, and the control of property. The advantages of being female are both less clear and less direct. Most women, until recently, have accepted their lower status as natural and inevitable.

The emphasis on the value of childbearing and child rearing as feminine tasks impresses upon women that their roles are complementary to those of men; that is, their function is to tend home and husband while productive labor is performed by men. The idealization of the mother figure in most major world religions is an example of this process. The proper place for a woman is by the hearth, tending the needs of her children and family. This is a sacred task, her calling in this world, comparable to men's duties outside the home (Tuchman, Daniels and Benet, 1980).

Girls and women often internalize the view that accomplishments of women are worth less than those of men. For example, females are more likely to discredit the achievements of women than of men if they are asked to evaluate articles written by academic specialists; when the identical article carried the name of a male author rather than a female, women students thought it better written and more informative (Goldberg, 1968). One of the most consistent findings in the social-psychological literature is the lower self-esteem and greater self-hatred of female respondents compared to males. Women, although this is not always true of young girls, describe themselves and other women in more negative terms than do men. This negative view of women by women can be offset, incidentally, by education and by contact with women of high status. Ferber, Huber, and Spitze (1979) found that women of higher education and those who had had experience with female bosses were least likely to prefer male bosses or professionals.

The evidence suggests that the reason that females describe themselves as ineffective and worthless is that they enact social roles of little power or worth. Even motherhood, although praised highly, offers few societal rewards, and usually makes women more dependent upon the support or protection of others. Whatever power and prestige are to be gained from the mother role must come through one's children, leading often to overmothering, dominance of the growing child, or living through the successes of one's offspring.

In contemporary society, it is often forgotten that until a few decades ago most women occupied statuses outside the home. They were active in the economy, the village, and the ongoing life of the community. Full-time motherhood was a luxury reserved for the wives of the rich, who often hired others to handle child-rearing and housekeeping tasks (Rossi, 1964). It was only in the post-World War II period in the United States, for example, that large numbers of families moved from cities into the newly developed suburbs of one-family homes. Within these houses, women were separated from one another, cut off from adult interaction and from involvement in the stream of life that characterized small towns and city streets. As a result, tasks associated with home-making and child care expanded to fill the time and energies of the full-time suburban wife/mother. Birth rates soared in the decade 1947–57 while the economy flourished on the manufacture of appliances for the home—washers, dryers, freezers, toasters, mixers, baby carriages, play equipment, furniture, a necessary second car, and, often taken as the symbol of suburban life, a barbecue grill. The suburban household is an almost purely *consuming* unit in which women are charged with maintenance of the home, its occupants, and its gadgets.

Nonetheless, strong feelings of discontent among women were evident in the mid-1960s, the date of the beginning of the second wave of the Women's Movement in the United States, Canada, and elsewhere in the industrialized world. Younger women came to feminism from their experiences in the other social movements of the 1960s, "Thinking we were involved in the struggle to build a new society, it was a . . . depressing realization that we were doing the same roles in the [civil rights] Movement as out of it: typing . . . making coffee . . . being accessories to the men" (Morgan, 1979). In addition, large numbers of women had remained in the labor force, others were seeking paid employment, the birth rate had once again declined, and female life expectancy continued to increase. Given these circumstances, it became increasingly difficult to claim that women should devote their entire lives to one responsibility—the care of young children—that now occupied less than one-seventh of their life span (Sokoloff, 1981). The foundations of gender stratification were brought into question. It is against this background that the current status of men and women in North America must be analyzed.

The Power Dimension. There is little question that the overwhelming majority of positions of power in North America are occupied by white males. Among the reasons given for this state of affairs are that women do not project images of leadership; that they are not socialized to be comfortable with power; and, in any event, they should not be distracted from exclusive devotion to their major homebound tasks.

There is also the suggestion that the presence of women in male groups would be disruptive; that is, it would encourage men to compete with each other for female attention (Tiger, 1969). It is quite possible that some men do not want to associate in a business-based peer relationship with a member of lower status, for this would diminish their own prestige.

Nonetheless, Figure 9-2 reflects changing attitudes toward women in public life. Although only 31 per cent of the American population would vote for a woman for president in 1937, by 1978, 76 per cent indicated they would do so. Yet no serious woman candidate for president has been put forward, and women candidates have difficulty raising money thus perpetuating one barrier to women in politics (*New York Times*, Oct. 14, 1980).

Women are also dramatically underrepresented in elected political offices at the federal, state, and local levels. As Figure 9-3 indicates, though women make up 51 per cent of the population of the U.S., women fill a very small percentage of political offices. In both Canada and the United States the political power structure is male dominated.

Although women executives in companies have made significant career gains in recent years, their levels of pay and areas of responsibility still do not approach those of most of their male counterparts. In 1980 the proportion of high-level executives who were female was 28 per cent. Yet women are unlikely

The majority of positions of power in the U.S. and Canada are occupied by white males.

Figure 9-2.
Would you vote for a woman President? How views have changed over the years. (Source: New York Times, *April 21, 1980. Gallup Organization, courtesy of Roper Center.*)

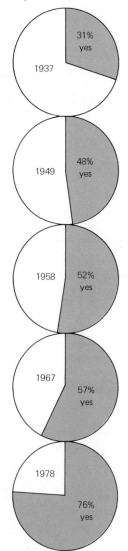

1937 — 31% yes

1949 — 48% yes

1958 — 52% yes

1967 — 57% yes

1978 — 76% yes

	Men%	Women%
U.S. Population	48.7	51.3
U.S. Senate	99	1
U.S. House	96	4
U.S. Supreme Court	100	0
Federal Judges	99	1
Governors	96	4
State Representatives	90	10
State Senators	95	5
Statewide Elective/ Appointive Offices	89	11
County Governing Boards	97	3
Mayors and Councilors	92	8
School Board Members	75	25

Figure 9-3.
Who rules the United States? (Source: *Center for the Study of Women in Politics, 1980.*)

to be at the top of major United States companies; only 1.5 per cent of the presidents, chairs, and vice chairs of these corporations were female (*Wall Street Journal*, Oct. 7, 1980). Clearly, the economic power system is also dominated by men.

Prestige. To the extent that prestige is measured by occupational status, the fact that women are absent from most high offices suggests that they do not, as a class, represent a prestigious stratum of society, although the *idea* of womanhood is venerated by political and religious leaders and teachings.

At the present, those occupations numerically dominated by women rank lower on prestige than predominantly male occupations. Furthermore, women are only rarely at the top of their occupational hierarchy, and generally have lower prestige than men in face-to-face work situations (England, 1979).

Property. It was not until 1860 that New York became the first state in the Union to pass a bill that granted married women the right to own property, to make contracts (though with her husband's consent), and to become joint legal guardian of their children.

In the area of financial credit, married women experienced discrimination and the inability to get credit in their own name until 1970 when the Equal Credit Opportunity Act (ECOA) made it unlawful for creditors to discriminate against any applicant on the basis of marital status.

Because more women entered the labor force during the 1970s than in any other decade of the twentieth century, the economic dominance of husbands has been challenged. Most research shows that working wives have more decision-making power in the family compared to those who do not receive pay from employment. Having one's own income is a crucial source of self-worth and self-assertiveness (Gillespie, 1971; Rubin 1975).

Yet a woman's employment is still more likely to be defined as secondary to the main breadwinning role of the husband, and her income is very likely to be smaller than his. In 1979, women full-time workers still had median earnings that were approximately 60 per cent of the median earnings of men in the United States and Canada. Within any given household, the difference is apt to be larger, with wives earning less than one-half their spouse's income. The saying that the more things change the more they stay the same seems to fit women's earnings in comparison to men's; there has been little change in the ratio of women's to men's earnings since 1939 (Norwood and Waldman, 1979).

To the extent that positions in stratification systems are linked to *achieved* statuses, the labor force participation of women is a crucial part of their overall rank in the society. To the degree that prestige, power, and property are allocated on the basis of *ascribed* characteristics, the position of women will invariably be inferior to that of men. The way in which achieved and ascribed statuses interact is therefore very important in determining the course of gender stratification. This point directs our attention to data on the economic roles of men and women.

The wages of full-time women workers are 40 per cent lower than those of men.

MEN AND WOMEN IN THE LABOR FORCE

An important trend of the past decade has been a steady increase in the labor force participation of women, most of whom, contrary to popular belief, are employed full-time. In the United States in 1979, three out of every four employed women held full-time jobs, and three of every four unemployed women were looking for full-time jobs (Norwood and Waldman, 1979). Recent increases in labor force participation have come largely from white women, the better educated, and those between the ages of 25 and 34, the years of most intense

In the last decade, there has been an increase in the number of women participating in the labor force, most of whom work full-time.

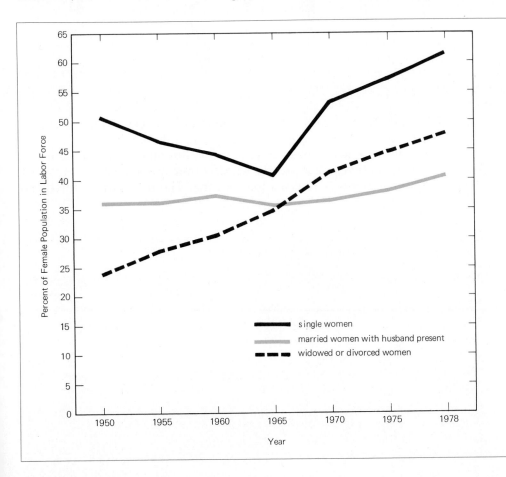

Figure 9-4.
Marital status of women in the labor force in the United States, 1950–78. Women in the labor force are shown as a per cent of the total female population. (Source: Statistical Abstracts of the U.S., 1979, U.S. Bureau of the Census.)

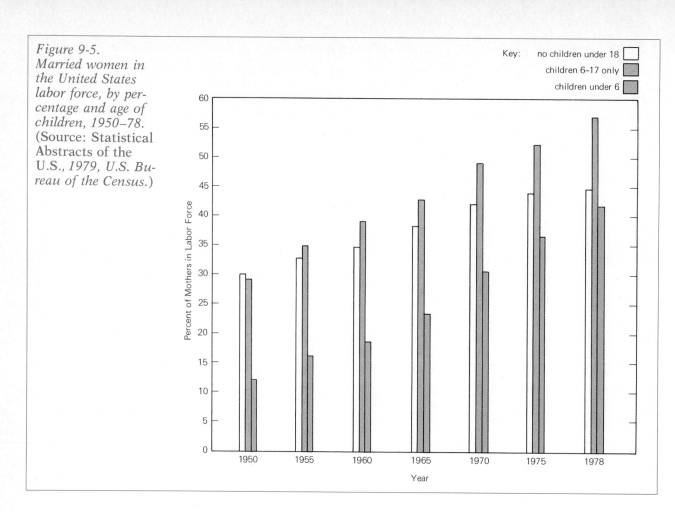

Figure 9-5. Married women in the United States labor force, by percentage and age of children, 1950–78. (Source: Statistical Abstracts of the U.S., 1979, U.S. Bureau of the Census.)

Key:
- no children under 18
- children 6–17 only
- children under 6

Percent of Mothers in Labor Force

Year

child rearing. Indeed, the fastest growing segment of the female labor force has been married women with young children. In an inflationary era, for many families a second income has been essential to maintain customary standards of living. The advantages of a second wage earner are shown in Table 9-1.

Women have many other reasons for working. The nonmarried (divorced,

Table 9-1. Median Income of Husband-wife Families in the United States, by Employment Status of Husband and Wife, 1979

Husband-wife families	Median income in 1979
All husband-wife families	$21,521
No earner	7,659
Husband employed only	17,791
Husband and wife employed	24,973
Male householder, no wife present	16,888
Female householder, no husband present	9,933

Source: U.S. Bureau of the Census, *Current Population Reports*, Series P-60, No. 125, "Money Income and Poverty Status of Families and Persons in the United States: 1979 (Advance Report), U.S. Government Printing Office, Washington, D.C., October 1980, p. 7.

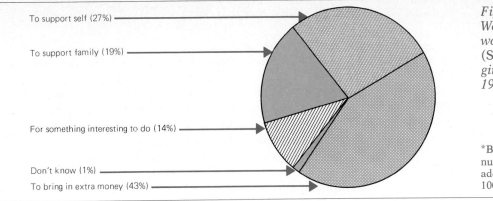

To support self (27%)

To support family (19%)

For something interesting to do (14%)

Don't know (1%)

To bring in extra money (43%)

*Figure 9-6.
Women's reasons for
working, 1980*.
(Source: Roper: Virginia Slims Poll,
1980, p. 237.)*

*Because of rounding of numbers, total percentage adds up to more than 100%.

single, and younger widows) are employed because they must support themselves. For others, the challenge and social contacts of a job are most important.

Women who are not in the labor force are also working, but not for pay. They provide a range of needed services for other family members—child care, food preparation, cleaning, laundry, and transportation—which then do not need to be purchased. Although Canada and many other modern societies give public recognition to the labor of homemakers in the form of family allowances, the United States does not.

The distribution of men and women in the labor force by occupation is very uneven, with some occupations typed as male, others as female. The largest single occupational category in which women are employed today is still clerical (stenographers, typists, and so forth). Today, women compose the following percentages of selected occupations in the United States:

99% of all secretaries-typists.

98% of all domestic workers in private households.

97% of all registered nurses.

92% of all bank tellers.

91% of all bookkeepers.

87% of all cashiers.

74% of all office-machine operators.

71% of all elementary and high school teachers.

11% of all physicians and osteopaths.

9% of all lawyers and judges.

3% of all engineers.   [Norwood and Waldman, 1979]

As you can see from this listing, those jobs in which women are most heavily concentrated do not afford opportunities for increased responsibility or promotion, and many utilize the same skills that are required for organizing homemaking and raising children. The majority of these jobs are among the lowest paying in the economy.

Concentrations of women in service and clerical employment are both cause and effect of gender-typing of jobs, based on beliefs about the qualities needed for the task and the relative abilities of males and females. Occupations in which women are most frequently found are culturally defined as requiring less

223

commitment and are accorded less prestige and lower pay. This is true of modern industrial societies in general, both socialist and capitalist (Coser, 1980). Indeed, in the majority of these countries, women represent a pool of cheap labor that can be used as temporary or replaceable workers in periods of economic expansion. The recent increase of women in the labor force throughout the world has been stimulated by mass technology. Such jobs require quickness and coordination but offer fewer career options, less union protection, and less job security (Barnet, 1980). Generally, women's unemployment rates are higher than men's; for example, in France, where women account for only about one-fourth of the labor force, they comprised more than one-half of those workers who were unemployed during the recession of the 1970s (Barnet, 1980).

The Women's Movement has been an important agent of change through **consciousness raising.**

Winds of Change . . .   It is important to recognize the Women's Movement as an agent of *consciousness raising*, that is, a means of making people aware of the lower status of women and the desire of many to claim equal rights and access

The Women's Movement as an agent of consciousness raising has been a means of making people aware of the lower status of women and the desire of many to claim equal rights. (Source: *Mary Ellen Mark, Magnum.*)

to positions of power and prestige. The most difficult task has probably been that of mobilizing large numbers of women who did not previously perceive themselves as disadvantaged. In fact, many still feel themselves to be privileged precisely because they do *not* have to compete in institutional spheres outside the home. To seek to change the relative statuses of men and women is therefore to evoke powerful forces of resistence. So powerful, in fact, that the Equal Rights Amendment to the Constitution will in all likelihood fail to be ratified by three-fourths of the state legislators within the time limit already extended by Congress.

The Equal Rights Amendment

Proposed Amendment XXVII
(Proposed by Congress on March 22, 1972)

Section 1. Equality of rights under the law shall not be denied or abridged by the United States or by any State on account of sex.

Section 2. The Congress shall have the power to enforce, by appropriate legislation, the provisions of this article.

Section 3. This amendment shall take effect two years after the date of ratification.

. . . **And Blasts of Opposition.** To question the validity or necessity of traditional patterns of gender-role socialization is to strike at the most deeply ingrained aspects of human behavior. Gender identity is, for many, the essence of self. Gender roles allow the individual to organize her or his own experience and to regulate action toward others. The claim that such roles and the stratification system built upon them are, today, more costly than beneficial has awakened powerful backlash forces. Those who oppose the redefinition of gender roles are drawn from many subgroups: (1) men and women who have deep investments in the *status quo,* including males who benefit from the services of a wife and the absence of serious competition to their self-image as effective leaders, and women whose involvements in the home give meaning to their lives; (2) business-sector organizations that would have to change their way of operating; and (3) religious groups whose beliefs strongly support the clear-cut division of tasks between men and women. Many church leaders, business managers, and individual men and women do not perceive any gains from change in the gender-stratification system, but, rather, foresee only the greatest harm to the values and institutional arrangements that have proven successful for them thus far.

The Future of Gender Stratification. What are the probabilities of change and in what direction might these occur? The overall political trend, in both the United States and Canada today, appears to be strongly conservative on what are called social issues. Yet in the educational sphere, positive long-term trends will probably continue. The proportion of women entering college and graduate schools has been steadily rising and does not appear to be abating. If economic prospects continue to worsen for those employed in higher education, the proportions of men who graduate from college and enter graduate schools of Arts and Sciences may actually decline relative to those of women. At the same time, graduate training in medicine, law, and business, although still largely male-

In education, the proportion of women entering college and graduate schools has been steadily rising.

dominated, are increasingly attractive options for women. The continued and growing presence of women in higher education—as students and teachers—will, in the long run, not only change the perceptions of leaders in these fields regarding women's abilities, but also change the content of subject matter to reflect the scholarship of academic women.

In the economic sphere, slightly larger numbers of female employees will be found at the management level, but the general distribution of women workers will most likely *not* change. The high-demand areas of the future will be the extremely technical occupations (which will continue to be male-dominated) and the service-worker, office/clerical sector (perhaps more female-dominated than ever). In sum, occupational stratification will remain much as before, with the general consequence of stabilizing the relative disadvantage of women in achieving prestige and incomes commensurate with those of men.

In the arenas of interpersonal relationships—courtship, dating, close friend-ships, and family life—changes are more difficult to measure. There is evidence of an increase in the inclination of men to assume joint responsibility for home-making and child care, but it is likely that women in the labor force will con-tinue to hold *two* full-time jobs.

Where the greatest change appears to be taking place is in the way that women think about themselves. Improvement in the mental health status of women between the early 1960s and the present has been attributed to the positive impact of the Women's Movement on their feelings of effectiveness and self-worth, and a broadening of choices (Srole and Fischer, 1978).

A new awareness of gender-role socialization and its effects has led to some changes in the way that parents now raise their children, but this is more likely

Table 9-2. Changes in Gender Stratification? Responses to the Question, Which Household Chore Should Both Boys and Girls Be Expected to Do, 1974 and 1980, by Sex of Respondent

Chore	1974		1980	
	Men	Women	Men	Women
Keep their own room clean	94%	95%	95%	97%
Make their beds	89	90	90	94
Wash or dry dishes	79	84	86	90
Help with grocery shopping	74	78	81	87
Help clean house	71	74	81	86
Carry out garbage	60	69	72	81
Do their own laundry	59	61	74	80
Help with cooking	53	63	68	76
Help with small repairs around house	47	60	60	73
Mow the lawn	40	54	56	70
Mend their clothes	36	39	50	56

Source: Virginia Slims Poll, 1980.

to affect daughters than sons. Few parents, including those identified with feminism, are prepared to make radical changes in their handling of male offspring. The changes that have taken place in parent expectations for their children are shown in Table 9-2.

In terms of personality, much is being written today of *androgyny*, the combination of feminine and masculine traits that are found in every individual. Several researchers (Bem, 1975; Livson, 1973; Spence and Helmreich, 1978) have found that adults with high scores on measures of androgyny are also more adaptive, flexible, competent in a variety of situations, and display higher levels of self-esteem compared to those with stereotyped, gender-linked personality styles. Apparently, the broader range of coping strategies available to androgynous women and men enhances feelings of self-worth and expressions of individuality.

It had long been thought, by social scientists as well as the general public, that femininity and masculinity were opposite poles of a single dimension; to be high on male-typed traits was to be low on female-linked ones. Personality test questions were designed and scored on the assumption that responses were either masculine or feminine.

> **Androgyny** refers to the combination of feminine and masculine traits found in every individual.

```
        Low _____ High

                 Nurturance

   (Masculine                    (Feminine
   Response)                     Response)
```

Androgyny, however, is measured in such a way that an individual can have *both* high or low scores on traits appropriate to either sex, as, for example in the cross-tabulation below:

		Assertiveness	
		High	*Low*
Concern for Others	*High*	Androgynous	Feminine
	Low	Masculine	Indeterminant

Adapted from Spence and Helmreich (1978)

The concept of androgyny also recognizes the extent to which personality traits are not fixed aspects of the psyche, but, rather, are activated to varying degrees by the situation. This suggests that a psychologically-healthy person is one who does *not* react in the same fashion to all stimuli but, for example, with anger if the situation warrants, or with patience under other conditions. The reaction is guided by a sense of the specific circumstances. Maturity is thus defined as the ability to change over time, to experience a broadening of capacities for dealing with others and with new situations, and to accept the many often confusing or conflicting aspects of one's own self. Individuals who lack this flexibility are thought to be poorly adapted to adulthood in a rapidly changing society.

Age Stratification

Age has been widely used as the criterion for entry or exit from valued statuses.

As an ascribed characteristic, age has been used as a criterion for entry into or exit from valued statuses in most societies. At the very least, adults have been distinguished from nonadults, although the precise boundary between the two categories has varied across cultures and through time. In some societies, a boy or girl assumes adult status upon physiological puberty. Other societies arbitrarily select a given age as the threshhold of adulthood—13 is a common age. In North America, the point of entry into adult statuses has varied historically. Today, as befits these complex societies there are different ages of majority for different roles: 18 for voting or enlisting in the armed forces, 18 to 21 for drinking, and 16 for females to marry, but 18 for males.

As part of the legacy of British common law, children are assumed to have diminished capacity for moral choices, and, therefore, are not held legally accountable for conduct that would be a crime if committed by adults. Conversely, certain behaviors that are illegal for young people are not indictable offenses for adults—running away from home, refusing to obey parents, and being sexually active, for example.

In most societies age, an ascribed characteristic, determines entry into or exit from valued statuses. (Source: *Michael C. Hayman, Photo Researchers, Inc.*)

Eventually, children become legally defined adults and therefore eligible for positions of power and prestige in the society. At some later time, these same individuals must give up important statuses. In some societies, relinquishing positions of power and prestige can be delayed indefinitely, as when the elders control property until their death. Only then can a son inherit the land required to support a wife and family. Such is the case in rural Ireland even today, which accounts for the very high ages of first marriage among the Irish (Stivers, 1976).

Other societies have provisions for the ceremonial transfer of power from one age group to another—*rites of passage* during which the young male is invested with adult status following some test of courage and strength. Similar ceremonies may mark the removal of elders from controlling positions (Foner and Kertzer, 1978). In modern industrial societies, just as arbitrary ages are selected for entry into certain roles, so too for exiting some roles—age 70 today for mandatory retirement in the United States and age 65 in Canada.

In other words, each society regulates the flow of individuals in and out of valued statuses through definitions of appropriate ages. These processes produce an age-related hierarchy of power and prestige (*age stratification*). Other variables, most notably gender and social class, determine a person's position in other stratification hierarchies at all ages. But age itself is an independent variable in allocating scarce social resources.

AGE GROUPS AND SOCIAL STRUCTURE

Every society is composed of age groups of different sizes and of a structure of age-related statuses. A model that illustrates the relationship between age groups and age statuses has been developed by Matilda White Riley and her associates (1972). This is shown diagrammatically in Figure 9-7.

The population of any society has a particular *age structure*, which is determined by (1) the number of births and deaths; and (2) the patterns of migration in or out of that society. Thus, at any one time, the population can be stratified into different-sized age groups. The populations of the United States and Canada are distributed by age and sex in a fashion fairly typical for industrial or postindustrial societies. The shape of the population, as shown in Figures 9-8 and 9-9, is produced by low birth rates and low death rates, and by little migration in or out of the society.

Rites of passage are ceremonies marking the movement from one age group to another.

The **age structure** of a society is determined by the number of births and deaths and the patterns of in and out migration.

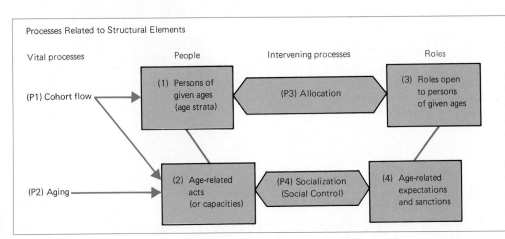

Processes Related to Structural Elements

Figure 9-7. The relationship between age groups and structure of age statuses. (Source: Matilda White Riley, Marilyn Johnson, and Anne Foner. Aging and Society, *Vol. 3, p. 9, New York: Russell Sage Foundation, 1972.)*

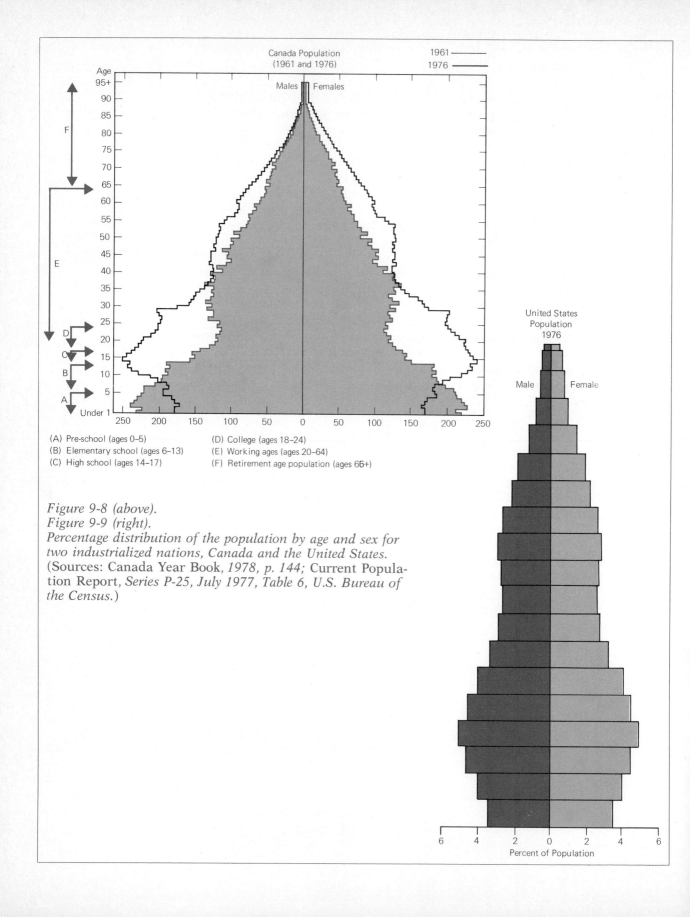

Canada Population
(1961 and 1976)

1961 ——
1976 ——

Males Females

Age
95+
90
85
80
75
70
65
60
55
50
45
40
35
30
25
20
15
10
5
Under 1

250 200 150 100 50 0 50 100 150 200 250

F

E

D
C
B
A

(A) Pre-school (ages 0–5)
(B) Elementary school (ages 6–13)
(C) High school (ages 14–17)
(D) College (ages 18–24)
(E) Working ages (ages 20–64)
(F) Retirement age population (ages 65+)

Figure 9-8 (above).
Figure 9-9 (right).
Percentage distribution of the population by age and sex for
two industrialized nations, Canada and the United States.
(Sources: Canada Year Book, *1978, p. 144;* Current Population Report, *Series P-25, July 1977, Table 6, U.S. Bureau of*
the Census.)

United States
Population
1976

Male   Female

6   4   2   0   2   4   6
Percent of Population

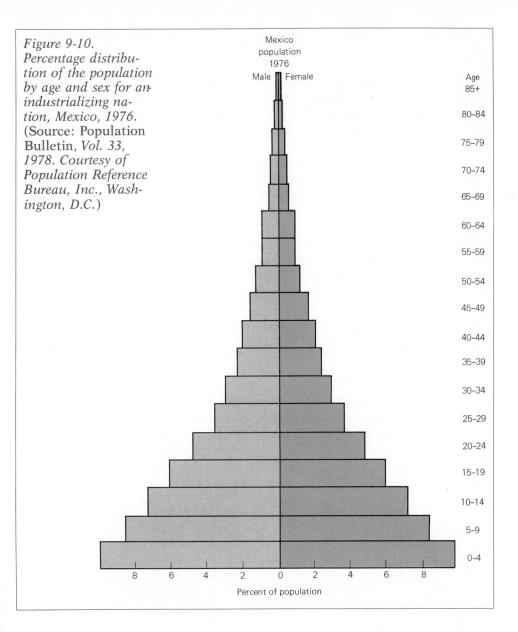

Figure 9-10. Percentage distribution of the population by age and sex for an industrializing nation, Mexico, 1976. (Source: Population Bulletin, Vol. 33, 1978. Courtesy of Population Reference Bureau, Inc., Washington, D.C.)

Mexico population 1976

Male   Female

Age

85+
80–84
75–79
70–74
65–69
60–64
55–59
50–54
45–49
40–44
35–39
30–34
25–29
20–24
15–19
10–14
5–9
0–4

8   6   4   2   0   2   4   6   8

Percent of population

Less modernized societies, however, have a very differently shaped population distribution. As Figure 9-9 shows, the population of these less industrialized countries is shaped like a pyramid, its shape reflecting high death rates combined with very high birth rates, processes that will be discussed in detail in Chapter 16.

Population pyramids, whether for industrialized or nonindustrialized countries, are graphic representations of the supply of males and females of different ages in a given society. Factors such as educational attainment, socialization experiences, and race and ethnicity will determine who fills many of the statuses in the social system. But much also depends on the number and types of statuses available to members of a particular age category (or *cohort,* that is

Population pyramids are graphic representations of the age structure.

all individuals who are born within a specific time period, for example, between 1960 and 1965).

Age Structure of Roles.   The statuses and opportunities available to people of different ages can be thought of as the *age structure of roles*. The number of jobs in the American and Canadian economy, for example, varies constantly. Much depends on technological factors, supply and demand, the existence of certain trade markets or raw materials, and so forth.

In the area of family life, it might seem self-evident that marriage roles will be available to all adults, but this is not necessarily the case. For example, after a war, there is often a shortage of marriage-age men, so that not all women will find husbands.

And so it is in all institutional spheres. The number and type of statuses and roles open to people of various ages differ, as do the number of individuals in each age stratum. Social institutions must then adapt to population shifts. This may be clearly seen in the current move to close classrooms and schools at the elementary level; there just are not as many school-age children as there were in the 1950s and 1960s. In fact, some elementary schools are being converted into housing for the increasing numbers of people 65+. Such changes in the population structure become a source of change in the social system (Waring, 1975).

Age-Related Capacities.   In many cases, biological factors limit an individual's ability to perform roles. The span of fertility, for example, is a biological given. Few females under the age of 12 or over age 50 can become mothers. The very old or very young will find it difficult to dig ditches. Professional athletes over age 40 are rare.

But for the most part, age limits are culturally and socially defined. It is because we equate beauty with youth that Miss Universe is so young. When airlines first hired stewardesses, there was an upper age limit that has now been extended, but the minimum age for female flight attendants remains around 20, and none are in their 60s. This is not because the job requires talents that are age-associated, but because incumbents are expected to be decorative. Another example of socially defined age limits is the age of consent for marriage. This varies from one place to another, has changed over time, and may be different for females than for males. Clearly, it is a belief about the appropriateness of sexual activity and not biology that account for these age criteria.

ROLE STRAIN AND ROLE SLACK THROUGHOUT THE LIFE COURSE

When individuals are excluded from statuses for which they perceive themselves capable, deviance may result. Much juvenile delinquency can be interpreted as premature attempts to play adult roles: driving, drinking, sexual experimentation, and so on. One recent study found that vandalism among middle-class teenagers was most clearly related to status needs among age peers in the roleless vacuum of late adolescence (Richards, 1979). So adolescence is a period of *role slack*, that is, when one's capacities are *under*demanded. Young adulthood is a time of *role strain* when the demands of work, marriage, parenthood, and civic responsibility can overburden the typical person (Goode, 1960; Wilensky, 1962).

Age structure of roles refers to available role opportunities in a society.

Age limits, for the most part, are culturally and socially defined.

Role slack occurs when a person's capacities are underdemanded.

Role strain occurs when too many role demands are made upon an individual.

Middle Age. Middle age has often been portrayed as a somewhat boring plateau between the stresses of young adulthood and the role dislocations and losses of old age. Only recently has middle age been considered a life-course stage worthy of serious analysis. Expressions of concern over a *mid-life crisis* for both men and women are very common today.

For women in middle age, the problems are most often those of role loss. Becoming middle-aged may lead to a sense of worthlessness in a society where females are valued for their youthful beauty. One's children have grown up and moved away, with the result that household tasks take less time and energy than at an earlier period. Many women are motivated to fill this gap by returning to school or work after decades of service to other family members. Increasing numbers will experience role loss through divorce or separation. After so many years outside the full-time labor force or in low-paying jobs, it will be difficult for many to find employment that offers more than a minimal standard of living (Rubin, 1979).

The middle-aged male also has his problems: reaching an occupational ceiling, experiencing loss of vigor, realizing that achievements have been lower than earlier aspirations, watching younger men take his place (Brim, 1976). A marriage based on rigid division of labor must be reconstituted when the children leave—a problem for both husband and wife. And men, too, may resent the changes taking place in their bodies and appearance (Lewis, 1981).

Old Age. Behind all these mid-life stresses and challenges lies the specter of old age in a contemporary Western industrial society. It is at the oldest age levels that the question of age-related capacities becomes both a major social and personal problem. When is an individual "too old" for certain roles?

Age-related capacities become a major social and personal problem at the oldest age levels.

It is at the oldest age level that the question of age-related capacities become a major problem. When is an individual too old for certain roles? (Source: Burk Uzzle, Magnum.)

Historically, this may not have been such an agonizing question. Very few people lived to be too old to carry out tasks of value to their group. Old women could still gather food and watch children and old men could recall information needed by the group. In very simple gathering-and-hunting societies, depending upon the availability of food, the frail elderly will be cared for or abandoned. This does not mean that young adults in these societies are heartless, but only that the group has developed norms and behaviors designed to increase the chances for group survival.

In more developed traditional societies, especially those based on plow agriculture or herding, the position of elders can be very powerful. It is the male head of the extended family who controls the flow of goods and services throughout the kinship group. He decides when land or cattle, or whatever signifies wealth, is passed down to younger family members. And it is the parents who choose marriage partners for their offspring, and who often continue to regulate the lives of married children. In the wider society, elders also monopolize positions of power in the religious and political realms.

The position of the elderly is based on their ability to **control** valued resources.

The difference in social status between elders in simple societies and those in more developed societies is certainly not due to some extraordinary change in human nature whereby obedience and deference toward old people suddenly disappear. The position of the elderly is almost entirely based upon their ability to *control* things of value to their children or to the society as a whole: economic assets, family loyalty, and information, to name the three most important. It is precisely these sources of control that old people lose in the course of modernization. That is, the lowered status of the elderly in industrial societies is linked to their lack of ability to command important resources either in the family or the society.

THE ELDERLY IN MODERN SOCIETIES

Old people in industrial societies tend to be disadvantaged on all major dimensions of stratification.

Along all three of the dimensions of stratification—power, prestige, and property—old people in industrial societies are disadvantaged. With industrialization, urbanization, and modernization of attitudes and behavior, old people lose the advantages enjoyed in all but the most simple societies.

In general, achieved statuses replace ascribed ones when education becomes important in preparing young people for adult statuses. Although it is still helpful to have family support and resources, offspring can make their own way through the occupational and educational systems; that is, few depend upon the inheritance of land or other assets. And even fewer would permit their parents to select a marriage partner—although parents may try to influence these choices. In short, old people can no longer command attention and deference on the basis of their control of family life.

Nor can the elderly command attention and respect from others on the basis of their continuing contributions to the society. As most workers today are employees rather than self-employed, they will retire at some age between 60 and 70. In the United States and Canada, retirement incomes are typically about half of earnings before retirement. The proportion of the elderly in the labor force, too, has been declining in the last 30 years. In both Canada and the United States, only about 12 per cent of those 65+ are in the labor force. In the United States, approximately 15 per cent of those 65+ live below or at the poverty level. Some few people in both societies will have high incomes in old

Conditions for high status	Conditions of old people in modern societies
1. Ownership and control of property needed by younger people.	Very few old people control the resources required by their offspring.
2. Command over strategic knowledge.	Old people's educational attainment is generally lower than that of younger people, and much less recent—in a society characterized by rapid technological change.
3. Old people serve as a link to the past in societies rooted in tradition.	Rapid social change and the "modern" mentality reduce dependence on tradition. It is the future that beckons, and the aged have little left.
4. The society is characterized by close-knit extended kinship groups.	Modern societies are characterized by the small nuclear family unit, living apart from other relatives and concerned with its own well-being. Older relatives are cut off from younger families.
5. The society is composed of small population clusters in stable communities.	Widespread mobility, and population movements off the land, into cities, and out again to the suburbs, have destroyed much of the stability of small communities. In all this flux, the elderly tend to be left behind in villages and the inner city.
6. An economic system characterized by relatively low productivity so that every pair of hands has productive value.	Industrial societies have high productivity economies in which machines replace hand labor, and where surpluses are generated. This relative *affluence* erodes the economic value of marginal workers (the aged, women and youth).
7. High mutual dependence in the family, community, and society.	The central features of modern society are individualism and a certain looseness of most traditional bonds.

These seven factors—personal and societal characteristics—will predict the social position of old people in any society. Their power and prestige will be highest where these seven conditions occur.

Source: Irving Rosow, "And Then We Were Old," *Transaction*, Vol. 2, No. 2, January–February, 1965, pp. 20–26.

Factors Affecting the Status of the Elderly in a Society

age, but large numbers will just manage to maintain an adequate standard of living (Hess, 1980).

Whatever political power the elderly have today comes from their numbers (about 10 per cent of both the total Canadian and the United States population) and the fact that they are more likely to vote than are members of the youngest age groups. It is largely in the areas of political and religious office holding that old people are still found in positions of power and prestige in modern societies. The election of Ronald Reagan at the age of 69 (the oldest person to be elected to a first term as President of the United States) is one such illustration of political staying power.

Although old people today certainly cannot command the power and prestige of another time or place, there is no reason to believe that younger people in the

There is little evidence that the change in traditional arrangements of caring for the aged has been detrimental to either the elderly or to younger people; in fact, relationships between generations may be more mutually satisfying today than in the past. (Source: *Peter Simon, Stock, Boston.*)

past were particularly pleased with traditional arrangements or that the aged today are without resources. In fact, it could be argued that relationships between generations today may be more mutually satisfying than in the past (Hess and Waring, 1978). Parents and their adult children can interact on a voluntary basis, with affection earned rather than demanded. Old people are not more often dumped into nursing homes, nor are their children any more negligent than may have been the case in the past.

Moreover, despite popular mythology, there was no golden age of extended family togetherness in the United States, Canada, or most other Western European societies. Where extended families are still found, as in Appalachia, there is little reason to believe that members are happier than those in nuclear families, and much evidence to the contrary.

THE POLITICS OF AGING

Old people and their supporters have achieved a number of political victories: a steady increase in Social Security benefits, Medicare, the Age Discrimina-

236

tion in Employment Act, and the Older Americans Act with its ever-expanding programs. No other category of persons in our history has been the subject of more extensive legislation. These gains have not necessarily been the outcome of political activism among the elderly, although there are a few national organizations of old people.

The major problem in organizing the elderly on their own behalf is not their lack of money or their physical limitations but the sheer *diversity* of the older population. Contrary to common belief that people tend to grow more conservative and more like one another in old age, those who are 65+ are less likely to agree on values and attitudes than are people in younger age categories. Having had a lifetime of unique experiences, and having seen so much of history unfold, the aged display an astonishing variety of viewpoints and interests. It should not be surprising that it has been so difficult to create a unified political base from which to launch an old people's movement (Ragan and Davis, 1978).

Not all old people were in favor of recent extensions of the age of mandatory retirement in the United States, and some would have preferred the age limit to be *lowered* rather than raised. Not all senior citizen organizations favored Medicare. And the wealthiest or most conservative among the elderly see no need for an Older Americans Act or for the Canadian New Horizons program. The more privileged elderly have only recently become reconciled to Social Security or to the Canada Pension Plan, and other programs once fought so bitterly as "socialistic."

It is no easier to organize older people around local issues. Where efforts are made to influence legislation and local ordinances, it is often others who speak for the aged: providers of services, adult offspring, and religious leaders. The Gray Panthers are the only prominent exception to this generally bleak picture of elderly activism.

This difficulty in creating a consciousness of kind means that the elderly have not yet made their age status an overriding identity—a point often overlooked by those using the minority-group perspective to analyze the aged. Yet, without greater political unity, the elderly will have a difficult time making further gains. As several political scientists have noted (*Society*, 1978), all the easy goals have been achieved. The legislation mentioned at the beginning of this section has assured the basics for survival to the great majority of old people. Further initiatives are unlikely because they could easily be perceived as occurring at the expense of younger age groups, who are already upset over increases in social insurance taxes. Another barrier to increases in funding for elders is that the old people who still remain without care, adequate incomes, or supportive services that would prevent institutionalization are most often members of minority groups without political clout.

All these considerations lead to the conclusion that "senior power" in the United States may have peaked, and that further legislation will continue to favor the more advantaged elderly. The next step—income maintenance at an adequate level, health-care delivery to the isolated, poor, frail, and supportive services that would enable people to stay in comfort in their own homes—may be a long time in coming. (For a commentary on similar Canadian problems, see Marshall, 1980.) To this degree, some subgroups of the old are doubly disadvantaged. Victimized by a lifetime of discrimination, being old is only the last stage, not the cause, of their neglect.

Old people and their supporters have gained a number of legislative victories, though their diversity presents problems in organizing.

The most needy among the elderly are most often those with little political representation and power.

Summary

Both gender and age are powerful determinants of one's social standing. Although one's sex status is ascribed at birth on the basis of anatomy, femininity and masculinity are achieved characteristics influenced by culturally defined expectations of appropriate behavior. The substantial variability within and between cultures in definitions of femininity and masculinity indicates that socialization and social structure are far more powerful than biological factors in determining attitudes, behavior, and temperament. Despite this variability in gender roles, studies indicate that whatever men do is valued more highly than women's work. This is the basis of gender stratification: the higher evaluation of male contributions to the group, and their consequent higher position on most dimensions of stratification.

To what extent does this differential evaluation and status stem from fundamental biological differences between females and males? The primates most resembling humans are least likely to display behaviors associated with biologically-based explanations of gender stratification.

Although most popular beliefs about male-female differences lack empirical support, they do influence people's behavior and attitudes. Research to date has identified only a few consistent gender differences. Most reported sex-linked differences refer to average scores for groups of males and females, and therefore mask the high degree of overlap.

Recent research on personality indicates that a combination of feminine and masculine traits is found in all persons but that through gender-role socialization, one set of characteristics is often suppressed. Adults with higher scores on measures of androgyny were found to be more adaptive, flexible, and competent in a series of situations calling for different kinds of reactions.

American and Canadian data indicate that the great majority of positions of power in high prestige occupations are occupied by men. Today, as more and more women have entered the labor force, the economic dominance of husbands has been challenged. Yet women who work full-time still earn only about two-thirds the income of men, and women college graduates make on the average 20 per cent less than male college graduates. Many occupations are typed as mostly male or female, and those jobs in which women are most heavily concentrated tend to pay the lowest wages and offer few opportunities for increased responsibility and promotion. These concentrations are both the cause and effect of the gender-typing of employment based on beliefs about the qualities needed for the job and the relative abilities of men and women.

Current developments indicate both support for and opposition to changes in gender stratification. Nonetheless, changes are occurring in the area of education, labor force participation, interpersonal relationships, parental expectations and, most dramatically, in the way women feel about themselves.

Age, as an ascribed characteristic, is used as the requirement for entering into or exiting from valued statuses. Social definitions of appropriate ages for role performances lead to an age-related stratification of power and prestige.

The population of every society has a specific age structure evolving from the number of births and deaths and its migration patterns. The resulting population pyramids represent the supply of males and females of different ages available to fill various social roles. Although biological factors set some limits on behavior, age limits are for the most part culturally and socially determined. When persons are excluded from roles that they believe they can fulfill, strain and deviance may result.

The social position of the elderly stems from their ability to control things of value to their children and to society—economic assets, family loyalty, and valued information. The elderly are a relatively powerless group in modern societies though their numbers are increasing and some do occupy powerful and prestigious offices in political and religious organizations.

The great diversity of political views and beliefs among the elderly make political unity based on age status difficult. Legislation providing the basis for survival to the great majority of old people has been enacted, but further provisions seem unlikely.

Suggested Readings

DAVIDSON, LAURIE, and LAURA KRAMER GORDON. *The Sociology of Gender.* Skokie, Ill.: Rand McNally, 1979. A timely analysis of gender role socialization and the impact of the family, ideology, stratification, the economy, ethnicity, and the Woman's Movement on continuity and change in gender roles. Although primarily concerned with the United States, the book includes a comparative treatment of gender roles in Sweden, China, and Israel.

HESS, BETH B., and ELIZABETH W. MARKSON. *Aging and Old Age: An Introduction to Social Gerontology.* New York: Macmillan, 1980. A detailed analysis of aging and old age utilizing a social systems and historical perspective. Includes an examination of the impact of ideology and beliefs about aging, the processes of aging, and the role of the aged in various institutional spheres.

MARSHALL, VICTOR W. (Editor). *Aging in Canada: Social Perspectives.* Pickering, Ontario, Canada: Fitzhenry & Whiteside, 1980. An anthology of articles dealing with various aspects of aging in Canada and implications for individuals, families, and the larger society, including the meaning of aging, work, and leisure, changing family contexts, health care, and the needs of and services for an aging population.

MEAD, MARGARET. *Sex and Temperament in Three Primitive Societies.* New York: Morrow, 1935/1963. A classic cross-cultural study of the way gender roles are defined in three traditional societies and in the United States.

RILEY, MATILDA WHITE, MARILYN JOHNSON, and ANNE FONER. *Aging and Society: A Sociology of Age Stratification,* Vol. 3. New York: Russell Sage, 1972. A landmark study of various aspects of aging and its interconnection with systems of inequality.

RUBIN, LILLIAN. *Women of a Certain Age: The Midlife Search for Self.* New York: Harper & Row, 1979. A sensitive account of major issues faced by maturing women—work and career decisions, identity formation, intimacy, changes in the mothering role, reevaluation of goals, and strains in the marriage relationship.

STEPHENSON, MARYLEE (Editor). *Women in Canada,* Revised. Don Mills: General Publishing, 1977. An anthology examining the roles of women in Canadian society with respect to their social status, political power, roles in the family, socialization, work, and careers, and the impact of feminism.

10 Racial, Ethnic, and Religious Minorities

*D*uring World War II, most of the Japanese-American population of the United States was interned in detention camps, and many Japanese-Canadians were relocated into interior regions of Canada.

When John F. Kennedy ran for President of the United States in 1960, his first campaign activity was to assure the public that, as a Roman Catholic, he would not be influenced by the Pope on matters of United States policy.

Refugees from Cuba, arriving in Miami, Florida in early 1980, were greeted by adults and children who wore white robes and pointed hoods and carried signs saying, "Keep America Pure."

These are only a few relatively recent examples of a long history of racial, religious, and ethnic intolerance (bigotry) in the United States and Canada. The symbolism of the Statue of Liberty welcoming the poor and huddled masses to the land of opportunity has often masked the difficulties experienced by members of racial, religious, and ethnic minorities.

Race, religion, and ethnicity are social categories that will influence social placement in any society. But societies do vary greatly in the degree to which the population is composed of different racial, religious, or ethnic groups. Some societies such as Denmark, Sweden, and Norway are culturally *homogeneous;* that is, members of the society are similar in racial stock, religious observance, and country of origin. As a consequence, such societies do not experience the difficulties of absorbing large numbers of people with norms and customs that differ from those of the majority. Recently, however, even Sweden has been shaken by attacks on "guestworkers" from Southern Europe and Northern Africa imported as unskilled or semiskilled industrial workers.

Other societies are culturally *heterogeneous;* that is, they contain large numbers of citizens who differ greatly in color and appearance, in beliefs and values, and in language and culture from one another and from a national ideal type. The Soviet Union has dozens of such nationality groups within its borders. So also, to a lesser extent, do Yugoslavia, Australia, New Zealand, South Africa, Israel, the United States, and Canada. In such societies, social order depends upon (1) how the diverse groups are brought into contact with one another (intergroup relations); and (2) the mechanisms for the allocation of scarce rewards (social justice). The basic theme of this chapter is how the ascribed statuses of race, religion, and ethnicity influence placement in major stratification hierarchies.

> Race, religion, and ethnicity are ascribed characteristics that influence social placement in all societies.

> Members of a **heterogeneous** society differ from one another in race, religion, national origins, and therefore often in beliefs, values, and language.

Minority Groups Defined

Minority groups are defined in contrast to a *dominant* segment of the population. The dominant group need not be a numerical majority. Dominance refers to *control* over central sectors of social life, including the power to define norms

> Minority groups are defined in comparison to a **dominant** controlling group.

and standards of beauty and worth. Thus, although white Anglo-Saxon Protestants (WASP) are a distinct minority of the American population, their influence on the culture, language, ideology, and law has shaped the nation. They are the Americans against which other groups are measured and evaluated. In contrast to the WASP ideal, nonwhites, non-Northern Europeans, and non-Protestants are distinguished by characteristics that not only set them apart but become cues for different, typically unequal, treatment.

There are four elements in the definition of minority group status:

1. *Distinctive ascribed traits* by which minority group members can be recognized.
2. *Differential treatment* on the basis of possessing this trait.
3. *Organization of self-image* around this identity.
4. *Awareness of shared identity* with others in the same group.

Minority group members belong to **subsocieties**.

Categories of individuals thus defined can be thought of as belonging to *subsocieties*. Participation in a subsociety fills three functions for its members: (1) providing in-group identity needed for self-definition; (2) maintaining patterns of primary group relationships (*Gemeinschaft*); and (3) interpreting the broader national society through the unique filter of minority group traditions (Gordon, 1978). In this fashion, minority group members can construct a sub-

Race: Some Problems in Definition

Although most of us speak of race as if we were certain of its meaning, it is almost impossible to give the term a scientific definition. There are two ways to classify racial groups from a biological perspective. The first is based on *phenotype*, or physical appearance such as skin color, eye shape, hair texture, or thickness of lips. Yet your own experience should demonstrate how arbitrary and inaccurate such classifications can be. There are no pure Negroid and Caucasoid types; both categories contain light- and dark-skinned populations, tall and short, long-headed and round-headed, straight-haired and curly. The range of variation within phenotype categories is too large to permit easy classification.

A second method for distinguishing races is based on *genotype*, or genetic makeup. This definition is also inexact. Human blood groups are determined by genotypes, but millions of combinations of blood groups exist. The closest that scientists have come to differentiating racial groups is to speak of the *relative distribution* of blood types; that is, one blood type will be more commonly found in one racial category than another.

From a scientific viewpoint, therefore, at the present time it is difficult to say that distinct races exist in a biological sense. Nor can racial differences in behavior and accomplishments be attributed to genetic potential. Rather, peoples of the world appear to possess similar biological potential for achievement. What varies is the opportunity structure. As a *cultural* construction, however, race is a powerful concept because what people believe to be real has real consequences, regardless of a lack of scientific validity. If members of different races are thought to differ in intellect and ability, the social system will reflect such expectations.

culture that protects and nurtures those who choose to remain within its network of primary and secondary ties. The cost of minority group membership, however, is often difficulty in entering mainstream social systems.

Both Canada and the United States contain minority groups distinguished along the dimensions of ethnicity, religion, and race.

Ethnicity refers to national background or cultural distinctiveness. Individuals and groups will vary in the extent to which the customs, language, and surnames of the country of origin are retained.

Religion refers to a set of beliefs and rituals associated with the sacred. Coreligionists recognize one another through shared worship and reverence for holy objects.

Race is much more difficult to define and is based upon the distribution of biological traits among populations.

Race and ethnicity are *ascribed* statuses. None of us can change from white to black nor from Puerto Rican to Polish ancestry, although some of us may successfully disguise these attributes. Religion is also an ascribed status but one that can be changed through conversion.

Social class, on the other hand, is an *achieved* status in modern industrial societies. By definition, access to positions of power, prestige, and property is controlled by the rules and actions of the dominant groups within a society. Members of various racial, religious, or ethnic minorities will encounter higher or lower barriers to achievement depending upon several factors, including these: (1) how closely they approximate the dominant culture in appearance and customs; and (2) the skills and talents (including education) they bring to the society. This means that the historical experience of various minority groups in North America will vary greatly, which makes generalizations somewhat difficult. For example, despite some similarities in their treatment within dominant institutions, the outcome for Jews and blacks in both the United States and Canada is very different. Blacks, because of their greater visibility in a predominantly white society, are much more likely to encounter barriers to social mobility.

> Access to power, prestige, and property is controlled by the dominant groups.

Ascribed Status and Stratification Hierarchies

In the United States, ascribed statuses, especially race, often serve as *caste* boundaries, limiting entry into mainstream positions of prestige and power. Over time, religion and ethnicity have become less powerful barriers to achievement than they were only a few decades ago. A Catholic (Al Smith) could not be elected president in 1928, but John Kennedy was in 1960. Recent United States secretaries of state were born abroad, one in Germany, the other in Poland. Jews and Italians now manage major corporations in both Canada and the United States; yet only a few decades earlier these same companies might not have hired them. In terms of the ability to achieve high positions in a society, some subgroups are more privileged than others. Table 10-1 presents in-

Table 10-1. Income in 1971 of Males 14 Years Old or Older, by Ethnic Origin United States (Ethnicity Listed From Highest to Lowest Median Income)

| Ethnic origin | Percent of males in income group | | | | Median income |
	Total	below $5,000	$5,000 to $14,999	$15,000 and over	1971
Total, all ethnicities	100.0%	37.9%	51.5%	10.6%	$6,905
Russian*	100.0	26.8	47.6	25.8	9,737
Polish*	100.0	27.8	58.3	14.0	8,366
Italian	100.0	30.3	58.6	11.0	8,072
English, Scottish, Welsh	100.0	33.6	51.9	14.5	7,774
German	100.0	32.4	55.3	12.3	7,693
Irish	100.0	33.3	55.1	11.5	7,530
French	100.0	34.8	56.8	8.4	7,146
Spanish	100.0	44.9	52.1	3.0	5,561
Other	100.0	43.1	47.7	9.2	6,119
Not reported	100.9	40.2	52.5	7.3	6,221

Source: *Current Population Reports*, Series P-20, 1972, Table 8.
* Includes high proportion of Eastern European Jews.

come data for different ethnic groups in the United States in 1971, the most recent year for which information was available. There is little reason to believe that the *relative* differences have greatly changed over the past decade although the dollar amounts will have risen significantly.

In Canada, too, ethnicity plays a role with respect to power, prestige, and

Table 10-2. Ethnic Group by Occupational Group, 1971 Canada

| Occupational group | Percent of ethnic group | | | | | | |
	British Isles	French	German	Hungarian	Italian	Jewish	Netherlands
Managerial, Professional, and Administrative	19.0%	15.8%	15.0%	16.1%	6.8%	29.0%	15.5%
Clerical and Sales	28.9%	23.4%	22.1%	18.2%	16.4%	43.0%	20.7%
Farming, Fishing, Forestry, Mining, and Related	7.0%	6.8%	13.8%	10.5%	2.4%	0.4%	15.2%
Manufacture, Processing, Machining, and Related	11.4%	15.9%	14.7%	19.7%	27.0%	8.4%	13.8%
Construction Trades	5.6%	6.9%	7.9%	7.2%	15.3%	1.7%	8.1%
Transportation, Material Handling, Other Crafts, and Equipment Operation	8.0%	8.0%	6.9%	5.9%	6.7%	3.1%	6.9%
Service	10.6%	11.2%	10.6%	11.9%	13.0%	4.9%	10.6%
Not Elsewhere Classified	9.5%	12.0%	9.0%	10.5%	12.4%	9.5%	9.2%
Total, All	100.0%	100.0%	100.0%	100.0%	100.0%	100.0%	100.0%

Source: *Perspective Canada*. Statistics Canada, Ottawa, 1974.

wealth. Table 10-2, presenting data for different ethnic groups in various occupations, indicates that persons of Jewish or British Isles ancestry are more likely to have white-collar occupations than individuals of Italian, Hungarian, Dutch, or French ethnic origins.

To understand these effects, some knowledge of the history of immigration to North America is required.

Roots of Racism:
European Settlers in North America

Canada and the United States have been largely populated only in the past two hundred years, primarily through the immigration of foreigners, who displaced the native or indigenous peoples who had entered the continent at least twenty thousand years earlier across a land bridge from Asia. But it was not long before the Native American tribes were reduced to the status of a racial/ethnic group inferior to the more "civilized" white newcomers. Because the culture of the white settlers was defined as superior to that of other people, the physical characteristics of other racial groups were taken as evidence of biological inferiority. Thus the white colonists rationalized their seizure of land and resources and the systematic destruction of the native cultures.

Both Canada and the U.S. were originally populated by **indigenous** peoples, the Native American Indians.

NATIVE AMERICANS IN NORTH AMERICA

A typical nineteenth-century view was expressed by President Andrew Jackson upon signing the Indian Removal Act of 1830:

> What good man would prefer a country covered with forests and ranged by a few thousand savages to our . . . Republic; studded with cities . . . and prosperous farms, embellished with more than 12 million happy people, and filled with all the blessing of liberty, civilization, and religion?
>
> [Quoted in Pearce, 1973, p. 57]

Treaties with Native American tribes could be ignored on the grounds that Indians were not entitled to equal status with white Americans, while government policy supported the forceful eviction of Indians from lands desired by white settlers. Even lands set aside to provide plots for each Native American eventually fell into the hands of non-Indians (Stevens, 1940). By 1978 approximately 53 million acres or 2.3 per cent of United States land was still managed in trust by the Bureau of Indian Affairs which controls land use. Because the Department of the Interior (in which the Bureau of Indian Affairs is located) has been interested in conservation rather than economic development of the reservations, a self-fulfilling prophecy of Indian economic backwardness has been realized (Guillemin, 1980).

Many treaties between the U.S. government and Native American tribes were broken because their lands were valuable to white settlers.

Contrary to popular belief, most Native Americans in the United States do not live on reservations. A majority live in metropolitan areas such as Los Angeles, Chicago, Seattle, and Minneapolis–St. Paul. Another large proportion live as farmers and migrant labor in the Southwest and North Central regions.

Demonstrations such as the occupation of Alcatraz Island have called attention to the broken treaties and unmet needs of Native Americans. (Source: Wide World Photos.*)*

Many Native Americans also live in New York state and northern New England.

Far from being on the verge of extinction, the Native American population has grown at a faster rate than that of the United States population as a whole, more than doubling between 1940 and 1970. The 1980 census will probably record slightly over one million (or .005 of the U.S. population) but there is so much controversy over who is or is not Indian that this figure is thought to be a gross underestimate, with some guesses as high as 15 million.

For those who remain identified as Native Americans, a new militancy is evident. Demonstrations, litigation, and publicity events such as the occupation of Alcatraz Island have called attention to the broken treaties and unmet needs of the American Indian. Several of the lawsuits have resulted in a return of native lands and/or million-dollar reparation payments. But it has been difficult for Native Americans to create a cohesive political presence because of the great diversity among tribes. There is no typical Native American, no one Indian culture, or language, or religion, or physical type.

The situation in Canada resembles that in the United States. The original inhabitants have been displaced, removed from their traditional sources of wealth, and subjected to negative stereotyping and discrimination. The Indian population of Canada, roughly 300,000 contains a large number of Inuit (Eskimo) who still populate the northern provinces, as well as tribes related to the Plains Indians of the United States, and the highly sophisticated cultures of the Pacific coast. Close to three-quarters of the Native American population in Canada live on reserves. Because of the high degree of independence allowed by provincial governments, Canadian Indians have not become as demoralized or militant as their counterparts in the United States. Nonetheless, the tribes are characterized today by inadequate economic resources, poverty, low educational attainment, poor health, negative self-image, and other symptoms of cul-

The great diversity among tribes has made political cohesion difficult for Native Americans.

tural disorganization. For example, life expectancy is 10 years lower than for other Canadians, suicides are six times the national rate, and admissions to hospitals for respiratory diseases are more than eight times the rate for all Canadians (Giniger, 1980; *Perspectives Canada*, 1980).

THE IMMIGRANT EXPERIENCE IN THE UNITED STATES

In response to the growing need for industrial labor, migration to the United States reached a peak in the last decades of the nineteenth century. By the 1920s, however, restrictive legislation effectively stemmed the flow of foreigners. Since then, relatively few individuals have been admitted, except under unusual circumstances.

European migration to the U.S. reached a peak in the late nineteenth century, reflecting a demand for industrial labor.

Between 1689 and 1754, the white population of the 13 American colonies increased from about 200,000 to one million, while over 200,000 blacks were imported as slaves. Convicts and impoverished European whites were among the early arrivals. So also were several hundred Jews and members of other persecuted religious sects. By the time of the American Revolution, the country's population was already racially, religiously, and ethnically diverse.

Up to the 1850s, most immigrants came from northern Europe. Although the Irish and German newcomers were in many ways culturally similar to the original settlers, their religious and political differences from the dominant group led to anti-Catholic rioting.

By the 1880s, the major streams of immigration came from Southern and Eastern Europe. Between 1875 and 1926, approximately nine million Italians

In the late nineteenth and early twentieth centuries, the majority of immigrants came from Southern and Eastern Europe. (Source: The Bettmann Archive.)

emigrated to the Americas, along with hundreds of thousands of Poles, Hungarians, Slovaks, Czechs, Rumanians, and Jews. Over 3.3 million Russians came to the United States between 1820 and 1950, and about 110,000 were admitted to Canada between 1910 and 1924.

These Southern and Eastern Europeans, primarily from peasant cultures, with their strange languages, religions, norms, and values, were greeted with fear and scorn. Native-born workers resented the newcomers who flooded the labor market and kept wages down. Protestants were hostile to both Roman Catholics ("papists") and Jews. The darker complexion and facial features of many newcomers were perceived as another threat to racial purity. The U.S. anti-immigration law of 1924 reflected both this fear of "inferior breeds" and the fact that the demand for low-skilled workers could be met without encouraging immigration (Parrillo, 1980).

IMMIGRANT EXPERIENCE IN CANADA

Despite the notion that the United States is *the* land of immigrants, Canada currently has a larger proportion of foreign-born population, as Figure 10-1 indicates.

Historically, the immigration policy of Canada was designed to encourage development of its vast agricultural resources while maintaining the country's essentially British character. Today, many Canadians are of Ukranian, Italian, Polish, Swedish, Danish, and Dutch ancestry. And in eastern Canada, there is also a flourishing Jewish community.

Although there was no official "white Canada" immigration policy, black and Asian settlers were not very welcome until the 1960s (Richmond, 1978). Since the 1960s, the proportion of immigrants from Europe has decreased and the percentage of newcomers from Asia, the Carribean, and other North and Central American countries has more than doubled, greatly diversifying the ethnic and racial composition. Although less than 3 per cent of the population are blacks, many of whom migrated from the United States over a century ago, increasing numbers of people from developing Third World nations have been admitted on temporary visas or as permanent residents.

The single largest ethnic/religious minority in Canada are descendants of French colonizers whose numbers have increased both by immigration and by a very high birth rate. Today, French-speaking (Francophone) Canadians comprise 26 per cent of the total population and 79 per cent of inhabitants of the Province of Quebec. Because French-speaking Canadians have been victims of discrimination in employment and other avenues to success, a powerful movement toward separatism and self-rule for Quebec has recently emerged. While English-speaking Canadians (Anglophones) traditionally have had a higher rate of upward social mobility than French-speakers, this had changed in Quebec by the 1970s. Not only were Francophones dominant in trade unions and blue-collar occupations, but they comprised a new middle class, concentrated in governmental jobs (Guindon, 1978; Laczko, 1978) although the private work sector remained under the control of Anglophones. Language became a rallying issue in Quebec when there were no more jobs available to French Canadians in the public sector. As a result, the economy of Quebec is split along language and ethnic lines (Guindon, 1978). A referendum on separatism and self-rule for Quebec was defeated in 1980, but further efforts may be expected if the economic

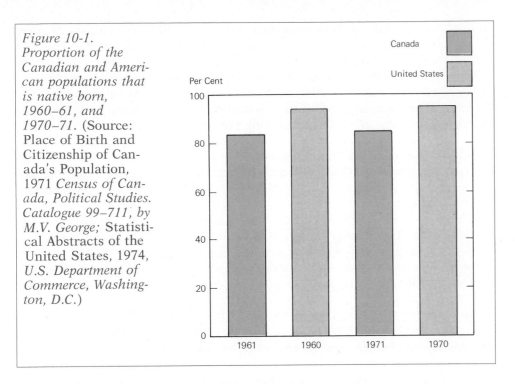

Figure 10-1. Proportion of the Canadian and American populations that is native born, 1960–61, and 1970–71. (Source: Place of Birth and Citizenship of Canada's Population, 1971 *Census of Canada, Political Studies.* Catalogue 99–711, by M.V. George; Statistical Abstracts of the United States, 1974, U.S. Department of Commerce, Washington, D.C.)

and social opportunities for French-speaking Canadians do not improve.

At the moment, the political and governmental dominance of French Canadians in Quebec has been effectively used to legislate bilingualism in the province and to secure educational autonomy for French-speakers.

Models for the Integration of Minority Groups

Our brief history of three centuries of migration to North America should explain the recurrent obsession of policy makers with the problem of how to weld such a diverse population into a cohesive whole. Social stability required the forging of a set of values and norms so that members of different groups could interact in an orderly fashion. Several models for the integration of minority groups have been proposed, among which are the *melting pot* and *cultural pluralism*.

THE MELTING POT MODEL

The model of the melting pot is based upon the belief that immigrants could and should, through exposure to the mass media and a common educational system, gradually lose their uniqueness and come to share a common language and culture, and enjoy equal opportunities for success in the New World. It was thought that in as much as all human beings were descended from Adam and

The **melting pot model** assumes that immigrants should lose their cultural uniqueness and become assimilated into the dominant American culture.

Eve, differences among them were the result of specific environments. In time, all would come to conform to American norms and beliefs, producing a homogenized collection of citizens.

Despite this ideological commitment to the melting pot, and despite the success of the public-school system in transmitting a common language and culture to millions of immigrants, ethnic minorities have, in many ways, remained "unmeltable." Not only was the melting pot ideology founded on a simplistic theory of human nature, but its supporters failed to take into account the crucial importance of race, religion, and ethnicity as sources of identity, self-affirmation, and community. There was also the tacit assumption that white Anglo-Saxon Protestant norms, values, and lifestyles represented the ideal to which others must subscribe.

At the very least, it was hoped that the children of minority-group members would become Americanized through an education consisting of civics, English, memorization of patriotic literature, and songs: "One part ability to read, write, and speak English; one part the Declaration of Independence; one part the Constitution; one part love for apple pie, one part desire and willingness to wear American shoes, and another part pride in American plumbing will make an American of anyone" (Smith, 1939, p. 115). In this sense, second- and third-generation immigrants have become strongly attached to American institutions and goals, and are often among the most vocal in expressing their patriotism.

To smooth the paths of upward mobility in the early part of this century, many changed their names to disguise religious and ethnic background. Elite universities were known to have quotas for "Jews and those whose names ended in vowels." Few minority-group members thought it feasible to run for political office, and even fewer were accepted into the management ranks of banks, corporations, or stock exchange firms. Americanization could go only so far in integrating minorities into the larger structures of society.

Yet, the persistence of ethnicity, race, and religion both as important facets of personal identity and as triggers for prejudice and discriminatory treatment led to a reconceptualization of the process of absorbing group members: *cultural pluralism* became the new ideal.

CULTURAL PLURALISM

The **cultural pluralism model** emphasizes the contribution of various immigrant cultures and the resulting cultural diversity of America.

The concept of the United States or Canada as "a nation of nations" emphasizes the unique contributions of various immigrant cultures to the diversity and vitality of social life. Cultural pluralism implies an acceptance or tolerance of diversity in relatively personal matters—food, family, religious rituals, community associations, and the like. It does not extend to *structural* changes that might produce parallel power systems within minority communities or that would lead to a large-scale change in the distribution of property, prestige, or wealth in the larger society.

It was once thought that under the impact of urban industrial life, later-generation minority-group members would gradually become *less* identified with background traits, until only surface differences remained, while their basic sameness as Americans would assure equal opportunity for success. Yet today there appears to be a resurgence of ethnicity expressed in a desire to discover and glorify one's roots. Not only is this search important for a sense of personal continuity and uniqueness, but the discovery of a shared past creates

The concept of cultural pluralism emphasizes the unique contributions of various cultures to the diversity and vitality of social life. (Source: Owen Frankin, Stock, Boston.)

bonds of mutual support among individuals who might otherwise feel isolated.

For some religious and ethnic groups this resurgence of awareness is possible precisely *because* the ascribed traits are no longer barriers to success. For others, the heightened identification with the past serves to cushion the continuing effects of prejudice and discrimination. For still other minority groups, the discovery and celebration of the past serve to mobilize members for political action. For example, slogans such as "Black is beautiful" and "I'm proud to be Polish" have strengthened identity with an individual's own ethnic/racial group. Formation of action groups such as the Chicano La Raza (literally, "the race") and the National Association for the Advancement of Colored People (NAACP) have heightened subcultural identification and also provided an avenue through which political pressure may be brought to bear on the dominant society.

Processes for the Integration of Minority Groups

There are several ways in which minority groups are linked to the larger society. These processes form a *continuum* from near isolation (*segregation*) to a blending into the dominant culture (*amalgamation*). This continuum is depicted in Figure 10-2.

Figure 10-2. Continuum of processes of absorption into majority culture.

Minority has low contact with majority culture.

Minority has high contact with majority culture.

Segregation Accomodation Acculturation Assimilation Amalgamation

De jure segregation is supported by law.

De facto segregation occurs in fact, though not necessarily by law.

Segregation refers to efforts to isolate minorities and may be of two types: *de facto* and *de jure*. *De jure* means supported by law; *de facto* means in actuality but not necessarily by law. An example of *de jure* segregation is the apartheid (apartness) policy of the Republic of South Africa, where a small minority of whites rules the country, and the majority—black and colored (racially mixed) Africans—have limited freedom of movement, either segregated on rural reservations or in clearly marked urban areas. Separate school systems, transportation, and public facilities are established by law for the different races, with the quality of nonwhite living arrangements distinctly inferior. Such an arrangement is similar to the legally-sanctioned separate facilities provided for blacks in the Southern United States up to the mid-1950s. Following a series of impor-

Through the process of accommodation *members of minority groups adapt to the majority culture without fully participating in it. Cubans in Miami, Florida, for example, have formed their own Spanish-speaking community. (Source: Michael Heron, Woodfin Camp and Associates.)*

Table 10-3. Steps or Subprocesses in Assimilation

Subprocess or condition	Type or stage of assimilation
1. Change of cultural patterns to those of host society	Cultural or behavior assimilation (acculturation)
2. Large-scale entrance into cliques, clubs, and institutions of host society on primary-group level	Structural assimilation (assimilation)
3. Large-scale intermarriage	Marital assimilation (amalgamation)
4. Development of sense of peoplehood based exclusively on host society	Identificational assimilation
5. Absence of prejudice	Attitude-receptional assimilation
6. Absence of discrimination	Behavior-receptional assimilation
7. Absence of value and power conflict	Civic assimilation

Source: From *Human Nature, Class, and Ethnicity* by Milton Gordon. Copyright © 1978 by Oxford University Press. Reprinted by permission.

tant Supreme Court decisions, *de jure* segregation in the United States is now prohibited. *De facto* segregation, however, remains.

Accommodation is the phase in which members of a minority become aware of the norms and values of the majority culture but do not necessarily internalize these. Individuals adapt to the majority culture without fully participating. For example, established Cuban residents of Miami can deal effectively with mainstream social institutions while remaining culturally and linguistically distinct.

Acculturation, sometimes called cultural assimilation, occurs when members of a minority group internalize the norms, values, and behavioral patterns of the majority society but are not admitted to more intimate groupings.

Assimilation, sometimes called *structural assimilation* to distinguish it from acculturation or *cultural* assimilation, refers to the entry of minority group members into the primary groups, associations, and major institutions of the majority society. The rate at which different minority groups become assimilated varies according to the visibility of physical differences and the degree to which culture traits depart from the majority ideal. It will, therefore, be easiest for light-skinned, English-speaking individuals to assimilate.

Amalgamation denotes the mixing of cultures or races to form new cultural and racial types. This is achieved through intermarriage. Rates of ethnic and religious intermarriage have increased greatly since 1960, but interracial marriages remain rare—less than 2 per cent of all marriages in the United States today.

The processes depicted in Table 10-3 highlight the complexity of the ways in which minority groups become part of the majority society. Segregation that is enforced by custom still regulates large-scale entrance into many institutional spheres as well as into primary-group relationships. Nor has identificational assimilation occurred, that is, the development of a sense of identity based

Accommodation occurs when a minority becomes aware of majority norms and values without internalizing them.

Acculturation occurs when a minority internalizes majority norms and values but is not permitted into intimate groupings.

Assimilation occurs when a minority enters intimate groupings and major social institutions.

Amalgamation occurs through ethnic, religious, and racial intermarriage.

Table 10-4. *Extent of Adaptation to American Core Society and Culture for Four Minority Groups— Blacks, Jews, Catholics, and Puerto Ricans*

Group	Type of assimilation						
	Cultural	Structural	Marital	Identificational	Attitude receptional	Behavior receptional	Civic
Blacks	Variation by class	No	No	No	No	No	Yes
Jews	Substantially yes	No	Substantially no	No	No	Partly	Mostly
Catholics (excluding black and Spanish-speaking)	Substantially yes	Partly (variation by area)	Partly	No	Partly	Mostly	Partly
Puerto Ricans	Mostly no	No	No	No	No	No	Partly

Source: From *Human Nature, Class, and Ethnicity* by Milton Gordon. Copyright © 1978 by Oxford University Press. Reprinted by permission.

entirely on membership in the majority society. Table 10-4 compares the level of assimilation for blacks, Jews, Catholics, and Puerto Ricans in the United States.

BARRIERS TO INTEGRATION

Institutional Racism. Segregated housing patterns are maintained at times by the practice of *redlining*, through which banks and other lending institutions

Gatekeepers and Homeseekers: Institutional Patterns in Racial Steering

Noting that the racially segregated housing patterns observed from 1940 to 1960 have remained virtually unchanged during the 1970s, Diana Pearce analysed the processes that maintain single-race neighborhoods despite the existence of Fair Housing laws and generally positive attitudes of whites toward the principle of racial integration in housing.

Pearce examined the behavior of real-estate agents, the gatekeepers of the housing market. Two homeseeking couples (who were in fact trained participant observer/interviewers), visited 97 real-estate agents in the Detroit area. Both couples had approximately the same income and savings. The husband was employed steadily in an occupation requiring a college education; the wife did not work. The only difference was that one couple was black and the other white.

The black couple was less likely than the white to be shown any home. Overall, the chances of seeing a house on the first visit to the real-estate agent were about 3 in 4 for whites but only 1 in 4 for blacks. Since fewer homes were shown to black couples, their range of selection was smaller. When blacks were shown a home, it was likely to be in either an inexpensive black neighborhood or an affluent suburb.

This research is described in Diana M. Pearce, "Gatekeepers and Homeseekers: Institutional Patterns in Racial Steering," *Social Problems* 20, Feb. 3, 1979, pp. 325–42.

refuse to make mortgage money available for housing in certain neighborhoods, especially those thought likely to deteriorate or decrease in value. This practice, albeit illegal, is used to limit the availability of money for housing in racially mixed neighborhoods. These real-estate and banking practices illustrate the concept of *institutional racism*. In many areas of social life, discrimination is built into the entire structure of norms and behavior and is reinforced by both formal and informal agents of social control. In the Pearce study, described in "Gatekeepers and Homeseekers," on page 254, all the agents were members of the National Association of Real Estate Boards, an organization that had opposed Fair Housing laws for many years. The realtors knew that other agents would cease to share information once the informal norms of *racial steering* were violated. Moreover, their business would suffer, as fewer and fewer whites would list their homes with an agency that had a reputation for placing black families in white neighborhoods. The agent who followed the law would soon be bankrupt.

Institutional racism appears also in the military, the educational system, religious organizations, voluntary associations, politics, and job-placement firms, among others. In sum, regardless of individual attitudes and legal norms, there are many *group* pressures that maintain segregation (Pinkney 1975; 1976).

Prejudice.   Other major barriers to complete assimilation involve *individual* rather than institutional responses. The two most important of these are *prejudice* and *discrimination*.

Prejudice refers to prejudgments regarding members of an ethnic, racial, religious, or other social category. Such attitudes are a form of *stereotypical thinking*, in which a single set of characteristics, unfavorable or favorable, are attributed to all members of a social category. Some examples of erroneous stereotyping include the characterization of whites as intellectually superior to nonwhites; of Jews as shrewd in business; of Chinese as inscrutable; of women as naturally dependent; and of the very old as senile. These beliefs feed prejudice and impair the ability to perceive others as unique individuals who may, or more often may not, resemble the stereotype.

Prejudice is also reinforced by *scapegoating*, or finding someone to blame for one's misfortunes. The term refers to the biblical practice of sacrificing a goat to appease the Lord for human sins. In contemporary society, scapegoating includes blaming the poor for being poor, feeling that rape victims were "asking for it," and holding a particular group responsible for national ills, as was the case in Nazi Germany where Jews were blamed for the country's economic collapse in the 1920s.

The origins of prejudice are complex. Factors associated with prejudice include these. (1) There is little or no contact with the minority group, so that false beliefs are not subject to correction. (2) As with other social attitudes, prejudice is learned, most often within a family and primary group context. (3) An individual's prejudices tend to conform to the norms of the community; that is, they are *institutionalized patterns* rather than personal quirks.

Willingness or unwillingness to have contact with a member of a minority group can be measured along a continuum of *social distance*. One way in which prejudice has been measured is by a set of questions (or *scale*) on which a respondent is asked to rate the degree of social closeness or distance she or he

Redlining is an illegal practice that occurs when banks do not make mortgage money available for home buying in certain neighborhoods.

Institutional racism is discrimination built into norms and behavior and reinforced by agents of social control.

Prejudice involves prejudging members of ethnic, religious, and racial groups.

Stereotypical thinking occurs when a set of characteristics is attributed to all members of a social group.

Scapegoating refers to finding a person or a group to blame for one's problems.

Prejudices are typically **institutionalized patterns** rather than personal quirks.

Table 10-5. Social Distance Toward Four Ethnic Groups
(Proportion Willing to Accept)

Relationship	English	German	German Jew	Black
Citizen	96%	87%	54%	57%
Employment	95	83	40	39
Neighbor	75	79	26	12
Friend	97	67	22	9
Spouse	94	54	8	1

Source: Adapted from Emory S. Bogardus, *Immigration and Race Attitudes*, New York: Ozer, 1971, p. 25.

would find acceptable with reference to various minority groups. Table 10-5 summarizes the results of a study in which respondents were asked whether they would be willing to accept members of four ethnic/racial groups in a variety of relationships that form a continuum of social distance, from most distant to very close, as follows: (1) as a citizen of the United States; (2) into one's workplace; (3) as a neighbor; (4) as a personal friend, and (5) as a spouse.

Discrimination is the **practice** of unequal treatment of people.

Discrimination.   Whereas prejudice is a set of attitudes, *discrimination* is the practice of unequal treatment of people. In many respects the two are closely related; prejudice leads to discrimination, and discrimination in turn reinforces prejudice in a vicious cycle, as shown in Figure 10-3, that limits opportunity and produces a self-fulfilling prophecy. Many years ago, for example, when Irish-Americans had low levels of educational attainment, they were denied opportunities for skilled training, which in turn confirmed the belief that "Irish are stupid." Yet prejudice and discrimination are two *separate* dimensions. An individual can be prejudiced without acting in a discriminatory manner. Conversely, individuals without prejudice against minority group members can act to deny them equal treatment.

As may be seen in Table 10-6, individuals are likely to act contrary to their attitudes when the situation is defined as appropriate. The real-estate agent who steers blacks may be without personal hostility toward the client. Conversely, the person who fears Jews may vote to admit them to his private club if other members are strongly in favor. Put simply, people tend to behave in such

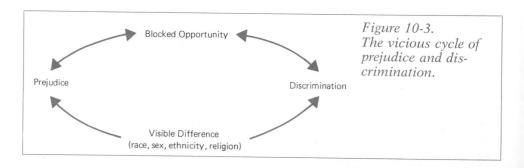

Figure 10-3.
The vicious cycle of prejudice and discrimination.

Table 10-6. An Illustration of the Relationship Between Attitudes and Behavior

		Attitude	
		Prejudiced	*Accepting*
Behavior	*Discriminatory*	—not only hates having strangers next door but actively attempts to prevent it (e.g., by cross-burning, organizations to retain exclusionary zoning laws, etc.)	—real estate agent/banker who does not care who lives where, but will not fight institutional racism/inequality
	Smoothing	—does not want strangers next door but will not do anything to prevent their moving in or their continued residence.	—meets goals of existing legislation, and does not object to strangers moving into neighborhood.

a way as to receive approval and validation from others in the groups to which they belong.

Table 10-6 also leads to the observation that discrimination can be reduced *without* attitude change by encouraging group norms that define such behavior as unacceptable. Because it is easier to change behavior than attitudes, policies altering discrimination are more successful in ending segregation than are attempts to reduce prejudice. Individual and institutional discrimination are often found together, as when norms permit and even encourage open displays of hatred.

Discrimination occurs through **individual acts** and through **institutional barriers.**

Impact of Prejudice and Discrimination. Not only do prejudice and discrimination have such obvious effects as the destruction of life, health, and property, but they have an impact upon the self. People who have been victims of prejudice and discrimination often internalize negative self-images, leading to low self-esteem and the devaluation of other members of the same minority group. In this way members of a minority may learn to act in ways that perpetuate the inequality or stereotype.

Not only is a toll extracted from the minority group that experiences prejudice and discrimination, but there are costs to the majority. In the case of active segregation, duplicate or parallel facilities, such as segregated school systems,

Arson

When Tom Porter, a 42-year-old corporate advertiser with IBM moved into a split-level home in a predominantly white neighborhood where housing values ranged from $70,000 to $100,000, he and his family were greeted by an explosion and fire only four hours after their arrival. While Mr. Porter was uninjured, his wife, two daughters, a niece, and a nephew required hospital treatment. Arson investigators found that gasoline had been poured into the kitchen and den of the house, and that the fire had been set by "professionals who knew what they were doing." The evidence strongly suggested that the fire was motivated by a desire to force the Porters out of a neighborhood in which they were perceived as undesirables.

This case of arson was reported by Lena Williams under the headline "Arson Destroys a Yonkers House After Blacks Move in," in the New York *Times*, Aug. 8, 1979, p. 1.

restrooms, and so forth must be provided. Furthermore, much human effort is wasted by members of the majority in maintaining their dominant position. This is a process that also affects the personality of those who discriminate or hold prejudices.

Fear of Displacement.   Prejudice and discrimination are most likely to be expressed by those who are most threatened by the success of minority-group members. They fear that they may be supplanted when others achieve equal status. For example, hostility toward immigrants in the nineteenth and twentieth centuries was most marked among members of the working class who felt, that entry of new groups into the labor market would reduce their ability to improve working conditions. Cummings (1980) found that white ethnic workers in direct competition with blacks in low-paying low-skilled jobs were more prejudiced against blacks than were white ethnic workers in higher-paying jobs.

Racial Minorities

BLACKS IN AMERICA

The first blacks in the United States arrived in Jamestown, Virginia in the early 1600s when a Dutch shipowner brought them from Africa and sold them to colonists. At that time the blacks had the same status as indentured servants and could, after a time, become freedmen. The status of slave as property rather than person evolved soon thereafter. As more slaves were imported, Southern agriculture became dependent upon their labor.

Such a system of inequality could be justified only by an ideology of racial differences equivalent to innate superiority/inferiority. Reconciling such a belief with the moralistic religious tradition of the white settlers required defining blacks as destined by God to serve the white colonists.

Between 1660 and 1860 at least 100,000 slaves fled to the North to join other relatively free blacks, but the majority remained nonpersons until the Emancipation Proclamation of 1863 during the Civil War. Between 1866 and 1877, under the protection of the United States military blacks enjoyed widespread participation in the economic and political life of the South. But Southern communities soon legislated *Black Codes* limiting these gains. The codes were enforced by intimidation from such groups as the Ku Klux Klan and the Knights of the White Camellia.

Black political and economic powerlessness was increasingly reinforced by resurgent racism reflected in *Jim Crow* laws that effectively segregated the races and denied voting rights to blacks. The key legal decision upholding segregation was rendered by the United States Supreme Court in 1896 *Plessy v. Ferguson:* "If one race be inferior to the other socially, the Constitution of the United States cannot put them on the same plane." A dual system of schools and access to public buildings remained intact until the *Brown* decision in 1954. It is only in the past two and one-half decades that blacks have exercised equal rights in the South.

Slavery as a system of inequality was justified by an ideology of racial superiority of whites.

Reacting unfavorably to economic and political gains made by blacks during the Reconstruction Era (1866–1877), Southern communities instituted Jim Crow laws which separated the races. (Source: Bruce Roberts, Photo Researchers, Inc.)

Migration North. Partly as a reaction to discrimination and violence, but largely in response to changing economic conditions, hundreds of thousands of blacks moved to the North in this century. Mechanization of Southern agriculture drastically reduced the need for field labor, and because machines are most efficient on large tracts of land, sharecroppers and tenant farmers were displaced. Between 1914 and 1924, approximately one million blacks migrated to urban industrial centers where there was demand for factory labor.

Changing economic conditions, discrimination, and violence led to the northward migration of blacks in this century.

Blacks migrated north in vast numbers because of the promise of a better life. Such hopes have not been fulfilled as illustrated by the conditions in this inner-city neighborhood. (Source: Stock, Boston.)

A black population that was 80 per cent rural in 1890 became 80 per cent urban by 1970. Once in the cities, blacks were confronted by *de facto* segregation in housing and education. Nonetheless, there were employment opportunities—especially during World War II and the economic expansion that followed. In many urban centers, thriving black communities developed in the 1930s and 40s. New York's Harlem, for example, was a center for musical and artistic talent during that era. Yet, as more relatively unskilled and uneducated Southern migrants moved into northern cities and as employment opportunities declined, life in the North became as difficult and oppressive as that once experienced in the South. Today a reverse migration pattern exists, with more blacks moving South, where new factories are being built, than are moving North.

Blacks and Stratification Hierarchies.   In 1978, 25.5 million blacks accounted for approximately 11 per cent of the total population of the United States. To what extent have American blacks moved into and up the stratification hierarchies? And to what extent can the term *caste* be used to describe separate and unequal status systems by race?

Power.   Although all legal barriers to black voting have been removed, participation rates of blacks are consistently lower than for whites. Some of this differential has been due to intentionally-constructed difficulties in registering

In recent years the political influence of blacks rose dramatically, as seen in this 1980 photograph of presidential candidate Ronald Reagan seeking the endorsement of the Rev. Jesse Jackson. (Source: United Press International.)

and voting in the South, but most is probably related to low income and educational attainment, which are associated with low voter turnout in general. Also, feelings of helplessness and alienation reduce motivation to vote ("What good would it do?").

The number of black elected officials has risen dramatically from about 1,500 in 1970 to 4,500 in 1978, over half of whom are city or county officials including the mayors of major cities such as Los Angeles, Atlanta, Newark, N.J. and Gary, Ind. Another 1,100 are on boards of education. (*Statistical Abstract*, 1979, p. 512.). Few blacks hold high positions in federal or state governments, although the proportions have been increasing slowly, as have the number of judges, medium-level civil servants, and law-enforcement officers. At the moment, these officeholders represent considerably less than the 10–12 per cent that would reflect the proportion of blacks in the population.

Property. In terms of employment, occupation, income, and wealth, blacks are greatly disadvantaged when compared to whites. As the last hired, blacks are typically the first fired when the economy turns downward. Thus in 1979, the yearly unemployment rates were almost twice as high for blacks as for whites.

As the last hired are also younger than those already established in jobs, the bulk of black unemployment occurs among young males who are precisely the age group requiring economic security to marry, raise families, and become attached to the labor force. The long-term consequences of their unemployment are incalculable and predictive of social unrest in the decades ahead.

Blacks are disadvantaged in terms of wealth, occupation, and income compared to whites—even at the same level of education.

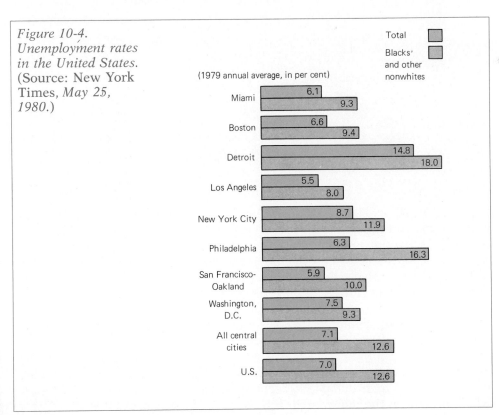

Figure 10-4. Unemployment rates in the United States. (Source: New York Times, *May 25, 1980.*)

Table 10-7. *Per Cent Nonwhite in Selected Occupations*

	1972	1978	*Percent change, 1972–78*
Professional, technical	7.2%	8.7%	+1.5%
Engineers	3.4	5.5	+2.1
Lawyers, judges	1.9	2.6	+0.7
Physicians, dentists	6.3	7.3	+1.0
Registered nurses	8.2	11.7	+3.5
College, univ. teachers	7.2	7.1	−0.1
Pre- & kindergarten teachers	13.3	15.7	+2.4
Athletes	6.4	4.0	−2.4
Managers & administrators	4.0	5.0	+1.0
Sales workers	3.6	5.0	+1.4
Clerical	8.7	19.5	+10.8
File clerks	18.0	23.4	+5.4
Secretaries	5.2	6.2	+1.0
Craft	6.9	7.5	+0.6
Operatives	13.2	15.0	+1.8
Manufacturing inspectors	8.8	11.8	+3.0
Textile operatives	15.8	25.7	+9.9
Transport	14.8	14.9	+0.1
Bus	17.1	21.1	+4.0
Truck	14.4	13.9	−0.5
Laborers	20.2	17.7	−2.5
Farm workers	15.1	15.7	+0.6
Service workers	18.5	18.5	0
Cleaning service	30.0	28.1	−1.9
Nursing aides, orderlies	26.9	27.6	+0.7
Fire-fighters	4.0	7.2	+3.2
Police	8.4	9.9	+1.5
Private household workers	40.6	33.0	−7.6

Source: *Statistical Abstract of the United States, 1979, p. 416–17.*

Moreover, 70 per cent of all unemployed blacks have never received any unemployment compensation (Urban League, 1980). Despite popular mythology, poor blacks are not predominantly on welfare: over half of all impoverished black households received no welfare assistance at all (Urban League, 1980). It is simply not true that federal and state programs for the poor provide an income cushion for most unemployed blacks or that men refuse jobs in order to collect welfare.

When employed, incomes of black workers lag behind those of whites. Among families with a full-time worker, black family income is roughly three-quarters that of a white family. For *all* families, black incomes today are under 60 per cent of that for whites. In part, these figures reflect the high proportion of black families headed by a female (40.5 per cent *vs.* 11.6 per cent white), many of whom are not in the labor force (U.S. Bureau of the Census, 1980).

Much has been written of the increase in proportion of black families that have moved into the middle class, but in most instances this move has required *two* wage-earners. A young black couple with two full-time salaries in 1977 earned about $1,300 more than the median income of a young white family in which *only* the husband worked (*Statistical Abstract*, 1979, p. 457). At the *same* level of education and occupational category, black wages are lower than those of whites. In fact, a typical white high-school dropout earns more than a college-educated black male. This is largely because of the differing employment opportunities for the two races. As Table 10-7 shows, nonwhites are most heavily represented in such relatively poorly paid professions such as nursing, kindergarten teaching, clerks, and service workers.

Prestige.   Given the political, income, and occupational data just presented, it becomes evident that sources of personal and social prestige are systematically denied to blacks in the United States. In the one area of most rapid gains, education, there is some indication that advancement may be more apparent than real. The proportion of black high school dropouts declined during the 1970s from 33 to 25 per cent, and the proportion of high school graduates going to college rose from 35 to 42 per cent so that blacks are now as likely as whites to go to college (New York Times, May 25, 1980). However compared with white high school graduates, a larger proportion are at two-year colleges and trade schools.

Conclusion.   The weight of evidence supports the *caste* model of black/white stratification, although debates over the relative importance of class and race continue. Some analysts (Wilson, 1978) claim that race *per se* is of declining significance relative to the overwhelming effects of poverty. Others cite continuing antiblack sentiment as a major determinant of the persistence of poverty itself. Moreover, the trend toward increased political and economic gains for blacks has been halted and even reversed as the overall economic situation has worsened. The costs of recession and inflation in the United States are disproportionately borne by the poor in general and blacks in particular.

ASIANS IN THE UNITED STATES AND CANADA

Asian-Americans are a heterogeneous category, containing people from diverse cultures and religious backgrounds and speaking different languages. Yet a tendency to classify all Asians together has dominated both immigration policy and popular attitudes. In this section, we shall describe some of the different Asian groups that have immigrated to the United States and Canada within the last 130 years, and the common and unique problems they have experienced as a result of both race and ethnicity.

Chinese.   Large-scale migration of Chinese to North America began in the mid-nineteenth century, stimulated by the Gold Rush of 1849 and the building of transcontinental railroads. By 1869, over 100,000 Chinese, the overwhelming majority of whom were young males, had entered the United States and Canada.

Because of their obvious physical and cultural differences and their willingness to work extremely long hours for very little pay, they were early victims of mob violence in both the United States and Canada. It was not uncommon for the "heathen Chinee" to be stoned in the streets, have his home burned, and to be beaten or hanged. In 1906, a Canadian mob destroyed the entire Chinese section of Vancouver.

Laws directed against the Chinese were quickly enacted, forcing them to live in specific sections of a city and limiting all geographic movement. In 1882, all legal immigration from China was halted to the United States, thereby creating an almost exclusively male society, segregated from the mainstream of American life. In Canada, entry was restricted by imposing a head tax of up to $500 for each immigrant until 1923, when Chinese were legally excluded (Lyman, 1974).

The anti-Chinese movement had a variety of unanticipated consequences. Chinese were restricted to a few urban ghettos, or Chinatowns that were essentially communities of homeless men. Social life was organized around three types of male associations: (1) the traditional family clan; (2) an immigrant aid society and (3) secret societies, or *tongs*, that functioned, in part, to organize and regulate illicit activities including gambling, opium, and prostitution. The creation of such cohesive associations within the segregated community accounts in part for the relative success of Chinese Americans once their isolation was ended in the early 1940s. The *mutual aid society* in which resources are pooled to support small businesses and to help those in trouble is one such example.

> The **mutual aid society** pooled resources to support small businesses and those in trouble.

Chinese Ethnics Today.   Following Pearl Harbor, the status of North American Chinese underwent an abrupt change: They were the "good" Asians in contrast to the "bad" Japanese. As *Time Magazine* of December 22, 1941, so delicately put it:

How to Tell Your Friends from the Japs:

Virtually all Japanese are short. Japanese are seldom fat; they often dry up as they age. Most Chinese avoid horn-rimmed spectacles. Japanese walk stiffly erect, hard-heeled. Chinese are more relaxed, have an easy gait. The Chinese expression is likely to be more kindly, placid, open; the Japanese more positive, dogmatic, arrogant. Japanese are hesitant, nervous in conversation, laugh loudly at the wrong time.

Thus did the Chinese gain acceptance—United States citizenship in 1943 and the entry of brides in 1946, ended the isolation of Chinese males. By 1970 sizeable Chinese communities were flourishing in New York and Hawaii as well as California.

There has also been a growing professionalization and high rates of upward mobility among those of Chinese ancestry. A high proportion of the younger generation have graduated from college and entered the fields of science, accounting, engineering, and drafting. Although some residential discrimination still exists, it is less difficult for Chinese than for Blacks to assimilate culturally. For instance, the Chinese/white marriage rate is considerably higher than the black/white rate.

Japanese Ethnics.   Kitano (1976) has suggested that the Japanese immigrant "came to the wrong country and the wrong state (California) at the wrong time (immediately after the Chinese) with the wrong race and skin color, with the wrong religion, and from the wrong country" (p. 31).

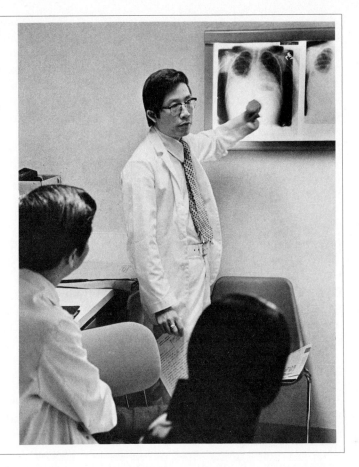

Americans of Chinese ancestry have high rates of upward mobility and growth in professionalization. (Source: *Guy Gillette, Photo Researchers, Inc.*)

The first large-scale Japanese immigration occurred between 1880 and 1924, when male laborers from rural backgrounds with limited education, found work as laborers on the railroads, in mining, agriculture, and canneries. Unlike the Chinese, however, they were permitted to bring their wives or prospective brides and to establish stable families. But as with the Chinese, agitation against the Japanese began to escalate as their success and numbers increased. In the United States, they were not permitted to own land; in Canada, they were prohibited from the professions and other occupations requiring licensing.

The first generation of Japanese-born immigrants, called *Issei*, were not highly assimilated. Yet their children, born in Canada or the United States and known as *Nisei*, were instilled with the value of education and of conformity to the norms and expectations of the majority culture. But after the outbreak of World War II, Japanese in North America were forcibly moved from their homes and relocated. In the United States, over 100,000 West Coast Japanese-Americans were placed in detention camps with guard towers and barbed wire fences. Their property was confiscated, sold, or stolen. Among the long-term effects of relocation were a reduction in the relative power of men over women in the family, weakening of control over offspring, and a reinforcement of sense of ethnic identity.

The large-scale Japanese immigration between 1880 and 1924 was stimulated by economic conditions.

The first generation of Japanese-born immigrants, the **Issei**, were not highly assimilated, whereas their children, the **Nisei**, are.

Japanese Today.   There were about 600,000 Japanese-Americans in the United States in 1970. There are also significantly more females than males. Third-generation Japanese-Americans rank highest of all nonwhite groups in educational attainment and income. In Canada, a sample of Toronto Nisei had an average family income almost twice the Canadian average for all ethnic groups (Makabe, 1976). Their occupational distribution is more varied than that of Chinese ethnics but they also are concentrated in ethnic businesses rather than in mainstream firms and corporations. Thus, although much social mobility within the Japanese-American and Japanese-Canadian communities has occurred, this is more a reflection of structural pluralism, where achievement has transpired within an ethnic group, rather than an indication of structural and marital assimilation into the majority culture.

The 1970s have witnessed the migration to the U.S. of people from the Philippines, India, South Korea, and Vietnam.

Other Asian Americans.   Since 1970, slightly more than 300,000 people from the Philippines, 150,000 from India, almost 300,000 South Korean, and over 100,000 Vietnamese have emigrated to the United States. Their arrival, like that of most new immigrants who are not of Northern European origin, has generated mixed responses. Asians now comprise over one-third of all entering peoples, with Koreans the most populous.

Ethnic Minorities

The great variety of nationality groups represented in the population is a defining characteristic of North American societies. To illustrate general themes in the immigrant experience as well as to provide an introduction to the fastest growing ethnic minority in the United States, our discussion will focus on the most recent entrants: Hispanic-Americans.

HISPANIC AMERICANS

Hispanic Americans include various cultural and racial subgroups sharing a common language. Major subdivisions are Mexican-Americans, Puerto Ricans, and Cubans.

Hispanic-American is a category comprising a large number of distinct cultural/racial subgroups bound together by a common language, Spanish (although even language patterns vary by country of origin). In 1979, over 12 million Spanish-speaking individuals were officially recorded as residing in the United States; and several million additional Hispanics are believed to have entered without official documents. Because of their high birth rate and the large proportion of young adults in the Hispanic population, it is likely that Spanish-speaking Americans will soon outnumber blacks as the single largest minority group in the United States.

In 1980 the three major ethnic subdivisions within the Spanish-speaking population are these: Mexican-Americans (Chicanos), roughly 60 per cent; Puerto Ricans, 14 per cent, and Cubans, approximately 6 per cent. The remainder are immigrants from other Central and South American countries, particularly the Dominican Republic and Colombia.

As Table 10-8 indicates, differences within the Spanish-speaking minority are striking, especially in terms of education, occupation, and income. There is a stratification system within the Hispanic population, based not only upon

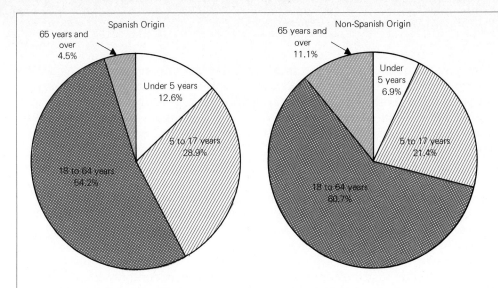

Figure 10-5.
Per cent distribution of the Spanish and non-Spanish origin populations, by age, March 1979. (Source: Current Population Reports, Persons of Spanish Origin in the United States, March 1979, Advance report, U.S. Bureau of the Census, series P-20, No. 347, October 1979, Figure 2.)

Table 10-8. Persons of Spanish Origin—Selected Characteristics: 1978

	Mexican	Puerto Rican	Cuban and other Hispanic
Characteristics			
Age: Under 18	43.0	46.0	36.4
18–34	31.1	27.8	27.5
65+	3.7	2.3	6.9
Years of School Completed			
Male: Less than 5	21.9	14.0	6.2
High School	36.6	26.0	56.9
College	4.8	5.1	18.0
Female: Less than 5	24.4	15.7	7.4
High School	32.1	36.0	55.1
College	3.9	3.6	10.3
Employment			
Male: White-Collar	18.5	26.2	36.4
Blue-Collar	63.1	52.3	47.8
Service, Farm	18.4	21.5	15.8
Per Cent Unemployed	9.6	11.7	8.5
Families Headed by Females	15.5	41.0	18.6
Family Income: 1978			
Under $4000	9.3	15.8	5.0
$4000–9999	26.0	42.2	24.5
$10,000–14,999	22.9	16.0	19.2
$15,000–19,999	17.4	12.1	16.6
$20,000–24,999	10.8	7.5	17.5
$25,000 and over	13.5	6.4	17.3
Median Income:	$12,835	$8,282	$15,326
Per Cent Below Poverty Level	18.9	38.9	16.3

Source: *Statistical Abstract*, 1979, p. 91, and *Current Population Reports*, Series P-20, #347, October 1979, p. 6.

these components of socioeconomic status but also upon skin color. Thus do race and ethnicity combine to determine the relative status of Spanish-speaking Americans, both within the stratification system of the wider society and within the prestige hierarchy of the Hispanic subculture. These internal divisions reduce the likelihood of the shared consciousness necessary to build an ethnic power base.

Chicanos. When the United States acquired its territories in the southwest, these areas had already been settled by Mexican migrants. Similar to the fate of Native Americans, a gradual pattern of economic and social subordination of the Mexicans developed as white Americans ("Anglos") migrated west (Moore, 1976).

Like many other ethnic groups who have not been accepted by the majority group, Chicanos tend not only to live in particular geographic areas, such as Southern California, South Texas, and New Mexico, but to live in distinctly Mexican neighborhoods or *barrios*. However, depending on the community in which they live, residential conditions range from highly segregated to almost completely nonsegregated living patterns (Moore, 1976). Although the stereotype of the Mexican farm laborer persists, relatively few Chicanos are rural residents—less than 20 per cent in 1979. Approximately 40 per cent live within the central city of metropolitan areas. Chicanos are less well educated on the whole than their Anglo or black age peers. This lack of education leaves many adults less capable of participation in the modern economy. Racial differences in school achievement are largely due to a conflict of cultures between home and schools, and, over time, many will simply drop out of a punishing situation.

The traditional Mexican family is an extended one, with the kinship group the main focus of obligation as well as source of emotional and social support. Within the Chicano family, gender roles are well defined. Both mothers and daughters are expected to be protected, subservient, and to dedicate themselves to caring for the males of the family. For the Mexican male, *machismo*, or the demonstration of physical and sexual prowess, is basic to self-respect, and is typically demonstrated before an audience of male friends but not family.

These traditional patterns function to protect Chicanos against the effects of prejudice and discrimination, but they also reinforce isolation from the majority culture, so that an upwardly mobile individual must choose between remaining locked into a semi-isolated ethnic world or becoming alienated from one's family, friends, and ethnic roots.

Puerto Ricans. Relative newcomers to the United States, Puerto Ricans began to emigrate because of the poor economic conditions on their island. By 1980, 1.7 million had settled in the United States, where two-fifths of these families have incomes below the poverty level, but where the expectations of economic success appear to be greater than in Puerto Rico.

While Puerto Ricans are often grouped with Chicanos, the two groups are very different in history, culture, and racial composition. Puerto Rico's culture is a blend of black and Spanish influences, with a heavy mixture of selected North American patterns. This is in sharp distinction to Mexico, where the population and its culture are composed of Spanish and Native American elements.

The Puerto Rican experience on the mainland has included a continuing struggle for stability and achievement in the area of education, politics, the arts, and community control. The Puerto Rican community has elected representatives to the U.S. Congress, New York and New Jersey state legislatures, and the New York city council. *Aspira* in education and the *Puerto Rican Forum* in community and civic affairs are but two strong organizations. Growing numbers of young Puerto Ricans are going into law, business, medicine, and teaching. Yet others continue to have difficulty on standardized English and math tests, drop out of school, and face unemployment. The Puerto Rican community in New York and other Eastern cities faces complicated problems in the area of physical and mental health care and housing (Fitzpatrick, 1976).

Though the wage gap between Puerto Rican family and white family median incomes has narrowed from one-half in 1969 to two-thirds in 1973, the U.S. Commission on Civil Rights in 1976 still concluded that even after taking into account factors such as language and job experience, "the evidence is compelling that racial, ethnic, and sex discrimination are barriers to job opportunities for Puerto Ricans." (1978.)

Cubans. Cuban immigration to the United States began in large numbers when Castro came to power in the mid-1950s. Between 1954 and 1978, over 325,000 Cubans were admitted as permanent residents in the United States. In early 1980, an additional 115,000 Cuban refugees entered the country in a sudden, somewhat chaotic exodus. While it is too early to determine how these new Cuban immigrants will fare in the United States, many earlier immigrants achieved success operating small businesses within Cuban communities.

Of all Spanish-speaking subgroups, Cubans are older, better educated, more likely to live in metropolitan areas but not the central city, and to have the highest median income. Much of their success, however, can be attributed to the educational and occupational characteristics with which the first wave entered America; theirs was a middle-class emigration in contrast to the Cuban newcomers of 1980 who are, on the average, younger, less educated, and relatively less skilled. The recent Cuban immigrants have also been received with greater hostility and fear and are likely to experience barriers to mobility within the established Cuban communities as well as outside.

Religious Minorities

We have dwelt at some length upon racial and ethnic minorities, and how ethnicity and race limit an individual's opportunity to achieve power, property, and prestige. Religion, too, has been a variable affecting self-identification as well as access to the good life in the modern society.

Religion is another characteristic affecting self-identification and access to power, prestige, and property.

PROTESTANTS
Both the United States and Canada are predominantly Protestant nations, numerically and ideologically. Although the framers of the Constitution explic-

Numerically and ideo-
logically, both Canada
and the U.S. are pre-
dominantly **Protestant**
nations.

itly declined the establishment of a state religion, being Protestant was an accepted precondition for economic and political leadership until very recently.

Because Protestantism has many forms, and embraces Episcopalian Wall Street brokers as well as African Methodist black sharecroppers, it is difficult to make general statements about social class. The various denominations can be roughly ranked in terms of the wealth of members, their levels of education, and occupational attainment. In this hierarchy, white Episcopalians are usually at the apex. Presbyterians, Congregationalists, and Lutherans are next followed by Methodist and Baptist congregations. In other words, the hierarchy of prestige within American Protestantism is from the most formal to the most spontaneous congregations, from whitest to darkest members, and from high socioeconomic status to low. Table 10-9 summarizes the differences in family income and occupational prestige for different socioreligious groups, including Protestant denominations, various Catholic ethnic groups, and Jews in the United States.

There are also regional variations: In the Philadelphia area, many of the most prestigious and wealthy families are Quaker; in Boston, many are Congregationalists or Christian Scientists; in Virginia, most are Episcopalian; in Texas, they are likely to be Methodist or Baptist.

Table 10-9. Religion, Mean Family Income, and Occupational Prestige in the United States among White Families, 1972–6

Socioreligious group	Mean income	Occupational prestige*
Protestants, All	*$10,120*	*45.9*
Episcopalians	14,100	48.4
Presbyterians	13,200	49.0
Congregationalists	12,045	47.3
Methodists	10,085	46.2
Lutherans	10,400	45.1
Baptists	9,245	45.8
Sectarians	8,080	45.7
Other Protestants	9,385	42.6
Catholics, All	*$10,820*	*43.8*
Irish	11,940	44.7
German	11,695	43.5
English and Welsh	12,900	49.7
French	10,120	45.6
Slavic	10,855	43.8
Polish	10,750	41.6
Italian	11,275	42.9
Spanish-Speaking	7,860	43.6
Other Catholics	10,610	43.6
Jews	*$14,350*	*50.0*

* The higher the rank, the higher the occupational prestige.
Source: Adapted from Wade Clark Roof, "Socioeconomic Differentials among White Socio-Religious Groups in the United States", *Social Forces*, 58, 1, 1979, Tables 2 and 3, 186–87.

CATHOLICS

Although Catholics enjoyed high prestige in such colonies as Maryland (whose founder was Roman Catholic), they were long regarded with suspicion by the dominant Protestant majority. As do the Protestant denominations, Catholicism embraces both the rich and the poor. The spectrum from the wealth of the Kennedys to the most recently arrived Mexican family is broad. There is a stratification hierarchy within American Catholicism that reflects the time of immigration, which also correlates with racial and ethnic factors. The internal status system is headed by the Irish and other Northern Europeans, followed by Southern and Eastern Europeans, with Hispanic groups at the base.

At one time, because of the different social class positions of the ethnic groups, it was a source of great agony to both families if an Irish Catholic sought to marry an Italian Catholic. As anti-Catholic sentiment has waned in the society as a whole, so also have many internal divisions within Catholicism.

The proportion of Catholics in the United States has risen dramatically over this century, from about 10 per cent of the total population in 1900 to about 25 per cent today. Most of the increase up to 1925 came through heavy immigration from southern and eastern Europe; after 1925, the growth of the Catholic population can be accounted for by their higher birth rates relative to non-Catholics. Since 1970, however, with the important exception of low-income Hispanics, the fertility of Catholic women has declined greatly. Today, the contraceptive behavior of Catholics is quite similar to that of the population as a whole. This change parallels other convergences between Catholics and non-Catholics in education, occupation, and income (Greeley, 1977).

To what extent does Catholicism remain a factor in social-class placement today? Probably very little. Remaining discrimination is more related to race and ethnicity than to religious preference. It had once been thought that the emphasis on community engendered by the parish church would impede the expression of individualistic achievement motivation among Catholics. And for some decades, the closeness of the religious/ethnic group, in conjunction with discrimination against Catholics, kept many young people from moving upward in the stratification system. These barriers now appear to be fully breached. Catholics are well represented today in politics, business, and higher education.

At the same time, the church provides a basis for identity and the development of primary group relationships. Despite considerable intermarriage, the majority of Catholics still marry within their faith, and large numbers continue to send their children to parochial schools.

JEWS

Jews have been in America since 1654. So long as their numbers remained few, they stirred little of the violent hostility that later emerged in the United States. Jewish immigration has had at least four distinct stages. The Spanish/Portuguese families that arrived in the 1600s were followed by a slow trickle of other escapees from religious persecution in Western Europe. In 1790 there were about 2,500 Jews in the United States, and 10,000 by 1830. Between 1830 and 1880, several hundred thousand Jews arrived from Germany, France and England.

Up to 1880, most Jews immigrating to North America were relatively educa-

*For a long time **Catholics** were regarded with suspicion by the majority WASP society.*

__Jews'__ immigration to the U.S. was linked to religious persecution in various parts of Europe.

ted, culturally sophisticated, and often skilled in finance. Aside from their religious customs, most were indistinguishable from other Americans. Many achieved great success in banking, retail trade, and clothing manufacturing. Large numbers joined the westward movement, establishing Jewish communities across the continent.

Between 1880 and 1920, however, an entirely different wave of immigrants arrived: peasant and village people from Eastern Europe, driven by the fear of massacre (Poles and Russians had initiated *pogroms* or "holy wars" against Jews). Two and one-half million fled to America before the immigration laws were changed in 1924. Compared to their Spanish and German predecessors, the newest Jewish immigrants were relatively uneducated, unskilled, and unsophisticated.

The fourth wave, between 1936 and 1946, consisted first of refugees from Nazi Germany and other European dictatorships. Only 150,000 were permitted to enter. These were generally high-ranking professional people who quickly fit into the American pattern. Then, in 1945–46, 100,000 destitute survivors of the European death camps were allowed to settle in the United States. In all, Jews compose 3 per cent of the United States population and a smaller percentage of all Canadians.

Among Jews, as with so many other minority groups, an internal stratification system exists, based on time of entry, correlated with ethnic origin and social class background: the Spanish are at the top, then Germans, then Eastern Europeans. In general, Jews have enjoyed success in the educational and economic spheres in Canada and the United States. They are disproportionately represented among college graduates, high-income earners, and professionals. (See Table 10-9).

There is, however, a sense in which success may erode the Jewish community. Historically, when faced with prejudice and discrimination, Jews were able to turn to one another in the close and closed communities that characterized Jewish life in Europe and North America. But upward mobility has dispersed the extended kinship group, uprooted individuals from the community, and encouraged individualistic achievement motivations. Intermarriage rates are high (perhaps 40 per cent) and the Jewish fertility rate is the lowest of any ethnic/religious group in the United States.

Emerging Themes in Group Relations

In this brief overview of racial, ethnic, and religious minority groups in North America, several themes emerge. Minorities meet resistance to achieving high status in the stratification system. They are subject to various degrees of prejudice and discrimination. There is a tendency to create status hierarchies even within the minority community, with different degrees of success in transferring these positions to the general stratification system. Members often rely on the support of the minority community. Their ethnic roots are important in conferring identity on minority members in our modern industrial society. Between the first and third generations of immigrants, great changes have occurred in all minority groups in the direction of approximating the patterns of dominant group norms and behaviors. Slowly, the effects of religious and ethnic distinctions have been minimized, but these are more superficial differences than are those of race or sex.

WHEN MINORITY GROUPS CLASH

If minority groups have similar histories of discrimination and low status in the United States, why do not the most disadvantaged join forces to challenge the control of dominant groups? One of the rallying cries of the 1960s was the need for a "coalition of the oppressed": women, blacks, Hispanics, homosexuals, and idealistic young whites. By the 1970s, these elements of a coalition had failed to stick together. Today, not only has each group tended to go its own way, but has often found itself in conflict with one or more of the other groups.

A short accounting should suffice: the women's movement has had some difficulty enlisting minority women to its cause, whereas gay women claim that their needs are being downplayed. American Jews, once the prime source of financial and organizational assistance to the black civil rights movement, have been deeply affronted by black support for the Palestinians. Blacks, on the other hand, found that Jewish goodwill often stopped short of pushing for their entry into graduate schools of law and medicine where Jewish young people might have to give up places to aspiring blacks. Competing claims for control of poverty programs have kept poor blacks and Hispanics from pooling their meager resources. Members of both groups must vie with one another for the diminishing number of unskilled jobs in the inner cities. The 1980 riot in Miami, Florida, although sparked by the acquittal of four white policemen in the death of a black businessman, was fueled by heightened resentment among blacks over the assistance being given to the Cuban refugees, many of whom would take jobs away from blacks.

When the economy is not growing, support is withdrawn from anti-poverty programs. Status fears are heightened, especially among those whose jobs are most threatened. It seems safe today to predict many more instances of clashes, verbal and physical, among minority groups. In a *zero-sum* situation, where one group's gain must be at the expense of another, each will be concerned only with its own goals. (Thurow, 1980) The ultimate effect, however, is that none will be strong enough alone to influence the dominant elites, and the possibility of major change in the structure of stratification is lost.

Summary

The chapter has focused on the experiences of racial, ethnic, and religious minority groups in the United States and Canada. Race, religion, and ethnicity are ascribed characteristics that influence the placement of groups and individuals in the stratification system of every society, though societies vary with respect to their cultural homogeneity or heterogeneity.

The experiences of minority groups are controlled by the dominant groups of the population. Minority-group status is defined in terms of four major elements: (1) distinctive traits identifying the minority group members; (2) differential treatment, stemming from that identity; (3) the organization of self-image based on this identity; and (4) awareness of shared identity with similar others.

The roots of racism in the United States and Canada date back to the treatment of the indigenous Native American population. By defining the culture of the white settlers as superior to those of other races, the land and resources of Native Americans were seized and their many tribal cultures systematically destroyed.

Non-Indian migration to North America dates back to the sixteenth century. Up to the 1850s most immigrants came from Northern Europe, but by the 1880s the majority were from Southern and Eastern Europe. Each new wave of immigrants had to deal with antiforeigner sentiments—fear, scorn, and discrimination. Despite the view that the United States is the land of immigrants, Canada has a larger proportion of foreign-born. The largest ethnic/religious minority in Canada is of French origin, comprising more than one-quarter of the total population of Canada.

How can diverse groups be welded together to form a nation? The melting pot model developed from the belief that immigrants could and should, through the influence of a common education and the mass media, lose their uniqueness and come to share a common language and culture and thereby benefit equally from opportunities for success. A second model—that of cultural pluralism—developed from the view that the United States was a nation of nations in which the unique contributions of various immigrant groups to the diversity and vitality of North American culture would be recognized. In actuality, minority groups are linked to the larger society along a continuum ranging from near isolation to a near-total blending into the dominant culture. Segregation, accommodation, acculturation, assimilation, or amalgamation are the major processes of minority/majority adaptation.

Barriers to integration reflect both (1) institutional patterns of discrimination built into the structure of norms and behavior, and which are reinforced by agents of social control, and (2) individual attitudes (prejudice) and behaviors (discrimination). Prejudice and discrimination have a strongly negative effect not only on people's lives, health, employment opportunities, housing, and income, but also on their self-images.

The historical experiences of blacks and Chinese imported to perform low-skill labor necessary for the development of the country are filled with systematic discrimination, hatred, and physical violence.

American blacks have made significant historical gains in political power, economic status, and prestige, especially since 1965, but there continue to be dramatic differences between the conditions of blacks and whites, indicating a caste model of racial inequality in the United States. Today, in fact, trends toward increased political and economic roles for blacks have stalled and even reversed as the nation's economic growth has slowed.

The Chinese, who came to work on the transcontinental railroads, were also victims of discrimination and mob violence. They adapted to the restrictive conditions of segregated urban ghettos by developing cohesive mutual-aid associations which were important in their upward mobility once isolation was ended.

The Japanese also came to North America to provide needed labor, and faced similar restrictive policies. During World War II over 100,000 were sent to detention camps. Japanese-Americans and Japanese-Canadians today rank high in terms of educational achievement and income while their occupational achievements have been concentrated in ethnic businesses rather than mainstream firms and corporations.

Currently, the fastest growing ethnic minority in the United States are Hispanic Americans—a large number of distinct cultural and ethnic groups sharing a common language, Spanish. Mexican-Americans (Chicanos), Puerto Ricans, and Cubans comprise the three major ethnic subdivisions.

Religion is another social category affecting self-image and access to power, prestige, and property. Although both Canada and the United States are predominantly Protestant nations, numerically and ideologically, the variation in wealth, education, occupation, and prestige within Protestantism is dramatic. Similar variation exists among Catholics and Jews reflecting the time of immigration, ethnic origin, and social class background.

Though religious and ethnic distinctions have become less important over time, institutional discrimination and personal prejudice continue to reinforce *racial* distinctions that perpetuate social inequality in America.

Suggested Readings

BALTZELL, E. DIGBY. *The Protestant Establishment*. New York: Random House, 1964. The classic study of the history, power, and lifestyles of the white Anglo-Saxon Protestant elite in the United States.

ISHWARAN, K. (Ed.). *Canadian Families: Ethnic Variations*. Toronto: McGraw-Hill Ryerson, Ltd., 1980. This anthology contains essays on the ethnic, cultural, and religious variations in family life among Canadian Indians, Greek, Polish, Japanese, Italian, French, Chinese, Dutch, and other minorities.

LADNER, JOYCE. *Tomorrow's Tomorrow: The Black Woman*. Garden City, N.Y.: Doubleday, 1972. A sensitive account of the experiences of black adolescents struggling against racism, discrimination, and poverty in an urban ghetto.

MOORE, JOAN. *Mexican Americans*. Englewood Cliffs, N.J.: Prentice-Hall, 1976, 2nd Edition. A recent and extensive *sociological* overview of the economic, political, religious, and familial experiences of Mexican Americans.

PARRILLO, VINCENT. *Strangers to the Shores: Race and Ethnic Relations in the United States*. Boston: Houghton, 1980. A comprehensive account of the experiences of the major immigrant populations in the U.S. including the older and newer European groups, Native Americans, Asian Immigrants, blacks, Hispanics, and other groups comprising the American mosaic.

PINKNEY, ALPHONSE. *Black Americans*. Englewood Cliffs, N.J.: Prentice-Hall, 1975, 2nd Edition. This thorough examination of the historical and contemporary experiences of black Americans, the black community, socioeconomic status, social institutions, deviance, assimilation, the black revolt and black nationalism should effectively destroy many stereotypes.

Woodward, C. Vann. *The Strange Career of Jim Crow.* New York: Oxford Press, 1957. Twenty-five years later, and still a first-rate history of racism in politics and the legal system in the United States.

(Source: *Woodfin Camp.*)

Part IV

Institutional Spheres

The next five chapters describe the major institutional spheres of social life: family, economic, political, educational, and belief systems. Over the course of human history, these areas of activity have become increasingly removed from their traditional source of control, the kinship group. In modern societies, economic, political, educational, and religious activities take place in specialized settings where individuals have statuses independent of family ties. The family itself has become specialized to a limited set of functions.

This process of institutional specialization and separation from kinship is called *structural differentiation,* as each sphere becomes a complex subsystem of the larger society. Thus, today, in North America, individuals parcel out their time and energies among these differentiated systems: going out of the home to work in an office or factory, attending school, electing lawmakers, worshiping with co-religionists, and engaging in family relationships to raise children and/or find emotional support.

In this set of chapters we will follow the historical development of institutional spheres and describe their structures in contemporary North America.

11

Marriage and Family Life

*I*t is not easy to speak objectively about the family or even to define it. It is the one institutional sphere with which every person is intimately familiar: it is our earliest environment, our refuge from the world, and a primary source of meaning and continuity. Emotions and values overlay our perceptions of family life.

Nonetheless, the family is similar to the other institutional spheres of any society; it is a set of norms and behaviors clustered around some essential activity. The family is a social product, devised by humans to ensure orderly reproduction and to meet intimacy and care needs. Family rules and roles vary from one culture to another and undergo change over time. Family life is neither divinely ordained nor instinctual. While built on certain biological and behavioral continuities with other primates, the human family is a social system based upon learned behavior.

Origins of the Family

As Kathleen Gough (1971) points out, "all primates share characteristics without which the family could not have developed. The young are born relatively helpless . . . and need prolonged care afterwards. Year-round sexuality means that males and females socialize more continuously among primates than among most other mammals . . . (And) a "division of labor" based on gender is already found in primate societies between a female role of prolonged child care and a male role of defense" (p. 761–2).

Yet without other characteristics not found in primates, humans could not construct family patterns much different from the loose ties that sometimes link chimpanzees. Gough lists such qualities as language, foresight, self-control, the ability to plan cooperatively, and adaptability through learning as the essential basis for emotionally close and enduring relationships between a given female and male. From the evidence of the Tasaday and other very simple societies we can also conclude that women and men originally shared many economic and family functions, and that power relationships were more egalitarian than in more complex societies.

Gough (1971; 770) concludes as follows:

> Together with tool use and language, the family was no doubt the most significant invention of the human revolution. All three required reflective thought, which above all accounts for the vast superiority in consciousness that separates humans from apes. In groping for survival and for knowledge, human beings learned to control their sexual desires and to suppress their individual selfishness, aggression and competition . . .
>
> The family was essential to the dawn of civilization, allowing a vast quantitative leap forward in cooperation, purposive knowledge, love and creativeness."

INCEST TABOOS AND THE DEVELOPMENT OF FAMILY

This description of the origins of the family emphasizes the crucial importance of the reflective mind that interprets signals from the body and selects appropriate responses. This means that human beings are able to control impulses, including sexual desires and jealousies. Such controls are internalized through a set of rules—formed through consensus among communicating individuals—regarding who can have sexual intercourse with whom. These rules are called *incest taboos*. Found in every human society, they specify precisely which members of the group can mate with others, typically forbidding sexual relations between parents and their offspring, and between brothers and sisters. Just who else is included varies widely. While there is evidence that some similar restraints are found in primate bands, incest taboos in human societies are often elaborate and arbitrary, varying from one group to another, and enforced by the weight of public opinion and internalized guilt.

Incest taboos are important for reasons other than the control of sexuality within a group. Lévi-Strauss (1969) considers incest taboos to be the foundation of group survival. By forbidding sexual relations within a given unit, the taboos force sons and daughters to marry *outside* their immediate family. In this fashion, alliances are made between one family and another; ties of kinship and obligation bring potential enemies together, the number of cooperative families in a society increases, and the group as a whole is strengthened. It is assumed that those bands of early hominids who invented effective incest rules were able to survive, both through the reduction of jealousy and the building of alliances. A third survival factor, unknown to early humans (in fact, unknown to most people until the work of Gregor Mendel a hundred years ago), lies in the genetic advantages of bringing new blood into a breeding group. Intermarriage increases the probability of genetic accidents while marrying out reduces the likelihood of mental and physical birth defects. The unintended consequences of incest taboos have been as powerful as the intended effects.

EXCHANGE FACTORS

Lévi-Strauss and others also suggest that the exchange of brides and grooms is the quintessential *social* relationship, serving as an example of all exchanges that bind together individuals and families in enduring social systems. If the leading males in various families, the reasoning goes, agree to relinquish sexual rights over their sisters and daughters, all other types of exchange follow. Underlying social action is the concept of *reciprocity*—that a privilege renounced or a gift given at one point in time obligates the recipient to return something of equivalent value at some future date.

THE PRINCIPLE OF LEGITIMACY

A third basis for marriage and family is described by Malinowski (1930) as "the principle of legitimacy," by which he meant that the function of marriage is to identify one man as responsible for the protection of a woman and her children, and for their placement in the social system. That is, since kinship is the fundamental organization of simple societies and since ascription is the primary means of allocating statuses, the role of the father in defining the social position of children becomes paramount. Note that the father need not be the

Incest taboos forbid sexual relations between specified family members.

The exchange of brides and grooms is a **social relationship,** binding together individuals and families.

The **principle of legitimacy** identifies one man as responsible for the protection of a woman and her children and for the children's placement in the social system.

biological parent. What is important is that there is a *social father,* an individual who assumes responsibility by virtue of a marriage ceremony.

Kinship in Cross-Cultural Perspective

Throughout this volume we have stressed the importance of family-based (kinship) relationships for the social structure of simple societies. Yet kinship systems vary from one society to another as well as through time. In general, there are five characteristics used to describe kinship systems: the number of spouses permitted at one time; who can marry whom; how descent and transmission of property are determined; where a couple lives; and the power relations within the family. The many differences between traditional and modern patterns is shown in Table 11-1.

CULTURAL UNIVERSALS AND VARIATIONS

The resolution of these five questions compose the family structure of a society. Elaborated over time, along with other rules governing courtship, child-

Table 11-1. Kinship in Cross-Cultural Perspective

	Traditional societies	*Modern societies*
How many spouses at one time?	One (monogamy) or Plural (polygamy): polygyny—many wives polyandry—many husbands	One (monogamy)
Who can marry whom?	Choices made by parents to enhance family power	Relatively free choice
Line of Descent	From males (patrilineal) From females (matrilineal)	Both equally (bilateral kinship)
Where couple lives	With groom's family (patrilocal) With wife's family (matrilocal)	Place of one's own (neolocal)
Power relationships	Various degrees of male dominance (patriarchy)	Greater equality (egalitarian)
Functions of Family	All embracing To protect the kinship group	Specialized To provide stable environment for child-rearing and emotional support
Structure	Extended	Nuclear
Focus of obligation	Blood relationships (consanquine)	Marriage tie and children (conjugal)

Ceremonies surrounding a marriage are universal. (Source: This page—Katrina Thomas, Photo Researchers, Inc.; Opposite page, top left— Elizabeth Hamlin, Stock, Boston; top right—Owen Frankin, Stock, Boston; bottom—Constantine Manus, Magnum.)

Marriage in pre-industrial societies protects and enhances the interests of descent groups.

rearing, divorce, and widowhood, these family systems present a fascinating panorama of human variability and adaptability. The precise way in which any society pairs off its young and organizes the relationships between parents and children varies greatly. Indeed, so varied are the courtship and marriage practices of different societies that it is impossible to provide any single explanation for the differences—neither region, land use, political systems, nor population factors can systematically account for these variations. Above all, the function of marriage in preindustrial society is the protection and enhancement of the interests of descent groups.

Ceremonies surrounding a marriage are also universal because the society as a whole has a stake in orderly reproduction. The rituals of the marriage ceremony symbolize the uniting of separate kinship groups through the exchange of gifts; the public nature of the marriage signifies the couple's responsibilities to

their society. For most people throughout human history, marriage has been less a personal than a familial and societal affair. Many of you will have had grandparents whose marriage was arranged by family elders, so common was this custom even in the twentieth century, and it remains today the preferred pattern in some of the world's societies.

While each society has developed and elaborated its unique solutions to the problem of orderly reproduction, there have also been master trends of change in family systems across time.

THE FAMILY IN CROSS-TEMPORAL CONTEXT

In modern societies, as other institutional spheres are differentiated from kinship groups in the course of sociocultural development, the form and functions of the family also change.

Extended Family Systems. Throughout human history and throughout most of the world today, the needs and interests of large family groups outweigh the needs or interests of specific individuals. The kinship or descent group is often referred to as an *extended family;* that is, a relatively large unit composed of a number of related households, either a father and his sons and their families, or the mother, her brother, her daughters and their families. Another type of extended family is that composed of a man or woman with plural marriage partners in societies where polygamy is practiced.

The **extended family** refers to a family group comprised of several related households.

The advantages of extended families are many: shared wealth and power, protection, and a supply of potential grooms and brides for alliances with other families. Horticulture and agriculture, remember, are based upon human labor and the ownership of land, so that over the many thousands of years that farming has been the major mode of adaptation to the environment, the extended family has been a central mechanism of survival. Before the rise of the modern nation state with public provision for the care of the young and old, guarantees of property rights, and education of youth, these tasks fell to the kinship group. In the absence of centralized governments for the maintenance of public order, each extended family guarded its own land and protected its members.

Nuclear Families. Each extended family is composed of nuclear units of a married pair and their minor children living together. This *nuclear family* will be more or less closely linked to other nuclear families in the kinship group in any society. In other words, the major distinction is not nuclear *versus* extended, but the degree to which nuclear units in the same kinship line share residence, resources, work, and responsibilities for blood relatives.

The **nuclear family** consists of a married pair and their children.

In general, extended family systems are typical of nonindustrial societies and the rural sectors of modern societies. In this sense, extended family systems are traditional while the nuclear family as an *independent* unit is considered modern. In fact, nuclear units are also characteristic of many simple societies, and were probably quite common in preindustrial Europe, contrary to popular belief.

Extended and nuclear family systems are *ideal types,* and in most societies elements of both patterns are present. In the modern context, nuclear family units, while maintaining separate residences, engage in extensive exchanges and mutually supportive relationships with other kin. Some social scientists (Sussman, 1959) use the term *modified extended family* to describe the modern type although *modified nuclear* seems to be more accurate in view of the high degree of independence of nuclear units.

There is another, more crucial distinction, however, between a modern and traditional family network: the primary focus of concern and affection. In the traditional extended family system, the blood line or kinship group is the source of rights and duties and the object of sentiment. What makes a family modern is not so much its structural isolation from other kin as its shift of focus inward to the married couple and their children. In more technical terms, relationships of blood (*consanguine*) are less central than the artificial bonds of marriage (*conjugal*). For example, if you were to receive two messages simultaneously, one reporting the grave illness of a parent and the other an accident to your spouse, to whose bedside would you go? In most traditional societies there would be no question that the duties to a parent, especially the father, super-seded all others.

Industrial development provides an encouraging environment for the development of relatively isolated, small family units. Workers and their families are able to pick up and move in response to labor force demands. A single family can also take advantage of the opportunities for upward mobility presented by achievement norms. Conversely, the protection against downward mobility offered by the pooled resources of an extended family are forfeited.

In anthropological terms the North American family is monogamous (one spouse at a time), based on relatively unrestricted choice of marriage partner, with descent and the transmission of property through both the mother's and father's blood line. The newlyweds establish their own household apart from other kin, and they increasingly share decision-making power within the marriage.

The Modern Family

The difference between traditional and modern family forms has been described as a progressive loss of function for the extended kin group. The nuclear family in a modern society is much less powerful or versatile than was the traditional extended family. In every institutional sphere, tasks once assumed by extended kin are now performed by outside agencies. In the *economic* sphere, as a rule, the family is no longer self-sufficient but dependent on wages earned by one or more adults who leave the home to work elsewhere. The Industrial Revolution dramatically changed the relationship between home and workplace (the two are now usually physically separate) and, consequently, the relationships among family members. Women and children lost their economic value and became dependent upon the earnings of the husband. The modern family is now primarily a *consuming* unit, highly dependent on the economic system beyond the home, over which they have little control.

> The family is no longer a self-sufficient **economic unit,** but dependent on wages earned outside the home.

In the *political* sphere, the rise of the modern centralized state reduces the need for protection once provided by extended kin. Armies, police forces, and courts replace the armed group of kinfolk. *Educationally* the public school system has been created to prepare individuals for the needs of an industrial economy. Few parents today could teach their children all of the specialized skills required for competence in a modern society. This task is turned over to presumed experts. So also are *religious* needs increasingly met by specialists in public places removed from the family setting.

As the extended family becomes less and less important as a source of goods and services, the young are freed from control by elders. At the same time, the challenges of modern life create a need for affection and emotional support that cannot be easily met by family members with whom one has relationships of unequal power or of sibling rivalry. Increasingly, then, individuals look to their marriage partners and their own children for such psychic rewards. The modern, conjugal family is specialized for emotional support and for the early so-

> With the decline of the extended family, the young are freed from control by elders.

cialization of offspring, that is, for gratification of expressive needs rather than the instrumental functions once provided by extended families.

Expressive needs are best met by a few affectionally-close individuals. Hence the importance of mate selection, not for the kinship-based needs of the past but for emotional compatibility. The *romantic love syndrome* (Goode, 1959) emerges as the new rationale for choice of a husband or wife. While love has always been a possibility in traditional marriages, rarely was it the sole reason for choosing a marriage partner. In the modern marriage, by contrast, love is the primary—indeed the only legitimated—basis for mate selection.

MATE SELECTION IN MODERN SOCIETIES

Compared with arranged marriages, it is fair to describe the contemporary North American model as one of free mate choice. At the same time, strong socialization pressures limit the type of person perceived as appropriate marriage material. Young men and women are not encouraged to choose across racial, religious, ethnic, or social-class lines. In many cases, the parents will have moved to a particular neighborhood precisely to channel the friendship contacts of their offspring.

Thus, while theoretically you could choose any one of the worlds' hundreds of million members of the opposite sex, you are confined to those you will actually meet. Furthermore, the expectations of parents and peers will affect who you choose to bring home for dinner. The general pattern has been for young people to select others who are very much like themselves in terms of social background.

Homogamy (*homo* = "like"; *gamy* = "marriage") is the technical term for the tendency of individuals to select a bride or groom from the same religion, race, ethnic group, and social-class stratum. People who are like oneself are easier to be with in many ways—values and attitudes are apt to be shared as a result of being products of a similar socialization experience. People who agree with us—who think and talk and have the same norms as we do—are very rewarding to be with; they verify our sense of rightness.

There are, then, a number of reasons why people tend to marry those quite like themselves, and data on divorce and happiness in marriage indicate a slight advantage to homogamous choices. *Heterogamy* (*hetero* = "different"), however, has its benefits—in vitality and the opportunity to learn other views and to discover new ways of perceiving. These challenges are often outweighed by the difficulties in communication and the probability of more areas of disagreement and potential conflict. Cross-racial marriages are especially vulnerable, but so also are marriages across religious lines or those that encompass wide differences in age or social class.

THE MARRIAGE MARKET

When marriages are not arranged by elders, individuals must make the best bargains they can. The choice of the word bargain was intentional because the mate-selection process in contemporary North America has many features of a marketplace, in which each potential partner must advertise her or his virtues just as any merchant does to attract buyers. The goal is to secure the most pleasing partner, as defined by personal taste, cultural ideals, and the expectations of parents and peers.

The **romantic love syndrome** focuses on love as the sole reason for choosing a mate.

Homogamy is the selection of a mate from the same religion, race, ethnic group, and social class.

Heterogamy refers to the crossing of religious, racial, ethnic, and social class lines in the choice of a mate.

The mate selection process in North America resembles a marketplace in which people make the best bargains they can.

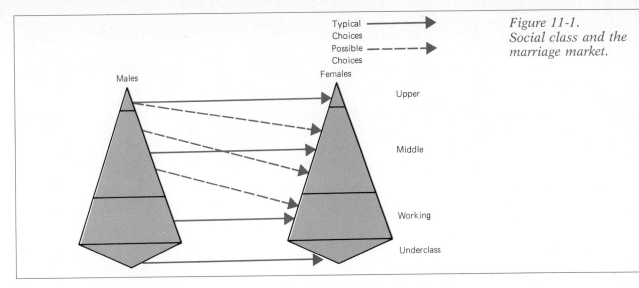

Figure 11-1.
Social class and the
marriage market.

Each individual has a value in this market through the possession of qualities desired by others. In most cases, a female's beauty and youth are the traits most valued by possible partners. In contrast, occupational goals and potentials are sought in males. Note that a female's value on the marriage market tends to decline with age, while a male's is likely to increase over time.

Social class is also an important variable. Although most people marry within the same stratum, men can marry down since their accomplishments usually place the couple in the status system. A female is urged to marry at the same or at a higher level than her father's. This pattern may change as women achieve occupational status in their own right and as family SES is determined by both parents' achievements.

EGALITARIANISM

The modern family is characterized by a reduction in traditional power differentials between husband and wife and between parents and children. In large part, this trend is the result of the many liberating currents in Western civilization stemming from the Enlightenment. It is difficult to maintain a commitment to freedom and equality in the general society while denying its exercise in the most intimate unit of the social system. Furthermore, affection is more likely to characterize the relationship of equals than that of persons in positions of superiority and inferiority.

Power differences between husbands and wives, as already noted, vary with the family system of a society. Historically, male dominance of females is related to the mode of subsistence—lowest in gathering bands, highest in agricultural states, and relatively low again in the late industrial era.

PARENTS AND CHILDREN

The increased freedom of youngsters is also related to two other modern trends: the influence of psychological theories of child development in this century, and the inability of contemporary parents to control fully the social placement of offspring. One long-term consequence of the work of Sigmund Freud and his followers is an intense concern with the effects of family life on infants and children. Self-conscious parents became fearful of repressing their offspring. The developing child was moved to the center of family life, and

289

"The Myth of the Vulnerable Child"

Models of child development in the twentieth century assign "an omnipotent role" to parents. It was assumed that if parents did certain things at particular moments, their children would be happy and successful; conversely, if the child was not happy or successful, the parents were at fault.

New research, however, suggests that parental influence on child development is considerably modified by both the child's own abilities to process information, organize meaning, and select behavior, and by the many other influences that impinge on the child. Moreover, there is very little scientifically derived evidence to support the thesis that "childhood stress must inevitably result in psychological damage."

The true test of the link between early experience and later mental health must be made with longitudinal data; that is, from the same individuals followed through time. In one study based on 200 cases interviewed in childhood and again at age thirty, the researchers had originally hypothesized that children from troubled homes would display problems as adults, while youngsters from homes judged to be happy would become well-adjusted adults. *Two-thirds* of these predictions were incorrect! The long term effects of both happy and unhappy homes had been greatly exaggerated.

To account for these findings, Arlene Skolnick rejects the idea that vulnerability or invulnerability to childhood experiences is an innate personality trait. Rather, the successful youngsters had *not* avoided but learned to cope with their family difficulties, often with the assistance of others (relatives, friends, the community itself).

This emphasis on coping capacities draws attention to the theory of *learned helplessness*. Individuals experience helplessness when faced with events over which they have no control or believe that they cannot control. Those who fight against helplessness learn a great deal about themselves. In fact, the absence of stress against which to measure one's capacities may be as damaging for the ego as being overpowered by events.

Since parental power can be modified by the child's abilities to deal even with unhappy experience, and by outside resources why has American psychology focused so obsessively on the mother-child relationship as if it existed in a vacuum? Skolnick notes the ideology of infinite perfectability through science that characterizes modern industrial life; given the correct techniques, the reasoning goes, parents could produce happy, adjusted offspring. Poverty is seen as the outcome rather than the cause of family difficulties. ". . . the standards of perfectability that have been applied to child-rearing and the family in this century have not only created guilt and anxiety in those who try to live up to them, but have also contributed to the neglect of (poor) children on a national scale" (p. 65).

Source: Arlene Skolnick, *Psychology Today*, February, 1978, p. 56–65.

dozens of best-selling books informed bewildered mothers about the correct way to raise children.

The child-centered family is not just a recent phenomenon. Historians of the family have traced an awareness of children's emotional needs over several centuries. As sanitation and public health improvements dramatically reduced infant death rates, a woman needed to bear only a few children since most would survive (in comparison to the eight or ten typically borne by most women throughout history and in much of the world even today). It then became possible to make emotional investments in one's offspring. So childhood emerged as a distinct phase of life, and the nurturance of infants became women's special domain.

These developments tend to enhance the importance of children within the nuclear family, no longer as potential marriage pawns but as creations in their own right. The close emotional bonds of the modern family coupled with the need for individual achievement lead to changes in relationships between the generations, from commanded respect for elders to earned affection. The mature young adult is one who can make his or her own place in society physically and psychologically independent of the parents.

FROM FAMILY OF ORIENTATION TO PROCREATION

The nuclear family is a self-destructing unit. If its task has been well-accomplished, the young are prepared to leave in order to form their own nuclear families. When the parents die, the original nuclear unit—called the *family of orientation* because it has provided guidance to its young—is dissolved, replaced by new nuclear families composed of the adult offspring and their spouses and infants—called the *family of procreation* because it is the source of the next generation.

The original nuclear family in which we are born and reared is the **family of orientation.**

The new nuclear family we start through marriage is the **family of procreation.**

Courtship and Marriage. To become fully adult, the adolescent must outgrow the dependencies of the family of orientation and be prepared to engage in close emotional relationships with members of the opposite sex. A large part of adolescence is spent in learning how to behave responsibly in sexual matters— a lesson not always easily learned in contemporary North America where so much prestige and status in the adolescent peer group depends on sexual adventurism.

Courtship socialization begins with a form of group dating among twelve- and thirteen-year-olds, where sets of boys and girls engage in a joint activity such as skating, going to movies, or just hanging out. Gradually, the numbers involved become smaller: perhaps three or four couples together, for comfort and protection; then, by late high school, double or single dating. As in simple societies, gifts are exchanged: bracelets, pins, rings. The difference is that the gifts are exchanged by the dating couple and not their families. Indeed, the families may be intentionally excluded from participation in these rituals.

Then follows a period of semi-engagement prior to the formal announcement made by the parents to the community at large. Up to this time, either young person could be released from the relationship, not without pangs but with relative ease. Once the public announcement is made, families and friends and the world in general are witness to the intention to marry; larger and more expensive gifts are exchanged. These customs reinforce the process, followed in most societies, of progressively bringing the weight of the community to bear on mate selection. Marriage is still too important to families and societies to be left entirely to the engaged individuals.

There are, of course, ethnic, religious, and social class differences in the precise ways in which courtship and marriage ceremonies are carried out within subcultures in the United States and Canada, but the great majority of first marriages in North America are similar in structure and function to those of any simple society. The marriage takes place in a religious setting, the father "gives away" his daughter, both families are well represented, and the ceremony is followed by a ritual feast for invited guests. Despite the popular belief that old-fashioned marriages are declining in importance, the data suggest otherwise. In fact, proportionately more North American young people marry today than ever before—almost 95% of both men and women will enter at least one marriage, and most will do so with a traditional wedding.

✓ The **family cycle** begins with marriage and the establishment of a nuclear household.

The Family Cycle. Having married and established a nuclear household, the great majority—again over 90%—will raise at least one child. Thus begins the life cycle of the contemporary conjugal family. In the two or three years of *aloneness together* before the arrival of an infant, both partners are typically in the labor force, saving for the future but also enjoying an active social life.

The *advent of the first child* brings profound changes to the relationship. First, the mother will most likely leave her job, reducing family income considerably. Her life revolves around the infant and its needs, often to the discomfort of the husband-father, who is now in competition for her attention.

✓ The **childbearing phase** today is completed while the parents are relatively young.

On the average, North American couples today have two children, spaced rather closely together within the first ten years of marriage. Since most parents will have married by their early twenties, this means that the *child-bearing phase* of the family cycle is completed when the parents are relatively young, in

Today, American couples are completing the child-bearing phase of family life while they are still relatively young. (Source: *Owen Frankin, Stock, Boston.*)

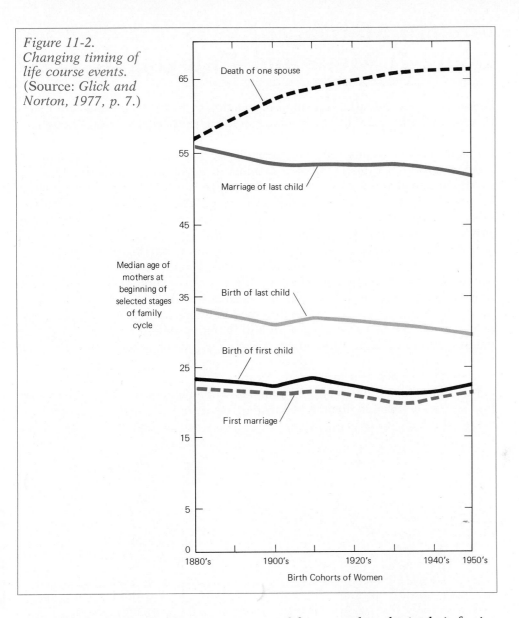

Figure 11-2.
Changing timing of
life course events.
(Source: *Glick and*
Norton, 1977, p. 7.)

Death of one spouse

Marriage of last child

Median age of
mothers at
beginning of
selected stages
of family
cycle

Birth of last child

Birth of first child

First marriage

1880's   1900's   1920's   1940's 1950's

Birth Cohorts of Women

contrast to the past when it was not unusual for a couple to be in their forties
when the last child was born.

   Child rearing today is essentially completed before the parents reach age 45.
Typically, the children will be in school full-time when their mother is 30–35,
with four more decades of life ahead.

   The *launching* or *empty-nest phase*, beginning when the last child leaves
home, has also been dramatically pushed forward. If the children are out of the
home before the parents reach age 50, and their life expectancy is now into the
eighth decade, a married couple has at least *two decades* of being alone together
again. This is a startling change, a phase of the family cycle that simply did not
exist for most couples before, when, less than a hundred years ago, it was as
likely as not that one parent would be dead before the last child left home.

The **empty nest phase**
begins when the last
child leaves home.

Modern Marriage: Doing It More and Enjoying It Less?

Despite the fact that all but a small proportion of North Americans will marry at least once and spend most of their adult life as married persons (although not necessarily with the original mate), great fears have been expressed regarding the stability of contemporary marriages. These fears are primarily based on the increasingly high rates of divorce in modern societies. (See Figure 11-3, for marriage and divorce rates in Canada and the United States.) Other factors commonly cited by survey respondents are violence in the family, women's labor force participation, and a general decline in morality (promiscuity, homo-sexuality, lack of religious values, and so forth).

Undoubtedly, there are strains in contemporary marriages that might not have existed to the same degree in earlier times. If one marries for love, chooses one's own mate, and is expected to provide emotional support in a relationship that could last for over five decades in a relatively isolated household, can there be any wonder that many couples find the task more than they can successfully accomplish? The fact that almost all adults marry should suggest that not all mates could have been well-chosen. Nonetheless, when asked about their current marriage, almost two-thirds of married persons indicate great happiness, and another 30 per cent are "pretty happy." Less than 5 per cent are "not too happy," but most of the unhappily married will have removed themselves from that condition through divorce, separation, or desertion. Then, too, people tend to define their situations as acceptable if they see no legitimate alternative.

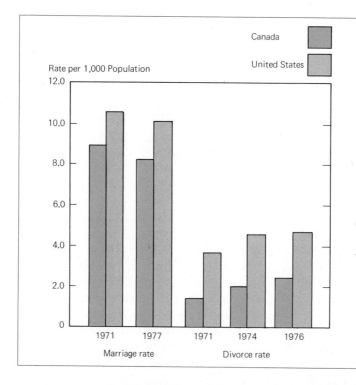

Figure 11-3. Marriage and divorce rates in Canada and the United States, 1971–77. (Source: Vital Statistics, Marriages and Divorces. *1976 and 1977.* Statistical Abstracts of the United States, 1977. U.S. Department of Commerce, Washington, D.C., *and* Perspectives Canada, *1980, III, p. 300.*)

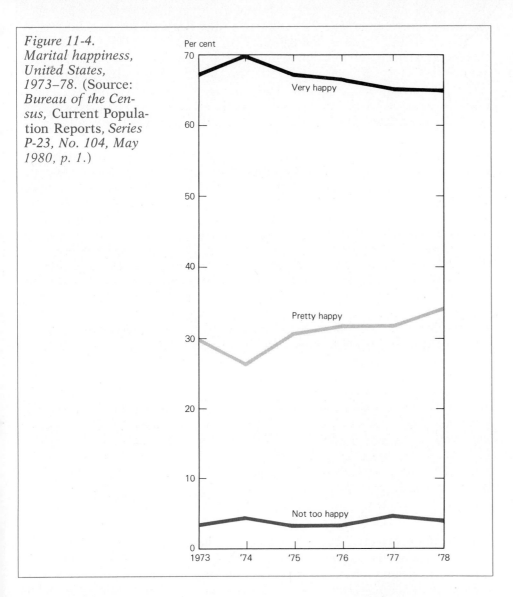

Figure 11-4. Marital happiness, United States, 1973–78. (Source: Bureau of the Census, Current Population Reports, Series P-23, No. 104, May 1980, p. 1.)

Although it is beyond the scope of an introductory chapter to cover all aspects of modern marriages, several features require further comment: the distribution of benefits in marriage, marital violence, and divorce and remarriage.

THE BENEFITS OF MARRIAGE

Functional theory would suggest that both partners benefit from the division of labor and exchange of affection that characterize modern marriages. In return for her devotion to household tasks, a wife receives social status, protection, economic security, and the opportunity to bear legitimate offspring. In return for being cared for and having children to carry on the family line, males are motivated to leave their homes each day to earn adequate incomes. Such a system also serves societal goals, providing willing workers and stable socialization environments.

Who Benefits from Marriage?

It is a common belief that males could do quite well without marriage but that a woman's life would be empty and unsatisfying without a husband. Reviewing the data on sex differences in mental health and expressed satisfaction with life, Jessie Bernard (1972) concluded that marriage actually confers greater benefits on men than on women. When compared with nonmarried men, husbands enjoy better mental health, physical health, and life satisfaction. When compared to nonmarried females, wives often display lower or equal levels of mental functioning. The happy-go-lucky bachelor and forlorn spinster of folk wisdom are products of our sex-role ideology, claims Bernard.

But Norval Glenn (1975) cites three national surveys that show married persons reporting much higher levels of happiness than do the nonmarried of either sex. If marriage is stressful for some women, it is profoundly satisfying to others. Since women who are satisfied with their marriages are more satisfied with all other aspects of their lives than are men, Glenn concludes that marriage is more beneficial to wives than to husbands.

Yet other data, reported by Gove and Tudor, (1973) found that since the mid 1940s higher rates of mental illness have been recorded for women than for men, reversing the trend before 1940, and that married women are most likely to be treated for mental illness. Gove and Tudor suggest that the isolation and lack of control over their lives experienced by nonworking married women in the suburbs, the repetitiveness of homemaking tasks, and exclusive responsibility for child care can be dangerous to one's mental health.

Other data presented by Gove (1973) compare death rates from various causes, by age, marital status, and sex, indicating that when compared with married men and women, non-married males are far more likely than are non-married females to die of a variety of causes that have some social component, such as suicide, homicide, accidents, cirrhosis, or diabetes. In fact, with respect to homicide, single women are at *less* risk than the married, largely because most murders take place within the family setting. These findings strongly suggest that marriage provides greater protection to men than to women.

From the perspective of conflict theory, however, such a basic harmony of functions cannot be assumed. Not only do family members have individual interests to defend, often at cross-purposes, but the family unit itself is not necessarily functionally suited to modern economic life. Increasingly, both husbands and wives are sharing domestic duties and responsibilities outside the home. Within the family, conflicts arising from the interaction of members as well as stresses from outside must be handled with minimal intervention from other kin or the community at large. The modern marriage can also be described as an emotional hothouse as easily as it can be called a true partnership of complementary individuals.

Under these circumstances, roles in the marriage are subject to negotiation, and the partners will bring different resources and aspects of power into their struggle to define the relationship. Control over the interaction will depend on such variables as the alternatives available to the partners, the type of support that can be expected from other people, and the financial status of partners. An idealized emphasis on the romantic/emotional elements of modern marriages has blinded many individuals to the very real struggles for power and self-definition that take place within the household. In general, it has long been assumed that women derive the greater benefits from marriage, that they have more at stake in maintaining the relationship, and, as a consequence, have less power within the relationship. Therefore, women are more likely than men to remain in destructive relationships, and to defer major decisions to their husbands.

These ideas have sparked a lively debate among sociologists of the family. Although it is generally agreed that men derive great power within the marriage from their economic roles outside the family, women are not necessarily powerless, especially those who also earn wages. Nor, as seen in "Who Benefits from Marriage" on page 296, is it clear that women derive the greatest benefits from marriage.

FAMILY VIOLENCE

The emotional closeness of modern family life has a darker side. People who are psychologically and emotionally dependent upon one another are also very vulnerable. Who can hurt you more deeply than the one who claims to love you? It is estimated that between 10–20% of American homes are arenas of interpersonal violence (Straus, Gelles, and Steinmetz, 1978). Although there are no comparable data that would permit comparisons between the level of family violence today and that of earlier times, it is quite likely that the home has always been a rather dangerous place, and it is safe to conclude that there will never be a time when family life is without risk. Throughout most of history, moreover, wives and children have been legally considered the possessions of the husband/father, without protection from the community except in extreme circumstances. Physical punishment of women and children as a means of discipline had widespread public support in North America. Only recently has the

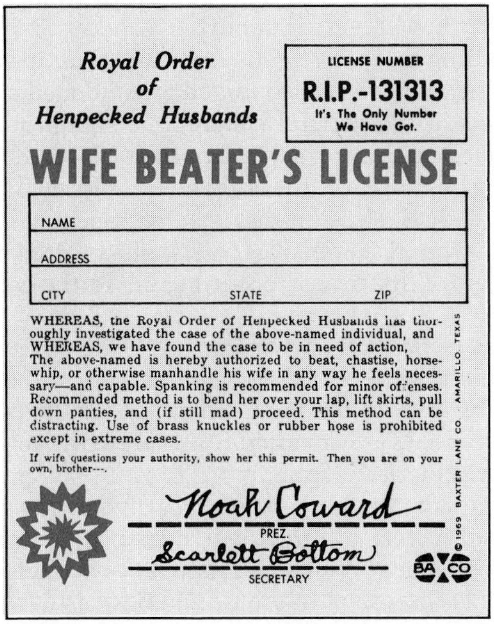

Family violence is the problematic side of the emotional closeness of modern family life.

Figure 11-5.
This "license" was the "funny favor" dispensed in a gum machine. It expresses cultural support for retaliating against the wife who henpecks.

Royal Order
of
Henpecked Husbands

LICENSE NUMBER
R.I.P.-131313
It's The Only Number
We Have Got.

WIFE BEATER'S LICENSE

NAME

ADDRESS

CITY   STATE   ZIP

WHEREAS, the Royal Order of Henpecked Husbands has thoroughly investigated the case of the above-named individual, and WHEREAS, we have found the case to be in need of action, The above-named is hereby authorized to beat, chastise, horsewhip, or otherwise manhandle his wife in any way he feels necessary—and capable. Spanking is recommended for minor offenses. Recommended method is to bend her over your lap, lift skirts, pull down panties, and (if still mad) proceed. This method can be distracting. Use of brass knuckles or rubber hose is prohibited except in extreme cases.

If wife questions your authority, show her this permit. Then you are on your own, brother---.

Noah Coward
PREZ.
Scarlett Bottom
SECRETARY

© 1969 BAXTER LANE CO · AMARILLO · TEXAS

BA▼CO

issue of domestic violence been brought into public debate. Beginning with concern over the abuse of children, attention spread to the phenomenon of battered wives, to husbands who are victims of violence, and, most recently, elderly members of the household subjected to abusive behavior.

In the case of child maltreatment, the abuser is typically the mother, often young, unknowledgeable, isolated, relatively poor, and without emotional or physical support from her husband or others. Unaware of how an infant develops, frightened by responsibility, under stress of poverty, and fearful of her husband, she expects the infant to behave in ways that the child simply cannot. The fact that premature infants and those with brain damage or physical problems are disproportionately represented among the abused strongly supports the thesis that unrealistic expectation leads to parental frustration. These infants are not only slow to develop but also do not easily produce the positive reinforcements—smiles, laughs, calm contentedness—that reward the parents' efforts (Lamb, 1978).

Yet domestic violence is most intensely directed at adult women. Some wives fight back, but most do not. Socialization to the female role is in large part learning to submit, to give, and to ask for little for oneself. Thus, many women believe that they must somehow be at fault if their husband is angry, that they deserve abusive treatment, and that it is they who have failed to maintain the marriage.

Violence manifested in the family often reflects the level of aggression in the larger society.

Roots of Violence.   Most researchers agree that violence in the family reflects tolerance of aggression in the society as a whole. Boys are taught to fight for their honor. Our most popular sports are periodically enlivened by players and fans attacking one another. Labor disputes often are marked by violence. International tensions are responded to with shows of strength. Rage breaks out in the inner cities. Millions of dollars are spent by American males on pornography that often features violence against women. White mothers scream at black children desegregating suburban schools. Police officers are in greater danger responding to domestic dispute calls than in pursuing thieves (Pinkney, 1972).

When violence is encouraged or condoned as a legitimate means of resolving conflicts in the societal sphere, one should not wonder that it appears in the interpersonal realm. Once applied, violence becomes an accepted means of dealing with others. The child who is physically punished learns that big people hit little ones, a lesson that may be repeated later on. If there is one consistent finding from research, it is this: violence does not serve to reduce tension or the probability that it will occur again. To the contrary, violence breeds violence.

DIVORCE AND REMARRIAGE

The number of marriages ending in divorce has increased steadily over the past several decades in both Canada and the United States.

In both Canada and the United States, the proportion of marriages terminated by divorce has risen steadily over the past several decades. The rise has been gradual in the United States, roughly following the curve of marriages as shown in Figure 11-6.

In Canada, the liberalization of divorce laws in 1968 was reflected in a rapid four-fold increase in the divorce rate as shown in Figure 11-7.

An additional number of marriages are informally dissolved through desertion and separation. In the United States, blacks are more likely to be separated than divorced, while whites are 2–3 times more likely to be divorced than sepa-

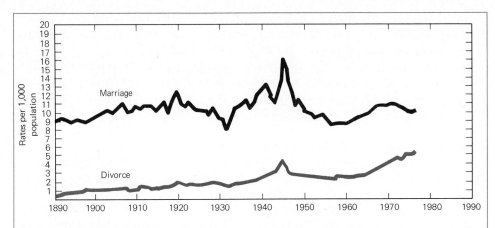

Figure 11-6.
Marriage and divorce rates, United States, 1890–1980. (Sources: U.S. Depart-
ment of Health, Education and Welfare, Public Health Service, "100 Years of
Marriage and Divorce Statistics, United States, 1867–1967," Vital and
Health Statistics, Series 21, No. 24, December 1973. U.S. Bureau of the Cen-
sus, Statistical Abstracts of the United States, 1977. Washington, D.C.: U.S.
Government Printing Office, 1977. U.S. Department of Health, Education
and Welfare, Public Health Service. "Births, Marriages, Divorces, and Deaths
for June 1978." As found in Marriage & Family Review, *Vol. 2, Summer,*
No. 2, Summer 1979, p. 36.)

rated. These data probably reflect differences in income and access to the legal system.

At any given moment, there will be more divorced women than men since men remarry sooner and at higher rates, reflecting the differential value of men and women on the marriage market. These differences are especially notable at older ages; remarriage rates for women over age 40 are considerably lower than those for males, whose remarriage probabilities do not change until age 65. In all, about 83 per cent of divorced men will remarry compared with 75 per cent of divorced women.

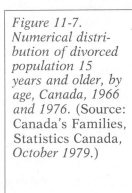

Figure 11-7.
Numerical distri-
bution of divorced
population 15
years and older, by
age, Canada, 1966
and 1976. (Source:
Canada's Families,
Statistics Canada,
October 1979.)

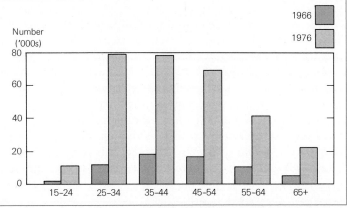

What accounts for such high divorce rates? At the most general level, divorce is the other side of the coin of free mate selection and the ideal of romantic love. If one marries for emotional support, psychological well-being, and affection, what rationale is there for continuing a relationship that provides none of the above and that may be damaging to mind and body? In other words, a marriage system based on expressive needs (rather than instrumental goals) must provide a means of dissolving unsatisfactory unions. All modern societies are faced with a similar problem, leading to liberalization of divorce laws, even in countries with strong religious opposition to divorce.

Further, women today have alternatives to remaining in an unsatisfactory marriage. Employed women and the single parent are not the statistical oddities that they were a few decades ago. As more women elect to leave a marriage, the stigma attached to such behavior lessens. While it is not easy to be a divorced person in a society created for couples, it is nonetheless a much less traumatic experience than in the past, especially for women.

The high divorce rates of the past two decades could also have been predicted from knowledge of the ages at which people marry. If there is one variable that consistently correlates with the probability of divorce and marital unhappiness it is *age at first marriage:* the lower the age for both males and females, the higher the risk of marriage failure (Schoen, 1975; Glick and Norton, 1979). What is there about early marriage that increases the likelihood of marital breakdown? Developmental immaturity is the most obvious variable, usually accompanied by withdrawal from school and entry into low-paying occupations. The combination of low income, low educational attainment, the cutting off of life options so early, and lack of emotional maturity, when added to the normal stresses of intimate relationships, produces a relatively unstable marital mix.

As for the factors protecting a first marriage, the most obvious is maturity. Completing either high school or college also helps, as does job stability and higher-than-median incomes for men. Once married, the most powerful predictive factor appears to be, quite simply, the number of years in the marriage—the longer the duration, the lower the probability of divorce. If we take all those who married in 1960, for example, 4 per cent will be divorced by the end of the first year, an additional 2.3 by 1962, 2.1 by 1963 and so on to 1.6 in 1969, and approximately 1.5 in the fourteenth year of marriage (National Center for Health Statistics, August 1979). The same pattern is found in all earlier marriage cohorts, indicating that there is *no* "second peak" in divorce rates once a couple reaches mid-life and their children leave home. Rather, with each added year, a marriage gains in strength as the couple confront and cope with the inevitable stresses of a modern marriage.

Although millions of children have been affected by their parent's divorces, the number of children per divorce is actually lower today than in the mid-1960s, largely because of declining birth rates, the tendency for divorces to occur early in a marriage, and the fact that troubled marriage partners often have fewer children than successful partners. Thus, in the United States today there are 1.03 children per divorced family compared to 1.32 in 1965. In Canada, in 1976, over two-thirds of divorced couples had either one or no dependent children.

The lower the **age of first marriage**, the higher the risk of marriage failure.

Minority Families

The family patterns described thus far in this chapter are those of the dominant culture. The nuclear family is an ideal to which most North Americans aspire. Many subcultural variations however, do exist. Whites of European background, French Canadians, and Hispanics often maintain extended households, although by the third generation the nuclear model is dominant. Poor families of all ethnic or racial groups depend on kinship ties and shared resources for their survival.

HISPANIC FAMILIES IN THE UNITED STATES

In keeping with the traditional patterns of their country of origin, and strongly supported by the tenets of Roman Catholicism, families of Spanish-speaking people in the United States contain large numbers of children. Since these families are also more likely than most to include other relatives, overall household size is large: in 1977, there were 3.47 persons per household among those of Spanish origin, 3.15 in black households, and about 2.80 in white households.

The power of males, especially the eldest, is traditionally extremely high within the family and outside. Friendships and other non-family relationships for women are discouraged. This type of traditional closeness and control over women and children is called *familism*.

There are hazards in describing the Hispanic family system since values often intrude. If it is suggested that familism and high birth rates could inhibit social mobility, or that Hispanic machismo could be oppressive to women, the researcher runs the risk of being labeled ethnocentric. Conversely, Hispanic writers, in reaction, tend to idealize precisely the same features, describing the Spanish-origin family as child-centered, warm, religious, and traditionally virtuous. As Mirande (1977) puts it:

> The basic difference between the two views . . . is not to be found in their substantive characterization of the family . . . but in their interpretation and evaluation of these characteristics. While the familistic orientation of Chicanos is universally recognized, critics see it as undemocratic, unAmerican and impeding individual achievement and advancement; supporters see it as a source of emotional and material support in a hostile and unrewarding world.

In time, however, mainstream Anglo values and behaviors, including the adoption of nuclear family patterns, will be introduced by younger family members, many of whom will travel the same paths of upward mobility as have members of other ethnic groups.

BLACK FAMILIES IN THE UNITED STATES

A great deal of controversy—and emotion—surrounds the discussion of family patterns among American blacks. To a greater degree than found among the white or Spanish origin populations, blacks are likely to live in single-parent families, to experience divorce, separation, desertion, widowhood, and singleness. This means that there is greater variation in the marital status and house-

Familism refers to a high degree of cohesion within the family group, and control of women and children by males and elders.

hold characteristics of blacks, and also that proportionately fewer will be living in intact nuclear families at any given moment. For example, in 1976, only 55 per cent of blacks lived in nuclear families compared to 80 per cent of whites.

The Inner-City Black Family: Matriarchal or Matrifocal?   Many scholars object to the use of the word matriarchy (female dominated) to describe the black family among the poor. A more accurate term is "matrifocal" meaning "centered on the women." The fact that black males are more likely to be unemployed or underemployed makes it extremely difficult for them to enact the traditional role of breadwinner. Moreover, the federal welfare system is arranged so that women with dependent children receive benefits only if there is *no adult male in the household.* Under such circumstances, the family fares better if the husband-father leaves. Many leave in order to seek employment elsewhere but are unable to move their wife and children to the new location.

The result is that a high proportion—over one-third—of black families are headed by women. This matrifocal system is held together by the extended line of female kin: mother, daughters, and their children sharing a household and pooling resources. If the women have power within this family group it is by default, and whenever men join the household they are typically accorded the status given males in our society.

Research into the nature and consequences of the matrifocal family system has taken two directions: one, exemplified by the work of Hill (1972) and Stack (1974), points to the strengths of the matrifocal pattern as a means of maintaining generational continuity, providing services to kin in general, and resisting the disintegrative influences caused by pressures outside the family. The second details outside pressures: unemployment, low pay assignment to demeaning tasks, residential segregation, and other institutionalized patterns of discrimination (Rainwater and Yancey, 1967). For both, the matrifocal family is a *response* to the conditions of poverty rather than the cause; that is, as "an adaptation necessary for survival and advancement in a hostile environment" (Hill, 1972:4). However, this emphasis on the matrifocal family of the urban ghetto has served to obscure the fact that a majority of black families are composed of husband-wife units that approximate the nuclear conjugal ideal of American culture.

The Black Stable Middle-Class Family.   An increasing number of black families are middle class in terms of education, occupation, and income of the adults. In 1950, for example, only 10 per cent of black families had incomes over the national median; by 1977 this percentage had risen to almost one-third.

These middle class black families differ somewhat from their white counterparts. The great majority are composed of *two* adult wage earners, often both professionals, whose *joint income* still falls short of that earned by one white breadwinner. Only among black couples under age 35, do two wage earners reach incomes comparable to those of white couples. Where only the male is employed, black family income is roughly two-thirds that of white single-earner families.

Not only is the typical black middle class family composed of two full-time labor force participants, but the relationships between husband and wife are typically more egalitarian than either dual-earner white families or single-

---

The **matrifocal** family system is best understood as a **response** to poverty rather than its cause.

The majority of black families are husband and wife units.

The great majority of middle-class black families include two adult wage earners.

earner black families (Willie, 1981). The reason for this is that the black husband and wife are likely to have equivalent educations and jobs, whereas dual-earner white families are characterized by greater differences in occupational level between husband and wife.

Alternatives to the Typical Family Model

As a result of the trends already discussed—later marriages, divorce, remarriage, women in the labor force, joint survival of married couples after the children have left home, and the probability of an extended widowhood—it is increasingly difficult to speak of "the American family" as a single dominant type. In fact, the ideal of a nuclear family, with children present and with only one wage earner, represents a decreasing proportion of Canadian families and a very small percentage of all families in the United States, as Table 11-2 indicates.

Clearly, government policies based on the universality of the nuclear family or on the one-earner model will not meet the needs of most families in the United States. In Canada, similar trends, although less strongly, are apparent: the divorce rate and female-headed households rose dramatically in the 1970s; the number of children per family is declining; and fewer households are shared by more than one nuclear unit (David, 1980; Malcom, 1980). Increasing numbers of dual-earner families have raised the average family income approximately 15% in the period between 1971 and 1976. Unlike the United States, Canada has a relatively comprehensive public policy supporting families: health insurance, child allowances, and social-service programs for all families rather than for only the poor or troubled.

The sharp increase in nontraditional family structures and the strong reaction to these changes have drawn attention to the many options surrounding courtship, marriage, and family life in modern societies. In this section we will

Table 11-2. Distribution of Adult Americans by Type of Household: 1977

Married, and living together, without children (either before or after children) or childfree	23%
Single, separated, divorced, widowed living alone	21
Head of single-parent family	16
Nuclear family, dual-earners, children present	16
Nuclear family, one earner, children present	13
Member of an extended family household	6
Cohabitating or experimental family unit	4
No-wage-earner nuclear family, children present	1
Total	100%

(Ramey, 1978).

briefly discuss a few of these—singleness, single-parenting, and alternatives to heterosexuality.

Many of the alternatives to the nuclear family model are a simple matter of *timing*. That is, the essential structure of family events remains fairly constant: most will marry at least once, have at least one child, and for most of their adult lives be members of a family of procreation, but do so at later ages or in a discontinuous fashion with periods of singleness between marriages.

SINGLENESS

Over the past two decades, the population of men and women in their twenties who are remaining single has increased.

Much evidence shows that over the past two decades in the United States, the average age at first marriage has reversed its previous decline. This means that more individuals between 20–29 are remaining single longer than was the case in 1960 or 1970 as illustrated in Table 11-3.

A number of population trends can partially explain this tendency to postpone marriage: (1) increasing numbers of women enrolled in higher education and enjoying expanding career opportunities; (2) widespread availability and acceptability of contraception; and (3) an excess of women at marriageable ages compared to men (the marriage squeeze). The squeeze occurs because the children of the baby boom years were preceded by smaller birth groups, so that if women prefer to marry men two or three years older than themselves, a shortage of men in the appropriate age groups will occur.

Certain attitudinal changes may be occurring as well (see Figure 11-8). Young people are less attached to the idea of early marriage than were their counterparts two decades ago. The greater freedom they enjoy in their contacts with one another reduces the need to marry in order to sustain an intimate relationship. Young adults embarked on careers might perceive marriage and parenthood as overly restrictive at this time of their lives. For many, goals of individual development and personal growth have, at least temporarily, replaced the more traditional one of settling down.

The range of life styles open to young singles has increasingly broadened (Stein, 1981), from the glamorous singles scene portrayed in the media (which

Table 11-3. Women and Men Remaining Single: United States, 1960–1980 (in Per Cents)

	1960	1970	1980	*Change from 1970 to 1980*
Women remaining Single:				
Ages 20–24	28.4	35.8	50.2	+ 14.4
Ages 25–29	10.5	10.5	20.8	+ 10.3
Men remaining Single:				
Ages 20–24	53.1	54.7	68.6	+ 13.9
Ages 25–29	20.8	19.1	32.4	+ 13.3

Source: U.S. Bureau of the Census, Marital Status and Living Arrangements: March, 1980. *Current Population Reports*, Series P-20, No. 365, Washington, D.C.: U.S. Government Printing Office, 1980.

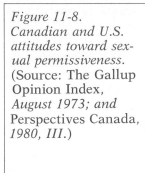

Figure 11-8. Canadian and U.S. attitudes toward sexual permissiveness. (Source: The Gallup Opinion Index, August 1973; and Perspectives Canada, 1980, III.)

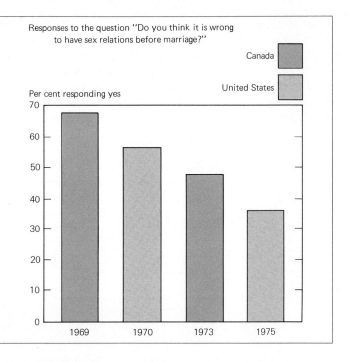

Responses to the question "Do you think it is wrong to have sex relations before marriage?"

Per cent responding yes

is often considerably less than glamorous to the participants) to patterns that vary little from those of married peers. Most do live in households of their own—thanks to their relative affluence—whereas many would have remained in the home of their parents at earlier times.

COHABITATION

In 1978, 2.3 per cent of all households in the United States were composed of an unmarried couple sharing a residence. This pattern is called *cohabitation*, and is technically defined as "a more or less permanent relationship in which two unmarried persons of the opposite sex share a living facility without legal contract" (Cole, 1977).

It is possible that large numbers of individuals have always cohabited but had heretofore been reluctant to disclose the arrangement to researchers. This is less true today. The United States Bureau of the Census estimated that about 1.8 million households were of this variety in 1981, tripling those counted in 1970. The most dramatic increase in cohabitation has occurred among those under age 25, especially college students, although it is likely that no more than one-fourth of all students are involved in this pattern (Lee, 1977).

Cohabitors appear to enjoy most of the benefits of marital intimacy and mutual care, and also to experience most of the difficulties that any two people experience in meshing their lives. From the studies reviewed in Macklin (1978), no evidence exists that cohabitors differ greatly from their noncohabiting peers, with the exception of having relatively low religious commitment. Cohabitors are no more likely than noncohabitors to have enduring relationships. About the same percentage of each category break up over a two-year period. Nor does cohabiting affect the probability of marital happiness—former cohabitors are no more or less likely than others to have stable marriages (Newcomb, 1979).

Cohabitation is the sharing of a residence by an unmarried couple.

These young people are *not* the products of broken homes or unhappy childhoods; they are not less involved in academic achievement; and they are only slightly less committed to marriage than are other students.

Macklin suggests that little can be predicted about an individual, about the quality of the relationship, or about its effects on later family behavior simply from the fact of having lived together without marriage. Cohabiting seems to be less a rebellion against the prevailing norms than a comfortable option that some people drift into in their yearning for intimacy.

SINGLE-PARENT FAMILIES

Data on single-parent families are often confusing. First, a single-parent family at one time may be a complete family at another. It is usually a temporary status. It is also necessary to distinguish several subgroups: the divorced, sepa-

In the United States, about one half of all children born today will spend part of their childhood in one-parent households. (Source: *Richard Kalvar, Magnum.*)

rated, widowed, or never-married parent. Moreover, family functioning will vary by the number and ages of children.

It is estimated that about one half of all children born today in the United States will spend some portion of their childhood in the one-parent situation, nine out of ten of these with their mother (Glick and Norton, 1979). Yet it is important to remember that prior to the divorce and in most cases at some time subsequently, these children will be in two-parent families. Overall, for the great majority, the proportion of their lives spent in intact families will still exceed the length of time spent in a single-parent household.

In the United States, single-parent households are typically at an economic disadvantage (Espanshade, 1979). If the children are very young, the parent may prefer not to work, becoming eligible for the federal program for Aid to Families with Dependent Children (AFDC) or for alimony payments plus child support from the former spouse. Alimony and child support judgments are, however, rarely carried out in full. Most ex-spouses are delinquent within a few years and enforcement is not a priority item for local authorities. Female-headed families in North America are four times more likely than those headed by men to live in poverty.

Many of the problems cited as evidence that divorce harms children are actually the effects of poverty. Low income also becomes an indirect cause of marital problems among offspring of divorced parents. The "transmission of marital instability," whereby children of divorce have higher rates of divorce than do children of intact families, is largely accounted for by economic pressures to leave school early and to seek security in marriage. Early marriage and low education are characteristic of children from single-parent homes, and are also correlated in general with marital instability (Mueller and Pope, 1977).

TEEN-AGE UNWED MOTHERS

Many single parents are themselves children in the sense that they are not legal adults. The teenage (15–19) birth rate in the United States, after leveling off in the early 1970s, has risen again despite widespread availability of contraception and abortion services, although the rate has declined for those aged 14 and younger.

Most social scientists agree that young people in North America are sexually active at earlier ages and in greater numbers than ever before—one-third of those aged 13–15, and over half of 15–19 year-olds in one national sample in the early 1970s (Sorensen, 1973). Moreover, among those who are sexually active, birth control knowledge and use, particularly on the part of young males, is quite low: only one-third took any precautions on the first occasion of sexual intercourse, but the figure rises to three-fifths of those with an ongoing sexual relationship.

Large numbers of teen-agers may have been sexually active in the past, but evidence is difficult to obtain. In any event, today's active teen-agers *can* become pregnant since the average age of first menstruation is now about 12-years-old (compared to age 16 in 1850). The great majority of Sorensen's (1973) sample claimed that they did not talk very freely about sex with their parents, and in many cases found that the parents could not provide useful information. Most felt that the type of sex education courses offered in the schools were of little value to them.

Why do so many unwed teen-agers choose to carry the fetus to term? Some hold religious scruples regarding abortion. For others, having the child may well signify an adult identity denied in the rest of their lives. Much of the stigma previously attached to illegitimacy has diminished and parents are more willing to assume responsibility for both daughter and infant than in the past. The fact that forced marriages are extremely unstable might convince the soon-to-be grandparents to provide a haven for their pregnant daughter rather than seek her marriage to a reluctant groom. In 1976 about half of unwed mothers aged 15–19 lived with both parents.

In general, the younger the mother, the more her life options are limited. Low educational attainment and low income, as we have described elsewhere, are the common characteristics of single-parent families. A teen-age never-married mother is likely to be particularly disadvantaged.

HOMOSEXUALITY

A homosexual life style is an alternative to the heterosexual family pattern for unknown numbers of North American women and men.

Other alternatives to the normative pattern of intact heterosexual families are associated with homosexual life styles. An unknown, and probably unknowable, number of North American men and women prefer sex partners of the same gender as themselves. One problem in counting homosexuals—apart from the issue of why Americans are so interested in counting them in the first place—is a matter of definition: How to measure sexual orientation? Is homosexuality to be defined strictly as behavior or as a self-definition. Clearly, there are many people who think of themselves as attracted to members of the same sex but who have not acted on that perception. Conversely, there are many who engage in homosexual acts while maintaining a basically heterosexual identity. Large numbers of homosexual men and women have at some time been married to someone of the opposite sex and have borne and raised children.

The homosexual population is composed of at least three subgroups: those who have not yet acknowledged their homosexual identity ("in the closet"); those who have always identified themselves as homosexual; and those who "came out of the closet" after heterosexuality had been attempted and found wanting. Since we cannot know how many individuals of the first category exist, estimates vary widely. Kinsey (1948) identified less than 5 per cent of adult males as exclusively homosexual, though the majority of male American adolescents will have had at least one homosexual encounter. An even smaller fraction of women are exclusive homosexuals, and less than half have ever had a homosexual experience. The commonly used figure for modern societies in general is one in twenty, or 5 per cent.

Origins of Homosexuality. Some medical researchers believe that a hormonal imbalance accounts for homosexuality, but none has yet shown a direct link between a physiological state and a particular behavioral outcome. Many men with low hormone levels are not homosexual and the great majority of homosexuals do not differ from heterosexual males in physiological functioning.

Mental health experts have long pointed to a particular family constellation as causal: a dominant mother and an ineffectual father. This finding, however, seems more to reflect biases in psychological theory than the family background of homosexuals. The same households produce both heterosexual and homosexual offspring, and it seems equally plausible that a brutal father would be a negative role model for many young males. A number of researchers have asked psychologists to analyze sets of personality test data in order to distinguish homosexual respondents from the heterosexuals. In almost every instance the mental health experts' decisions were no more accurate than if the data sets had been sorted by a non-professional (Jay and Young, 1979). Nor is it possible for most observers to identify homosexuals accurately on the basis of speech, dress, or mannerisms. The very great majority of homosexuals are utterly indistinguishable from the population in general. In 1973, the American Psychiatric Association removed homosexuality from its list of diseases of the mind.

But if not a matter of biological or psychological determinism, what processes produce homosexual rather than heterosexual individuals? Sociologists tend to believe that homosexuality, like heterosexuality, is learned in much the same fashion as any facet of sexuality, through experience, labeling, and internalization of self-definitions that, in turn, affect further behavior, and so on in a cycle that gradually reduces alternative avenues of sexual expression (Gagnon, 1977; Simon and Gagnon, 1967).

Challenging the powerful social controls against homosexuality are the emergence of the Gay Rights Movement and a gay sub-culture. (Source: Charles Gatewood, Magnum.)

For example, the male child whose pubertal development is delayed may be teased by others and filled with self-doubt. These feelings inhibit masculine behavior or lead to difficulties in acting out heterosexual roles. Such failures reinforce the doubts. If, at the same time, chance homosexual encounters prove less anxiety-producing, the youngster may well come to prefer these experiences. In other words, a long chain of events, making heterosexuality problematic while encouraging homosexual activity, must occur with few counteracting experiences. For most young people, successful heterosexual encounters are carefully nurtured by parents, peers, and cultural forces so that most adolescents emerge as heterosexual adults.

That few theories of female homosexual development yet exist probably reflects a lesser concern with females in general as well as the great fear of male homosexuality that dominates thinking on the subject. This fear, *homophobia*, expresses deep insecurities among men regarding their masculinity in any society in which women have been the sole and exclusive raisers of the young. So strong is the cultural aversion to homosexuality in North American culture, and so powerful are the social controls against the expression of sexual interest in other men, the wonder must be that as many as 5–10 per cent of the male population will find the homosexual option attractive enough to forfeit approval by family and friends, and to run the risks of job loss and harassment. The homosexual option has been enhanced by the emergence of a supportive Gay Rights Movement and a visible subculture.

Homophobia refers to the strong fear of homosexuality.

Male-female differences within the homosexual subculture. While homosexual couples do not necessarily recreate the gender role differences found in heterosexual relationships, with a dominant "male" and subservient "female," gender role based differences between the ways in which males and females pursue homosexual intimacy do exist. In general, homosexual males have many more partners, remain in any one relationship a shorter length of time, and engage in a wider variety of sexual experiences than do female homosexuals. Lesbian relationships are more emotionally intense, more permanent, and less varied. As with women in general, female ties tend to be nurturant, expressive, and mutually supportive. Conversely, true to the male stereotypes in our culture, the male homosexual scene is frequently characterized by exploitiveness, instrumentality, prestige and power needs, and impersonality (Humphreys, 1972; Levine, 1979; Wolf, 1979).

There are differences between the ways in which men and women pursue homosexual relationships and between the male homosexual and lesbian subcultures.

Is homosexuality a threat to the family? Despite the new gay activism, greater public tolerance, and increasing areas of legal protection, it is unlikely that the homosexual life style will attract more than the 5 per cent of exclusive homosexuals and another smaller percentage of persons drifting in and out of the subculture. Opponents of homosexuals seem to imply that the homosexual scene is so attractive that other people must fear exposure to it—an attitude that suggests doubts about the strength of heterosexual identity. A more likely possibility for increasing the ranks of homosexuals is that heterosexuality based on gender inequality may become a progressively less attractive option, particularly for women.

The debate on homosexuality has been misdirected in one crucial respect. The underlying assumption in most of the discussion is that homosexuality is so overriding an identity that every other aspect of the individual is affected. This is not the case. Just as heterosexuality does not obsess most other people, coloring their every thought and act, the homosexual's preference in sex partner is but one part of a complex personality and social actor. The problems of daily life—work, leisure, comfort and safety, companionship, death, and taxes—beset the gay as well as the straight, and in many ways are rendered harder for the homosexual to resolve because of job discrimination and social stigmatization.

REFLECTIONS ON ALTERNATIVES TO THE NUCLEAR FAMILY

The alternative patterns explored in this part of the chapter vary in the degree to which they have been voluntarily pursued. Singleness, child-free marriages, cohabitation, and open homosexuality can be more or less consciously chosen, with many persons and couples simply drifting into the status over time. Others will have set out to defy cultural expectations and to create the lifestyle with which they feel most comfortable. Single-parenthood, also, may be a conscious choice, particularly for adolescents; for others, it is the undesired outcome of a divorce or death of a spouse.

None of these alternatives involves more than a small fraction of North American adults at any one time. Over the individual's lifetime, however, many years will be spent outside a nuclear family: singleness before marriage, a period of marriage without children, perhaps several years as a single parent, and, for women, an extended widowhood. Although many perceive the alternative patterns as competitive to the nuclear family, it would be more accurate to consider both nuclear family living and its alternatives as life-course contingencies.

The overwhelming proportion of American adults will spend the greater part of their adult years in a nuclear family of procreation. At various moments in the life course, other options will be taken, some because they appear more attractive at the time, and some because of events beyond one's control. Far from dying, the North American family appears to be alive and well as human beings devise a variety of structural forms to meet enduring needs for intimacy. Rather than condemn nontypical forms or attempt to force people into a single mold—much like trying to put the genie back in the bottle—public policy could greatly strengthen family life through provisions for the economic security and social-service needs of teenagers, single parents, widows, and the poor in general.

Summary

As with other institutions, the family system is a set of norms and behaviors clustered around the essential activities of reproduction, socialization, protection, intimacy, and care. Family-based relationships are essential features of the social structure of societies. Though these kinship systems vary from one society to another and over time, they can all be described in terms of five basic characteristics: (1) the number of spouses permitted at one time; (2) who can marry whom; (3) how lines of descent and the flow of resources are determined; (4) where the couple lives; and (5) power relations within marriage and the family.

The major temporal shift has been from relatively large extended family systems composed of a number of related households, to the nuclear family system composed of a married pair and their children. The nuclear family is a less powerful and versatile unit than the extended family, as an increasing number of tasks once assumed by the kinship group are now performed by outside agencies. Yet the stresses and demands of modern life create needs for affection and emotional support which most people seek from their marriage partners and their children. The modern family has thus become a specialized agency of interpersonal support and primary socialization of children.

The modern family is also characterized by reduced power differences between husbands and wives and between parents and children. These changes toward egalitarianism have been influenced by broader liberal trends, legal changes, the influence of psychological theories of child development, and a decline in parents' abilities to control the social mobility of their children.

Marriage and parenthood continue to be almost universal among North Americans—almost 95 per cent marry at least once and about 90 per cent become parents. Marriage and parenthood thus continue to be strongly preferred and to be associated with positive feelings.

Although marriage rates continue at record highs, there is widespread fear for the future of the North American family due to increasing frequency of divorce, a growing awareness of family violence, and the perception of a general decline in morality. The emotional intensity of marriage sometimes erupts into family violence directed most often against women and children. Rather than relieving tension, violence tends to breed further brutality.

When marriages no longer yield emotional support and affection, partners separate and divorce. An increasing number of contemporary marriages end in divorce, even though a large majority of these men and women will remarry.

Recent research on North American families indicates a substantial variety of alternatives, including single men and women living alone, unmarried men and women living together, single-parent families, and homosexual life styles. Research on these alternatives and on minority families suggests that there is no one ideal or universal North American family model. Public policies seeking to meet the needs of families must recognize the validity of diversity within the family system today.

Suggested Readings

BERNARD, JESSIE. *The Future of Marriage.* New York: Bantam, 1973. An informative and lively summary of the sociological research on marriage and the family.

BURR, WESLEY, REUBEN HILL, F. IVAN NYE, and IRA L. REISS (Eds.). *Contemporary Theories about the Family* (2 Vols.). New York: Free Press, 1979. A comprehensive collection of essays on the modern family, including the effects of social change, interaction patterns, marital problems, childrearing, and the various theoretical models used to study the family.

GOODE, WILLIAM J. *World Revolution and Family Patterns.* New York: Free Press, 1963. This is a landmark study of the relationship between industrialization, modernization, ideology, and changes in the family life in China, Japan, India, Middle East, parts of Africa, Western Europe, and North America.

ROSS, HEATHER L. and ISABEL V. SAWHILL. *Time of Transition: The Growth of Families Headed by Women.* Washington, D.C.: Urban Institute, 1975. The economic and social situation of children and mothers in single-parent families is thoroughly examined.

RUBIN, LILLIAN BRESLOW. *Worlds of Pain.* New York: Basic Books, 1976. This description and analysis of working-class families, marriage, and intimate relationships is based on in-depth interviews by a sensitive researcher.

SKOLNICK, ARLENE. *The Intimate Environment: Exploring Marriage and the Family.* Boston: Little, Brown, 1978 (second edition). One of the best of the fine marriage and family texts available. A very clear and lively analysis of the family, class and ethnic differences, gender roles, love and sexuality, parenthood, childhood, socialization, and the future of the family.

STEIN, PETER J. (Ed.). *Single Life: Unmarried Adults in Social Context.* New York: St. Martins, 1981. An anthology examining the variety of single lifestyles with sections on work, health, parenting, intimacy, aging, living arrangements, and social class, gender, age, and racial differences.

STRAUS, MURRAY, RICHARD J. GELLES, and SUZANNE K. STEINMETZ. *Violence in the American Family.* New York: Doubleday, 1978. Presents the most complete analysis of the context, prevalence, causes, and consequences of violence against wives, children, and husbands.

WILLIE, CHARLES V. *A New Look at Black Families.* second edition. Bayside, New York: General Hall, 1981. The strengths and problems of black families are thoroughly and compassionately presented in this landmark essay.

12 Economic Systems

When the General Motors assembly plant opened at Lordstown, Ohio, in 1966, the first workers hired were men who left other local employment for the promise of higher wages, but the monotony of factory work led to high turnover rates once the best jobs were taken by the oldest employees.* With a work force increasingly composed of young men out of high school, the plant operated through the late 1960s, turning out about 60 cars per hour, and plagued by absenteeism, lateness, and shoddy workmanship. When the Vega model was introduced in 1970, a management team from GM decided to make Lordstown a showplace factory. The plant was closed for several months and a new, automated assembly line introduced in which machines replaced workers. When the men returned to work, the line was geared to 100 cars an hour with the aid of welding robots. A typical worker had 36 seconds in which to complete a complex set of motions before the next unit appeared on the line. Three hundred and fifty workers were laid off.

Claiming that GM had violated a clause in the union contract by changing the conditions of employment without consultation with the union, the workers filed grievances and passed cars down the line with parts missing and other acts of sabotage. Finally, the workers went on strike. After much negotiation, the union agreed to the speed-up of the line in return for rehiring the laid-off workers and settlement of back-pay and other economic issues. But the basic conditions of work remained unchanged. As one worker put it: "The guys are not happy here. They don't come home thinking, Boy, I did a great job today and I can't wait to get back tomorrow. That's not the feeling at all . . . He's not concerned at all if the product is good, bad, or indifferent." (Terkel, 1972). But it was 1972 and jobs were not all that easy to find. Besides, the pay was still better than a lot of other semi-skilled jobs.

Lordstown has become a symbol of the condition of modern labor and the problems of decreasing productivity in a late industrial economy. The incident raises issues of automation, alienation, worker satisfaction, and the role of management, all of which will be discussed later in this chapter, but that cannot be understood fully without some understanding of the nature of the economic system as a macrosystem.

Origins and Functions of Economic Systems

Economic behavior originates in the attempts of any human group to adapt to its environment. The term "mode of subsistence" refers to the primary means of surviving in the particular geographic location of that group. Gathering, fish-

Economic behavior stems from people's attempts to adapt to their environment.

*The details of the Lordstown incident are taken from Stanley Aronowitz, *False Promises: The Shaping of American Working Class Consciousness*, New York: McGraw-Hill, 1973; and Studs Terkel, *Working*, New York: Avon Books, 1975, pp. 256–265.

ing, hunting, herding, horticulture, agriculture, and industrialism have been the major means whereby human groups have survived.

Over the course of human history, simple economic techniques are often replaced by adaptations involving a more extensive division of labor. Some societies will develop new modes of subsistance through necessity or contact with other groups. Other societies remain essentially unchanged. A variety of economic systems characterize contemporary cultures: The Tasaday still subsist on gathering, Bushmen hunt, Tungus herd reindeer, Eskimo fish, Trobrianders practice horticulture, Yucatan Mexicans are agriculturists, and Western Europe is industrialized.

As societies evolve, such simple modes of subsistence as gathering are replaced by industrialization and complex division of labor. (Sources: left— John Nance/Panamin, Magnum; right—Dave Sagarin, Editorial Photocolor Archives.)

Figure 12-1.

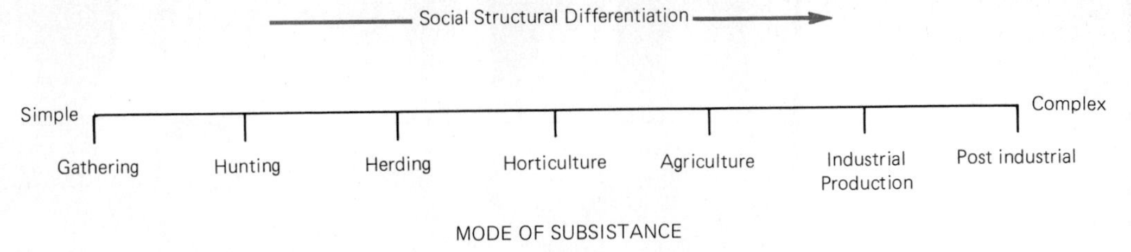

Social Structural Differentiation →

Simple ——————————————————————————— Complex

Gathering   Hunting   Herding   Horticulture   Agriculture   Industrial Production   Post industrial

MODE OF SUBSISTENCE

described as "st...
government poli...
omy by channeli...
subsidies to far...
loans to firms su...
sociologists to re...
poor" (Marshall...
whereby progra...
for the nonpoor...

Conversely, ot...
economic proble...
medical care and...
been more respo...
cial welfare prog...

Current politica...
of government r...
so much excessi...
vate interferenc...
of resisting pow...
lems in the eco...
decently for our...

Inflation occur...
and services bein...
little money in c...
plentiful. Capital...
traction because...
and because the...
can be reconcilec...

Another devel...
sumed natural b...
Conglomerates d...
same line of busi...
do not necessari...
several other kin...
sectors is concen...

One additiona...
corporations. The...
a number of diffe...
nations. The prol...
affect the econom...
operations. The b...
lished for compa...
made on the basi...
The twenty larges...
12-1—which also...
proportion of tot...
ages range from...

M...
syste...
all go...
this...
ruble...
syste...
else...
many...

M...
excee...
and s...
item,...
rema...
fall. T...
with...
agree...
by en...

CONS...

Co...
"eate...
hold...
produ...
the se...
their...
becon...

Mc...
tasks...
for e...
with...
stantl...
versa...
symb...
analy...
prope...
presti...
other...

In...
indus...
The d...
proce...
as we...

The above diagram is intended to illustrate the broad *general* thrust of economic-system development through human history. Increasing complexity is not necessarily better than simplicity; indeed, members of most simple societies have more leisure time than do contemporary Americans, and there is evidence that the economic situation of many Africans has declined in the past few decades even as their societies undergo modernization.

Once established, a mode of subsistence tends to become elaborated; the original patterns (folkways) are endowed with moral virtue (mores) and ultimately supported by a set of impersonal rules and sanctions (law). This is the process of *institutionalization* whereby a particular economic adaptation becomes the way of the group, and affects other areas of activity, such as family structure and interaction, ideology, and power relationships. Nonetheless, economic change has come to most societies in the form of greater specialization within the group and between one society and others. Nationwide markets have replaced village exchange systems.

These processes of specialization and involvement in a world economy are as descriptive of the United States and Canada as of Burma or the Congo Republic. From a society of agricultural villages, all four nations have developed economies in which agriculture is a declining sector while mining and manufacturing now link them to an international market system. And within all four, the rate of economic change varies from region to region; small farms, fishing villages, and factory towns coexist with modern cities and industries.

Components of Economic Systems

The economic system of any society consists of norms and statuses relating to the *production*, *distribution*, and *consumption* of resources.

PRODUCTION

There are three levels of production, each associated with a different mode of subsistence.

Primary production refers to extracting things of value from the ground or water. Fishing, agriculture, and mining are all primary modes of production.

Secondary production is economic activity that involves turning raw materials into some other commodity. Weaving, basketry, and pottery were the earliest *manufacturing* activities—quite literally, since *manus* is Latin for "hand" and *facere* means "to make." Today, of course, hands have been replaced by machines, but in principle there is no difference between working wet clay into a pot and making dacron out of fibers.

Tertiary (third level) production involves the provision of *services* rather than

Institutionalization occurs when a given mode of subsistence becomes the way of life of a group.

Primary production extracts resources directly from the earth.

Secondary production transforms primary resources into another commodity.

Tertiary production creates services rather than goods.

The major diff
between capit
socialist syster
extent to whic
nomic activity
lated by politi
thorities.

Under capitalis
means of produ
and distributio
privately owne
operated for pr

Table 12-1. The Twenty Largest United States Multinationals: 1980

Company	Foreign revenue (millions)	Foreign as % of total
1 Exxon	$56,999	72.1%
2 Mobil	27,401	60.3
3 Texaco	26,023	67.9
4 Ford Motor	19,106	43.9
5 Standard Oil Calif	17,490	58.4
6 General Motors	16,751	25.3
7 IBM	12,244	53.6
8 Intl Tel & Tel	11,579	52.6
9 Gulf Oil	11,102	46.4
10 Engelhard Minerals	9,790	54.1
11 Citicorp	7,287	66.8
12 General Electric	4,997	21.7
13 BankAmerica	4,728	50.0
14 Conoco	4,709	36.1
15 Dow Chemical	4,672	50.5
16 Occidental Petroleum	4,573	47.4
17 Chase Manhattan	3,786	62.3
18 Standard Oil Indiana	3,725	19.7
19 EI du Pont de Nemours	3,357	26.7
20 Xerox	3,316	47.2

Source: Forbes, July 7, 1980.

Standard Oil of Indiana. For eleven of the twenty corporations, at least half of their 1980 earnings came from foreign sources.

SOCIALISM

The distinctive characteristic of **socialism** is the use of political planning to promote greater economic equality in the society.

The original theorists of capitalism viewed the economic system as operating free of political intervention despite the fact that through all of human history economic and political power have been intertwined. What distinguishes socialism from other economic systems is the stated goal of using political planning to promote a more equal distribution of goods and services among members of a society.

Marxism. Contemporary socialist theory owes much to Karl Marx's analysis of capitalism's successes and failures. In fact, Marxist analysis is based on the idea of a dialectic or set of contradictions in the economic realm that leads to a new structure. Marx had predicted that the very success of capitalism in the accumulation of wealth among a few accompanied by increased misery among the many would soon drive the middle-class intellectuals and small-business owners (or bourgeoisie, pronounced *boor-zwah-zee*) into the ranks of the working class (proletariate) where they would provide leadership for the overthrow of capitalism.

Marx assigned priority to the economic system in determining the shape of other institutions. He was keenly aware of the many manifest and latent ways in which religious, political, familial, and educational patterns support and reinforce particular economic systems. For example, Marx and his colleague, Freidrich Engels, saw the bourgeoise family as a miniature social system in which the male head of household acted toward his dependents as an owner toward employees, reinforcing capitalist relationships. Among the proletariat, family survival required that members accept whatever wage labor was offered to them, children and mothers especially.

Marx examined the links among institutional spheres, with special emphasis on the economic base.

The social system, to Marx, was a seamless web of relations between and among the institutional spheres, a view that most modern sociologists share, though some may question one part or another of the many ideas that he developed and modified over several decades, and that still remain the subject of lively debate in the social sciences.

Much of his economic and political theory has not stood the test of time. The workers of the world have not united (in fact, North American workers are extremely nationalistic). The union movement in North America has been more moderate than Marxist; the middle class did not become proletarianized but, rather, expanded faster than the laboring class. And while still highly concentrated, wealth has recently become slightly more evenly distributed in most western societies precisely because of social welfare policies and economic planning. But Marx could hardly have forseen all these developments, many of which occurred as a *response* to his analysis.

We are, however, left with much of value from Marx's analysis of the link between the economic and the political:

> The importance of Marx's economic interpretation of history can hardly be exaggerated. It brought to light the enormous weight of economic forces, such as technology, transportation, the supply of raw materials, the distribution of wealth, finance, and the formation of social classes, in past and present politics, in law, and in the formation of moral and social ideals. Whether he exaggerated the importance of economic factors is of little moment, for their importance is certainly great. His emphasis upon them closes once for all the gap between politics and economics left by the earlier liberal utilitarianism. It is probably not an exaggeration to say, by his development of this suggestive hypothesis, Marx was the most important social philosopher in the world of the nineteenth century (Sabine, 1937).

It was this insight into the centrality of economic relationships that has spurred the development of a socialist perspective—not necessarily Marxist, but located precisely at the intersection of politics and economics to which Marx drew attention.

Contemporary Socialism. Socialism refers to the theory and practice of state intervention in economic processes in order to ensure equitable distribution of goods and services. The crucial difference between a socialist and a capitalist economic system is the answer to the question: "Who controls economic decision making?" Socialism, to attain its goals, must be linked to political democracy so that the voting public can hold decision-makers responsible. Capitalist theory and practice, on the other hand, insists that only market mechanisms must guide decisions of economic leaders, and that these forces in the long run will benefit all members of the society. Political intervention can only impede the "invisible hand."

Socialism has taken many forms in contemporary societies. At one extreme, as in Eastern Europe and the Soviet Union, a nondemocratic government claiming to represent all the people has taken over control of the means of production. According to Marxist doctrine, oppression should cease because there would no longer be two classes, owners and workers, but only owner-workers. The recent strike of Polish workers demanding the right to form unions not dominated by the Communist Party is evidence that many workers still feel oppressed. Moreover, inequality remains stubbornly entrenched in these countries although the degree of income and prestige stratification is less extreme than in the nonsocialist past. Critics of socialism are also quick to point out that productivity in socialist economies is often lower than in comparable nonsocialist economies. There are status distinctions between managers and workers, communist party members and others, skilled labor and peasants, and between university graduates and the less educated.

A less complete form of socialism is practiced in Norway, Sweden, and Denmark. Here, state planning is primarily concerned with the distribution of services, while large sectors of production remain in private hands, subject to market forces. This arrangement is often called a welfare state. Health care, higher education, income, housing, and social services are provided in such a manner as to minimize status and class differences. However, it must be remembered that most of these countries, in comparison to the United States and Canada, are relatively small and homogeneous nations where a high level of concern for one another can be more readily generated than in countries with large racial, religious, and ethnic minorities (and, therefore, less sense of shared fate). Nonetheless, Canada has a national health insurance program and has moved toward greater equality in the distribution of other services than has its southern neighbor. But paying for the welfare state entails a relatively high rate of taxation as illustrated in Table 12-2.

To put the tax issue into perspective, the high costs of quality housing, medical care, and higher education in the United States probably absorb at least the same proportion of income as do taxes in Sweden, for example.

Table 12-2. Taxes as a Per Cent of GNP in Various Countries, 1976

Developed countries	Recent average tax	Less developed countries	Recent average tax
Sweden	43	Spain	21
France	38	Jamaica	17
West Germany	35	Columbia	16
United Kingdom	35	India	15
Canada	32	Philippines	11
United States	32	Nigeria	9 1/2
Switzerland	23	Mexico	7
Japan	21	Afghanistan	6

Source, McGee (1977), p. 152.

Socialism and the Reduction of Inequality. There is some evidence that direct government intervention reduces differences among income groups (Stack, 1978). Also, where there is a political party with socialist goals in a democratic political structure, differences in income and access to higher education are minimized (Hewitt, 1977).

Both Stack and Hewitt were testing the generally accepted thesis that sheer industrial development alone will generate greater income equality in any society, and that democratic political systems inevitably lead to a reduction of inequality. Not so, say both researchers. Industrialization without government involvement does not appreciably affect stratification systems (Stack), and political democracy does not reduce inequality unless the voters use their power to support political parties committed to that goal (Hewitt).

But the record of societies that are considered Marxist—the Soviet Union, the People's Republic of China, and Eastern Europe—is mixed:

> . . . a socialist economy is not incompatible with rapid economic growth and the reduction of inequalities in income and living standards. Failures include (1) the persistence of very high levels of political inequality, (2) the persistence of workers alienation, (3) the persistence of sex inequalities, (4) the persistence of rural/urban inequalities, and, perhaps most serious of all, (5) the failure of the new societies to give birth to the new socialist man. (Lenski, 1978)

Each system—capitalism and socialism—has its strengths and drawbacks; neither is divinely ordained; both are historical developments; and the future of each is more a political than an economic matter. The link between the political and the economic and the many ways in which the same political system can have different economic consequences are summarized by Titmuss (1974) as ideal type models of modern political economics:

1. "Residual Welfare" model in which the state intervenes only after the private market and individual resources have been exhausted. This description fits the United States where public-assistance programs are expressly designed to afford temporary relief for "failures" and the "deserving needy." In addition, many residual welfare programs benefit the private market—housing subsidies to landlords and medical reimbursements to physicians, for example.

2. "Industrial Achievement/Performance" model where government and welfare policies reinforce the free enterprise economic system by encouraging work, productivity, and other industrial virtues. Other aspects of the American political economy fit this model as well—work incentive programs, job training, refusal of welfare to adult males without jobs, and so forth.

3. "Institutional Redistributive" model describes societies in which services and goods are provided in such a manner as to unify the society. Reduction of gross inequality, assured well-being in old age, family assistance before an emergency, and life-long health care are some of the policies that should lead to a reduction of tension and conflict in a society. Sweden perhaps comes closest to this model, although other Western European countries and Canada are moving in this direction.

The Organization of Work

DIVISION OF LABOR

Within any economic system, work is divided through specialization of tasks. This division of labor is minimal in simple societies. Among the Tasaday, both men and women, children and adults, pick berries and catch fish. But among the Bushmen of the Kalahari Desert, both age and sex are the basis of specialization, with young women gathering fruit and digging roots, young men hunting, and the elders maintaining the campsite, watching children, and offering advice.

Economic systems vary in the extent of **division of labor** or specialization of tasks.

Labor is divided among the Bushmen of the Kalahari Desert by age and sex: young men hunt, young women gather, and elders maintain the campsite. (Source: *Marvin E. Newman, Woodfin Camp and Associates.*)

In a complex society such as the United States or Canada, there are hundreds of occupational specialties, all carefully ranked in terms of skill, income, and prestige. The United States Department of Labor publishes a *Dictionary of Occupational Titles* containing about 20,000 entries.

This extreme specialization of labor led many sociologists, from Emile Durkheim to Talcott Parsons, to perceive modern society as potentially fragmented, with each person being socialized to a particular version of the general culture. The major problem for modern societies becomes the creation of a sense of community and shared values among so many different kinds of specialists. For Max Weber, the increasing division of labor and rationalization (breaking into smaller and smaller tasks) of everyday life spelled the end of liberal humanistic impulses; when all is rationalized and demystified, some essential element of liberty is lost. And for Marx, it all leads to *alienation*, feeling cut off, one from the other, and each from the products of her or his labor. At the extreme, members of modern society can become alienated even from themselves; that is, to feel detached from one's own activity, like a robot, just going through the gestures of living—an orientation referred to as *self-estrangement*.

Extreme specialization of labor can lead to fragmentation and **alienation** in modern society.

All would agree that modern economic systems involve ever-finer divisions of labor. The factories were designed to bring laborers *out* of the home into a place where the machines could be more efficiently attended. Eventually, the factories adopted an *assembly line* mode of organization; each step in a complex task was isolated and one worker did just that one set of activities and no other. The relationship of a worker to the finished product was stretched to near invisibility. An instructive example would be the difference between a shoemaker and a worker in a shoe factory. The former completes the whole task, and the finished product has the shoemaker's distinct stamp of individuality. The latter is responsible, say, for attaching the heel to each shoe as it moves down a conveyor belt. As a consequence, the factory worker has little sense of creative accomplishment in the finished product. In fact, the assembly line system can breed resentment among workers, increasing their feeling of alienation from their own labor.

On the **assembly line**, workers continually perform one set of tasks at a pace set by the line.

The Happy Worker: Myth or Reality? Despite dehumanizing trends in the modern mode of production, North American workers continue to express high levels of satisfaction with their jobs—between 75 and 80 per cent over the past several decades (Converse et al., 1980). But these proportions vary with the type of employment. Worker dissatisfaction is highest in jobs that are closely supervised, routinized, yet involving the mastery of complex tasks (Kohn, 1976). Under these circumstances, many researchers have found that workers are characterized by feelings of powerlessness, self-estrangement, normlessness, cultural isolation, and meaninglessness (Blauner, 1964; Seeman, 1972; and Kohn, 1976). These dimensions have become the definition of the concept of alienation. Thus, when workers feel that they cannot control the pace of their work, or that their tasks are without purpose, they become bored or even angry, and lose any sense of pride in their labor. These attitudes often spill over into nonwork areas of life such as family relationships and leisure activities.

Worker satisfaction is linked to the degree of self-direction permitted in the job.

It is important to note that these findings point to the way in which jobs are paced and controlled as the crucial factors, and not to advanced technological work in general. Where workers can exercise self-direction and contribute to decisions regarding their product, even on the assembly line, satisfaction and morale are generally high. And productivity increases along with the quality of workmanship. This lesson is currently being applied in many plants in North America and Western Europe, following a model widespread in Japanese industry and currently referred to as "Theory Z" (Ouchi, 1981). Traditional practice focussed on short-range profit making, and a rigidly controlled work force. Encouraging worker participation in goal-setting, and seeking their advice on matters of technical competence, managers using Theory Z increased the efficiency of their plants and reduced absenteeism and turnover. Conflict theorists, however, would suggest that the workers had simply been coopted and that essential control and profits remain in the hands of a managerial elite.

Other experiments in extending worker control include abolishing the assembly line and giving small groups of workers the responsibility for producing the finished product through whatever division of labor they decide upon. This system has been successfully tried in Swedish automobile factories—the product is of very high quality, but the costs are also high. *Job rotation* is another technique for relieving boredom and for enlarging the worker's view of his or her role in the productive process by taking on one another's tasks. Private ownership and worker control—or *workplace democracy*—has led to high productivity and worker satisfaction in a large manufacturing firm in Holland, as reported by Rothschild-Whitt (1981) who saw it as a "promising new model of worker self-management" within a capitalist framework. In general, job enrichment programs involve the following features: autonomous work groups, responsibility for quality, challenging assignments, financial rewards for learning, reduction or elimination of supervision, self-government, and elimination of status symbols such as separate parking lots or eating facilities for white- and blue-collar employees (Shepard and Voss, 1978).

One compelling conclusion from recent research into worker satisfaction is that *intrinsic* satisfactions such as the opportunity to use skills, freedom to plan work, to try new things, and to take pleasure in the finished product are by far the more important elements in overall worker morale than, as has often been assumed by management, either level of pay or job security. And also contrary to most previous beliefs, the search for intrinsic satisfactions is as strong among manual workers as among white-collar employees (Gruenberg, 1980). There are not two different types of worker, characterized by different levels of education and needs for achievement, but, rather, workers who find themselves located in jobs that either provide intrinsic satisfaction or do not. In the latter case, extrinsic rewards will come to be valued.

Thus, while the overall level of worker satisfaction may have remained high over the years since the Second World War, data from surveys taken between 1958 and the mid 1970s indicate that the components of satisfaction have changed dramatically. Whereas income and job security ranked highest before 1970, these are now less important than intrinsic rewards such as a sense of accomplishment and demand for challenge (Converse et al., 1980).

The replacement of human labor by machines is **automation**.

The ultimate in impersonal production is *automation*, the replacement of human labor by machines. Although the initial cost of such machines is very high, depending upon the wage scale in the society, the machine will, in the long run, be cheaper than human power. Machines have additional advantages: they do not complain and they do not strike. As a case in point, seasonal crops in

North America are picked by migrant workers who travel from one area to another throughout the harvest season. Migrant labor is the least expensive segment of the labor force: no Social Security taxes and records, payment by the piece rather than day or week, and the workers are often unregistered aliens or persons of very low status who will be willing to work under any conditions. Agitation on behalf of migrant labor has led to legislation improving their working conditions, providing schooling for their children, and raising the min-

Do They Really Do It Better in Japan?

The current difficulties of the United States automobile industry have led to an increasing interest in the organization of work within the Japanese factory where job turnover and quality control are much less problematic than in North America. Much has been written in the popular press about how Japanese workers are guaranteed life-time employment, receive many non-work benefits, and are given a great deal of responsibility on the line. This paternalism—the company acting as parent—is thought to be an extension of traditional Japanese patterns of obedience to authority (to the Emperor, to bosses, and to one's father). This view is a great oversimplification according to Robert E. Cole, one of the leading authorities on the Japanese factory system. Cole notes the many ways in which tradition has been used to solve uniquely modern problems, and how much has been borrowed from the industrial West to create a rather unique system in *some* sectors of the Japanese economy.

Comparing Japanese and United States rates of intragenerational mobility (job promotion) and job transfers (from one employer to another), Cole found that the structural patterns in the two countries were quite similar but that the *rate* of such job changes in Japan were only half that of the United States. That is, Japanese male workers are much less likely to be promoted but will, on the average, remain with an employer for twice as long.

There are a number of reasons why the Japanese worker will stay despite the low promotion possibilities. Employment is made attractive through career development programs, housing and recreation facilities provided by the employer, and the feeling that one is being treated as a human being with a contribution to make to the company and society. However, Cole also notes that because of weak unions, employers have great power, reinforced by business-oriented conservative governments, and that the owners retain the gains from increased productivity. Moreover, the system so admired by Western visitors pertains to the largest firms only, and the wage and benefit differential between these industries and those in areas of low-skill labor are even greater than in the United States. Finally, jobs in the high-security industries are available only to young men, which means that once a worker is hired, he will tend to remain with that employer. The conditions of work are pleasant, job rotation is frequent, and the employee gradually moves upward by ability and seniority—much the same pattern, suggests Cole, as the career of a college professor.

Source: Robert E. Cole. *Work, Mobility, and Participation.* Berkeley: University of California Press, 1979.

imum wage. This has made the migrant labor force increasingly expensive, so that many growers are turning to machines to harvest their crops. The end result has been a decline in the need for migrant labor, an unintended and undesired consequence of the manifest desire to improve their lot.

Effects Are Disputed as Migrants Continue Ohio Tomato Walkout

Columbus, Ohio, Oct. 21.—Both sides claim success after the second harvest season of a strike by migrant farm labor in the tomato fields of Northwest Ohio.

Migrant farm laborers struck the canners and growers in this area, which is the second leading one in the nation, for higher pay and better working conditions.

The growers say that they reaped almost a full crop this fall by using mechanical pickers. The worker's organization says that much of the crop was lost because wet weather precluded use of the machines.

The workers, organized by the Farm Labor Organizing Committee, based in Toledo, picketed the fields, waving banners and crucifixes. They drove in dusty pickups and campers through the county's tomato and soybean fields.

The growers responded by buying tractor-pulled mechanical pickers.

Despite the high cost—$40,000 for each piece of equipment—75 percent of the $28 million Ohio tomato crop was mechanically harvested this year, as against 29 percent last year, according to agricultural extension agents in the county.

The number of migrant workers declined from 4,000 last year to 1,200 to 1,500 this year.

The Campbell Soup Company, with a large plant in Henry County, signed contracts with only those farmers who had invested in machinery. The other major Ohio canner, Libby-McNeill & Libby, also urged its growers to mechanize (*New York Times*, 10/22/79, A-11).

LABOR AND THE LABOR MOVEMENT

In the classical Marxist analysis, laborers competed with one another in a market that was oversupplied with workers relative to the jobs available. Under these conditions, employers could offer the lowest wages for which anyone would work. For workers, the solution lay in organizing employees so that all could demand higher wages or all refuse to work.

Given the oversupply of unskilled workers in the early days of the factory system, such organizing was extremely difficult and largely unsuccessful. The modern labor movement in North America took shape in the 1880s and was the object of repression by the government as well as the business sector. After decades of violence, unions in the United States and Canada finally succeeded in organizing large number of workers. In both countries, workers with specialized skills joined the trade unions that became the American Federation of Labor (AFL) or the Christian Union in Quebec. These were the elite of the labor movement, and organizing was relatively easy since they had a monopoly on skills needed by employers. The great mass of semi- and low-skilled workers were harder to organize, but eventually formed the Congress of Industrial Organizations (CIO). In 1955, in the United States the two were combined to create one dominant union, the AFL-CIO.

The history of the early days of unionization in both Canada and the United States makes fascinating reading: moments of triumph and tragedy, bravery and cowardice, and a remarkable set of leaders whose names are all but unknown to students today. It is hard to realize when political candidates consult union leaders and vie for their support, that only a few decades ago unionists were thought to be radical subversives hellbent on destroying capitalism and the American Way. It was not until 1944 that a charter of legal rights for workers was established in Canada (Abella and Millar, 1978). In fact, some contemporary sociologists claim that United States unions are simply another conservative factor in the economic system, having been *coopted* (brought into the mainstream power structure). For example, the former head of the United Auto Workers became ambassador to the People's Republic of China; his successor sits on the Board of Chrysler Corporation; yet their predecessor had been harassed by the government and jailed for his union activities. In Canada, the unions have remained relatively uncoopted, playing a more active role in opposition to the growth of corporate power than in the United States (Willcox, 1980).

Some sociologists claim that labor unions have been **coopted** into the economic power structure.

It was not uncommon in the early decades of this century for children to work in mines and sewing factories ("sweat shops") seven days a week, twelve hours a day, for pennies, and under dangerous conditions. In 1911, one hundred and fifty women and girls died in a fire at the Triangle Shirtwaist Factory in New York City. The event created a surge of public support for the unionization movement. A recent memoir of one of the Triangle workers (who began work at the age of eight) describes their conditions:

> . . . we started work at seven-thirty in the morning, and during the busy season we worked until nine in the evening. They didn't pay you any overtime and they didn't give you anything for supper money. Sometimes they'd give you a little apple pie if you had to work very late. That was all. Very generous.
>
> What I had to do was not really very difficult. It was just monotonous. When the shirtwaists were finished at the machine there were some threads that were left, and all the youngsters—we had a corner on the floor that resembled a kindergarten—we were given little scissors to cut the threads off. It wasn't heavy work, but it was monotonous.
>
> . . . The employers were always tipped off if there was going to be an inspection. "Quick", they'd say, "into the boxes!" And we children would climb into the big boxes the finished shirts were stored in. Then some shirts were piled on top of us, and when the inspector came—no children.
>
> . . . The employers didn't recognize anyone working for them as a human being. You were not allowed to sing.
>
> We weren't allowed to talk to each other.
>
> . . . You were not allowed to have your lunch on the fire escape in the summertime. The door was locked to keep us in. That's why so many people were trapped when the fire broke out.
>
> . . . My pay was $1.50 a week no matter how many hours I worked. My sisters made $6 a week; and the cutters, they were the skilled workers, they might get as much as $12. The employers had a sign in the elevator that said: "If you don't come in on Sunday don't come in on Monday," You were expected to work every day if they needed you and the pay was the same whether you worked extra or not.
>
> Conditions were dreadful in those days. We didn't have anything. If the season was over, we were told "You're laid off. Shift for yourself".
>
> . . . There was no welfare, no pension, no unemployment insurance. There was nothing. We were much worse off than the poor are today because we had nothing to lean on; nothing to hope for except to hope that the shop would open again and that we'd have work.

I stopped working at the Triangle Factory during the strike in 1909 and I didn't go back. The union sent me out to raise money for the strikers.

. . . There was so much feeling against unions then. The judges, when one of our girls came before him, said to her: "You're not striking against your employer, you know, young lady, You're striking against God", and sentenced her to two weeks on Blackwell's Island, which is now Welfare Island. And a lot of them got a taste of the club.

After the 1909 strike I worked with the union, organizing in Philadelphia and Cleveland and other places, so I wasn't at the Triangle Shirtwaist Factory when the fire broke out, but a lot of my friends were.

I'm quite sure that the fire was planned for insurance purposes. And no one is going to convince me otherwise. And when they testified that the door to the fire escape was open, it was a lie! It was never open. Locked all the time. One hundred and forty-six people were sacrificed, and the judge fined Blank and Harris (the owners) seventy-five dollars!

The Way it Was, Pauline Newman, New York Times, September 1, 1980

Actually, even today the unions represent a small proportion of all workers in the United States. Only about one-fourth of all those employed in industry and government are dues-paying members of unions. The largest number of *non*-union employees are female office workers, who have traditionally resisted unionization—due to pressure from employers (female office workers are in great supply) and also a function of gender-role socialization to passivity and "ladylike" behavior. Interestingly, after being refused union membership until 1950 black workers are now more likely to be union members than are their white counterparts. From the beginning of the labor movement in the United States, blacks were excluded from apprentice programs and most craft unions. Echoing the feelings of most Union leaders and workers, Samuel Gompers, founder of the AFL, felt that nonwhites were really not the equals of white males (Stearn, 1971). Anti-female sentiments have been equally widespread. The first woman member of the AFL-CIO Executive Council was appointed in 1980. Unions composed of mainly female workers, such as in the garment industry, have always had primarily male officers.

> The largest group of **nonunion employees** are women office workers.

Many manufacturing operations have relocated from the northeast to southern and border states (and even to Third World countries) because of the low proportion of unionized labor and the consequently lower payroll. Southern and border states have been very generous in tax abatements to the relocated industries. This has led to a major organizing efforts by the unions among textile workers in these states. A union-supported boycott of the J. P. Stevens textile company was a long, drawnout, and sometimes violent affair. The Stevens boycott had been less effective than the one waged by Cesar Chavez's United Farmworkers against lettuce and grape growers and the Teamsters Union in California. In general, boycotts are difficult to sustain over long periods, and require the cooperation of the buying public, most of whom have no immediate personal stake in the outcome.

An additional problem is the fact that many rank-and-file workers believe that their union leaders have become too much a part of the establishment, looking out for their personal power interests rather than those of the workers. Dissident groups have developed within the ranks of teamsters, steel workers, and miners. Moreover, the fact that union leaders endorse certain candidates or policies does not necessarily bind their followers; in recent elections, many

Table 12-3. Union Membership, United States 1977

Per cent in each group who are union members

	Male	Female
White	28.9	14.5
Black	35.3	23.5

Earnings:

Weekly average non-union	$221
Weekly average union-workers	262
Construction workers	343

Geographic distribution (% of labor force in the area who are union members):

Middle Atlantic States	35.9 (high)
West South Central	14.9 (low)

Type of employment:

Blue collar	43%
White collar	18%
Service	19%

Range:

Railroad	82.5%	Agriculture, etc.	12%
Metal & Auto	72%	Textile	11%

Source: Department of Labor, Bureau of Labor Statistics, Report 556 (April, 1979).

Mobilizing public opinion, Cesar Chavez led a successful boycott of California produce, in order to gain higher wages for farm workers. (Source: Christopher Brown, Stock, Boston.)

workers have voted against their union's endorsed candidates. Despite criticism of their leadership, the overwhelming majority of union members in a recent national survey expressed satisfaction with their union: 25% were very satisfied, 48% satisfied, 17% dissatisfied, and 10% very dissatisfied (Kochan, 1979).

The two main goals of Western labor movements are the upgrading of workers and the elimination of inequality.

Organized Labor and the Reduction of Inequality.   The ideology of Western labor movements rooted in socialist theory proclaims two sets of goals: the upgrading of workers and the elimination of inequality within the laboring segment as well as in the society as a whole. In Europe, these goals are embodied in socialist political parties such as England's Labor party, France's Socialists, or West Germany's Social Democrats. In the United States and Canada, however, organized labor has typically formed alliances with nonclass-based political parties. The Liberal Party and the recently formed New Democratic Party in Canada and the Democratic Party in the United States have, since the 1930s, tended to be favored by organized labor and other wage workers. Conversely, the Progressive Conservatives in Canada and the Republicans in the United States have become identified with business and employer interests. In neither North American country has a specifically labor-oriented government been elected. As a consequence, some gains for workers have resulted from specific unions' support for specific candidates. These gains have been most uneven, with some labor groups enjoying special influence at particular historical moments.

Most of the labor movement's victories have been achieved through **collective bargaining** with employers.

Most of the victories of the labor movement have been made by individual unions through *collective bargaining* with employers. Under these circumstances, unions representing the most skilled segments of the labor force have made proportionately greater gains for their members than have the unions bargaining on behalf of less skilled and more easily replaceable workers. The end result is a *highly stratified* labor force. Without a Labor Party banner under which to unify and resolve differences, each labor union does the best possible for its members, even at the cost of jobs or income to other unionized workers, and especially to the nonunionized.

How well has the union movement in the United States reduced inequalities within the working class? Using census data on income, race, and occupation, and Department of Labor Statistics on union membership, E. M. Beck (1980) concludes that in the period 1947–1974 the effects of unionism were primarily to maintain the favored economic status of white workers relative to blacks. Income inequality by race was not greatly reduced by union membership or by unionization in general.

An additional barrier to equality within the labor force is the creation of differentiated labor markets, that is, separate pools of workers for different types of employment.

The **dual economy** has two distinct sectors of workers for different types of employment: core industries and peripheral businesses.

The dual economy theory (Averitt, 1968) states that in advanced capitalist economies two distinct sectors can be identified: (1) a core composed of large-scale industrial and mining corporations characterized by high productivity, high profits, monopolies, unionization, and intensive investment of capital; and (2) a peripheral sector of small firms with low productivity and profit, nonunionized work force, low rates, intensive use of manual labor, and relatively free competition. The incomes of both owners and workers in the core sector are quite high. Peripheral entrepreneurs, on the other hand, have few resources for growth and little political power. Workers on the periphery will have similarly risky employment opportunities and a lower wage scale than workers in the core sector (Beck, et al., 1978). This is true for all industrialized societies.

Segmented Labor Markets. The low-skill, labor-intensive nature of the peripheral sector is associated with a labor force disproportionately composed of women and members of low-status minority groups. In other words, gender and race often distinguish two types of labor pools—one composed of white males who move into core sector jobs with relatively high pay and some mobility potential; the other composed of women, blacks, and Hispanics of either sex, who are channeled into low paying and often temporary or seasonal employment.

The concept of a segmented labor force or split labor market refers to the fact that even where skills and education are the same, blacks and women tend to have lower status jobs and consequently lower incomes (Bonacich, 1975). Once employed, moreover, additional discrimination effects classify jobs filled by

A **segmented labor force** develops when women and nonwhites have lower status jobs and income than white men, although their skills and education may be the same.

Sex and race separate the labor pool: white males move into jobs with high pay and opportunity for advancement while women, blacks, and Hispanics are directed toward low-paying, temporary, or seasonal employment. (Source: Ellis Herwig, Stock, Boston.)

women or blacks and Hispanics differently from similar jobs held by males and whites (janitor as opposed to cleaning woman; or guard v. matron; or administrative assistant v. executive secretary).

Many analysts of dual sector and segmented labor pools refer to these phenomena as products of advanced capitalism, suggesting that in a planned economy such distinctions within the labor force will be minimized. Yet data from the Soviet Union (Swafford, 1978) and other East European socialist states (Lenski, 1978) clearly display the same differences between male and female incomes regardless of skill and education level that are found in the United States and Canada.

Nor is a segmented labor market necessarily an outcome of industrialization (whether capitalist or socialist). It appears that some groups have been assigned the dirty work of any society, from the days when Pharoahs used Israelite slaves to build the Pyramids. It should not surprise us, then, that Mexican-Americans now pick grapes in California, or Yugoslavs clean the streets of German cities, and Turks perform the menial tasks in Swedish factories.

EMPLOYMENT AND UNEMPLOYMENT

Employment itself is linked to ascribed characteristics not connected to ability: age, sex, and race.

The state of being employed, as well as the type of job held, is related to characteristics that are not necessarily related to ability: age, sex, and race. In early 1979, in the United States, almost two-thirds of all noninstitutionalized persons over the age of sixteen were in the paid labor force. Fifty-nine per cent were employed and almost 6% were unemployed. The remaining one-third were primarily home makers or retired individuals.

But employment and unemployment are not evenly distributed among subgroups as Table 12-4 illustrates.

In Canada, in 1978, 78 per cent of males 15+ were in the labor force, compared to 48 per cent of females, (*Perspectives Canada* III, p. 304)

Young people (16–19) and those 65+ have relatively low labor force participation rates. In general, also, the higher one's educational attainment, the more likely to be employed.

Hardcore Unemployment. In the United States today, black teenagers are the hardest hit by unemployment—two in five between age 16–19 compared with one in five white young persons. Many blacks and Hispanics, at all ages,

Table 12-4. Employment Status of United States Population 16+, May, 1979

	Male (%)		Female (%)	
	All	Black/other	All	Black/other
In Labor Force				
Employed	72.3	61.6	47.2	46.4
Unemployed	5.0	10.6	6.8	12.6
Not in Labor Force	21.3	26.8	49.2	46.7

Statistical Abstract of the U.S., 1979, p. 394.

are labelled "structurally" or "hardcore" unemployed because there are few appropriate jobs in their geographical area or because they lack the education, skills, experience, or motivation to secure and maintain employment.

Federal programs to counter structural joblessness have been only partially successful. Since overall business growth has been very slow since 1977, few jobs are opening up. Moreover, the areas where jobs are being created are outside the central cities and the Northeast in general, where most hardcore unemployed live. The major funding program for jobless poor people, CETA (Comprehensive Employment and Training Act), pays for public employment and training of individuals for a period of 18 months, after which it is hoped that the trainee will find a job in the private sector. This has not occurred, however, and critics of CETA claim that people should be trained directly for private-sector employment through subsidies to firms that will hire eligible workers. But there is little indication that the private sector is willing or able to absorb these workers. In any event, job training programs are no longer being funded by the federal government.

Explaining Employment Differences. A theory popular among economists today explains employability and earnings in terms of human capital, that is, the training and skills that an individual brings to the labor market (G. Becker, 1967). This is essentially a functionalist approach, and has been challenged by data indicating that both blacks and women receive *lower* returns that white males on years of education, training, and skill.

The conflict perspective would lead to the question: who benefits from unemployment and from sex and race differentials in employment? High unemployment rates in general tend to favor management in wage negotiations. To the degree that the government or outside forces can be blamed, attention is deflected from management mistakes and inefficiencies leading to economic failure, as when layoffs of automobile workers in 1980 were attributed to unfair business practices by Japanese car makers, to environmentalists, and to the Carter Administration, rather than to the manufacturers' unwillingness to build small, fuel-efficient, less costly automobiles in the late 1970s. When jobs are scarce, hostility is aggravated among those in the least secure positions. Economic downturns are accompanied by increases in racial conflict and, most recently, by claims that women are taking jobs away from more qualified men. These divisions within the working class also serve the interests of corporate owners and managers by personalizing the issue rather than focusing on the structural features of the economy responsible for unemployment swings.

A structural analysis of the economic system would focus on the segmented labor market and core/periphery sector differences to explain variations in earnings and employment histories among subgroups. Researchers using this type of analysis claim that *where the worker is located in the economic structure* is a more powerful explanatory variable than the characteristics of the workers proposed in the human capital model (Tolbert, Horan, and Beck, 1980). Workers in the peripheral sector are channeled through hiring practices and other gatekeeping activities (school tracking and guidance, entry into training programs, and personal policies), regardless of talent or intelligence, largely on the basis of ascribed characteristics.

> The **human capital** theory explains employability and earnings in terms of an individual's training and skills.

Summary

This chapter focused on the origins, functions, and structures of economic systems, and on the way work is organized in contemporary North America.

Economic behavior develops as people cope with their environment. Groups and societies have dealt with their subsistence needs in a number of ways that gradually become institutionalized; that is, endowed with moral virtues and supported by norms and the law.

The economic system of any society involves the production, distribution and consumption of resources. Capitalism and socialism represent two major economic systems in contemporary industrial societies. The basic difference between them is the extent to which economic activities are regulated by the government and by ideology.

Although the concept of the free market and perfect competition remain part of capitalism, the economic Depression of the late 1920s led to increased governmental intervention in the workings of the economic system. Contemporary North American economies consist of free markets within limits set by governmental regulations. Through its budget powers the federal government can stimulate certain sectors of the economy while maintaining inequality in other sectors.

Karl Marx focused on the primary importance of the economic system in shaping all other social institutions, and on the ways in which religious, political, family, and educational systems reinforce the dominant economic system. The interdependence of institutional spheres is generally acknowledged by social scientists, and has formed the basis of socialist ideology. Although the form of contemporary socialism varies, differences among income groups have been reduced through government involvement in the economy, but many inequalities remain.

In any economic system, work is divided among specialists. This division of labor is minimal in simple societies and highly specialized in complex societies. Modern industrial societies are characterized by an ever finer division of labor, for example the development of the assembly line accompanied by the increasing replacement of human labor by machinery. Although most workers express satisfaction with their jobs, some will become alienated as a result of loss of control over the pacing and conditions of their labor.

The economic system itself is divided into various subsystems. One of these subsystems involves unionization. The history of unionization in North America is a mixture of victories and defeats. Two major sets of goals are sought by the organized labor movement: the upgrading of workers as a category and the elimination of inequality within the labor force itself. While individual unions have achieved victories through collective bargaining, the skilled segments of the labor force have made greater gains than have the unions representing less skilled and more easily replaceable workers.

Employment and the type of job held are related to age, sex, and race, which are ascribed characteristics not necessarily related to ability or job performance. Women and blacks, when compared to white males with comparable training, skills, and education, are less likely to be employed, and generally receive lower wages, fewer promotions, and are found in lower ranked occupations.

Suggested Readings

ABELLA, IRVING and DAVID MILLAR (eds). *The Canadian Worker in the Twentieth Century* (New York: Oxford University Press, 1978). Partly based on interviews with elderly workers and documents from the early days of the union movement in Canada, this collection of readings traces the history of unionization, the living conditions of workers, and the situation of working women.

CLEMENT, WALLACE. *Continental Corporate Power: Economic Linkages between Canada and the United States* (Toronto: McClelland and Stewart, 1977). The structure of North American corporate power is systematically described and analyzed in this volume that has influenced Canadian and U.S. scholars.

CONNOR, WALTER D. *Socialism, Politics, and Equality: Hierarchy and Change in Eastern Europe and the USSR* (New York: Columbia University Press, 1980). A well-balanced assessment of progress toward equality and continuing hierarchy and inequality in the USSR and Eastern Europe.

FRIEDMAN, MILTON and ROSE FRIEDMAN. *Free to Choose* (New York: Avon, 1981). The Friedmans present the case for contemporary free enterprise in a format and style that has made this book a best seller in paperback as well as hard cover.

HARRINGTON, MICHAEL. *Socialism* (New York: Bantam, 1972). This is a highly readable account of the historical roots of socialism, its theoretical foundations and its contemporary forms.

SOKOLOFF, NATALIE. *Between Money and Love: The Dialectics of Women's Home and Market Work* (New York: Praeger, 1980). A review of various theoretical and empirical approaches to the study of women and their work, gender roles and the labor market, and the relation of women's roles as mothers in the home to their paid work in the marketplace.

STEPHENS, JOHN D. *The Transition from Capitalism to Socialism* (London: Macmillan Press Ltd., 1979). The theme of the transition from capitalism to socialism is traced through the writings of Marx, Lenin, and others. The book includes comparative discussions of political changes in Western Europe, the USSR, Sweden, Britain, France and the U.S.

TERKEL, STUDS. *Working* (New York: Random, 1972). In the words of the book jacket, "people talk about what they do all day and how they feel about what they do"—frankly and fascinatingly.

13 Politics and Power

"*P*ut not your trust in princes," warns the psalmist of the Bible. Over two thousand years later, the British historian Lord Acton wrote: "*Power tends to corrupt, and absolute power corrupts absolutely*". And yet the absence of political order—anarchy—has been equally feared throughout human history. The tension between forces of freedom and control is an enduring aspect of social life.

Power, as defined by Max Weber, is the probability that an individual or group can realize its own goals even against the opposition of others in a particular action. Note that this definition is social rather than personal; that is, power is less an attribute of an individual than it is a possibility within a social situation—at work, at home, in daily interactions as well as in town halls, or Washington and Ottawa. *Political sociologists* study the underlying dynamics of power and control among competing groups. Their concern is with "who rules, why, and how?"

In this chapter we will begin with a macrolevel consideration of the origins and development of political systems in terms of functional theory before dealing with the uses of power from an essentially conflict perspective.

Origins and Functions of Political Systems

Political institutions are patterned statuses and roles developed by each human group to meet the need for internal order and external defense. To ensure that necessary tasks are carried out, some individuals are given power to enforce the norms. In the simplest societies, age and sex are the minimal bases for power differences: Elders give orders to juniors, and males to females.

At the societal level, the essential problem of order is that of coordinating the activities of individuals and groups, and for this, *institutionalization* of social control functions is required. When two or more kinship groups live together, some mechanism for resolving disputes must be devised. This is the origin of political institutions: arrangements for rule-making and enforcement that have priority over other loyalties within the society. The larger the society, the greater the specialization of tasks, and the more problematic becomes the maintenance of social order. Thus, the course of sociocultural development is also the history of the elaboration of political institutions, from the temporary leader of a hunting band to the current governments of North America.

THE MAINTENANCE OF ORDER

Each society will develop some mechanism for transforming normative agreement into enforceable rules. Recognition of the authority of the father in

Formal bodies of lawmakers exist in all modern societies. Pictured here are the Israeli Parliament, the Knesset, and the capital, which houses the U.S. Congress. (Sources: top—Owen Frankel, Stock, Boston; bottom—Rhonda Galyn, Photo Researchers, Inc.)

the family or eldest male in the kinship group brings with it the power to punish violators of the norms and reward those who conform. In larger societies, councils of elders would define rules, listen to complaints, make judgments. Today, in all modern and most developing societies, formal bodies of lawmakers exist—Congress, Parliament, Cortes, Knesset, and so on—whose efforts are typically reinforced by an administrative apparatus, judicial system, and an increasingly complex pattern of statuses involved in *norm enforcement:* police, magistrates, courts, jails, prisons, and secret-service agents.

THE DEFENSE OF THE GROUP

The second major function of the polity is to provide for security from external enemies. It is a peculiarity of history textbooks that periods of warfare have received most attention, thus exaggerating the military aspects of the political system. In North America, periods of warmaking have been relatively few, and large standing armies were unknown until the last four decades. But since the end of the Second World War, defensive and offensive capabilities have absorbed an ever larger amount of public funds and political attention. Defense-related expenses will account for almost 30 per cent of the total government expenditures of the United States in 1982. Throughout the world, governments are spending eight times as much for research on new weapons as on solving energy problems (*New York Times,* Sept. 6, 1980, p. 3).

Providing security from external enemies is a major function of the polity.

Political Institutions in Complex Societies

The formal organization of a society—its government—is linked to the other institutional spheres through a set of basically mutually supportive exchanges. In general, political institutions provide a protective environment for business, family life, religious observance, and educational pursuits. In return, groups and individuals give expressions of loyalty to the government. The Pledge of

The government is linked to other social institutions through mutually supportive exchanges.

Individuals express their loyalty by such patriotic gestures as displaying the flag. (Source: Patricia Hollander Gross, Stock, Boston.)

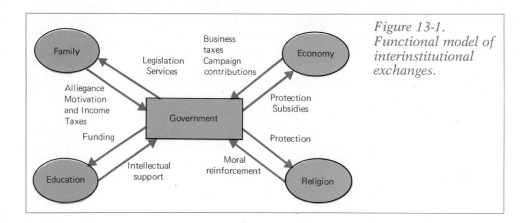

Figure 13-1. Functional model of interinstitutional exchanges.

The **state** is the primary support of the economic system.

The **political economy** refers to the interconnection between the political and economic spheres.

In **totalitarian systems** the right to dissent is minimal.

Democratic systems are more tolerant of dissent and opposition.

Allegiance is recited in schools; the National Anthem sung before sports events; families display the flag and provide personnel for the armed forces; and religious leaders are often strong supporters of the political establishment. The link between the economic and political sectors has especially fascinated sociologists. For many social scientists, the political organization of modern societies—the *state*—is the primary support of the economic system, whether capitalist or socialist. Despite the extensive overlap of political and economic subsystems, the state has a number of unique characteristics and a sphere of relatively autonomous activities.

TOTALITARIAN AND DEMOCRATIC STATES

Just as economic systems vary along a continuum of central planning, political systems can be arranged along a continuum of individual rights: at one pole are *totalitarian* states in which the right to dissent, as expressed in competition between political parties, is minimal. *Democratic* polities are characterized by a relatively high level of tolerance of dissent and the right to organize in opposition.

Contemporary totalitarian states come in a variety of forms: military, civilian, and religious, and are most frequently found in the Third World where the dislocations of modernization have destroyed the traditional political order while the preconditions of democracy (literacy, economic stability, egalitarian ideology) have not been established. In many cases, democratic processes have been tried but found to be too ineffective in maintaining order, especially in times of economic breakdown. This leaves the path open for a dictator who promises to restore law and order and to have the trains run on time. In still other totalitarian states, ideological considerations are paramount; for example, the belief that one group—members of the revolutionary elite, or Communist Party, or Moslem Clergy, for example—can best rule in the interests of all.

Democratic systems are also varied, differing mainly in the structure of political parties and voting procedures. Not all democracies allow all adults to vote, and there is no guarantee that democratic processes produce more competent or honest rulers than any other system. The major advantage of the democratic system is that rulers can be periodically held accountable and replaced.

With these basic considerations in mind, then, let us turn to the more basic dimension of power that both underlies the formal organization of a society and regulates the relations of individuals and groups.

POWER

Cultural norms and social structural arrangements ensure that some statuses will command greater power than others, and that power will be unevenly distributed across subgroups within the society. The question of who is able to exercise power, to occupy statuses in the formal political system, or to claim the allegiance of others, is called the question of *legitimacy*. It is assumed that those who are ruled will follow orders only when they perceive the exercise of power as legitimate, that is, in accordance with the norms of the group or the desires of the ruled.

Legitimacy. Again, it is to Max Weber that sociologists turn for their terminology and theory: "All ruling powers, profane and religious, political and apolitical, may be considered as variations of, or approximations to, certain pure types. These types are constructed by searching for the basis of legitimacy which the ruling power claims" (Gerth and Mills, 1958).

Authority is the legimate exercise of power, and Weber describes three ideal types of legitimate authority.

Authority is the legitimate exercise of power. ✳

1. *Charismatic authority*. The word "charisma" is Greek for "gift" and has come to mean a special talent or quality within an individual, often thought to be divinely given. Charismatic authority, says Weber, is not based on the position held but upon some perceived extraordinary quality of a person that leads others to submit to that person's will.

Charismatic authority is based on perceived personal qualities. ✳1

Since charismatic authority is based on personal characteristics, there is always the problem of building an organization that can continue the cause after the gifted person has died (and charismatic leaders, because of the high emotion they generate, for and against, are likely to have relatively brief lives). This is the problem referred to by Weber as "the routinization of charisma." The divine gift must be translated into everyday structures, but in doing so, becomes noncharismatic. The leaders who follow a charismatic figure have to work harder to win the allegiance of the ruled.

Among the few historical figures who can be thought of as charismatic are Jesus, Mohammed, Mahatma Gandhi, and Martin Luther King, Jr.—all, it should be noted, men of religion. Charismatic authority, notes Weber, is essentially irrational because it is not always linked to the established structures of the society, and followers are asked to comply on the basis of faith—faith that can be disappointed when anticipated miracles do not occur.

2. *Traditional authority* is based upon a mind-set that invests habitual routine with the strength of unquestioned norms of conduct: "This is the way it has always been, therefore this is the way it must always be". Weber singles out *patriarchy*—the rule of fathers, husbands, elders, masters of the household, lords, princes and all forms of nobles, and especially the sovereign—as the archetype (ideal form) of traditional authority.

Traditional authority is based on habitual routine.

Since traditionalism is based upon the absolute acceptance of the norms while leaving a large area of arbitrary control to the patriarchal figure, it, too, is irrational; that is, it is not based upon universal standards or grounded in reasoned argument among the ruled.

Charismatic leaders, such as the Rev. Martin Luther King, Jr., President John F. Kennedy, and Cuban Premier Fidel Castro, exhibit personal qualities which aid their exercise of authority. (Sources: top left—Wide World Photos; top right—United Press International; bottom—Romano Cagnoni, Magnum.)

As with charismatic leadership, traditional rulers are faced with the problem of choosing successors. Since the basis of authority is still an attribute of the person—maleness, age, prowess in battle, among others—traditional leadership must also be routinized. But unlike charismatic authority, the traditional leader derives power from the people's willingness to follow tradition. Succession, therefore, tends to become a matter of tradition also, from father to son, or nearest male heir. Thus are royal families created and maintained.

3. *Legal authority* is based upon an impersonal bond between those who hold office and those who submit to that authority. The limits of power are established by laws, recognized norms that members of a society debate and set and agree to obey. "The legitimacy of the authority," writes Weber, "becomes the legality of the general rule, which is purposefully thought out, enacted, and announced with formal correctness" (p. 299).

This, to Weber, is rationality: limited rule, universally applied. In the political sphere, then, limited representative democracy is more rational (though not always more effective) than the arbitrariness of traditional rulers or the appeal to faith of the charismatic leader.

Legal authority is based on impersonal norms established by law. ✳3

THE EXERCISE OF POWER

Legitimacy also relates to the willingness of members of a society to take orders from others—once the basis of authority has been established. Political systems can be arranged along a continuum representing freely-given legitimacy and that which is coerced (forced). Note that some dictatorships will be legitimate (though not democratic) because the ruler has been able to claim traditional or charismatic authority. Yet even in democratic systems, leaders must seek public approval for their policies and programs, to assure reelection or at least the continuation of one's party in power. Thus, the manipulation of public opinion is an important element in the exercise of power in most modern polities.

Public Opinion. Attempts to control public perception can be very subtle. In a democracy, using the trappings of office to influence opinion or distributing public funds to reward some groups while withholding favors to others have proven highly effective. When Richard Nixon, during the Watergate hearings, was trying to persuade the public that he had done no wrong, he appeared on television in the Oval Office with the Great Seal of the Presidency behind him, an American Flag at his side, and a pile of officially stamped notebooks on his desk—who could doubt his legitimacy?

Two other techniques have been used in democratic as well as totalitarian states: propaganda and censorship.

Propaganda is the selective release of information favorable to actions taken by the ruler(s) of any state. During wars, propaganda has been used to generate public support for the war effort. During the war in Vietnam, for example, information favorable to the United States was quickly passed along to the news media while stories that would reflect poorly on the American military were not disclosed, on the grounds that such knowledge would lower support for the war.

Propaganda is the dissemination of information favorable to actions taken by the governing authorities. ✳

Usually, a relatively free press should be the strongest bulwark against such manipulation of the public, but the media are also dependent on officials for information, and uncooperative reporters can be shut out of future stories. In

Through propaganda, governments can maintain high levels of public support and create enthusiasm for official policies. (Source: Editorial Photocolor Archives.)

the United States, owners and operators of radio and television stations must have their licences renewed, and in both Canada and the United States newspaper editors have personal or political interests that often coincide with those of people in high office. Moreover, the commercial media depend on advertising revenue, and advertisers often have their own political agendas. Also, at moments of national crisis the press tends to be restrained in criticisms of government.

<u>Censorship</u> is the practice of controlling the flow of news through *forbidding* the disclosure of certain information. Again, the most obvious cases occur in wartime, when claims of national security are invoked. But censorship can also occur in a democracy in peacetime.

Surveillance and the Chilling of Dissent.   In countries that do not have constitutionally guaranteed *civil liberties* (which are rights residing in individuals, even against the state), governments can control behavior through the police and other means of watching citizens. These are common tactics in totalitarian states, but they have also been used in democratic societies. During the 1960s, the Federal Bureau of Investigation tapped phones, opened mail, used agents in

Censorship is the practice of forbidding the disclosure of certain information.

Civil liberties are rights belonging to individuals even against the state.

In 1979 the federal government asked the courts to forbid publication of a magazine article that told how easy it was for a reporter to find information necessary for building a nuclear weapon (provided, of course, that one had the complex technology and reactors to do so). A lower court agreed to issue an injunction *before* the magazine was published, the first instance in our history of *prior restraint*. Since all the data for the article had been gathered from publicly-accessible sources, it was very difficult for the government to continue to claim that national secrets were being published or even that the information would help others construct a nuclear weapon; any country capable of doing so could get the required assistance from any one of a half-dozen other nations.

After several months, the government dropped its case, and the *Progressive* published its article. But for these several months one small segment of the United States press experienced peacetime censorship.

When that issue of the *Progressive* finally came out, a prison warden clipped the article from a magazine intended for an inmate. It is against prison rules to allow inmates information on bomb-making. When it was pointed out that it was highly unlikely that a prisoner would have the necessary equipment to manufacture nuclear weapons, the warden relented and allowed the entire magazine to be read.

disguise, and photographed people who attended anti-war rallies. A high school student who wrote to the Socialist Workers Party of the United States for information for a term paper had her mail watched for many years thereafter.

Most Americans do not realize that guarantees of civil liberties were designed by the creators of the Bill of Rights to protect citizens against the state's great powers to chill expressions of discontent. Recent polls indicate that the majority of those questioned would approve the surveillance and denial of civil liberties of several kinds of groups.

A Gallup Poll commissioned in 1980 found that 37 per cent of the respondents thought that present curbs on press freedom were "not enough," 30 per cent "just right," and 17 per cent "too strict" (the rest had no opinion). The same survey found that 75 per cent of those polled (including 60 per cent of those with college educations) *did not* know what was in the First Amendment (*NY Times*, Jan. 18, 1980, p. A10).

For your information:

Amendment I (1791)

Congress shall make no law respecting an establishment of religion, or prohibiting the free exercise thereof; or abridging the freedom of speech, or of the press; or the right of the people peaceably to assemble, and to petition the Government for a redress of grievances.

In general, tolerance of dissent and nonconforming behavior is directly related to educational level, so that increased tolerance between the 1950s and today in the United States is largely accounted for by the extension of higher education. Conversely, tolerance is negatively associated with measures of religiosity (Nunn, Crockett and Williams, 1978).

Coercion, Repression and Genocide. At the extreme end of the continuum of social control, some governments maintain order by the forceful restraint of

349

Coercion is the use of force to ensure compliance.

Repression is the use of arrest, imprisonment, and executions to control dissidents.

Genocide means the systematic slaughter of an entire race or category of people.

dissent. *Coercion* refers to the use of force to ensure compliance. The threat of the use of force can be equally effective if citizens believe that such force can and would be used. This is why only one or two highly publicized cases are required in order to secure the obedience of most citizens.

Repression or *suppression* involves the use of imprisonment, executions, and house arrest to control dissidents. Those defined as troublemakers are simply removed from where they can make trouble. This is a common technique in the Soviet Union today.

The ultimate means of enforcing one's rule is to do away with opposition altogether. *Genocide* literally means "to kill an entire race of people." It was practiced by the Third Reich toward Jews in Europe, and by the government of Iran with respect to the Kurdish people.

POWER IN RELATIONSHIPS

Why do individuals remain in relationships in which the power differentials appear to be profoundly unbalanced—slaves, citizens in dictatorships, wives in brutalizing marriages, and so forth? One consideration is the availability of alternatives, another is the cost (effort, risk, consequences of failure). It does little good to rebel if further repression is the only outcome. Many people accept tyrannical rule as a lesser evil than anarchy. For still others, a lack of personal freedom is an acceptable price for not having to cope with difficult decisions. Consent of the ruled can be induced by raising the costs of dissent. Terror, involving secret police, political imprisonment, and the use of torture, is a common means of escalating the cost of noncompliance in totalitarian societies. Lesser threats, such as the inability to find employment, are common even in democracies, as in the blacklisting of media personalities during the anti-Communist crusades of the 1950s in the United States.

Consent of the ruled is gained by raising costs of dissent or reducing benefits of disobedience.

Compliance can also be assured by shaping interactions so that individuals believe that they are to blame for their unhappiness. For example, teenagers are defined as disobedient if they object to their treatment.

Power relationships result from **negotiations** among participants.

In this sense, power relationships result from *negotiation* among participants in a social action. At both the macro- and microlevel, claims Anselm Strauss (1978), social order is constantly being changed or maintained by a bargaining process among interacting groups and individuals. The social structure is at once the outcome of negotiation and the context for further exchanges.

But it is important to bear in mind that negotiators do not bring similar resources to the process. This is clear, for example, in the relationships between agents of government and individual citizens, between college administrators and students, or between employers and nonunionized employees. Less obvious, perhaps, are power differentials in everyday life, as demonstrated by who can touch whom or impose on the other's personal space—behaviors described as "body politics" (Henley, 1977).

Societies marked by great differences in wealth and power are relatively unstable.

It is probably fair to state that societies marked by extreme differences in wealth and/or power are relatively unstable and that increasingly repressive actions are needed to keep the masses from rebellion, as recently seen in Iran, Argentina, Korea, and Eastern Europe.

David Kipnis (1976) has described the major corrupting influences of power that operate on both the societal level and that of everyday relationships: (1) the desire for power becomes an end in itself; (2) powerholders cannot resist using institutional resources for personal gain, betraying the trust of others and perverting the public good; (3) powerholders receive false feedback, are isolated from reality, and develop an exalted sense of self-worth; (4) all this leads to the devaluation and avoidance of the less powerful supported by an ideology of natural superiority/inferiority.

Political Participation

A common frame of reference for the discussion of political behavior is the actual participation of individuals in the process of selecting their rulers. Since the major distinction between a democratic or totalitarian polity is the existence of opposition parties (and, by extension, relatively free elections), involvement in the political process varies from society to society in terms of who can take part and to what extent.

In the United States and Canada, participation is possible at many levels: One can run for office, become active in the campaigns of others, contribute money to candidates, vote, or fail to vote.

OFFICE HOLDING

Although the United States and Canada have very different methods for selecting candidates, the results at the federal level are comparable: executive, administrative, and legislative bodies composed almost exclusively of middle-class white males. In both countries, religious, ethnic, and regional characteristics no longer serve as absolute barriers to candidacy for national office. Of the last two prime ministers of Canada, one was a Westerner, the other a French-speaking Catholic. In the United States, a Catholic became president in 1960 and a Southerner in 1976. Other bases of stratification remain relatively intact: particularly race and gender.

The time and money involved in running for office in the United States limits the number and type of individuals who can afford to campaign. Also, many politicians and voters perceive males—especially white middle-class men—as more authoritative than women. Thus, few women or members of racial minor-

Table 13-1. Members of U.S. Congress: Selected Characteristics, 1969 and 1979

	Male	Female	White	Black	Asian
Representatives					
1969	425	10	424	9	2
1979	417	16	414	16	3
Senators					
1969	99	1	97	1	2
1979	99	1	98	—	2

Source: Statistical Abstract of the U.S., 1979, p. 509.

Table 13-2. *Women Holding State and Local Public Offices, 1975 and 1977*

	State executive & judiciary	State legislature	County commissions	Mayors	Township and local councils
1975	226	610	456	566	5,365
1977	207	696	660	755	9,195

Source: *Statistical Abstract of the U.S.*, 1979, p. 513.

ities are encouraged to seek nomination or, if nominated, become successful candidates.

In general, women still report strong resistance to their participation in electoral politics, difficulties in raising money, and a greater need to have family support than do men (Marilyn Johnson, 1980). Nonetheless, female and black representation at the state and local levels has increased dramatically in the past few years, although state and national offices are as difficult as ever to achieve.

Table 13-2 may underestimate the number of female officials since it does not include school boards, where women often outnumber male members.

As for blacks in the United States, the figures are similar to those for women: higher at the lower levels of government (See Table 13-3) (Hamilton, 1978).

Despite these striking gains, women and members of racial minorities are greatly *underrepresented* in positions of power, and the more so as the real power of the office increases. In this fashion, the stratification hierarchy of power is substantially reproduced. People without power in the economic or interpersonal spheres are not perceived as appropriate incumbents of positions of political power, and without legitimate authority, they are indeed powerless, thus reinforcing the original perception.

Campaign activity is engaged in by only a small proportion of individuals in the United States and Canada. Political participation is usually assumed to be

Campaign activity in the United States and Canada involves a very small proportion of the population.

Table 13-3. *Number of Black Elected Officials, 1970–1979*

	1970	1974	1977	1979
U.S. Senators, Representatives	10	17	17 ⎫	
State Legislators, Executives	168	239	299 ⎭	315
Mayors	40	108	162 ⎫	
Other Local Officials	559	1,142	2,335 ⎬	2,647
Judges, Magistrates	114	172	247 ⎭	
Police Chiefs, Law-enforcement Officials	47	111	200	486
Members of Local School Boards	362	767	1,251	1,136

Source: Joint Center for Political Studies, Washington, D.C. in Hamilton (1978) p. 22; and *Statistical Abstract of the U.S.*, 1979, p. 512

determined by individual interest and beliefs (Campbell, et al., 1969). But recent research suggests that volunteering to help in a campaign requires more
effort than simply going to the polling booth. Orum (1976) raises the possibility
that factors external to the individual can be as important as level of interest in
accounting for entering the public arena as an active worker for a candidate or
cause. Using Canadian data, Zipp and Smith (1979) tested the hypothesis that
campaign activity is stimulated when the individual is recruited by friends, and
found that personal contact increased the likelihood of becoming active by 50
per cent. In other words, a person's social network must be taken into account
in explaining who volunteers to work in a campaign, and how they are selected.
Individuals do not act in a vacuum, but are embedded in social systems that
affect political behavior as well as most other activities.

Voting is the minimal act of political participation, and in those societies
where voting is not mandatory, many citizens do not bother to go to the polls or
even register for the right to vote.

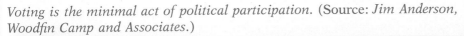

Voting is the minimal
act of political partici-
pation.

Canadians are far more likely to register and to vote than are citizens of the
United States. In the elections of May 1979, for example, 76 per cent of eligible
Canadians cast their ballots; percentages ranged from 81 in Prince Edward
Island to 60 in Newfoundland. This lowest figure for Canadian provinces was
higher than the 53 per cent who turned out for the 1980 presidential election in

Voting is the minimal act of political participation. (Source: Jim Anderson, Woodfin Camp and Associates.)

Table 13-4. *Voting Age Population in the United States: Percentage Registered and Voting 1968 and 1980*

	Per cent registered		Per cent voting	
	1968	1980	1968	1980
Totals	74.3	66.9	67.8	59.2*
White	75.4	68.4	69.1	60.9
Black	66.2	60.0	57.6	50.5
Spanish-origin	—	36.3	—	29.9
Male	76.0	66.6	69.8	59.1
Female	72.8	67.1	66.0	59.4
North & West	76.5	67.9	71.0	61.0
South	69.2	64.8	60.1	55.6
18–20 yr. old	44.2	44.7	33.3	35.7
21–24	56.4	52.7	51.1	43.1
25–44	72.4	65.5	66.6	58.6
45–64	81.1	75.8	74.9	69.3
65+	75.6	74.5	65.8	65.0

Source: *Statistical Abstract*, 1979, p. 514, adapted from Tables 836 and 837. *Current Population Reports*, Voting and Registration in the Election at November 1980, Series p. 20, No. 359, Washington, D.C., 1981.
*This is higher than the 53 per cent reported in the press due to sampling error in the CPR surveys.

the United States. In non-presidential election years, voting rates in the United States dip below 50 per cent; only 46 per cent voted in the congressional elections of 1978.

As you can see from Table 13-4, both registration and actual voting varies by race, gender, region, and age. Education is also a powerful factor; the higher the years of completed schooling, the more likely one is to be registered and to vote. Least likely to vote are the young (18–24), Southerners, those with less than a high-school education, blacks and Hispanics.

Most baffling of all is the low participation of persons 18–24. When the voting age in federal elections in the United States was lowered to 18 in 1972, it was thought that this symbol of political maturity would encourage young people to express their dissatisfactions through the electoral process. But this age group is the most mobile segment of the population, and many have not been in one place long enough to qualify for voting. Young people are also changing statuses from student to worker, from single to married, from child-free to parent, and their attention may not be on politics, although issues of war and peace most directly affect young people, and inflation and taxes are especially hard on those just beginning occupational and marital careers.

Nonvoting has often been considered a sign of alienation from mainstream society. As Emile Durkheim has pointed out, those individuals with the most ties to other people are most likely to preserve their stake in the society. Voting is one means of protecting investments in social order and of controlling one's

Up until 1920, the majority of United States adults did not vote because they *could not*. With the passage of the Women's Suffrage Amendment—a mere 60 years ago—all noninstitutionalized citizens over age 21 were legally entitled to vote, and only since 1972 have those 18–21 been granted this right. Yet in every presidential election since 1920, the percentage of *non*voters has been greater than that voting for the winning candidate:

Although the proporiton of nonvoters has steadily increased since 1960, the actual percentage varies greatly from one election to another, and was higher in 1920, 1924, and 1948 than it is today.

Nonvoters, as already noted, tend to come from the more disadvantaged strata in terms of income, occupation, education, employment, and race. The nonmarried (who are also likely to be aged 18–24) have a lower voting rate than the married, adding further support for the Durkheim thesis.

Why Not Vote?

Most nonvoters—79%—do not vote because they are not registered (26.5% were ineligible because of residence and filing requirements; and 52.5% because they were "not interested in registering"). Of the remaining 21%, slightly more than half were unable to (primarily due to illness or travel) and the remainder were not interested.

In 1976, 38 million adults failed to register. One-third of these were unable to register because they were not citizens, too ill, lacked transportation, or could not meet eligibility requirements. Two-thirds were not interested, over half of these because they forgot or did not get around to it. The rest didn't care about the candidates or politics in general.

As a result, only 27.2% of all adults elected the man who became president in 1976, and in 1980 an even smaller proportion elected (26%) Ronald Reagan.

Source: Charles E. Johnson, Jr., *Current Population Reports*, Series P-23, No. 102, April 1980.

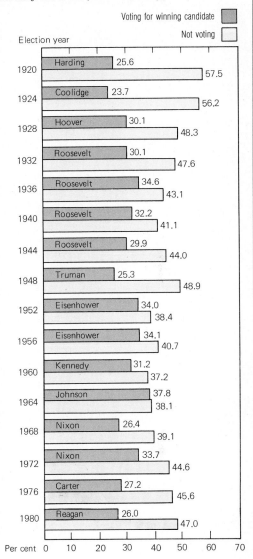

Non-Voting Americans

Per Cent Voting for the Winning Candidate and Per Cent Not Voting: 1920 to 1980 (After universal suffrage)

Voting for winning candidate ▓
Not voting ☐

Election year

Year	Candidate	Voting for winning	Not voting
1920	Harding	25.6	57.5
1924	Coolidge	23.7	56.2
1928	Hoover	30.1	48.3
1932	Roosevelt	30.1	47.6
1936	Roosevelt	34.6	43.1
1940	Roosevelt	32.2	41.1
1944	Roosevelt	29.9	44.0
1948	Truman	25.3	48.9
1952	Eisenhower	34.0	38.4
1956	Eisenhower	34.1	40.7
1960	Kennedy	31.2	37.2
1964	Johnson	37.8	38.1
1968	Nixon	26.4	39.1
1972	Nixon	33.7	44.6
1976	Carter	27.2	45.6
1980	Reagan	26.0	47.0

Per cent 0   10   20   30   40   50   60   70

fate. Thus, those who are employed and well educated, in mature adulthood, and members of the dominant race are most likely to vote, to run for office, and to take part in campaigns. And, consequently, they also tend to benefit most from political decisions (See box on "Non-Voting Americans").

POLITICAL SOCIALIZATION

The motivation to register and to vote and one's political attitudes and affiliations are learned behaviors. *Political socialization* refers to the influences and experiences through which attachment to the political system and to a political party are formed. Since each 18-year-old does not confront the political system as a blank slate, the major controversy in the study of political socialization has

Political socialization refers to the experiences that influence involvement in the political system and party affiliation.

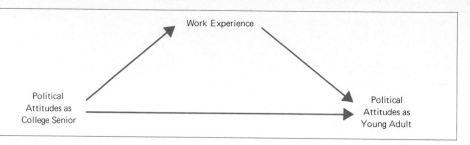

Figure 13-2.
A model of political
socialization.
(Source: Adapted
from Lorence and
Mortimer, 1979.)

been over the relative impact of (1) early learning in the home, community, and
school system, or (2) adult experiences that can lead to reexamination of adolescent political attitudes. Some research indicated relative stability of political
orientation from adolescence to adulthood (Sears, 1975), while other findings
indicate that early socialization has a limited effect in the face of later experience (Niemi and Sobieszek, 1977).

In a test of these two hypotheses, Lorence and Mortimer (1979) found that the
pattern of political socialization involved a complex interplay of early and later
experiences, as illustrated in Figure 13-2. For this sample of college-educated

Early socialization has a
strong effect on later
political orientation.

men, the straight line between attitude as a college senior and attitude as young
adult indicates a strong *direct* effect of early socialization, or stability in political orientation. But there was also a tendency for work experience to have some
effect, often reinforcing the original orientation because conservative students
chose careers in the military and business sectors while liberal college men
turned to the legal and academic professions.

In general, wealth is associated with conservatism. But the effects of education are mixed; on the one hand, a college education is associated with higher
income and success in business, and there is a correlation between these variables and a preference for the Republican Party. On the other hand, a college
education is also associated with liberalized attitudes and increased tolerance,
both associated with Democratic Party reference.

In both Canada and the United States today, traditional links between social
class and political party preference are eroding, partly due to the lack of class
consciousness in general, and partly because the real differences among strata
are decreasing. Thus, many members of the working class strongly endorse
conservative social values while some youth from affluent families embrace
radical politics.

The Structure of Power in America

"Who Rules?" is a question over which social and political scientists have
waged a great and lengthy debate. Two major paradigms have guided this research: the Elite model and the Pluralist model. Both perspectives attempt to
account for the distribution of power in "mass society" defined as one in which
traditional bases of authority have been replaced by distant bureaucracies, and
where primary groups (neighborhoods, communities, or ethnic and religious
organizations) no longer serve as buffers between the masses and their rulers.
The question of who rules has centered on whether there are many different
competing and mediating bases of power (*pluralism*), or whether most crucial

decisions are made by members of a very small group of leaders numbering perhaps a few thousand (the *power elite*).

POWER ELITES

A conflict model of political systems would assume that the state in a capitalist society is controlled by members of the same class that dominates the economic system. On the one hand, the state facilitates the accumulation of wealth by an economic elite (Szymanski, 1978); and on the other, capitalist goals and interests have shaped the government in terms of policies and personnel (Wolfe, 1977). The basic thesis is that there *is a ruling class*, a "national upper class" described by Domhoff (1967) as owning a disproportionate amount of the country's wealth and yearly incomes, whose members control banks and corporations, and through this economic power, the foundations, elite universities, mass media, the executive branch of government and its regulatory agencies, the legal system, and the law enforcement bureaucracy (See Figure 13-3).

This formulation owes much to a controversial book by C. Wright Mills *The Power Elite* published in 1956. The essence of Mills' thesis was that the leaders of the major spheres of influence—business, government, military—are products of a similar class background and socialization experience. Without having to prove a conspiracy or even contact between those who control various sources of power, Mills makes the claim that these leaders think alike and will have the same conceptions of personal and social good. Therefore, they will tend to make decisions that are mutually supportive and that reinforce the high positions on stratification systems already enjoyed by members of their social class. But warnings about concentration of power need not apply only to capitalist societies and institutions. Even hierarchies originally dominated by the nonelite ("the people"), such as trade unions and political parties, will, over time, tend toward hierarchy. This is the "Iron Law of Oligarchy" (see Box on p. 358) proposed by the political theorist, Robert Michels (1876–1936).

The crucial factor for Mills and others was the extent to which all hierarchies are headed by members of the same social stratum. The interpenetration of elites seems as inevitable as hierarchy-formation; that is, those with power in one sphere of activity can exert influence on other areas of social life. The same process appears to be at work in Canada. Porter (1965) uses the image of a "vertical mosaic" to suggest a phenomenon similar to Mills' power elite, and Clement (1975) traces the ties between a corporate elite (business, media, and so forth) and the Canadian political parties. In both countries, labor organizations finance and support candidates of the Liberal and Democratic parties,

> The **ruling class** thesis refers to a national upper class who own and control a disproportionate amount of wealth and power.

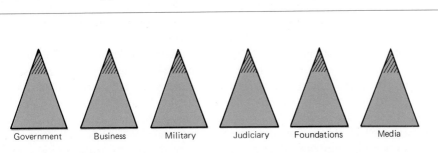

Figure 13-3.
The power elite is composed of members of the upper and upper middle class who have achieved the highest possible positions in each of these centers of power.

Government   Business   Military   Judiciary   Foundations   Media

The Iron Law of Oligarchy by Robert Michels

"By giving themselves leaders, the workers create with their own hands new masters." Michels was referring to worker-based political parties in Europe in the early decades of this century, but his analysis is also applicable to other political and economic organizations. When a small group is set up in leadership positions, it becomes an elite decision-making body. An oligarchy is "the rule of a few." When these few must decide for the many, they bear responsibility for those decisions and therefore have a crucial stake in the outcomes. This leads to disruption in communication between the top and the base of any organization, with the leaders manipulating information that supports their decisions, and avoiding information that might question their wisdom. The leaders have a full-time commitment to their rule; the rank-and-file are only periodically concerned.

A similar process has been noted with respect to other high offices. The phrase "terrible isolation of the presidency" tends to make tragic that which can be a self-imposed protection from adverse criticism. Regardless of how democratic the original goals of the leaders, the mere fact of being a leader reinforces oligarchic tendencies and a consequent gap between leaders and followers. This would not, of course, be unexpected in societies based on elitist principles, where the differences between rulers and the ruled are rationalized as being inherent or divinely ordained. Michels' insight was to apply the principle of oligarchy to avowedly nonelitist organizations such as trade unions or socialist political parties. And, we may add, to the leadership of democratic states.

while business groups support and finance the Conservative and Republican parties.

Is there a power elite? The question would seem to be empirically verifiable, but the relationship between economic and political power is not always clear. For example, Michael Useem (1978) traces the existence of an "inner group" of the capitalist class from survey data on over 1,300 individuals who serve as directors of corporations, socialize at the same exclusive clubs, serve on community boards and national commissions, raise money for special causes, and guide their children's educational and marriage choices. But these interlocking memberships and displays of cohesion did not necessarily lead to greater unity in pursuing class-based interests in the political sphere than was evident among more peripheral executives. Similarly, Gwen Moore (1979), using interview data from 545 leaders of major political, economic, and social institutions in the early 1970s found "considerable integration among elites in all major sectors of American society" but not "a cohesive ruling group acting in concert to further common interests" (p. 689). In other words, a ruling class clearly exists, but its political unity is open to question.

One form of elite penetration outside the party process is exemplified by the two-way traffic in top personnel between the government and business sectors. Governments call upon the services of business leaders, and executives with high posts in government bureaus that control certain industries, upon leaving government employment, take high-level jobs with the very firms they just regulated. In the United States, for example, between 1944 and 1970, two-thirds of former commissioners of the Federal Communication Commission took jobs with a firm previously regulated by the FCC (Greene, 1973).

Yet, is it not also the case in societies as large and varied as the United States and Canada, characterized by regional diversity and heterogeneous populations, that political and economic interests of the various strata may not coincide? The sheer number of business interests suggests that to speak of "big business" is misleading except at the most general level. Actual firms and business sectors are often in direct competition for resources and markets. Moreover, the fact that individuals are in the same social stratum does not necessarily means they will share all goals, although there is evidence that contacts made at elite schools or through family connections and exclusive social clubs are important factors in getting things done in business and government. Recognition of the essential diversity of interest groups in mass society has led to an alternative model based on the concept of diffusion of power.

THE PLURALIST MODEL

The pluralist model contends that political power is distributed among a number of groups and subsystems (Riesman, 1950). Quite apart from the Constitutional division of authority into legislative, executive, and judical, as well as federal, state, and local, the pluralists claim that within any of these divisions, competing segments ensure that no *one* group or class of individuals can have control of the decision-making processes.

The concept of *countervailing forces* in the pluralist argument suggests that competing power blocs (or coalitions) will form to limit the exercise of power of any other group that appears to become overwhelmingly strong. For example, while business interests exercised uncontrolled power in the nineteenth century, the rise of unions and of government intervention ultimately served to constrain big business. And when the unions began to gain great strength, the Taft-Hartley Act and other legislation was enacted to curb big labor. And today we find that big government is once more under attack from business interests. In this view each center of power—business, government, and labor, for example—acts as a buffer against uncontrolled expansion of the others, so that a dynamic balance is maintained, as illustrated in Figure 13-4.

> The **pluralist model** assumes that power is distributed among a number of groups and subsystems.

> **Countervailing forces** are competing power blocs that limit the power of any one group.

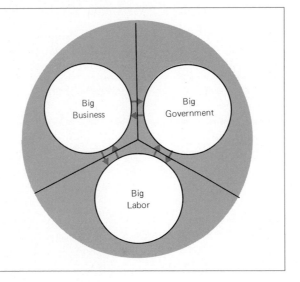

Figure 13-4. Model of countervailing forces. If one sector should begin to grow in power, the other two would be likely to expand to meet the threat of being overwhelmed, creating barriers to further growth.

Big Business

Big Government

Big Labor

Critics of pluralism stress the idealistic nature of the belief in countervailing forces, claiming that, in fact, members of the same social stratum are making crucial decisions in all these subsystems so that the end result is to increase the power of the upper middle class and the wealthy (Lukes, 1974; Parenti, 1978).

Some of the most important differences between the two models have been summarized by Kornhauser (1961) in Table 13-5.

Kornhauser discusses the insights and blind spots in the two models. Mills exaggerates the autonomy of the elite from other interest groups or from internal limits, while Riesman fails to appreciate the great power differentials between competing groups—a neighborhood consumer's organization is no match for Consolidated Edison. Yet both analyses converge on one conclusion: there is an absence of effective political action at all levels, especially among the relatively powerless.

Table 13-5. Two Portraits of the American Power Structure

Power structure	Power elite (Mills)	Pluralist (Riesman)
Levels	a) unified power elite b) diversified and balanced plurality of interest groups c) mass of unorganized people who have no power over elite	a) no dominant power elite b) diversified and balanced plurality of interest groups c) mass of unorganized people who have some power over interest groups
Changes	a) increasing concentration of power	a) increasing dispersion of power
Operation	a) one group determines all major policies b) manipulation of people at the bottom by group at the top	a) who determines policy shifts with the issue b) monopolistic competition among organized groups
Bases	a) coincidence of interests among major institutions (economic, military, governmental) b) social similarities and psychological affinities among those who direct major institutions	a) diversity of interests among major organized groups b) sense of weakness and dependence among those in higher as well as lower status
Consequences	a) enhancement of interests of corporations, armed forces, and executive branch of government b) decline of politics as public debate c) decline of responsible and accountable power—loss of democracy	a) no one group or class is favored significantly over others b) decline of politics as duty and self-interest c) decline of effective leadership

A comparison of the power elite vs. the pluralist model is provided by a series of studies of local politics. In the 1950s, Floyd Hunter examined the structure of power in a community through the use of the *reputational method*. Selected citizens were asked to submit lists of community leaders that were then screened by another panel until 40 names stood out. These forty were asked to select the top ten from among themselves. Hunter (1953) verified the existence of a "community power structure" of interlocking memberships and influence, primarily drawn from the business sector. This study, along with many others conducted in the late 1950s and early 1960s, is often cited in support of the power elite position.

But in 1961, Robert Dahl published an intensive study of decision making on three types of issues in New Haven, Connecticut, in which he compiled separate lists of social and economic "notables" and found very little overlap. To Dahl, it appeared that a number of elites exercised power at the level of local government, and that their interests did not necessarily coincide. From his data, he found that decision-making was essentially decentralized and closer to a pluralist than an elitist model. Similar findings have been reported by other researchers of community power. Then in the late 1970s, Domhoff (1978) presented a reanalysis of one of the issues studied by Dahl: urban renewal in New Haven. Using the same type of data augmented by interviews and content analysis of official documents, Domhoff maps networks of influence leading to the conclusion that a business-based ruling class determined the fate of public policy in New Haven. Moreover, Domhoff traces this web of influence from the national to the local level.

Dahl's book was titled *Who Governs?* and Domhoff's work was called *Who Really Rules?* The differences found in the two studies suggest that the researcher's expectations can influence how data are interpreted. Undoubtedly, future community power studies will add new perspectives on the question of who rules. Much will depend also on the size and history of the community being studied; the governance of a small town is likely to differ from that of a large city.

All critics can agree with Mills and Riesman that, in general, the great mass of citizens are politically inactive and nowhere more so than among the poor. The urban poor, especially, appear powerless against the business and political groups that rule a city. Over the past decade much has been written of a new movement to organize urban neighborhoods into effective political entities, able both to provide local services and to fight City Hall on behalf of those without direct power.

COMMUNITY ACTION

The debate over who rules may be seen as an extension of the argument between the functional and conflict interpretations of social order. As guiding ideas, or *restraining myths* (Hamilton, 1975), these perspectives shape the definition and perception of social issues, and inevitably become politicized. Thus, the conflict/elite perspective is rooted in Marxist theory and the politics of the left (oriented toward structural change), while the functionalist/pluralist view is associated with politics of the right (oriented toward stability and maintaining the status quo).

A.C.O.R.N.

Two of the most successful social action organizations have been Massachusetts Fair Share, a state-wide association with several dozen local chapters, and ACORN (Association of Community Organizations for Reform Now).

ACORN's offices are in New Orleans, but it sends organizers anywhere they are invited. There are ACORN affiliates in almost 20 states involving over 2500 low- and moderate-income families. Both ACORN and Massachusetts Fair Share have had greatest success organizing against utility rate increases, tax inequities, and health care delivery problems.

ACORN has as its ultimate goal the redistribution of economic and political power from the elite to the great mass of ordinary people through localized decision making:

> We organize people around issues which will point to the structural foundation of society from which unequal distribution of goods and services derives. We organize neighborhood groups to build a base of constituents which can wield power in its own right. It is the wielding of this power which will ultimately bring about the change.
>
> Therefore, in coalition with groups whose self-interests are related to, but not the same as ours, our interest is not in specific or immediate reforms; instead our purpose in such participation is to build political power for the 70 percent of the nation's population that remains powerless.

[Rathke, Borgos and Delgado, 1979, p. 35]

It remains to be seen whether or not this version of radical change will be any more successful than efforts in the 1960s.

In the 1960s the best-known efforts to organize the powerless were directed by Saul Alinsky. In Chicago, Rochester, and other urban centers, Alinsky taught the poor, largely black, residents of the inner city how to organize themselves, to demonstrate, boycott, and build local associations. A latent benefit of this activity was the creation of a sense of effectiveness among largely alienated populations—showing that together they could indeed accomplish certain goals.

Alinsky's work was eclipsed by the turmoil of Vietnam and the peace movement, followed by the current period of public indifference to the cities. But Alinsky had left a legacy: a body of thought and action that could guide later attempts to bring power back to the people at the grassroots (or, in this case, asphalt) level. In the late 1970s, many of the idealists of the antiwar and civil rights movements turned their attention away from the highest levels of power to the lowest—the urban neighborhood.

As with self-help groups in general, neighborhood organizations are a means of bridging the enormous gap between semi-isolated families or individuals and the bureaucratic structures "out there." This quest for community is an enduring theme in sociology, and nowhere more crucial than in complex societies.

The creation of local organizations in the 1970s has been issue-centered: health care, housing, utility rates, and street safety have been popular concerns. There are perhaps several thousand such organizations in the United States today, involving several hundred thousand citizens. Since each is locally-oriented with a particular set of salient issues, the building of coalitions has only now begun.

THE FUTURE OF ELECTORAL POLITICS

Pluralists often describe the many competing power constituencies as "veto groups" that, if not able to realize all their goals, can at least singly or in coalitions succeed in depriving others of their goals. The health of a democracy in this model depends upon the viability of a large number of veto groups. This is what makes democracy appear so inefficient when compared with totalitarian governments.

To theorists of the power elite, such groups are stratified by command over resources, so that in reality, people of wealth are able to influence elections disproportionately to their numbers. In recognition of this problem, laws passed in the 1970s have limited the amount of money that any one individual can give to a political candidate, and presidential elections are now partly financed by federal funds. The Supreme Court, however, has recently ruled that *private* (nonparty) political activity in support of a candidate is a form of speech that is protected by the First Amendment. The result of this ruling has been the proliferation of Political Action Committees (PACs).

Political Action Committees. The original PACs were union-oriented. The major American unions collected voluntary contributions from members that became a "war chest" to be used on behalf of candidates. Today, similar groups have been formed by business and other special interest groups. Since the wealth of corporate leaders is far greater than that of unions, the PACs organized around business interests are now a powerful force in American politics.

> **Political action committees (PACs)** are special interest groups formed by citizens, unions, business associations, and other organizations.

Initiative and Referenda. One current movement, intended to allow citizens the right to overrule their local legislatures, advocates the use of citizens' initiatives and referenda. Under this system, if a sufficient number of citizens sign valid petitions, certain questions can then be put before the public in a legal election. The originators of the initiative movement devised this technique as a means for ordinary people to reassert their control over the legislative process that are often dominated by lobbyists. One major target thus far has been local tax rates, spurred by the stunning success of an initiative to reduce property taxes in California in 1978 ("Proposition 13").

One ironic result, according to a private research firm, has been to allow corporate interests to influence the initiative process through their ability to outspend most citizen's groups. One example cited was an attempt to block construction of an oil storage terminal in Long Beach, California in 1979. The citizen's group spent $17,000 against an oil company's $860,000. But where citizen groups' funds are equal to or greater than that spent by corporations, the corporate position lost. As one observer put it, "The golden rule of politics prevails—he who has the gold rules" (*New York Times*, Aug. 20, 1979, p. A 17).

> **A referendum** submits proposed or actual laws to the direct vote of the electorate.

Single-Issue Interest Groups. But money is not the only resource needed to exert power in elections. Passion is another. The mid-1970s in the United States saw the rise of a new political phenomenon: the single issue interest group. This is an organization with but one goal to which members are intensely devoted to the exclusion of any other interest. This means that compromise—the normal give and take of a democratic polity—is impossible. Further, no matter how many other issues a candidate and interest group members might agree upon, if he or she refuses to support *the* single issue, interest group members will work

> The **single issue interest group** is an organization with one goal.

The 1970's saw the rise of a new political phenomenon, the single-issue interest group. (Source: Stock, Boston.)

Fragile Federation

Canada, like the United States, is a federation (of Provinces rather than States) linking an industrialized East with an agricultural/mining West and Center. In both countries, the early influence of British culture and immigration has been dominant, persisting to this day in the basically WASP composition of economic and political elites. In both countries, native populations were displaced and then ignored (although less bloodily in Canada than in the United States), and in both nations the movement westward and the beginnings of industrialism created a need for labor that was filled by immigrants from Europe.

Among the important differences are those of political structure and economic development. The shape of the Canadian confederation is currently in the process of renegotiation between the federal government and provinces seeking greater autonomy. This development is being resisted by those who fear it will further impede the creation of national unity. Cultural domination first by England and then by the United States, in addition to regional, ethnic, and religious divisions, has made it difficult to establish a uniquely Canadian culture and identity.

With respect to the economic system, Marsden and Harvey (1979) trace how Canada's colonial ties to England were replaced by those to the United States so that, despite industrialization, Canada occupies a position on the periphery of the world system. That is, Canada operates much like a colony for the core manufacturing economy of the United States. This secondary status is increasingly resented by Canadians, whose sense of national identity may be thereby enhanced. Current attempts to stem the flow of United States imports, including television programs and advertising, are designed both to protect Canadian industry and promote Canadian cultural artifacts.

But by far the most significant social/political development in recent Canadian history is the "quiet revolution" of the 1960s and 1970s that transformed the French-speaking citizens of Quebec into a self-conscious elector-

to defeat the candidate. Many of these single issues are morality-based and, therefore, presented in absolute terms, as, for example, the matter of homosexual rights, gun control, abortion, and environmental concerns.

Political Polarization. The rise of single-issue constituencies will bring profound changes in the distribution of political power in the United States. Until, now, the power of fringe groups—those holding extreme views on any issue—had been limited by "cross-cutting" loyalties and affiliations. That is, most citizens have a number of sources of identity and concerns, some of which negate the influence of others. For example, North American Jews have traditionally been very liberal on issues such as civil liberties and civil rights. But a wealthy Jew may find himself or herself sharing the more conservative views of income peers. The existence of both these pressures on the same person serves to reduce the probability of becoming extremely liberal or extremely conservative; in fact, the individual may decide to not become politically active at all.

So, too, with most North Americans, religion, ethnicity, education, occupation, and income may be all associated with competing viewpoints. But where

Political polarization occurs when characteristics such as religion or ethnicity consistently divide the population into the same interest groups.

ate. During this period, the liberal government created many middle-level white collar jobs for the French speakers, the province became urbanized, and the church lost much of its control over health and education. As a result, a revolution of rising expectations affected both the new French-speaking middle class and members of the working class who also desired a share in the new wealth and mobility. The Parti Quebecois (PQ) was founded in the late 1960s as a vehicle for these aspirations, and by 1976 the PQ won a majority of seats in the Provincial legislature.

Among the many grievances of Quebecers (and francophones in general) was the fact that speaking English was a prerequisite for prestige jobs anywhere else in the country. The introduction of *bilingualism* (a recognition of the equal importance of French and English in government and education) as federal policy did not appease supporters of the PQ. Once in power, the PQ made French the only official language in the Province of Quebec, restricted access to English language schools to very few children, and increased tax rates on high income earners. The net result has been the flight of English-speaking families out of Quebec, thus opening up more positions and housing to French-Canadians. But the flight of the anglophone middle-class and businesses has also reduced the Province's tax base, and working-class militants are complaining that the PQ is a tool of the middle class (Deutsch, 1980).

For all their desire to maintain a French-speaking polity, Quebecers did not wish to secede from the Canadian Federation, and in 1980, voted down a proposal for greater sovereignty vis-à-vis the rest of the nation. Yet while secession appears to be a dead issue at this moment, Canada's provincial leaders—in the mineral-rich West as well as Quebec—continue to have difficulty defining just what their relationship with the federal government should be. The Canadian polity is in the process of profound change as great as that which created the Federation in 1867 and secured full independence from Great Britain in 1931.

these characteristics consistently divide members of the society into the same groups, *polarization* can occur. In Canada, for example, French-Canadians differ from English-speaking Canadians not only in ethnic identity but in religion, education, occupation, and income, with the French-speaking segment generally disadvantaged in access to institutions of power and privilege. When societal issues continually divide the population in this manner, extremist politics are a frequent result, as in the case of Northern Ireland today.

The Future of the North American Democracies. To what extent will the changes currently under way in the United States and Canada affect distribution of power in the political sphere? At first glance, the direction of change appears to be toward increased diffusion of power from the federal to more localized levels, and perhaps toward more widespread public participation through involvement in single-focus interest groups. At the same time, these are fragmenting developments, creating deep divisions among citizens by lessening the importance of overriding goals and the compromises required to sustain broad social order.

If the power of economic and social elites is diminished, what forms will the new distribution of power take? Will democracy be served through multiple power centers? Will new elites arise as suggested by the iron law of oligarchy? Many decades ago, the Italian social scientist Vilfredo Pareto (1848–1923) noted that although new blood periodically refreshes the elite strata, the behaviors characterizing powerholders do not change all that much over time. Pareto described this process as "the circulation of elites," expressing an essentially pessimistic view of the possibilities of democratization in modern societies.

Other observers are more optimistic, seeing in the current economic crises and political turmoil in democratic societies an opportunity for a real dispersion of power—the 1960s cry of "power to the people" has not lost its appeal.

Summary

Politics refers to the organization of power relationships in a society. Political institutions are patterned statuses and roles developed in each society to provide internal order and external defense. The government, the major political institution, is linked to other social institutions through mutually supportive exchanges. The connections between the economic and political sectors—the political economy—is of particular interest to sociologists. In both capitalist and socialist societies, the state is the primary support of the economic system.

Under totalitarianism the right of individuals and groups to dissent is minimal, while under democracy there is much greater tolerance of the right to dissent and organize in opposition.

Power refers to the ability to achieve one's set of goals regardless of others' wishes. When institutionalized in the political system, power gains legitimacy. Max Weber identified three ideal types of legitimate power: charismatic authority, traditional authority, and rational-legal authority. Power is exercised in modern states through various policies, including the manipulation of public opinion, propaganda, censorship, surveillance, coercion, repression, and even genocide.

Power can also be observed in interpersonal relationships. Consent of the ruled by the more powerful is gained by raising the costs of dissent. Power relationships are negotiated but people do not hold equivalent resources. For example, citizens have less power than the government, college students have less power than college administrators, and employees have less power than employers.

Two major models seek to identify the structure of power in the United States and Canada. The power elite model assumes a homogeneous national upper class which controls great amounts of economic, political, and legal power. The pluralist model assumes that power is distributed among a number of groups and that these competing groups prevent any one group or class from one-sided control. Substantial disagreement regarding the power structure exists, yet both models agree on the limited political influence of the masses. The debate over who rules is an extension of the differences between the functional and conflict models of social order.

Electoral politics in the United States is currently being reshaped by the emergence of Political Action Committees (PACs) and other special interest groups. Corporate interests have usually been able to control local initiatives by outspending citizen groups. The growth of single-issue interest groups focused on morality-based issues has led to the process of political polarization. While cross-cutting loyalties and affiliations have historically limited the power of fringe groups, political polarization is bringing about profound changes in the distribution of political power in both the United States and Canada where divisions between East and West and between French- and English-speaking populations are also polarizing the political system.

Suggested Readings

CLEMENT, WALLACE. *The Canadian Corporate Elite: An Analysis of Economic Power.* Toronto, Canada: McClelland and Stewart, 1975. A powerful description of the role of Canadian economic elites in shaping and controlling the structure and processes of Canadian society.

LIPSET, SEYMOUR MARTIN. *Political Man: Essays on the Sociology of Democracy.* New York: Doubleday, revised edition, 1981.

MILLS, C. WRIGHT. *The Power Elite.* New York: Oxford University Press, 1956. Mill's classical statement identifying the power elite at the "command posts" of business, government, and the military.

OSSENBERG, RICHARD J. (Ed.). *Power and Change in Canada.* Toronto: McClelland and Steward, 1980. This set of essays applies the conflict perspective to a number of facets of Canadian political and economic life.

WOLFE, ALAN. *The Limits of Legitimacy: Political Contradictions of Contemporary Capitalism.* New York: Free Press, 1977. An examination of the ways in which capitalist goals and interests have shaped governmental policies, and how political support for social welfare programs conflicts with the needs of corporations.

14 *The Educational System*

In 1968 in the Ocean Hill–Brownsville section of New York City, black parents and white teachers fought in the streets and courts over who would control hiring and promotions; the teachers struck, and the ill-will generated by that controversy still pervades the school system. The black parents sought to make the schools responsive to the needs of their children; the white teachers fought to retain their power.

In 1974, as the West Virginia mining district of Kanawha County was about to adopt new textbooks, a group of angry, religiously-oriented citizens claimed that the new books were filled with blasphemy—dirty words, pictures of urban slums, and the theory of evolution. Buildings were fire-bombed, buses attacked, and lives threatened as Kanawhans sought to maintain control over what their children learned (Page and Clelland, 1978).

In 1976, the government of Quebec passed legislation that officially limited access to English-language schools to children who had one parent that had also attended an English-speaking elementary school in Quebec. All other children must attend schools wherein French is the *only* language. In this way, Quebekers seek to transmit their culture.

In all three cases, social class as well as cultural differences were involved. In Ocean Hill–Brownsville, poor parents sought to break the monopoly of educational elites that they perceived as providing inferior education to their offspring. The Quebec and Kanawha parents, conversely, fought to retain a traditional culture and class based values against mainstream influences that others thought would better prepare children for the modern world (Billings and Goldman, 1979). All three events demonstrate the crucial role of education and its control in the lives of parents as well as their children.

Educational activities are an extension of the socialization process that originates in the family. Since family members often cannot teach all that a child may require in order to become a productive adult, other agents of the community take over the task. The more complex the society, the less family-bound is the educational system.

Formal education extends the socialization process begun in the family.

In simple societies, such as the !Kung, a boy will begin to practice hunting with a stick or make-shift bow and arrow, stalking spiders and spearing salamanders. Female children will accompany their mothers on the daily round of foraging for berries and digging roots; some will help with the care of infants. Both boys and girls will learn through observation and practice.

In societies characterized by greater specialization, family members often retain control over crafts or strategic information, as in apprenticeship programs today. But many other occupations are not so easily handed down from parent to child, or else they require long periods of specialized training. For such occupations, the earliest schools developed—for scribes in China, philosophers in Greece, priests in Judea.

In modern societies, the education system has become highly specialized.

Higher education is no longer just for the priveleged few; there are now approximately 3,000 public and private two-year and four-year colleges and vocational schools. (Source: Woodfin Camp.)

The Functions of Education

As an extension of the socialization process, educational systems share the major tasks of transmitting the culture and preparing young people for adulthood. In addition, a number of other societal and personal needs are met through the school system: the acculturation of immigrants, the maintenance of cultural integrity (as in Quebec and Kanawha County), and the generation of new knowledge at the university level. These are all *manifest functions:* specific stated goals of the education system.

Specific stated goals of the education system are its **manifest functions.**

There are also *latent functions* served by schools and universities. The phrase "hidden curriculum" has been used to refer to the nonacademic lessons learned in educational settings. Schools are channels of social placement, serving gatekeeper functions in the expansion or maintenance of stratification hierarchies.

Latent functions refer to unspecified outcomes such as gatekeeping and the hidden curriculum.

TRANSMITTING THE CULTURE

A major function of education is the transmission of culture.

In a society that is both structurally differentiated and heterogeneous in terms of population, the culture is almost impossible to define. Each person can know only a part of the total experience of various subgroups. The problem of developing a standardized educational system and a core curriculum has never been completely solved. One of the benefits claimed for local control in both the United States and Canada is precisely this lack of uniformity. In the United States, for example, there are about 16,500 separate public school administrative divisions representing very different populations and subcultures, with control over funding, staffing, and some aspects of the curriculum. Under these

The version, or vision, of the United States conveyed through social science textbooks has changed over time. Frances Fitzgerald, a journalist, has charted these variations in the style and content of public school history textbooks since 1800.

In the nineteenth century, schoolbooks were often written by clergymen whose piety, patriotism, and WASP outlook pervaded the texts. This ethnocentrism lasted well into the twentieth century, even as millions of immigrants added an authentic variety to the population. History was the story of great statesmen and generals and of a "manifest destiny" embodied in white, Protestant, male heroes.

Very little was written of the immigrant experience, of oppression of racial minorities, of anti-Catholicism and anti-Semitism, of political corruption, of poverty in the midst of affluence, or of the use of force against union organizers.

By the time of the Great Depression, however, it was impossible to ignore these facets of American history. The most popular problem-oriented textbook of the 1930s ran into fierce opposition from business interests, patriotic associations, and church groups who felt that it was unAmerican to criticize capitalism or blame the economic system for poverty.

After World War II, patriotism and pride were again the dominant themes. This was the era of anti-Communist fervor associated with Senator Joseph McCarthy. In one junior high school textbook, students were solemnly urged to resist Communist influences and even to report subversive activities to the FBI.

The 1960s brought new pressures on textbook publishers to include material on nonwhites and racial unrest. Then came the women's movement to challenge the masculine bias of textbook writing and content. Today, Native Americans, blacks, women, immigrants, and the labor movement are presented more accurately than before.

But other changes in the nature of textbook publishing and selection could reduce diversity. School textbooks are now adopted on a district or even statewide basis. No longer can a publisher print a number of unusual texts that might appeal to a few local boards or a specialized audience. Most primary and secondary school books are now put together by committees of writers and reviewers, aimed at offending the fewest possible interest groups. Fitzgerald concludes that today's history textbooks are a more accurate reflection of the past than were those printed before 1960, but by this very token, without a single viewpoint or colorful theme; they are in fact, quite dull, and subject to political pressures.

Source: Frances Fitzgerald, *America Revisited*, Boston, Little Brown, 1979.

circumstances, it is difficult to achieve consensus on what every young person should know. For the most part, the task of presenting a common culture has fallen on the writers and publishers of textbooks. Decisions made by writers of these books, by publishers, and by school boards that select them mean that what is learned by school children is filtered through many layers of value and potential bias. In other words, education is also a *dependent* variable with its content shaped by considerations of social control, religious values, and profit-making.

Education may also be understood to be a **dependent** variable shaped by factors of social control, religious values, and profit-making.

ACCULTURATION OF IMMIGRANTS

The public schools have been relatively successful in acculturating diverse immigrant populations.

It was once thought that North America's immigrant populations would become acculturated rather easily, with the schools serving as "melting pots." And the public schools did absorb large numbers of non-English speaking people, successfully transmitting minimal skills in English and an introduction to modern industrial society. Part of this success is due to the particular historical era in which most acculturation took place. The period between 1880 and 1920 was one of enormous economic expansion in the United States, capable of absorbing unskilled and semi-skilled workers. City school systems were staffed with young, bright, and idealistic teachers, and most students were committed to learning whatever was necessary to succeed in the "land of opportunity."

The fact that the same school systems are having less success with Hispanic and black youngsters today must also be placed in historical perspective. The types of student, the teachers, the buildings, and the supportive environment are very different. There is no labor market for those without a high school education or for many *with* the diploma. Family and neighborhood supports for students are sometimes lacking, and young people are less inclined to accept the claims of educational authorities than they were in the past.

TRAINING FOR ADULT STATUSES

The educational system helps prepare students for work, family, and community roles.

A third major manifest function of the educational system is the preparation of individuals for the roles they will perform as adults in the community, family, and workplace. From the first day in elementary school to the last, students are taught the virtues of their society. Civics courses are among the most repeated elements of the curriculum. Citizenship is also taught indirectly through involving school children in charity drives, walk-a-thons, cake sales, and car washes. The first community into which the child must be integrated is, of course, that of the school itself. The child learns to follow orders without question, to show respect to authority, and to accept the rules of classroom competition.

Throughout their years in elementary and secondary schools, young people are presented with direct and indirect training in traditional family roles. Their earliest reading portrayed the idealized suburban lives of Jane and Dick, whose mother is a homemaker and whose father leaves the home each day to earn a living for the family. Very little material was presented to suggest that most women, often including their own elementary school teacher, work for pay outside the home; or about divorce, although about one-third of the students will have been personally affected. What is called *sex education* was typically a short course in reproductive biology rather than a discussion of the responsibilities of sexual activity and married life. This was true until recently. In the 1970s changes in the public schools resulted in a truer picture of the diversity of family life. These changes are currently under attack as some groups seek to have the schools revert to a more traditional portrayal of family life.

Good work habits such as hard work, diligence, and competitiveness are rewarded, while tardiness, laziness, sloppiness, and indifference are discouraged, if not actively punished. Those who do exceptionally well are publicly honored and identified as outstanding examples of the quality of the school. School organizations are geared to preparing students for further training and future work careers.

STRATIFICATION FUNCTIONS

Schools prepare young people for eventual adult occupational positions through a "filtering process" whereby students are channeled into one curriculum rather than another. The high school guidance counselor assumes a central role in this process, along with parents and peers.

The Great School Debate. Critics of the educational system claim that the schools operate to sort out young people into winners and losers (Bowles and Gintis, 1976). Children from certain minority groups are rarely encouraged to take college preparatory courses; for example, Polish and Italian students in the 1930s, and Hispanic and black youth today. Colin Greer (1973) argues that the public schools have actually operated to freeze the low status of New York City's most oppressed groups.

A report for the Carnegie Council on Children (de Lone, 1979) concludes that social class, race, and sex are more predictive of educational career and eventual income than are IQ, motivation, or early childhood training, and that the schools in fact reproduce social inequality from one generation to another.

On the other side of the debate, Diane Ravitch (1974) cites the many successes of the public school system in fostering upward mobility. The schools, she notes, have always been a target of political struggle as each minority group strives to use them for its benefit. If blacks and Hispanics appear to be less successful in manipulating the system, Ravitch suggests this results from the greater range of problems these students bring into the classroom than others have brought.

In general, children of the middle and upper strata score higher in aptitude tests. They are also more likely to remain in school *regardless* of their test scores, than are the offspring of the less affluent. The division of students into different tracks or programs occurs today at an earlier stage in their school career than it did only a decade ago. Social class, race, and sex of the student are all associated with track placement and, hence, with the length and quality of education received.

The Great School debate illustrates the difference between a conflict and functionalist interpretation of data. From the conflict perspective, status groups compete to maintain or improve their class positions through control over educational opportunity and the dominant ideas in the culture (Persell, 1977; Collins, 1979). The functionalist viewpoint stresses the importance of academic competition in separating the worthy from the less able, creating a hierarchy of talent or *meritocracy* based on individual ability.

Sponsored and Contest Mobility. In a 1960 essay titled "Sponsored and Contest Mobility in the School System," Ralph Turner described two ideal types of social mobility norms within the educational system. *Sponsored mobility* occurs when decisions are made early in the educational career to separate certain groups of students and to keep them separated throughout their school years. This can take place through early tracking or through dual systems of private and public education. *Contest mobility* refers to a more open and meritocratic school situation in which students are not totally segregated on the basis of intellectual ability, and in which there is the possibility of movement in and out of particular programs.

Schools filter students into different curricula.

Radical critics claim that the schools reproduce social inequality by sorting out young people into winners and losers.

Middle- and upper-strata children are more likely to remain in school, regardless of test scores, than are children from less affluent families.

Under **sponsored mobility**, some students are separated from the others very early and prepared for eventual success.

Contest mobility refers to a meritocratic educational system.

The Structure of Opportunity in School

While much has been written about tracking, few empirical studies have been conducted on the actual track system of a given high school. One such recent study was conducted in one high school in the Northeast that was 99% white and 80% lower middle or working class.

Rosenbaum found that students were generally tracked by ninth grade and remained in that track throughout high school, and that tracking was consistent across courses (that is, a high track placement in math was associated with the same placement in English, and so forth). Moreover, most college track students were accepted to four-year colleges while virtually no noncollege track youngster went on to a four-year college.

It was not that students on the noncollege track did not desire a college education, or that their courses were so very different from the college bound, or that their scholastic achievement was so much lower. Many had been poorly informed of their chances, selecting the noncollege track without realizing that the future was being foreclosed. By not telling students what was happening, the school authorities reduced pressure for track changes while encouraging the perception of free choice.

From these findings, Rosenbaum suggests a third mobility norm in our education system: *tournament mobility*, whereby ". . . when you win, you only win the right to go on to the next round; when you lose, you lose forever." While paying lip service to the contest norm, most school personnel encouraged sponsored mobility, and by keeping students mystified as to the real nature of their choices managed to create the tournament situation.

Source: James Rosenbaum, *Social Forces*, Vol. 57, No. 1, 1978, pp. 236–250.

High prestige colleges and universities perform a crucial function in maintaining the stratification system.

Higher Education and Social Mobility. The role of colleges and universities in maintaining the stratification system is crucial. For many decades the graduates of high prestige, private colleges and universities in the United States and Canada formed a religious, social, economic, and political elite. Even today, about one-third of those running the nation's largest corporations are graduates of these universities. Physicians, attorneys, judges, lawmakers, and Episcopal ministers are also likely to be from the half dozen top-ranked institutions.

The success of the upper class in placing their children, regardless of their academic ability, in the elite institutions, has led some sociologists to suggest that this process has replaced the traditional method of handing down family property.

What Higher Education, particularly the elite universities, does offer upper-class students is the set of personality skills and values required for acceptance in upper-class social circles and the elite business world. Studies of top corporate management reveal that promotion is less a matter of intellectual capacity than self-confidence in the ability to orchestrate the work of others, and a willingness to make difficult decisions. Paralleling these results, studies of American higher education confirm that schooling helps cultivate similar personality traits. It is not surprising, then, to find that corporate recruitment policies rely on college credentials less as a measure of a job applicant's technical abilities than as an index of the applicant's motivation and character. (Useem and Miller, 1977)

Attending any type of college is strongly associated with family income in both the United States and Canada (Bureau of the Census, April, 1981; *Perspectives Canada, III*, 1980). Young people from relatively affluent families are en-

"I said it's not often one gets one's chimney swept by a person with a B.A. from Sarah Lawrence." (Source: *Drawing by W. Miller;* © *1979 The New Yorker Magazine, Inc.*)

rolled in college at double the proportion of those from families with incomes below the median. And despite the great increase in college enrollment of the past four decades, it is still the case that an average student from a high income family stands a better chance of entering and completing college than does the intellectually gifted offspring of the less wealthy. (Nelson and Nock, 1978).

Students from middle income families are most likely to attend state supported colleges and universities, where their educations are subsidized by taxes paid by all families, including those that cannot afford to send their children to four-year colleges. It is largely at the community college level that nontraditional students are welcomed. Relatively low costs, part-time programs, evening and weekend sessions, and geographic convenience make the community college accessible to a wide range of student. Actually, these two-year colleges often provide smaller classes and closer interaction with instructors than is possible in introductory courses at four-year schools.

The stratification of institutions of higher education is represented in Figure 14-1.

The higher ranked the institution, the higher the standards for admission and the higher the fees. As might be expected, proportions of female students, minority group members, and working class young people decrease as the prestige of the institution rises. Thus, community colleges typically have more women

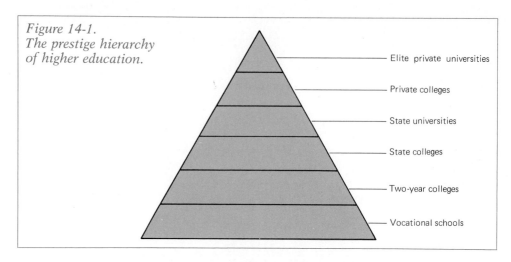

Figure 14-1.
The prestige hierarchy
of higher education.

- Elite private universities
- Private colleges
- State universities
- State colleges
- Two-year colleges
- Vocational schools

than men, a wider age range, relatively more members of racial and ethnic minorities, and large numbers of young people who also hold full-time jobs. In other words, the student body in two-year colleges more closely reflects the democratic ideals and cultural diversity of the society than does the student body of more exclusive institutions.

Critics of the community colleges have come from the Marxist rather than the elitist perspective. For example, Pincus (1979) argues that the two-year college *limits* rather than enhances the mobility potential of working class, non-white, and female students by directing them toward the dead-end vocational preparation courses that serve the training needs of local industry. The college transfer curriculum is reserved for middle class white students. In this way the stratification hierarchy of the larger society is reproduced through the expansion of higher education.

DEVELOPING NEW KNOWLEDGE

Industrial societies are dependent upon the production of scientific and technological information. Throughout human history, knowledge has been the monopoly of specially-trained persons: witch doctors, storytellers, scribes, teachers, wise men and women, and, in historical societies, academics. For the greater part of our history, religious institutions were the repositories of knowledge in the West. With the surge of scientific interest during the Renaissance and Reformation, followed by the Great Age of Enlightenment, secular universities became research centers, devoted to the production as well as transmission of knowledge.

Universities help develop new knowledge through research and teaching.

Today, North American universities are major teaching and research institutions. The research function has expanded greatly in recent decades, as graduate students are required to perform original research, and professors must publish academic papers in order to be promoted. In the United States, financial support from the government or from private businesses and foundations is the lifeblood of many graduate departments today, often also influencing research priorities.

These many functions of education—manifest and latent—are reflected in the structure of the modern educational system.

The Structure of Education

In modern societies, the educational subsystem has become highly differentiated, not only from other institutional spheres, but internally as well. Where
there was once a one-room schoolhouse, there are now age-graded separate
classrooms divided among elementary, intermediate, junior high, and high
schools. Where once a few colleges educated the sons of the well-born, there are
now thousands of public or private two- and four-year colleges and universities
in North America.

This structural differentiation also reflects changes in the content of education itself. The vast increase in knowledge available to members of modern
societies leads to specialization and compartmentalization both within schools
and between different types of institutions.

In the earliest grades, a homeroom teacher leads the children through a variety of activities. As the student moves from first through twelfth grades, the
structure of the classroom also changes, with the compartmentalization of subject matter reflected in the fact that the student goes to the specialist's room
rather than having the teacher come to the homeroom.

Partly because of the large number of children in most school districts, and
partly as a response to contemporary theories of child development, the career
of a schoolchild today is composed of discrete stages: kindergarten, first
through fifth grade, sixth through eighth, and ninth through twelfth. Typically,
the buildings housing these grades are separate from one another, often in different parts of the district.

Specialization is most marked in the array of *post-secondary* institutions
available to high school graduates: vocational training schools, apprenticeship
programs, two- and four-year colleges, universities, and research centers. There
is truly something for everyone, including those over age 35 enrolled in college
or in the thousands of adult education programs offered by local school systems. There are post-secondary schools for almost every occupational specialty
from hair dressing to music and art.

Specialization is great-
est in the range of post-
secondary institutions
available to high school
graduates.

Inclusiveness. In October 1979, about half of the United States population
between ages 3 and 34 was enrolled in school.

In Canada, over six million, or one-fourth of the *total* population, were enrolled as full-time students in 1977.

In *numbers*, the school population of North America almost doubled between
1950 and 1970, as the baby boom children entered the system and remained
through high school. But since 1970 the school-age population has declined
numerically, reflecting the low birth rates from 1965-on and reduced immigration. It was expected that increasing proportions of high school graduates in the
1970s would continue their education, but even this percentage has actually
decreased. In the United States, fewer than one-half of 18–19-year-old high
school graduates were enrolled in college in 1978 compared to slightly over 50
per cent in 1970. This decline has occurred among young males only. Women at
all ages and men aged 25–34 had *higher* enrollment percentages in 1978 than in
1970. A similar increase in women's enrollment in higher education was reported for Canada, from 38 per cent in 1966 to 45 per cent in 1977.

Recently there has been a dramatic increase in the enrollment of older students in colleges and vocational schools. (Source: Ellis Herwig, Stock, Boston.)

There has also been an influx of older students (35+) into colleges and vocational schools. In the United States close to 1.4 million individuals age 35 and over (primarily women) are working toward academic degrees or certificates (U.S. Bureau of the Census, April 1981).

PRIVATE AND PUBLIC SYSTEMS

The educational system in the United States and Canada is composed of both public and private schools.

As in many other democracies, there are two educational systems in both the United States and Canada—one supported by public taxes and open to all eligible, the other paid for by private subscription. Private education in North America is primarily of two types: *parochial* schools that are operated by religious groups; and *preparatory* schools that typically attract children from affluent families.

The most extensive system of **parochial education** is controlled by the Roman Catholic Church.

Parochial Schools. By far the largest and most extensive system of parochial education in North America is operated by the Roman Catholic Church: over two thousand schools enrolling over three million students in the United States, and almost three thousand schools with an enrollment of a million and a half students in Quebec. The fastest growing sector of the parochial school system in the United States today involves conservative Protestant Christian schools. These schools are highly traditional, emphasizing discipline, rigid gender role distinctions, and the teachings of the *Bible*. The functions of parochial schools go beyond controlling the content of education and insulating students from competing values and mores; they also limit the range of friendship choices and ultimately influence mate selection.

Other Private Schools. A system of elite elementary and college-preparatory schools, colleges, and universities operates in both the United States and Can-

378

ada to provide expensive and academically excellent educations to the sons and daughters of "good families." Enrollment in such exclusive schools is a sign of family wealth and prestige. Shielded from contact with children of other classes, introduced to the brothers and sisters of one's prep school friends, encouraged to date others with the same educational background, upper class young people typically make the appropriate choice of mate. In this fashion, the class structure is quite literally reproduced in successive generations. The shared experience of elite education is also the basis of adult friendships and of entry into a network of business contacts, permitting members of this class to keep their dominant position in the hierarchies of wealth and power.

> Private schools help reproduce the class structure in successive generations.

Public Education. The history of public education in North America illustrates the link between the value system, the educational system and the economic system. When the two broader forces—values (equality, fairness) and economic system requirements (need for skilled employees)—have coincided, public education has expanded both in the numbers of young people attending and in the length of time they must remain in the system. Historically, public education in North America, was necessitated both by ideals of democracy and by the westward movement of populations beginning in the early 1800s. Be-

> The link between dominant values, the economy, and the educational system is illustrated in the history of public education.

The largest network of parochial schools (school operated by religious groups) in North America is run by the Roman Catholic Church. (Source: Owen Franken, Stock, Boston.)

tween 1850 and 1950 the expanding needs of the economic sector led to raising mandatory school ages and to increased emphasis on vocational training. And since 1950, in both countries, the public education sector has mushroomed, especially at the higher levels, in response to the growing need for managers and technicians in a modern economy.

In The Classroom

The structure and functions of schooling are macrosystem phenomena. Another sociological perspective on education is the examination at the microsystem level of the classroom. The interaction between teacher and students creates a classroom climate that affects the children's behavior and self-perceptions. Conversely, the composition of a classroom has effects on the teacher. This interplay constitutes the social system of the classroom.

> The educational system in the United States is designed to reward achievers, placing students in constant competition with one another.

The school system of the United States is designed to reward high-achieving individuals. From early on, the children learn that one's own success may depend upon the failure of others. Since there can only be a few best pupils, the students are in constant competition *with one another*. Nonetheless, suburban schools have proven very successful in their task of preparing young people for achievement.

Not too long ago—as late as the early 1950s—urban school systems in the United States also had an enviable record. But with the great exodus of mid-

Pygmalion in the Classroom

In a well-known experiment, the researchers were able to administer an intelligence test to all students in one elementary school that divided each grade into three classrooms (above average, average, and below average). From these classrooms, Rosenthal and Jacobson selected the names of one-fifth of the students *at random*. Homeroom teachers were told that these students were "bloomers" who would soon experience a spurt of intellectual development.

At the end of the school year, eight months later, all students were re-tested. Although the "bloomers" were actually no different in ability from their classmates at the beginning of the school year, most showed improvement in IQ scores on the second testing. Some bloomers showed little gain but others had raised their scores by 10 points or more. The researchers concluded that teacher expectation had subtly affected the children's performance, a classic example of the *self-fulfilling prophecy*. When asked to describe their students at the end of the year, teachers ranked the bloomers as more interesting, curious, appealing, affectionate, well-adjusted, and happier than their classmates.

Source: Robert Rosenthal and Lenore Jacobson, *Pygmalion in the Classroom: Teacher Expectation and Pupils' Intellectual Development*, N.Y.: Holt, Rinehart, and Winston, 1968.

The interaction between teacher and student creates a classroom climate that affects the children's behavior and self-perception. (Source: Cary Wolinsky, Stock, Boston.)

dle-class whites to the newly built suburban housing developments, the school population of the larger cities changed dramatically. The schools that had so well served the immigrants of the early twentieth century were inherited by the children of working class blacks and white ethnics who remained in the cities.

THE URBAN SCHOOL

Not only has the school population changed, but so has the structure of the teaching profession. Teachers today are most often unionized; school administration is bureaucratized, with layers of authorities. Moreover, the economic life of major cities has been transformed by a second exodus to the suburbs—of light manufacturing, offices, and corporate headquarters.

Unlike the past, the urban public school system must absorb a higher proportion of children of the very poor, keep them in the schools for longer periods of time, and prepare them for labor markets that are narrowing.

By all accounts of those who have taught in the inner-city schools, it is a difficult task. The staff often feel unable to control their environment. The students are frequently rebellious, feel put down, and see no useful purpose to remaining in the schools. Conflict is common: white students against blacks, blacks against Hispanics, pupils against teachers, teachers against community boards, and community boards against the central board of education. The schools reflect and sometimes magnify all the tensions in the surrounding environment of adults, and little learning can be accomplished under such circumstances.

Yet this picture of inner-city schools as a battle ground may be overdrawn. Some schools and many pupils do manage to accomplish their goals. Many more could, according to the research of Ronald Edmonds (1979) and his colleagues. Children learn in many ways, and there is no single foolproof method for teaching. The more successful schools in Edmonds' study differed from one another in many respects, but the common features were: a) strong administrative leadership within the school, b) a climate of expectation in which no child was permitted to fall below minimum levels, and c) an orderly and quiet atmosphere (though not rigid or oppressive). Similar characteristics were found to give private school children an educational advantage in a recent report by James Coleman (1981).

In other words, the learning difficulties of inner-city children in school are not matters of personal characteristics or family background or a "deprived cultural context." Rather,

> We can whenever, and wherever we choose, successfully teach all children whose schooling is of interest to us. We already know more than we need in order to do this. Whether we do it must finally depend on how we feel about the fact that we haven't so far. (Edmonds, p. 32).

The social system of the classroom, and the larger system in which it is embedded, has much to do with the failure of the urban schools to serve the needs of their current pupils.

COMPETING PHILOSOPHIES OF EDUCATION

Open Classroom Movement. Building on the work of the educational philosopher John Dewey, reformers have sought to encourage the active, creative, individualized talents of school children through particular learning environments. In the 1960s this became the open classroom movement. It was thought that once the apparatus of the classroom—walls, confined working spaces, chairs in a row, the teacher's desk in front and at a distance—was eliminated or rearranged, the children's minds would also be liberated from constraint. And for many pupils this was the case. Allowed to follow their interests with guid-

The **open classroom** encourages the development of the creative talents of school children in an unconstrained supportive setting.

In the 1960's the "open classroom" movement sought to liberate students from traditional restrictions, with the hope that this would nurture individual abilities. (Source: Elizabeth Hamlin, Stock, Boston.)

ance and support, these children blossomed intellectually and socially. Others found it difficult to work in the relatively unstructured environment of the open classroom. Also, many teachers were not trained for this approach, and could not handle the children. Parents, too, were dismayed at a classroom so different from their own experience, and so seemingly disorganized. In general, the open classroom flourished in the middle class suburban schools, where children were being raised along similar lines anyway.

Yet it was the minds of disadvantaged children that school reformers sought to liberate. A series of books highly critical of urban school systems in particular appeared in the mid-1960s, with titles such as *How Children Fail* (Holt, 1964), *The Way It Spozed To Be* (Herndon, 1965), and *Death at an Early Age* (Kozol, 1967). These were scathing indictments of teacher indifference in a system designed to control rather than free its children. Perhaps the most influential book of that period was Charles Silberman's *Crisis in the Classroom* (1970) which described the school system as "a vast wasteland."

Back to Basics. But by 1970 counter-trends were already developing, and test scores were dropping. A consensus was developing on the "problem of the schools" with precisely the *opposite* interpretation of the situation from the authors just mentioned. Politically and religiously conservative groups attacked secular humanism; others spoke of lack of discipline and permissiveness; and many were disturbed over the power of teacher unions. The one motto that united so many different critics was Back-to-Basics, by which is meant discipline, emphasis on traditional subjects, and the inculcation of respect for authority. Many inner city parents and educators have found the emphasis on structure and basics to be highly successful learning techniques. At this writing, the back-to-basics movement appears dominant among parents and taxpayers. One outcome of their success is the current call for more testing of students *and teachers* or "accountability."

> The **back-to-basics** trend centers on discipline, respect for authority, and an emphasis on traditional subject matter.

Quality, Inequality, and the Schools

Educational systems are shaped by the needs and nature of the broader systems in which they are embedded. And school children are often expected to solve problems with which their parents have failed to cope. Thus, the schools have borne much of the brunt of the demand for racial equality in the United States, and of separatist passions in Canada.

SCHOOLING AND RACIAL EQUALITY IN THE UNITED STATES

The issue of racial equality illustrates the enduring tension between different aspects of the United States' value system: quality and individual merit on the one hand, equality and social justice on the other.

> The goal of racial equality spotlights a contradiction in the American ethic—individual achievement and merit vs. equality and social justice for all.

School Desegregation. The continuing value conflict between the twin goals of justice and freedom has centered on the schools as both creators of inequality and as potential vehicles for equal opportunity. In 1954, the Supreme Court of

The Supreme Court in 1954 decided that racial segregation created by local authorities was unconstitutional and was to be abolished.

the United States decided that where local authorities had created a racially segregated school system, this was, in and of itself, a violation of the Constitutional guarantee of equal treatment under the law and must be dismantled "with all deliberate speed."

Over twenty-five years later, after much deliberation and very little speed, the record on desegregation is mixed. Southern school districts slowly complied. But thousands of white school children were taken out of the public system and placed in private schools. And within the schools, as we have seen, tracking can effectively separate the races, with white children disproportionately assigned to the higher tracks. The black children in integrated schools are often rendered invisible (Rist, 1978).

In the North, unlike the South (where *de jure* segregation had been common), the schools were becoming racially separate through the movement of white families to the suburbs over the past three decades. By 1980, most urban school systems in the North were overwhelmingly nonwhite, while the suburban schools remained almost totally white. To the degree that such dual systems were not the result of legislation (that is, the drawing of school district lines) but of population trends (*de facto*), could they be considered unlawful? In general, the courts have insisted upon the desegregation of urban schools, a move that requires extensive busing of school children.

Busing has created additional problems. Parents who wish to avoid both busing and interracial contacts have simply moved out of the district. "White flight" is one latent consequence of desegregation orders, leaving the school district with even fewer white children to be integrated.

School desegregation and its busing requirements have often brought violence in the streets and in the schools, as in Boston for over a decade. In other cases, school districts have successfully integrated with minimal disruption due to a great deal of public-relations work and the cooperation of community groups. But many politicians feel that there are votes in resistance to busing, and most public opinion polls bear this out.

As for the long-term consequences, Coleman (1977) claims that the pursuit of the manifest goal of an integrated education has the latent consequence of creating greater segregation to the detriment of nonwhite students. A "tipping point" of 30 per cent nonwhite enrollments appears to accelerate the flight into the suburbs (Levine and Myer, 1977; Giles, 1978), but the exodus of whites into the suburbs has been a rather steady process since 1950 regardless of other factors. It is difficult, therefore, to assign a particular percentage to that part of white flight caused by school integration.

Other commentators (Rossell, 1978) have reviewed the evidence cited by Coleman and others, and found few long term negative effects on students or communities from court-ordered desegregation. Much depends on the specific history and composition of school districts, the support of influential individuals and groups, and the absence or presence of demagogues.

Solutions. Under threat of court orders, school systems have undertaken a variety of approaches to reduce segregation and to stem white flight.

Magnet schools attract high ability students by offering specialized educational programs.

Magnet Schools One way to keep white youngsters in inner city schools is to offer an unusual educational experience. Magnet schools, as the word implies, attempt to attract students of high ability to a particular program offered only

On the basis of standardized tests of intelligence, some social scientists (for example, Jensen, 1969) believe that the abilities being measured are largely inherited, and that, therefore, some racial groups are inherently superior to others. A majority of social scientists and experts on genetics argue that inherent tendencies are expressed in social contexts and that intellectual functioning is the outcome of the *interplay* between innate ability and learning experiences in a particular environment.

Moreover, reported IQ differences refer to *group averages* and therefore cannot be used to prejudge a given individual. In general, most human abilities are distributed in much the same way among all racial and ethnic groups; that is, roughly the same proportions of each subpopulation will score superior or average or below average. In the case of standardized IQ tests, there is some evidence that items reflect a middle class, white experience of the world.

In addition, intelligence is probably not a single trait but a bundle of abilities that individuals possess in differing combinations of varying strength at different ages. Intelligence is a complex set of capacities only partly measured by performance on IQ tests.

For all these reasons, conclusions about the intellectual abilities of any racial or ethnic group are probably more *political* than scientific. The IQ controversy has been used to rationalize differential educational treatment of blacks and Hispanics. For example, researchers in California were struck by the large numbers of Mexican-American and black children referred to classes for the mentally impaired. Although the youngsters had IQ measurements well below average, they were actually neither feeble-minded nor retarded. They could not understand the tests. A majority were quite capable of caring for themselves, of sustaining social relationships, and of dealing with the world outside of school (Mercer, 1973). On the basis of interview data, observations, and medical examinations, most of the students were reassigned to regular classes.

Other research has shown that early intervention can dramatically affect the subsequent development of intellectual skills, as seen in the long-term gains registered by Head Start children in the United States (Hunt, 1979).

In a study of mental abilities and environmental forces among children from five ethnic groups in Canada, Marjoribanks (1972) found that environmental factors appeared to account for a greater share of the group differences than did ethnicity alone. The various ethnic environments stressed different aspects of learning and achievement, so that each group had a slightly different "profile" of abilities on test performances.

---

in that school, such as music and art, science, athletics, or special teaching technique for which many parents will consider busing worthwhile.

Grade differentiation Another way to divide children into desegregated units is to have specific schools for each grade. That is, school X is for all kindegarten through second graders in the district; school Y is for third through sixth; and school Z is the intermediate school. This way, all children will have some years in their neighborhood school and other years away, so that the burden of busing is more equally distributed.

Grade differentiation divides a district's students into separate schools for certain grade levels.

Merging school districts If whites are in the suburbs and nonwhites in the cities, one integration method involves the merging of school districts so that both sets of children are in the same district, with busing to create racial balance among all the schools in the new district.

Enrichment of nonwhite schools If integration cannot be achieved, then a compensatory enrichment of the inner-city schools could at least provide equal, if separate, education. This course of action requires the willingness of taxpayers to support extra levies for other people's children.

Programs for the Handicapped. How fair is an educational system that teaches only those who can come to school and meet the expectations of classroom teachers? If the constitutions of most state governments guarantee a free public education for all, what are school districts to do about their physically and mentally handicapped youngsters? For many years the physically handicapped have been coached at home for a few hours a week. Emotionally disturbed youngsters have either been labeled "uneducable" or sent to special classes, and the mentally retarded have rarely received all the educational services from which they could benefit. Only recently have parents of handicapped youngsters organized to exchange information, initiate lawsuits, and petition school boards. This pressure has resulted in legislation mandating appropriate education for the over eight million handicapped young people in the United States, of whom about half are actually receiving such services.

The major problem, of course, is that special education is more expensive to provide than the normal classroom experience. Classes must be small and teachers carefully selected, equipment must be purchased, and regular evaluations provided. When communities feel burdened by taxes, the local school budget is often the first to be cut, and since most parents do not have handicapped youngsters, special education is apt to be defined as a frill. Since state law often protects the special programs, cuts must be made elsewhere, causing some antagonism between the parents of handicapped children and other taxpayers.

Mainstreaming Another technique involves the integration of handicapped children into the regular school program. Not only does this normalize the experience of the handicapped but also gives other students the opportunity to learn about and interact with those who differ from them, reducing stereotyping and stigmatization. But mainstreaming is difficult to implement. Without

> The handicapped are one group that has traditionally been neglected by the educational system.

> **Mainstreaming** involves the integration of handicapped children into the regular school program.

Table 14-1. Handicapped Children Receiving Special Services, United States, 1978

Type	Number
Speech Impaired	1,227,000
Learning Disabilities	969,000
Mentally Retarded	945,000
Emotionally Disturbed	289,000
Deaf and Hard of Hearing	87,000
Visually Handicapped	36,000
Cripples and Other Health Impairments	224,000

Source: Statistical Abstract of the U.S., 1980, p. 362.

Integrating handi-capped students into regular school programs both normalizes the experiences of the handicapped and gives the other students the opportunity to learn about and interact with people who seem "different". (Source: *George Whiteley, Photo Researchers, Inc.*)

additional help—both training and the provision of classroom aides—many teachers cannot cope, while the nonhandicapped and their parents feel cheated. In some cases, mainstreaming has increased negative attitudes and added to the strain of the handicapped pupils; in other instances, actual and potential benefits have outweighed these drawbacks.

FINANCING AND FAIRNESS

Directly or indirectly, the issues and controversies surrounding the United States educational system are related to the method of financing schools: the local property tax. People who pay school taxes want to control that system, and they want to see results—high test scores, college admissions, and their children prepared for occupational competence. Many school districts are willing to pay for quality education; other districts cannot afford it.

The deterioration of city school systems is linked to a shrinking tax base, due to the exodus of businesses and to the low taxable incomes of the remaining residents. At the other extreme, suburban school districts have the tax base to provide a full range of instructional and recreation programs. This growing disparity between wealthy and poor school districts led to a series of state supreme court decisions in the 1970s that declared unconstitutional the property tax as a basis for school funding.

Enrollments and Costs. This increased concern over the financing and the content of education comes at a time of *declining* enrollments due to the low birth rates of the 1960–80 period. The number of children in elementary grades has steadily declined and so will the secondary school population by 1986. These losses will be relatively greater in the public than private schools. Similar population trends affect the enrollment of Canadian students (Figure 14-2). In both countries, the numbers of college students will remain somewhat constant in the 1980s, slightly up in the United States and slightly down in Canada.

At the same time, however, the number of teachers in both countries will *not* decline and will even continue to rise. In the sphere of higher education, most

387

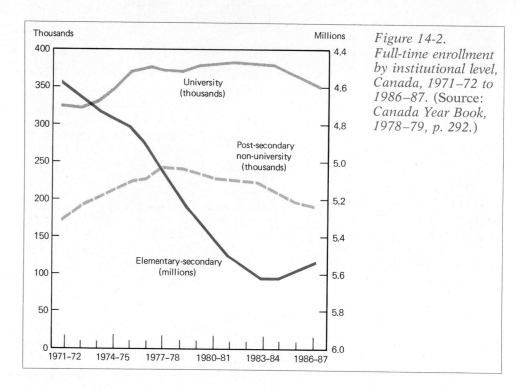

Figure 14-2.
Full-time enrollment
by institutional level,
Canada, 1971–72 to
1986–87. (Source:
Canada Year Book,
1978–79, p. 292.)

importantly, costs have steadily risen. In 1979 in the United States, inflation alone accounted for an 11 billion dollar increase in a total expenditure on education of over $150 billion. Much of the resentment directed at teachers' unions and the demand for accountability stem from taxpayers' awareness of rising costs and the perception that they are paying more and getting less.

A Report Card for the Educational System

As might be expected of so varied an institution with so many personal and societal functions, the educational systems of the United States and Canada have received both high marks and failing grades.

 Successes:

The establishment of a universal and comprehensive school system in nations characterized by diversity in student backgrounds and needs.

Basic assimilation tasks performed by the elementary schools in the first half of the twentieth century.

A postsecondary educational system with a wide range of options, and potentially available to most high school graduates.

Jencks reviewed data on achievement tests (which must be distinguished from IQ tests) since the 1920s. Scores rose steadily up until the mid-1960s but have declined over the past fifteen years. However, current declines are far lower than the earlier gains. Jencks summarized the data in this manner:

> All in all, four conclusions about standardized tests seem justified. First, these tests measure a narrow range of skills and information—often narrower than their labels imply. Second, despite these limitations, it is probably true that today's high school students know less about literature, history, politics, and the physical environment than students knew a decade ago. In addition, today's students probably have fewer of the complex skills they would need to repair these deficiencies. Third, while high schools have many legitimate objectives besides teaching traditional academic subjects, there is no reason to suppose that they are doing a markedly better job in achieving these objectives than in teaching academic subjects. Fourth, these problems are not apparent until students reach about fifth grade (p. 35).

But what are the causes? Conservatives point the finger at "humanistic" innovations of the 1960s. The teachers' unions blame the tests as being too reliant on rote learning of the back-to-basics type, and the public often cite television, a general permissiveness in the society, broken homes, busing, and student indifference.

Yet, as Jencks points out, critics speak as if the societal context has remained unchanged. In many areas, today's students are far more sophisticated than those of the past. In the high schools—where most of the score declines have taken place (*not* in the elementary schools)—an increasingly bored or rebellious student body faces a teacher corps increasingly unsure of its authority. When neither students nor teachers feel that their task is important, Jencks suggests, the mastery of complex skills does not seem worthwhile. The lowered test scores, then, reflect the fact that students are "serving time" in high schools.

Jencks feels that the demand for minimum competency testing might just serve a useful purpose—not for the reasons advanced by testing advocates, but simply to give the impression that high schools do have something of importance to teach. Minority-group students would not necessarily lose out, either; those who earn diplomas would know they had accomplished something of value. The basic problem, says Jencks, is "getting adolescents to respect knowledge and intellectual rigor."

Source: Christopher Jencks, *Working Papers*, July/August, 1978, pp. 30–41.

Failures:

Inequality remains built into the dual and parallel school systems. The social class structure is continually reproduced through the length and type of schooling the individual's family can afford. Even as the educational level of all groups has risen, the relative position of racial and ethnic subgroups is unchanged.

Millions of North Americans cannot read or write sufficiently well to address a letter correctly or to understand a bus schedule.

In the United States since the mid-1960s, scores of high school students on standardized achievement tests have steadily declined. This has led many commentators to declare that the schools have failed. The situation appears to be more complicated than any one-factor explanation.

A recent study of 5,000 student scores on achievement tests in Canada (Powell, 1980) concludes that "almost all existing test procedures are defective" because they are based on the concept of one right answer, a way of thinking rooted in the religious curriculum of the past. This mental set, claims Powell, is inappropriate for a scientific age in which skepticism, openmindedness, and relativism are required to form and test hypotheses. The smartest students, he remarks, often over-read the questions and score poorly, so that test score declines could reflect the obsolescence of the testing technique or a more modern cast of mind among students.

THE PUBLIC'S PERCEPTION

In both Canada and the United States there has been a marked drop in parents' satisfaction with the quality of their children's education, as seen in Figure 14-3. A recent Gallup poll (*Newsweek*, April 20, 1981), however, found that 47 per cent of respondents rated the schools as excellent or good, and 60 per cent felt that their childrens' education was better than their own elementary and secondary schooling, while 74 per cent rated their childrens' teachers as excellent or good.

Supporters of the public schools can point to hundreds of exceptional schools and school systems throughout the country, to a commitment to provide education to previously neglected subgroups, and to an enviable record of personal and public service: most young people emerge from the system knowing most of the basics required for coping with a modern society.

There are, however, enough parents mistrustful of the public school system to support a growing network of private academies and parochial schools. This suggests that *pluralism* in education might be the vogue of the 1980s: special

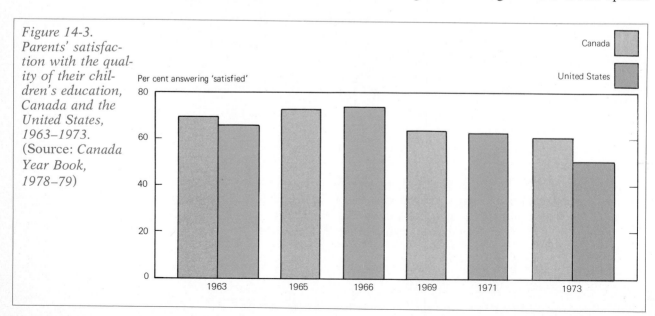

Figure 14-3. Parents' satisfaction with the quality of their children's education, Canada and the United States, 1963–1973. (Source: Canada Year Book, 1978–79)

schools for various types of young people. It is also likely that as more taxpayers place their children in the nonpublic system, pressures will build up for public support of the alternative schools—in the form of tax deductions, shared busing, schoolbook loans, and so forth. In which case all taxpayers would subsidize the private education of a few.

The growth in nonpublic school enrollments suggests an educational pluralism in the 1980s.

The Voucher Movement.   At one extreme, the idea of a voucher system is being revived. Originally intended to offer alternatives to parents of inner city children, voucher plans are now supported by religious groups, conservative causes, and economic elites.

The voucher system would operate this way. School tax monies in a given district would be redistributed to families as tickets (receipts or vouchers) entitling each child to a certain number of dollars toward an education in any type of school located in that area. This would encourage the establishment of all types of educational enterprises, so that each child could be placed in an environment most conducive to her or his abilities. To ensure some fairness, names would be drawn randomly for those schools with limited enrollments. Many children would benefit from a more individualized education, but they would also lose an opportunity to learn with a varied set of peers.

The voucher system would allow families to spend a given amount of tax money for any type of school available.

Many analysts expect that the public school systems will respond to this pressure by becoming more differentiated within school districts. That is, particular public schools will specialize in certain programs and learning techniques, just as private schools do now.

It is safe to conclude that public education in the United States is faced with a major challenge, and may not survive in its present form. The public schools, particularly those in the central cities, may be left with only the most difficult students to educate with ever-decreasing resources. Private and parochial schools can select their student body and screen out the hard-to-teach, thus providing a more favorable environment for learning.

The Future of Higher Education

Following the dramatic growth of higher education of the 1950s and early 1960s, the rate of increase has begun to slow in both Canada and the United States, where between 20 and 25 per cent of the population 18–24 are enrolled in post-secondary schools. Actually, the rate for males has remained constant in the late 1970s with almost all the increase due to the entry of women, part-time students, and persons over age 25.

In part, the decline in the rate of college enrollments reflects the passing of the baby boom generation, the same phenomenon that is leading to the closing of elementary and secondary schools throughout the two countries. But why haven't increasingly higher proportions of high school graduates chosen to continue their education? Even with the network of community colleges in both countries, fewer than half of each year's high school graduating class in 1978 proceeded to higher education. Traditionally, female enrollments have been lowered by marriage or employment, but it is they who are now entering college at a higher rate than their male age peers. A small proportion of male high school graduates will enter the armed forces, but the larger number go directly into the labor force where they perceive that experience and hard work will ultimately bring them success.

The college population in Canada and the United States, then, continues to be composed primarily of middle-class young people. The major changes have been in the sex ratio of undergraduates, and the age distribution of students in general. Black enrollments in the United States had increased throughout the 1970s but appeared to have leveled off at about 10 per cent. In many cases, the enrollment of blacks and of young people from working class backgrounds has been possible because of educational loans and grants provided by the federal government, programs that are in the process of being cut back or phased out by the Reagan administration.

Once in college, the student is faced with a more intense competition for grades than in high school, especially if one's goal is graduate school. The most popular fields of study today, reflecting a more sober economic situation than in the 1960s, are business, prelaw, and computer technologies. Of decreasing interest to college students are the traditional subjects that once formed the core of a college education: humanities and the social sciences. The new culture of technology seems to have won out against the old culture of humanistic studies.

For now, however, the trend in both the student body and the faculty is toward greater emphasis on increasingly narrow skills, following the general societal pattern of specialization and upgrading of technical competence. A return to the broader goal of instilling a general education and introduction to all aspects of the culture seems rather distant in a society entering the post-industrial age.

Summary

Formal education is an extension of the socialization process begun in the family. As societies become more complex, family members are less able to teach their children all that is necessary for adult participation in the society.

The functions of education include: transmission of the culture to children; acculturation of immigrants; training for adult statuses in the community, workplace, and family of procreation; maintaining the stratification system; and developing new knowledge.

Schooling in North America is both an avenue of upward mobility and bulwark of the status quo. The educational system is itself a stratified hierarchy of private and public schools, elite universities and community colleges, vocational schools, and research centers.

Schools also constitute a microsystem of goals, values, rules, roles, and expectations. Students in both urban and suburban schools learn about competition, success, and failure as they interact among themselves and with their teachers. Teacher expectations shape a child's self-image and can encourage or inhibit classroom performance.

Educational systems are linked to other social institutions and have become a major arena in the struggle for racial equality in the United States, and for ethnic and regional equality in Canada. School desegregation and busing, education of the handicapped, and fairness in school financing are all controversial issues in the United States, placing the public school system is some jeopardy.

Overall, the record of educational systems in North America is mixed. Both countries have established an extensive system of public schools that eased the assimilation of waves of immigrants; a broadly available and diversified system of post-secondary schools now enroll students from the full range of ethnic and racial minorities and age groups. At the same time, inequality continues to be reinforced, millions of North Americans cannot read or write sufficiently well to enter the mainstream, and achievement test scores of high school students in the United States have declined over the past decade and a half. Parents' attitudes display ambivalence: a general decline in satisfaction with the schools combined with continued confidence in teachers and the feeling that their children are receiving a better education than they had.

Nonetheless, changes are taking place at all levels of the educational system, from a demand for more variety in the elementary and secondary schools to the effects of declining enrollment growth and government funding for higher education.

Suggested Readings

BOWLES, SAMUEL, and HERBERT GINTIS. *Schooling in Capitalist America* (New York: Basic Books, 1976). A radical analysis of the educational system in the United States, which is shown to preserve economic inequality and the existing class structure.

CARLTON, RICHARD A., LOUISE A. COLLEY and NEIL J. MacKINNEN (eds.) *Education, Change, and Society: A Sociology of Canadian Education.* (Toronto: Gage, 1977). A series of insightful articles dealing with many aspects of education in Canada.

Carnegie Council on Policy Studies in Higher Education, *3000 Futures: The Next Twenty Years for Higher Education* (San Francisco: Jossey-Bass, 1980). An economic, demographic, and social-policy analysis of the issues confronting American higher education through the year 2000.

GORELICK, SHERRY. *City College and the Jewish Poor: Education in New York City, 1880–1924* (New Brunswick, N.J.: Rutgers University Press, 1981). This recent monograph reexamines the history of higher education for poor Jewish students in New York City, and the myth of social mobility through higher education.

KATZ, MICHAEL B. *Class, Bureaucracy and Schools: The Illusion of Educational Change in America* (New York: Praeger, 1971). The author argues that the American system of urban education—universal, tax supported, free, bureaucratically organized, class biased and racist—has remained basically unchanged since the 1880s.

LEACOCK, ELEANOR. *Teaching and Learning in City Schools* (New York: Basic Books, 1969). A dramatic demonstration of the crucial importance of teachers' expectations in influencing the success and failure of white and black students in middle- and lower-class schools.

ZWERLING, L. STEPHAN. *Second Best: The Crisis of Community College* (New York: McGraw-Hill, 1976). This readable historical and first-hand account of the educational process in two-year colleges includes policy suggestions for implementing the "heating up" as opposed to the "cooling out" function of community colleges.

15 Belief Systems

*I*n Professor Peter's *Quotations for Our Times,* the following appear:

> Religious awe is the same organic thrill which we feel in a forest at twilight, or in a mountain gorge.
>
> —William James

Put God to Work for you and maximize your potential in our divinely ordained capitalist system.

—Norman Vincent Peale

Theology is an effort to explain the unknowable in terms of the not worth knowing . . . it is not only opposed to the scientific spirit; it is opposed to every other form of rational thinking.

—H. L. Mencken

A philosopher is a blind man in a dark room looking for a black cat that isn't there. A theologian is the man who finds it.

—Laurence J. Peter

The Sociological Study of Belief Systems

How can the same human activity be awesome, materialistic, wrong-headed, and capable of uncovering the unseen? What is there about religious yearnings that evokes such a range of comment? And how can such beliefs be subjected to scientific analysis?

Because belief systems involve faith and emotions, they appear to be unsuitable for critical examination. Nonetheless, sociologists *do* study belief systems, and have been interested in this phenomenon from the beginning of the discipline—both Comte and Durkheim had much to say about religion, although what they said was very different. Comte was a man of the Enlightenment who would substitute a secular (of this world) ideology—the scientific study of society—for the religious faith of the past. Durkheim saw the function of religion as a celebration of society itself. Religious ideas and rituals, according to Durkheim, were ultimately based on the collective experience of the group and functioned to unite and reaffirm the solidarity of its members.

DURKHEIM ON THE ELEMENTARY FORMS OF RELIGIOUS LIFE

Since "human institutions . . . [are] founded in the nature of things"—that is, rooted in experience—Durkheim proposed that the origins of religion must lie in society itself. What other frame of reference or categories of thought were available to early humans? In the first place, beliefs, like language or any other symbol system, depend upon the *agreement between minds* for their meaning. Secondly, the content of belief systems—the objects worshipped, the ceremonies enacted, and the ideals revered—all express the *unity of believers*. In these ways, says Durkheim, social life itself is being celebrated. Shared beliefs, in turn, provide a way for individuals directly to experience the abstraction "society."

Therefore, Durkheim concludes: "At the foundation of all systems of belief and of all cults . . . are a certain number of fundamental conceptions and ritual attitudes, which, in spite of the diversity of forms which they have taken, have the *same objective significance and fulfill the same functions* everywhere . . . . There are no religions that are false. All are true in their own fashion; all answer, though in different ways, to the given conditions of human existence" (Durkheim (1912), emphasis added). We must clarify at the out-set that sociologists do not examine the truth value of any religion; these are questions for the philosophers and theologians. Sociologists explore the consequences of religious beliefs. That is, they do not ask "Is it true or false?" but rather, "What happens because people believe it?" The latter is an empirical question, the former is not. In fact, the essence of belief systems is that they deal with ultimate issues that cannot be answered scientifically. The sociological study of belief systems, however, can be as objective and value-free as the analysis of any other institutional sphere. The sociology of religion is based on the assumption that beliefs are a social product, a universal element of culture whose content varies from one time and place to another.

Sociologists examine the **consequences of shared beliefs.**

DEFINING BELIEF SYSTEMS

Much of the debate among sociologists involves identifying the universal aspects of belief systems. What, for example, are the essential components and processes that allow us to link such diverse phenomena as cannibalism, Calvinism, and communism? And how are individual needs meshed with social necessity?

One definition that spans individual and group processes has been offered by J. Milton Yinger (1969) Religion is found where (1) there is an awareness of and interest in the continuing, recurrent, permanent problems of human existence; (2) where rites and shared beliefs relevant to that awareness . . . exist; and (3) where there are groups organized to heighten that awareness and to teach and maintain those rites and beliefs. 'What I have described," says Yinger, "is a three-level definition combining an individual character aspect (awareness and interest), a cultural aspect (shared rites and beliefs) and a social structural aspect (groups)."

Belief systems are based on the human condition of wonderment, consist of doctrine and rituals, and unify a community of believers.

Such a definition applies to any system of belief and not necessarily those dealing with the supernatural or divinities of some kind. The basic elements in such systems are the human condition of wonderment, beliefs and rituals, and a community of believers. When these are found in conjunction, regardless of content and practice, a *belief system* exists, whether essentially religious or not. If the beliefs and rituals adequately meet human needs, and if they also foster a sense of solidarity among believers, that system is functionally equivalent to any other.

The minimal conditions for a belief system are as follows: (1) A human need for meaning, comfort, or transcendance that leads to (2) an organized and internally-consistent set of beliefs and rituals that are (3) shared by members of a group that recognizes its uniqueness.

Religions are types of belief systems; however, belief systems need not be religious. (Source: Thomas Hopker, Woodfin Camp & Associates.)

FUNCTIONS OF BELIEF SYSTEMS

Systems of beliefs and ritual thus fill both individual and group needs. At the personal level there is a need for meaning—something to believe that gives your life value and continuity. There is also the anxiety that attends events over which humans have little control—disasters, accidents, even the timing of life and death. And then there are the moments in the life course fraught with danger or mystery—puberty, marriage, childbirth, aging.

Both tragedy and joy require some definition: Why has this happened to me? These events, remember, do not come with meaning attached; through conversations with others we define what is happening to us, and why. Belief systems are one such attempt to interpret the world. Individuals turn to faith and worship in times of both great personal misery or happiness.

These are often not only times of personal fearfulness, but points at which the unity of the group is placed under stress. At the group level, belief systems allay anxiety and bring members together. Group identity is often symbolized by an

Beliefs and rituals fill both individual and group needs.

object of nature—rocks, trees, animals—called a *totem*.(The Star of David, the Maple Leaf and the Bald Eagle are functional equivalents of the totems that many tribes and clans use to describe their group) much as a member or a follower of sports teams in North America might say, "I'm a Bear, or North Star, or Viking."

(Many of the world religions also serve a "cooling out" function; that is, beliefs and rituals can soften anger at injustice. The poor, especially, need to feel that their lives have some value. If it is the will of God, or Allah, or some other deity that some should suffer now in return for blessing in the next world ("the last shall be first"), hard times are easier to bear. Exceptions are revolutionary ideologies that attempt to *awaken* the sense of injustice and which, in order to do so, must claim that established religious beliefs are barriers to true con-

(Totems serve to symbolize and focus group identity,)in this case, Native American Indians. (Source: Craig Aurness, Woodfin Camp & Associates.)

The Rain Dance

The Rain Dance of several Native American tribes has long been an object of amusement to American schoolchildren (everyone knows that dancing can't bring rain!). Yet these same children regularly pray for things they want, including good weather as well as Christmas presents. Actually, the purpose of the Rain Dance is two-fold. Its *manifest function* is to activate rituals that influence the supernatural or uncontrollable aspects of life. But the *latent functions* of the Rain Dance immediately affect members of the group. By coming together for the dance ceremonies, and by chanting and acting out traditionally-hallowed patterns, individuals experience the unity that binds them. As Durkheim might point out, the ritual is an affirmation of the society.

If one thinks about the condition under which a rain dance is necessary— drought—it is obvious that personal anxiety and social strain will also be present. Under these circumstances what better way to generate cohesion than through a ceremony that symbolizes the strength and continuity of the group? The Rain Dance, then, is effective at one important level of social life, although it may not always bring rain.

sciousness) This is the context of Marx's statement that religion is the opiate of the masses, lulling them into a false consciousness that their status is divinely ordained and that it cannot be changed by human action. In the view of many contemporary conflict theorists, religion continues to be part of an oppressive cultural superstructure, controlled by members of the privileged classes for the benefit of maintaining the *status quo*.

DYSFUNCTIONS OF BELIEF SYSTEMS

(A basic assumption of most belief systems is that one and only one doctrine reflects the truth. If each belief system is *the* revealed Word, then others must be wrong. Moreover, those in possession of the one and only truth are often under an obligation to spread the Word.)

(For this reason there is always potential conflict among those who hold different beliefs. Because there is little room for compromise, religious wars have been among the most bloody and long-lasting in history.)Western history is filled with instances of religious persecution, forced conversion, and wholesale slaughter despite the fact that most faiths extol love and brotherhood, at least among believers. (Belief systems tend to unify the faithful but divide them from all nonbelievers who, by definition, are unfaithful and therefore often intolerable.)

Within a given society, the existence of two religions is often associated with conflict as, for example, in Northern Ireland, Nigeria, and Canada today. The United States has avoided major *sectarian conflict* (interreligious strife) by elevating tolerance of religious practices into a legal and moral principle.

Article VI of the Constitution of the United States:

No religious test shall ever be required as a qualification to any office or public trust . . . .

The First Amendment states, in part:

Congress shall make no law respecting an establishment of religion or prohibiting the free exercise thereof.

The major dysfunction of belief systems is the potential conflict among individuals and groups with different beliefs.

Major **sectarian conflict** has been avoided in North America by incorporating religious tolerance in legal and moral principles.

399

Northern Ireland's continuing conflict illustrates a common dysfunction of belief systems: intolerance for those outside the group. (Source: *Jim Anderson, Woodfin Camp & Associates.*)

But the First Amendment has not kept anti-Catholic and anti-Semitic passions in check; United States history, too, is filled with episodes of religious persecution and discrimination. The Ku Klux Klan was founded to save the nation from the degenerating influence of Catholics and Jews as well as blacks.

In the rest of the world, for centuries, missionaries and colonial administrators, unable to perceive native beliefs as legitimate, have tried to "convert the heathen" by imposing western religions. Although functional for European powers, colonialism and missionary activity were frequently dysfunctional for the native peoples. In many instances, missionaries were successful in converting the natives, but assisted in the destruction of the culture at the same time. Belief systems, remember, emerge from the experience of the group and express the uniqueness of its believers. When indigenous beliefs are supplanted by religions with no connection to their lives, members of a preliterate society lose a sense of cohesion and of personal anchorage. They become, in a real sense, rootless.

These examples illustrate a major sociological principle: that the same social pattern can be both adaptive and maladaptive depending on the context and the specific group involved. What is functional for a subgroup may not be so for the larger society. Thus, a belief system can increase solidarity within one group, but be a source of division in a society with several different sets of beliefs and believers. Nor do religions invariably allay personal anxiety; the anthropologist A. R. Radcliffe-Brown (1964) suggests that rituals and beliefs can generate a sense of insecurity and danger where none need exist. That is, if people were not so afraid of violating taboos or of a failure of faith they might be less anxiety-ridden and less in need of religious solace.

Nonetheless, in all human societies a minimal set of beliefs exist that (1) provide a meaning to life; (2) explain the unknown; (3) reduce tensions of important transitions in the life course; and (4) generate a sense of solidarity among believers. Belief systems are a means of adaptation devised by humans to sup-

A social pattern can be both functional and dysfunctional depending on the context and groups involved.

port the ongoing life of the group and to meet certain personal needs. That is, people create gods; or, as Voltaire, the French philosopher, put it: "If God did not exist, it would be necessary to invent him".

STRUCTURE OF BELIEF SYSTEMS ✓

Every religion or ideology has three essential components based on these personal and societal needs.

1. An *origin myth* (the word myth is not used to imply falsity but to indicate that the events being described happened at a much earlier time and cannot be verified). The origin myth is a tale of how the group originated, such as the story of Creation in Judaism and Christianity, or the anthropology of Marx's associate Friedrich Engels explaining the origins of private property. Both serve the same function of creating a history that makes sense of the present.

2. In the present, there are *rules of conduct* to be followed: proscriptions (prohibitions) and prescriptions (recipes for the good life) to guide the individual. These codes of conduct serve to reinforce social order—as, for example, the Ten Commandments or most of the *Koran*, the holy book of Islam.

3. The third element of belief systems is a *vision of the future:* a mission such as spreading the good word, waiting for the Second Coming, leading the Revolution, and so forth. The sense of destiny unifies all true believers and gives meaning to both individual existence and human history.

The same three elements are found everywhere, in the religions of simple as well as complex cultures, among believers in scientific explanations as well as followers of mysticism, of astronomers and astrologists alike. And of militant antireligionists. As the economist Joseph Schumpeter (1942) describes it, "Marxism *is* a religion. To the believer it presents, first, a system of ultimate ends that embody the meaning of life and are absolute standards by which to judge events and actions; and, secondly, a guide to those ends which implies a plan of salvation . . ." It appears that belief systems of one sort or another are *universal* elements of social structure. The earliest evidence comes from grave sites of the Neanderthal (*H. sapiens neanderthalensis*) populations and suggests that ritual burials preceded the advent of modern human populations by more than 100,000 years.

The Origins of Belief

The question of the origins of belief systems and religious behavior is one that has intrigued scholars as well as the general public. Among the many educated guesses are these: awe at power of nature, fear of death, the need to interpret dreams, guilt over the wish to kill one's father, and original sin. Nor can we overlook the possibility of some deep impulse to mysticism as a basic human trait; that is, a need to escape the limits of one's own senses. This drive toward *transcendence* is described by the social critic Lewis Mumford (1956) in these terms:

Every belief system has an origin myth, rules of conduct, and a vision of the future.

The limited goals of peace, order, power, security, wealth, knowledge, would be only disheartening mirages that left the thirsty soul dry, if they were regarded as life's ultimate consummations. . . . If 'Be yourself' is nature's first injunction . . . 'transform youself' was her second—even as 'transcend yourself' seems to be her final imperative.

Most contemporary social scientists, however, follow Durkheim and look to the nature of social life itself. In this view beliefs emerge from human interaction, so that religion and society are coterminous (exist together). Without going so far as to claim that society worships itself, the social scientist must pay attention to the particular structure of a society and its culture to understand why certain beliefs and rituals are elaborated.

For example, one plausible reconstruction of the origins of religion focuses on economic uncertainty experienced by people dependent upon crops. Would the gods bring seeds to life again? Would the harvest be sufficient? The link between human fertility and that of nature should lead to veneration of female objects, and indeed, the earliest artifacts of a clearly religious nature are tiny sculptures of females in an advanced state of pregnancy, such as the Venus of Willendorf.

These sculptures are often referred to as fertility figures, and are assumed to represent a female-centered worship among early agriculturalists. There is also evidence of females with important ritual functions in more culturally-developed societies—Vestal Virgins, for instance, and Druid priestesses. Since religions are reflections of social systems, some scholars have concluded that these practices signify a relatively egalitarian social order.

Yet the major world religions today are strikingly dominated by male imagery: the Father reigns supreme, through chosen Sons. The leaders of the biblical Hebrews are called the Patriarchs; Christianity is extremely masculine in its symbols, doctrine, and power structure; Islam, similarly, is almost exclusively male-oriented. Although Eastern religions—Buddhism, Hinduism,and Shintoism—are less stridently masculine, woman's role in ritual is extremely limited. These regularities in religious dogma and practice, originating in *agricultural* societies of the Near and Far East, strongly reflect the patriarchal social systems of the time and place of their origin.

Yet despite such universal similarities, it is the diversity and richness of beliefs and rituals that fascinate the social scientist. In preliterate societies, especially, the elaboration of ritual and the application of magic are often more complex than in modern societies. If one were to classify societies on the basis of belief systems rather than mode of subsistence, it is the industrial nations that are more simple in their rituals and belief systems.

Cross-Cultural Perspectives

Whatever the origins, and however rooted in the experience of the group, belief systems are capable of endless variation—in detail, if not in outline.

In all societies there are two very different sets of behaviors and objects: one set is the *sacred*, somehow imbued with holy, divine, mystical, or supernatural force; the other realm is the *profane*, encompassing behavior that is unholy, earthly, understandable in its own terms. In every society, also, some individuals are designated as responsible for the sacred objects. Religious roles are among the very first to emerge in human history.)

There is an ethnocentric tendency to consider the religious behavior of preliterate people as evidence of a lower or fundamentally different level of intelligence. The anthropologist, Lucien Lévy-Bruhl, in his *How Natives Think* (1926), spoke of a "prelogical" mode of thought of people immersed in magical explanations because they could not grasp the rational meaning of events. Strong opposition to the view that there are two different ways of thinking linked to cultural development was expressed by another anthropologist, Bronislaw Malinowski.

Caught in the South Pacific during World War I, Malinowski lived with and carefully observed the life of Trobriand Islanders over an extended period. Malinowski's interest in *latent function* (unrecognized consequences of behavior) led him to conclude that *magic* was goal-directed activity in contrast to *religion*,

Sacred behaviors and objects are associated with divine, mystical, and supernatural forces.

Profane behaviors and objects are unholy, everyday, and understandable in their own terms.

Rational knowledge cannot always predict outcomes, and many people find solace in religion. (Source: Katrina Thomas, Photo Researchers, Inc.)

Magic is goal-directed activity whereas **religion** expresses the value of tradition in a society.

which was an expression of the value of tradition in the society. Moreover, Malinowski claimed that the Trobrianders had a great deal of scientific knowledge, although it was not organized as is scientific information in a modern society. The natives had an especially keen and rational grasp of boat-building, sailing, planting, and jewelry-making, for instance. The difference between Trobriand and modern religious behavior was not a difference in mentality but in the scope of knowledge. Two Trobriand examples are particularly illustrative of this difference:

> When fishing in the lagoon, which is a calm area of water protected from the ocean by a ring of land, there was very little magic or ceremony involved in the outfitting and departure of canoes. But beyond the ring of land, in the ocean where high winds and sudden waves were an unpredictable hazard, the departure of the vessels was laden with ritual . . . .
>
> At life crisis events associated with danger or awakening of strong emotions, magic is invoked. Birth is surrounded with rituals to ward off evil. But, unlike most other societies, there are no puberty rites in the Trobriands because this biological moment does not signify a crisis in the life of individuals or the group since sexual activity begins in childhood. But love is something else, and the threat of misdirected passion must be countered by powerful magic formulas (1954).

Malinowski's point is clear: Magic is evoked where rational knowledge cannot predict the outcome. And these are precisely those moments in which members of modern societies, also, cross their heart, rub a rabbit's foot, light candles, and pray.

Baseball Magic

Trobrianders are not the only persons to invoke magic when the outcome of an activity is uncertain. So also do contemporary athletes.

A former player, George Gmelch describes a number of rituals, taboos, and fetishes practiced by professional baseball players. Such behavior is rarely displayed in the act of fielding because the outcome is a matter of individual skill under the control of the player. In hitting and pitching, however, outcomes cannot be rationally calculated, and *ritual* behavior is common. Players often repeat the precise order of motions, or wear the same clothes, or eat the same food that they did on a day when they performed exceptionally well. Gmelch describes his own experience:

> In hopes of maintaining a batting streak, I once ate fried chicken every day at 4:00 P.M., kept my eyes closed during the national anthem and changed sweat shirts at the end of the fourth inning each night for seven consecutive nights until the streak ended. (p. 40).

Taboos include not mentioning a no-hitter while the game is in progress, avoiding certain foods associated with a poor performance, not shaving, or staying away from women before a game. Popular *fetishes* involve rubbing sacred objects, wearing talismans, tapping the bat three times, and any of the repeated patterns of twitches and tics you may have noticed among pitchers and batters.

Source: George Gmelch, Transaction, Vol. 8 June, 1971, p. 39 ff.

Belief Systems and Social Change

Since belief systems deal with the eternal (either truth is everlasting or it is not truth), most religions are inherently conservative, quite apart from the conflict theorist's view that established religions reinforce the political and economic structures of inequality. Yet religions can be agents of social change. New movements are continually being formed within established religions, even in simple societies. Typically, a charismatic leader introduces change in the traditional forms of religious practice, or becomes the founder of a new religion, as, for example, both Jesus and Mohammed.

Karl Marx emphasized the priestly, conservatizing functions of religion. Max Weber studied the dynamic aspects of belief systems and the relationship between religion and other institutional spheres. Weber spoke of the *routinization of charisma*, whereby the prophetic mode is transformed into worldly organization. The resulting bureaucracy often becomes the deadening structure described by Marx. In other words, many religions have originated as forces of social and political change, but will, if successful, eventually become the new establishment.

Routinization of charisma describes the transformation of the dynamic, prophetic mode into bureaucratic organization.

There is a basic tension between religion and its emphasis on the holy on the one hand and the world as it is, full of imperfection and temptations, on the other. Jealousy, hate, lust, greed, and other assorted human passions always threaten to turn one away from contemplation of the perfect good. Religious leaders must continually warn and rebuke the less faithful. Some religions, claimed Weber, survive by maintaining an other-worldly stance; that is, the members remove themselves from the everyday world into religious communities separate from the rest of society (as for example, the Hutterites and Amish of modern America). Or as Confucians and Orthodox Jews do, believers can create two spheres of activity with different rules for each. Thus, the Orthodox Jew may hold a job and be devoted to secular business concerns for part of the day, but in the rest of his or her activities follow a purely religious way of life.

Priests and Prophets

Max Weber distinguishes the *priestly* from the *prophetic*. In general, priestly functions involve dealing with the specific tradition of the faith in which the priest is a trained and ordained leader. In religious terms, the priest is a conservator, and in political terms, often supportive of the existing structure of power. The prophet, on the other hand, is a charismatic figure, usually risen from the ranks of untrained laypersons, and witness to a revelation calling for a new order. As the bringer of this new order, the prophet is by definition at odds with established authorities. The prophet may be a simple teacher of the new law as was Jesus, or may seize political power as did Mohammed. Therefore, priests represent traditional values, and may actually be the inheritors of a prophetic movement. Prophets disrupt the social order, and, as disturbers of the peace, leave themselves vulnerable to passions both for and against their prophecy.

Christianity and Islam: A Chronicle Of Two Cultures

Birth of Christ

A.D. 29
Crucifixion,
Resurrection,
Ascenscion

c.70–100
Gospels
written

312
Constantine
converts to
Christianity

800
Charle-
mange
crowned

1054
East-West
schism

1096
Second
Crusade
begins

1323
Thomas
Aquinas
canonized

1517
Reformation:
Luther posts Theses

1533
Calvin's
conversion

1534
Establishment
Anglican Church

1545
Counter-Reformation:
Council of Trent

1834
Spanish
Inquisition
abolished

1869–70
Vatican
Council I

1962–65
Vatican
Council II

Centuries
Christian
Dates

| 1 | 2 | 3 | 4 | 5 | 6 | 7 | 8 | 9 | 10 | 11 | 12 | 13 | 14 | 15 | 16 | 17 | 18 | 19 | 20 |

Islamic
Dates

637
Umar enters
Jerusalem

622
Hegira from
Mecca to Medina

A.D. 610
Mohammed's
revelation

969
Fatamids
conquer
Egypt

1187
Saladin
captures
Jerusalem

1258
Rule of Ab-
basids ends

1520
Suleiman rules
Ottoman
Empire

1453
Ottomans
capture
Constantinople

1648
Taj
Mahal
completed

1922
Ataturk
abolishes
Turkish
sultanate

1960
OPEC
formed

1979
Ayatollah
Khomeini
rules Iran

Egyptian-
Israeli
peace
treaty

Here are some
key events in
the ongoing
stories that
are the worlds
of Islam and
Christianity.

(The New York Times Magazine, January 6, 1980.)

NATIVISTIC MOVEMENTS

In times of extensive or rapid social change, the power of established authorities to interpret the world and provide guidance may be weakened. These are the historical moments when charismatic figures are likely to emerge and find a mass following: for example, the Old Testament prophets, Mohammed, Jesus, the Ayatollah Khomeini, and Wovoka of the Plains Indians.

The Ghost Dance Religion. By the late 1880s, the buffalo had long since disappeared from the Great Plains. Native Americans were being forced onto reservations, as white settlers took their land and destroyed the Indians' culture base. For a short period in 1870, a version of the traditional Ghost Dance, an extremely hallowed celebration of Indian culture uniting all those who share a way of life, swept through the tribes. By 1888, when disorientation and anger were widespread among the Plains Indians, the Ghost Dance Religion was revived under the influence of Wovoka, a prophet who taught the tribes a new dance that he claimed would resurrect dead ancestors and replenish the land with animals for hunting. The Dance spread rapidly, along with a hatred of whites and a renewed pride in Indian ways. A particularly enraged group of Dakotas under Chief Sitting Bull fought the United States Army at Wounded Knee and was thoroughly defeated. Although the Ghost Dance religion persisted for another few years, Native American culture and society in the United States were effectively destroyed.

The Ghost Dance is an example of nativistic revival movements that arise when a culture is disintegrating under the impact of profound change. In the

Nativistic revival movements arise when a culture is disintegrating.

Pacific Islands disrupted by war and colonialism, islanders have built airstrips for the arrival of planes full of plenty (remembered from the Second World War). These *cargo cults* express the breakdown of a traditional order, a yearning for the wholeness of the past, and a magical reliance on, quite literally, the "God in the Machine" (Worsley, 1968).)

MODERNIZATION

Throughout the world today, however, the most powerful forces of social change are those associated with *modernization*. The implications for religion are profound because modernism is in many ways a challenge to faith. The effect of modernization on belief systems has been varied: Nonreligious ideologies such as Communism or Nazism gain prominence while at the same time rapid social change leads to nativistic movements such as the wave of Islamic revivalism in Iran, and of Christian fundamentalism in the United States.

The modern age is also characterized by *world religions*, representing the triumph of a very few major faiths in spreading across the world, absorbing other religions and converting millions:

Modernization, the most powerful force of social change, has dramatic implications for religion.

Table 15-1. Estimated Membership of the Principal Religions of the World. Statistics of the world's religions are only very rough approximations. Aside from Christianity, few religions, if any, attempt to keep statistical records; and even Protestants and Catholics employ different methods of counting members. All persons of whatever age who have received baptism in the Catholic Church are counted as members, while in most Protestant churches only those who "join" the church are numbered. The compiling of statistics is further complicated by the fact that in China one may be at the same time a Confucian, a Taoist, and a Buddhist. In Japan, one may be both a Buddhist and a Shintoist.

Religion	North America[1]	South America	Europe	Asia	Africa	Oceania[2]	Total
Total Christian	231,099,700	158,980,000	348,059,300	89,909,000	137,460,300	18,112,600	983,620,900
Roman Catholic	131,631,500	147,280,000	182,514,300	47,046,000	53,740,000	4,475,000	566,686,800
Eastern Orthodox	4,189,000	552,000	50,545,000	1,894,000	15,255,000	380,000	72,815,000
Protestant	95,279,200	11,148,000	115,000,000	40,969,000	68,465,300	13,257,600	344,119,100
Jewish[3]	6,641,118	727,000	4,082,400	3,203,460	294,400	84,000	15,032,378
Moslem	249,200	238,300	8,283,500	433,001,000	134,285,200	103,000	576,160,200
Zoroastrian	250	2,000	6,000	224,700	600	—	233,550
Shinto	60,000	92,000	—	55,004,000	—	—	55,156,000
Taoist	16,000	12,000	—	31,088,100	—	—	31,116,100
Confucian	96,100	85,150	25,000	173,940,250	500	42,200	174,189,200
Buddhist	155,250	195,300	200,000	260,117,000	2,000	16,000	260,685,550
Hindu	81,000	782,300	260,000	515,449,500	483,650	841,000	517,897,450
Total	238,398,618	161,114,050	360,916,200	1,561,937,010	272,526,650	19,198,800	2,614,091,328

1. Includes Central America and West Indies. 2. Includes Australia and New Zealand, as well as islands of the South Pacific. 3. Includes total Jewish population, whether or not related to the synagogue. NOTE: Because of war and persecution, there are about 18,000,000 refugees throughout the world who are not integrated into religious statistics of the land of their temporary residence. Source: *Britannica Book of the Year, 1978.*

Religious Organization

Sociologists have a vocabulary for types of religious organizations.

Church: An association of believers that has a clear structure of offices and places of worship, that is, a high degree of institutionalization. Churches are recognized entities in the social system. Thus, we can speak abstractly of the Catholic Church or Protestant Church in North America. This usage is more general than reference to a specific church such as the First Baptist Church of Boston. Although Jews worship in Temples and Moslems in Mosques, we can also speak of the Jewish or Moslem Church as a religious organization.

Ecclesia: Refers to the situation of a state or established church. Most members of the society will be members of the one church, and the church hierarchy and political leadership are mutually protective of each other's interests. For example, the Anglican Church is the established church of England and, for most of its history, of Canada; Judaism is the state religion of Israel; Catholicism of Italy; and Islam of Egypt. Typically, political authorities are more powerful than religious leaders in modern societies; but there are a few instances of *theocracy* in which religious leaders also control the political apparatus, such as Iran under the Ayatollahs after the fall of the Shah in 1979.

Denomination: An organized religious group *within* church, as for example, the Methodist and Baptist branches of Protestantism, or the Reform movement within Judaism. Denominations have their own hierarchy, ritual style, and version of the truth. Often, denominations have developed through *schism* (division) within an established church, out of which a new religious group is formed that varies somewhat but not entirely from the mother church.

Sect: A group that separates from a denomination, usually over a matter of theological interpretation and practice. Evangelicals within Protestant denominations often build their own places of worship while remaining a part of the larger religious body. Over time, a sect may attract enough members and find sufficient differences with the established hierarchy to become a full-fledged denomination in its own right. Among Moslems, for example, local conditions have produced many different versions of Islam, usually described as sects but actually much closer to denominations and in some cases to ecclesia. This has led to a great deal of internal conflict in the Moslem world.

Cult: The term used to describe religious groups even smaller in number and less organized than sects. Cults are often based on immediate emotional experience rather than the thought-out theology of most world religions. Ecstatic (emotional, revelation-oriented) practices such as snake-handling, talking in tongues (glossolalia), and uncontrollable body movements are frequent features of cult behavior.

Secularization. The great transition from traditional to modern societies involves, among other trends, the triumph of science, rationality, technology, and belief in the powers of the individual. These traits are components of *secularization*. The focus is on this world, on human beings coping with prob-

√ **Secularization** involves the triumph of science, rationality, and technology.

lems of life and death, of order and meaning. Science, of course, need not be considered in opposition to revealed widsom; there are always ultimate questions that science cannot answer. For example, the well-known astronomer Robert Jastrow (1978) notes that although scientists are now fairly certain that the solar system began with a Big Bang about eight billion years ago, we will never be so certain about the moment before the great explosion; therefore, who can say that some divine power was not present in the origin of our world? And if scientists were to find out about the moment before the Big Bang, what of the moment before that one? There is always one more question and, with it, one more area in which faith can take precedence over science.

Nonetheless, the areas of life in which rational answers and solutions have replaced faith or magical practices is ever-widening. The difference between the Trobrianders and ourselves is that our technology permits us to foresee and prepare rationally for more potential problems. Yet, for all the sailing technology at our command, a sudden storm capsized dozens of the best-made yachts and drowned many first-rate sailors in the Irish Sea in 1979. A Trobriand seaman might suggest that more attention should have been paid to magic rituals, and who can prove otherwise?

It is the rational way of thinking (the *secular mind*) that most conflicts with religion. The belief that human beings themselves can change the conditions of their lives is a profound challenge to the belief in divine providence. If a machine breaks down there is little benefit to praying for it to resume operating, but a great deal to be gained by reading the technical manual and making appropriate adjustments. The secular mind, moreover, is characterized by *consumption* values—enjoyment of the here and now, guided by a vision of the good life on earth rather than in the next world. Central, also, to the secular orientation is an emphasis on the *individual*. Personal qualities, self-direction, and individual responsibility for one's conduct are linked to success in contemporary industrial societies.

A secular orientation emphasizes the personal qualities and self-direction of the **individual**.

Thus, the secular mentality and the organization of modern life appear to diminish the prospects for religious control over behavior or deep commitment to religious values. However, as we shall examine later in this chapter, religious fervor has not disappeared, and faith has not been entirely replaced by science. In fact, there is some evidence of a resurgence of religious beliefs and practices that deny the validity of scientific explanations of theological questions.

Organized Religion and Religious Behavior in Contemporary North America

PARTICIPATION AND ATTENDANCE

The Yearbook of American and Canadian Churches, 1980, containing the most thorough and recent data on organized religion in North America, (see Table 15-2), reports the following:

Table 15-2. United States Churches and Members, 1980

	Number branches reporting	Number of churches	Number of members
Buddhists	1	60	60,000
Eastern Churches	17	1,583	3,632,555
Jews	1	3,500	5,781,000
Old Catholic, Polish National Catholic, Armenian Churches	9	421	808,684
Protestants	186	300,676	73,704,162
Roman Catholic	1	25,542	49,602,035
Miscellaneous	7	1,188	160,340
Totals	222	332,970	133,748,776

Source: The Yearbook of American and Canadian Churches, 1980, p. 231.

Three-fifths of the total population of the United States are formally affiliated with a church.

In Canada, the population is more evenly divided between Protestants and Catholics—roughly ten million of each. Other sizeable minorities of Canadian church members include 300,000 Jews, 220,000 Greek Orthodox, and 200,000 members of the Pentecostal Assembly.

Catholics compose the largest single church in both societies although all Protestant denominations combined form a majority. The proportions of Catholics in North America has steadily inceased, through selective immigration in the United States up to the 1920s, and by relatively higher fertility rates in both countries since then. In the United States, and increasingly in Canada, as more Catholics move into the middle class, their birth rates approximate those of the Protestant majority. In order to do so, however, many Catholic couples now engage in contraceptive behavior forbidden by the Catholic hierarchy. The resulting feeling of guilt have led many to avoid churchgoing although they remain "communal Catholics" (Greeley, 1977).

In general, in modern societies, religion as an ascribed characteristic loses significance as a determinant of social placement although personal religiosity can remain very high. For example, Gallup poll data in the United States for 1978 found that 57 per cent of a national probability sample of 7500 adults said religious beliefs were "very important" and another 27 per cent said "fairly important." Only 15 per cent indicated that religious beliefs were "not too" or "not at all" important to them. The subgroups most likely to endorse the importance of religious beliefs are women, nonwhites, Southerners, older people, people from small towns and rural areas, and those in lower income and educational strata (Jacquet, 1980, p. 270) Moreover, of all institutions in the United States, respondents ranked organized religion highest on trust or confidence (see Table 15-3).

Despite such avowals of faith, churchgoing in North America has declined steadily over the past quarter century.

Catholics compose the largest single church in North America, but Protestant denominations combine to form the majority religion.

Table 15-3. *Confidence in institutions, United States 1979*

Institution	Per cent expressing "a great deal" or "quite a lot" of confidence
Organized Religion	65%
Banking	60
Military	54
Public Schools	53
Newspapers	51
U.S. Supreme Court	45
Television	38
Organized Labor	36
Congress	34
Big Business	32

(Jacquet, 1980, p. 270)

This trend continued into 1979 when the most recent Gallup poll data reported that 40 per cent of adults "attended regularly." Catholics were most likely to have attended regularly (52 per cent) and Jews the least (20 per cent), with Protestants in between (40 per cent). Women attend more frequently than men, nonwhites than whites, and Southerners and Midwesterners more than those on either coast. Attendance also increases with age. These data could reflect real generational/cohort differences in religious behavior, suggesting that today's young people will not become more involved as they age. Alternatively, the life events that turn people toward religious observance—marriage and parenthood, a death in the family, marital and occupational difficulties—have not yet been fully experienced by those under age 30. Possibly both trends are at work so that aging is associated with the probability of attending religious service, but with each incoming cohort of adults doing so at a slightly

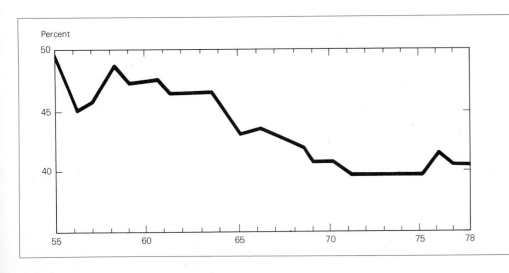

Figure 15-1. *Percent of adult population attending religious services, United States, 1955–78.* (Source: *Jacquet, 1980, p. 269.*)

A 1978 Gallup poll reported that 84 per cent of adults said religious beliefs are very important or fairly important in their lives. (Source: Watriss-Baldwin, Woodfin Camp & Associates.)

lower rate than the one before, thus producing the fairly constant rate of 40–45 per cent for the past fifteen years.

There are other trends that could explain the low attendance and membership rates of many young people in both Canada and the United States. One of these involves not secularism itself so much as its effect on *intermarriage* (Greeley, 1978). Religious commitment takes place in a social matrix in which ideology or beliefs are less important than interpersonal relationships. Intermarriage places many couples in a potentially conflict-filled situation that can be avoided by reducing the importance of religion in their lives. Young people, especially those with generally liberal attitudes, account for the increase between 1960 and 1978 in those checking "none of the above" when asked about religious affiliation (Hadaway, 1980). The religious commitment of North Americans has been diluted by both the secularization of religious life and, paradoxically, the religionization of public life.

CIVIL RELIGION IN THE UNITED STATES AND CANADA

North American societies are almost unique in the heterogeneity of their religious sector. Perhaps only the Soviet Union encompasses as many religious minorities. But no other nations permit the range of religious expression found in Canada and the United States, and protected by custom and the law.

Given the variety of religious expression in North America—from mainstream churches to obscure sects—how can the need for a unifying belief system at the societal level be met? This is the question posed by the sociologist Robert Bellah, who finds the functional equivalent of a common faith in an *American civil religion*. Bellah (1970) describes the elevation of secular ideals and history to a quasi-religious level. In the United States, the motto "In God We Trust" and the phrase "one nation under God," although not extolling any specific religion, lend an aura of sanctity to the nation's leaders and institutions. With certain modifications due to the history of Canada as a colony of Great

✓ The potentially conflicting situation stemming from **intermarriage** can be reduced by decreasing the importance of religion.

✓ The elevation of secular ideals and religious tolerance in the U.S. has produced an **American civil religion.**

412

Britain and its unique French-speaking Catholic minority, Fallding (1978) has analysed a civil religion in Canada in very similar terms.

Despite religious diversity, we can unite around the moral mission of our society. The idea that God has somehow blessed this continent is also exalted on secular holidays such as the Fourth of July and Denomination Day. Political leaders call upon "God's will or wisdom" or "divine help." These beliefs serve the essential functions described by Durkheim as the sanctification of the social order and the integration of its members. The more diverse the religious communities within the society, the greater the need for such an "ideological umbrella."

Yet Bellah (1970) does not claim that nationalism has replaced religion; rather,

> I conceive of the central tradition of the American civil religion not as a form of national self-worship but as the subordination of the nation to ethical principles that transcend it and in terms of which it should be judged.

Other analysts are less optimistic; they fear a loss of authentic spiritual commitment in a vague sea of secular religiosity where the important attribute is to have a religious affiliation rather than to live fully one particular set of beliefs (Herberg, 1960).

Thus the great paradox of contemporary *mainstream churches* in Canada and the United States: widespread religiosity combined with declining membership in the regularly established churches. The term "mainstream churches" refers to historical institutionalized bodies such as Greek or Roman Catholic, or major Jewish and Protestant denominations.

Recent attempts to make the church more relevant to modern life styles by using the vernacular (everyday speech) or replacing hymns with folk songs, and calling the pastor by his or her first name, have alienated those who prefer the traditional forms, and who desire a profoundly moving experience from their devotions. Peter Berger (1969) claims that religions must meet a human need for *transcendence*, that is, helping worshippers rise above the humdrum of daily life and to feel part of an unbroken chain of experience. In fact, the more routinized and rationalized that everyday experience becomes in modern societies, the more urgent is this desire for a mystical awakening. According to Berger, secular faiths cannot meet this need because the very nature of secularism is earthbound. People seek to understand the everlasting, not the here and now. They do not wish to be presented with moral dilemmas but to be insulated from them.

Religions meet a need for **transcendence** of one's daily life.

Contemporary Trends in the United States and Canada

THREE DECADES OF CHANGE

The 1950s and the "Death of God." The long period of social stability, cultural blandness, and personal prosperity in North America from 1945 to the early

1960s (and to the end of that decade in Canada), produced many deceptive postulates: that economic growth was endless, that democracy would sweep the world, that the American Dream was available to all willing to work for it, and so forth. As Max Weber predicted, the world seemed demystified, rationally mastered, and all problems capable of technological solution.

Out of these perceptions came the thesis that "God is dead," and that nonrational religious experiences—revelations, possession by the Devil, speaking in tongues, and the like—were holdovers from a superstitious past that would soon disappear altogether as mainstream churches became more humanistic, and oriented toward this world and its problems. Religious holy days had become commercial holidays, and "the American Way of religion" seemed triumphant.

The 1960s and Social Activism. By the early 1960s, it appeared that the churches were without a mission: no heathens to conquer, not many souls to save, few Princes of Darkness with which to do battle. Then came the challenge of the civil rights movement in the United States. Black leaders sought and found allies among those who had long preached brotherhood and justice—members of the religious establishment. That the civil rights movement was spearheaded by black clergy added special impact to their plea for religious support. And the mainstream churches responded positively. No civil rights demonstration in the 1960s was without its ranks of nuns, rabbis, priests, and ministers. The National Council of Churches budgeted several million dollars to its Commission on Race and Religion (CORR) founded in 1963. CORR organized the mammoth march on Washington in August 1963, lobbied for civil rights legislation, and conducted summer programs in Mississippi in 1964 ("the ministry of reconciliation"). The passage of the Civil Rights Act of 1964 owes much to pressures exerted by mainstream churches (Clark, 1970).

No sooner had the churches responded to the demands for equality and justice for blacks, than the moral dilemmas of the Vietnam war became apparent. Again, many clergy—though in smaller numbers than for the civil rights movement—joined antiwar demonstrations. Altogether, the 1960s were a decade of social activism unparalleled in modern church history. Younger clergy, especially, were exhilarated by their roles in the fight against racism and what they perceived as an unjust war.

Their parishioners were considerably less thrilled. While church leaders were engaged in protest, rank-and-file church members grew increasingly upset at decisions being taken without their consent, and many disapproved of the causes to which their clergy were drawn, resenting the time away from the pulpit as well as the money and effort diverted from local needs.

The 1970s and Retrenchment. By the end of the 1970s, membership in the National Council of Churches declined, contributions decreased dramatically, lawsuits were threatened questioning NCC's tax-exempt status, and several public opinion surveys showed clearly that a majority of citizens did not feel that the clergy should engage in direct attempts to change the society (Hadden, 1969).

Off the streets and back in the pulpit, many ministers, priests, and rabbis were able to redefine their mission as service to their particular congregation rather than to abstract concepts or to groups outside their immediate responsibility. The dilemma of choosing between serving one's flock, the primary responsibility of a minister, or serving broader goals of peace and justice was resolved in favor of saving souls. The prophetic functions that had inspired clergy in the 1960s gave way to an emphasis on priestly duties. Fallding (1978) notes a similar shift in the mainstream Protestant churches of Canada, though with a time lag of several years.

Even with the new thrust in North American religion—away from social involvement and toward pastoral duties—the mainstream churches have not regained their previous strength in terms of membership and contributions. Much vigor has been drained off by the rise of evangelical fundamentalism and the emergence of a variety of sets and cults in the 1970s.

Evangelical Fundamentalism.   The enduring human need for transcendence is today often coupled with fear of losing control over a way of life. Certain groups such as Southern whites, socially conservative midwesterners, and members of religiously traditional denominations (e.g. Missouri Synod Lutherans, Southern Baptists) may be especially upset by secularism.

In the United States today, the growth of fundamentalist sects among whites, advocating absolute adherence to the words of the *Bible*, has been aided by a network of religiously-oriented radio and television stations. This "electronic ministry" reaches millions of listeners weekly.

The term *evangelical* connotes an emphasis on salvation and dramatic witness to the presence of a divine spirit. The concept of being *born again* is central to the Protestant Evangelical doctrine; it means having an experience that changes the course of one's life through an acceptance of the Lord. A public affirmation of this rebirth brings the weight of the community to bear on future conduct. Thus, in both white and black evangelical congregations, the large gathering of believers in which members stand up and announce their commitment is a particularly effective means of meeting personal and group needs for salvation and reinforcement of belief.

> **Evangelical** faiths emphasize salvation and witnessing the presence of a divine spirit.

> To be **born again** is to have an experience that changes one's life through an acceptance of faith.

The new primarily white churches and sects have been well-financed. From the proceeds of his radio and television appeals, for example, Oral Roberts has realized enough money to build an entire university campus. There is no question that evangelicism is big business. It is also increasingly powerful politically.

From a social-scientific perspective, the evangelical-fundamentalist movement can be considered as a nativistic revival. As indicated in Table 15-4, evangelicals, both black and white, are likely to live in the South, to have limited educational and occupational attainments, to be elderly, to come from small towns, to be women, and to be drawn from lower-status Protestant denominations. Whites with these characteristics may feel that their traditional culture is being threatened by satanic forces, and that the solution is a return to the values and behaviors of the past. To hope that by retaining prayers in schools and censoring texts one's children will be protected against the evil forces of modernism may seem futile. But an enormous faith and conviction here translates into economic and political power for the "Christian Right."

Fundamentalists can also tap a general well of disillusion over American society and policies. The ambiguous end to the Vietnam War, the new sexuality,

Table 15-4. Evangelical Christians: Who Are They? Evangelicals, as defined in this Gallup Poll, are those 1) who describe themselves as "born-again Christians" or as having had a "born again" experience, 2) who have encouraged others to believe in Jesus Christ and 3) who believe in a literal interpretation of the Bible or accept the absolute authority of the Bible. Chart shows the percentage of various groups who meet all three criteria.

Total		19%
Sex	Women	22
	Men	15
Race	Non-whites	36
	Whites	16
Education	Grade school	30
	High school	19
	College	12
Region	South	33
	Midwest	16
	West	13
	East	10
Political affiliation	Southern Democrats	39
	Republicans	22
	Northern Democrats	15
	Independents	14
Religion	Baptists	42
	(All Protestants)	28
	Methodists	18
	Presbyterians	16
	Lutherans	10
	Catholics	6
	Episcopalians	4
Age	50 years and older	22
	30–49 years old	19
	25–29 years old	15
	18–24 years old	13
Occupation	Clerical and sales	25
	Manual workers	21
	Not working	21
	Professionals	11
Community size	Under 2,500 residents	26
	2,500–49,999	20
	50,000–499,999	17
	500,000–999,999	14
	1,000,000 or more	14

Gallup Poll N = 3000
New York Times September 7, 1980, p. A-39.

"Christian Voice" is a new political action committee using the network of religious television and radio stations to support conservative candidates for federal office. Until recently, most white Protestant conservatives had been very conscious of the division between church and state; indeed, their creed was one of remaining aloof from the earthly struggles of politics. Today, however, feeling that they have lost control of the forces determining the quality of their lives, some fundamentalists have followed their leaders into direct intervention in politics.

"Christian Voice" has met with instant success. For example, a government decision to cut off funds to private schools that failed to meet federal guidelines for racial integration or that maintained separate curricula for male and female students brought at least one hundred thousand letters to Congress. As a result the Department of Health, Education, and Welfare plans to withold funds.

On the eve of the 1980 presidential election, a group of fundamentalist ministers calling itself "Moral Majority" was formed to support candidates for political office who held "Christian positions" on such issues as: Women's Rights (against), public support for private schools (for), evolution (against), school prayers (for), homosexual rights (against), defense spending (for), and the Panama Canal Treaty (against).

As a result, the entire issue of church/state relations in the United States has once more become a major topic of debate.

political paralysis at the federal level, and the economic crises of advanced capitalism all cry out for explanation and correction. The root causes of these phenomena are extremely complex and hardly reassuring to people seeking certainty. Therefore, it is both logical and comforting to believe that a return to faith, to patriarchal families, and to the individualist ethos of early capitalism will solve all problems. If the fault lies with Eastern intellectuals (George Wallace's "pointy-headed" bureaucrats), hippie-type young people, and immoral women, then the solution is to remove these groups from political power. Thus, what began as a movement to save individual souls can become a crusade to purify the nation. Moreover, the fundamentalists' power within their denominations has been increasing. For example, at the June 1979 convention of the largest Protestant denomination, Southern Baptists elected an extreme religious and political conservative as their new president. In terms of membership and money, the fundamentalist/evangelical churches and sects have been gaining rapidly while mainstream religious bodies have experienced yearly declines. These trends strongly support the thesis that mainstream churches dominated by upper middle-class northeastern intellectuals have failed to meet a need for transcendent experience or to reduce status anxiety among large numbers of the less affluent and less worldly. In other words, there are social status as well as purely doctrinal differences involved in the phenomenon.

The New Cults. Another source of defection from mainstream religion is the variety of new cults attracting large numbers of young adults. Although far less important numerically, religiously, and politically than the fundamentalist movement, the cults have great shock value because of the sometimes bizarre

417

behavior of believers and because of the fear generated among parents of converts. Some of the modern cults are offshoots of the fundamentalist movement, others derive from Eastern religions, still others center on the supernatural, and at the opposite extreme, on one's own self. In addition, a number of expressly political cults have developed among members of powerless minorities.

Fundamentalist cults.   The Jesus People or "Jesus Freaks," Jews for Jesus, Campus Crusade for Christ, and Children of God are part of Protestant revivalism discussed in the last section, but aim at a younger age stratum than, say, the Missouri Lutheran Synod. By giving a contemporary air of communalism to their practices, these groups offer a religiously-grounded alternative to those young people who, in the 1960s, might have been drop-outs or acid heads. Persons in their late teens and early twenties are also increasingly attracted to religious practices and organizations based on non-Western belief systems.

The Eastern cults.   The late 1960s were also a period in which Eastern religions became popularized in this country. In the past decade, many million

Since their popularization in the late 1960s, various Eastern religions have attracted many adherents in the United States. (Source: *Peter Southwick, Stock, Boston.*)

Americans have taken an active part in one or another form of Eastern religious devotion. Exact numbers are difficult to derive since some individuals are members of several cults at different times, and the organizations tend to exaggerate their membership.

The most widespread Eastern influence has been Transcendental Meditation (TM), a practice of disciplined contemplation and relaxation that achieved sufficient respectability to be accepted in several public school districts. TM cen-

Religions of the Far East

In contrast to religions originating in the Near East—Judaism, Christianity, and Islam—the major belief systems of Southeast Asia and the Far East are more contemplative, oriented to nature, and polytheistic (accepting many gods). The questions posed by such religions as Buddhism, Hinduism, Shintoism, and Confucianism are these: "What is my place in the universe?" "Which path shall I take to happiness?" "What is the way of harmony?" "What is life?" There is an element of searching and seeking in these questions that is very different from the insistence on received doctrine of Islam or Christianity: "*This* is the way!"

Three elements of Eastern Religion that have great appeal to young people in the United States today are (1) the emphasis on self-discipline (not unlike early Calvinism), (2) a belief in the unity of all life, that is, humans *and* nature, past *and* present, and one person to another, all linked together in one chain of life, and (3) experience is more highly valued than intellect. Thus, knowledge comes from an opening of the mind to feeling and intuitive understanding.

Hinduism and Buddhism in India, Confucianism in China, and Shintoism in Japan are, however, very different from one another in history and precise doctrine.

The great theme of _Hinduism_ is that of an everlasting cycle of life in which all things are reincarnated (born over and over again), and the grand goal of human existence is to transcend this endless cycle through contemplation that brings perfect peace from earthly passions.

Buddhism is based on knowledge of right conduct and enlightenment through suffering and contemplation, with the goal of *Nirvana*, a complete emptying of the self so that Buddha's insights can enter and free the individual from the cycle of reincarnation.

In contrast, _Confucianism_ is founded on a reverence for the past, and is full of precepts for behavior, much like Western religions. The key concept is *piety* (respect and righteousness), first expressed in the family as the worship of ancestors and obedience to parents, then extended to the state. Subjects shall respect their kings, children their parents, wives their husbands, and younger siblings their elders. Friend to friend is the only egalitarian relationship in the Confucian hierarchy.

Shintoism, the indigenous religion of Japan, is based on the belief that divine forces of nature (Kami) exist in the sun and moon, rivers, trees, and animals. Shinto has been greatly influenced by Buddhism and Confucianism, and has proven open to a variety of elements (including faith healing).

ters are found in every large town and city, attracting basically middle-class participants of all ages. The more rigorous forms of Eastern mystical devotions—Zen Buddhism, Yoga, and Hare Krishna—attract a very small and select group of relatively young, affluent, and college-educated seekers of truth.

Between the popularity of TM and the limited appeal of Zen and Yoga, lie the charismatic mystical cults that have Eastern leaders and religious elements but that are also heavily infused with Western (often commercial) influence. Examples are the Divine Light Mission headed by an adolescent guru, Maharaj Ji, for example, and the Unification Church of Reverend Sun Myung Moon, whose followers are known as "Moonies."

The Unification Church has aroused the most controversy of any contemporary cult for its alleged brainwashing of members, who leave everyday life in order to live together and to work solely for the glory of Reverend Moon. Having no other reference group, the Moonies become extremely dependent upon the Church leadership, and having given up all other sources of gratification, members find meaning and pleasure exclusively through their association with one another.

Parents who have attempted to kidnap their children from the Unification Church have met with mixed success. Some offspring are grateful, others extremely angry. There are important Constitutional questions regarding the legality of kidnapping an adult from a voluntarily chosen course of action (Robbins and Anthony, 1978). Middle-aged parents find it difficult to understand how their offspring could become totally dedicated to a Korean businessman who claims to be the Messiah. Yet most converts are legal adults exercising their First Amendment rights of freedom of association.

Why Join? If the cults are as dangerous or outlandish as many parents and other commentators think, why have they been so attractive to American youth, many of whom are among the most affluent and well-educated segment of our population. Harvey Cox, the theologian, in his *Turning East* (1977), offers the following explanations, most of which also apply to those who join Western fundamentalist cults (Doress and Porter, 1978).

> ✓ The young join cults for several reasons, including acceptance and community, immediate experience, and authoritative guidelines.

1. The cult provides *acceptance,* friendship, and community. Those who are attracted to cults are likely to say that they feel lonely and unloved (a sentiment that brings great agony to their parents). Since late adolescence and early adulthood are periods of searching for future commitments, before marriage and career choice, young people who are uprooted from their homes and living in the temporary shelters of a large city or college are especially vulnerable to such feelings.
2. Cultists are looking for *immediate* experience. For many, the world has been filtered through the intellect or through parental interpretations. This need for direct encounters with reality may also account for other features of contemporary youth culture such as motorcycling and drug use.
3. Some members are seeking an *authoritative guide.* Unable to deal with family-based authority, but also incapable of constructing their own priorities of choice, many young people need someone to make these decisions for them. The cults that emphasize discipline and adherence to the leader's orders will be very attractive: What a relief to find truth, order, meaning, and an end to confusion!

4. A small group of believers have arrived at their decision to turn East out of the perception that Western civilization is corrupt and/or dying. For these individuals the Eastern religions represent the *wave of the future,* and a return to wholeness and to nature almost destroyed by Western technology.

It is not only the young who thirst for simple and clear answers to the problems of daily life in a rapidly changing society. There are cults for older people, too.

Out-of-this-world cultism. Although there have been periodic predictions of the end of the world from the beginning of recorded history to the present, today's believers are unique in embracing contemporary technology. The newest versions feature invasions from outer space, the arrival of Unidentified Flying Objects (UFOs), and extrasensory perception (ESP) phenomena. Millions of Americans, old as well as young, believe in astrological predictions, and more millions attend movies about exorcism, possession by the Devil, haunted houses, and so forth. Paperback books on the supernatural were best sellers in the late 1970s. But only a few people actually join cults centered upon out-of-the-world phenomena.

When prophecy fails. Obviously movement leaders who predict the end of the world at a specific date have thus far been in error (though they may not be at some future date). Nor have nativistic revivalists been overly successful in turning the clock back. What happens to the movement when prophecy fails? This question was posed by Leon Festinger, Henry Riecken, and Stanley Schacter (1966) in a study of members of a sect who confidently awaited the predicted end of the world. When the expected event failed to occur, group members were faced with *cognitive dissonance*—the mental discomfort associated with holding mutually exclusive perceptions and ideas: "the world will end" and "it didn't." To relieve the dissonance, the mind must resolve the discrepancy between these perceptions.

The dilemma can be solved by foresaking one belief or the other; in this example, to convince oneself that the world has really ended but will take a different form than that expected, or, conversely, that the belief was mistaken in the first place. It is very difficult to admit that one is wrong, especially if the belief has been deeply held and one's life has been organized around it. A third way to reconcile conflicting attitudes, beliefs, or perceptions is to rework the connection between them. In the case of failed prophecy, the "true believers" can attribute the failure not to the deity or divine spirit directing events from on high, but to actions of the humans below. Either they failed to reckon correctly the exact time of the final moments, or they hadn't believed strongly enough to convince the higher powers to proceed with the divine plan.

Thus, cargo cultists, ghost dancers, and members of prophetic sects can continue in their faith while empirical evidence contradicts their expectations. This very faith becomes precisely that which distinguishes true believers from those who have sold out to modernization.

Self-awareness cults. Some cultists wait for spaceships and others turn inward. Alongside the new evangelicism and interest in the supernatural there has been a dramatic upsurge of groups dedicated to the cultivation of the self (Schur, 1976; Stone, 1978). This search for the authentic self is often carried out

Cognitive dissonance is experienced when an individual must deal with mutually exclusive ideas and perceptions.

with the same fervor and commitment as the search for religious transcendence. Charismatic leaders, supportive belief systems, and rituals are as important among true believers of self-awareness as among followers of Reverend Moon or the electronic ministry.

Based on the work of Carl Rogers and Abraham Maslow, The Human Potential Movement, claiming that each individual has untapped resources of creativity, has not only influenced the practice of psychotherapy in North America but has also spawned hundreds of commercially successful organizations such as National Training Institutes, Scientology, Synanon and EST (Erhard Seminar Training). Some individuals move from one group to another, "seeking to find themselves" and others. Encounter groups have a social component both as part of the treatment and its cure. The group as enforcer of the new norms is a well-known feature of behavior-changing organizations such as Alcoholic Anonymous (AA) and its many imitations.

Political cults.   The 1970s were punctuated by public fears and fascination with the headline-producing actions of members of political cults: Black Panthers, the Symbionese Liberation Army (SLA), and the People's Temple are perhaps the three most striking examples. All three are rooted in the civil rights agitation of the 1960s, becoming increasingly militant as the pace of improvement in the conditions of poor blacks became increasingly slow. Shoot-outs, imprisonment, and internal quarrels eroded whatever strength the Panthers and SLA could command.

The People's Temple, however, grew in numbers, wealth, and commitment throughout the 1970s. A biracial group of believers in the charismatic Reverend Jim Jones, members of the People's Temple followed their leader to Guyana in South America, where they established the community of Jonestown based on a mixture of Christianity and Marxism.

In November 1978, the world was shocked to learn of the mass suicide in Guyana of 911 adults and children, members of the People's Temple. In an effort to explain such a bizarre, unprecedented event, most analysts examined the personality of Jim Jones, or the characteristics of his followers—both of which were unusual. But however interesting these details might be, they can explain only why some people chose to join the People's Temple; nothing in these personal data can account for the mass suicides of almost one thousand individuals.

Sociologists Rose Laub Coser and Lewis Coser (1979) chose to focus on the *structural* elements of The People's Temple and the settlement of Jonestown, which they define as a utopian commune, one of many such attempts to create an ideal community in the midst of a social order perceived as corrupt or immoral. Moreover, communes "have an innate tendency to become . . . *greedy institutions."* Greedy institutions are those that absorb all the energy and passion and loyalty of individual members.

In what respects was Jonestown "a greedy institution in the jungle," and how can this account for its ultimate destruction?

1. *Isolation.* Not only in Guyana, but in branches of the Temple in the United States, Jones sought to create a barrier between his people and the outside world. Members had to give up all outside contacts and possessions. No news came in and no messages went out. Temple members were com-

pletely dependent upon Jones for information. Under these circumstances, members could not test reality against any independent source. Their cognitions were shaped entirely by Jones.

2. This isolation was reinforced by *secrecy*. Temple members were never told precisely what was going to happen next, generating high levels of anxiety. Orders came suddenly and were to be obeyed without question.

3. Within the community, Jones managed to break up couples and families. He insisted on *celibacy* for all but himself, and proceeded to have sexual relationships with large numbers of men and women. The ultimate effect was to destroy stable dyads among members, making each person dependent upon Jones alone for affection.

4. Jones further introduced *catharsis sessions* in which individuals were humiliated, denounced, and forced to strip physically and emotionally. Mistrust of other members was reinforced at the same time that self-esteem was destroyed.

This situation was also Jones's downfall. His followers could not call upon psychic reserves to unite against an outside threat when it came in the person of a United States representative investigating complaints from some constituents with relatives in Jonestown. Zombie-like, emptied of interpersonal commitments, children and childish adults could only follow Jones's orders to drink the poisoned Kool-Aid rather than seek their own survival.

Reflections on the Future of Belief Systems in North America

The major lessons of the past several decades seem to be: first, that science and rationality have not successfully replaced mysticism or the need for transcendent meaning felt by large numbers of North Americans, young and old alike. Second, in societies characterized by cultural pluralism and rapid change, forms of belief and ideology are also varied. The search for meaning embraces both the entire cosmos and the depths of self.

In these currents of change, mainstream churches have been perceived as relatively distant, elitist, and routinized in comparison to the churches, sects, and cults offering a more immediate emotional involvement. The experience of *conversion* is exhilarating; confusion and anxiety are transformed into inner calm and certainty. The lost and lonely find a "home" in the community of believers. Much the same can be said of those joining secular social movements and crusades, but with one crucial difference. For many, if not most, of those attracted to religious sects and cults, the precise beliefs being espoused may be relatively unimportant—*believing* and *belonging* are the salient factors (Roof, 1978). Adherents to social reform movements, on the other hand, are more likely to be recruited on the basis of ideology. For both types of believers, the existence of a supportive group is essential for the maintenance of motivation and adherence to the cause.

Conversion is an experience which transforms confusion and anxiety into inner calm and certainty.

In other words, attraction, recruitment, involvement, and commitment are social as well as personal phenomena. Interpersonal ties have a great deal to do with who joins what (Stark and Bainbridge, 1980). Parents are, of course, the first and most powerful influence on religious identity. Adolescents and young adults are more likely to follow friends into cults and sects than to seek out a particular faith on their own. And among adults, one's spouse and friends have a marked effect on the type and level of religious attachments (Greeley, 1978).

The question for the future, then, is whether either the mainline churches or the civil religion of modern North America can retain sufficient force and meaning to serve a unifying function in pluralistic societies founded on tolerance and supported by a general core of nondenominational values. The evidence indicates that while there has been a long term trend toward religious tolerance and liberalized social attitudes (Steiber, 1980), the recent rise of privatized, evangelical, and fundamentalist sects may reverse these currents of secularization. Recognizing this trend, many heretofore liberal mainstream churches are becoming more conservative in terms of doctrine, ritual, and goals, with increased emphasis on the private rather than public dimensions of belief and faith (Berger, 1969). Moreover, this shift is not a matter of social class, education, ethnicity, or community size, but of the individual's embeddedness in a particular local community (Roof, 1978). A need for shared faith and bonds of fellowship, which are associated with localism have eclipsed the emphasis on meaning, intellectualism, and liberal activism of the mainstream churches. Far from being dead, the religious sector is very much alive in modern North America, and the outcome is far from clear.

Summary

All belief systems have certain elements in common—the human experience of wonderment, doctrines, rituals, and a community of believers. Systems of beliefs fulfill individual and group needs—the individual is provided with explanations that make life meaningful, while the group is provided with beliefs that relieve anxiety and bring members together.

Every belief system includes three essential elements—an origin myth, rules of conduct, and a vision of the future. Beliefs, according to sociologists, emerge from social life. Society and religion are closely intertwined. Every society differentiates between sacred and profane behaviors and objects. Modernization and secularization have had profound effects on religion. The secular way of thinking with its emphasis on science and rationality, challenges beliefs in the divine, and in values based on faith.

Although religious beliefs continue to be important for a majority of the population, churchgoing has declined steadily over the past 25 years in North America. The great variety of religious expression in North America has led to the emergence of a civil religion. The last three decades have witnessed important changes in the involvement of organized religion in the secular affairs of society. The social stability and prosperity of the 1950s which seemed to leave the churches without a mission were followed by the challenge of social activism and the civil rights movement of the 1960s, and the anti-war movement of the 1970s, supported and led by many clergy. The 1970s saw a retreat from activism and the prophetic function, and a return to more priestly and pastoral duties.

Although mainstream churches have not been able to regain their membership and financial strength, the growth of evangelical fundamentalism and the rise of new sects and cults testify to a deep need for religious engagement and expression. The evangelical emphasis on salvation has attracted substantial numbers of converts. These new churches and sects are primarily white, well-financed, commercially successful, and increasingly powerful politically in their support of conservative candidates and issues.

The many new cults, attractive to large numbers of young people, further deplete the ranks of mainstream denominations. While the new cults are often opposed by parents and social commentators, young recruits are attracted by an accepting and friendly community, authoritative guides to truth and meaning, and the belief that the cults represent the wave of the future. By contrast, social reform movements emphasize political ideology and good works. For all believers, a supportive group context is crucial for generating motivation and commitment to the cause.

Suggested Readings

BERGER, PETER L. *The Sacred Canopy: Elements of a Sociological Theory of Religion* (New York: Doubleday, Anchor, 1969). An elegantly written examination of the complex relations between religion and society, and the increasingly private nature of belief and faith.

COSER, ROSE LAUB, and LEWIS COSER. "Jonestown as a Perverse Utopia," *Dissent*, Spring 1979, pp. 158–163.

COX, HARVEY. *Turning East* (New York: Simon & Schuster, 1977). Insightful examination of the processes and motivations underlying the growth of Eastern and Western fundamentalist cults.

CRYSDALE, STEWART and LES WHEATCROFT (eds.) *Religion in Canadian Society* (Toronto: Macmillan, 1976). A stimulating set of essays examining religious diversity in Canada.

DURKHEIM, EMILE. *The Elementary Forms of Religious Life* (New York: Free Press, 1965/1912). The classic analysis of the functions of religious beliefs and religious rituals, what they represent, and how they contribute to the integration of the social order.

MALINOWSKI, BRONISLAW. *Science, Magic and Religion* (New York: Anchor, 1954). The noted anthropologist analyzes the functions of magic, religion, and science in the South Pacific Trobriand Islanders society.

SHAFIR, WILLIAM. *Life in a Religious Community: The Lubavitcher Hassidim in Montreal* (Toronto: Holt, Rinehart & Winston, 1974). An ethnographic and sociological examination of the lifestyles of a community of orthodox Jews in a French-Canadian city.

WEBER, MAX. *The Protestant Ethic and the Spirit of Capitalism* (New York: Scribner, 1958/1920). Weber's classic and controversial analysis of the importance of secularized Protestantism on the development of capitalist production in the West.

(Source: *Magnum Photo.*)

Part V

Contemporary Issues

In the five chapters which constitute Part V of the text we examine several major contemporary issues. Chapter 16 describes population changes and the quality of health care in North America. Chapter 17 deals with various kinds of criminal behavior including juvenile delinquency, white collar crime and corporate crime, the police, and the legal system that administers punishments. Chapter 18 focuses on the growth and development of cities and suburbs in North America, the quality of life, and the contemporary urban crises.

The final two chapters examine the origins and processes of social and cultural change. Collective behavior and social movements described in chapter 19, often signal major changes in social structure, culture, and individual lives. The broader implications of social change, modernization, and a glimpse of the future are considered in chapter 20.

16 Population and Health

*I*n 1976 two out of every five people in Africa, Asia, and South America were under age 15, compared to one in four in North America.

A child born in North America today can expect to live over seventy years, in contrast to just under fifty years in most of Africa and Asia.

In the nineteenth century, the average number of children born per mother was five; at the present time, it is around two.

In 1880, less than 2 percent of the world's population lived in cities of 100,000 or more; by 1960, that figure was 20 per cent, and today it is almost 40 per cent.

Introduction

Above are only a few examples of world-wide population changes in the last century. In this chapter, we shall examine shifts in the size and composition of populations, the spatial (geographic) distribution of people, and patterns of health, illness, and death that occur as societies modernize; that is, move from preindustrial to industrial and postindustrial economies. To most North Americans, population problems are associated with nations other than their own: for example, the overpopulation of developing Third World countries; the several-year famine in parts of Africa; and the high infant death rate in Cambodia and Afghanistan. But the life chances of individuals and the social structure of the United States and Canada are just as thoroughly linked to the growth, composition, and distribution of the population as are those more crowded, less modernized, and less economically developed nations. All are affected by population changes, which in turn have an impact upon the social and economic fabric of society. This chapter describes some of the dynamics of population change and their effects on personal health and quality of life.

As noted in Chapter 12, based upon the nature of its economic system, a society can be described as *preindustrial, industrial,* or *postindustrial.* In the *preindustrial* society, fishing, agriculture, and mining predominate as the mode of subsistence. In an *industrial* society, machine technology for the manufacture of goods is dominant. The *postindustrial* society is characterized by increased growth of the services sector, including finance, trade, transport, recreation, health, education, and government. If labor and capital are the chief structural features of industrial economies, the production of information and knowledge are hallmarks of postindustrial economies (Bell, 1973). As you will see in this chapter, changes in the size, composition, and distribution of populations are closely allied with industrial development. Demography (from the Greek *demos,* or people), is the study of the characteristics and patterns of change of human populations. Before examining some of these shifts, let us define some of the basic terms and sources of data used by demographers.

Commonly Used Demographic Terms

Birth rate: the number of births within a specified time period divided by the total population within that time period, multiplied by 1,000. This may be visualized as:

$$\frac{\text{total number of births, Canada, 1981}}{\text{total Canadian population, 1981}} \times 1,000 = \text{Canadian birth rate, 1981}$$

Death rate (mortality rate): the number of deaths within a specified time period divided by the total population within that time period multiplied by 1,000. Thus:

$$\frac{\text{total number of deaths, United States, 1981}}{\text{total United States Population, 1981}} \times 1,000 = \text{U.S. death rate, 1981}$$

Life expectancy: the average length of life remaining to a person at a given age, typically at birth.

Natural increase: the birth rate minus the death rate.

Fertility rate: the number of live births within a specified time period divided by the population of women between the ages of 15 to 49 (the years most likely to be childbearing) multiplied by 1,000. Thus,

$$\frac{\text{number of live births, Canada, 1981}}{\text{number of Canadian women aged 15 to 49, 1981}} \times 1,000 =$$

Canadian fertility rate, 1981

The fertility rate is a more refined measure of births than the birth rate which is based on total population of all ages and both sexes, rather than only women likely to give birth.

Infant mortality rate: the proportion of deaths to live births of children below one year of age to live births in the population, that is,

$$\frac{\text{number of deaths below age 1 in 1981 in the U.S.}}{\text{number of live births in 1981 in the U.S.}} \times 1,000 =$$

Infant mortality rate, U.S., 1981

The infant mortality rate is regarded as a sensitive indicator of health and economic development, and is also important in determining life expectancy.

Migration: the movement of people into (immigration) or out of (emigration) a given geographic area. Migration is an important variable in the growth or decline of regional or national populations.

Net migration: the difference between in-migration (immigration) and out-migration (emigration) of a geographic area within a specified time period.

Population growth: the sum of natural increase (birth minus deaths) and net migration.

Demographic transition: the change from populations characterized by high birth, high death rates; to high birth, low death rates; to low birth, low death rates; to population stability (zero population growth). This transition typically accompanies modernization.

SOME BASIC DEMOGRAPHIC CONCEPTS

Demographers commonly use two types of numbers to describe populations: *absolute numbers* and *relative numbers*. *Absolute numbers* are the actual count of people, of births, deaths, marriages, and so forth. For example, the statement that 16.4 million Canadians live in urban areas describes a characteristic of the population in absolute numbers. Although useful, absolute numbers have their limitations. The United States, for example, has a population about ten times larger than that of Canada, so that a comparison of the absolute number of urban residents in Canada to those in the United States would tell us little about similarities or differences in the concentration of people in urban versus rural areas in the two nations. It is for that reason that demographers often use *relative numbers*, such as percentages, rates, and ratios, that summarize statistical information and control for differing population size. Relative numbers are derived from absolute numbers and are especially useful when we compare the behavior of a given population at two or more points in time or when comparing two or more societies at the same time. Some of the more common demographic terms are defined in "Commonly Used Demographic Terms" on page 430.

Absolute numbers are actual counts of people, births, marriages, deaths, and so forth.

Relative numbers refer to proportions of certain types of people in the total population.

SOURCES OF DATA USED BY DEMOGRAPHERS

Census. The desire to count the number of people who were born, died, or resided within a geographic area is very old. While we do not know when the first population statistics were collected, ancient Greece, Rome, and Egypt all gathered information about their populations, often for taxation or military purposes. *Censuses* are basically inventories of the entire population at a given time, and provide valuable information about the characteristics of each person in a specified geographic area.

Today in the United States and Canada, a census, required by law, is taken every ten years. The first census in the United States was gathered in 1790, the most recent one in 1980. In Canada, a national census has been made since 1851, with more limited surveys every five years since 1956. Although in both nations everyone is required by law to answer census questions, not surprisingly the information is subject to error; some individuals find its questions too difficult to answer; others, despite guarantees of confidentiality, are concerned about privacy; and some (especially the very poor and members of ethnic minorities) are difficult to locate and thus are never counted. A typical national census in the United States and Canada has been estimated to have about a 3 per cent error, meaning that its information is about 97 per cent accurate. Censuses taken in developing nations, where the population may be more difficult to locate and where illiteracy is greater, are much less accurate.

The kinds of information collected in a census reflect not only the complexity of the society and its values but also the uses to which the material will be put. In 1790, when the first census workers in the United States compiled data on a given area, questions were few and publication of the results immediate. Census-takers nailed the information they had collected to store walls so that each citizen could check to be sure the information was accurate and only five questions were asked: number of free white males 16 years of age or older, number of free white females, number of free white males under 16, number of other free (nonwhite) persons, and number of slaves. This simple information gave an indication of number and location of potential voters and nonvoters by race,

Censuses are inventories of an entire population in a specific area.

A census is taken every ten years in the United States and Canada.

1
APPORTIONMENT OF CONGRESS

The U.S. Constitution requires the apportioning of seats in the House of Representatives based on the population of each state. Therefore, an accurate count of the population is necessary to determine whether a state should gain or lose representatives.

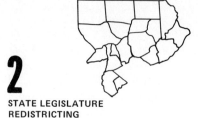

2
STATE LEGISLATURE REDISTRICTING

State legislative districts also are dependent on census population totals to assure fair representation. Other election and administrative boundary lines often are based on census statistics. It's the fair way to make sure each voter carries the same relative weight as every other voter in the state.

3
FEDERAL AND STATE AID PROGRAMS

A significant part of local government's budget is based on revenues received from the state and federal government. Many of these aid programs use census statistics as a fair way to distribute funds. Examples: revenue sharing, community development, health, education, highways, job training, school lunch program, economic development.

4
POPULATION FACTS

Each population question on the census questionnaire produces statistical totals which are important for drawing a statistical profile of the community—age, race, sex, marital status, educational level, ethnic background, occupation, employment status, income, veteran status.

5
HOUSING FACTS

The 1980 census also will measure the status of housing: the number of rooms, types of heating and cooking fuels, value of the property or rent paid, plumbing facilities, utility and other costs. These census facts provide a statistical profile of living quarters and help each community plan for future housing needs.

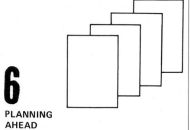

6
PLANNING AHEAD

Without accurate information, decision makers in government, private Business or civic organizations could not plan ahead. The census gives the community facts on which to base future actions in many activities in years to come.

Figure 16-1.
Census impact on the community. (Source: *Fort Myers* News Press, *1980.*)

sex, and age. By 1890, not only had the complexity of questions increased, but they mirrored national concerns of that era about the morality, physical characteristics and health of the population, including such questions as: "Are you a tramp, syphilitic, or habitual drunk?", and the head size (large, average, or small) of any mentally retarded persons in the household. The 1980 United States Census focused on information of practical use to the government in congressional reapportionment (which can be done only on the basis of decennial (10-year) census information), as well as assessment of the housing, income, family size, and other components of quality of life. Figure 16-1 shows some of the current uses of census information in the United States.

Sample surveys are based on a small but representative part of a population.

Sample Surveys. In both the United States and Canada, sample surveys, or mini-censuses, based on a small but representative sample of the nation or of a region, provide updated information that supplements the census, and is not otherwise available on a national basis. This survey technique has the advantage of giving relevant information at a relatively low cost within a short period of time. In the United States, for example, data on unemployment and house-

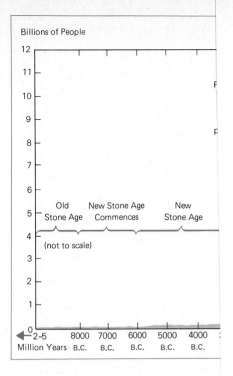

Population growth occurs in or
most of human history, the number
number of deaths. It is *lowered mo*
responsible for the demographic tra

THE DEMOGRAPHIC TRANSITION

The *demographic transition* was t
led to an increase in the world popu
lation growth for two reasons. First
lation more slowly by death. Seco
adults are likely to survive through
cline in mortality rates that began i
ated in the eighteenth and ninetee
social and economic changes, inclu
that enlarged food supplies, thus re
nutrition resulting in greater resista
proved living conditions as a resul
dustrial revolution; and (4) better he
lic health and sanitation measures s
nineteenth and early twentieth cent
acterized the demographic transitio
birth rates causing a surge in popu

It takes several decades before b
offspring will survive infancy and c
number. The trend toward lower b
urban couples for whom large num
mobility and improved standards of
provide in an agricultural, tradition
along with death rates, little or no

hold composition are gathered monthly from a panel of approximately 50,000 households.

Vital Statistics.   Vital statistics are records of births, deaths, divorces, marriages, and other significant events that are recorded as they occur. Such records traditionally were collected by parish churches and, in some parts of Europe, date back to the eleventh century. It was not until the latter half of the nineteenth century, however, that most Western European countries began systematic civil (governmental) registration of these events, although the church records of births and deaths for past centuries continue to provide fairly reliable information about patterns of marriage, births, and deaths for previous eras. In both the United States and Canada, vital statistics are collected on a state, provincial, or territorial basis, and summarized by the national government. Unfortunately, not all areas are equally thorough or accurate in their record keeping so that data on marriages and divorces, for example, are actually estimates.

Migration Statistics.   Another source of information used by demographers is migration statistics. In some nations, very close counts of both internal and international migration are kept. In the United States and Canada information is collected primarily on immigration into the country; these data are useful in assessing the changing characteristics of the population as well as net migration, that is, the gain or loss of population through international migration.

The Growth of Populations

The process of modernization among human societies has been accompanied by profound changes in population processes and the social meaning of population statistics. For the first hundreds of thousands of years when people were hunters and gatherers, the world population probably never exceeded 10 million people. In contrast, the world population in 1980 was approximately 4.5 billion, and is increasing at a rate of about 74 million people per year. In other words, every five days another million people are added to the population. This increase is even more dramatic when you realize that it took two to five million years for the population to reach one billion in 1800! Demographers and other social scientists are concerned that today's growing population will place tremendous pressure on natural resources, the physical environment, and the social fabric of society. Table 16-1 summarizes world population growth and rates of increase.

How did this change come about? As Table 16-1 suggests, population size is closely tied to the availability of food and to the level of technology of a group. The shift from food gathering and hunting to food growing meant that larger numbers of people could be supported, but world population increased only slightly over the 10,000 or more years of basic agriculture. It is only with the industrial revolution of two hundred years ago that the large sustained rise in world population has taken place.

Vital statistics are records of important events such as births, marriages, and deaths.

Migration statistics measure the population flow within a society as well as movement in or out of the country.

Demography is the statistical study of human populations, shifts in the population, and the social meaning of population statistics.

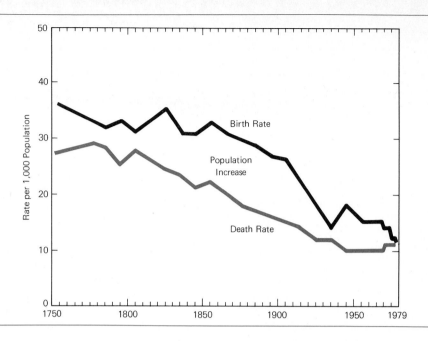

Figure 16-3.
Birth and death rates, Sweden, 1755–1978. (Source: "Our population predicament: A new look," Population Bulletin, Vol. 34, No. 5, December 1979, p. 11.)

In 19
milli
searc

Tab

Ye

1
10
5
2

To

* A
tim
Sou

Malthus and Exponential Population Growth

The stage of high birth rates and lower death rates is sometimes called the *Malthusian* period of population growth, after the British clergyman, Thomas Malthus (1766–1834). A demographer, social reformer, and opponent of contraception, Malthus suggested that there was a close relationship between the number of people and the amount of food available. Observing the high birth rates in late eighteenth century England, Malthus predicted that the number of people would soon overtake the available food supply because population increases in a *geometric progression,* doubling itself every twenty-five years. Agricultural production, however, increases in an *arithmetic progression,* adding a constant quantity to present production every twenty-five years. Thus, Malthus predicted runaway population growth in which a population of one million would increase to two million after twenty-five years, four million after 50 years, eight million after 75 years, and so on to about 1,000 billion after 500 years. Food, however, would merely increase by adding the quantity presently produced every twenty-five years, so that after 500 years it would be no more than twenty times greater than at the present time. Population would grow a million-fold; food production only twenty-fold. Geometric increase of population is called *exponential growth.*

Malthus proposed that positive checks to halt this population disaster must be taken, and advocated celibacy and late marriage; otherwise, harsher, natural restraints like war, famine, disease, and malnutrition would limit population growth through death. While Malthus correctly predicted the rise of population at a swift rate, he did not consider that improved technology would cause agricultural production to increase much more rapidly than he predicted, nor did he realize that couples might voluntarily limit the size of their families through means other than sexual abstinence. The concern about rapid population growth and its effect on agriculture, natural resources, and quality of life initially voiced by Malthus, however, remains a major issue today.

The overcrowded and unhealthy conditions on many Native American reservations reflects the link between socio-economic status and life expectancy. On the reservations, infant mortality is almost double that of the general population (Michal Heron, Woodfin Camp & Associates.)

country; when national averages were taken, as in Table 16-3, the fact that there are a number of well-off people obscures the plight of the poor. In countries such as Chad, where the overwhelming majority of the population is very poor and plagued by famine and disease, the results are much plainer: the population dies at a relatively rapid rate.

To summarize, although life expectancy has increased in most nations of the world, this is most marked in modern, industrialized nations. Those nations still undergoing the transition from a preindustrial to an industrial mode of subsistence continue to have higher rates of infant mortality and lower life expectancies than modernized countries. To a large extent, this reflects the lower standards of living, poor sanitation, and minimal incomes in developing nations; it also mirrors less efficient agricultural production and lack of money with which to purchase food and technology from other countries.

BIRTH AND FERTILITY RATES

Social scientists and demographers have been intrigued with the decline in births and fertility that has accompanied the demographic transition in industrialized nations. (You will recall that *birth rates* are calculated by dividing the total number of births within a given time by the total population, and *fertility rates*, considered a more accurate measure, by dividing the total number of births by the number of women of childbearing age). Most demographers have

MORTALITY

Although e
frequency wi
age likelihood
the demograp

Life Expe
average leng
around 30 ye
ancient Rom
such events a
were commo
land caused
try. Malnutri
diseases, also
century death
in industrial
age groups; i
1900, only ab
average life e
close to 73 pe

Table 16-3.
Gross Natio

Country
Industrialize
Canada
United Sta
United Ki
Sweden
West Germ
Netherlan
Developing N
Nigeria
Zambia
Chad
Saudi Ara
Iran
India
Pakistan
People's R

Source: Abridge

GROWTH OF THE POPULATION I

In 1610 the population of both
handful of white Europeans, and a
probably not over several hundred
ada was estimated at about 24 mil
According to 1981 population esti
proximately 229 million—an increa
nations, two sources of growth we
deaths (*net increase*), and (2) a su
migration). (Population Reference E

With 4.5 million people in 1790, t
inhabitants by 1810, and by 1850 th
of Canada today. In 1900, the Unite
Most of this rapid rise in the numbe
century; percentage increases betwe
shows that the growth of inhabitar
per cent each decade! Immigration
1900, approximately 22.7 million in

In Canada, most of the populatio
years. While part of this increase is
Canada in 1949, much has been du
recently, especially in Quebec. For e
were recorded in Quebec for severa
Canada, 1979). Today, however, Que
any Canadian province. Migration
growth; between 1901 and 1911, 1.
per cent increase in population dur

The history of both countries has
Originally, the two nations had prec
ing the dominant mode of produc
from rural to urban locations. Table
and preindustrial form of economic

Table 16-2. Shifts from Rural to Ur
Canada, 1910–11 Through 1980–8

Year	Ur
1910–11	45
1920–21	51
1930–31	56
1940–41	56
1950–51	64
1960–61	69
1970–71	73
1980–81	74

Source: Overbeek, 1980, Tables 11 and 13 and F
*Estimates

This demographic transition is most clearly illustrated in data for Sweden 1755 to 1978, as seen in Figure 16-3.

As Figure 16-3 shows, until the late eighteenth century, both birth and death rates were high. While the majority of married women gave birth to many children, infant mortality and the death of women in childbirth were quite common. In the early nineteenth century, the death rate fell gradually, followed by a decline in births some five decades later until both were at low levels in the 1930s. After the post-war baby boom of 1945 to 1965, birth and death rates continued their historical decline. Sweden's population today has stabilized at a bare replacement level, which, if continued for several decades, would produce *zero population growth*. The United States and some Canadian provinces are approaching a similar condition. By 1976, the fertility rate in both countries had fallen below the *replacement level* of 2.1 children per woman, which is the level at which parents replace themselves in the population. (The extra .1 in the 2.1 figure is used by demographers because some children die before reaching the age of childbearing, and others who survive will not have children).

A very different demographic transition characterizes the less industrialized areas of the world. Through the introduction of public health measures (especially sanitation) and medical technology from industrialized nations, a dramatic reduction in mortality rates has occurred within decades rather than centuries, and developing nations are experiencing an unparalleled population growth. High birth rates have continued while infant and overall mortality

Zero population growth represents a situation of no natural increase in the population.

Developing nations are characterized by high population growth.

Family planning has helped the fertility rate in North America to fall below the replacement level of 2.1 children per woman. If this trend continues for several decades, zero population growth will result. (Source: Lynn McLaren, Photo Researchers, Inc.)

rates
natio
The d
graph

*The combination of high birth
clining infant mortality rates I
ened severe food shortages in (
tions. (Source: Jason Lauré, W
& Associates.)*

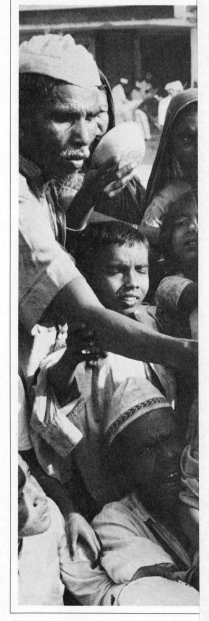

*Figure
United
tion—p
2050. S
highest
timate;
lowest;
III are
with II
zero po
growth,
lar to c
rates. (
Bureau
sus, 198*

Differences in mortality
rates among societies
reflect variation in
causes of death.

Populatio
estimate I
of nations
geographi

Life expectancy and
mortality are strongly
influenced by one's so-
cial class membership.

until their 65th birthday and the average life expecta
74 years. Much of this gain is the result of reduction
rate.

In developing nations, however, despite some declin(
expectancy remains relatively low, as is shown in Tab

Why is there such a marked difference in both life exp
infant mortality rate (which, you will recall, is a signific
ing life expectancy) between industrialized nations and

Causes of Death. A major factor in differential mort;
in causes of death. In industrialized nations, there has b
in mortality at all ages from acute illnesses such as diar
losis, influenza, small pox, or typhoid, and an increase
communicable, degenerative conditions such as hea
chronic disorders. In both Canada and the United St.
cancer are currently the leading causes of death, and la
In contrast, the major causes of death in nations tha
modernize are similar to those in the United States or
ago. For example, in Iran, the leading causes of death
parasitic illnesses, diseases of the respiratory system su
chitis and tuberculosis, and unspecified diseases of e;
1980).

The decline in acute and infectious diseases as lea(
modernized nations is closely associated with a rise in i
living, including better diet and improvements in sanit
ogy, too, has played a role, although there is some evid
tion of such medical treatments as antibiotics and inoc
little effect upon the decline of infectious disease in thos
industrialized by the beginning of the twentieth cent
seems that infectious diseases in most Western Europea
nations were already declining at a rapid rate prior to 1
medical techniques (McKinley and McKinley, 1977), a
case in Third World countries today.

Social Class. Another factor associated with mortal
bership. Life expectancy is influenced by such variable:
tion; for example, in the United States, among famili(
than $3,000 per year and where the household head has
formal education, the infant mortality rate is about 14(
the national average. A similar picture is found in Car
Americans in both countries highlight some of the links I
status and life expectancy. On the reservations, infant m
that for the general population; people live in very overc
the majority get their water from potentially contamina
1974: *Perspectives Canada*, 1980).

The inequalities of power, wealth, and prestige withi
ferential distribution of infant mortality and life expecta
has many poor people, but it also has a middle class ar
rich live a life isolated from the conditions that plagu

concluded that the higher survival rates for children provided an incentive for
limiting family size, because it was no longer necessary to have large families to
ensure that one or two children would live to adulthood. Furthermore, as
modes of economic production became more complex, and increasing levels of
education were required for social mobility, large numbers of children became
more of a liability than an asset. Child labor laws reduced their ability to contribute to the family income, while compulsory education laws required that
they be supported until a certain age. Then, too, improved contraceptive techniques became widely available in most industrialized nations as early as the
1880s.

Actually, there is evidence that attempts to limit family size in one way or
another have characterized most societies throughout history. The relatively
late age of marriage common in Western Europe until the last century or so was
one such restraint; other methods included infanticide, particularly of females,
abandonment, and starvation. Eighteenth-century European observers noted
that the deaths of children were often welcomed, as when parents wished
openly and loudly for their children to die or leave home, and when small pox, a
major cause of infant and childhood mortality, was known as the "poor man's
friend" (van de Walle and Knodel, 1980). The point here is not that earlier
generations of parents were more unfeeling or heartless than those of today,
but that, contrary to popular belief, children were not always viewed as an
asset, either to the nobleman or farmer with limited wealth, or to the landless
industrial worker. In the absence of more effective methods of birth control,
infanticide by neglect, death through disease, and child abuse relieved women
from the excessive strain of working all day in industry or agriculture, and at
the same time assuming all child care duties. Infant mortality also relieved men
from the support of very large families (van de Walle and Knodel, 1980).

This reduction in family size was not necessarily related to industrialization.
Although both birth rates and fertility rates declined in England only after
considerable urbanization and industrialization had taken place in the late
nineteenth century, a similar reduction occurred at about the same time in less
industrialized Hungary. Indeed, the first sign of fertility decline occurred in
nonindustrialized France a century earlier, when the majority of the population
was rural, poor, and Catholic (van de Walle and Knodel, 1980). This suggests
that economic development is a sufficient but not necessary cause for fertility
decline; also important are social values.

In most Western nations one hundred years ago, women who married in their
early 20s and survived their childbearing years could expect to bear six to eight
children, four to six of whom would probably live to marriageable ages themselves. Yet birth rates tended to be somewhat lower than we might expect because many women married rather late, and others died or were widowed during their childbearing span (van de Walle and Knodel, 1980). Nor did all women
marry. Despite the fact that we think of remaining single as a new lifestyle
associated with being modern, between ten and twenty-five per cent of Western
European women a century or so ago remained unmarried, as compared
to somewhat under 10 per cent today. A typical demographic pattern in Western Europe in the mid-nineteenth and twentieth centuries is illustrated in
Figure 16-6.

Comparing women in the nineteenth and twentieth centuries, it is obvious

Historically most socie-
ties have attempted to
limit family size.

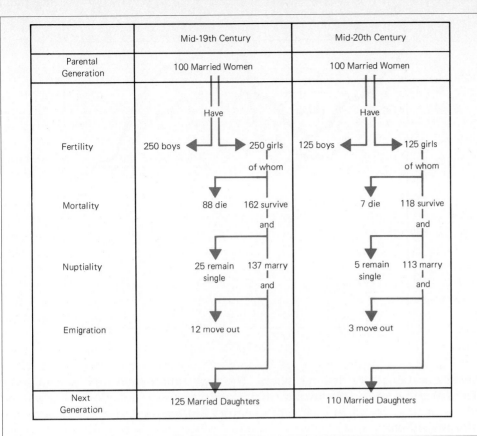

	Mid-19th Century	Mid-20th Century
Parental Generation	100 Married Women	100 Married Women
	Have	Have
Fertility	250 boys ← → 250 girls	125 boys ← → 125 girls
	of whom	of whom
Mortality	88 die 162 survive	7 die 118 survive
	and	and
Nuptiality	25 remain single 137 marry	5 remain single 113 marry
	and	and
Emigration	12 move out	3 move out
Next Generation	125 Married Daughters	110 Married Daughters

Figure 16-6. Typical demographic patterns in Western Europe, mid-nineteenth and twentieth centuries. (Source: van de Walle and Knodel, 1980, Fig. 1, p. 4.)

that, despite fairly high levels of mortality, nonmarriage, and international migration, substantial population growth did occur. But at the same time, fertility—the number of children per family—was declining. However, while women were bearing fewer children, these offspring were more likely than ever to survive to adulthood and marry. Thus, instead of the 25 per cent gain in population observed within one generation a century ago, there was a 10 per cent gain in population in the middle of this century.

Fertility has continued to decline throughout the industrialized countries. While there was a temporary increase in births—the baby boom of 1947 to 1963—fertility rates remain relatively low. One of the most interesting facts in recent demographic history is the similarity of fertility patterns in the United States and Canada (Figure 16-7).

The picture for nations that are just beginning to modernize is very different, however. For example, in 1979, the birth rate in Nigeria was 50 per 1,000 population, just slightly above the birth rate of 46 per 1,000 for Africa as a whole; in Latin America, the birth rate was 35 per 1,000, and in Southeast Asia, it was 36 per 1,000. Compare these with rates for industrialized nations: Europe, 14 per 1,000, and North America, 15 per 1,000 (Population Reference Bureau, 1979). For modernizing nations, high fertility remains a major problem. Yet evidence from the European experience with declining fertility suggests that a well-designed and socially acceptable family planning program may reduce birth rates rapidly in preindustrial and modernizing societies. The argument that large families are needed to provide care for parents in old age (that is, children as insurance policies) in societies without formalized social welfare systems is

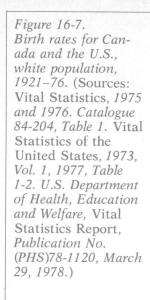

Figure 16-7. Birth rates for Canada and the U.S., white population, 1921–76. (Sources: Vital Statistics, 1975 and 1976. Catalogue 84-204, Table 1. Vital Statistics of the United States, 1973, Vol. 1, 1977, Table 1-2. U.S. Department of Health, Education and Welfare, Vital Statistics Report, Publication No. (PHS)78-1120, March 29, 1978.)

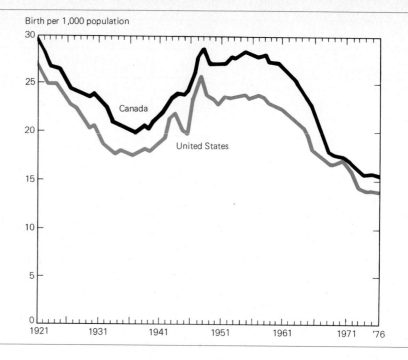

being questioned by demographers. The high infant mortality rate in some Third World countries today may in part reflect parents' reactions to unwanted births, just as it did in eighteenth century Europe (van der Tak, Haub, and Murphy, 1979).

MIGRATION

Migration is the third important component in population change and has a direct impact upon the size of a population. Migration describes the movement

Figure 16-8. Pushes, pulls, and mediating factors in migration.

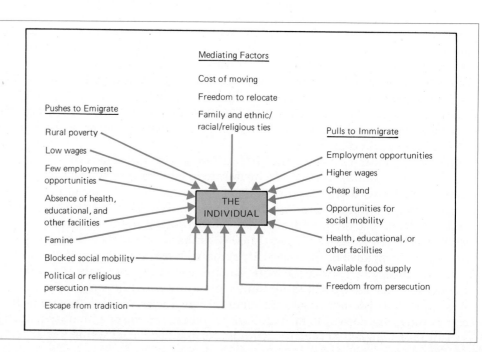

of people in space, a change in usual place of residence when an individual crosses political or administrative boundaries, such as moving from one state or province or nation to another. Why do people choose to migrate? Peterson (1975) has proposed several broad reasons, including: (1) *primitive migration*, occurring when people are unable to cope with natural or climatic forces, such as drought, famine, or exhaustion of water supplies; (2) *impelled* and *forced migration*, typically due to political pressures, such as were experienced by Jews in Nazi Germany in the 1930s, or conservative Cubans from Castro's regime in the early 1960s; (3) *free migration*, in which individual choice plays a role, such as in the movement westward in the United States and Canada; and (4) *group migration* and *mass migration* where large numbers of people, sharing a common characteristic such as ethnicity or religion, relocate. The Irish in the nineteenth century and such religious groups as the Hutterites, Mennonites, and Amish are illustrations of entire groups forced to move in order to improve their living standards or maintain a unique way of life. These migration categories often overlap; most migrants may choose to leave their place of origin for more than one reason. For example, communities of Hutterite migrants from Europe came to North America not only to maintain a way of life (group immigration) but also to avoid religious persecution (impelled or forced immigration).

Who migrates? While much depends on the historical period and the distance traveled, demographers have observed that migrants are predominantly young unmarried males when the distance is great and when migration has a pioneering quality. In general, migrants tend to be young unattached adults who lower the age structure of the country they enter while raising that of the place they leave. Figure 16-8 illustrates some of the pushes and pulls toward migration.

> **Net migration** is the number of migrants entering a country less the number leaving.

Composition of the Population

While size of populations, fertility, mortality, and migration are all important aspects of a population, they are affected by and reflect two basic population characteristics: *age* and *sex*. Both these variables are directly related to fertility and mortality, for only women of a certain age can bear children, and older people (or in some nations, infants) are much more likely to die than other age groups. And, as just noted, age and sex are also related to migration.

POPULATION PYRAMIDS

Demographers often summarize the age and sex of a population by *population pyramids*. Population pyramids represent the age and sex composition of a country at a given point in time. Differences in the age and sex distribution of economically developed countries such as the United States, Canada, and Sweden, and less developed nations such as Mexico and India may be observed in the population pyramids shown in Figure 16-9. As you look at these population pyramids, you will notice that a vertical line divides the number of males, shown on the left side of the chart, from the number of females, shown on the right. The figures on the scale at the bottom gives the numbers (in millions) of

> **Population pyramids** summarize a country's age and sex composition.

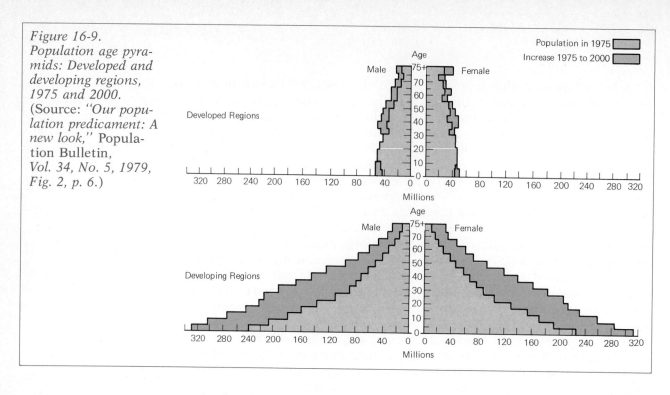

Figure 16-9.
Population age pyra-
mids: Developed and
developing regions,
1975 and 2000.
(Source: "Our popu-
lation predicament: A
new look," Popula-
tion Bulletin,
Vol. 34, No. 5, 1979,
Fig. 2, p. 6.)

Population in 1975
Increase 1975 to 2000

people of each sex; and horizontal bars represent age groups in five-year inter-
vals. This way of summarizing population is used in all population pyramids,
regardless of the country or region.

In Figure 16-9, the inner population pyramid for developing countries in
1975 is typical of nations growing because of the reduced infant and childhood
mortality. The outer pyramid shows how the age and sex composition of the
population will look in the year 2000, assuming current levels of fertility and
mortality. Compare the pyramids for developing countries to those for developed nations and you will see the differences in the age and sex distribution of
modernizing versus modernized nations.

Population pyramids are affected by the three basic processes described in
the previous section: births, deaths, and migration. Immigration and emigration may produce bulges or dents in the age and sex structure of receiving and
sending countries. Special conditions also affect population pyramids; for example, in the U.S.S.R., a large number of deaths occurred during World War II.
This produced a shortage of both males and females, thus affecting the marriage rate, birth rate, and sex composition of the population.

WHY ARE AGE AND SEX IMPORTANT?

Although ultimately a matter of historical events and individual choice, the
combination of births, deaths, and net migration at any particular point in time
produces a certain number of males and females within each age group. These
age groups make up the population pyramid of a nation. Knowledge of the age
and sex structure of a population is important for several reasons. First, it provides information about the actual and potential size of the labor force; for
example, developing nations, such as those illustrated in Figure 16-9, must produce more to support their younger members; developed nations, with a relatively large retired population, must also produce to support nonearning members of society.

Dependency Ratios.   The age and sex composition of a population permits calculation of the *dependency ratio,* that is, the ratio of those under 15 or over 65 years of age to people aged 15–64. The dependency ratio is often used as a measure of the economic well-being of a nation as it describes the proportion of income earners (or potential earners) to those not producing income. Since only those in the labor force pay taxes and earn income to support children or the elderly, a nation with a very high proportion of old or young must produce more to support its members.

The **dependency ratio** reflects the proportion of the population earning an income compared to those not producing income.

Age, Sex, and Lifestyles.   Furthermore, information about age and sex composition allows us to understand various aspects of political and economic life. For example, when the proportion of males in a population is greater than that of females different lifestyles and types of social control emerge. In frontier Canada, as well as the United States, when unmarried males comprise the majority of the local population, high levels of drinking, fighting, and prostitution were likely to occur, so that accidents and violence become concerns for law enforcement (Marsden and Harvey, 1979). In family-oriented cities and suburbs, where the sex ratio is about equal, social and economic behavior are family-oriented. As Marsden and Harvey (1979) observed, "local government and voluntary associations adjust their activities to the prevailing demographic conditions and tasks" determined by the age and sex composition of a population.

Birth Cohort.   Another key aspect of the age structure of a society is a *birth cohort,* that is, a category of people born within a certain time period. Each birth cohort varies in its original composition and will change as a result of mortality associated with sex, social class, ethnicity, and race. What members of a particular age cohort share is a common history that affects their life chances, including ability to achieve work statuses, education, marriage, and to earn incomes. The interplay between birth cohort, opportunity structure, and social change is illustrated by the fate of Americans born in the decade or so after World War II.

A **birth cohort** is composed of all those born in the same time period.

In the 1940s, demographers observing a century-long decline in the United States fertility rate predicted a continuation of this trend. This prediction was based upon the accepted sociological observation that increasing urbanization and modernization produce a shift from a traditional to a modern way of life. As part of this process of modernization, it was expected that individualism would flourish; women would be freed from exclusive repsonsibility for family tasks as specialized institutions absorbed many home-based functions; and widespread use of effective contraception would make small families the norm. What actually happened, of course, was a bumper crop of babies: over a decade of high fertility before the trend reversed. What had gone wrong in the predictions?

As we can now see, the theory was essentially correct, but failed to take into account temporary fluctuations in response to special conditions. After the war, marriage rates soared, and both the young newlyweds and other couples separated by the war proceeded to produce infants. But this was not a return to the romanticized large families of traditional societies; rather, for women marrying during the baby boom, the babies came sooner and faster than for their parents, who had actually delayed fertility because of the economic conditions of the Great Depression. What was different between the generations was the age at marriage and the timing of births.

A variety of reasons for this headlong rush into early marriage and closely spaced births have been advanced. The unparalleled economic expansion after 1945 created favorable mobility opportunities for the relatively small number of young men (the depression birth cohort) then entering the job markets. The availability of GI mortgages and other funding made home ownership relatively easy, and the post war suburbs were developed. At the same time, there was a revival of a profamily ideology espoused in women's magazines and by psychoanalysts, sociologists, and anthropologists. This theme had lain dormant in our culture for some time.

Yet, by the early 1960s, the enchantment had worn off, the fertility rate began to decline, and the downward trend resumed. But the effects of the baby boom years will linger on throughout the life course of the cohort.

What does it mean for an individual to have been part of the temporary baby bulge? Because the baby boom cohort is so very much larger than either the depression cohort of the 1930s or the 'baby bust' cohort of the mid or late 1970s, its members can expect problems and frustrations not experienced by those born before or after them. There are simply more people of the same age competing for the same things. For example, members of the baby boom have had to cope with overcrowded classrooms and teacher shortages throughout much of their education. Those entering the job market have found that jobs are not easy to get. Once employed, they can expect to earn less compared to older workers than have other generations of young workers, since experienced older workers are relatively few in number and can command higher salaries.

Job advancement opportunities will be less assured than for their parents. There are fewer senior positions available in comparison to the number of applicants. Housing and home ownership, too, will be more difficult to secure as large numbers of prospective new home buyers compete for existing housing stock and drive up costs. Housing today is far more scarce and expensive for the new home buyer than a decade ago.

Even in old age, being a member of the boom cohort will have an impact upon individual lives. In 1981, about one quarter of the Federal budget will go to support the elderly and their dependents. When the baby boom elderly are at their peak in 2025, this figure could reach at least 40 per cent of the budget. These senior boomers will make extra demands on the Social Security system at a time when the still-employed labor force is likely to be much smaller than it is today.

In sum: throughout their lives, members of the baby boom cohort will find that the quality of their lives has been affected by being members of a large age cohort caught between two smaller ones. They will have to cope with the problem of rising expectations during a period of relatively slow growth. Because there are more boomers, their chances for wealth may be less than for either their parents or their much younger siblings. And in old age they will place an extraordinary burden on their small number of offspring who must support their parents' retirement as well as their own children's education (Bouvier, 1980).

Population, Economic Development, and Quality of Life

REGIONAL DIFFERENCES IN GROWTH IN THE UNITED STATES

The Rise of the Sunbelt. While there is no general agreement as to which states make up either the sunbelt or the snowbelt in the United States, Biggar (1979) has proposed that a useful definition of the sunbelt is "those southern and western states with a mild climate, recreational facilities, and expanding job opportunities in industries and services." These states are shown in Figure 16-10, which also shows the most important streams of interstate sunbelt migration between 1965 and 1970.

Within the past two decades, sunbelt states have received almost half of all

During the past two decades the mild climate and ample job opportunities of the Sunbelt have attracted about 50 per cent of all interstate migrants in the United States. (Source: Burk Uzzle, Magnum Photos, Inc.)

CONTEMPORARY ISSUES

✓ About half of all Americans migrating to another state over the past two decades have moved to the sunbelt.

interstate migrants in the United States; as 41 per cent of those who moved from the snowbelt of the North and North Central States chose the sunbelt. Among people already living in the sunbelt, about 51 per cent moved to other sunbelt states (Biggar, 1979).

Why the sudden attractiveness of the South and Southwest when for most of this century migrants had streamed out of the South into the industrialized North? By 1950 snowbelt states had entered a postindustrial era and many

Figure 16-10. Salient streams of general interstate sunbelt migration, U.S., 1965–70. (Source: Jeanne C. Biggar, "The Sunning of America: Migration to the Sunbelt," Population Bulletin, Vol. 34, No. 1, March 1979, Fig. 3, p. 18.)

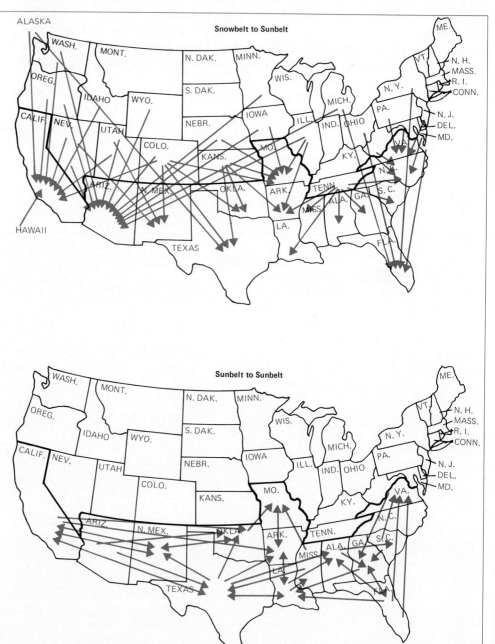

Table 16-4. Sunbelt Unemployment: June 1980 Rates

U.S. Average	7.8%	Texas	6.0%
North Carolina	7.4	Oklahoma	4.4
South Carolina	8.5	New Mexico	8.1
Georgia	7.6	Colorado	6.0
Florida	6.6	Utah	5.4
Alabama	9.5	Arizona	6.7
Mississippi	8.6	Nevada	6.4
Louisiana	7.8	California	7.3

Source: *Wall Street Journal*, Sept. 3, 1980, p. 29.

industries moved to the South, where taxes were lower and there was a ready labor pool of workers for labor-intensive, low-wage manufacturing, such as textiles and clothing. Furthermore, the South was attractive because of its low rates of unionism among workers. Unionism in the sunbelt is about one half of that of the United States as a whole, and all but three sunbelt states have "right-to-work" (anti-union) laws. The result of this is that workers traditionally have been willing to work for lower wages than those in the North and North Central states. After years of living in a largely economically underdeveloped region, sunbelt workers were less concerned with high wages than with simply having jobs (Biggar, 1979).

Many snowbelt residents have been attracted to the newly expanding area of the United States despite generally lower wages. Employment opportunities are greater, the environment is relatively free of urban blight, taxes and energy costs are lower. The sunbelt promises a more rural, less congested, cleaner environment in which to live and raise children—precisely the initial attraction of the suburbs in old, industrial cities. Even large sunbelt cities provide a less frenetic way of life. And for many, particularly older people, the warmer climate is a major benefit.

Who migrates to the sunbelt? While recent data on the characteristics of those who move will not be available until the detailed results of the 1980 Census are published, sample survey data show that interstate movers are relatively young (15–44), considerably better educated than the general United States population, and more likely to be employed in professional, technical, and managerial occupations than the population of the nation as a whole.

Migrants to the sunbelt tend to be younger, better educated, and in professional and managerial occupations.

The industrial development and in-migration of people to the sunbelt has resulted in a more equitable distribution of income among the various states. In the South, per capita income rose from 79 per cent of the national average in 1960 to 90 per cent in 1976. Unemployment in the sunbelt has also been lowered to below the national average. Yet there is some indication that the bloom is off the rose and the sunbelt is losing its immunity to recession, as Table 16-4 shows.

Furthermore, the number of jobs available, a significant index of employment and unemployment, has been dropping in the sunbelt. Added to this is the fact that, despite its rapid economic growth, the South still had more than twice as many people below the poverty level in 1977 when compared to the

Northeast. Texas, the bellwether of economic growth for the region, had one-fifth of its almost 13 million residents at or below the poverty level (Biggar, 1979). The very poor have not benefitted from the sunning of America.

In sum, the growth of the sunbelt has reduced regional inequities, both in income and in population. (See Figure 16-11.) As the sunbelt has grown and become part of the mainstream of the American economy, the snowbelt has declined. As Biggar (1979) has pointed out, this equalization has been a mixed

Figure 16-11.
Preliminary 1980 U.S. Census results showing shifting patterns of growth and regional inequalities. (Source: New York *Times,* December 25, 1980, p. 28, *from the U.S. Bureau of the Census.)*

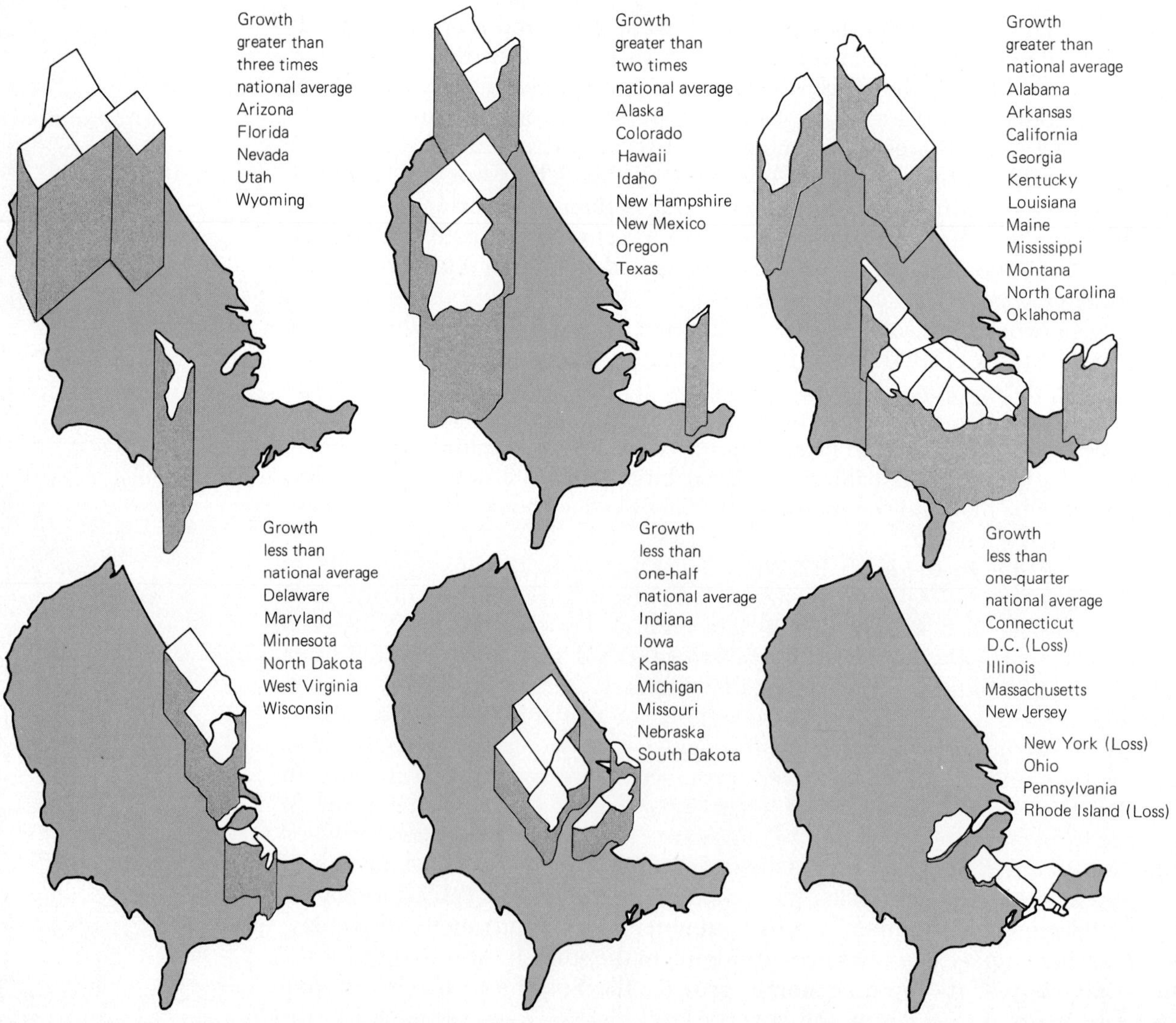

Growth greater than three times national average
Arizona
Florida
Nevada
Utah
Wyoming

Growth greater than two times national average
Alaska
Colorado
Hawaii
Idaho
New Hampshire
New Mexico
Oregon
Texas

Growth greater than national average
Alabama
Arkansas
California
Georgia
Kentucky
Louisiana
Maine
Mississippi
Montana
North Carolina
Oklahoma

Growth less than national average
Delaware
Maryland
Minnesota
North Dakota
West Virginia
Wisconsin

Growth less than one-half national average
Indiana
Iowa
Kansas
Michigan
Missouri
Nebraska
South Dakota

Growth less than one-quarter national average
Connecticut
D.C. (Loss)
Illinois
Massachusetts
New Jersey
New York (Loss)
Ohio
Pennsylvania
Rhode Island (Loss)

blessing, where competition for Federal dollars may pit the declining snowbelt against the rising sunbelt, thus creating new sectionalism.

In addition, the very conservatism and low tax rates of the sunbelt that made it attractive for business may sow seeds of decay, where reluctance to provide mass transit, better schools, city planning, and more services will create problems now faced by the decaying cities of the snowbelt (*Washington Post*, 1/15/78). "The challenge for planners is to direct . . . growth in such a way that the sunbelt states can continue to provide the quality of living which the new migrants seek to enjoy" (Biggar, 1979).

REGIONAL IMBALANCE IN CANADA

Growth of the Major Cities.   While the major cities in the United States have been losing population to the sunbelt, suburbs, and small town and rural areas, the proportion of Canada's population in the major metropolitan centers has increased steadily through the 1970s (*Canada Year Book* 1978–1979). (See Figure 16-12.) The industrial boom following World War II produced major shifts in residence toward urban centers. This was due, in part, to the mechanization of agriculture. Calgary, Alberta showed the highest rate of growth between 1971 and 1976; the greatest gains in absolute numbers of people were made by Toronto and Vancouver. Generally speaking, Canadians have migrated from economically-declining areas into more prosperous ones, thus producing deep regional differences in wealth and power that persist to the present day (Cuneo, 1978). Table 16-5 summarizes some of the regional differences of Canadian society.

What has occurred in Canada is an interregional imbalance, where the rich

In the 1970s the proportion of Canada's population in urban centers increased.

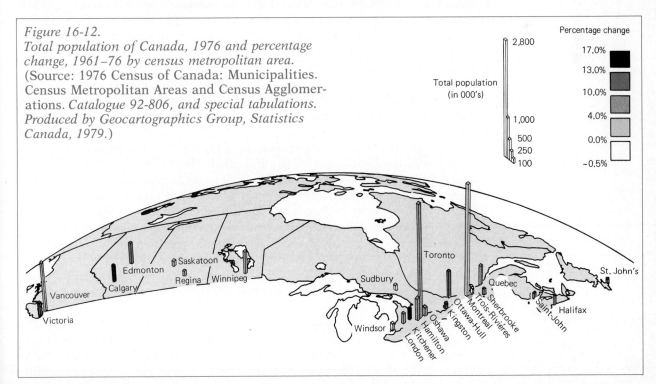

Figure 16-12.
Total population of Canada, 1976 and percentage change, 1961–76 by census metropolitan area.
(Source: 1976 Census of Canada: Municipalities. Census Metropolitan Areas and Census Agglomerations. *Catalogue 92-806, and special tabulations. Produced by Geocartographics Group, Statistics Canada, 1979.*)

Table 16-5. Regional Aspects of Canada's Contemporary (1965) Class Structure. (%)

Occupational class of respondents who are heads of households	National	Atlantic	Quebec	Ontario	Prairies	British Columbia
Working Class	56%	62%	58%	57%	44%	61%
Old Middle Class						
Rural	9	12	6	6	21	3
Urban	16	14	16	16	17	17
New Middle Class	19	12	20	21	18	19
Total	100	100	100	100	100	100
	(3660)	(385)	(1443)	(1064)	(528)	(240)

Source: Cuneo, 1978.

provinces get richer, the poor poorer. For example, incomes in the Maritime provinces are only 76.5 per cent of the national average; these provinces are also the most rural (Clement, 1978). Conversely, the principal industrial provinces, Ontario and Quebec, containing 62 per cent of Canada's population in 1976 (*Canada Year Book*, 1978–1979), are not only the two most urban but also are among the most resource-rich regions of the nation (Campbell, 1978) with Ontario incomes over 110 per cent of the national average. Thus, they are able to meet much of their need for natural resources with in-province products, and this process decreases the ability of many other provinces to trade with them (Campbell, 1978).

Most recently, the oil-rich Western Provinces have become centers of growth, demanding greater local control of their revenues. The entire federal structure of the nation is currently being renegotiated between the central government in Ottawa and the provincial capitals of the West. Further population and business shifts westward are expected to characterize the coming decades. The upshot of this has been to increase many interregional differences, so that the most highly paid and skilled workers are attracted to the richest provinces, and regional disparities in income and standards of living are more marked (Cuneo, 1978).

In sum, parallel tracks of concentration of people in urban areas appear to be developing in the United States and in Canada. In the United States, preliminary 1980 census data indicate that there is a trend to population sprawl, where more people are moving to formerly rural areas and to smaller towns (*New York Times*, 9/30/80). The most recent Census projections estimate that the sunbelt population will comprise 43 per cent of the nation's population by the year 2000, given current rates of growth. In Canada, the picture is less clear; both the provinces with the greatest level of industrialization and urbanization and those in which new wealth is being created are attracting migrants from poorer, rural areas (Gertler and Crawley, 1976).

POPULATION PATTERNS IN MODERN AND DEVELOPING NATIONS

In contemporary society, what are some of the ways in which population statistics can provide information about the economic organization and degree of modernization of a particular society? In this context, it is more useful to think in terms of *nations* rather than societies; nations are distinct political entities on which data are more or less routinely collected, but a society is not necessarily identical with political boundaries. For example, Nigeria contains several societies, each with its own culture, language, and social structure.

Mode of Subsistence. One obvious way that a nation may be defined as preindustrial, industrial, or postindustrial is by its mode of subsistence. The higher the proportion of the labor force engaged in agriculture, the more likely is a society to be preindustrial. Table 16-6 presents data on the proportion of the labor force employed in agriculture in six Latin American nations and the United States to highlight the variation in the mode of subsistence in developing, industrial, and postindustrial countries.

As you will notice as you read Table 16-6, in all seven nations there was a decrease in the proportion of people employed in agriculture over an eleven-year period, indicating movement away from agricultural economies. Yet there are marked differences among the countries that give clues about their level of industrialization. The United States, a postindustrial society, has by far the lowest proportion of its labor force in agricultural work, and this percentage is declining. Argentina and Chile, both of which are industrial economies, rank next. Mexico has begun to industrialize at a relatively rapid rate; agricultural employment declined by almost 11 per cent during 1965–76. Bolivia, the Dominican Republic, and Paraguay, while gradually industrializing, still have over half of their labor force employed in farming and are thus much closer to the ideal type of preindustrial society in which the primary mode of subsistence is land-based. Information on the broad type of employment of a population, such as agricultural or nonagricultural, is therefore a ready clue to a nation's stage of economic development.

Urban-Rural Population. The proportion of the population that resides in urban or rural locales also tells us about the level of modernization and technol-

Table 16-6. Percentage of The Labor Force Engaged in Agriculture in Six Latin American Countries and the United States, 1965 and 1976

	Percentage of labor force in agriculture		
Country	1965	1976	Net change, 1965 to 1975
United States	5.1%	2.6%	−2.5%
Argentina	18.2	14.2	−4.0
Chile	26.9	20.5	−6.5
Mexico	50.3	39.6	−10.7
Bolivia	58.2	52.2	−6.0
Paraguay	54.5	50.4	−4.1
Dominican Republic	63.8	58.2	−5.6

Source: Abridged from *Statistical Abstract of Latin America*, Vol. 19, table 405, p. 48.

ogy of a nation. Less economically developed countries are far more likely to have higher concentrations of people in rural areas and villages precisely because they are less industrialized. Urbanization describes the process in which there is a rise in the proportion of the total population concentrated in cities and suburbs. While urban concentration provides a rough indicator of the extent to which industrialization has occurred, it does not tell us how these urban dwellers earn their living. For example, both the United States and Argentina are urbanized, yet the United States is postindustrial, with much of the labor force employed in service occupations rather than manufacturing. Measures of urbanization, therefore, do not allow us to distinguish an industrial from a postindustrial country.

QUALITY OF LIFE

Health is an important indicator of the quality of life in a society.

While a variety of indicators of quality of life among populations in modernizing and modernized nations have been developed, such as *per capita* income, gross national product, level of education, and literacy, one of the most important is the health status of the population. Health is closely linked not only to the level of industrial development of a country but to the age and sex composition of its population, and to the distribution of power, wealth, and prestige.

The social meaning of health varies among societies.

Health.   Both *health* and *illness* are straightforward words, but they have been given different meanings in various time periods and societies. Thus, health is culturally defined; that is, what may be considered normal or healthy in one society is considered abnormal in others. This is not to say that disease is not real or that causes of illness cannot be identified but rather that members of a society develop norms about whether a specific condition is to be viewed as illness or not. For example, yaws, a disease that produces skin disfigurement, is so common in some developing areas of the world that people without its blemishes are considered odd looking. Moreover, some illnesses will be identified as respectable, such as heart disease, or not respectable, such as venereal disease.

Industrial and technological change, too, may produce new disorders that were unanticipated. For example, the rapid urbanization of nineteenth century London led to inadequate sanitation and contaminated water supplies, which, in turn, gave rise to a cholera epidemic that killed large numbers of city dwellers.

More recently, traces of such chemicals as PCB, which has been linked to cancer, skin diseases, and reproductive disorders, have been found in the waters of Midwest states. Members of the United States military involved in atomic bomb tests during World War II are believed to be at a greater risk of cancer, as are those who sprayed Vietnam with Agent Orange. The point here is that each economic stage of development and technology has had its own pattern of health and disease as well as its own way of treating it. Yet all diseases share certain common socially undesirable consequences; they are either painful to the individual or handicap him or her in the performance of social roles. Finally, in most nations today, disease is generally recognized as requiring some sort of treatment intervention.

Throughout most of human history, most human illness was caused by microscopic organisms, such as bacteria, viruses, and fungi. As you will recall from the discussion of mortality rates earlier in this chapter, there has been a dramatic shift in causes of death, one indicator of the level of health and nutrition in a society. In modernized nations, the major illnesses are chronic ones, and most are not caused by microorganisms, nor are they communicable. In both the United States and Canada today, children under six years of age are most likely to have acute, infectious diseases; the frequency of these conditions declines thereafter.

The study of the patterns of the occurrence of specific diseases, disabilities, and defects within a population is known as *epidemiology.* Social epidemiologists are particularly concerned with the distribution of illness in a social context; that is, how the life styles of individuals and groups relate to the appearance or disappearance of diseases. They have also been concerned with analyzing the interplay between a specific disease agent (such as bacteria or viruses), the individual, and the social and physical environment. The uses of epidemiology are many, and the findings from epidemiological studies have increased knowledge of patterns of both illness and health, as well as explain the differential rates of illness within a population. For example, in 1854 a London physician, John Snow, observed that there were sharp differences in the numbers of people who contracted plague among different districts of London. He was able to trace the epidemic to contaminated water sources from which those people with the highest incidence of plague got their water. More complex epidemiological studies have been undertaken to understand the factors influencing contagious and disease resistance. Tuberculosis, for example, is

Epidemiology is the study of the patterns of occurrence of illness in a population.

The Sick Role

One concept used by sociologists to describe the behavior of the sick person and his/her relationships to physicians or other therapists is that of the *sick role.* An ideal type, this concept was introduced by Talcott Parsons (1951) to take account of the changes in role relationships that occur in illness and has the following characteristics: (1) The sick person is defined as incapable of usual role and task behaviors due to incapacity beyond his or her control; (2) Accordingly, s/he is exempted from normal responsibilities; (3) In return, since illness is an undesirable state, the patient is obliged to seek competent help from disease specialists; and (4) To follow the instructions of physicians or other therapists in order to get well as soon as possible. The sick role is only conditionally legitimated; that is, the sick person is granted exemption from normal role behaviors only as long as s/he works at getting well. The activity of complying with medical instructions and treatment replaces normal activity but is not expected to be a long-term role.

Like all ideal types, the model of the sick role is a fixed standard against which different kinds of behavior in illness may be measured. Not all people are equally prone to take the sick role; about 22% of the American population accounts for three-quarters of visits to physicians (USDHEW, 1975). Number and persistence of symptoms, ability to recognize symptoms as well as their perceived seriousness, and the extent of social and physical disability all are determining significant factors in determining whether and how one will play the sick role. Social and cultural factors also are important, as are availability of information and treatment, and the state of medical knowledge.

Table 16-7. Life Expectancy at Birth for Selected Countries by Sex and Number of People Per Physician (1975-1979)

Country	Life expectancy		Number of people per physician
	Males	Females	
Sweden	72	77	600
Netherlands	71	77	600
Canada	69	76	600
United States	68	76	600
India	42	41	410
U.S.S.R.	64	74	300

Source: *Statistical Abstract of the United States,* 1979, table 1550, table 1547; *Statistics Canada; Health: United States,* 1975, tables CD.1.22a and 22b.

due to a particular kind of bacteria, but its contagiousness has been found to depend not only upon exposure to the germ but to general social conditions and the health state of the individual who was exposed. With the rise of the industrial revolution and increased migration from rural to urban locales where dramatic changes in life styles, such as overcrowding, close physical contact among many people, poor hygiene, malnutrition, and bad sanitation, took place, vast increases in the numbers of people contracting tuberculosis deaths occurred. Isolation of these social factors led to their correction, and tuberculosis began to recede as a major killer. Changes in lifestyle were thus directly involved in both the rise and decline of this disease.

Paradoxically, although the United States spent about 9 per cent of its gross national product (GNP) on health care, Americans do not have as long an average life expectancy as do members of other industrialized nations.

While there is some relationship between the thousands of people per physician and life expectancy, this alone does not explain why, for example, Canadians, Swedes, and the Dutch have longer life expectancy at birth. The answer to this problem lies with both the organization, accessibility, and affordability of medical care (see Table 16-7).

The Organization, Financing, and Accessibility of Health Care Services. While many models for the organization of health care have been proposed, three are particularly relevant to contemporary North American patterns of present and future health service: the *professional model*, the *central planning model*, and the *health maintenance organization model.** The *professional model*, most prevalent today in the United States, has as its most outstanding feature the power and influence that physicians exercise over the structure, practice patterns, and regulation of performance of health care, itself organized around the central role of the individual medical practitioner in the doctor-patient relationship. Most physicians working within the professional model operate essentially as small businesses, that is, as members of solo or partnership practices loosely

The **professional model** is based on physicians' control of health care.

*This discussion is summarized from Elwood, 1978.

bound to other physicians through referral practices, informal communication and friendship networks, hospital affiliations, and medical society membership. Payment for health care is fee-for-service, where fees are determined by members of the profession on the basis of customary costs within a given geographic area and medical specialty. Competitive pricing is usually limited to medical products suppliers and health insurance companies. Regulatory controls are focused on the activities of individual practitioners rather than on the profile of medicine as a whole and are dominated by practitioners. Emphasis on quality assurance has traditionally been on controlling inputs into the system, that is, the quality of medical training and licensure. Licensing of physicians is controlled by the profession itself, and licensing and regulation of hospitals is also vested in professional health care groups. Distribution of health manpower has been determined by training, practice opportunities and individual preferences rather than by policy determinations of need or salaried job openings.

In contrast to the professional model is the *central planning model*, based on the concept of public control over the planning and allocation of health staffing and resources. Within the central planning model, all medical care is provided through non-competitive geographically organized health systems in which a central planning agency or health authority is responsible for the coordination of health resources including practitioners and facilities within a defined region. While the pattern of such health systems varies from country to country, many resemble the 'planetary' form of organization developed in Sweden, where there is one health center per 15,000 people which revolves around a district hospital (one per 60,000–90,000 population), in turn revolving around a central hospital. The central hospital answers to the regional medical center (one per million population) which is responsible to a government agency or agencies. In sum, services in this model are organized on the basis of population and governmental estimates of service needs; physicians are incorporated into the system either on a salary or by formal contract. The geographic distribution of physicians is controlled through regulation, assessed needs, and vacant positions. Although fee-for-service practice is not discouraged and physicians may see private patients, this is the exception. Payment for health care may be from a variety of sources, including government insurance and appropriations, private health insurance, and consumer out-of-pocket expenditures. In Sweden, for example, national, county, and municipal funds, compulsory national health insurance and direct payments by patients finance health care, while in England, health care is almost entirely financed on the national level through general tax revenues.

The third model, the *health maintenance organization (HMO)*, is an almost uniquely American pattern of health care delivery, based upon prepayment for services and the assumption that competition among competing HMOs will result in improved, cost effective, and efficient health services. That is, high quality and cost effective services will be assured to patients through a capitation (per person pre-paid costs) payment high enough to cover costs of health services if these are provided efficiently and with good judgment, keeping in mind what sorts of procedures might be expected in the average case. A variety of different structures and funding patterns have developed among HMOs, but all provide a full range of services, such as preventive, outpatient and in-patient treatment, hospitalization, tests, x-rays, and so forth, to voluntarily enrolled

The **central planning model** is based on public control over health care.

The **HMO** is based on prepayment of health care and competition over services.

subscribers who pay a fixed pre-paid premium. The HMO model is more flexible than the central planning model as it is based upon the notion of free enterprise and competition among HMOs, where those most able to compete effectively will survive and less efficient or effective ones will be driven out of business. To date, however, there has been relatively little competition among HMOs; rather, most organizations of this type have competed not with each other but with physicians in solo or partnership practice. Some HMOs have been criticised for setting up restrictive membership where poor health risks are denied membership with the result that those people most in need of health services are not eligible for coverage (Lennox, 1980).

The controversy surrounding the organization and financing of health care in the United States is considerable. Those who support greater governmental intervention in the health care area have argued that planning at the national level is necessary since providers have vested interests which may not necessarily coincide with the needs of the population as a whole. The individual consumer is neither well informed nor foresighted enough to anticipate, plan, and save money for his or her health needs adequately. Furthermore, without national health insurance and governmental regulation of health care, the differential distribution of health services that now exists in the United States would not be overcome. For example, in Mississippi, there were only 105 physicians and 30 dentists per 100,000 population in 1977, but in New York State, there were 243 physicians and 76 dentists per 100,000 (*Statistical Abstract of the United States*, 1979, p. 107).

Opponents of government intervention in health care have argued that government involvement would bring about a lowering of the quality of care and limit professional autonomy. Physicians, because of their technical expertise, are in the best position to assess the need for health services, and the laws of the market will discourage exploitation by a few greedy individuals. The individual consumer, not an agency or regulatory board, is in the best position to plan for financing his or her own health care.

A major issue intertwined with the ways in which health care should be organized is its financing. Health care costs have risen dramatically since 1967, the base year on which prices are calculated. While the consumer price index as a whole rose from 100.0 in 1967 to 214.7 in 1979, medical care costs increased to 236.3 and the major increases within this category were for hospital rooms (369.3) and physicians' services (240.7). In 1978, national health expenditures were 192.1 billion dollars, or 9.1 per cent of the gross national product of the United States, and were paid by a variety of sources, including direct payments by consumers (29%), private health insurance such as Blue Cross-Blue Shield (25.5%), and government insurance including Medicare and Medicaid as well as appropriations (37.5%) (*Statistical Abstract of the United States*, 1979, p. 100).

A comparison of health care expenditures in the United States and the United Kingdom in the last few years indicated that the United Kingdom spent almost 3 per cent less of its gross national product than did the United States on health care, that its per capita spending for health care was much lower (a difference of about $463 dollars), its infant mortality rate lower, and number of hospital admissions lower (Malone, 1978). Several factors account for the unremarkable health care record of the United States despite its larger expenditures. These include high administrative costs of United States insurance plans

(14% as compared to 6% in the U.K.—Malone, 1978) as well as alleged medical waste and mismanagement, including unnecessary surgery, x-rays, and other tests; and an estimated one billion was lost through fraud and abuse in the health care industry (*Society*, 1978). Contrary to common beliefs about the British National Health System, its costs are relatively low and its services have greatly improved the health status of subscribers. Very few British wish to see the system replaced by the U.S. model (Malone, 1978).

Significant socioeconomic differences associated with minority group membership affect life expectancy, illness and disability risks and the health care received. Overall, nonwhites are more likely to have more days of disability but fewer physician visits than whites in the United States; this is largely a result of their lower socioeconomic status. A similar health picture has been observed among Indians and Eskimos in Canada, but, since they account for a relatively small proportion of the population, their limited access to health care makes little difference in national figures. In the United States, in 1977, people of all races with family incomes under $5,000 per year averaged about 33 disability days per person as compared to about 13 days among those with family incomes of $15,000 (*Statistical Abstract of the United States*, 1979, Table 185); and poorer people are also least likely to have either private or public health insurance (Ibid, Table 154).

There are also sex differences associated with health and disease. While high rates of maternal mortality are absent in industrialized nations, women throughout their lives have higher rates of illness but longer life expectancies. There are apparently biological differences between the sexes that favor longevity among women. Therefore, a society's sex ratio is related to the rates of illness and death.

Minority group membership affects one's life expectancy, the probability and severity of disability, and the health care received.

The Environment. Another aspect of quality of life that has been of increasing concern in recent years is the quality of the environment, especially in industrial and postindustrial nations. As the population of the world has expanded at a rapid rate, the fear that natural resources will be depleted and that the air and water will be polluted has occupied both popular and scientific attention.

The condition of the environment is another index of the quality of life.

It is an oversimplification, however, to believe that modifications to the environment are new events. There has been a long history of human depletion of the natural environment, beginning with hunting, gathering, and agriculture, when natural vegetation was replaced with crops, lands were overgrazed, and forests were felled. As humans began to construct cities and to urbanize, they transformed the environment still further, utilizing natural resources and polluting the environment in the drive toward industrialization.

One group of concerned scientists has predicted that industrial and postindustrial societies will soon collapse completely due to the loss of nonrenewable natural resources, such as usable land for agriculture, oil, and natural gas (Meadows, *et al.*, 1972). According to this argument, termed the "doomsday approach" by its critics, natural resources will drop dramatically during the last decades of this century, leading to rapid declines in production and in food per person. Pollution will continue to accompany industrial growth, and overpopulation to destabilize the developing nations.

If this argument is correct, how can the doomsday effect of modernization be

Concern with the quality of the environment has gained both popular and scientific attention in the United States today. (Source: Paolo Koch, Rapho/Photo Researchers, Inc.)

averted? Meadows suggested a variety of measures, some of which are already being implemented in the United States and Canada: (1) stabilizing populations so that birth rates equal death rates; and (2) shifting focus from the production of material goods to a service economy. Other strategies include: (3) reducing pollution to one-quarter the 1970 rate; (4) reducing consumption of nonrenewable natural resources to one-quarter the 1970 value; (5) channeling capital from industrial to food production; (6) emphasizing methods to restore eroded or infertile soil; and (7) improving the efficiency and lifespan of industrial facilities such as steel mills and power plants so there will be less waste of resources.

Summary

Demographers study the characteristics and distribution of populations. Censuses, sample surveys, vital statistics, and migration statistics are the major sources of data used by demographers. Censuses are inventories of the entire population of a country; in Canada and the United States they are conducted every ten years. Mini-censuses, or sample surveys, provide updates over shorter periods of time. Vital statistics are records of births, deaths, divorces, marriages and other important events. Migration statistics are counts of movements within a society or in and out of the country.

Changes in population size are linked to availability of food and the level of technology in a society. Population growth increased slowly over the many thousands of years before the industrial revolution which set the stage for a dramatic and sustained rise in the world population. The first stage of the demographic transition is characterized by lowered death rates accompanied by continuing high birth rates, leading to a surge in population growth. Several decades later, as birth rates also decline, the pace of natural increase in the population also slows.

Mortality rates, birth and fertility rates, and migration are the major components of population change. Mortality declines at the youngest ages are reflected in large increases in life expectancy (the average length of life one can expect to live) that ultimately lead to reductions in birth rates. Immigration and emigration patterns also affect the age distribution of the population in both the receiving and sending societies. The age and sex composition of a society are summarized by demographers in population pyramids shaped by the combination of births, deaths, and overall migration at a specific point in time.

There are substantial regional differences in population growth in North America. In the United States the sunbelt region has attracted migrants from other states, while the snowbelt areas have lost population. A number of economic, social, and personal factors underlie this trend, though most recent data indicate a slowing down of the sunbelt's rapid economic growth.

In general, also, United States cities have been losing population to their suburban fringe areas. In contrast, the proportion of Canadians living in the major metropolitan centers has increased steadily through the 1970s. As Canadians migrated from economically declining areas to more prosperous ones, regional differences in wealth, political power, and standards of living have intensified. The development of the more rural provinces may reduce regional inequities.

Health is an important indicator of the quality of life in any society, and is closely related to the level of industrialization, the distribution of power, wealth, and prestige within the society, and the age and sex distribution of its population. The social meaning of health is culturally defined and varies among societies. For example, though the United States spends about 9 per cent of its gross national product on health care, life expectancy is not as long and infant mortality is higher than for several other industrial societies. Even in modern societies with national health insurance programs, such as Canada, health care is not evenly distributed. Lower social class and minority group membership remain important determinants of life expectancy, the incidence and severity of disability, and the amount and type of services received.

The quality of the environment is another index of the quality of life. The past two decades have been a period of increasing concern over air and water pollution and the depletion of natural resources by members of industrialized societies. Many scientists predict grave consequences for health and standards of living, while others speak of technological breakthroughs. But there is evidence that world-wide fertility and birth rates have declined and that population control is being accepted in many developing nations. Nonetheless, the world's population continues to increase by several million people a day, though at a slower rate than a decade ago, and industrial pollution is spreading across the developed areas of our planet.

Suggested Readings

EHRENREICH, BARBARA, and DEIRDRE ENGLISH. *For Her Own Good: 150 Years of the Experts' Advice to Women* (Garden City, N.Y.: Anchor, 1979). A penetrating and provocative historical analysis of the struggle between women and the medical and psychiatric establishments.

KOTELCHUCK, DAVID (Ed.). *Prognosis Negative: Crisis in the Health Care System* (New York: Vintage Books, 1976). The staff of the Health Policy Advisory Center (Health/PAC) provides an extensive analysis of health care institutions, health care personnel, and government intervention in the health system of the United States.

OVERBECK, JOHANNES. *Population and Canadian Society* (Toronto: Butterworth, 1980). In this comprehensive overview, population developments in Canada are compared with data from the United States, other industrial nations, and Third World countries.

PAGE, JOSEPH, and MARY-WIN O'BRIAN. *Bitter Wages* (New York: Grossman, 1973). Members of Ralph Nader's research group identify the social and structural factors that result in occupational hazards and injuries and the lack of protection of workers in the United States.

VAN DER TAK, JAN, CARL HAUB, and ELAINE MURPHY. "Our Population Predicament: A New Look," *Population Bulletin*, 34:5, December 1979. This extremely readable monograph examines the demographic transition in industrial and industrializing nations, as well as probable directions of change in the remainder of this century.

WRONG, DENNIS. *Population and Society* (New York: Random House, 1976). Wrong's discussion of major demographic concepts and the dynamics of population growth is both concise and comprehensive.

17 Crime and Punishment

*I*n 1980, a 26-year veteran of the United States House of Representatives was convicted of bribery and conspiracy in the ABSCAM scandal, in which Federal Bureau of Investigation agents had posed as representatives of an Arab sheik seeking admission to the United States. He was convicted for taking a $50,000 bribe to ensure the sheik's entry into the United States without inquiry by immigration officials.

In March 1980, a firebomb exploded in the Vancouver, British Columbia, branch of the Canadian Imperial Bank of Commerce. This was the fifteenth blast in this city over a ten-week span. Since most targets were banks or government offices, it was thought to be the work of politically-motivated terrorists.

In Beverly Hills, California, a group psychotherapy session was interrupted when another man joined the group. Saying, "Gimme your money or I'll kill you," the armed man fled after collecting about $900 from members of the therapy group.

In September 1979, an unidentified sniper shot a fifteen-year-old black high school athlete while his football team was playing a scheduled game in Charlestown, a white section of Boston, Massachusetts. The boy is now almost totally paralyzed.

What do these different events have in common? Some involve violence, some are politically motivated, and others involve power or greed. What these acts share is one thing: They are against the law. Conduct in violation of the law is *criminal behavior*. These examples illustrate the great diversity of crimes and criminals, and of reasons why a given act comes to public attention. The fact that there is no one cause of crime or criminality is of particular interest to sociologists. As we saw in Chapter 6, since every society has its rules, it also has its deviants and agents of social control. The amount of crime in any given society will depend upon both (1) the range of conduct constrained by law; and (2) the effectiveness of control mechanisms.

How is a crime different from other forms of deviant behavior? While many types of deviance elicit only informal sanctions, *crimes* are those deviant acts arousing such strong feelings among members of a society that they are officially prohibited. Individuals who pursue unlawful conduct are targets of formal and official sanctions, including arrest, prosecution, and punishment. In this chapter, you will read about different types of crime in contemporary society. You will see that crime is a *social construct*, a product of social interaction. The mechanisms by which crime is controlled are also discussed: the police, the courts, jails, and prisons.

Criminal behavior is conduct in violation of the law.

The level of crime in society is a result of both the range of behavior constrained by law and the effectiveness of control.

The Role of Law

In modern societies, the *law* of the state or province is the formal embodiment of rules enforcing conformity. In simple societies these are matters of custom and informal sanctions. Social norms become laws when their violation is met by action exercised in a socially approved, predictable way by an authorized third party; that is, norms are enforced by impersonal agents of the people as a whole, who are empowered to act as accuser and judge.

Behavior contrary to the interests of social order is punishable under **criminal law,** while behavior contrary to the interests of private individuals is punishable under **civil law.**

A distinction is usually made in contemporary law between *criminal* and *civil.* Conduct believed to be against the interests of the society or state is sanctioned under *criminal law;* conduct against the interests of private individuals is punishable under *civil law.* This distinction is not as neat as it sounds. For example, consider the act of assault which is directed against a specific individual but which is also a threat to the public interest, inasmuch as individuals want to feel that they are generally safe from assault. Assault therefore involves both a criminal and a civil violation of law (Quinney and Wildeman, 1977).

The criminal law is one set of rules and regulations in society and overlaps norms of the family, church, and other institutional spheres. Many criminal behaviors have been so defined since the days of Moses in the Bible. Others are relatively new additions: dope pushing, airline highjacking, and income-tax evasion. What is crime in one time and place is not crime in another. For example, prior to the American Civil War, slavery was legal in the United States. Today, slavery is not only against the law in North America but anyone treating another individual as a slave is subject to imprisonment.

Durkheim observed that crime is functional by generating social cohesion and setting normative boundaries.

It is unlikely that there was ever a society without crime. Durkheim pointed out that crime is necessary to all societies for its *latent functions* in generating social cohesion and setting boundaries of normative behavior. What does vary is the definition of crime; this is in large part a result of which groups have sufficient power to enact their norms into law.

The concept of crime as a wrong against society is very old, although punishment was often left to the injured individual or family rather than to agents of the state. Retaliation, or "an eye for an eye," was an early and exact form of social control. This rule, although bloody, ensured that no greater punishment would be assessed than the harm done, and was actually a first step in creating the balance scales of justice. With the rise of nation states, the right to punish wrong-doers was taken away from individuals and families to become a state monopoly. When sanctions are applied universally to all who commit a given act, we can speak of the rule of law.

How Norms Become Laws

The **social injury theory** assumes that laws are passed to protect members of society from harm.

At least three theoretical explanations have been proposed to explain how norms are translated into law: (1) the *social injury;* (2) *consensus;* and (3) *conflict.* The *social injury approach,* perhaps the most common-sensical of the three, is based on the assumption that all laws are passed to protect members of society from harm. Laws are therefore rational attempts to reduce the frequency of actions injurious to the public welfare or morals or interests of the state. This approach is vague as it does not answer the questions: *what* are injurious or harmful actions? And, *who* decides what is injurious and harmful?

The *consensus* model is built upon the idea that norms become law because they are a crystallization of custom, a reflection of the social consciousness or the public mood. Laws thus reflect public opinion and are a kind of barometer to social values within a society. While there may be conflicts over certain points, such differences will revolve around relatively minor issues. Basic agreement will occur over the important issues. This is a *functionalist* view, evolving from the work of Durkheim and his successors. The emphasis is upon social cohesion; whatever conflict and competition may occur between groups within a society ultimately results in the strengthening of social norms embodied in law.

> **Consensus theory** assumes that laws reflect customs, social consciousness, and public agreement regarding appropriate behavior.

In contrast is the *conflict* approach, of which there are two interpretations. The first is the *economic perspective,* stemming from the influence of Karl Marx, that emphasizes the links between the economic interests of deviant and nondeviant members of society. Basic to Marx's view of crime was the economic influence of the criminal upon bourgeois interests. Crime not only drains off an unwanted group from the labor force but creates jobs for others: judges, lawyers, legal scholars, and a diversity of crime-detection experts.

> **Conflict theory** assumes that laws serve the interests of the dominant class.

More recently, Quinney (1974) has enlarged upon this theme, proposing that the legal system serves the interests of the ruling class instead of society as a whole. He summarizes the conflict perspective on how laws are created as follows: (1) Since societies contain different economic interests, and since views of right and wrong vary immensely, both individuals and groups want to maximize their own self-interests by passing laws; (2) groups and individuals differ in their access to power within a society: (3) thus, many activities that are actually dangerous to the public are rarely labeled as criminal (for example, automobile designs, wars, radioactive waste disposal) while most laws are enacted because they reflect the political, economic, and ideological interests of

Table 17-1. A Model of Theoretical Perspectives as They Relate to Types of Criminal Behavior

Criminal behavior explained by theory	Theoretical perspective		
	Social good	Consensus (functionalist)	Conflict
Acts dreaded by most (for example, murder)	Yes	Yes	Yes
Acts of threat to many vested-interest groups (for example, theft)	No	Yes	Yes
Acts threatening special-interest groups (for example, nuclear power plant sit-in)	No	No	Yes

specific power groups (for example, laws against loitering or defacing property). In short, *economic power* is a strong determinant of what becomes law.

A variation upon this theme is proposed by the *culture conflict* school. Rather than emphasizing the economic differences among groups, culture conflict theorists stress differences in *values*. From this perspective, economic class interest is only one of a number of lines of division within a society. When the community has disintegrated into competing factions and custom is no longer sufficient to maintain conformity, law is imposed by the strongest faction at a given time, and represents the will of the most powerful interest group (not necessarily the majority). Table 17-1 summarizes the types of criminal behavior taken account of by each of these three theoretical perspectives.

Each perspective emphasizes a different aspect of the legal system. Yet any given system is the outcome of the interplay of consensus, conflict, and the need for order.

The **culture conflict** model stresses **value** differences and assumes that laws reflect the values of the most powerful groups.

Theories of Criminal Behavior

One of the most basic questions that people ask about crime, regardless of its type, is "What causes some people to become criminals while others remain law-abiding citizens?" Of the sociological explanations proposed for deviant behavior, three are especially relevant to crime: *differential association, anomie,* and *opportunity structure.*

Differential Association Theory.   The differential association theory, proposed by the American criminologist Edwin H. Sutherland (1883–1950), was a logical extension of the argument that human behavior is learned and that therefore criminal behavior develops through the same processes as any other form of behavior. The theory of differential association may be summarized as follows.

The theory of **differential association** assumes that criminal behavior is **learned** behavior.

1. Criminal behavior is learned in social interaction with others and has no unique biological or genetic roots.
2. It is within *primary groups*, rather than from the larger society that one learns motives and techniques for committing crimes; reasons for conforming to or violating particular rules, and what behavior is permissible in which situation.
3. An individual becomes a criminal when definitions favorable to the violation of law outweigh unfavorable ones; that is, one becomes a criminal because there are more factors favoring such activity than there are opposing it.
4. Those differential associations most likely to result in criminal behavior are frequent, long lasting, intense, and occur relatively early in life.
5. Learning criminal behavior involves the same processes of learning as any other behavior. For example, people who value money could become robbers, stockbrokers, or physicians. There is thus *no* value or need-pattern unique to criminals as opposed to noncriminals. The individual becomes

criminal when reinforcement for lawbreaking is stronger than for remaining law abiding.

Anomie Theory. As detailed in Chapter 6, *anomie theory* focuses on the social-structural properties producing criminal behavior when individuals are denied access to the means of achieving legitimate success (Merton, 1957). The child growing up in the slum who internalizes the belief that material wealth is the most desirable goal in life usually encounters difficulties in realizing that expectation through conventional, legitimate channels. The tension experienced by those who seek socially valued goals but are barred from acceptable ways to achieve them is resolved through *innovation,* by which illegal means are substituted for legal ones. Criminal behavior is one response to the differential distribution of opportunities for success.

Albert Cohen (1955) expands anomie theory by suggesting that delinquent and law-abiding behavior both depend largely upon one's sociocultural environment and social interaction. The reason that *delinquent subcultures* develop primarily among juveniles in the poorer classes is because these youngsters are relatively inept at competing effectively in a middle class world (Cohen, 1955). When they enter school, they are measured by middle-class norms that have not

Anomie theory focuses on the effects of a lack of fit between socially-valued goals and legitimate means of achieving these.

Subcultures such as street gangs tend to develop because they provide a confirmation of identity and a sense of excitement. (Source: Eladio J. Ballestas, Photo Researchers, Inc.)

Table 17-2. Types of Delinquent or Criminal Subcultures Likely to Develop Owing to Differential Opportunity

Delinquent subculture type	Focus of activity within subculture		
	Acquisition of property and money	Violence and gang war	Drug use, alcohol use
Criminal	Yes	No	Nc
Conflict	No	Yes	No
Retreatist	No	No	Yes

been emphasized in their prior socialization. Thus the children of the poor fall short and, unable to compete successfully within the school setting, they seek success elsewhere: in the activities of the gang where they find a confirmation of identity and a sense of excitement.

Opportunity Structure Theory.   Delinquent or criminal subcultures have their roots in the lack of fit between culturally learned aspirations among lower class youth and the limited possibilities of attaining success (Cloward and Ohlin, 1960). Three types of delinquent subcultures may arise from *blocked opportunity structure.* These subcultures are summarized in Table 17-2. Each of these subcultures stresses a different career pattern and source of status and gratification: for the criminal, property and wealth; for the conflict-oriented, violence; and for the retreatist, the means of complete withdrawal from both deviant and conformist pressures. These theories of criminal behavior have been used to explain the incidence of "crime in the streets" rather than "crime in the suites." Public concern with crime has been almost exclusively directed to offenses committed by the poor. But social learning and opportunity can also affect criminal behavior among the nonpoor, as will be noted throughout this chapter.

> **Delinquent and criminal subcultures** originate in the discrepancy between aspirations and blocked opportunity structures.

Crime in North America

Crime in the Streets.   Fear of crime is common in both the United States and Canada. In the United States, at least 40 per cent of the population report they are afraid to walk alone in their own neighborhood at night (Book of Criminal Justice Statistics, 1973). Most feared in both nations are *street crimes,* that is, acts that directly threaten one's person or property. In this section we shall review some of the most common types of crime in the streets.

In the United States, two major sources of data are used to determine the extent of crime. The first is *Uniform Crime Reports,* compiled by the Federal Bureau of Investigation from information submitted by city, state, and county police units on the number of offenses known to them. Seven reporting categor-

ies, selected because they are regarded as among the most serious law violations, form the basis of the F.B.I. Crime Index. These crimes include: (1) murder and non-negligent manslaughter; (2) forcible rape; (3) robbery; (4) aggravated assault; (5) burglary; (6) larceny; and (7) motor vehicle theft. Excluded from the index are embezzlement, con games, forgery, and other types of fraud or white collar crimes.

In Canada, comparable data on crime, compiled by almost every police force in that country, are generated through Uniform Crime Reports submitted to

Table 17-3. Crime Rates for Selected Offenses Reported to the Police in the United States and Canada, 1978

	Rate per 100,000 population	
Crime Reported to Police	United States	Canada
Murder	9.0	2.6
Forcible Rape	30.8	8.5
Robbery	191.0	83.7
Aggravated Assault	256.0	—*
Burglary	1,424.0	1,185.9
Larceny/Theft	2,744.0	2,671.7
Motor Vehicle Theft	455.0	354.0

Source: *Statistical Abstract of the United States*, 1979, Table 291, p. 177; *Perspectives Canada III*, Table 9.1, p. 158.
*Comparable data not reported.

Statistics Canada. Table 17-3 summarizes crime rates for index crimes in the United States and various offenses in Canada that correspond roughly to the index crimes in the United States.

Although Uniform Crime Reports are widely used by the police and mass media in both nations to measure increases and decreases in crime, they have two major shortcomings. (1) Not all crimes are reported to the police, for many victims do not want to take the time and effort to lodge a complaint. Some may be fearful of reprisals if an offense is reported, and still others do not feel that it will do any good. Thus official statistics greatly underestimate the number of crimes. (2) The data reported by various local units are not always comparable. States, provinces, and municipalities differ in definition, in reporting tech-

Table 17-4. Victimization Rates of Crimes Against Households, 1977. (Rates per 1,000 Households)

Household characteristic	Burglary			Larceny			Motor vehicle theft		
	Total*	White	Black	Total*	White	Black	Total*	White	Black
All households	89	84	122	123	124	116	17	16	21
Homeowner	74	72	102	113	112	116	14	13	23
Renter	115	110	139	142	148	116	23	24	20
Households with income of—									
Under $7,500	102	94	129	109	110	103	12	13	8
$7,500–$14,999	86	81	134	135	134	142	17	16	28
$15,000 and over	27	83	104	135	136	130	22	20	56

*Includes other races not shown separately.
Source: *Statistical Abstract of the United States*, 1979, Table 297.

niques, in willingness to do the required paperwork and in deliberate falsification. While we do not know how much crime is not reported or how much reported criminal activity is not recorded, one Canadian study estimated that on the average, only about 20 per cent of all crimes were reported to the police (Courtis, 1970). Comparable data from the United States suggest that 28 per cent of major offenses were ever reported to police authorities (Skogan, 1976). It seems clear that far more crimes are committed than are ever brought to the attention of law enforcement agencies.

A majority of crimes committed in both Canada and the United States are not reported to the police.

Nonetheless, the data do provide a very rough indication of the number of crimes considered most serious by officials as well as of the types of activities in which law enforcement agencies are engaged. Because of their unreliability, however, they are not very useful in assessing changes in the volume of crime. What official crime rates do describe is the amount of criminal activity that comes to the official attention of the police and how it is labeled.

To supplement the incomplete information provided by *Uniform Crime Reports*, a second source of information, the *National Crime Survey* which relies upon information received from victims, has been developed in the United States. While the National Crime Survey has the advantage of direct reports from victims during sample surveys of the general population, it also has disadvantages, for no one knows the extent to which respondents may conceal, exaggerate, or minimize crimes of which they have been the target.

Typical of the Survey data is Table 17-4. From this table, you can see that (1) blacks are more likely than whites to be victims of burglary, and (2) households with lower incomes are more likely to be burglarized, as are renters of either race. Despite popular mythology, it is the poor, rather than the rich, of either race who are more likely to be burglarized, probably because opportunity is greater and police surveillance less. Larceny (theft of property or other valuables without use of force) follows a different pattern: the poor are least likely to be victimized because there is so little to take.

Violent Crimes. Of the seven index crimes, four are violent: murder and non-negligent manslaughter, forcible rape, robbery, and aggravated assault (including attempts to kill). Comparing the homicide rate for the United States with that for Canada and selected European countries indicates the magnitude of violence in the United States (see Table 17-5 below).

Table 17-5. Selected Homicide Rates. (Per 100,000 Population)

Country	Year	Total	Male	Female
United States	1976	9.1	14.5	4.0
Canada	1975	2.7	3.6	1.8
Sweden	1976	1.3	1.5	1.0
United Kingdom	1976	1.1	1.2	1.0

Source: *Statistical Abstract of the U.S., 1979*, Table 300, p. 182.

The typical homicide
victim in the United
States is male, black,
and young.

The typical homicide victim in the United States and Canada is male, and, in the United States alone, is black. In 1977, the homicide rate per 100,000 was 53.6 for black males and 12.0 for black females in comparison to 8.7 for white males and 2.9 for white females. Typically, too, victims are young; homicide ranks as the second leading cause of death in the 18–24-year age group in the United States.

Many explanations have been proposed for the high rate of homicide in the United States, including the strong tradition of violence surrounding racial conflict, the labor movement, and the settlement of the west. Some sociologists have suggested that there is a *subculture of violence* in the United States in which overt physical aggression is the norm in some kinds of social interactions among members of certain subgroups (Wolfgang and Ferracuti, 1967; Wolfgang, 1958). Working-class youth and those from ethnic groups stressing masculine honor are more likely to learn to resolve conflicts through violence than are young people from middle-class homes. Yet there is an element of blaming the victim in the theory of subcultural violence. The prevalence of homicide among young black males (and, to a lesser extent, young black females) indicates intolerable levels of frustration, poverty, and blocked opportunity. To term this a subculture of violence may be descriptive but it is not explanatory. Figure 17-1 presents a more expanded diagram of factors involved in the relatively high American homicide rate.

Physical aggression is a
behavioral norm in the
subculture of violence.

Property Crimes.   The volume of crimes against persons seems small in comparison to property crimes. In 1978, over 3 million burglaries, 5.9 million larcenies, and almost one million cases of motor vehicle theft were reported to the police, and these data may underestimate the actual incidence of such offenses by at least one-half. Victims often feel it is not worth the trouble to report the crime, especially if the loss was small or not recoverable through insurance.

Property crimes are
much more common
than crimes against persons.

Who commits property crimes? With the exception of burglary (a more specialized and "professional" crime), property crimes are committed by young males with limited educations who are disproportionately drawn from minority groups. At least, these persons get arrested and taken to court. Relatively few middle-class thieves are processed through the courts. They are more likely to be labeled as mentally disturbed and funneled into psychiatric treatment or, if juveniles, sent to special schools when detected.

At every age in both Canada and the United States, males are more likely to be arrested and charged with a crime than are females, although there is some suggestion that this pattern may be changing (see Figure 17-2).

Female Criminals.   Until recently, very little had been written about the female offender. The number of women arrested and imprisoned has been far lower than the number of men. In 1978, women accounted for only about 16 per cent of those arrested in the United States and 10 per cent in Canada. The number in prisons is also very low, a fact contributing to the very high cost of their incarceration which ranges between $6,000 and $20,000 per year (Baugh, 1979).

A variety of theories have sought to explain the relative absence of female criminals, including such contradictory ideas as that the female offender is a biological or psychological oddity, rebelling against the natural passivity of her

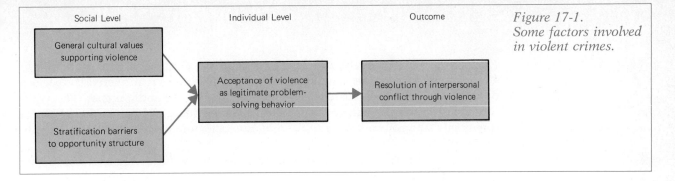

Figure 17-1.
Some factors involved in violent crimes.

Social Level

General cultural values supporting violence

Stratification barriers to opportunity structure

Individual Level

Acceptance of violence as legitimate problem-solving behavior

Outcome

Resolution of interpersonal conflict through violence

sex; that she is innately more vicious and cunning and thus less likely to be detected; that she is more conforming, more moral, more religious, and thus not easily tempted; and that she has less social support from peers for criminal activity and thus less opportunity.

That differences in the type and patterns of crime for women may be a result of gender socialization has also been proposed. As Freda Adler (1979) commented: "We go crazy and we go criminal along the well-worn paths that our 'mazeway' has constructed for us . . . . How else can we understand the female

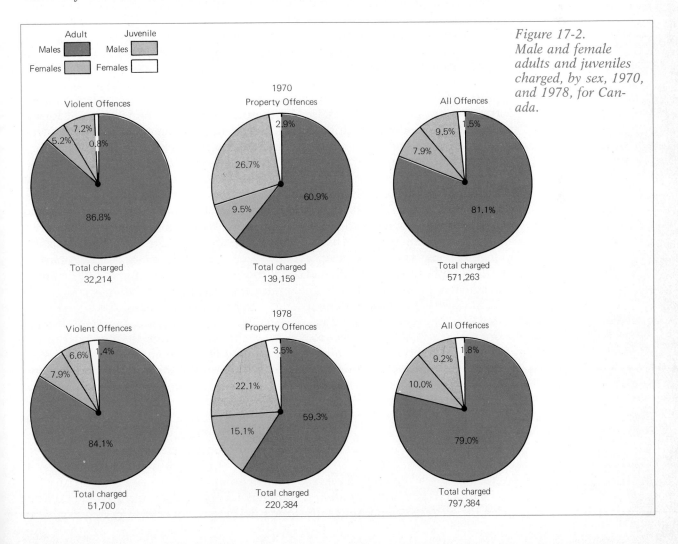

Figure 17-2.
Male and female adults and juveniles charged, by sex, 1970, and 1978, for Canada.

Adult   Juvenile
Males   Males
Females   Females

1970
Violent Offences   Property Offences   All Offences

7.2%   2.9%   1.5%
5.2%   0.3%   26.7%   9.5%
86.8%   9.5%   60.9%   7.9%
        81.1%

Total charged   Total charged   Total charged
32,214   139,159   571,263

1978
Violent Offences   Property Offences   All Offences

6.6%   1.4%   3.5%   1.8%
7.9%   22.1%   9.2%
84.1%   15.1%   59.3%   10.0%
                79.0%

Total charged   Total charged   Total charged
51,700   220,384   797,384

(or for that matter, male) offender except in the context of her social role?" It is difficult to commit a major crime, such as burglary or armed robbery, if one has not been trained to move with stealth or to handle a gun. The types of crimes in which women have been involved include prostitution, larceny (primarily shoplifting), vagrancy, and domestic violence—all linked to gender role.

Has the nature of female criminality changed with the advent of the women's movement? Both Canadian and United States data show a gradual increase in the proportion of women arrested within the last decade. The increase, however, has been almost entirely accounted for by greater female participation in such petty property crimes as larceny, fraud, and forgery (Simon, 1979: Steffensmeier, 1980). Relatively few women are arrested now or have been arrested in the past for commission of violent offenses such as assult or homicide.

Exaggerated protection of women (chivalry) seems relatively unimportant today in crime reporting. Using data from the United States National Victimization Survey for 1972–76, one investigator reported that for serious offenses, women are more likely than men to be reported to the police. And male victims are more likely to do the reporting than are female victims (Hindelang, 1979).

Since women are probably no more nor less moral than men, the rise in female rates of larceny, forgery, and other property crimes appears to reflect increased opportunities to commit such acts rather than any basic personality changes. Moreover, women who are arrested for criminal activity rarely express feminist sentiments. To the contrary, the few crimes of violence perpetrated by women are closely tied to their roles as mothers, wives, and lovers. Traditional gender roles still dominate the lives of female and male offenders. Nor is there a female subculture of crime (Steffensmeier, 1980).

Organized Crime.   For many Americans, the *Godfather* movies sum up what they know about organized crime: It is Sicilian-led, run by close-knit families, ruled by a patriarch who exerts almost complete control over his family and who demands secrecy while loyal lieutenants kill troublesome enemies in restaurants, warehouses, and barber shops. The words "Mafia" and "Cosa Nostra" have become synonymous with the concept of organized crime in America.

It is both difficult to define and to separate fact from fiction about criminal syndicates or organizations. The major sources of information are Congressional hearings, court testimony, data from informants, and journalistic accounts. The simplest definition of *organized* or *syndicated* crime is continued, organized endeavors to accumulate wealth in defiance of the law. Or, in the words of the President's Commission on Law Enforcement and Justice (1967), "a society that seeks to operate outside the control of the American people and their governments" in which "thousands of criminals" work within complex organizational structures.

Organized crime has three distinguishing characteristics. (1) Its members supply goods and services not otherwise available such as loan sharking, gambling, and narcotics. (2) In order to carry out illegal activities without interference, public officials and others in positions of power are bribed and otherwise corrupted. (3) Violence is used to enforce compliance.

Organized crime is neither a new nor solely Sicilian phenomenon in the United States. When immigrants found that the streets of urban America were

Organized or **syndicated** crime is committed by members of formally-structured groups operating outside the law.

Organized crime involves the delivery of illegal services to noncriminal customers, the corruption of public officials, and the use of violence.

not paved with gold, and when discrimination and prejudice reduced access to legitimate economic opportunities, illegal activity provided a readily available, if crooked, ladder of social mobility. Successive immigrant groups have found that crime often brings success. In the United States, during the latter part of the nineteenth century, organized crime was dominated by Irish and Germans. By the turn of the century, Eastern European Jews emerged as gang leaders, and by the late 1920s, Italians began to displace the others in syndicated crime. Because they were among the last immigrants, Italians found it particularly difficult to break out of the slums. Crime has always been an attractive alternative to poverty in the urban ghettos of America.

If the syndicates are ladders of social mobility, then blacks and Hispanics, as the minorities most likely today to be excluded from legitimate opportunity structures, should become increasingly involved in organized crime. Limited evidence suggests this is true, although thus far the operations of blacks and Hispanics have been limited to narcotics, gambling, protection, and extortion primarily within ghetto areas (Ianni, 1974). As white ethnic criminals move into legitimate businesses their low-prestige, illegal activities are handed over to the next immigrant group in succession.

For obvious reasons, the amount of money amassed and invested by organized crime is unknown. Estimates of the profit from illegal gambling alone ranged from $7 billion to $50 billion in 1967, and remains high despite the spread of legalized gambling. The accumulation of unrecorded wealth has in fact sparked governmental concern: Money buys power. Crime syndicates are able to manipulate the value of shares on the stock market, to control prices of retail goods, to evade regulations on the quality of goods produced, to avoid payment of income taxes, to secure government contracts without competitive bidding, and to influence the activities of trade unions. The combination of investment in legitimate businesses and corruption of officials is possible only because of vast amounts of working capital.

Organized crime makes its money from its ability to fill a need for illegal services: gambling, loan sharking, narcotics, and prostitution. Less frequently mentioned are the phony home repair racket, hijacking and other large-scale thefts coupled with fencing or selling illicitly acquired goods, skilled arson, planned bankruptcy, and murder.

Crime in the Suites: White-Collar and Organizational Crime

White-collar crime is a term coined by Edwin Sutherland to describe "a crime committed by a person of respectability and high status in the course of his occupation" (Sutherland, 1949). Although we have titled this section "white-collar and organizational crime," we want to stress the point that, while the two are often confused with each other, they are separate entities. *White-collar crime* denotes legally prohibited activity by nonviolent means to obtain or avoid loss of money or property or to secure a professional or business advan-

White-collar crime refers to illegal activities committed by persons of high status, usually by nonviolent means.

tage. *Organizational crime* refers to illegal actions undertaken by legitimate corporations—bribery, price fixing, and tax evasion—for corporate rather than personal advantage. To class both types of criminal activity as "white collar" simply indicates the middle-class nature of the crimes (for money, no violence) and the criminals (white-collar, tie, and three-piece suit).

White-Collar Crime.   White-collar crime is committed for personal advantage by individuals in the course of their employment. The bank executive who embezzles funds, the physician who performs unnecessary surgery, the businessman who pads his expenses, the teacher who conceals a second source of income from the Internal Revenue Service, and the promoter of fraudulent land schemes are all white-collar criminals.

The extent of white-collar crime in the United States and Canada is unknown because the crimes are extremely difficult to detect, often have no identifiable

White-Collar Crime: Fraud and Swindles

Each era has produced its own set of master swindlers whose illegal activities have netted them millions of dollars. One of the oldest swindles involves paying high cash returns to early investors in a get-rich scheme before leaving the scene with the remainder of the money. A master of this method in the 1920s was an American financier named Charles Ponzi, who took in over $15 million dollars on the slogan "50% return in 45 days, double your money in 90." Small investors flocked to make their killing. Ponzi's investments included a brokerage firm, a mansion, a limousine, and an excellent wine cellar. Exposed by an article in the *Boston Post*, Mr. Ponzi was indicted on 86 counts of larceny and mail fraud for which he served a 10 year sentence (Slocum, 1962). Similar schemes emerge every year, including the 1980s craze for money pyramids.

Many frauds and confidence games are on a much smaller scale. The Business Opportunities column of the *National Enquirer* (7/22/80) contains the following. Only the names and addresses of the advertiser have been changed.

REVERSE THE aging process with an amazingly simple method that's proven successful. Brochure $1.00 plus self-addressed stamped envelope. Taylor Made Publications, 1222b A Street, Anytown, U.S.A.

UGLY FAT disappears quick. Stuff your mouth all day. Works 100%. No gimmicks, no pills, calories, or carbohydrates to count. Mysterious secret of weight loss finally revealed. Works a lifetime. Send $2.00 to Fat Off, Box 555, Home Valley, U.S.A.

EARN HUNDREDS weekly stuffing envelopes. Request free information. MAGIC, Box 123, Big City, U.S.A.

AVOID WRINKLES. Secret technique! $3.00. Box 1024, Small Town.

Each of these ads plays upon vanity or greed, and promises an unlikely, simple solution to a difficult problem. As P. T. Barnum the circus founder, claimed many decades ago, "There's a sucker born every minute."

victims, and involve fairly complex financial dealings. Although white-collar crime does not evoke the degree of fear created by crime in the streets, it powerfully impacts on the social fabric, affecting hundreds of thousands of citizens, and generating public mistrust of business and officials as the costs of multimillion dollar frauds are passed on to the public. Billing on government contracts for services that were not performed, cutting back on construction materials below the required specifications to make a higher profit, doubling the bill to insurance companies, and filing false income tax returns ultimately raise prices and lower the standard of living of all citizens.

White-collar crime, like any other, is defined differently from time to time. As a recent historical example, up until 1967, the physician in the United States who performed an abortion—except when the mother's life was in danger—was liable to criminal prosecution; today the physician is engaging in the legitimate practice of medicine. Changes in social norms have led to the redefinition of many other professional behaviors. On the other hand, technology, the mass media, and economic affluence have created the possibility of new forms of white-collar crime: consumer fraud while pandering to status needs or appealing to greed. The increasing complexity of modern society also enhances the white-collar criminal's options for developing relatively profitable schemes and lessens the likelihood that the criminal will be detected. To the average victim of white-collar crime, the means for redress are so technical, lengthy, and expensive that most find it easier to ignore than to fight: after all, no one got mugged.

> White-collar crimes are difficult to detect, without violence or identifiable victims, often involving complex financial arrangements.

Organizational Crime. Organizational crimes differ from white-collar crimes in one important aspect: they are not engaged in for personal gain but in the course of one's role as an employee or corporate decision maker (Dershowitz, 1961). For example, the bank vice-president who embezzles millions to cover gambling debts is a clear-cut example of a white-collar criminal. John Dean, G. Gordon Liddy, and other members of the Watergate conspiracy during the Nixon administration were corporate criminals as were the executives of Lockheed, Exxon, and some 200 other American firms who have systematically bribed agents of foreign governments in defiance of United States law. Their activities were undertaken to fulfill organizational rather than purely personal goals. Price-fixing and informal agreements to divide markets are other forms of organizational deviance.

> Organizational crimes are carried out in one's role as an employee and not for personal gain as in white-collar crime.

Does it make sense to think of an organization as deviant? Americans have a national preoccupation with the individual actor as the root of societal evil, and prefer stories about greedy, mentally ill, or corrupt people to analyses of widespread social conditions or interlocking social and economic interests. Yet what at first appeared to be the self-seeking motives of former President Carter's younger brother, Billy, who accepted sizeable "loans" from the Libyan government in 1980, were far more complex. Whatever Billy Carter's personal motives, he was merely an individual actor in an intricate organizational web, involving a foreign government and United States business interests.

Ermann and Lundman (1978) cite four conditions of organizational deviance.

1. *An organization is deviant when its policies violate the expectations of the public,* that is, its external norms.

2. *The deviance must be supported by internal norms that conflict with its formal goals.* If a corporation or government bureau is more concerned with its own survival and power than with producing a public good or service, its internal norms may be in conflict with formal goals. Watergate is an excellent example.

3. *The deviant internal norms of the organization must be supported by the power elite of the organization.* This is an important point. The frequent "rip-offs" within an organization by its employees and workers' ways of short-cutting or evading institutional norms are *not* set by the power elite; at best they are tolerated. In other cases, the deviant internal norms are supported at the highest level, as in bribery of foreign officials and the systematic illegal domestic spying by the Central Intelligence Agency and Federal Bureau of Investigation in the 1960s.

4. *The deviant behavior must be supported by (a) recruitment of willing personnel, (b) socialization to the internal organizational norms, (c) a pattern of rewards for compliance to these norms, and (d) support from peer groups and elites within the organization.* In short, corporate deviance, like other forms, is not only learned and rewarded but supported within the organizational structure.

Many legitimate acts committed by corporations would be considered criminal if committed by individuals.

Although many corporate actions are not considered criminal according to existing law, these same acts would be crimes if they were committed by an individual. It is estimated that industrial corporations cause approximately 100,000 deaths per year through negligence and deliberate action—a homicide rate about five times that committed by individuals in the United States. For example, in one plant, asbestos concentrations that cause lung disease and cancer were found to be ten times the permissible amount; yet the company was fined only $210 and the violations were listed as "nonserious" by government inspectors. While no overt crime was committed, about one-half the long-term workers in this plant have developed symptoms of fatal asbestos lung disease (Swartz, 1975).

Business organizations have prime responsibility to their stockholders, and their goal is to make a profit. Governmental agencies and legislative bodies, however, are expected to serve the general public. Blau and Scott (1962) have proposed a useful framework for analysing both types of organizations and their deviant acts. They distinguished two types of deviance: deviant action contrary to the interests of the *prime* beneficiaries (for example, stockholders) or to the *secondary* beneficiaries (employees, public) of the organization.

The *prime beneficiaries* of a corporation such as ITT, Ford Motor Company, or Mobil Oil are its stockholders; the prime beneficiaries of a political party, a fraternal organization, or a labor union are its members. For government, the prime beneficiaries are the public. Offenses against prime beneficiaries can take many forms: diversion of union pension funds to build resorts; use of corporal punishment in the public schools; maintenance of a hospital for the convenience of staff rather than patients; and release of confidential Internal Revenue information to the White House staff for political purposes.

Secondary beneficiaries include employees of an industry or corporation, consumers of almost every manufactured product, and the general public. All may be endangered when the organization deviated from standards of industrial safety or when it evades paying taxes. For example, in 1975, ten major United States corporations paid no corporate taxes on over one billion dollars of income; another two dozen paid less than 10 per cent. Although the corporate tax rate was fixed at 48 per cent, these companies took advantage of tax incentives and various write-offs so that the corporate sector has been paying a decreasing share of running the country. While the proportion of federal receipts from corporate income taxes was 22.7 per cent in 1967, by 1975 it was only 14.4 per cent (*Congressional Record*, 1976). If corporate America pays a very small share of the costs of running the United States, individual citizens must replace every revenue dollar lost through the tax loopholes available to corporations. While this behavior is not unlawful, a conflict theorist might argue that it is legalized crime in which individuals and small businesses are sacrificed to the economic interests of an elite.

Since organizational deviance has not been appreciably lessened by laws or regulation from outside, or by surveillance from within, we must conclude that the benefits outweigh the costs of such activity. Corporate crime, like any other, provides goods and services at a profit. Unless the demand for such benefits declines or alternative sources are found, such activities will continue.

Crimes Without Victims

Crimes without victims are sometimes known as vice or crimes against morality; that is, they are not directed against a person or property but are believed to endanger or offend the moral fiber of society. Yet moral standards in complex societies are mixed and constantly changing; what offends one group's morality may be acceptable to another. Because no victim is involved in such offenses as pornography, prostitution, gambling, drug use, and consensual sex acts between adults, many people have argued that these acts should be decriminalized. The prosecution of such behavior wastes the time and resources of police and court personnel, and serves only to stigmatize the few who are arrested.

Crimes without victims violate moral standards but those involved are willing participants.

Victimless crimes are also those likely to lead to corruption of law enforcement personnel. Vice squads are the most vulnerable unit in any police department. The range of discretionary power here is often so great that the officer can be bribed to arrest X and not Y, or to raid one home and not another. There is also the possibility that the officers' subjective evaluation of different kinds of people will dictate who is picked up on vice charges. In all these ways, the ideal of equal treatment under the law is systematically and regularly violated by the very agents of law. That victimless crimes remain on the statute books reflects a complex set of economic as well as value-laden issues.

Prostitution or the Selling of Sexual Favors. Although there are male prostitutes whose clients are primarily homosexual, prostitution is usually a female occupation in the United States, Canada, and most of the Western World. The number of prostitutes in the United States or Canada is unknown. In 1976,

56,694 arrests for prostitution and commercial vice were made in the United States; 71 per cent involved women, often the same ones arrested several times over the year.

Almost always the prostitute is arrested and not her male customer. Although primarily a woman's occupation, prostitution is dominated by males; police, primarily men, exercise political power; pimps (procurers) exercise physical and psychological control; and clients wield economic and physical power (Heyl, 1977). As Heyl (1977) commented: "It may well be that the oldest profession is the most sexist of them all."

As long as prostitution is considered a danger to public morality, there are many individuals and groups benefitting from this belief. Clean-up campaigns win public support for politicians and police officials. Prostitution squads of the police earn their living by arresting prostitutes and may augment their incomes with bribes from women attempting to avoid arrest. The judiciary system collects fines from processing prostitutes while bondsmen receive fees for posting bail money. Ultimately, prostitution would disappear if large numbers of males were not eager clients, yet rarely are they blamed for the existence of prostitution.

Nonetheless, prostitution as an organized business is apparently declining. As Adler (1979) has pointed out, there are now a large number of "daytimers"— ex-models, unemployed actresses, homemakers, and students—who work part-time as prostitutes to augment their income. These may be the vanguard of a group of female entrepreneurs who are beginning to replace the small-time pimp and his stable of girls (Adler, 1979). The bulk of the business, however, remains under the control of organized crime groups.

Gambling. Like prostitution, gambling is believed by many to taint the morality of the public. Arguments against gambling include its links to organized crime, its bribery and corruption of public officials, and its destructive effects on families. The desire to gamble, to take a chance, to get a large reward for a small investment, is very widespread. Again, we have no accurate statistics on the number of people who gamble illegally nor how much they spend. Statistics for 1976 indicate that there were 65,437 gambling arrests in the United States; some of these arrests, as with prostitution, include multiple counts of the same people.

Despite these arguments, churches have long used bingo games as a means of raising funds, and by 1976, 44 states had some form of legalized gambling, such as state lotteries and casinos. In Atlantic City, New Jersey, where casino gambling was recently legalized, tax revenues of approximately $18 million were anticipated for the year 1980. The New Jersey casinos reported winnings of $5 million per day in early 1980. But the major objections remain: involvement by organized crime, potential bribery of officials, and economic ruin of families of gamblers—whether the gambling is legalized or not. While legalized gambling is increasingly prevalent, it is unlikely that it will replace illegal gambling which still provides better odds and tax-free winnings to both players and organizers.

Drug Use. Another controversial crime without victims is use of drugs not prescribed by a physician but acquired illegally, although supporters of

---

While prostitution is primarily a woman's occupation, it is dominated by men: pimps, police, and clients.

tougher laws argue that users are victimized by their very dependence on drugs. The link between drug use and commission of violent offenses has also been cited as a reason for maintaining strict drug laws, but much of this relationship disappears when the social status of the user is taken into account. In other words, while many poor criminals are drug users, many middle-class users do not commit crimes. Although the number of people addicted to narcotic drugs is unknown, several studies indicate that rates of addiction are higher among physicians and nurses than among the poor.

Since there is so much popular mythology surrounding drug use, it is difficult to provide a short review of fact. To begin with, most research evaluating the impact of drug use has been poorly designed, and facts about the effects of marijuana, heroin, cocaine, and other substances have been politicized both by those who support tighter control of drugs and those who support decriminalization or legalization of some or all substances. What is clear is that the illegal drug market is a primary source of income for organized crime.

We do not know the number of people who habitually use drugs, nor do we know how many people use them recreationally. Use of substances is age-related; the majority of American college students may have tried marijuana or have friends who have tried it, but their parents are much less likely to fit into either category. Patterns of drug use also vary; during the 1960s, heroin, marijuana, and LSD were most often discussed in the popular press; today, cocaine appears to be increasingly popular.

Juvenile Delinquency

Juveniles may come to the attention of the law enforcement system for three reasons: (a) they have committed a crime, (b) they are neglected or abused, or (c) they have committed a status offense which is an act that would not be considered in violation of the law if committed by an adult. Truancy, use of alcohol or tobacco, running away from home, being a potential runaway, being ungovernable (incorrigible) are all status offenses. According to *Uniform Crime Reports*, of the 665,781 children under the age of 15 who were arrested in 1976, 26 per cent were arrested for larceny, 12 per cent for burglary, and 10 per cent as runaways.

Males are three times more likely than females to be arrested for juvenile offenses. More white than nonwhite young people are arrested, but nonwhites are disproportionately represented, composing 30 per cent of juvenile offenders. The fact that children from low-income and working-class homes have higher arrest rates than those from more affluent homes could reflect a real difference in delinquent activity or the tendency for police and other authorities to attach the delinquent label to poor youngsters.

When self-reports of delinquent behavior are compared with official records, the data suggest that official reports produce more extreme racial, class, age, and sex differences than do self-reports (Elliott and Ageton, 1980). In terms of social class, some studies find no differences, while at least one shows more serious delinquency among higher status boys (Williams and Gold, 1972).

Males are three times as likely as females to be arrested for juvenile offenses.

Table 17-6. Arrests of Juveniles and Young Adults, by Age, for Selected Offenses in 1976

Offense	Percentage of those arrested			
	Under 15	Under 18	Under 21	Under 25
Murder	1.3	9.2	24.2	42.6
Forcible Rape	4.2	17.3	35.8	57.2
Robbery	9.2	33.5	56.5	76.0
Burglary	19.2	51.5	71.4	84.3
Gambling	.6	3.9	11.9	22.2
Curfew and Loitering	27.3	100.0*	100.0	100.0
Runaways	39.1	100.0*	100.0	100.0

Source: Federal Bureau of Investigation, Uniform Crime Reports, 1976. Washington, D.C.: U.S. Government Printing Office, 1977, p. 183. *Not offenses past the age of 18.

Table 17-6, drawn from *Uniform Crime Reports,* shows the cumulative percentages for arrests by offense charged and age group. Reading across the table, you can see that 1.3 per cent of the arrests for murder and nonnegligent manslaughter were of persons under the age of 15, 9.2 per cent were of those under age 18 (which means that 7.9 per cent were between the ages of 15 and 17), and so on. Curfew and loitering arrests were exclusively of juvenile offenses. In general, crime is an activity of young males, and one that most grow out of by their early twenties.

The Police and Law Enforcement

The police have both formal and informal power as agents of social control. As formal agents, they are charged by the state with the detection and control of criminal behavior. As informal agents, they exercise a great deal of discretion in deciding which offenses and offenders will receive attention and how they will be processed and charged. Officers may also settle challenges to their authority on the spot rather than invoking the sanction of arrest (Werthman and Piliavin, 1967).

The police and other law enforcement agents such as the F.B.I. are newcomers to the North American scene. In the seventeenth and eighteenth century, crime detection and control were relatively simple processes, executed by constables, sheriffs, justices of the peace, watchmen, and private citizens. With increased urbanization, however, municipal police forces, roughly modeled on the city of London police, were organized to maintain public order among the masses of immigrants and laborers.

The police are *enforcers,* not definers, of rules. Howard Becker (1963) distinguished enforcers, who do not necessarily have any personal stake in the partic-

The police are the **enforcers,** not definers, of the law.

ular law to be upheld, from the *moral entrepreneur* who is a crusader with a heavy investment in the social control of certain types of behavior defined as morally reprehensible. The enforcer is a bureaucrat committed to the duties of an office, not a reformer or legislator (Becker, 1963). Whether a police officer considers a given act to be dangerous or morally reprehensible should be irrelevant; his or her job is to enforce the law.

A **moral entrepreneur** has a strong concern with morally correct behavior.

From the perspective of conflict theory, the police in any society are hired agents of the rich and powerful, charged with keeping disruptive elements under control. Functionalist theorists, believing that the government represents the people, assume that law enforcement agents use force only upon imperfectly socialized individuals who must be restrained in order to maintain public order.

The actual conduct of police work, however, is governed by rules established within the organization as well as by law. Police bureaucracies are unique in some respects. The status of police officer demands not only conformity to organizational norms and rules but aggression and risk-taking on the job. Far more than any other public employee, an officer is under constant pressure from a variety of sources. As a member of a hierarchial organization, the officer must conform to the quasi-military discipline and norms of the department while maintaining sufficient flexibility to handle a variety of situations where there is no certain outcome, and where the threat of danger is always present. Furthermore, as the police are formal agents of social control, they are often not well-liked within the community. Many police officers conceal their occupation from their neighbors and prefer to wear plain clothes rather than their uniforms to and from work in order to avoid stigma, harassment, and even violence (Niederhoffer and Niederhoffer, 1978).

The officer's status is ambiguous, partly connected to the underworld, and partly linked to civilian life. Faced with hostility in both worlds, a high degree of social solidarity develops among members of a force. The police form an in-group, united against a variety of out-groups. This social cohesion is also strengthened by the threat of physical violence and death. While only 123 law enforcement officers were killed in the line of duty in the United States in 1978, the fear of sudden violence and death is a constant of police work. Accordingly, there is a strong reliance upon other officers for physical as well as psychological and social assistance. Police spouses and children often find themselves cut off from the greater part of the officer's life, a situation aggravated by irregular hours and shifts. As a consequence, the incidence of domestic violence, and marital problems, is high among police families.

Police Corruption. Corruption refers to acts contrary to public expectation involving deliberate engagement in or support of illegal activity. Corruption is, therefore, a violation of the trust placed in formal agents of social control. Tendencies toward corruption are built into the law enforcement system, as we noted in discussing victimless crime.

Police corruption is a violation of public trust.

Police work often calls for techniques of questionable legality such as reliance on informants, use of entrapment (trapping someone into committing an offense), and other forms of subterfuge ranging from the unmarked car of the highway patrol to the undercover work of an agent infiltrating the ranks of the American Nazi Party. Since the law enforcement agent would arrest the offender, it is also likely that a certain number of law breakers, ranging from speeders to members of organized crime, would attempt to bribe police officers.

A wave of police corruption scandals in the United States began to come to light in the 1970s, the most publicized of which was initiated by Frank Serpico, whose reports of corruption in the New York City Police Department made him the subject of a book and film. An investigating commission found that police corruption was widespread, ranging from "grass-eating", or minor nibbling from the purses of local merchants, to "meat-eating", or aggressive seeking and consumption of very large amounts of cash. The police, like other groups charged with social control, stand at "the invitational edges of corruption."

"The Invitational Edges of Corruption"

This study of the role of narcotics agents provides further insight into the broader structural problems of legal regulation. The narc is part of a bureaucracy formed to enforce laws against the manufacture, sale, and use of illegal substances. In most cases, the illegality consists of obtaining drugs without a physician's prescription.

There are many similarities between the legal and illegal markets for drugs. Both involve willing buyers and sellers; both are regulated by organizations whose mission is to make a profit; and both have an internal structure that seeks to reduce the kinds of sanctions used against them. The major difference between illicit and licit markets is the type of regulation: legal activities are licensed or inspected; illegal activities are controlled and patrolled by law enforcement agents. Accordingly, agents of law enforcement are viewed by illegal merchants as objects to be manipulated. This places a high level of stress upon the individual agent and can lead to his/her corruption.

Manning and Redlinger observed certain typical patterns of corruption among narcotics officers: (1) taking bribes; (2) becoming a drug user (offender) and thus, under the control of the illegal industry; (3) use of entrapment indistinguishable from drug peddling; (4) confiscation and appropriation of property that is diverted to the personal use of the law enforcement agent; (5) illegal search and seizure, in which suspects had evidence planted on them or additional drugs were added in order to "make a bust"; and (6) unwarranted use of violence (sometimes called physical therapy) on suspects.

Over time, the regulatory agency becomes indistinguishable from the business it seeks to control. Bribery, the use and buying of the product to be regulated, illegal surveillance and spying, dependence on informants, and expropriation of seized property characterize both. The invitational edges of corruption for narcotics agents are very real but not qualitatively different from those for other law enforcement agents. Nor are they appreciably different from the possibilities of corruption available to those who regulate legitimate business activity.

The police officer is not very different after all.

Source: Peter Manning and Lawrence J. Redlinger, in Paul Rock (ed.), *Politics and Drugs.* New York: Dutton/Society Books, 1976.

Trial and Punishment: The Judicial Process

The judicial process has three principal participants: the prosecutor or district attorney, the defense attorney, and the judge. They are assisted by many other actors in supporting roles but essentially the trial process is a *triad,* in which the prosecutor represents the interests both of society and any aggrieved parties, the defense attorney represents the accused, and the judge stands for impartial justice. Within the courtroom, two adversaries, the prosecutor and the defense attorney, argue before an allegedly impartial third party. While one cornerstone of the American and Canadian legal systems is the right to trial by a jury of one's peers, most trials, especially for minor offenses, take place before a judge without a jury.

The three principal parties in the criminal justice system process are the prosecutor, the defense attorney, and the judge.

COURT SYSTEMS IN THE UNITED STATES

There are two court systems in the United States: one for adults and the other for juveniles.

Adult Criminal Courts.   There is no unified system of criminal courts in the United States but rather a dual hierarchy of federal and state courts. At the top

The right to be tried by a jury of one's peers is guaranteed by the American legal system. (Source: Wide World Photos.)

of both the federal and state hierarchies is the United States Supreme Court, which hears appeals from both the lower federal courts and from state supreme or appeals courts.

Juvenile Courts.   The juvenile court system developed as a separate social control agency designed to keep children and adolescents from undergoing the stresses of adult criminal procedures and to emphasize the goal of treatment rather than punishment. Since the juvenile court judge was presumed to represent the interests of the child, legal safeguards provided to adult criminals were not thought necessary. However, over the last 15 years, the United States Supreme Court made several rulings which reduced the informality of the juvenile justice system. Precisely because the juvenile court was informal, it lent itself to arbitrary decisions; indeed whether a judge can act both as an agent of social control and an advocate for the child is open to question. Accordingly, today, juveniles who are charged with a crime have the following rights that were previously denied to them: (1) to know the nature of the charges against him or her; (2) to have legal counsel; (3) to confront witnesses; and (4) to avoid self-incrimination. These rights do not extend to status offenses such as truancy, running away, or unmanageability.

> The juvenile court system is designed to protect juveniles from the stresses and labelling of adult criminal procedures.

PROCESSING THE CRIMINAL

Just as the judicial system is complex, so is processing of the person accused of a crime. At every step in the process, decisions are made that influence the fate of the person suspected of committing a crime. After being arrested and charged with a crime, if the suspect cannot post (pay) bail, the suspect goes to jail to await trial. During this time, the accused might be advised to plea bargain ("cop a plea"), that is, plead guilty to a lesser charge. *Plea bargaining*, an agreement between the prosecution and the accused to reduce the charges if the defendent pleads guilty, is very controversial; its critics claim that it is used to the disadvantage of the poor or uneducated. By pleading to a lesser charge, the accused is promised a lighter sentence; at the same time, the prosecutors are able to clear cases and secure convictions, both of which are indicators of success in controlling crime, and the public is spared the costs of a trial.

> **Plea bargaining** is an agreement between the prosecution and the accused to reduce the charges in exchange for an admission of guilt.

What determines the type of sentence given to an offender? Although the range of penalties is set by law, judges have some flexibility. Public demands for fixed and firm penalties are often opposed by criminologists as leading to greater inequalities in the system. It has been noted, for example, that judges with limited options are likely to send people to prison (Nagel, 1980). On the other hand, sentencing policies are not always based upon considerations of the law. In fact, the single most important determinant of a state's prison population is the availability of cells. When more cells are available, more people are sentenced to prison (Nagel, 1980). Thus court practices are tied to the availability of prison space, so that as more prisons are built, proportionately fewer offenders are diverted to other programs.

STIFFER CRIMINAL PENALTIES—DO THEY MAKE A DIFFERENCE?

One proposed solution to the high rate of crime is to make punishment harsher and to let the public know it. Whether heavier punishments reduce the incidence of crime is hotly debated. Research data indicate that the type of offense is an important factor; some types of illegal acts are more easily deterred by the thought of punishment than others.

For example, a study of the impact of stiffer penalties for drunken driving in Great Britain showed that traffic fatalities were significantly reduced as a result (Ross, Campbell, and Glass, 1970). Automatic breath tests to those suspected of drunken driving or involved in an accident and mandatory punishments, including fines, loss of driver's license, and imprisonment, were instituted. When traffic fatality statistics before and after the new law were compared, a dramatic reduction in the monthly casualty rate was recorded. In this case, a widespread publicity campaign may have deterred drunken people from driving, but similar campaigns do not always have the expected results.

To assess the impact of publicity about the death penalty King (1978) undertook a study of the relationship between public awareness of executions and the homicide rate in South Carolina. Homicides neither increased nor decreased significantly with public awareness, nor did the actual occurrence of an execution have a demonstrable effect as either a brutalizing or a deterring factor.

A similar pattern has been observed with increased penalties for rape and attempted rape (Schwartz, 1968). A particularly brutal rape case in Pennsylvania led to the enactment of harsher punishments for this crime. Analysis of the available statistics on the incidence of forcible rape or serious injuries to victims found that the new law and the publicity surrounding its enactment had no effect. It appears that crimes of violence are not likely to be affected by harsher punishment, although minor offenses, such as drunken driving, are sensitive to stronger sanctions.

As we consider the deterrent effect of punishment for various types of crime, it is worth keeping in mind the differential application of penalties according to ascribed and achieved status characteristics of the offender. For example, in 1969, Federal courts convicted 502 people for tax fraud (averaging $190,000 per person convicted), but only 19 per cent were sentenced to prison. Those who were sent to prison had terms averaging 9.5 months. During the same year, these courts convicted 254 people for burglaries of federal property and banks, and almost 4,000 people for interstate motor vehicle theft. Sixty per cent of

There is no compelling evidence that harsher punishment reduces the level of crime.

Harsher punishment seems to have little effect on violent crimes, but a stronger effect on minor offenses.

"Which are you—a victim of society or a crook?" (Drawing by Ed Arno; © 1979 The New Yorker Magazine, Inc.)

these were sentenced to prison, for terms averaging over 20 months. Non-whites serve much longer sentences than whites convicted of the same crime; Federal Bureau of Prisons data show that, in 1970, the average sentence for non-whites convicted in drug cases was almost two years longer than that for whites. Similar patterns were observed for other offenses. Nor has this picture changed appreciably within the last decade. With a few exceptions, the stiffest criminal penalties are given out not to those who commit the most serious or costly crimes but to those who lack the power, wealth, and prestige to maneuver the judicial system to their own advantage.

The Debate over the Death Penalty. Throughout much of human history, offenders who disrupt social order have been dealt with harshly—with exile or death the ultimate sanctions. And for many years, up until 1967, the death penalty was an accepted element of the criminal justice system of the United States. *Capital punishment* is another term for application of the death penalty (from *capo*, "head"). In 1967, the United States Supreme Court rendered void most state statutes regarding capital punishment on the grounds that the laws were too vague and unevenly applied. Many social activists had hoped that the court would declare the death penalty a "cruel and unusual punishment" forbidden by the Fourth Amendment to the Constitution. The court refused to go this far and set more rigorous standards for judges and juries. Table 17-7 presents the kind of data that persuaded the court of racial bias in the application of the death penalty.

Between 1968 and 1978, only one execution took place in the United States

Capital punishment is the application of the death penalty.

Table 17-7. Prisoners Executed Under Civil Authority: 1930 to 1978
[*Excludes executions by military authorities. The Army (including the Air Force) carried out 160 (148 between 1942 and 1950, 3 each in 1954, 1955, and 1957, and 1 each in 1958, 1959, and 1961). Of the total, 106 were executed for murder (including 21 involving rape), 53 for rape, and 1 for desertion. The Navy carried out no executions during the period. See also Historical Statistics, Colonial Times to 1970, series H 1155—1167*]

Year or period	Total[1]	White	Black	Executed for murder Total[1]	White	Black	Executed for rape Total[1]	White	Black	Other offenses[2] Total[1]	White	Black
All years	3,860	1,752	2,066	3,335	1,665	1,630	455	48	405	70	39	31
1930–1939	1,667	827	816	1,514	803	687	125	10	115	28	14	14
1940–1949	1,284	490	781	1,064	458	595	200	19	179	20	13	7
1950–1959	717	336	376	601	316	280	102	13	89	14	7	7
1960–1964	181	90	91	145	79	66	28	6	22	8	5	3
1965–1967	10	8	2	10	8	2	—	—	—	—	—	—
1968–1976	—	—	—	—	—	—	—	—	—	—	—	—
1977–1978[3]	1	1	—	1	1	—	—	—	—	—	—	—

— Represents zero. [1]Includes races other than White or Black. [2]25 armed robbery, 20 kidnapping, 11 burglary, 8 espionage (6 in 1942, and 2 in 1953), and 6 aggravated assault. [3]No executions in 1978.
Source: *Statistical Abstract of the United States, 1979,* Table 341.

The U.S. Supreme Court, the highest Federal Court, consists of nine judges whose decisions are final and take precedence over those of all other judicial bodies in the country. In 1981, Sandra Day O'Connor was appointed to the Supreme Court, the first woman in the history of the United States to serve in that capacity. Justices are appointed by the President, confirmed by the Senate, serve for life and may be removed from office only by impeachment. (Source: Bill Fitz-Patrick, The White House.)

while the Court reviewed revised state laws. Today, several hundred prisoners are on death rows awaiting their socially-sanctioned death. These prisoners are there because of strong public opinion in favor of reinstituting the death penalty. Arguments in favor of capital punishment are based on two theses: (1) that the death penalty *deters* the commission of crime; and (2) death is a justifiable act of *retribution* on the part of agents of the state.

Deterrence. Fear and reported increases in crime rates have revived the belief that the harshness of a penalty will deter potential criminals, or ensure that one person, at least, will never commit another crime.

Opponents of the death penalty are quick to note that evidence to support the deterrence thesis is less than convincing. Indeed, most studies show no statistically significant murder-rate reduction due to the application of capital punishment (King, 1978; Bailey, 1980). Moreover, since most murders are crimes of passion committed against members of one's own family or friends, it is difficult to estimate how many would have been avoided through rational calculation of the punishment.

Supporters of capital punishment believe in its **deterrence** effect on potential criminals.

495

Retribution. In this view, executions are a visible means of redressing (balancing out) a social wrong. Somehow, members of a society feel avenged when they can see that a crime has not gone unpunished, regardless of the deterrent effect of the punishment. In other words, imprisonment or the death penalty is not applied to control the wrongdoer as much as for the general public. This is an extension of Durkheim's thesis that punishment is a means of reaffirming the moral norms of the community.

Opponents of the death penalty suggest that retribution is a dangerous motive for taking life in the name of the state because the latent message is, "See, we can kill him, too," thereby doing little to bolster a belief in the sanctity of human life. Publicized executions, from this perspective, are barbaric spectacles, evoking hate-filled emotions, and ultimately weakening the moral norms, especially when the penalty is selectively employed, as Table 17-7 illustrates, against certain subgroups.

But logical arguments over the manifest function of capital punishment are probably less important than a recognition of its latent consequences: to solidify the group against the threat of evil, and to reaffirm the essential virtue of those who do not need to use violence to secure success.

Prison Life

HISTORY OF AMERICAN PRISONS

The contemporary prison system in the United States has been influenced by two contradictory philosophies: *rehabilitation* and *punishment*. *Punishment* literally means the infliction of pain or penalty; *rehabilitation* denotes restoration to a former state of health. The penal system is caught between these two perspectives, attempting to rehabilitate and punish at the same time.

Within the past decade, controversy over the prison system has reemerged. At the same time that many claim that the prison system is too soft, there is renewed interest in rehabilitation programs. As of 1974, the most recent year for which data are available, 88 per cent of the 592 state prisons had a remedial education program, and 81 per cent had vocational training (*Statistical Abstract of the United States, 1979*). While these programs vary in quality and extent, they represent an attempt to stress the reform aspect of incarceration, probably stimulated by recent court decisions on overcrowding and ill treatment, and by riots against these conditions. As Schoen (1979) recently pointed out, "Virtually every prison in the country has been subject to a lawsuit, some so grandiose that a state's entire correctional system has been put into receivership." Some prisons have been forced to close because of inadequate and inhuman conditions. The contradictory heritages of punishment and salvation still coexist within the contemporary prison system of the United States.

PRISONS AS TOTAL INSTITUTIONS

Prisons and jails are *total institutions* (Goffman, 1961a) in which diverse human needs are handled by a bureaucratic organization that promotes group living. Prisons and jails have certain common features with military bases,

monasteries, mental hospitals, and nursing homes. As Goffman defined it, a total institution is a place where there is a breakdown of the barriers that typically separate sleep, work, and play. Ordinarily, these activities are carried out in different places, with different role partners and under different authorities. In the total institution, all aspects of life are conducted under the same authority and in the same physical locale. Furthermore, the total institution encourages batch living, where each person must carry out his or her activities in the presence of others, where everyone is required to do the same thing, and where all activities are closely scheduled and predictable, based on the needs of the institution and its staff. Inmates are stripped of preconfinement identities: clothed in prison garb, shaved, given a number, and subjected to other ceremonies of degradation and depersonalization.

Total institutions, such as prisons and jails, control and monitor all aspects of life.

While total institutions may be categorized according to their purpose—protection of the inept, isolation of dangerous persons, rehabilitation of the ill, and so forth—they are all *resocializing* institutions, designed to change people and their sense of selfhood (Goffman, 1961). Every total institution is a *mini-society* for its residents, and prisons are no exception. While there is an immense variety among prisons, ranging from the maximum security walled prison of Sing-Sing to the minimum security prison farm of Chino, California, all share certain characteristics: (1) restriction of personal freedom; (2) limited choice of work; (3) impersonality; (4) social distance between prisoners and prison officers and guards; (5) single-sex setting.

These structural aspects of the prison generate a subculture among inmates that is very different from that of the prison personnel. The subculture of prisoners includes such rules for behavior as: play it cool, do your own time, don't get involved; be tough; never inform on fellow inmates; don't sympathize with officials or accept their word. Inmates construct a definition of the situation

Abbott was placed in a reformatory at age 11, sent to prison at age 18, and by the age of 29 had been incarcerated for 18 years. He has served time in several different prisons for such crimes as issuing a check with insufficient funds, fatal assault while in prison, and bank robbery. Here are some excerpts from his letters to the novelist Norman Mailer:

"I've looked through steel bars so long it's odd not to see bars everywhere . . . . Walking through the gate into any unit is exactly like walking into a room lined with animal cages. Any prisoner has a full view of any other prisoner in his cell. All day there are arguments and threats hollered all over the place. It is not too different, really from the monkey house at the zoo."

"You try only to keep yourself together because others, other prisoners, are with you. You don't comfort one another; you humor one another. You can't stand the sight of each other and yet you are doomed to stand and face one another . . . . You must bathe together, defecate and urinate together, eat and sleep together."

"It's the prison system . . . that drives us to outrages on one another. We are not animals but we are herded like animals . . . . You can't know how sad I feel when I realize the source of, and the nature of, the involuntary pride and exhilaration all convicts feel when they are chained up hand and foot as though they were vicious lions . . . . They make killers out of pussycats like that . . . . The world is focused on us for a moment. We are somebody capable of threatening the world in some way—no matter how small a way."

In 1981, while on parole, Abbott stabbed and killed a waiter outside a New York restaurant, claiming that he thought himself about to be attacked. On January 22, 1982, Abbott was convicted of manslaughter.

Source: Excerpted from "In Prison": Jack Henry Abbott, *New York Review of Books*, XXVII, 11, June 26, 1980.

that rationalizes their conduct and reinforces the values of their subculture. Very few will be resocialized to the norms of straight society without exposure to competing norms, the opportunity to learn skills for success in the outside world, or contact with family.

Both staff and inmates must adjust to the requirements of institutional order. As Conrad (1973) pointed out, these accommodations "are inconsistent with rehabilitation . . . . In any prison, regardless of the hazards to safety, the discomforts and irritations of the present occupy the attentions of everyone". and irritations of the present occupy the attentions of everyone".

CONDITIONS IN PRISON: WHOSE FAULT?

Total institutions exert total control, and, given the public's low evaluation of inmates, this control can become tyrannical. Inmates' property may be destroyed, reading censored, associates monitored, visitors limited, and very lives threatened (Greenberg and Stender, 1972). What makes conditions in prison so difficult? Is it the character of the prison officials who brutalize prisoners? Or is it the prisoners themselves who, by their past histories, have demonstrated that they need to be restrained with strong measures? Both of these questions are framed along dispositional reasoning; that is, that there is a predisposition among certain individuals to act in certain ways. An alternative approach is the *situational view:* it is the social situation and the particular statuses and roles assigned to individuals that produce certain kinds of behavior. Remember the experiment described in Chapter 5 in which mentally healthy volunteers, all similar in personality traits and attitudes, were randomly assigned the role of

X **Dispositional** and **situational** reasoning are two conflicting explanations for the behavior of inmates.

prisoner and guard. The experiment had to be halted within a week because of emotional breakdowns among the "prisoners" and sadistic behaviors among the "guards." The mock prison experiment provides insight into the real world of the prison. One's status in the social structure of the prison—prisoner or guard—was both a determinant of behavior and of beliefs about the self. Against the context of this experiment, such events as prison riots become more understandable. One of the most savage prison riots in United States history occurred in the New Mexico State Penitentiary in 1980, leaving 33 inmates dead, 80 injured, and $82 million worth of damage to the prison (Boston *Globe*, 2/17/80). Unlike the Attica Prison riot in 1971, in which 32 inmates and 11 correctional officers were killed by state police bullets, all the deaths in the New Mexico Penitentiary were of inmates by inmates. Overcrowded, with 1,136 men in space designed to accommodate 850, this penitentiary had been the site of unrest for several years. The rioting prisoners soon took control of the prison and, rather than killing guards, began to murder and mutilate informers (inmates who had traded information for privileges).

The prison experience increases tension and hatred among prisoners, while overcrowding and other conditions provide the immediate pretext for riots. As data in Table 17-8 suggest, many state prisons are old (13 per cent were built before 1899), understaffed, and with wide variation in their annual operating expenditures. Are there alternatives? In 1973, the Commission of Standards and Goals for Criminal Justice observed that "the correctional system to date appears to offer minimum protection to the public and maximum harm to the offender" (quoted in Schoen, 1979). Yet, in response to public demands for

Overcrowding and violence are the basic conditions of prison life. (Source: *Susan S. Perry, Woodfin Camp and Associates.*)

Characteristic and per cent of all institutions					
Year of initial construction		*Full-time prison staff*		*Annual operating expenditures*	
Before 1899 and unknown	13%	Less than 20	42%	Less than $200,000	29%
1899–1923	10	20–99	23	$200,000–1 million	34
1924–1948	31	100–299	15	$1 million–$3 million	14
1949–1969	40	300 or more	11	$3 million or more	15
1970–1973	6	unknown	9	Unknown	8

Source: *Statistical Abstract of the United States, 1979*, Table 333.

larger and more secure prisons, massive building programs are underway in almost every state. It is estimated that construction expenses for each bed today are $100,000, plus operating costs of about $20,000 to $25,000 per year. This is an expensive solution, over twice the cost of a Harvard education.

Alternatives to building include: (1) community-based programs except for the most dangerous offenders; (2) small correctional facilities where there is a high level of social interaction between staff and inmates, and employment for which prisoners are paid competitive wages, and from which they pay income taxes and the costs of their incarceration; (3) home-like surroundings which one may decorate as one chooses; and (4) short-term home furloughs. The alternatives have been used with success in several European countries.

But the basic problem that has plagued the prison system since its inception in the United States and Canada remains: Should prison attempt to treat and rehabilitate? Or is the function of the prison to cause pain and discomfort on the "eye for an eye" principle? The two positions are not easily reconciled.

Summary

Every society has its rules and conformists as well as its deviants against whom negative social sanctions are applied.

Crime, a particular type of deviant behavior, is defined as conduct against the law. Certain types of behavior are labeled as crimes when there are sufficiently strong feelings that these actions must be officially placed off limits and violators punished.

While definitions of what behavior is criminal vary from time to time and from one society to another, it is unlikely that there was ever a society without crime. Identification of behavior as off limits has a dual function: it strengthens the norms of a society and it ensures that those norms are protected.

Various explanations of criminal and delinquent behavior suggest that crime is a social construct and is learned behavior. Not all criminals receive the same penalty for the same crime; those who are of a lower social status and members of a minority group are more likely to be imprisoned or executed than those of higher social status or whites.

The experience of prison has negative consequences on a large number of inmates. Criminals who are sentenced to institutions are largely cut off from non-criminal models of social behavior, and socialized to pro-criminal activity in prison. Accordingly, they often learn the techniques, language, attitudes, and behaviors of other criminals.

Whether the threat of punishment has a deterrent effect remains a hotly debated question. Some criminologists have argued that certainty of punishment is a more important deterrent than severity. Others have argued that it depends upon the offense; those crimes that are relatively minor, and nonemotionally charged, are deterred by certain punishment while more serious crimes of passion, such as murder, are rarely inhibited by the thought of certain punishment. Still others have proposed that retribution, not deterrence, is necessary.

All these factors have led to a basic contradiction in approaches to handling the offender. The penal system, in both the United States and Canada, has been trapped between two contradictory philosophies: deterrence and punishment on the one hand, and rehabilitation on the other. Yet there is little consensus about the norms of justice, and debates about whether the punishment should fit the crime continue. Interestingly, those most likely to support an "eye for an eye" type of punishment are those least likely to be arrested and imprisoned for a crime. Consistently, the law enforcement system has come down hardest on those with little power, wealth, or prestige.

Suggested Readings

GINGER, ANN FAGAN. *The Law, the Supreme Court and the People's Rights* (2nd Edition) (New York: Barron's, 1977). Ginger traces the historical development of civil liberties, civil rights, and the rights of criminal defendants under the United States legal system.

JACKSON, GEORGE. *Soledad Brother: The Prison Letters of George Jackson* (New York: Coward-McCann, 1970). This dramatic first-hand account illuminates the experiences of those who defy the agents of law enforcement.

JOHNSON, JOHN M., and JACK D. DOUGLAS (Eds.). *Crime at the Top: Deviance in Business and the Professions* (Philadelphia: J.P. Lippincott, 1978). This collection of 21 essays explores the nature of deviant business and professional practices in everyday life including land-sale frauds, price fixing, stock-market manipulations, and deceiving the elderly.

McCAGBY, CHARLES H. *Crime in American Society* (New York: Macmillan, 1980). A readable overview of the many forms of criminal activity in the United States: organized, white-collar, organizational, and street crime.

MOORE, JOAN. *Homeboys: Gangs, Drugs and Prison in the Barrios of Los Angeles* (Philadelphia: Temple University Press, 1980). The Hispanic barrio provides the setting for Moore's account of drug dealing, youth gangs, and imprisonment. Implications for social policy are carefully drawn.

QUINNEY, RICHARD. *Critique of Legal Order: Crime Control in Capitalist Society.* (Boston: Little, Brown, 1974.) A hard look at the criminal justice system and the control of crime from a conflict perspective by a leading criminologist.

RETTIG, RICHARD P., MANUEL J. TORRES, and GERALD R. GARRETT. *Manny: A Criminal-Addict's Story* (Boston: Houghton Mifflin, 1977). An integrated theoretical perspective is used to develop the life history of Manny Torres from his youth as a member of a gang, becoming a drug addict, a criminal, a convict and eventually a parolee, told in Manny's own words.

18 Urban and Suburban Life

*D*ifferences of opinion about the vices and virtues of urban life are probably as old as the first ancient city. Ruins or traces of cities have been found by archeologists in the Near East, Asia, and West Africa. From these remnants, it is estimated that cities evolved about 6000 years ago as centers of government, agriculture, commerce, and/or religion.

This chapter surveys what happens to social institutions and social interaction as city life becomes the prevailing pattern and as rural and village life declines. In order to understand the impact of the city upon social institutions and value systems, you will also learn about the growth of the city and suburbs, and some of the problems associated with urban and suburban residence in North America at the present time.

Urban life has been associated with assertiveness, masculinity, intellect, power, and danger; the suburbs and countryside with domesticity, rest, closeness to nature, and safety. Although these lifestyles are social inventions, it is the city that has been singled out by critics as the height of artificiality. For example, Thomas Jefferson commented that American cities were "pestilential to the morals, health, and liberties of man" and viewed a then rampant yellow fever epidemic as a blessing in disguise that would reduce the urban population (Fischer, 1976).

Four interwoven themes have dominated debates on the merits of urban or rural life: (1) nature versus art, where the city may be described as either more civilized or depraved than the hinterland; (2) familiarity versus strangeness, where the city is associated with the new, the different, the unexpected; the rustic with familiar things and people; (3) community, or *Gemeinschaft*, relations exist in the rural area as opposed to the impersonal *Gesellschaft*, social relations that dominate urban life; and (4) tradition versus change, in which the countryside is the stronghold of traditional values, the city the site of secular, tradition-shattering values and social norms (Fischer, 1976). These four themes illustrate an historical ambivalence toward the city. On the one hand, the city symbolizes freedom, progress, excitement, and innovation. On the other hand, it is seen as contrived, lonely, stressful, and ugly. By and large, the evidence suggests that both rural and village life have been romanticized by most North Americans who long for the relative simplicity and isolation of the countryside. Thus, according to a 1972 Gallup poll in the United States, 32 per cent of those surveyed indicated they would prefer to live in a small town, 23 per cent on a farm, and 31 per cent in a suburb, if they could live anywhere they wanted. Only 13 per cent chose the city. Yet the majority of North Americans—about three quarters, live in what are defined as urban areas. If city life is so unattractive, how can this pattern be explained? The major reasons for migrating to or remaining in the city have been associated with modernization and division of labor. In industrialized societies, the urban setting has traditionally provided not only a more differentiated occupational structure but greater economic opportunity and more and better jobs.

Figure 18-1.
The development of the city in historical perspective.

Migratory bands   Rural/Farms   Cities

Human Evolution   10,000 Years Ago   5,000 Years   Today

Archaeologists estimate that cities evolved approximately 6,000 years ago. Pictured here are the ruins of Petra, an ancient city in Jordan. (Source: Hubertus Kanus, Rapho/Photo Researchers, Inc.)

Growth of the City

URBANIZATION

A major step in the process of modernization has been *urbanization,* or the concentration of large numbers of people of diverse occupations and backgrounds in cities. Only in the past hundred years has urban life been the norm for the majority of the population. The development of machine technology and the expansion of the factory system and mass transportation enhanced the growth of large cities following the Industrial Revolution. Although major cities have existed at least since the days of the Old Testament, the societies in which they were located remained primarily rural, with most members engaged in village agriculture and crafts.

Before 1850, no society or nation was predominantly urban. In 1900, only England was an urbanized nation. Yet by 1980, all industrialized societies were highly urbanized, a process that is accelerating worldwide. Figure 18-2 shows the rapid growth of population in towns of 20,000 or over for four nations since 1850 when relatively few people lived in cities of that size. Despite the different rates of urbanization during various time periods, industrial nations such as Argentina, postindustrial ones such as the United States, and industrializing countries such as Brazil and Mexico all show an increase in urbanization that is associated with technological change.

There are three major characteristics of *urbanization:* (1) density of population, and either (2) size of the population in a geographic area or (3) varieties of statuses. Generally, the larger the number of people with different ascribed and achieved status within a defined geographic space, the more likely are we to describe the area as urban. In the urban environment, overt symbols of power, prestige, and wealth—the size of one's home, the neighborhood in which one

Urbanization involves the concentration in cities of large numbers of people of differing occupations and backgrounds.

The three major characteristics of urbanization are density, size, and heterogeneity of the population.

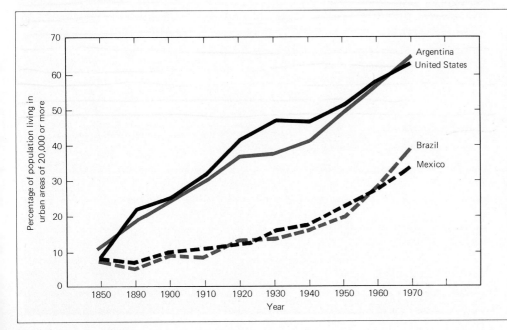

Figure 18-2.
The process of urbanization in the United States, Argentina, Mexico, and Brazil, 1850–1970. (Source: Statistical Abstract of Latin America, Vol. 19. Los Angeles: University of California at Los Angeles, Latin American Center Publications, 1978, Table 627, p. 81. Data selected from a larger table.)

lives, the car one drives, and the clothing worn—are more important in defining one's status and identity than in more rural localities. In the countryside or small town, one's family history, economic position, and personal characteristics are well known by others; overt status symbols have far less meaning.

Urbanization does not hinge on some magic number or absolute size or density. Rather, it is a continuum, a matter of degree (Wirth, 1938; Davis, 1959; Redfield, 1947). For example, in many agricultural villages in India the average number of people per room is greater than that found in some of the largest cities. Yet they are not urbanites; the geographic area that they inhabit, the size

Urbanization is a matter of degree rather than absolute numbers, size, or density.

These two views of San Francisco, California, show the urbanization that has taken place since 1850. (Source: Photo Researchers, Inc., and Peter Menzel, Stock, Boston.)

Table 18-1. Rural and Urban Life: Typology and Continuum

Characteristic	Rural—————Urban
Heterogenity of population	Low —————— High
Availability of organizations and services	Low —————— High
Division of labor	Low —————— High
Potential anonymity of individual	Low —————— High
Predominant nature of social relationships	*Gemeinschaft* —————— *Gesellschaft*
Predominant type of social control	Informal —————— Formal
Degree of status ranking on the basis of overt symbols	Low —————— High

Note: an *ideal type* of rural society is described under the heading "rural," and an *ideal type* of urban society is described under the heading "urban." Since ideal types are rarely seen in real life, the lines between "rural" and "urban" indicate that there is a continuum on each of the dimensions listed.
Source: Adapted from Butler, 1976, p. 266

of the village population, and the degree of division of labor are all too small. Some of the differences between rural and highly urbanized life are summarized in Table 18-1.

This typology is based on characteristics that may not exist in their pure form but that indicate the major differences between rural and urban ways of living, and that appear to some degree in real-life situations.

Statistical Definitions of Urbanization.   While sociologists do not universally agree about the definition of the term "urban," a variety of definitions have been developed by demographers who have used *population size* as a yardstick. There are several advantages to this criterion, one important one being the availability of accurate data on population size in many countries. Furthermore, since large communities are more diverse and provide greater opportunities for different lifestyles, occupations, living arrangements, and so forth, population size may have an effect on other aspects of social life. Knowing the size of the population of a city thus allows us to make some guesses about what life may be like there. Keep in mind, however, that what may be a reasonably accurate guess about lifestyles and behavior in one part of the country or about one nation may not be accurate about another, since social norms and values are more important factors than sheer size of the population.

Demographers in the United States describe geographic areas as urbanized if they have 2,500 inhabitants or more, and in Canada as urbanized if there are 1,000 or more inhabitants. Often metropolitan areas such as Toronto, Vancouver, San Francisco, Boston, New York, and Washington, D.C. spill beyond their municipal divisions and encompass smaller cities, towns, and even some rural and semi-rural areas. To describe such units, demographers have introduced the term *metropolitan area.*

Standard Metropolitan Statistical Area (SMSA) is the term used by the United States Census Bureau to denote a largely nonagricultural, continuous geographic area containing a city or set of twin cities of at least 50,000 people.

Population size is often used as a measure of urbanization in statistical definitions.

Census Metropolitan Area (CMA) is used by the Canadian Census to describe a continuous built-up area of 100,000 population or more. While neither term fully captures the diversity of the areas within its boundaries, both convey the notion of an urban rather than rural or village locale.

URBANISM

Akin to the concept of urbanization is *urbanism*. While urbanization generally denotes the factors of size, density, and heterogeneity of a population within a spatial location, *urbanism* is a social phenomenon or way of life, in which traditional lifestyles associated with rural and village life are replaced by norms and individualistic styles of behavior (Redfield, 1941).

Many sociologists have been appalled by the effects of city life. For example, Louis Wirth (1938), in a classic essay on urbanism, proposed that the density and diversity of large cities have negative psychological and social consequences. Urban life exposes one to a barrage of stimulation that is difficult to handle. Primary group ties are increasingly difficult to maintain, as individuals engage in temporary and segmented role relationships. In turn, both social control mechanisms and informal support networks are loosened. Left to face their difficulties alone, city dwellers are more vulnerable to suicide, alcoholism, mental illness, and criminality. More recently, this view has been supported by Milgram (1970) who claims that the urban environment produces "psychic overload" that is difficult for most individuals to handle easily.

This portrait of the negative impact of urban life has been seriously challenged. There is, for example, no evidence that mental illness is more common in the city than elsewhere (Srole, 1972), nor that deaths from alcoholism are higher (Gove, Hughes, and Galle, 1979). Primary group ties are not weakened; indeed, contact with kin is as frequent among urban dwellers as among rural residents. (Wilensky and Lebeaux, 1965; Berry, 1973). Suicide rates and use of stress-reducing drugs are now slightly *higher* in rural than in urban areas (Gove, Hughes, and Galle, 1979). As Dewey (1960) pointed out, urbanism is *not* a way of life confined to the city; rather, it is a trait associated with whole societies and not simply population size and density.

An urbanized society is characterized by patterns of behavior, social structure, and ideologies that are worldly, dynamic, civilized, and highly literate (Dewey, 1960). Ruralized societies, on the other hand, are ones in which ritual, tradition, kinship loyalty, and stability are valued, even among those living in the city. For example, in medieval Europe, as in preindustrial nations today, life was largely ruralized, with few differences in social institutions, quality of life, or intellectual vitality between the city and the country.

In modernized nations, urban-rural differences once more diminish. Whether you live in New York City, Vancouver, Yellowknife, or Peoria, you are living in an urbanized society. Even the most remote farm is touched by information diffused from urban areas via television, films, books, radio, and newspapers. Interaction between city and rural residents has also been promoted by national highway systems. (Firey, Loomis, and Beegle, 1950). While the term urbanism has been traditionally used to describe the ways of thinking and acting of people in the city, it is more than that. Urbanism also means cosmopolitanism (from the Greek, *Kosmos*, or "world"), where ways of thought, values, and innovations flow from metropolitan to rural areas and are spread throughout

Urbanism refers to various aspects of the way of life in cities.

the society. Similar constructions of reality are shared by residents of city and the countryside. The occurrence of urbanism is thus closely linked with the development and expanding influence of the city.

The Development of the North American City

The growth of the city has been particularly dramatic in North America. In the United States in 1790, there were only 3.9 million people, or an average of 4.5 people per square mile. Values and belief systems were dominated by traditional, rural patterns except in a few cities. There were no cities with a population as large as 50,000, and only 5 per cent of the people lived in towns of more than 2,500. By 1870, the United States population was 25 per cent urban, and by 1920, 50 per cent. In 1981, the total population was approximately 229 million or about 73 people per square mile, three-fourths of whom live in urban areas as defined by the census (Population Reference Bureau, 1981).

In Canada, a comparable growth of urbanization has occurred, albeit at a later date than in the United States. In 1851, 13 per cent of Canadians lived in urban areas; as of 1981, 76 per cent of the 24 million population were urban residents. All provinces, with the exception of Prince Edward Island, have more than half their inhabitants in urban areas, and Ontario and Quebec have at least four out of every five people living in densely settled areas.

In neither country is the population evenly distributed among geographic regions. For example, the island of Manhattan in New York City has an average density of 75 thousand people per square mile, and 23.6 million others live within a 10-mile radius (Hauser and Schnore, 1965). Close to three in every ten Canadians live in the three largest metropolitan areas of Toronto, Montreal, and Vancouver. Population estimates for 1977 show that the density of people in the United States is greatest in counties within 50 miles of coastal shorelines, as Table 18-2 indicates.

Table 18-2. Population of the United States per Square Mile Residing in Counties Within 50 Miles of Coastal Shorelines and Remainder of the United States

Shoreline	Average number of people per square mile
Atlantic	407.7
Pacific	198.7
Great Lakes	221.9
Gulf of Mexico	119.8
Rest of the United States	40.5

Source: *Statistical Abstract of the United States*, 1979, p. 10, Table 7.

A megalopolis consists of overlapping metropolitan areas within a small geographic region with many social, economic and transportation links.

Because so many people are concentrated in relatively small geographic areas, increased attention has been paid to the super-metropolitan region, characterized by social, economic, and transport links between overlapping metropolitan areas. Described by Gottman (1961) as *megalopolis* (from the Greek, *mega*, "large," and *polis*, or "city"), one such stretch is "Bo-Wash," an almost continuous area of urban and suburban communities extending from north of Boston to just south of Washington, D.C. and from the coast of the Atlantic Ocean to the Appalachian foothills—a large region indeed.

Although predicted by some urban scholars as the wave of the future, the megalopolis has grown during the last decade at a slower rate than expected as the United States population has shifted from the large metropolitan areas of the Northeast and North Central areas to the promises of sun, fun, and expanding industrialization of the sunbelt states (Biggar, 1979). The most rapidly developing regions in Canada have been Alberta and British Columbia where peo-

Some Descriptive Models of Urban Ecology

Studies since the 1920s have shown that cities in most Western industrialized nations develop according to one of three basic models: (1) the *concentric zone*, (2) the *sector*, and (3) the *multiple nuclei*.

The *concentric-zone* model (Burgess, 1925) described the city as a series of circles built around a central core (zone 1) that contains the cultural center and business district. Just beyond the central core lies the zone of transition, encompassing both industrial and commercial activity and residential slums, transient rooming houses, cheap hotels, and other rundown dwellings. Zone 3 contains housing for blue-collar workers as well as shops designed to meet their needs while zone 4 is comprised of single family detached houses, where white-collar workers reside and satellite shopping centers develop. Zone 5, the commuter's, is bounded by the richer residences of zone 4 but also includes suburbs, estates for the wealthy and near rich, industrial plants, and local workers' housing. Based largely upon observation of Chicago and similar, older, industrial cities, the concentric zone model describes the spatial arrangement of some, but not all, large cities.

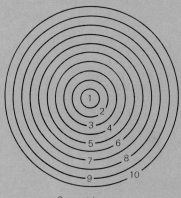

Concentric zone

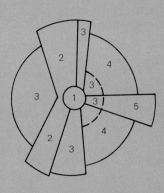

Sector

ple have been lured by the wealth of oil, natural gas, and new industry. The Canadian Northwest, like the American sunbelt, has experienced rapid economic growth and in-migration of people.

Reasons for Rapid Growth of Cities. Sociologists generally agree that there are several conditions required for the growth of cities: (1) an agricultural base able to produce food surpluses that can support both the rural and urban population; (2) an efficient transportation system; and (3) provision of jobs and services in urban areas attractive enough to pull people from the countryside (Davis, 1959; Taylor, 1980). Urbanization is thus closely tied to modernization and industrialization, machine technology, and division of labor.

Prior to the Industrial Revolution, the majority of people farmed the land to support both themselves and the minority in the city. At the end of the American Civil War, about one third of the population was still engaged in farming.

> The rapid growth of cities is linked to modernization, industrialization, technology, and division of labor.

Pittsburgh and New Orleans, for example, resemble more closely the *sector* model (Hoyt, 1939) where certain physical aspects of the city, such as transportation routes, unusual scenic beauty, or geographic barriers modify the shape and growth patterns of cities. Cities thus become divided into a number of sectors, radiating from the central business district. Those areas best situated for industry or trade because of their location will expand in one sector, residential areas along another route.

The third model of urban ecology is the *multiple nuclei* (Harris and Ullman, 1945). Unlike the concentric zone and sector theories, the multiple nuclei approach is based on the assumption that the city has not just one but several nuclei or centers, each of which is devoted to different activities. Similar land uses tend to cluster, and like attracts like. Thus, one nucleus may be devoted entirely to financial activities, another to manufacturing, another to government, and so forth. The specialized facilities within a given area attract those who support it, and the city becomes differentiated.

Each of these three models is here illustrated graphically.

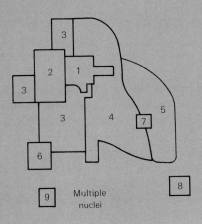

District

1. Central business district
2. Wholesale light manufacturing
3. Low-class residential
4. Medium-class residential
5. High-class residential
6. Heavy manufacturing
7. Outlying business district
8. Residential suburb
9. Industrial suburb
10. Commuters' zone

Multiple nuclei

After World War I, as tractors and other power-driven equipment reduced the amount of manual labor required for agriculture, migration from the farms increased. In 1979 alone, about 37,000 self-employed farmers sold their land to commercial farming corporations (agribusiness), continuing a 44-year trend toward fewer, larger, and more efficient farms (*New York Times,* December 29, 1979). Farmers now account for a scant 3.6 per cent of the United States population. It is not surprising that the spatial distribution of people has shifted and that land uses have changed dramatically.

THE ECOLOGY OF THE URBAN SCENE

The term *human ecology* was coined by Robert Park in 1921 to describe the physical relationship between people and land use. Park and his associates at the University of Chicago observed a series of phases in human ecology. In small-scale, primarily rural societies, there are few specialized land uses in either city or country. When distinct areas are allocated for specific uses, these are generally clustered. In the contemporary metropolitan center, however, specialized land use is the norm, often enforced by zoning regulations that control what kind of use may be made of land. Neighborhoods are designated as industrial, business, multi-family, or single-family dwellings.

Although the growth of most cities has not been shaped by official policies, classical social ecologists such as MacKensie (1926) have noted processes common to urbanization in many societies. These include: (1) *concentration;* (2) *segregation;* (3) *invasion;* and (4) *succession. Concentration,* the first phase of urbanization, occurs when large numbers of people settle in a relatively small space. This leads to overcrowding, in turn promoting decentralization of activities so that people and industries spread from the center of the city to outlying areas.

With decentralization of activities comes *segregation,* or ecological differentiation, where specific activities become spatially identified with particular areas of the city, and are physically isolated from others. In this fashion, the city becomes characterized by an observable financial district, retail trade center, and residential sector, each separate from the others.

Cities are never static. Any differentiated area is open to *invasion* by new activities or populations. For example, industries may encroach upon a residential neighborhood, a warehouse district can be converted into luxury condominiums, or a traditionally black neighborhood may be repopulated by Puerto Ricans. Once this process of ecological invasion is more or less complete, *succession,* where one activity or group of people supplants another, has occurred.

From a conflict-theory perspective, this description of urban development has been criticized as deterministic. That is, technology and land uses have been treated as almost predestined processes in urbanization rather than as the results of social inequality and conflict (Tabb and Sawers, 1978). Conflict theorists have proposed that the present physical forms of the city merely reinforce and reflect economic, ethnic, and racial stratification (Gordon, 1978; Castells, 1976). In short, rather than a gradual, social evolutionary process, urbanization is shaped by political and economic forces. Gordon (1978) has proposed that urbanization in capitalistic societies has been governed by three basic stages in the development of capital formation.

Human ecology describes the physical relationship between people and land use.

Concentration occurs when large numbers of people settle in a relatively small area.

Segregation, occurs when specific activities take place in specific areas of the city.

Differentiated areas are subject to **invasion** by new populations and activities.

Succession is the completed cycle of ecological invasion.

Table 18-3. Stages of the Economy and Type of City Growth

Stage of capitalism	City type
Commercial accumulation of wealth———→	Commercial city (mixed land use)
Competitive accumulation of wealth———→ through manufacturing and industry	Industrial city (large factories and slums in city)
Corporate accumulation and monopoly———→ of wealth by conglomerates	Corporate city (no vital central core)

Source: Summarized from Gordon, 1978.

As Table 18-3 shows, the industrial city corresponds most closely to the concentric zone model, while the corporate city resembles the multiple nuclei model of classical ecology (see Figure 18-3). In contrast to the functional explanations offered by traditional demographers, a conflict approach highlights the following processes (Gordon, 1978):

FROM COMMERCIAL TO CORPORATE CITY

In North America prior to 1850, cities were organized around craft manufacturing, commerce, transportation, or politics. These early urban centers more closely resembled the medieval city than the contemporary metropolis. Dominated by informal street life, random placement of streets, shops, and dwellings, the haphazard arrangements of buildings and people promoted spontaneity in social relationships. Only as land became more expensive did the urban grid of rectangular or square city blocks begin to develop and specific land uses become identified.

By 1850, the commercial city began to be replaced by the *industrial* city, dominated by the factory, the railroad, and the slum. The large industrial city is particularly suited to two functions: (1) economy of scale, that is, large numbers of workers could be employed within a single factory or series of factories and a surplus labor pool built up within the city to meet expanding needs; and (2) enforcement of labor discipline. In the large city, the working classes were more isolated from the middle and upper social strata. As economic and residential differences increased and social cohesion lessened, the industrial city became an ethnically, racially, and economically segregated place to live.

The industrial city just described was relatively short-lived. By the beginning of the twentieth century, industrial plants were being built in vacant areas outside the central city. Whole industrial satellite cities, such as Gary, Indiana, which was developed by United States Steel, emerged. Decentralization of industry was aided by the availability of electrical power lines, trucks and highways, and the automation of manufacturing, processes that developed even more rapidly after World War II. The introduction of assembly line production demanded a different kind of industrial plant. Rather than the old, multistory factory of the industrial city, the vast one- or two-story building, where a large number of employees could work on an assembly line on the same floor, was more cost-efficient. Between 1899 and 1901, industrial employment in twelve of

Large **industrial** cities emerged in response to the need for ready pools of disciplined laborers.

the thirteen largest industrial districts in the United States increased 100 per cent faster in outlying, new, industrial suburbs than within the city itself (Ashton, 1978).

While technology promoted development of the city (Banfield, 1974), conflict theorists have been quick to point out that the suburbanization of industry predated many technological innovations. Gordon (1978) has proposed that suburbanization of industry began precisely to reduce and avoid labor-management conflict. As the trade union movement organized in the industrial city, factory owners found it advantageous to erect an isolated mill or plant in a new suburb, thereby reducing the potential contact their employees might have with union organizers and workers in other factories. Relocating industries from the central city had other economic advantages for the owners—reduced taxes and shorter commuting time. The flight from the city in order to reduce municipal tax payments persists today as industries increasingly relocate outside central cities and out of the Northeast altogether.

Industries have moved out of the inner cities for economic, political, and labor-related reasons.

An additional factor promoting industrial growth outside the central city was a shift in the political power base. The old commercial city and the early industrial city had been largely dominated by political leaders closely related to the social and economic elite. As central cities grew, and migrants from rural areas and from abroad streamed into the city, the old economic elite found its power eroded by the new political machines, dominated by and seeking votes from these newcomers. Not only was the machine more responsive to the needs of its worker constituency than to the elite, but it was often corrupt (Ashton, 1978). Inability to control political machines based on urban workers' votes provided additional incentives for owners to relocate industry beyond the city limits (Mollenkopf, 1978).

THE GROWTH OF THE CORPORATE CITY

The corporate city developed when manufacturing was decentralized and economic power consolidated in smaller towns and cities.

The corporate city began to evolve as manufacturing was decentralized and capital consolidated in the early 1900s. It was not until the 1920s, however, that economic power were sufficiently centralized that skyscraper business and financial districts developed within the central city (Gordon, 1978; Blumenfeld, 1964). Two parallel transformations took place in the urban locale: at the same time that industry was relocating to the periphery of the city, the old downtown shopping district was gradually taken over by office buildings serving as focal points of power for the administration of industry and the development of service industries such as banks, life insurance companies, and so forth.

The typical corporate cities of the United States, however, are not the old industrial centers such as New York, Detroit, or Chicago, but the newer cities in the sunbelt, such as Dallas, Phoenix, Atlanta, and Houston. In Canada, similar shifts have occurred with the Western cities of Edmonton, Regina, Calgary, Winnipeg, and Vancouver experiencing rapid growth. With few identifiable factory districts within the city, the working class scattered, and suburban shopping malls replacing the downtown shopping area, the corporate city resembles the multiple nuclei model proposed by Harris and Ullman (1945): the fragmented metropolis.

With a few notable exceptions, the central city is no longer the source of technological innovation; rather, industrial parks in suburbs and strip cities are more likely to produce such change. Silicon Valley, a large area well outside

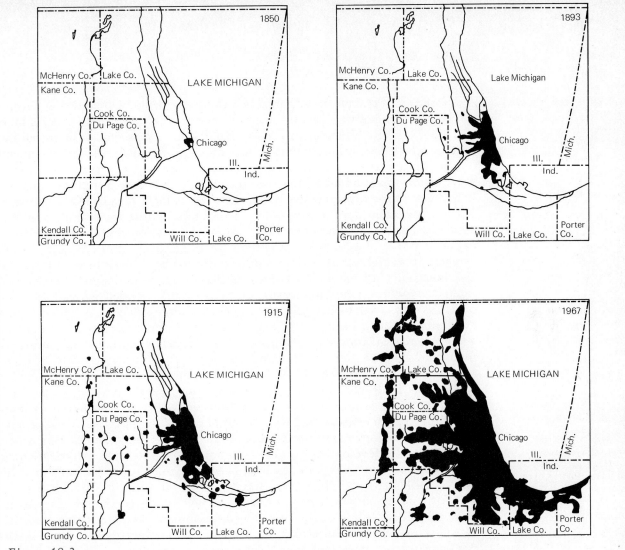

Figure 18-3.
Phases in the growth of Chicago, Illinois. (Source: *Abridged from Sternlieb and Hughes, 1980.*)

the municipal limits of San Francisco, and Route 128, beyond the initial ring of suburbs of Boston, are two such sites where mass industry and large labor pools have been replaced by high level technology firms employing white-collar technicians and managers who live nearby (Sternlieb and Hughes, 1980).

Figure 18-3 summarizes the development of one city, Chicago, Illinois, as it changed from a commerical city in 1850 to a corporate city in 1967. In 1850 Chicago covered a small geographic area on the shore of Lake Michigan. By 1893 the city had begun to send streamers outward, and there were also a few isolated factory suburbs. By 1915, the development of suburbs and exurbs was even more pronounced. In 1967, Chicago's metropolitan area included not only a large, continuous area in Illinois and Indiana, but a series of outlying districts. The growth and development of these outlying districts, suburbs, is examined in the following section.

The Suburbs

A suburb is part of the metropolitan area, often linked to the central city's economic and social activities.

A suburb is part of a metropolitan area beyond the political boundaries of a city but bound to the central city by economic and social links (Boskoff, 1970; Martin, 1956). Although they are the most rapidly growing sector of metropolitan areas in North America, suburbs are not unique to the modern era. Both ancient and medieval cities had their suburbs, but they were unlike suburbs in contemporary industrial and post-industrial societies in that they were most often inhabited by the very poor who lived outside the walls of the city. Recent United States Census data for the twenty-five largest metropolitan areas indicates that residential segregation by income, education, occupation, and race is more pronounced in the suburbs than in the central cities (Farley, 1977). As described in Chapter 10, racial, ethnic, and sex discrimination by real-estate agents, builders, mortgage lenders and others have tended to ensure that suburbia is almost exclusively white (U.S. Commission on Civil Rights, 1978). The result of these practices has been to produce a doughnut complex, where the hole in the doughnut is a deteriorating central city, while the doughnut itself a prosperous suburban region, in sharp contrast to the suburbs of preindustrial and early industrial society.

SUBURBAN LIFE

Growth of the Suburbs. Suburbanization began to accelerate in the last part of the nineteenth century as both a result of relocation of industry to the suburbs and technological change (Gordon, 1978; Ashton, 1978; Yeates and Garner, 1976). Prior to development of the automobile, introduction of the streetcar made suburban development possible. It was not uncommon for land speculators to build streetcar lines from the center of the city to outlying districts where they had bought land in order to attract people anxious to escape the noise and filth of the city to new housing developments (Ashton, 1978). Once the new development had been sold, the land speculators encouraged municipalities or private corporations to purchase the streetcar line.

Suburbanization resulted from the expansion of the highway system, spread of housing developments, and dispersion of industry.

A major impetus in the spread of suburbia was the mass production of automobiles that began in the 1920s. In 1900, only 10 per cent of the American population lived in suburbs; by 1929, the population of suburbs was growing twice as fast as that of central cities. Construction of new highways with public

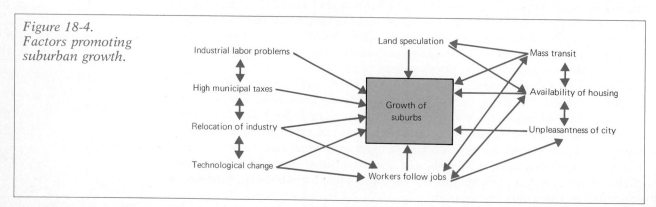

Figure 18-4.
Factors promoting
suburban growth.

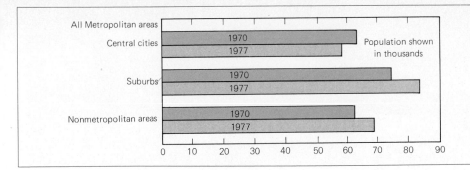

Figure 18-5.
Shifts in population
from 1970 to 1977.
(Source: *Sternlieb*
and Hughes, 1980,
p. 51.)

funds also made suburban life more convenient for large numbers of commuters.

There is, however, no single explanation for the rapid suburban growth within the last fifty years. Rather, it is the outcome of an interactive process in which living conditions, political factors, taxation, relocation of industry, and other events including technological change contributed to suburban expansion. This is shown graphically in Figure 18-4.

After World War II, suburbs began to expand rapidly as upwardly mobile veterans took advantage of low-cost mortgage programs as well as the opportunity for publicly-financed higher education. Today, more Americans live in suburbs than in central cities or nonmetropolitan areas, and many never leave their suburb except to go to work. Between 1970 and 1977, the population in central cities declined and the suburban population increased, as is shown in Figure 18-5.

What is the lure of suburban life? One major reason for the growth of suburbs is a shift in capital investment patterns so that new facilities (hospitals, universities, recreation complexes, office buildings, shopping centers, etc.), more efficient than old ones, have been increasingly located outside the central city (Sternlieb and Hughes, 1980). At the same time that new facilities have relocated outside the central city, few new jobs have been generated inside the central city. Accordingly, both people and jobs have drifted to the suburbs. Yet the central city still employs large numbers of people who commute daily from their suburban homes. For example, studies of journey-to-work patterns among Toronto commuters indicate that the average worker spends about one hour per day commuting (Yeates and Garner, 1976). Those in higher-status occupations, such as professionals, managers, and proprietors, commute longer distances to work each day than do manual or clerical workers (Yeates and Garner, 1976), presumably because they can afford the housing and transportation costs associated with living a greater distance from the work place. Clearly, job location is an important factor in the choice of suburban versus central city living, but it is not the only one.

Advantages of Suburban Life. Several generations ago, proponents of suburban life claimed to have the best of both worlds: being close enough to the city to take advantage of cultural and educational activities yet enjoying the wholesomeness, peace, and tranquillity of the countryside (Taylor, 1980; Fischer, 1976; Howard, 1965). Both Canadian and American life have been marked by a separation between public and private spheres, domestic and social pursuits, and male and female activities (Saegert, 1980). The suburbs provided one way in which these differences might be more fully accommodated as

517

The opportunity to own a home in an environment oriented toward family life has attracted many North Americans to the suburbs. (Source: Bill Owens, Magnum Photos Inc.)

well as an opportunity to own a single-family dwelling and to raise a family in an outdoors environment.

Suburban life is dominated by its family orientation. As you can see in Table 18-4, 41 per cent of all families living in suburbs in 1977 in the United States had children under the age of 18: a rate higher than in either nonmetropolitan or central city areas.

Stated advantages of suburban life include tranquility, a clean environment, and strong family orientation.

The advantages, then, of suburban life are several. The suburbs are more removed from the noise and crowding of the city, yet relatively close to its activities. At the same time, there is more room in which to follow leisure pursuits, to enjoy outdoor activities, and to raise children. Permitting less anonymity than the city, suburbia is also more homogeneous, where people of like backgrounds and interests choose similar districts in which to live. Home-

Table 18-4. Percentage of Families With Children Under the Age of 18 in Central Cities, Suburban, and Nonmetropolitan Areas, 1977, in the United States

Area of residence	Percentage of families with children under 18
Central Cities	26%
Suburbs	41
Nonmetropolitan and Rural	33

Source: Adapted from Freeman, 1980, p. S8, Table 2.

"Suburbia: The New American Plurality"

On the basis of a survey conducted by Louis Harris and Associates in 100 different communities throughout the United States, *Time* reported that there are at least four different types of suburbs. While suburbia is stereotypically viewed as the territory for the middle and upper classes, this is an oversimplification. The four types of suburbia identified are as follows:

1. *The affluent bedroom community* is inhabited by professionals, executives, and other white-collar workers who are predominantly white, Protestant, Republican homeowners with relatively high incomes.

2. *The affluent settled community* contains white-collar workers with slightly lower incomes who are less likely to own their own homes, and who are predominantly white, a mix of Protestant and Catholic, and slightly more likely to vote Republicans than Democratic.

3. *The low income, growing community* is home for predominantly skilled, semi-skilled, and unskilled workers whose incomes are substantially lower than those in the affluent suburbs and whose residents typically vote Democratic.

4. *The low income stagnant community* is inhabited primarily by unskilled and service workers of mixed ethnicities. This type of suburb has the lowest proportion of commuters to the central city.

While the typology developed by *Time* is just one of a number of possible ways in which to view the differences among suburbs, it is useful in highlighting the vast differences that exist among such communities. Regardless of the typology used, each type of suburb has its own form of social life and tensions, while residents share the advantages of more leisure time at home, greater interest in the neighborhood, and more social involvement with neighbors than do most central city dwellers.

Source: *Time*, 97, March 15, 1971, pp. 14–20.

---

ownership is usually made possible by the availability of mortgage money for single-family dwellings, a deeply-valued goal of many North Americans.

Disadvantages of Suburban Life. Yet for all its advantages, suburban life also has its hazards. Public transportation is generally poor, sometimes nonexistent, so that a second, even a third, car is required to shop, visit friends, and pick up children. Paradoxically, the trend to suburban residence has persisted despite high energy costs since 1974; husband-wife families in particular are still drawn to the suburbs (Sternlieb and Hughes, 1980).

Services may be difficult to reach as well. Transportation to the central city is often limited so that cultural and educational opportunities, while relatively near, are often inaccessible. While hospitals, shopping plazas, office parks, and restaurants are abundant in many suburbs, they too are not accessible by foot. Nor are there many services for different age groups. Much suburban development has been planned for couples with small children so that playgrounds and barbecue pits abound. Yet, as the suburban population has aged, few resources or activities may be geared for them; the old, teenagers, singles, and one-parent families have been left out of the planning equation. Ideologically and ecologically, suburbia remains the stronghold for rearing young children in a dual-parent family. (Ridgeway, 1981).

The very homogeneity of the suburb, initially one of its attractions for many

Stated disadvantages of suburban life include lack of public transportation, scattered services, isolation, and homogeneity.

home buyers, has proved to be a disadvantage for some. As more and more suburbs have developed and become entrenched communities, they have also become increasingly stratified according to income, ethnicity, and race. Despite a tendency for suburbs to also become employment communities, a status hierarchy of "good" versus "mediocre" versus "poor" suburbs remains (Stahura, 1979). The movement to suburbia during the last two decades has occurred at a slower rate for both female-headed and minority households than for white husband-wife households. Blacks are only one-third as likely and Hispanics half as likely to live in suburbs as are white families. (U.S. Commission on Civil Rights, 1968). The result of these trends has been to reduce cultural diversity.

Because of their relative homogeneity, the suburbs have often been criticized as promoting conformity. Conformity is more likely in suburbia, but whether suburbia promotes conformity or conformists merely select suburbia remains an open question (Gans, 1967: Fischer, 1976). The sameness of suburban life is reinforced by the lack of opportunity for young people to meet people different from themselves, and it has been suggested that suburban schools sustain a narrow view of the world where students are prepared to live in a conforming, bureaucratic society (Wynne, 1977).

Suburban life encompasses qualitatively different experiences for women and men.

Quality of Life.   Suburban life is a series of tradeoffs in which men and women have qualitatively different experiences. Saegert (1980), in a study of relatively wealthy urban and suburban couples, found that the average urban woman in this sample differed from her suburban counterpart in that she placed a higher value upon working outside the home (whether or not she was employed), resembling both urban and suburban men in this regard. Suburban dwellers of both sexes were more satisfied with their home as a place to raise children, to do work they enjoyed, to have fun, and as a space to use freely, while city residents of both sexes were more involved in work-related and cultural pursuits. The domestic character of the suburbs seems evident.

Research in both the United States and Canada (Saegert, 1980; Michelson, 1977) accents the differences in quality of life for men and women in the suburbs. For example, men are generally more likely than women to want to move from the central city; for them, suburban life represents both a status symbol and a retreat. Women are more likely than men to find themselves bored, and to report that their spouses spend less time with them, the children, and other family members (Michelson, 1977). These gender related differences cut across socioeconomic lines, and both white collar and blue collar women have reported that moving from the central city to suburbia reduced rather than enhanced the number of close ties with family and friends (Gans, 1967; Saegert, 1980).

Suburban women, like rural women, must rely more often upon their own resources and upon their immediate families for sources of pleasure and amusement. In this context, it is interesting to note the large increase in the proportion of suburban wives who, sooner or later, seek outside employment (Michelson, 1977). Just as the city has been condemned for producing psychic overload (Milgram, 1970), suburbia has been accused of producing psychic underload (Popenoe, 1977).

The Crisis in American Cities

ROOTS OF THE URBAN CRISIS

Since 1970, the number of people living in central cities has declined about 1 per cent per year, while the suburban population has increased on the average of 1.5 per cent yearly. Not only are fewer people living in the central cities, but those that remain are increasingly poorer: in 1969, the median family income of central city dwellers was 83 per cent of that of suburbanites in the United States, but by 1977, this figure had dropped to 79 per cent. Furthermore, while suburban family income kept pace with rising inflation, central city family income did not. The Consumer Price Index rose by 65 per cent between 1969 and 1977, and median suburban family income increased at about the same rate (66%). Among central city families, income fell below the rate of inflation by 9 per cent *New York Times*, 5/23/80). The vicious cycle begun earlier became evident by the end of the 1970s; more people, businesses, and jobs had deserted major metropolitan city centers, leaving the area increasingly less attractive and encouraging the flight of those who could still afford to move.

Since 1970, population has declined in the central cities and increased in the suburbs.

Migration Patterns. Between 1920 and 1960, millions of rural residents had migrated to the city in search of jobs, leaving hundreds of depopulated rural areas behind them (Biggar, 1979). By 1970, this stream of rural to urban movers was relatively small, partly because there were few people still living in rural areas and partly due to the rapid growth of non-metropolitan areas and newer cities in the sunbelt (Biggar, 1979; Sternlieb and Hughes, 1980). Most hard hit by losses in population have been the largest metropolitan areas, with two million or more people. In sharp contrast to the in-migration to these largest urban centers during the 1960s, these areas lost 2.2 million people through out-migration between 1970 and 1976 (Biggar, 1979).

Shrinking Tax Base. There are a number of reasons for this exodus from the central city, including the attractiveness of suburban life, the relocation of new industries into suburban and Sunbelt areas, and the cheaper cost of labor in noncentral cities. As migration from large metropolitan centers has accelerated, the municipal tax base for these cities was reduced. To counteract the financial losses resulting from a smaller tax base, many central cities have had to raise property and other taxes. These increased taxes in turn have encouraged out-migration from the central city into suburbs or other parts of the country, as is here shown diagramatically.

The exodus from central cities has resulted in a substantial shrinking of the tax base.

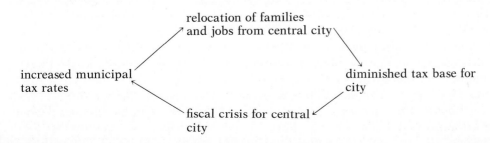

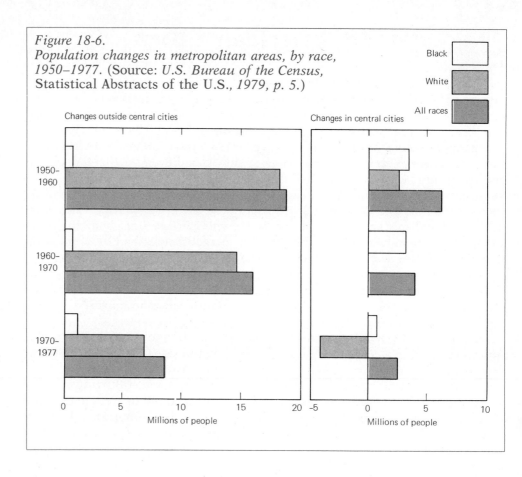

Figure 18-6.
Population changes in metropolitan areas, by race,
1950–1977. (Source: *U.S. Bureau of the Census,*
Statistical Abstracts of the U.S., *1979, p. 5.*)

Black

White

All races

Changes outside central cities

Changes in central cities

1950–1960

1960–1970

1970–1977

0   5   10   15   20   –5   0   5   10

Millions of people

Millions of people

The upshot of this process is that the elderly, the poor, women, female-headed families, and minority groups—precisely those most disadvantaged economically—have remained in the city. Younger, white, more educated, husband-wife families have departed to the suburbs or to the Sunbelt. Figure 18-6 summarizes some of the major population changes in metropolitan areas by race between 1950 and 1977. As you will notice in this figure, between 1970 and 1977, the numbers of whites in central cities declined dramatically.

The cities most affected by decline are the older, more industrialized centers of the North and East.

What Cities Decline. Must all large cities decline in a postindustrial society? The answer would appear to be "no." Those cities most affected are the oldest and most industrialized, built at a different phase of economic development. Of the 50 largest cities in the United States, 25 are old cities and 25 relatively new. Gordon (1978), analyzing the current urban crisis, found that shrinkage in the labor force and in jobs between 1960 and 1970 occurred in 16 cities, all but two of which were old cities. Furthermore, ten of the eleven cities with the highest municipal expenditures were old as were fourteen out of the sixteen cities in the most serious fiscal trouble and with the greatest municipal debt (Gordon, 1978).

Although this study is based on data for 1960 and 1970, Nathan and Fossett have suggested that older cities have continued to decline throughout the 1970s, where "the rich got richer and the poor got poorer" (*New York Times,* July 7,

1980). For example, Boston and Baltimore both lost population at a greater rate between 1975 and 1977 than during the 1960s. Preliminary Census Bureau data for 1980 show that the population within the city limits of Boston fell 21.4 per cent in the 1970–1980 decade (*Boston Globe*, July 14, 1980).

It seems clear that cities developed during the industrial phase of a society may not adapt easily to a postindustrial economy. The resources that make a city prosper as a manufacturing center may be dysfunctional for a postindustrial economy. Ringed by more affluent, predominantly middle-class residents, urban dwellers in decaying cities are limited in their abilities to expand or change the character of the core city. There is neither money nor space to do so.

CONSEQUENCES OF THE URBAN CRISIS

Municipal Fiscal Crises. In March 1975, when the worst economic depression since 1929 occurred, New York City found that it would no longer be able to continue to borrow from banks or money funds—the city was having difficulty repaying past loans and presented a poor credit risk. The fiscal collapse of New York seemed imminent. Commentators observed that the city had been living beyond its means, that it had done too much for its citizens, and that high municipal wages and welfare payments had created an unbearable drain on municipal funds (Newfield and Du Brul, 1978; Tabb, 1978). To reduce the squeeze, these expenses must be reduced. Not so, argues Tabb (1978), who suggests that municipal unions and the welfare population were *not* the cause of the fiscal crunch.

While per capita costs for all municipal functions were about $400 higher in New York than in other high-cost cities such as Boston and Baltimore and almost $1,000 higher than Los Angeles or Chicago, this comparison fails to take account of the different types of municipal services provided by the different cities (Tabb, 1978). That is, New York City provides some services that are supplied elsewhere by state, county, school board, special districts, and other nonmunicipal units. Furthermore, Philadelphia, Newark, and Baltimore have more municipal employees per capita than New York City where labor costs are not abnormally high (Tabb, 1978).

Rather than too much service, there may be too much inefficiency and favoritism to particular individuals and power elites (Newfield and Du Brul, 1978). Thus, in 1976, the municipal government failed to collect over $1 billion in taxes, fees, and fines that were owed; for example, landlords who had received loans to rehabilitate vacant buildings through a municipal loan program owed at least $107 million, (Newfield and Du Brul, 1978). Moreover, the banks, rather than lending money to the municipal government, decided to sell off New York City bonds in order to reduce their own risks in a chaotic money market.

New York City's fiscal plight is part of a larger, world economic crisis as well as of national policies that have penalized the old industrial city. As Newfield and Du Brul (1978) pointed out, the farm subsidy program that hastened the mechanization of agriculture has also led to the creation of a large labor pool of unemployed workers who migrated to the older industrial cities prior to 1970. Rising energy costs have hurt both the Northeast and the North Central States. New York's crisis is a complex phenomenon being experienced to lesser degrees by many older cities in which industry and capital have moved out to more attractive investment areas, leaving behind urban social problems. The concentration of poor, minority groups, elderly, and female-headed households is a *consequence*, not a cause, of the money problems of older cities.

Unemployment. That a large number of urban residents are unemployed has been a topic of national concern since the early 1970s. Between 7 million and 8 million Americans were unemployed in 1980, with an average length of unemployment of about 15 weeks (U.S. Commission on Civil Rights, 1980). Women and minority males were most likely to be unemployed; throughout the 1970s, the unemployment rate among blacks has been twice that of whites. Over 30 per cent of black teenagers in the labor market were unemployed throughout the 1970s. Women and minority males are most likely to be unemployed because they are both the objects of discrimination and possess fewer skills and less experience. Manufacturing jobs, historically the mainstay for urban manual workers, have dwindled. Even when jobs are available, women and minority group males are likely to have much lower incomes than white males (Freeman, 1980). The net result of the exodus of more and more factories from the large industrial cities is that more and more families remaining in the central cities live below the poverty level. This is shown graphically in Figure 18-7.

One effect of high unemployment rates has been an increase in the number of welfare recipients; what Piven and Cloward (1971) have called a "relief explosion", following from the large migration of agricultural workers to the cities between 1945 and 1964 and the subsequent flight of whites and jobs. The welfare rolls expanded in response to civil disorder as a means of soothing the poor in those cities most torn by rioting (Piven and Cloward, 1971). More people who were eligible for welfare were stimulated to apply and were able to receive benefits in these areas. This is, however, a very different picture from that found

> Unemployment dispro-
> portionately affects teen-
> agers, minority group
> members, and women
> heads of household.

> One effect of high unem-
> ployment has been an
> increase in the number
> of welfare recipients.

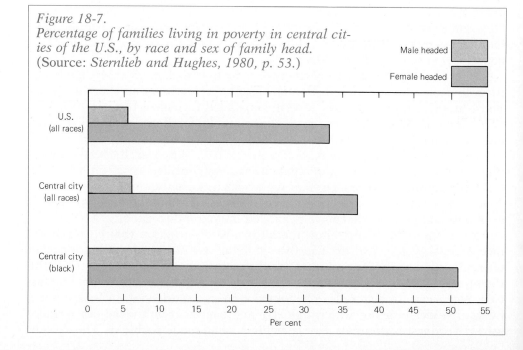

Figure 18-7.
Percentage of families living in poverty in central cities of the U.S., by race and sex of family head. (Source: *Sternlieb and Hughes, 1980, p. 53.*)

Table 18-5. *Average Monthly Aid to Families With Dependent Children (AFDC) Payment, for Selected Urban and Rural States, 1978*

State	Average monthly payment to families
Population more than 60% urban	
New York State	$375
Michigan	$337
Massachusetts	$323
Wisconsin	$319
Washington State	$307
Texas	$108
Population less than 60% urban	
Georgia	$107
South Carolina	$ 88
Mississippi	$ 61
U.S. Average Payment, 50 states	$254

Source: *Statistical Abstract of the U.S.*, 1979, Table 569, p. 354.

in sunbelt states, where welfare payments remain small and more difficult to obtain, as Table 18-5 illustrates.

The relief explosion begun in the late 1960s has increased with the economic recession of the late 1970s. Despite the passage of such programs as the Comprehensive Employment and Training Act (CETA), providing a number of training programs aimed at welfare recipients, women have remained most affected by poverty in the city. Preliminary evidence on the CETA program suggests, that fewer women than men are likely to be trained for well-paying jobs. Furthermore, women are more likely than men to be unsuccessful in obtaining a job after training (Freeman, 1980). Especially likely to live in poverty are black, female heads of households in the city. The poor are trapped, both in city and countryside, in a vicious circle yet unresolved by economic policies (Tussing, 1974; Piven and Cloward, 1971).

Housing. The concentration of minorities and women in the central city is reinforced by the availability of affordable housing in the oldest and most deteriorated neighborhoods (Downs, 1979). Minority and female-headed households were only about two-thirds as likely to be living in their own home in 1976 as were white intact families (U.S. Commission on Civil Rights, 1978).

Several factors contribute to the lower rates of home ownership for minorities and women. As Werner, Frej, and Madway (1976) have pointed out, even when annual income, assets, outstanding debts, monthly debt burden, and the number of years in present occupation are held constant, minority rejection rates for mortgages are considerably higher than are majority rates. Similarly, women mortgage seekers experience discrimination in lending practices by banks (Werner, Frej, and Madway, 1976). A second factor that has contrib-

Minority groups and women are more likely to live within the central city.

Disinvestment, or red-lining, occurs when lending institutions refuse to invest in neighborhoods perceived as deteriorating.

uted both to low home ownership rates and to deteriorating central city housing is that of *disinvestment* (sometimes called redlining), where lending institutions refuse to invest in neighborhoods that are perceived as deteriorating or likely to deteriorate in the foreseeable future. The withdrawal of mortgage funds from a particular neighborhood can effectively kill that area.

Overcrowding (usually defined as more than one person per room in a dwelling unit) also is frequent in low-income, female-headed or minority inner-city housing, as is the lack of essential housing elements such as a flush toilet, hot water, central heating, complete kitchen, and easy access to the dwelling unit from outside (U.S. Commission on Civil Rights, 1978). Yet inner city housing is

Traveling in and out of urban areas for employment is a world-wide phenomenon. Here, a woman leaves the Brazilian capital, Brasilia, after a day's work.
(Source: *Rene Burri, Magnum Photos Inc.*)

not cheap by any means; in both Canada and the U.S., poor people spend a larger percentage of their income on housing than do the nonpoor. Fifty-eight per cent of Canadian families in the bottom 20 per cent of the income distribution spend more than one quarter of their income on housing, while 90 per cent of the families in the top fifth of income spend less than 20 per cent (Yeates and Garner, 1976). In the United States, over two-thirds of female-headed households and over one-third of all minority households spent over 25 per cent of their income on rent (U.S. Commission on Civil Rights, 1978).

The quality of inner city housing is often very poor, essentially because investors want to realize the maximum amount of income on a short-term basis (Yeates and Garner, 1976). That is, because investors in inner city housing may be uncertain about the future of the neighborhood, they are unwilling to improve and maintain the property. The risk is too great. As the quality of their housing declines and landlords abandon upkeep, residents find it impossible to maintain essential services or provide security.

Block busting, too, may create problems in certain neighborhoods. This process works as follows: A real estate agent and a developer may work together to assemble land for future redevelopment. As a first step, the developers begin to purchase properties in an area they plan to revamp. Step two occurs when the real estate agent or other hired manager begins to operate these newly purchased properties as apartments or rooming houses for low-income groups. These properties deteriorate rapidly as no repairs are made, and long-term residents of the area are likely to panic and sell. As owners prepare to sell, their homes are bought by the developers. Thus a vicious cycle is set into motion; as more people move out, the neighborhood becomes unsafe; fire insurance may be cancelled, and even more owners sell because their property is uninsured. Demolition of some houses by the developer may further discourage ownership by the remaining residents in the neighborhood. The cycle is thus completed. The abandoned neighborhood is now ripe for redevelopment and eventual profits and the owners can secure low-cost government loans for this purpose. This process is not uncommon in both the United States and Canada (Yeates and Garner, 1976).

Block busting occurs when real estate agents and developers buy property at low prices, redevelop an area, and sell at a high profit.

DEALING WITH THE CRISIS

Analysts of problems of the city, such as housing, unemployment, and fiscal crises, have proposed a variety of solutions. Conservative writers such as Banfield (1974) believe that urban ills stem from too much government intervention in the private market; that the assumption that all people are created equal has led to programs that merely increase the problems of the city; and that what is needed is a policy of *benign neglect* which will lead to the disappearance of these problems over time (Banfield, 1974).

In sharp contrast to this approach, conflict theorists claim that the very structure of North American social and economic institutions makes it impossible to solve these problems; that Capitalism is based upon the notion of scarcity and surplus; and that in order to preserve current power relations it is necessary to maintain unequal distribution of goods and wealth (Gordon, 1978; Piven and Cloward, 1971). Therefore only radically different approaches to the problems of the city will directly affect the poor, since programs developed to date are by definition inadequate, a mere drop in the bucket to muddy the basic conflict between rich and poor. In the following sections, various solutions to the urban crisis are reviewed.

Regionalization is a method to contend with the problem of imbalance between the impoverished central city and the more affluent suburbs.

Regionalization. Any large city faces the problem of how to pay for necessary services when jobs and taxable incomes cross the city line into other towns. As more affluent families flee to the suburbs and as industry withdraws from the central city, the fiscal tax base of the central city is reduced. The central city can no longer support the services its residents require, while the suburbs can pay for more services than their population needs (Yeates and Garner, 1976, p. 433). To restore the balance between the central city and its suburbs and to reduce competition between nearby locales for industry and tax dollars, *regionalization* has been proposed as a solution that would recognize the interdependence among units in the total metropolitan community (Chinitz, 1965; Wood, 1961). *Regionalization* refers to the concept of creating area-wide governing bodies to handle area-wide problems such as water supply, sewage, highway construction, parks, property assessment, transportation, and so forth. Local municipalities might or might not remain responsible for provision of schools, fire departments, and other services.

Although regionalization is not a new concept—Boston, Massachusetts attempted to regionalize in 1896—it has not been popular in the United States. Even when the metropolitan area is located within one county, agreements among the various municipal governments are difficult to negotiate and implement, and considerable revamping of existing local governmental structures is required. In Canada, the idea has met with more success; as of 1954, regionalization was adapted in the metropolitan area of Toronto, when the Municipality of Metropolitan Toronto was created. Charged with performing functions that previously had been provided by 13 districts, the Municipality has made progress on several issues, including education, water supply, sewage disposal, control of air pollution, uniform law enforcement, and public transportation (Yeates and Garner, 1976). While less progress has been made with respect to housing, urban renewal, health and welfare, the system is firmly established and remains viable if not perfect.

Gentrification refers to the migration of more affluent families back into the central city.

Gentrification. At one time, the *gentry* were the wealthy who fled the problems of the city to their country estates. In recent years, a new type of gentry has been identified: those middle and upper income individuals who leave the suburbs to move into the city. *Gentrification* is the term used to describe the migration of these people into urban centers and their renovation of existing housing. A recent phenomenon, gentrification is associated both with the expansion of high-paying jobs at the headquarters of multi-national corporations located in the central city, and with changing lifestyles (Markusen, 1980). Increasing numbers of professional husband-wife couples are employed in the city, and fewer will have more than one or two children. The city remains attractive to young singles with relatively high incomes and an interest in the arts and entertainment (Markusen, 1980). Census data, for example, indicate that a majority (over 60%) of all singles live in large cities; among those 35–54 years of age who have never married, the greatest concentration is in cities of 50,000 or more (Carter and Glick, 1976).

Accompanying gentrification has been *urban homesteading*, where rundown

Boston: A City of Two Tales

Boston is a city known for its "b"s: Brahmins (elite families), brainy academics, beans, busing, blue-collar workers, and political bosses. As this assortment suggests, Boston is a city of contrasts and contradictions. While it has become a center of urban restoration and business development within recent years, it is still torn by ethnic tension and poverty. For example, Quincy Market and Faneuil Hall Marketplace, both historic landmarks, have been redeveloped into a series of expensive shops and restaurants that attract about one million visitors per month; some hotels are booked two years in advance; more renewal projects are planned, including the renovation of a former Navy Yard into luxury housing. Gentrification abounds in formerly deteriorated neighborhoods such as the South End and Dorchester where Victorian houses are being restored by members of the middle- and upper-income groups.

This very process, however, has created further tension. In those areas where gentrification and urban redevelopment has been most pronounced, the long-term, low-income residents have been displaced. Invasion has been followed by succession, but many have been forced to relocate in less desirable neighborhoods where they have no close ties. To make this process more problematic, Boston is a series of segmented, ethnic and racial communities where the life style of the wealthy WASP elite is very different from the ethnic loyalties of Irish-American South Boston. In recent years, intergroup tensions have centered on racial lines. Busing of school children has been a central point of controversy for both blacks and whites.

What the future holds for Boston is unclear. As John O'Bryant, the first black to be elected to the Boston School Committee, commented, "We have a long, long way to go. Yet Boston is no worse than other cities in this country. I would not discourage anyone from settling here."

Source: *Newsweek*, June 9, 1980, 49–51.

Urban homesteading refers to the sale of rundown housing for low prices with the understanding that the buyer would rehabilitate it for personal use.

housing units were placed on the real estate market for very low prices, with the understanding that the buyer would rebuild the dwelling for his or her own use. Some units were sold for as low as $1! Redevelopment of such property was made easier for the buyer through low-interest, government-subsidized loans.

Yet neither gentrification nor urban homesteading have solved the cities' woes. As some commentators on current developments in the city have noted, despite optimistic reports and the physical evidence of construction in some rundown neighborhoods, an increase in office rents, and housing rehabilitation, it is far from clear that many older cities have become economically prosperous. To the contrary, they may not have yet hit the bottom of their economic decline (New York *Times*, July 7, 1980).

The Future of Cities

For all of the problems of cities, they are likely to survive in one form or another. There are goods, services, opportunities for economic and social mobility, and cultural diversity that can be found only in the city which will continue to make it attractive as a place in which to live and work.

The **eumenopolis** is a continuous series of cities interconnected nationally and worldwide.

What will the city of the future be like? A variety of models have been proposed. Doxiadia (1968) has suggested that by 2150, there will be a *eumenopolis* (from the Greek for worldwide city). The *eumenopolis* is essentially a strip city development, interconnected nationally, continuously, and worldwide. Can you imagine a eumenopolis extending from Toronto through New York City and Washington, D.C. to Atlanta?

While this kind of linkage provides social and economic connections throughout a nation, continent, or worldwide, it does not address some of the issues of quality of life that have concerned many urban sociologists and planners who have also examined how space and territory are used. Space is both a physical area and a social construct, defined by its particular use and the type of social interaction that takes place within it. In both urban and suburban areas, space is more likely to be divided according to its social function than in the rural environment. In other words, social conditions, physical construction, norms, and values dictate the ways that space is used or territories identified. For example, restaurants, bars, and clubs are physical spaces designed to promote social interaction; motel lobbies, office complexes, and bus stations are not. The physical construction of an urban or suburban space to enhance or discourage social interaction will determine the kind of social behavior that takes place, and reflects the values of that society.

In metropolitan areas in North America, privacy is highly valued and associated with high social status so that the greater one's power, wealth, and prestige, the more privacy is one accorded. The officers of a corporation occupy more physical space than do junior executives, who in turn have more privacy than secretaries. Assembly-line workers are more likely to use a large, common washroom, whereas high-ranking employees have a key to a special executive toilet. Privacy is also closely tied to ideology; on many Israeli Kibbutz, where communal living and work are consciously desired there is little private physical space. Husband and wife have a private bedroom, but children live communally, while dining, kitchen, toilet, and other facilities are shared by all kibbutz dwellers.

Viewing the contemporary urban scene, critics such as Jacobs (1961) and Newman (1972) have proposed, paradoxically, that the emphasis on single function dwellings and privacy has resulted in a deterioration of the quality of urban life. As large numbers of smaller buildings have been replaced by high rises, often with only one function such as office or apartment, spatial areas have been created with very high density of people at some hours of the day but very low at others. The result of this single function use of space has been to lessen the strength of informal social controls that operate in multiple-use spaces to keep the area safe, pleasant, and interesting. In multi-purpose neighborhoods, as in small towns and the countryside, vandalism and theft are less common because intruders are easily recognized. The spatial segregation of urban areas is particularly problematic for the very young, the very old, the poor, and the physically handicapped. They are bound to a limited area for most of their activities. Yet many of these spaces are not easily defended, for they are constructed in a way that minimizes social interaction and reduces the possibility of surveillance and sense of neighborhood. For example, playgrounds in multiple-story housing projects may be designed at ground level where it is difficult for parents to oversee. Apartments are designed with a central elevator shaft and long corridors, both of which inhibit development of social cohesion within the building.

One proposed solution to single-function urban spaces has been the *"arcology"* complex, in which mile-high buildings are constructed that provide a setting for one's entire life (Solari, 1969). Each of these complexes would contain offices, housing units, schools, churches, and shops. Outside the complex, the natural landscape would be preserved for recreation. This scheme would promote satisfactory social interaction, encourage social cohesion, and allow cities to be built in a variety of places, including in space, at sea, or in traditional city locales.

The **arcology** complex is constructed to provide a setting for one's entire life.

Other solutions that have been proposed include satellite cities and garden cities. Also viewed as total environments, these towns would be relatively small—between 50,000 and 300,000 people—and provide all the necessities of life. With a low density of people per square mile, both residential and industrial sites would be included, reducing commuting time and emphasizing pedestrian travel.

Satellite cities and garden cities are relatively small and include both residential and industrial sites.

Whether the city of the future will take the shape of any of the above proposals depends on a willingness to plan for residential development. Thus far, neither the United States nor Canada has had a comprehensive urban planning policy. Instead, in both nations, there has been a set of "uncoordinated, often contradictory, essentially random public policies and programs . . . . Thus, if in the past urbanization has been governed by any conscious public objectives at all, these have been, on the one hand, to encourage growth, apparently for its own sake; and on the other, to provide public works and public welfare programs to support piecemeal, spontaneous development . . ." (Berry, 1973). How we construct cities of the future will be closely related not only to the economic situation but, more importantly, to our social structure and value system.

Summary

In this chapter, we have looked at what happens to social institutions, social interaction, and to the individual as urbanization becomes the norm for the majority of the population. While city life has been criticized as strange and different, impersonal, untraditional, and more artificial than that of the countryside or suburbs, the lifestyles associated with all three locales are social constructs. The diversity of the city promotes social differentiation, creativity, and change.

Despite the romantic view held by most North Americans regarding the virtues of country life, the majority of people in both countries, as in most industrialized nations, live in urban areas. Since World War II, more and more individuals live in suburbs, popular for their relative peace and quiet, spaciousness, encouragement of leisure pursuits, and advantages for raising children. But suburban life also has drawbacks: transportation is generally poor, services may be difficult to reach or not available at all, and the very sameness that initially attracted people to suburbia may produce conformity and boredom, especially among teenagers, the elderly and middle-aged women.

Older cities have been beset by a number of problems in the last few decades, including shrinking population, smaller tax bases, high rates of unemployment, and relocation of industry. Many major cities have attempted to counter these difficulties by subsidizing new construction, promoting gentrification and urban homesteading, and seeking new sources of capital. It seems unlikely, however, that the old, industrial city will continue to prosper unless further social changes are made.

A variety of ways in which the city of the future might be constructed have been proposed, all of which are designed to reduce some of the problems of present-day cities. The future of North American cities depends on the decisions made by voters, legislators, and owners of capital. City planning, like all other social planning and deliberate social policy, reflects a series of choices between competing values and interests. Decisions about size, location, type of construction, transportation, parks, schools, and use of space to promote or reduce social interaction will reflect both the power interests and the norms and values of the society in which they occur.

Suggested Readings

ALLON, NATALIE. *Urban Life Styles* (Dubuque, Iowa: William C. Brown, 1979). These insightful ethnographic essays are based on Allon's participant observation in three urban settings: dieting groups, health spas, and singles bars.

FISCHER, CLAUDE S. *The Urban Experience* (New York: Harcourt, Brace, Jovanovich, 1976). This survey of the social and psychological consequences of urban life includes chapters on the historical development of cities, neighborhoods and the family in urban areas, the growth of suburbs, and concludes with speculations about the future of urban areas.

GORDON, DAVID (Ed.). *Problems in Political Economy: An Urban Perspective* (2nd edition) (Lexington, Mass.: D.C. Heath, 1977). The editor has gathered a comprehensive set of essays illustrating the radical, liberal, and conservative perspectives on education, employment, housing, poverty, welfare, crime, health, and the quality of urban life.

NEWFIELD, JACK, and PAUL DU BRUL. *The Abuse of Power: The Permanent Government and the Fall of New York* (New York: Penguin Books, 1978). The authors develop the thesis that a secret government of financiers, developers, backroom politicians, union leaders, and businessmen run the cities through a system of "legal" graft, and demonstrate how this "permanent government" brought about the financial collapse of New York City in the late 1970s.

SUTTLES, GERALD D. *The Social Order of the Slum: Ethnicity and Territory in the Inner City* (Chicago, Ill.: University of Chicago Press, 1968). A classic work on the social organization of the slum, in this case the high delinquency area around Hull House on Chicago's Near West Side. Suttles examines the development of behavioral standards, arising from the specific life experiences of the residents, that take precedence over the moral standards of mainstream society. (Winner 1969 C. Wright Mills Award of the Society for the Study of Social Problems.)

TABB, WILLIAM K., and LARRY SAWERS (Eds.). *Marxism and the Metropolis: New Perspectives in Urban Political Economy* (New York: Oxford University Press, 1978). As an example of current applications of conflict analysis, this collection of essays examines the relationship between various urban problems and the economic base of late industrial and postindustrial societies.

19

Collective Behavior and Social Movements

*I*n both the United States and Canada in 1980 there were several cases of rock-music fans trampling one another to get into or out of concert halls, brawls at sports events, schoolchildren engaging in mass hysteria, sudden runs on consumer goods rumored to be in short supply, street demonstrations for and against homosexual rights, sit-ins at nuclear power plants, attempts to disrupt municipal services by striking workers, and acts of defiance to authority by Native Americans.

How can the theories and concepts of the social sciences make any sense of such a grab bag of activities? These are all examples of *collective behavior*, a category that includes such diverse social actions as crazes and fads, panics and outbursts of mass hysteria, mobs and riots, crowds of all types, the effects of rumor and public opinion, social movements and revolutions. What these phenomena have in common with the other behaviors examined in this book is that they involve interacting individuals who influence one another whether or not they are in actual contact (Brown, 1965). What distinguishes incidents of collective behavior from other types of social action is the relative absence of formalized norms and shared values.

Collective behavior, therefore, is not group behavior as we have described it in Chapter 4, even though a number of persons are responding to a common situation or stimulus. Collective behavior is more spontaneous, more loosely structured, more purposeless than most social action. Yet we have also suggested that no social situation remains totally unstructured for very long. Rather, collective behavior is characterized by *emergent* norms, flowing from events as they unfold and as participants define their behavior.

There is no easy formula for specifying what is or is not collective behavior; it is largely a matter of degree. At what point, for example, does a revolutionary mob become an organized force for change? How spontaneous are lynching parties? Does the fact that so much collective behavior is strange, unexpected, and often bizarre blind observers to basic elements of structure?

As a minimal definition, collective behavior consists of noninstitutionalized activities that can be a response to, as well as a cause of, normlessness or change, and that typically "occur when values and institutions are in flux" (Dreier, 1974). In this chapter we will explore the manifestations of collective behavior that have most relevance for the study of social change. Other types of collective behavior—fads, crazes, and fashions—are more properly considered as fleeting aspects of popular culture.

Collective behavior refers to crazes, panics, fads, crowds of all types, mobs and riots, social movements, and revolutions.

Emergent, rather than established, norms characterize collective behavior.

Types of Collective Behavior

How can events as diverse as reacting to rumors and engaging in rebellion be linked? One approach is to arrange types of collective behavior along such dimensions as a) spontaneity vs. structure, b) short vs. long term, c) expressive vs.

instrumental, and d) unconscious vs. conscious goals. For example, a continuum of spontaneity might look like this:

Spontaneous | hysterical outbursts, panics & rumor behavior / publics / crowds / riots / social movements / revolutions / Structured

HYSTERIA, PANICS, AND RUMOR

In general, events that are spontaneous are also short-lived, expressive in nature, and without conscious goals. Rumor behavior, many kinds of crowds, and outbreaks of mass hysteria share these attributes. So seemingly unstructured and spontaneous are these types of collective behavior that they are often described as irrational. While it may be difficult to predict outbreaks of rumor and hysteria, these events are not random or baseless. There are social, structural, and historical causes underlying much of what appears unpredictable and without reason. Most cases of mass hysteria, for example, can be traced to

These people at a rock concert are exhibiting collective behavior: *spontaneous, loosely structured, and relatively free of formalized norms.* (Source: *Jeff Albertson, Stock, Boston.*)

Some manifestations of collective behavior are important primarily for what they tell us about popular taste at a particular moment. Three of these—crazes, fads, and fashions—can be classified according to their duration, extent of public participation, and social significance:

Crazes are periodic outbreaks of unexpected and often outlandish behavior, such as swallowing goldfish, sitting on flag poles, playing with hula hoops, walking pet rocks, or piling into phone booths. These activities are rarely intended as profound social statements although something can be read into almost any type of behavior. In the late 1960s several incidents of 'streaking' (running naked in public) were interpreted as protests against conventional mores.

Fads are somewhat more enduring than crazes, and also appeal to a wider audience. Adult roller skating, bongo drums, earth art, and social message T-shirts or bumper stickers are typical recent examples.

Fashions are more enduring, widespread, and socially significant than either crazes or fads. Trend-setters define what is 'in', and networks of influence carry the message. The direction can be from the top down, as in the case of 'designer clothes' for the wealthy being copied in ready-to-wear versions, or from the masses up, as in the case of blue jeans and T-shirts.

Distinctions of dress and adornment are insignia of social status. In a society without an hereditary aristocracy, it may be necessary for the higher strata to be distinguishable from the lower in some very obvious way. Blumer (1974) suggests that in a classless society, fashion would be irrelevant, and in a caste society, unnecessary (since status distinctions are quite clear on other grounds).

Fashion may also serve to establish individuality, as when a particular item of dress or adornment becomes a personal statement, a way of standing out from others. This function is especially significant in a society in which individualism is valued but individuality less encouraged.

In societies where personal adornment is discouraged—such as religious communities, communist nations, Puritan New England, and Iran under the Ayatollohs—fashion can even be a subversive element. Soviet authorities regularly condemn western fashions in dress and music among the young.

---

environmental stress. The seventeenth-century New England schoolgirls who claimed to be possessed by witches were probably suffering from a combination of puberty, sexual repression, and boredom (Boyer and Nussbaum, 1974). Nor were the targets of their accusations—unmarried older women who were not fully integrated into Puritan society—randomly selected; they were marginal people, feared for their nonconformity.

Similarly, just a decade ago, hysteria swept through the French city of Orleans, spurred by rumors that Frenchwomen shopping in stores owned by Jewish merchants were being drugged and sold to brothels in the Near East. Weeks passed before the police and press could convince townspeople that the women mentioned in these stories were all alive and well and still living in Orleans (Ianiello, 1969). It is doubtful that such a rumor would be believed or even circulated in a place without a history of antisemitism.

Panics, too, are grounded in real fears and anxieties. The people trampling over one another to escape a sinking ship are acting out of an immediate appre-

Panics occur when people respond to an immediate sense of danger. (Source: Wide World Photos.)

hension of danger. In other cases, fears are based on more generalized beliefs that unknown and uncontrollable forces are at work in the world.

A rumor is a piece of information from anonymous sources that is passed from one person to another without being confirmed or verified. Spreading a rumor is a form of collective behavior, and the rumor itself is a key element in many other collective events (panics and riots especially). Some rumors may be intentionally planted by those with a particular goal in mind, but most are

X
*A **rumor** is information passed from person to person without being verified.*

"The Martians Are Coming! The Martians Are Coming!"

At 8:00 PM on Sunday, October 30th, 1938—Halloween—actors of the Mercury Theater began their radio presentation of H. G. Wells's novel *The War of the Worlds.* Although some listeners knew they were hearing a radio play that dealt with science fiction, so perfectly did an actor mimic an announcement that an unidentified flying object had landed in Grover's Mill, New Jersey, that millions of people fled their homes to escape the Martian invasion. As it happened, much of the audience had not tuned in at the beginning of the program, but about ten minutes later, because a competing radio show was featuring a rather poor singer. What listeners heard for the next half hour or so was a dramatization of Wells's account of how the Martians fought a battle with United States troops in the Watchung Mountains of New Jersey, then moved on to New York City where the population was quickly overcome by poison gas, and where, by the time of the half-hour station break, only one survivor was left.

The second half of the program was never broadcast. Panic had swept the country: bus and train terminals were mobbed; phone lines swamped; rumors of casualties widely circulated. Yet only one person had actually been injured, and none of the subsequent law suits claiming damages was upheld in court.

Source: This section is based on John Houseman, "The Men from Mars," 1948.

unconscious distortions of normal communications that tend to reinforce existing prejudices.

The life of a rumor can be compared to the child's game of "pass it on," where, with each telling, some features are embellished and others forgotten. In his early classic studies of rumor, Gordon Allport (Allport and Postman, 1947) demonstrated the way in which the original story is reshaped by the attitudes and expectations of successive tellers, as when a picture of a white man threatening a black is often reversed in the telling. Allport notes that the natural history of a rumor will depend upon a number of factors: its *content* (is it plausible? interesting?), the *number of people involved* (how many times the rumor is retold), *chain of communication* (who tells whom), and *attitudes* toward the subject matter (prejudice, vested interests, hidden agendas). The rumor about the "missing women" of Orleans, for example, became increasingly detailed regarding which shops were involved; the content—white slavery—was sufficiently lurid to assure interest; the form by which it was spread—word of mouth—added plausibility ("If everyone is talking about it, there must be some truth to it"); and people's readiness to believe the worst of Jewish merchants made them extremely gullible.

The evolution of a rumor depends on its **content, the number of people involved, chain of communication,** *and* **attitudes** *towards the subject matter.*

In other situations such as a milling crowd, rumors fill a void in situations where verifiable data are not available, and allow members of a group to give shape to a vague or ambiguous situation (Shibutani, 1966). Rumors serve to organize perception and to spark collective action. When people are acting in unstructured and normless conditions, they are especially vulnerable to any plausible definition of the situation.

PUBLICS

Unlike the other collective phenomena discussed in this chapter, a public is composed of individuals who are not in the same place at the same time, but who are reacting to a common stimulus in a similar fashion. For example, Richard Nixon's concept of the "silent majority" referred to an assumed public of people who felt strongly about supporting the Vietnam war but who did not take to the streets to demonstrate their approval of his policies. Nixon's reelection campaign was targeted, through the media, to activate this vast public.

A public *consists of people who are not in the same place at the same time, but who react similarly to certain stimuli.*

Advertising of all types is designed to create a public for a product, whether a bar of soap or a politician. Other publics consist of individuals with some pre-existing common interest—the environment, gun control, Canadian separatism, or civil rights, for example—whose opinions may be formed individualistically but whose commitment can be galvanized to action by particular events reported in the media.

An unorganized public can become an *interest group* when members feel strongly enough to move beyond letter-writing and seek out others with similar feelings. This latent capacity for action in publics enhances the potential power of the media. The importance of publics in modern societies cannot therefore be overestimated. Until recently it was very difficult, if not impossible, to reach all members of the society simultaneously; today, it can be done at any given moment. Ultimately, mass society is based upon the willingness of publics to support the social order. As Kingsley Davis (1949) stated over three decades ago: modern society "rests preeminately on public opinion and public behavior . . . (which) help greatly to give modern society its dynamic quality."

The **interest group** *develops out of an organized public.*

CROWDS

In contrast to the loosely linked collective phenomena of rumors, panics, and expressions of public opinion, another set of relatively spontaneous and temporary behaviors is typically characterized by greater mass, consciousness, and *emergent* qualities; that is, these forms have the possibility of becoming organized groups. Crowds of various types are closer to being authentic social groups than are the collections of individuals who pass along rumors or succumb to hysteria.

A *crowd* is a temporary gathering of individuals brought together by some common concern or activity, and in which there is an awareness of the presence of others. The scope of a crowd is therefore limited to the particular actors in one place at one time. Yet a crowd is not a group in the sense of having structure, such as a division of labor with patterned roles. Rather, members of the crowd lose their identities as distinct persons when they blend into an undifferentiated mass. Under these circumstances, says Davis (1949), "they yield easily to impulses that otherwise would be restrained." In other words, one can literally as well as figuratively become "lost in the crowd" and therefore released from the norms that typically regulate behavior among individuals.

> A **crowd** is a temporary gathering of individuals brought together around a common activity or concern.

Types of Crowds. There are many different kinds of temporary collections of people, from the shoppers in a supermarket at a given moment to a lynch mob. Not all crowds exemplify collective behavior—some encounters are too brief, and others too structured. For example, both casual and conventional crowds test the limits of our definition of collective behavior.

> ✗ Four types of crowds are identified: **casual, conventional, expressive,** and **acting.**

   ✓ *Casual Crowd.* An accidental assemblage of people who happen to be pursuing individual goals in the same place at the same time (such as shoppers, travellers, or strollers) who share a common focus for a moment or so—as witnesses to a fight, for example.

   ✓ *Conventional Crowd.* Those gathered as spectators or audiences at events governed by established norms, such as religious services or theatrical performances. Here behavior is relatively patterned and therefore predictable.

But both these types of crowd have the potential for being transformed into a different kind of crowd such as those described by Blumer (1951):

   ✓ *Expressive Crowd.* When participants vent strong feelings with outbursts of emotion, normative restraints disappear, and a previously conventional audience can become an expressive crowd. Expressive behavior has no other goal than the release of emotion. Spectators at sports events often release joy or hostility by such acts as tearing up the turf in victory or throwing bottles in anger. Even a relatively sedate concert audience will turn nasty if a star performer fails to appear, and people have been trampled at religious meetings.

   ✓ *Acting Crowd.* Acting crowds have some goal beyond mere ventilation of feeling. Fueled by the belief that only action outside the norms can accomplish those aims, the acting crowd may be transformed into a mob engaging in *riot* behavior.

   ✓ *Riots.* Far from being an unusual event, riots have occurred with some regularity in American history, from the Boston Tea Party to Attica State Prison. By far the most common type of mob action in the United States has been the *race riot.* Thousands of blacks were lynched in the South before, during, and after the Civil War; hundreds, perhaps, thousands of Chinese "disappeared" in the

> ✗ The **race riot** has been the most common type of mob action in the United States.

West. White mobs caroused through the streets of black sections of several Northern cities in the 1860s and 1940s; and acting crowds of white parents have damaged buses and thrown objects at black schoolchildren in Boston and elsewhere in the 1970s.

The black ghetto riots of the mid-1960s—in Cleveland, Detroit, the Watts

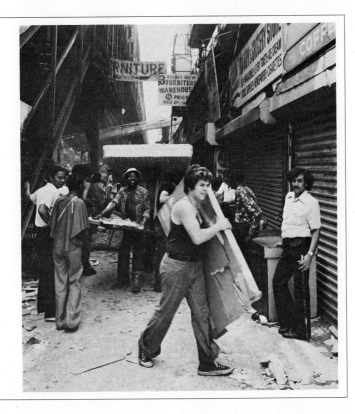

section of Los Angeles, and Rochester, New York—were not race riots in the same sense as those mentioned above. Black mobs did not attack white residential areas but directed their violence at white-owned business within the ghetto and at other symbols of white control of the political and economic life of the inner city. Even as late as 1980, black rioters in Miami remained essentially within their part of the city, though by this time there were few nonblack targets in the area.

Not all mob action is negatively evaluated in the United States; much depends on who is involved and who does the judging. Students, blacks, and prisoners are usually defined by the media as rioters. Strikers, desegregation protesters, or National Guard troops that are out of control are rarely described as rioting although identical behaviors are being observed.

1,000 + 1,000 = 5,000— Estimating Crowd Size

One goal of a protesting crowd is to convince the public at large that the cause is a popular one, and one dramatic technique for creating that impression is the *demonstration*. Organizers announce their intention to conduct a "massive rally" at some strategic site, usually the grounds near the Washington Monument. Then the numbers game begins. Organizers have a vested interest in the highest numbers, while opponents win propaganda points when the expected crowds fail to materialize. The media prefer the larger counts because this reinforces their decision to cover an event. Police and sanitation personnel are tempted to inflate figures to make their tasks appear more heroic.

The politics of crowd counting is demonstrated in this excerpt from Sturges' analysis.

On October 3, 1970, 20,000 persons (or perhaps 200,000) attended a March for Victory rally in Washington, D.C., led by fundamentalist Christian minister Carl McIntire.

Park police estimated 20,000 at the Monument Grounds. Mr. McIntire refused to give a crowd estimate, although he had predicted a turnout of 500,000 as recently as Friday.

Justice Department observers estimated 15,000 to 20,000 persons attended the afternoon rally at the Monument Grounds.

The *Washington Post* counted 7,150 persons marching at 4th Street and Pennsylvania Avenue. The marchers joined others already assembled at the Monument. The first word was not to be the last. Undaunted, the religious weekly *Christian Beacon* (edited by Carl McIntire, D. D., litt. D.) insisted in its October 8 issue "the estimated attendance was between 200 and 250 thousand."

Estimating crowds, as Sturges reports, is largely guesswork strongly influenced by value judgment and situational factors. The same size crowd looks larger when it fills a small place than when spread out in a larger area. On the other hand, it is easier to take an accurate count in a limited space than one without clear boundaries. Since only a certain number of bodies can occupy a given territory, the density of a crowd can be mathematically calculated—if anyone really wants to know.

Source: Gerald D. Sturges, *Transaction Society*, 1972.

✗**Common Elements of Crowd Behavior.** Given the great variety of crowd phenomena—in size, duration, cohesion, and goals—are there any common elements that allow the observer to describe crowd behavior in general? Turner and Killian (1972) suggest that the following characteristics are found to some degree in all crowd situations:

Lack of certainty regarding what should be done.

A feeling that something should be done.

A diffusion of this feeling among participants.

Creation of a particular *mood* based on the communication of this uncertainty and urgency.

Vulnerability to suggestions for a course of action to relieve anxiety created by the mood.

Relaxation of customary restraints on behavior.

The specific content and subsequent course of action will depend on the unique situation. Crowd behavior is, by definition, less predictable than that governed by norms and structured statuses. For all these reasons collective behavior has fascinated social scientists. And not surprisingly, the models developed for understanding these phenomena have also been varied and somewhat incomplete.

MODELS OF COLLECTIVE BEHAVIOR

What turns an otherwise stable aggregate of individuals into a group of twitchers or a rampaging mob? Several theories have been advanced to explain such seemingly antisocial behavior. Because collective behavior takes place outside the expected rules of interpersonal conduct, its causes and consequences represent a breakdown of social order. In this fashion, the mainsprings of social action are often revealed more clearly than when people behave in a predictable manner. The taken-for-granted world of values and norms that hold a society together are illuminated, while attempts to restore order test the legitimacy of authorities. And, throughout, the meanings attributed to events by participants and by authorities highlight the social construction of reality. Further, many explanations of collective behavior bridge the fields of sociology and psychology. In other words, individual motivations and cognitions are important elements in several of the models to be described, and the study of collective behavior is often framed in a social-psychological perspective.

Contagion theories are essentially social-psychological in their focus on the individual's definition of the situation. The basic argument is that individuals can lose their personal identity in the anonymity offered by a crowd of strangers or, at the very least, feel free of ordinary normative restraints on behavior. A sense of personal responsibility for one's actions gives way to a collective will ("the crowd did it"). Since crowds are by definition unstructured, some confusion results ("what are we doing here? who's in charge?"). A rumor may run through the crowd, or someone may emerge to impose meaning. The directionless situation increases individual susceptibility to suggestion ("Oh, so that's what it's all about"). One person imitates another, and soon the crowd is swept up ("Let's get 'em!"). In the nineteenth century, a fashionable theory held that

✗ **Contagion theory** focuses on the individual's sense of reality in a crowd situation.

only a thin veneer of socialization covered the primitive urges of human beings, so that the crowd situation offered an opportunity for this uncontrolled creature to emerge (LeBon, 1896).

The **emotional reaction model** focuses on how the intensity of crowds develops.

A more sophisticated version of social contagion theory is Blumer's (1951) *emotional reaction* model: a) an initial stage of aimless milling, in a situation of relative anomie, leads to anxiety; b) followed by a focusing of attention on a theme or leader; c) once a sense of direction is developed, members of the group mutually reinforce that definition of the situation. This *spiraling of intensity* creates an acting crowd.

Brown and Goldin (1973) point out that contagion theories are based more on value judgment than on observation. Not all acting crowds become uncontrollable mobs or threats to law and order, although when defined as such, violence may indeed result, as is often the case in public and police reactions to motorcycle rallies (Shellow and Roemer, 1966). These theories overlook the orderly and rational elements of crowd behavior and fail to specify how emotions are transferred from one person to another.

Payoff matrix refers to the perceived costs and benefits received from different courses of action.

The rational and seemingly irrational aspects of crowd behavior can be reconciled, as suggested by Brown (1965), if we assume that people perceive certain costs or benefits from different courses of action; that is, they operate in a *pay-off matrix*. The basic situation in an acting crowd is described as "one of communication among persons having a similar conflict of mind, between an impulse which is socialized and one that is not, with the physical possibility of acting out the unsocialized impulse . . . free of punishment and guilt." When it appears that one has more to gain than lose by choosing the unsocialized option—for example, trampling someone in order to get out of a burning building as opposed to respecting the rights of others and going up in flames—a panic is likely. The fact that so many others are reacting in the same way lends an air of correctness and inevitability to the occasion.

Emergent Norm Theory. A more sociological model assumes that persons in unstructured situations seek to impose some sort of rational order on events. The crowd is not a collection of anomic individuals but a field for evolving norms and relationships, as participants interact and gradually develop rules of conduct and give meaning to their activity (Turner and Killian, 1972). The outcome of collective interaction is determined by this *emergent construction of realities* (Wright, 1978).

An emergent construction of realities emphasizes the interaction of participants in developing norms of conduct and meanings.

This model receives support from studies of the civil disorders of the 1960s. When first reported in the media, the ghetto riots were portrayed as the work of 'riffraff,' mentally unstable and criminal elements among the poor, an interpretation that absolves the rest of the nation from any responsibility for the conditions that make riots possible or logical. But more careful analysis of arrest data and patterns of destruction indicate that rioters were not the most deprived or alienated, and that the crowds exercised great discretion over which buildings to damage (Moinet, 1972; Berk and Aldrich, 1972).

In other words, there is often an economic or political agenda underlying apparently aimless mob actions. Although the crowd is the immediate agent of destruction, the roots of the riot may be found in the larger society and its institutions. Yet, not all mobs are characterized by shared beliefs or even the hope of calling attention to perceived injustice, as the following typology indicates.

A Typology of Riots.   Gary Marx (1970) proposed a property space for classifying riots, based on two dimensions: (1) whether or not the riot has a specific goal (instrumental/expressive), and (2) the presence or absence of a unifying ideology (generalized belief).

Goal Orientation

		Instrumental	*Expressive*
	Yes	**A** Change-oriented riots	**B** Hate riots
Generalized Belief			
	No	**C** Situational riots	**D** Issueless riots

Examples of cell A are food riots and revolutionary mobs. Lynching parties and mass actions against religious minorities fall in cell B. Prison riots are directed at changing immediate conditions of existence, but without a shared set of beliefs (cell C), while violence following sports events or rock concerts lacks both ideology or specific goals (cell D).

The "Value-Added" Approach.   A more extensive and detailed sociological theory of collective behavior has been presented by Smelser (1962, 1968). In the "value-added" model, Smelser proposes six stages or determinants of collective behavior. Each step must be present for the next stage in the sequence to occur; when all are present, the course of collective action can be predicted; when one or more elements is missing, the probability of collective action is reduced. The term "value-added" suggests that at each stage the range of options is progressively narrowed.

> The value added model lists six steps in the development of collective behavior.

The six conditions that are both necessary and sufficient to produce some type of collective behavior are:

1. *Structural conduciveness* refers to the way in which social institutions are organized that either permit or inhibit the expression of collective behavior. In a totalitarian state, for example, a political protest rally would be highly unlikely. Or, if urban poor lived in air-conditioned private homes, large numbers of young males would not be in the streets on a hot summer evening and the probabilities of a riot would be reduced.

2. *Structural strain* involves the introduction of tension into the situation. Tension stems from conflicts, ambiguities, and inequities of social structure that are perceived by individuals as deprivations and injustices. Feelings of fear, anxiety, and expressions of hurt are the personal consequences of structural strain. Residents of inner cities and members of minority groups are structurally situated to experience conditions leading to a sense of injustice.

3. *Growth and spread of a generalized belief* occur with the emergence of explanations for one's intolerable situation. The source of strain is identified, "whitey," "the power elite," "them." Certain characteristics are attributed to those responsible; and appropriate responses are indicated. Through their shared interpretation of the situation, individuals are prepared for joint action.

In the case of ghetto riots, white-owned businesses that have been identified as taking money out of the neighborhood are targeted for retaliation.

4. *Precipitating factors* are dramatic events that lend credibility to the generalized belief. The events need not have actually occurred; a rumor will serve to precipitate crowd reaction if the rumored event fits into the world view already produced by ideology. Most of the urban violence of the 1960s was ignited by incidents of police brutality against blacks that were further embellished by rumor. If this newest confirmation of their definition of the situation comes at the same moment that milling crowds are in the streets, the effect can be similar to putting a torch to a powder keg. No outside agitators are needed when the ground has already been well prepared by countless incidents of degradation.

5. *Mobilization for action* occurs when direction is given to the crowd ("let's go!"). At this point, one or several leaders may emerge to specify the action to be taken. For the individual, mobilization refers to the person's availability and willingness to be recruited into the proposed activity. In terms of the payoff matrix: when the impulse to express anger and hurt conflicts with the impulse to restraint, under conditions of relative anonymity in a situation in which others are urging action, the aggressive option is increasingly attractive and the riot is on.

6. *Social control factors* refer to the responses of authorities. Crowds can be encouraged or discouraged from a given course of action by the way the situation is handled by politicians, the police and courts, and the media. The application of force can stifle or inflame a crowd. Authorities can respond by acknowledging the grievances and taking steps to reduce further strain, or attempts can be made to coopt protest leaders or to mediate disputes. The ultimate fate of the collective action is shaped by interaction between crowd participants and the agents of social control.

In the case of the ghetto riots of the 1960s, the immediate reaction of state and local authorities was to call out the National Guard, which stopped the violence before it could spill over into white residential areas. The federal level response was to allocate many millions of dollars for job training and temporary relief in those cities with the greatest riot potential (Button, 1980). From 1968 on, however, government policy has turned increasingly conservative, with the allocation of funds determined by "law and order" considerations rather than by the grievances of potential rioters.

Smelser's formulation has stimulated much research and has been successfully applied to a number of studies of collective protest (for example, Lewis (1980) on the Kent State University incident). The theory has also been criticized on various grounds. Since collective behavior spans phenomena from the trivial (fads and crazes) to the profound (revolution), and from the transient (episodes of mass hysteria) to the relatively enduring (social movements), theoretical models must be fairly abstract. And since it is more important to understand events that actually shape the social order, theories that focus on change-oriented phenomena—protest, social movements, and revolution—deserve special consideration and are the subject of the remainder of this chapter.

Resource Mobilization.   The most powerful attack on social-psychological theories of collective behavior, has been mounted by those who emphasize factors of *resource mobilization*. As described by McCarthy and Zald (1977), resource mobilization theory focuses on (1) the social supports available to pro-testers, and (2) the tactics used by agents of control. It is *not* assumed that shared grievances and generalized beliefs—both social-psychological variables—are necessary conditions for the emergence of social movements.

Resource mobilization theory begins with the assumption that in modern industrial societies there is always enough generalized latent discontent to pro-vide the base for protest. In fact, issues can be manufactured out of this free-floating anxiety, without any preexisting specific grievance or ideology (these will come later, to rationalize behavior). Note, however, that the focus remains on individuals.

The mobilization perspective is given historical depth by Tilly (1978) who argues that a great transformation in the nature of collective action has taken place with the rise of the modern nation state and capitalism because the inter-est groups that control economic and political structures have changed. Collec-tive action is no longer organized on the basis of 'natural groups' as exemplified by the peasant revolts of the sixteenth century, but has become formalized into secondary groups that recruit membership, raise funds, and agitate for change. Thus, today, street demonstrations among people with generalized feelings of powerlessness can be organized around almost any specific issue: the elderly against utility rate increases, inner city poor against hospital closings, renters against landlords, prisoners against the food served to them, students against rising tuition, and so on.

Tilly (1978) combines a mobilization model of individual choice with a broader *polity model* of class conflict derived from Marx. Mobilization refers to collective action as the result of individuals pursuing their narrow self-interests under specified cost/benefit conditions: "What will this do for me?" is the cen-tral question. To this relatively conservative view Tilly adds the concept of class

Resource mobilization theory stresses the sup-ports available to pro-testors, and the tactics used by social control agents.

The **polity model** adds the concept of class struggle to the individ-ual choice aspect of the mobilization model.

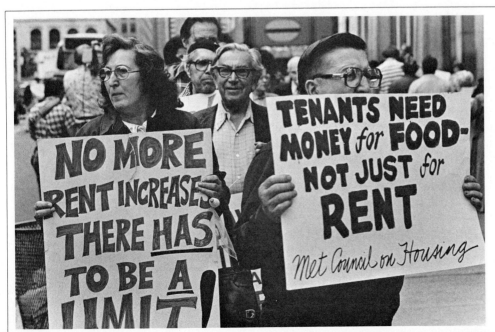

In modern industrial societies demonstra-tions among people with feelings of powerlessness can be organized around a number of specific issues. (Source: Fred Lombardi, Photo Researchers, Inc.)

struggle between those with access to the system's rewards and those without. Collective behavior thus reflects an unending conflict over claims to the benefits bestowed by the system under *zero-sum* conditions: what one group has must be at the expense of another. Revolution and violence are the result of shifting political coalitions rather than of a malfunction of a stable system (as in functional theory) or of felt deprivation on the part of participants (as in social psychological theories).

In a series of publications, Gamson (1975, 1980) applies the mobilization perspective to a broad range of protest groups and in so doing, combines functional and conflict theory. To be successful, a group that is challenging the status quo must solve two functional problems: a) maintaining the commitment of members for eventual activation, and b) solving problems of internal conflict within the movement.

Gamson (1975) listed four factors associated with success of a protest movement: centralization, bureaucratization, selective incentives for participants, and the willingness to use violence. The absence of any or all of these positive features just mentioned, or experiencing violence, and factionalism (the splintering of members into subgroups) are associated with failure. Crises that threaten political stability in the society and that mobilize participants while weakening adversaries are also favorable to movement growth (Piven and Cloward, 1977; Goldstone, 1980).

With these theoretical perspectives in mind, let us now turn to a detailed analysis of social movements.

Social Movements: Beliefs and Action

Social movements represent organized attempts to bring about or resist social change.

Social movements represent organized attempts to introduce or to resist social change. McCarthy and Zald (1977) distinguish among social movements, social movement organizations, and social movement industries:

Social movement is defined as "a set of opinions and beliefs in a population" expressing a preference for changing elements of the social structure or its system for allocating scarce rewards. A *countermovement* is a set of opinions and beliefs in a population that is opposed to the goals of social movement.

Social movement organizations are the formal structures designed to achieve the goals of a movement or countermovement.

Social movement industries arise when a number of organizations can unite around a single issue.

Contemporary social movements, including those based on a belief in equality for blacks, women, homosexuals, French-speaking Canadians, for or against nuclear power or the legalization of marijuana involve broad constituencies on each side of the issue, specific formal organizations to realize these goals, and coalitions with a variety of other organizations.

Social movements can be organized to introduce change, or, as in this example, to resist it. (Source: *United Press International Photo.*)

Countermovements should be considered in relation to the movements against which they emerged, that is, as part of a *dialectic process*. Dialectic refers to the conflict of opposites that ultimately creates a new reality which, in turn, creates contradictions and new challenges, and so forth through time. Movement and countermovement are therefore intertwined in a dynamic relationship that creates a changed environment. Moreover, countermovements share many characteristics of social movements in general. Mottl (1978) identifies a four-stage life cycle for the countermovement very similar to the developmental sequence of the primary social movement presented later in this chapter.

1. Resistance to change.
2. Mobilization of protest.
3. Transformation to militancy.
4. Reinstitutionalization of *status quo* if successful; continued low-level resistance if failing.

Countermovements can only be understood by studying the movements which influenced their emergence.

CLASSIFYING SOCIAL MOVEMENTS

Social movements can be classified by a number of features, the most important of which are duration, goals, and tactics.

Duration. Blumer (1974) distinguishes those social movements that represent broad, secular currents of change *(general)* from those that are more limited in time and place *(specific)*. An example of a general movement is the gradual expansion of civil liberties (freedom of speech, assembly, and belief) in North America. Specific movements for and against have emerged periodically, including the Free Speech Movement at the University of California, Berkeley

Social movements can be identified by several characteristics, including **duration, goals** and **tactics.**

in the early 1960s, and periodic book burnings and anti-obscenity campaigns that seek to limit some forms of publication. The overall trend has favored the civil libertarian position, although this may not be the case for specific countries at specific moments in history.

Goals.   Goals range from limited change to complete overhaul of the social structure, from total resistance to change to dropping out of the system altogether. In general, *tactics* are determined by the nature of the goals.

Reform movements are associated with a desire for change within the system that can be accomplished without radical restructuring of institutions. For example, extending constitutional guarantees of equal treatment to blacks or homosexuals involves relatively simple legislative or judicial actions. Tactics selected are those most likely to influence legislators or public opinion: demonstrations, electioneering, use of the media, and endorsement by leading figures in government and popular culture.

Revolutionary movements are based on the belief that only fundamental changes in values and social structure can accomplish desired goals. With such a belief, extraordinary tactics are not only permissible but often preferred as a means of attracting media attention, and for spreading uncertainty and fear among the populace. Hijacking, fire bombs, and other forms of terrorism are associated with contemporary revolutionary movements throughout the world: the Red Brigades in Italy, Palestinians in the Middle East, Catholics in Northern Ireland, the Weatherman faction of Students for a Democratic Society in the United States in the 1960s, and the Front de la Liberation de Québec in Canada in the 1970s.

But not all revolutionary movements depend on violent tactics. The separatist movement among French-speaking Canadians is directed at structural change in the federal system of Canadian government. And the most successful revolutionary movement in recent history was relatively bloodless: the seemingly all-powerful Shah of Iran was removed through collective protest designed to disrupt all normal activity and paralyze the country. The violence came later, once the revolution was completed. It remains to be seen whether the nonviolent union movement among Polish workers will lead to radical change in the political and economic structures of that country.

Resistance movements are those designed to forestall change. The resurgence of the Ku Klux Klan and emergence of other "backlash" organizations in the United States today demonstrates widespread resistance to the civil rights and civil liberties goals of the general movements already mentioned.

Utopian movements are directed toward the creation of an ideal society among a selected group of true believers, with the hope that the limited example will serve as a guide to more extensive change in the society. Ironically, the word "utopia" means "no place," in recognition of the impossibility of a perfect society. Yet individuals have sought to create just such a social system in reality as well as in imagination. Utopian idealism is most often realized in the social organization of a *commune,* an intentional community separated from the larger society and composed of those who have made an ideological commitment to realizing movement goals. Utopian movements, although rare and somewhat exotic, are living laboratories for the study of collective behavior. They flourish at particular historical moments, are subject to all the contingen-

---

X **Reform movements** work for change within the system.

X **Revolutionary movements** work for fundamental change of the system.

X **Resistance movements** emerge to forestall social change.

Utopian movements seek the creation of an ideal society among a group of believers.

cies of survival of any movement, and because participants must live with one another all day, every day, are vulnerable to internal disintegration. Ideology and leadership become extremely important to maintaining the commitment of members and for resolving disputes (Kanter, 1972).

Although communes have been part of the North American scene since the founding of the two nations, one of the most startling embellishments of the astonishing decade of the 1960s was the surge of communalism among young Americans. The structural conduciveness of economic affluence, the availability of mood-changing drugs, and an eventual disenchantment with political protest all heightened the appeal of "dropping out" (Gardner, 1978). The commune movement was diverse, colorful, often amusing, sometimes dangerous, and ultimately not very successful. For many young people, the commune was meant to be a temporary part of their lives, and so it was. Yet many others, old and young, are still engaged in serious attempts to create alternative communities. The keys to success appear to be commitment and structure (Kanter, 1972; Gardner, 1978) and an unswerving belief in their myths (Hall, 1978). Without structure and common agreement on goals, the commune drifts into anarchy. Isolation from other social systems leaves members totally dependent on one another, which can enhance mutual caring or lead to authoritarianism and paranoia, as in the case of the People's Temple or Synanon (Lang, 1978).

WHO JOINS SOCIAL MOVEMENTS?

Do different types of movements attract different types of people? Are some individuals more likely than others to participate in collective protest and social movements? Common sense suggests that movements would attract people who are ideologically predisposed to movement goals or, that they have more to gain than lose from participation. Social-psychological theories often assume the availability of a pool of relatively discontented people waiting to be mobilized, but few researchers have explored the actual process of recruitment.

It has also been noted that movements draw recruits from populations that are relatively marginal or socially isolated. Among the characteristics associated with movement participation are geographic mobility, lack of family ties, recent status change, status inconsistency, and personal maladjustment. It is the young, the unattached, and the relatively rootless who are more often found carrying placards in street demonstrations than are people fully enmeshed in work and family. In the student protest movements, for example, first-year and transfer students were overrepresented in contrast to students more anchored in the specific college.

However, this social psychological profile of movement participants ("they're just a bunch of kooks and malcontents") did not accurately reflect the characteristics of men who took part in ghetto riots, nor does it describe the women engaged in antifeminist activity or participants in the antibusing movement (B. Useem, 1980).

A sociological approach, however, is less concerned with personal attributes of members than with the process that links them to a particular movement. *Recruitment* to a movement is not a random, chance event. Some individuals may be more susceptible than others, such as the rootless and unattached, but they rarely seek out membership. More often, participants are introduced to the movement (its beliefs and its organization) by other people. Real isolates

> Social movements often draw recruits from populations that are **marginal** or socially **isolated**.

Persons who are rela-
tively unattached are in
a position of **structural
availability** for recruitment to social move-
ments.

are outside any network of influence. Snow et al. (1980) argue that being relatively unattached (nonmarried, underemployed, and so on) only frees an individual to explore new lines of action. These persons are then in a position of
structural availability for recruitment because there are so few other competing
demands on time and energies. Whether or not they actually are introduced to a
movement depends on their social networks, how many and what kinds of
friends or acquaintances they have.

> Our findings indicate that the probability of being recruited into a particular
> movement is largely a function of two conditions: (1) Links to one or more move-
> ment members through a preexisting or emergent interpersonal tie; and (2) the
> absence of countervailing networks.

In a study of antibusing activists in Boston, Bert Useem (1980) found that
isolates were *less* likely to join the protest movement than were people firmly
embedded in a network of like-minded friends and neighbors. *Solidarity* preceded movement activity and reinforced the feeling that whites were being neglected and manipulated, thereby justifying protest behavior.

In other words, the "how" of recruitment—tells us more about who joins
what than does an analysis of the reasons—the "whys"—that participants give
for joining. Reasons for participation are often supplied *after* an action, in order
to rationalize what has already happened (Snow et al., 1980).

PHASES IN THE DEVELOPMENT OF SOCIAL MOVEMENTS

Social movements have
a life course or natural
history.

A number of schemes have been constructed for describing the "natural history" or *life course* of a social movement (for example, Gettys, 1937; Hopper,
1950; Zald and Ash, 1969; Blumer, 1974). Although different terms are used, all
these models distinguish at least four major phases from the inception to the
dissolution of a social movement: (1) a preliminary period of personal discontent and vague unrest in the society; (2) the crystallization of concern and the
construction of information networks; (3) formation of organizations to embody
movement beliefs; and (4) either the institutionalization of the movement's
goals or its decline through attrition of membership.

Phase one begins with
widespread feelings of
deprivation and **discontent.**

Phase One.   Widespread feelings of discontent and/or awareness of deprivation on the part of individuals are often associated with conditions in the larger
society: economic crises, wars, migration, technological change, natural disasters, and so forth.

Some social movements—*nativistic revivals*—arise when a group's traditional culture is disrupted, dramatically changed, or destroyed. Other movements occur not at the lowest ebb in a group's fortunes, but when conditions
have begun to improve, when the gap between anticipated benefits and the
actual pace of social change generates a *revolution of rising expectations* (Davies,
1962). Some support for this thesis is found in the history of the French and
Russian revolutions, in the Quebec separatist movement in Canada, and in the
civil disorders of urban United States in the late 1960s.

Absolute deprivation
occurs in the absence of
the basic necessities of
life.

For the individual, feelings of deprivation may be absolute or relative.
Absolute deprivation occurs when one is without the basic necessities of survival. When both material and emotional needs (respect, dignity) are frustrated, individuals may feel there is nothing to lose by joining a movement. But

deprivation can also lead to feelings of powerlessness and a withdrawal from active coping. For this reason, the extremely poor may not participate in movements undertaken on their behalf.

Relative deprivation is felt by those who compare their situation with some previous or expected state of well-being and perceive that they have lost or not gained what they feel to be legitimately theirs. Countermovements such as taxpayers' revolts and antibusing campaigns are composed of people who feel threatened with loss of social status—power, prestige, or relative wealth in relation to other groups. Relative deprivation also involves comparing oneself with others considered one's equals, and concluding that one is being treated unfairly ("I'm as good as they are"). Anti-discrimination movements develop from feelings of relative as well as absolute deprivation.

In the first phase of a social movement, however, these feelings are not clearly articulated nor widely shared. The initial reaction is to blame failure on oneself or on fate. The type of leader likely to emerge at this period is the *prophet* (to believers) or the *agitator* (to agents of social control).

Phase Two.   In the second phase of a social movement, discontented individuals realize that there are many others who share their anger or dismay. Here is where the media are crucial to the crystallization of a movement; publicity gives voice and a legitimate presence to what had been vague and unfocused emotions.

Recognizing that one is not alone is a necessary but not sufficient condition for the emergence of a social movement. To transform personal feelings into public issues, individuals require an *ideology* that explains the structural sources of their concern and provides an agenda for action. A movements' belief system presents an alternative construction of reality capable of mobilizing individuals. For example, the ideology of white supremacy serves this purpose for a countermovement composed of American Nazis, the Ku Klux Klan, and members of the National States Rights Party.

A second essential ingredient in this phase is the construction of a communications network—newsletters, special-interest magazines, and the development of local units or cells of like-minded individuals. In this phase of a movement, leadership tends to be of the charismatic variety able to articulate the yearnings of the discontented, and to attract media attention. The leader embodies the dream.

Phase Three.   The *mobilization* or *formalization* stage occurs when movement members acquire the resources needed to create an organization; namely, money, active participation of a critical mass, and generalized social tolerance or at least the absence of repressive controls.

This is the stage at which a movement is transformed into a social movement organization, and when charismatic leadership is reinforced or replaced by managerial types. In Weber's terms, the movement is partially demystified and subject to the challenges of survival in a more or less hostile environment and the need to maintain the commitment of participants.

It is at this point that *resource mobilization* becomes crucial. No matter how discontented individuals may be, and no matter how powerful their beliefs, unless they can effectively meet the functional requisites for social system sur-

---

Relative deprivation is felt by those who compare their existing situation with a previous or expected state of well-being.

In phase two personal discontent becomes a public issue, usually coinciding with the development of an **ideology.**

Phase three consists of the **mobilization** or **formalization** period during which an organization is created.

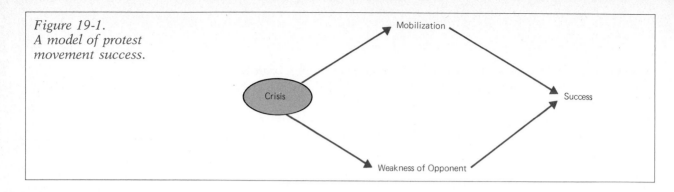

Figure 19-1.
A model of protest
movement success.

Crisis → Mobilization
Crisis → Weakness of Opponent
Mobilization → Success
Weakness of Opponent → Success

Important aspects of **re-source mobilization** are the **emergence of a dominant leader**, the **development of a bureaucratic structure**, and the **accompanying centralization of powers.**

vival, the movement will not succeed. Goal attainment depends on dealing effectively with other groups, deflecting the forces of social control, resisting cooptation, and avoiding factionalism. According to Gamson (1975) *centralization of power* and the *emergence of a dominant group or leader* tend to solve the problem of internal conflict within the movement, while the *development of a bureaucratic* structure sustains the movement even when members are not activated.

It also helps if those opposed to the movement are relatively disorganized. Goldstone (1980) and Piven and Cloward (1977) suggest that the weakness of opposing forces is at least as important to success as is the creation of structure within the movement (see Figure 19-1).

√ Phase four consists of the movement's **institutionalization.**

✗ **Phase Four.** Institutionalization occurs when movement beliefs become part of the taken-for-granted world, and when movement goals are embodied in relatively stable organizations. At this point there are two aims to be achieved: a) recognition of movement organizations as legitimate representatives of these goals, and b) producing benefits for members (Gamson, 1975).

Organizational Success. There are dangers in becoming fully organized and accepted. One is the problem of goal displacement, whereby maintaining the formal structure displaces the original goals of the movement. Leaders of movements can also be coopted by being drawn into mainstream power structures, perhaps spending as much time with legislators and government officials as with their own constituency. Above all, the tendency toward oligarchy must be resisted. These dangers are conservatizing influences (Zald and Ash, 1969), as leadership passes to bureaucrats whose loyalty is to the organization, in contrast to the charismatic leader's devotion to the cause. Organizational success and its consequences, therefore, may destroy a movement.

Substantive Success. A social movement also loses momentum when substantive goals are achieved. The coalition formed to press for women's suffrage in the United States disappeared overnight once the Nineteenth Amendment was passed in 1920. Four decades later, a new feminist movement emerged to settle the unfinished business of the first.

Substantive Defeat. Early successes of social movements provoke counter-movement activities and organizations. The socialist movement of the 1930s in the United States was effectively crushed by a combination of government action, public fear, and internal dissension. The Women's Christian Temperance Union (WCTU) enjoyed the victory of the Prohibition Amendment before experiencing thorough defeat with its repeal.

In many cases, some movement goals will be realized but not others. This presents problems for the continued activation of member commitments. Some participants will feel vindicated and cease to be active in the movement. Leaders must continually emphasize the unmet goals while the opposition points to what has been accomplished and claims that it is sufficient. Manipulation of public opinion is crucial in this respect. For example, both the civil rights and women's movement today are foundering on the public perception that their major goals have been accomplished.

Organizing the Poor for Fame and Profit: The National Welfare Right Organization

Of all the social movements spawned in the 1960s none might seem more improbable than an organization of welfare recipients claiming their legal entitlements to adequate allowances and respectful treatment. The view of most nonpoor, then as now, is that welfare beneficiaries should be grateful for what a generous society chooses to give them. Up until 1965, only about half of those eligible for Aid to Families with Dependent Children (AFDC) had enrolled, either from ignorance or indifference. This was the situation that social scientists Frances Fox Piven and Richard Cloward sought to change dramatically. By informing people of their rights and then mobilizing them to pursue their claims, Piven and Cloward's goal was to overload the welfare system to such an extent that the federal government would have to become responsible for a nationwide program likely to be more favorable to welfare recipients than the current system.

Piven and Cloward (1971) favored the tactics of mass demonstrations and creating the maximum feasible trouble for local agencies, with the latent function of providing an opportunity for effective collective action to those whose previous experiences had reinforced tendencies to alienation and withdrawal. This ideal of a "poor people's movement" as a spontaneous grass-roots protest was not shared by other leaders of the urban poor. They preferred a more formal type of organization, and the National Welfare Rights Organization (NWRO) was formed in 1966 under the direction of people experienced in the civil rights movement. At its peak, a few years later, over 20,000 welfare mothers (mostly black) were involved.

As Piven and Cloward (1977) describe its subsequent history, NWRO illustrates the problems of goal displacement and cooptation. Having created an organization designed to capture media attention, its leaders became public figures. Organization-centered goals replaced those of directing benefits to the poor; scarce funds were used for office salaries, and energies were devoted to enhancing the power of its leaders. As a consequence, the welfare mothers withdrew their support, and the movement collapsed in the general wave of antiwelfarism of the 1970s. In this case, organization was clearly not sufficient to activate and sustain commitment from the rank-and-file, nor to overcome resistance from outside. Critics of Piven and Cloward (Roach and Roach, 1978) claim that NWRO—in theory and practice—was flawed from the beginning, a "road to a dead end," and that the poor would have done better to work through the organized labor movement rather than to divide the working class.

Frances Fox Piven and Richard Cloward, *Poor People's Movements*, New York: Pantheon, 1977, and Jack L. Roach and Janet K. Roach. "Mobilizing the Poor: Road to a Dead End." *Social Problems*, Vol. 26, No. 2, 1978.

SOCIETAL REACTIONS TO SOCIAL MOVEMENTS

The success or failure of a social movement also depends on variables external to the movement. In many cases, groups in power will be supportive of movement goals, once convinced of its legitimacy or power. Politicians are quick to pick up winds of change, as witnessed in the 1970s by increasing support of the antiwar movement and declining commitments to civil rights and the Equal Rights Amendment in the United States. The Quebec Separatist Movement and the environmental movement are countered by partial measures designed to deflect the full force of movement demands.

Repression and **cooptation** are techniques of social control that suppress or contain the movement.

In general, agents of social control can utilize two basic strategies: *repression* and *cooptation*. Jailing, deportation, harassment, and the ultimate use of armed force have all been used to repress movements defined as subversive. These tactics have been very effective in destroying left-wing movements and militant racial organizations (such as the Black Panthers) but only moderately and temporarily effective against right-wing movements such as the American Nazis or the Klan, reflecting value judgments made by political leaders and law enforcement officials regarding the potential harm of a movement.

Cooptation refers to bringing former dissidents into the established leadership structure. A black civil rights leader who becomes a presidential advisor, or a feminist elected to Parliament, becomes part of the power elite against which she or he had previously fought. Even where such gains are more apparent than real, it is the public perception that is important. A few visible acts of cooptation can give the impression that movement goals have been accomplished, thus reducing public support for further gains, while also depleting movement leadership.

To illustrate many of these universal problems and processes of collective protest, we will examine three contemporary movements—that against nuclear power, and those for women's equality and for homosexual rights—that embrace activists in both Canada and the United States. A brief case study of the black civil rights movement in the United States may also have implications for a society as heterogeneous as that of Canada.

Some Current Social Movements: Dilemmas and Directions

THE PROTEST MOVEMENT AGAINST NUCLEAR POWER

The anti-nuclear-power protest movement (ANPM) is an offshoot of the larger environmental movement. It is composed largely of younger activists who became impatient with the slow, establishment-oriented activities of the parent movement. As analysed by Barkan (1979) ANPM illustrates many of the organizational difficulties discussed throughout this chapter, particularly in four areas of controversy within the movement.

Goals: Single-Issue vs. Multi-Issue Protest. ANPM activists have generally chosen to limit themselves to opposition to nuclear power plants, avoiding

other issues such as nuclear weapons, thus reducing the chance of forging a more broadly based alliance.

Tactics: How to Define Nonviolence.   ANPM is committed to nonviolent civil disobedience as a matter of principle (their major objection to nuclear power is its potential for physical harm to citizens), and as a strategy likely to win public support. *Civil disobedience* involves nonviolent aggression: occupation of premises, sit-down strikes, and demonstrations. The moral dimension of civil disobedience is the willingness to be arrested or roughed up for one's opposition to public policy.

> **Civil disobedience** is nonviolent but generally illegal action.

More militant subgroups accuse the mainstream organization of selling out, then break away, often conducting guerrilla actions provoking violence from the authorities that can either enlist sympathy or alienate the public.

Consensus and Affinity Groups.   Following the Quaker method of securing group approval of any course of action, the ANPM adopted the process of *consensus* rather than majority rule. Consensus requires that an issue be discussed until all present agree on a given response. This is a very time-consuming process although essential for solidarity. *Affinity groups* of a dozen or so self-selected individuals carry out the decisions arrived at by consensus. "Affinity" means likeness or closeness, and affinity groups are composed of persons who have some special bond, making the group extremely supportive.

> **Consensus** requires discussion of an issue until all present agree on a given course of action.

> **Affinity groups** are composed of people with a common bond.

Each of these choices strengthens internal cohesion but lessens the effectiveness of the movement in mobilizing to counter the ability of power companies to influence legislators and manipulate public opinion.

THE MOVEMENT FOR HOMOSEXUAL RIGHTS (GAY RIGHTS)

There are special difficulties involved in organizing for gay rights. Whereas it is not illegal to be against nuclear power or speak French or to be female, it is

557

Organizing for gay rights is complicated by hostility toward gays, and the illegality of homosexual acts.

often illegal to commit homosexual acts. Few minority groups have experienced the extreme prejudice and discrimination still directed against homosexuals in North America. Homosexuals have been refused religious sacraments, fired from jobs, beaten by thugs, broadly ridiculed and humiliated, and, until recently, diagnosed as mentally ill and forbidden entry visas in the United States.

As a consequence, most homosexuals remain in a self-enforced state of secrecy. To organize would require public acknowledgment of one's sexual preference, and could lead to the loss of job, friends, respect in the community, and safety. Yet, if homosexuals do not announce themselves and join together in protest, how can the public view of homosexuals as effeminate men and masculine women be changed?

To overcome these barriers some means of communication had to be created, a leadership structure established, and an ideology developed that would justify and rationalize homosexuality, bring people out and into the streets, and provide an agenda for action. It would be difficult to overestimate the forces of social control: fear alone has kept millions from acknowledging their homosexuality.

Conditions for Emergence. A gay rights movement could not have emerged without the major changes in the climate of sexual expression that accompanied the social protest movements of the 1960s, but the precipitating or galvanizing event could not have been predicted. A gay bar off Christopher Street in New York City was routinely raided by the police one evening in 1969, when, much to the surprise of everyone, the patrons resisted and pushed the police back into the street, an incident that became for gays the functional equivalent of the Boston Tea Party. Over the next several years, local groups were formed in almost every major city and campus in North America, linked by newsletters, magazines, and an informal communications network.

Ideology. An ideology of homosexual rights must counteract negative societal definitions, explain the nature of homosexuality, reinforce a positive identity, and activate a commitment to action. This is done by stressing the normalcy of most homosexuals, and by claiming the right of privacy for nonpublic acts between consenting adults. With regard to housing and jobs, homosexuals seek the same equal protection of the laws that has been applied to other minority groups.

Tactics. Gay rights activists have applied the full range of protest group tactics, from normal electoral politics in San Francisco to confrontation and demonstrations elsewhere in the United States and Canada.

Internal Divisions. The Gay Rights Movement is no more unified than any other protest group. Female homosexuals (lesbians) are angry with the anti-female bias and exaggerated "macho" characteristics of some leaders of the movement. Radicals refuse to work within the legal/rational system. The willful flaunting of exaggerated behaviors by a visible few and the entire sado-masochistic scene tend to undercut the public support carefully built up by movement leaders.

Organization. The major organizations speaking on behalf of the movement are the *National Gay Task Force* in the United States, and the *Canadian National Gay Rights Coalition*. Both function as coordinating committees maintaining communications through national newsletters. Essentially, the movement is decentralized, with autonomous local groups, including Gay Caucuses in many professional organizations and on many campuses.

The goals of local organizations are as much social as political, providing a supportive environment for the stigmatized. Homosexual clubs affirm the identity of members and encourage others to come out, reinforce the belief in their essential goodness, and identify the external sources of their discontent.

A flourishing gay subculture now characterizes most large cities in the United States and Canada. In the more liberal, mainline denominations, gay churches have been institutionalized. The recent publication of a number of books written by or for homosexuals has both spurred general interest in gay lifestyles and created a literature lending weight and artistic legitimacy to the movement.

Yet much remains unfinished. Most North Americans remain unconvinced that homosexuality is as valid as heterosexuality. Resistance mounts and the harassment continues: In Canada, two men were recently indicted and convicted of the crime of kissing on a Toronto street, steam baths were raided, and a member of a government commission was dismissed solely on grounds of his being a homosexual.

THE WOMEN'S MOVEMENT

Of all the social movements of recent decades, two appear to have had especially widespread and irreversible effects: the civil rights movement and the women's rights movement.

Emergence. From a generalized discontent in the 1960s, the new feminist movement emerged with the realization by individual women that their condition was not due to some personal failing but was the result of forces in the culture and social structure that limited and shaped their lives. Their consciousness was awakened by such books as Friedan's *Feminine Mystique* (1963). A commission on the Status of Women appointed by President Kennedy published a report in 1963 documenting widespread discrimination against women in the United States, and encouraged the formation of state-wide networks of activists. In Canada, a 1970 *Report of the Royal Commission on the Status of Women* similarly documented extensive inequality. An additional element in the emergence of the new feminism was the experience that many younger women were gaining in the other protest movements of the 1960s, including being treated as sex objects.

Organization. Once the legal, structural, and ideological bases of the movement were formed, it was only a short step to formal organization. The National Organization for Women (NOW) was established in 1966 by several former members of the Commission on the Status of Women. Since that time, dozens of other organizations have been formed at the national, state, and local levels in Canada and the United States. Yet the movement as a whole remains essentially unorganized (some would suggest disorganized), without central leadership or administration in both countries. In large part, this was a conscious decision. The ideology of the movement is relentlessly nonhierarchical and antielitist. To build a typical structure of superordination and subordination would negate the meaning of feminism.

Goals. Another reason why there is no single organizational structure is that the goal of equality is so broad that there is room to debate over what to achieve, when, and how. As a central symbol, feminists in the United States have chosen the Equal Rights Amendment (ERA) but there are some factions that feel the amendment is either too much, or not enough, or simply irrelevant. For the more radical segment of the movement in both countries, heavily influenced by Marxism, the goal is nothing short of the complete restructuring of the capitalist state. However, a majority would be gratified to achieve legal equality and control over their own bodies.

Tactics. As might be expected from this description, tactics vary across a spectrum from lobbying legislators to street theater and massive demonstrations. Interestingly, the feminists have been less violent than their opposition, who have fire-bombed abortion clinics. Feminists have sought to influence target groups directly and indirectly through the media and public opinion. Media attention, very heavy in the early days, helped spread the message to women who might otherwise have felt isolated, but focusing on the most flamboyant issues and personalities has often worked to trivialize the movement.

The women's movement is extremely diversified in goals, style, tactics, and organization.

Internal Differences. The women's movement is extremely heterogeneous: gays and straights, Marxists and reformists, whites and nonwhites, and special interest subgroups such as union women, athletes, career professionals, politicians, homemakers, single parents, and so forth. Freeman (1975) has also described a basic division within the movement between an "older branch" and a "younger" one. The older branch prefers to work through established channels for reformist change, and through bureaucratic organizations. The younger branch is not only typically composed of younger women, but emphasizes grassroots organizing for specific local goals, and is basically concerned with 'consciousness-raising' among individual members of small friendship groups (see also Cassell, 1977). In the long run, it may be this underground channel of personal change and mobilization that will have the greater impact on the course of feminism in North America.

Balance Sheet. While falling short of enactment of firm guarantees of reproductive freedom in both nations and of the ERA in the United States, the movement has accomplished much. But the gains have been slow and uneven. Perhaps the greatest change has been in the general perception of gender roles. It seems unlikely that either men or women will think about themselves and their relationships in the same way as before the movement.

THE CIVIL RIGHTS MOVEMENT: AN UNFINISHED PROTEST

The history of black protest in the United States begins with slave revolts in the eighteenth century and continues to this very day in a variety of forms. The modern civil rights movement that emerged in the mid-1950s in the South has been analysed by Sherman and Wood (1979) in terms of six factors necessary and sufficient for protest movement success:

1. Structural conditions. As blacks moved from the rural South to the urban North in the period 1940–45 in response to employment opportunities, their situation improved with regard to jobs, income, education, and awareness of power. That is, absolute deprivation was lessened, especially in Northern cities.

2. Felt deprivation. Relative to whites, however, blacks remained deprived in terms of housing, education, jobs, and pay, and the level of relative deprivation continued to increase through the following decades.

3. Ideological crystallization. Awareness of the gap between the ideals of democracy that large numbers had fought for during the war and the reality of their condition led many blacks to the realization that such inequity should be openly protested. The chief architect of this ideology was Rev. Martin Luther King, Jr., who argued for *nonviolent tactics and reformist goals.* King directed his call to action to both the blacks experiencing deprivation and to those whites who recognized the moral dilemma of continued segregation in the land of the free. Both the goals (reform) and tactics (nonviolence) would make civil rights activism acceptable to large numbers of whites.

4. Precipitating events. The 1954 Supreme Court decision that the "separate but equal" doctrine was inherently unequal and therefore unconstitutional was one of the events that precipitated protest. Then, in December 1955, a black woman, Rosa Parks, was arrested in Montgomery, Alabama for refusing to go to the back of a bus where there were special seats for blacks, just one of the endless petty harassments endured by blacks in a segregated society.

5. Mobilization. The black community responded to Rosa Parks's arrest with a show of solidarity—a boycott of public transportation in Montgomery that caused enormous losses to white-owned businesses. Reverend King provided charismatic leadership, rallying blacks to continue the boycott and reinforcing the effectiveness of nonviolent tactics. Sit-ins and silent marches followed throughout the South. When agents of social control resorted to violence, the sights and sounds appeared on national television, mobilizing the commitment of many whites. In 1963, hundreds of thousands of supporters rallied in Washington—the emotional high point of the movement.

Subsequently, overt resistance to civil rights declined, important legislation was passed at all levels of government, and antiblack organizations went underground (to reemerge in the late 1970s).

Organization. At the national level, there are several long-established civil rights organizations such as the National Association for the Advancement of Colored People and the Urban League. Both are reformist and highly-respected organizations staffed by middle- and upper-stratum blacks (although many of the founders of NAACP were whites).

Martin Luther King, Jr.'s organizational creation was the Southern Christian Leadership Conference, primarily led by churchmen. Dozens of other localized or special interest associations have been established in the past two decades. Yet there is no one overarching organizational structure to the civil rights movement, and, on occasion, leaders of these various groups have been in conflict over goals, tactics, and funding.

> The civil rights movement has changed the status of American blacks and altered race relations throughout the U.S.

Internal Divisions. The major internal divisions are between reformists and militants, and between a middle-class leadership stratum and the less affluent, less articulate black population. The difficulty of organizing this latter segment was illustrated by the fate of the National Welfare Rights Organization.

Balance Sheet. The civil rights movement has realized impressive gains in politics, the law, education, and public accommodations. In a real sense the legal structures of segregation and discrimination have been dismantled. It is equally true that massive resistance to black advancement remains, that *de facto* segregation continues to separate the races, and that discrimination still circumscribes the lives of blacks, poor and nonpoor alike.

At the moment these backlash forces have stalled the civil rights movement, which is also in some organizational disarray. The assassination of Martin Luther King was a blow from which the movement is only now recovering. Further, economic system failures have reduced the possibility of continued upward mobility and placed black and white workers in conflict with one another for existing jobs. But to the extent that the moderate leadership fails to sustain gains already made, while the objective conditions of many blacks continue to deteriorate, the stage is set for a new, more militant grassroots movement.

Our examination of collective behavior, and the analysis of contemporary social movements especially, should be placed in the broader context of social change. Many manifestations of collective action—some types of rumor-mongering and rioting, for example—occur because individuals feel threatened by change or seek to induce it. Conditions of normlessness are common in modern societies because so many changes take place in all aspects of life, and in increasingly shorter periods of time. Such instability breeds confusion and dismay, creating the anomie that is a precondition of collective behavior.

Social movements are more directly implicated in the study of change, as a conscious attempt to end some unacceptable condition or to bring about a new order, or to resist change. We have not yet dealt in detail with those movements that are explicitly revolutionary. Such movements provide a bridge to our last chapter: Modernization and Social Change.

Summary

A range of behavior, including crazes and fads, panics and mass hysteria, mobs and riots, crowds, rumor and public opinion, social movements, and revolutions are included in the study of collective behavior. Collective behavior can be classified by the degree to which it is spontaneous or structured, short-term or long-term, expressive or instrumental, and goal-oriented. Spontaneous events such as hysteria, panic, and rumors tend to be short-lived, expressive, and lacking clearly stated goals. A more cohesive form of collective behavior characterizes crowds, temporary gatherings of people brought together by some common activity.

Several theories of crowds and other collective behavior have been developed, including contagion theories, the emotional reaction model, emergent norm theory, the value added model, and the resource mobilization model.

Social movements are organized attempts to introduce or to resist social change. The success of social movements often produces counter movements—the two are interlinked in a dynamic relationship that changes the social environment. A major distinction exists between reform movements aimed at change within the social system and revolutionary movements which seek basic changes in values and in the social system itself. The goal of resistance movements is to forestall change, while that of utopian movements is to establish an ideal society through the example of a small group of true believers.

Social movements tend to develop through four phases: (1) an early period of personal discontent and general unrest in the society; (2) the crystallization of concern and creation of networks of information; (3) the development of organizations based on movement beliefs; and (4) either the adoption of the movement's goals or its decline. The success or failure of social movements is a result of both external and internal factors. Four current social movements are analyzed: the protest movement against nuclear power, the movement for gay rights, the women's movement, and the civil rights movement. These struggles for social change continue, despite substantial opposition to each.

Suggested Readings

FANON, FRANTZ. *The Wretched of the Earth* (New York: Grove Press, 1968). Fanon's discussion of colonialism and revolutionary protest has been very influential among intellectuals in the developing nations.

FREEMAN, JO. *The Politics of Women's Liberation: A Case Study of an Emerging Social Movement and its Relation to the Policy Process* (New York: McKay, 1975). In this provocative volume, Freeman traces the development of the contemporary women's movement and its implications for social policy, from a social movement perspective.

HUMPHREYS, LAUD. *Out of the Closets: The Sociology of Homosexual Liberation* (Englewood Cliffs, N.J.: Prentice-Hall, 1972). The many links between individual choices and collective movements for social change are explored.

KING, MARTIN LUTHER, JR. *Stride Toward Freedom: The Montgomery Story* (New York: Harper & Row, 1958). This is the noted civil rights leader's first-hand account of the struggle toward desegregation and the attainment of justice for blacks in the years before the Montgomery boycott brought national attention to the movement.

PIVEN, FRANCES FOX, and RICHARD A. CLOWARD. *Poor People's Movements: Why They Succeed, How They Fail* (New York: Vintage, 1979). An insightful examination of the successes and failures of four protest movements—those of unemployed workers, industrial workers, and the civil rights and welfare rights movements.

SMELSER, NEIL J. *Theory of Collective Behavior* (New York: Free Press, 1963). This is a sociological classic, presenting a systematic step-by-step model of collective behavior and social movement development. This volume is an important starting point for any theory of social protest.

Useem, Michael. *Protest Movements in America* (Indianapolis: Bobbs-Merrill, 1975). Useem's treatment of protest movements in the United States is a fascinating panorama of human hopes and follies, stunning successes and utter failures.

20 Modernization and Social Change

N o culture, not even that of simple societies such as the Tasaday, is exactly the same today as it was five hundred or even five years ago. Even if all members of a society were to resist any change from within and insist that everything be done as it always has been, there are forces beyond their control that make such continuity highly unlikely. Climate changes can affect the mode of subsistence; famine and disease can diminish a population; wars and invasions destroy existing social structures; and contact with other societies introduces new and different cultural traits. *Social and cultural change* refers to the processes whereby values, norms, institutionalized relationships, and stratification hierarchies undergo transformation over time. *Cultural changes* occur in the areas of norms, beliefs, values, and technology. *Social change* affects the patterns of interaction and institutional arrangements within the society. The two are so closely interwoven that we shall use the terms interchangeably in this chapter.

Social and cultural change are the processes whereby values, norms, institutions and relationships undergo transformation.

General and Specific Change

The course of change in any given society will depend upon specific historical events. For example, the emergence of African nation-states produced change for the Ik, as did a chance encounter with a trapper from outside alter the Tasaday, and as three hundred years of immigration, territorial expansion, and modernization altered Canada and the United States.

One of the major controversies in social theory is concerned with the existence of a *cumulative trend* over the many thousand years of human history. The basic model we have adopted in this book assumes that there has been a general development from simple to more complex social systems, from small bands of gatherers with their limited material culture to the social and technological complexities of modern industrial and postindustrial societies. In proposing this model, we recognize that such a development is not characteristic of every society, for chance factors play an important part in specific outcomes. Yet, when the history of all known societies is added together, there is a general pattern: certain technologies and types of knowledge do not emerge without a set of prior conditions. In that sense, any social system is an outcome of all that has gone before within it, as well as the impact of external forces. Nonetheless, more complex social orders tend to follow simpler ones in time, although many forms may exist simultaneously. On the North American continent today, for example, one can find hunters and trappers, herders, traditional religious agricultural communities—such as the Amish or Hutterites—as well as industrial cities and residential suburbs.

A cumulative historical trend assumes a general development from simple to more complex societies.

You should also keep in mind that not all institutional spheres necessarily become more complex as societies become more intricate. As we have seen, kinship and belief systems are more elaborate in simple societies than in mod-

Traditional communities such as the Amish co-exist in the United States with a modern complex society. (Source: *Talbot Lovering, Stock, Boston.*)

The Mountain People

For countless generations, a hunting and gathering tribe called Teuso inhabited a stretch of mountainous land in East Central Africa. Nomadic bands of Teuso tracked big game in a yearly cycle that brought them past food gathering and watering sites and back to their main grounds. The Teuso were careful never to take more from the land than necessary, so that animals and plants could be replenished for the following year's cycle. The Teuso were well adapted to their geographical and physical environment, maintaining a careful balance between population and resources.

Teuso society was characterized both by the high level of cooperation required for hunting and the relative equality of the sexes associated with the women's important contributions to economic security. As in most hunting/gathering cultures, relationships were informal and flexible. Few distinctions were made on the basis of wealth or power within the society. The Teuso were described by the anthropologist Colin Turnbull as an open and friendly people.

Following World War II, however, major changes were imposed upon the Teuso from outside. New countries were formed in central Africa as nationalism replaced established colonial rule. Leaders of these emerging states sought to build cohesive nations out of the numerous tribal units within their new and arbitrary boundaries. The Teuso, now called the Ik, found that their traditional hunting grounds had been incorporated into a National Park within which they were forbidden by law to pursue the animals that had been at the center of their way of life. Governmental officials sought to convert the Ik into farmers who would stay in one place, rather than remain migratory hunters and gatherers. The land selected for the Ik was a rocky area with little rainfall and since the tribe had no tradition or technology

ern ones where both spheres have been considerably reduced in scope. When kinship loyalties and religious authorities no longer control the conduct of daily life, other institutions are developed or changed to handle the tasks of regulating social order, socialization, and the provision of material and emotional satisfactions. For example, in modern societies, the government, educational establishments, and the conjugal family manage tasks that were once controlled through kinship networks and religious organization.

THE RISE OF THE NATION-STATE

The nation as a distinct unit of social organization is relatively new as the dominant source for group identity, communality, and loyalty. For most societies throughout human history, nationality meant little; rather, residential locale, kinship, and ascribed status were the bases for social cohesion. *Nationalism,* or a shared belief by a large number of people that they have something in common powerful enough to seek political unity, became a tool welding together heterogeneous populations only within the last 400 years or so. Nationalism provides a sense of "we group" with which very different individuals and subgroups may identify; it may also hasten processes of economic development and social change.

The **nation** is a distinct unit of social organization providing group identity, communality, and loyalty.

Nationalism refers to a consciousness of shared identity among members of a politically distinct territory.

suitable for farming, disaster was inevitable.

Indeed, when Turnbull revisited the tribe in the 1960s, he found a people who had become "as unfriendly, uncharitable, inhospitable and generally mean as any people can be." What we think of as normal bonds of affection and compassion had disappeared. Under the threat of starvation, each member of the society acted in terms of immediate self-interest, even snatching morsels of food from a child or ill person.

Turnbull's interpretation is that the Ik are victims of "progress," by which he means modern technology that outstrips human efforts to adapt through social and cultural change. Once a mode of subsistence has been drastically altered, all the relationships built upon that base collapse. Social order disintegrates; meaning is lost. Turnbull goes one step further, suggesting that, in such dire circumstances, a more elemental human nature emerges, and that the Ik may represent the fate of all of us as relationships are increasingly dehumanized in the pursuit of technological superiority, so that social relationships become superfluous to survival.

Our interpretation is somewhat less gloomy. Certainly, major subsistence changes affect every other aspect of life, *including personality.* But the story of the Ik may not illustrate a basic human nature dominated by ruthless self-interest as much as the general proposition that humans are basically neither competitive nor cooperative. Rather, they are shaped by the cultures and social systems they have devised to adapt to their environments.

More specifically, the Ik illustrate the themes of this chapter: the causes and consequences of change at both the macrolevel of culture and social structure, and the microlevel of interaction and personality.

Source: Colin Turnbull, *The Mountain People.* New York: Simon and Schuster, 1972.

While the existence of strong, relatively stable monarchies promoted the rise of nationalism in Europe, at least two other factors favored the concept of the nation state as a foundation for political authority and self-identity: capitalism and colonialism. Indeed, for many countries, the growth of capitalism coincided with the emergence of nationalism; as capitalistic economies developed, there was a search for wider markets and raw materials to be exploited. This was especially pronounced in countries such as England, France, Germany, the Netherlands, and Spain.

With the discovery of the New World, traders and settlers from Europe entered territories whose inhabitants had little sense of national identity. Many lands like the North American continent had native populations organized into tribal, geographically dispersed, and culturally and linguistically dissimilar societies. The lack of national identity among native inhabitants of these new lands encouraged greater nationalistic fervor within the European countries that claimed and colonized other continents. More integrated forms of social organization were developed with patterns of mutual loyalty and dependency between colonists and the sending nation. Thus, the stage was set for the emergence of a nationalism that transcended allegiance to local community, region, or clan.

This was not the pattern among Third World societies, however. By the early 1900s, four nations—the United Kingdom, the United States, Germany, and France—owned about 85 per cent of all capital invested abroad (Chirot, 1977). Furthermore, about 86 per cent of the population in Africa was controlled by European states, and 42 per cent of the population in Asia was under the political rule of colonialists (Chirot, 1977). By the early 1950s, however, a new wave of nationalism emerged in precisely those countries that had been dominated by European and American economic and political power only a few years before. As a new, indigenous, middle class was formed in Third World nations, its members had learned not only the general forms and uses of colonial nationalism but the bitter fact that their own career aspirations were limited by it. Not surprisingly, the new nationalism was filled with non-Western content and anti-colonial sentiment. For the Third World, nationalism became a liberation movement where the common element was not language, culture, shared social institutions, or economic expansion, but anti-colonialism.

In the Third World, nationalism has become a liberation movement strongly based on anti-colonialism.

This new surge of nationalism, encouraging the break-up of old stratification and authority structures, has stimulated diversified, independent economic growth. Yet, because of the internal diversity and old tribal loyalties of many Third World nations, nationalism has different meanings to various social strata and cultural groups within the same country. This may create instability in some developing nations because while the established middle classes tend to favor independence without radical change, old elites will desire a return to an idealized past, whereas new intelligentsia and workers press for radical social change.

VARIATIONS IN CHANGE

Although nationalism has been a recent and potent factor in social and cultural change, it does not determine the course of any particular society. The general processes of specialization and differentiation that characterize the broad sweep of sociocultural development cannot shape the specific fate of a nation or group. Some societies will undergo rapid transformations, whereas others remain relatively untouched by currents of change. Human history is a graveyard of vanishing cultures. The Tasaday will disappear for want of marriage partners; the Ik may disintegrate from lack of social bonds; the Inuit of Canada are in the process of profound cultural change; and the heirs of the warriors of the Great Plains languish on reservations. Throughout the world, native bands that have survived for thousands of years are faced with the prospect of adapting to new circumstances, including nationalism.

In the Near East, previously isolated herding and agrarian societies are in the process of rapid and sudden growth, modernization, and nationalism; Saudi Arabia is one example. The rate of change may be more than the existing culture can support, so that a counter movement, seeking a return to traditional ways, emerges as in Iran today.

Within a given culture, not all change is in the direction of increased complexity. Some cultures emerge from prehistory to become highly sophisticated nation-states before undergoing a long period of decline and reversion to more simple communities. For example, ancient Egypt had a highly specialized and differentiated social structure, yet for many centuries thereafter existed as an unorganized basically agrarian territory controlled by a succession of other nations. But, as in the Egyptian case, some of these societies experience a rebirth as a modernizing nation.

In other words, each society has its unique trajectory of development; that is, it occupies some part of the continuum of social complexity and has its own specific rate of change. No two may be alike in these respects, and the probabilities of further growth are not determined but subject to historical forces.

Sources of Change

Let us examine the sources of specific social and cultural change, the mechanisms whereby change is adopted or resisted, and the major theoretical statements regarding the nature of social change.

EXTERNAL SOURCES

There are four external sources of social and cultural change: (1) environmental changes, ranging from drought to war, that shift the balance between a population and its physical environment; (2) invasion; (3) culture contact; and (4) diffusion. Each of these is described in this section.

Environmental Changes.   Many natural events, such as disaster, disease, climatic shifts, and the like, upset the balance between population and environment. Starvation, migration, and changes in the mode of subsistence are all possible solutions, and each involves readjustments in the social relationships built upon people's previous adaptations to their environment. The incidence of the tornados and hurricanes that periodically strike our continent are small-scale North American examples of the types of natural catastrophe that regularly occur in Asia and Africa.

Environmental changes include both natural events, and conditions precipitated by human beings.

Other disastrous situations are produced by humans rather than nature; environmental degradation of land and water is one example. Overuse and over-kill of resources, as in the case of land that is overfarmed so that it loses its nutrients, or the countless species of fish and wildlife that have been depleted, are other illustrations. In these cases, a customary mode of subsistence no longer supports the group. Wars and the bombing that now accompany hostilities can rapidly destroy the economic base and social bonds of civilian populations.

Invasion of one group's territory by other groups or nations is a major source of change.

Invasion.   Invasion of one's territory by other tribes, colonial powers, or economic interests is a major source of change. If members of the society remain in place, more powerful forces will attempt to impose their culture and forms of social organization. For example, in the European colonies of Asia and Africa, the language of the colonizing country was adopted (or imposed, in some cases) as the official language, the education system was patterned entirely after that of the ruling nation, and missionaries introduced a new belief system.

If the group flees to another geographic location, other changes must be made. The !Kung of central Africa once occupied more productive land than the dry deserts upon which they now hunt dwindling herds, and they have had to adjust accordingly. Many native tribes in the Philippines have been pushed further and further back into the rain forests as logging companies cut their way into the jungle.

Culture contact with people from other societies is the most pervasive source of change.

Cultural Contact.   By far the most constant and pervasive source of change comes through simple *culture contact* with members of other societies. Through the ordinary activities of hunting or herding, one tribe will impinge upon the grounds of another; or contact will be deliberately established for the purpose of trade or exchanging marriage partners; or the contact will be imposed by invading or expeditionary forces. By whatever means, one group learns about how the other has coped with the tasks of survival. New knowledge is thus available, although whether or not it is adopted will depend upon a variety of factors, including the history of the receiving culture and the force with which the new group promotes change.

Diffusion is the spreading of cultural items from one society to another.

Diffusion.   Diffusion is the process by which items of culture spread from one society to another through culture contact. Not all traits are equally likely to be accepted by members of another society. In general, technology is most easily diffused, for it is a matter of simple observation whether or not a new technique is more efficient than another. Conversely, nonmaterial items of culture, such as beliefs or values are much less readily adopted. After all, who can so quickly tell whether one tribe's gods are more effective than another's?

Yet not even proven methods for increasing a group's food supply will be accepted if the new technique is thought to involve radical changes in other aspects of culture. The introduction of a new item of culture has many consequences, similar to the ripples produced by the throwing of a stone into a pond. A major change in one institutional sphere has effects on all the other relationships between group members and may be resisted by those who fear both the immediate and long-term effects. During the early days of the factory system, for example, equipment was sabotaged by workers, quite literally, when a *sabot* (a French word for shoe) was thrown into the machine. Typically, however, the superior effectiveness of a gun compared to a spear or bow and arrow, for example, can be easily demonstrated and is soon adopted. But this will require a change in all the rituals surrounding the old way of hunting and perhaps some shift in power relationships within the group, eventually altering its system of social stratification.

The term *cultural lag* (Ogburn, 1922) is used to describe the time period between the introduction of a new technology and the many other adaptations that must follow in the areas of values, norms, and social relationships. Take the case of the introduction of the mass-produced automobile in North America in the 1920s whose effects on other parts of the social system are still being felt: the distribution of the population between city and suburb, patterns of work and leisure, and even courtship behaviors have been radically changed by the ability of most individuals to own their own automobiles. The physical environment has also been altered, as superhighways, drive-in theaters, and shopping

Cultural lag refers to the gap between a change in technology and a corresponding change in values, norms, and social relationships.

The introduction of mass-produced automobiles in the 1920s has had an enormous impact on the social system of America. (Source: Joe Munroe, Photo Researchers, Inc.)

malls sprawl across the land. Moreover, the full effects of pollution from fuel emissions may not be felt for many decades.

A particularly violent form of diffusion occurs when one group is conquered by a more powerful one, and traditional patterns are intentionally destroyed while new ways are forcibly imposed. The colonization of Asia, Africa, and South America was frequently accompanied by efforts to convert the natives to Western morals and beliefs. In North America, *internal colonization* effectively destroyed native cultures. In many cases, this destruction was intentional, a means of reducing the power of native leaders to resist invasion of their territory. In other cases, it was the result of ethnocentric arrogance, the assumption that our ways were vastly superior to those of simpler societies. Nor has violent diffusion been confined to the distant past; when the U.S.S.R. invaded Afghanistan in 1980, already fragile tribal societies were further divided, and modes of subsistence altered. Clearly, whether diffusion is imposed through conquest or adopted voluntarily, it is a powerful force for change.

If the major source of sociocultural change is diffusion, and diffusion depends on culture contact (whether voluntary or forced), then the rate of change will vary according to the geographic location of the group. It is no accident that the elaborate civilizations of ancient times evolved among societies located on major rivers, such as the Nile, the Tigris, and the Euphrates, or sea lanes (around the Mediterranean), or trade routes of any kind. In such locations, contact and diffusion enlarge the potential cultural base, thereby increasing the likelihood of cross-fertilization of ideas and practices. All these factors in turn enhance the vitality and adaptability of social arrangements. Out of such ferment came many of the most important discoveries and inventions of human history: the alphabet, number systems, navigational aids, efficient construction techniques, and so forth, all many thousands of years before the year 1 A.D.

On the other hand, bands, tribes, and societies outside the path of culture contact will change much more slowly because their culture base remains relatively narrow, limiting the probability of both discovery and invention. In some cases, such as the Amish in North America, the group will intentionally isolate itself from outside influences in order to preserve a traditional way of life. Orthodox Jewish and Christian religious sects have similarly sought to protect themselves against corrupting contacts with the larger culture. This is a major function of religious schools for their children; just as an immigrant generation enthusiastically sent their offspring into the public school system to absorb the new culture, these traditionalists gladly insulate their offspring from contact with it.

INTERNAL SOURCES.

Discoveries and Inventions. Internal sources of change are those developed by members of a society out of existing culture traits. A distinction is often made between *discoveries* and *inventions*, both of which are internal sources of change. A *discovery* involves the awareness of some aspect of nature that already exists but had not been perceived before, such as the laws of relativity, the infection theory of disease, Jupiter's moons, or subatomic particles. *Inventions* involve the combination of existing elements of culture in a novel fashion. Think of all the items of knowledge and technology that had to be put together in a new way to produce the space vehicle that has discovered the moons of

Discoveries occur when a pre-existing condition is first perceived.

Inventions use existing cultural elements to develop new forms.

Jupiter or the atomic accelerators that enabled discovery of the existence of subatomic particles.

✓**Innovation.** The term innovation—something new—is used to encompass both discovery and invention, for the two processes are frequently intertwined. A few crucial innovations in culture during prehistoric eras were probably essential to the survival of the species. Fire, the wheel, ways of keeping track of the seasons, and animal traps, for example, may have been discovered in only one or two places and then diffused throughout the inhabited world.

Once innovations are diffused and accepted, a group increases its cultural base, that is, the total inventory of traits that encourage further discoveries and inventions. Therefore, the likelihood of innovation is directly related to the size of the culture base; in other words, the more there is to work with, the greater the probability of recombining elements into something else. This is why the *rate of change* is greater in modern than in preindustrial societies, particularly preliterate ones. Inventiveness is not related to differences in intelligence among the peoples of the world; rather, it is associated with the accumulated knowledge of the group. There is a Latin saying that "pygmies placed on the shoulders of giants see more than the giants themselves"; this well describes the innovative advantages of those living in modern societies (Merton, 1967).

The **rate of change** is greater in industrial than preindustrial societies.

✓**Population Shifts.** An often overlooked source of change is variation in the size and composition of a society's population. Groups too small, too isolated, or too malnourished to reproduce successfully will either die off or move from their niche to make contact with other people or improved food supplies. Other societies become overpopulated in relation to their subsistence base; for example, starvation in Eastern Africa and parts of India and Cambodia is responsible for the disintegration of cultural patterns and social organization as people crowd into the refugee camps for survival. Population pressures in the country of origin are cited as a major impetus to migration to North America; the potato famine of the 1840s in Ireland is one such example. Both the sending and receiving countries are altered by migration patterns.

Population shifts refer to the variation in the size and composition of the population.

Within any society, the relative size of different age groups can produce important changes. In Chapter 18, we traced the effects of the Baby Boom generation on every institutional sphere as this birth cohort moved along its life course: from expansion of the educational system to clogged avenues of upward occupational mobility. And, in their old age, this cohort will strain the Social Security and pension systems undoubtedly producing still more changes in the social fabric. Since this very large cohort is being followed by a very small one in Canada, the United States, and much of Western Europe, other effects are likely, such as a reduction of educational institutions but less strain on the home-building industry and increased opportunity for upward mobility.

Yet, the rapid rate of change in modern societies will bring widespread societal changes regardless of the size of the population cohorts through the sheer passage of time. As a birth cohort moves through the social structure from childhood to eventual extinction, its own peculiar characteristics and unique historical experience will modify the social system (Riley and Waring, 1976). In other words, just as the existing structures and patterns of a society affect its members, these individuals alter the institutions through which they pass.

Social Change and Modernization

FROM PREINDUSTRIAL TO POSTINDUSTRIAL SOCIETY

What do such disparate countries as the Soviet Union and the United States and Canada have in common that can shed light upon social change and trends in contemporary societies? With different languages, cultures, forms of economic organization and political ideologies, the answer would seem to be: "Very little." Yet, both are examples of modern societies built upon the concepts of rationality and bureaucratization of authority. Strange as it may seem, the political ideology of a nation may have little to do with a modern social structure. Rather, modernization is a social process whereby a society becomes more internally differentiated and complex, and where science and technology guide change. As societies become modernized, they may be said to converge; that is, they become more alike with respect to their social structures, status hierarchies, and power and authority relationships. Nonetheless, they retain their unique historical and cultural features.

Within the past thirty years, as social scientists have become increasingly aware of Third World nations, more and more attention has been turned toward studies of the process of modernization. Primarily, the modernization model has been used to describe the shift from preindustrial, agricultural modes of subsistence to industrialized ones. Eisenstadt (1966) has suggested that the sociocultural change associated with modernization has two important aspects: (1) *mobilization*, or the process by which old patterns of social, economic, and psychological commitments are weakened and people thus become available for socialization to new patterns; and (2) *social differentiation*, that is, a shift from diffuse to specialized roles (Eisenstadt, 1966).

Modernization as a master trend is linked to three other trends already discussed: urbanization, industrialization, and secularization. Concentrations of workers and consumers, engaged in the production and distribution of specialized goods and services, and guided by rational-legal norms compose the modern society. As you will recall, Max Weber's concept of *rationality* refers to a type of social action in which traditional and emotional bases for behavior are replaced by a belief in a logical relationship between means and ends. Characteristic of industrialized societies, this highly practical view emphasizes the introduction of predictable and systematic procedures, the backbone of which is a cause-effect model. This has been the basis of new technologies in the economic system, culminating in the replacement of physical labor by machines. Rationality as a basis for political and economic authority, according to Weber, paved the way for the accelerated social change that characterizes modern societies.

Yet legal-rational power is a relatively new concept whose development parallels the rise of European industrial society and of the nation-state. To understand the ways in which the sociocultural changes associated with modernization occur, recall some of the contrasts between *preindustrial* and *industrial* societies. Preindustrial societies have economies based on extraction from natural resources. Industrial societies are characterized by an economic and social organization based on machine technology and large-scale systems of production. The development of capitalist economies from the sixteenth century onward, coupled with technological, cultural, and political systems that en-

Rationality is based upon the belief in a logical connection between means and ends.

couraged profit, gave some countries tremendous advantages in economic development.

Investment and risk-taking spread Western financial power throughout the world, so that a few industrialized nations dominated the remainder of the world. These economically dominant nations are now beginning to enter a new phase of development: *postindustrialization*. Postindustrial and industrial societies differ in one important respect: while both are industrialized, in postindustrial economies, the majority of the labor force is no longer employed in manufacturing but in providing services (Bell, 1973). The service sector includes government, management, education, and health care, among other occupational categories. Bell has identified five components of postindustrial societies: (1) a change from a goods-producing to a service economy; (2) the great importance of professional and technical workers; (3) emphasis on theoretical knowledge as the basis for policy formation and change; (4) the planning and control of technological growth; (5) the creation of a new intellectual technology based on statistical and logical techniques and problem-solving computers.

In **postindustrial economies** a majority of workers are engaged in services rather than in manufacturing.

How do postindustrial societies differ from others? Essentially, they are an extension of trends found in industrial societies but having different emphases. In postindustrial nations, the organization of science and technology is paramount; however, in industrial societies, manufacturing and productive capacity traditionally have been emphasized. As Bell (1973) commented, "If industrial society is defined by the quantity of goods as marking a standard of living, the postindustrial is defined by the quality of life as measured by services and amenities . . . deemed desirable and possible for everyone." Thus, while the index of steel production is a common measure used to assess the rates of economic growth of industrial societies, the proportion of scientific and technical workers and the amount of funds spent on research and development are more meaningful descriptions of change to a postindustrial phase.

The major problem in postindustrial society is not economic growth but that of efficient organization and codification of knowledge: "the most besetting dilemma confronting all modern society is bureaucratization" and the tendency to *goal displacement* when organizational rules are established largely for the benefit of bureaucrats (Bell, 1973).

Bell argues that in postindustrial society, a premium is placed on knowledge, technical skill, and managerial abilities as bases of power. Acquisition of capital is no longer as important as in industrial society, nor is ascribed status necessary for access to power or wealth. Education and skill provide ready routes to wealth, power, and prestige (although interpersonal influence remains very useful).

Power in postindustrial society is based on knowledge, technical skills, and managerial abilities.

There are many observable consequences of this concern with knowledge and technical skill. Although there is a new technical elite, this elite is dependent to a large extent upon industrial and government support or subsidy. This, in turn, has created problems in management: who owns the sciences and the scientists? While their knowledge is indispensible in rapidly changing postindustry, their authority and autonomy remain vaguely defined. While the power and importance of science has risen, so has the power of the bureaucrat. Science and technology are objects of management—not always to the satisfaction of science or the general public.

Modernization and the Self

What happens to the self in modernized societies? Modern society presents a series of contradictions. Life can be satisfying and pleasing to the individual because of the diversity and differentiation that characterizes a complex society. Yet isolation and frustration are more likely to occur in rapidly changing urban societies than in traditional ones. Contemporary urban life in particular is characterized by precision and impersonality, but also a "highly personal subjectivity" (Simmel, 1950). In other words, a different kind of consciousness develops among urbanized people; what sociologist Georg Simmel called the "blasé attitude," more familiar to most of us as the urban state of indifference that marks encounters with strangers in public places such as buses, subways, movie theaters, and so forth. This indifference is a survival mechanism developed by each individual to withstand the constant stimulation by other people, sights, smells, noises, and activities that occur in a modernized, complex society. What is unique about modern urban dwellers is precisely this ability for highly selective perception designed to screen out personally meaningless or unpleasant stimuli.

This reserve has both positive and negative aspects. On the positive side, it guarantees a degree of anonymity unknown in suburbs, small towns, and rural areas, or in less complex societies, and thus allows the individual greater freedom of movement and lifestyle. One may act without the fear of negative sanc-

Despite the diverse opportunities that modern societies offer the individual, feelings of isolation and frustration often accompany change. (Source: *The Museum of Modern Art/Film Series Archives.*)

In urban areas, a state of indifference can serve as a survival mechanism to withstand constant stimulation. (Source: *Donald Dietz, Stock, Boston.*)

Toward a Subcultural Theory of Urbanism

Why is there such a range of behavior in large urban centers? Many sociologists have suggested that this variation is an indication of anomie; primary group relationships break down and social norms are lost in the vast impersonality of the city. Fisher suggests that the emphasis on alienation, impersonality, isolation, and dehumanization in the urban setting fails to take account of the positive and dynamic aspects of city life.

Briefly, his argument is as follows:

A large population in a given area results in urban differentiation, that is, subcultures linked to social class, age, special interest, place of origin/ethnicity, and to occupation. Generally the more urban an area is, the more intense and meaningful its subcultures are to its members. This is just the opposite of isolation and normlessness attributed to city life. The development of numerous and distinct subcultural beliefs, norms, values, and institutional patterns encourage members to maintain social ties with the group, thus promoting internal cohesion.

This process is not static; the more urban a place is, the more likely is diffusion of subcultural traits from one group to another. There is a constant exchange of information, norms, and values among members of competing subcultures. The results are a wider range of human behavior and greater possibilities for identification with one unique subculture.

Source: Claude S. Fisher, *American Journal of Sociology, 80:6, 1975.*

tions that exists in smaller, more traditional settings. On the negative side, the anonymity of the urbanized, modern society may increase loneliness, especially for individuals unable to make connections with others of similar interest and concerns.

The multiple sources of subcultural identity available to city dwellers may have a fragmenting effect on the individual.

The very range of possibilities for subcultural identification in the urban environment can be fragmenting in their effects. The individual confronted with a wide range of choices may no longer be totally embedded in his or her social group. Social differentiation in modern society could be so fragmenting that individuals feel somehow incomplete or lacking a clear identity. Whether the totally-acting person—the self—is ever fully explained by the sum of one's statuses and roles, the point remains valid: extreme differentiation and separation of roles may be unsatisfying for the self.

Indeed, as we have emphasized throughout this book, the very self of individuals is related to their positions in social structure in a mutually reinforcing manner. The self is always a product of a particular type of social structure. For example, from the Marxist perspective, the mode of production shapes the self. The alienation that results from a worker's relationship to the modes of production under industrialism permeates her or his very being. Change processes thus consist not only of structural and cultural shifts within a society but also involve psychological changes.

Complex societies provide a greater range of roles than are available in tradition-based or developing nations. Shifts from traditional primary relationships (*Gemeinschaft*) to relationships based on rational self-interest (*Gesellschaft*) enable people to live in distinctly different social worlds.

Much of the self is formed through the actions and reactions of others toward us. The complexity, diversity, and sometimes unpredictability of others' responses to one's self in modern, urban societies are far greater than the relatively stable interaction in a small town, village, or hamlet. The self, then, must be in a state of exaggerated reflexiveness; each of us must constantly read and process cues from others to an extent not required in less complex society.

The effect of social structure on personality has been described by David Riesman (1950). Contrasting three different ideal types, each associated with a particular level of industrial development, Riesman identified the *tradition-directed* self, whose behavior was governed by customs; the *inner-directed*, whose behavior was governed by an internal gyroscope and who was the prototype of the capitalist or worker in industrial society; and the *other-directed*, who is equipped with a psychological radar with which to scan the environment for appropriate messages to guide one's behavior. The other-directed individual, suggested Riesman, is characteristic of postindustrial society. Constantly anticipating new roles and aware of the need to adapt swiftly, the other-directed differs from the other two types in being less certain of how to behave under all, or even most, circumstances.

The reactive-adaptive self is a mixed blessing. The ability to adapt one's self to a variety of situations allows the individual to anticipate and prepare for changing roles. Yet it may also result in anxiety and a crisis of the self. The self is constantly being constructed and reconstructed to fit varying statuses and roles; who and what one is is not readily identifiable. Consumer goods become commodities to establish status: part of what Goffman has called one's "identity kit," or "I am what I wear and use."

During the 1970s, a variety of commentators became alarmed over what they described as an obsessive self-centeredness among Americans–a turning inward with the sole goal of individual survival and happiness. This marked a major change from the 1960s dominated by outward-looking political activism.

Much of the concern about this "new narcissism" (after the youth in Greek legend who fell in love with his own reflection) has been expressed in psychiatric terms. Thus, the concept of the "narcissistic society" is based on the assumption that self-absorption is a realistic mode of adaptation to the tensions and anxieties of modern life. But as Roberta Satow, a sociologist and a practicing psychoanalyst, points out, these concepts perpetuate the feeling that the only thing we can change is ourselves. When the blame for the selfishness of the "me generation" is focused on individuals, attention is drawn away from the shortcomings of social institutions. We must keep in mind that the social structure is composed of *institutionalized* relationships that predispose individuals to develop narcissistic personalities, rather than simply of narcissistic personalities who comprise a society. Until we realize that exaggerated self-concern is a response to the problems of social arrangements, psychological explanations and individual, clinically-oriented solutions will predominate, and inhibit change in the social structure.

Source: Roberta Satow, *Psychology Today*, October, 1979.

In sum, personality is mobilized as a resource in modern society, and the self is rationalized. Success, achievement, conscious control, and self-improvement are primary goals. The self, as the "me" orientation that dominated the United States in the 1970s illustrates, becomes treasured above all else as an object to be manipulated.

Accepting Change

As we have noted, not all change is immediately accepted, nor are diffused traits, however superior they may appear, universally welcomed. The new item must be compatible with the existing culture of the receiving society. Innovations must be perceived as meeting a need or conferring a benefit that outweighs the costs of changing behavior. Moreover, in any society there will be people with a *vested interest* in maintaining the *status quo;* that is, who derive power, prestige, or wealth from the existing arrangements, and who typically are people with great influence in the group. No African witch doctor could have resisted medical missionaries any more thoroughly than members of the American Medical Association fought against Medicare for the elderly between 1945 and 1965. Or, one might ask why it has taken so long for automobiles produced in the United States to be equipped with emission control devices, and why the American automobile industry has lagged so far behind other nations in producing compact, more fuel-efficient vehicles? In sum, what vested interests are preserved in resisting change?

Change is promoted or resisted by individuals who occupy statuses in social

People who benefit from existing arrangements have a **vested interest** in the **status quo.**

Agents of change are individuals who occupy positions through which they can influence the direction of change.

sytems. Some status incumbents are more influential than others as *agents of change.* If the tribal chief or shaman (wise person) adopts an innovation, others are likely to follow. In any society, there are trend setters and gatekeepers who can influence the direction of change.

Although in modern societies the media play an important part in the introduction of new items, formal and informal interpersonal channels of communication remain as important for North Americans as for Australian aborigines. *Social networks* carry the message from one person to another. In an early study of the diffusion of innovation in medicine, Coleman et al. (1957) found that a new drug was more readily adopted by physicians who were more profession-oriented and more integrated into a network of local physicians than by physicians relatively isolated from their medical peers and patient-oriented. Both types of physicans had been exposed to information about the new drug at the same time, but the rate of prescription of the product varied by the doctor's role in social/professional networks. The first to advocate the drug, because of their reputations as professional leaders, gave the weight of their prestige to its endorsement; others followed, with the most isolated physicians being the last to adopt.

Acceptance of specific social changes thus depends upon many factors including: (1) whether the new trait or idea is consistent with what already exists in the culture; (2) the perceived costs of adopting the new item or giving up customary modes of thinking and behaving; (3) the resistance generated by those with vested interest in the *status quo;* (4) generalized fear of the long term consequences of change; and (5) the influence of change agents.

Indeed, not all agents of change are appreciated. Many are labeled as troublemakers or heretics, and are subject to social control and negative sanctions. Ridicule is an effective technique (Bella Abzug), as are imprisonment (Galileo), assassination (Martin Luther King, Jr.), and execution by the state (Sacco and Vanzetti). When such forces of social control are brought into play, broad currents of change may be temporarily suspended and short term changes halted as well. The ability of an agent of social change to be effective depends upon the social context in which he or she acts. For example, the idea that the earth was the center of the universe remained a portion of official Church doctrine throughout the middle ages despite evidence from astronomers to the contrary. Those who attempted to shake this tenet were dealt with harshly, since the centrality of the earth was a deeply treasured religious belief.

Types of Change

As noted earlier in this chapter, the *pace* and *extent* of change required by the introduction of new elements will vary greatly.

INCREMENTAL CHANGES

Incremental change is a long gradual process in which one modification is followed by another.

Some changes are part of a broad secular trend whose ultimate impact is unknown. Alterations in social life proceed by small steps or increments. *Incremental change* may go unnoticed for long periods until, finally, a major transformation has occurred. For example, the agricultural revolution of pre-history was not a revolution in the sense of sudden dramatic shifts in the mode of subsistence, but a long gradual process in which one modification was followed by another, affecting all institutional spheres. The same can be said of the Industrial Revolution, some elements of which were evolving in Europe long before the introduction of factories. The cumulative outcome, however, *is* a radical departure from the past. In Quebec, a silent revolution occurred over many decades resulting in the emergence of a French-speaking managerial middle class in 1970s, with widespread ramifications in the Province and Canada as a whole.

In general, modern societies are characterized by master trends toward increased political participation, civil liberties and civil rights, sexual privacy, secularization, and increased educational attainment. But these results of incremental change are *not* as inevitable as may once have been thought. Modern industrial states can also be marked by political repression, religious fanaticism, and a reduction in personal choice and freedom, as in Eastern Europe and the Soviet Union today. In Canada and the United States, long term changes in the status of women, increased tolerance of religious and other minorities, and greater family privacy appear to be firmly established although subject to temporary setbacks. As described by Davis (1980) from an examination of public opinion polls over the past decade, we are currently witnessing "conservative weather in a liberalizing climate": that is, within the long-term trend toward increasingly liberal attitudes, there are moments when the direction of change is reversed. Of course, such shifts could be the beginning of climate change.

The inevitable succession of birth cohorts and their flow through the social system are also important sources of unplanned change. This is particularly the case in modern societies where the social system itself undergoes rapid alterations so that even if cohort characteristics did not change greatly, cohort members would be moving through a different set of structures than did those who preceded them or who will follow. In actuality, causes and effects of change are interactive; that is, the cohort modifies the social system and the culture, while being influenced and shaped by the existing structures. For example, the characteristics of today's old people are very different from those of the past. Thanks to Social Security and Medicare, most are able to live independently in the community. This has led to the expectation that communities will provide certain social services previously supplied by family (housing, nutrition, transportation, recreation). Once these services are in place, future cohorts of the elderly will take them for granted and be even less dependent upon their children in old age. The implications for family relationships are profound (Hess and Waring, 1978).

Another type of incremental, unplanned change occurs in the sphere of ideology. Members of a society at any one historical moment see the world through the lens of a particular model of reality (Kuhn, 1962). This world-view, or *paradigm*, organizes reality as, for example, the concept of an unchanging natural universe that dominated medieval thought: "this is exactly how it was at the moment of Creation." Gradually, however, bits and pieces of information accumulated that failed to conform to this paradigm until finally a new conception of the natural universe emerged: evolution through natural selection. This new paradigm was being developed by several different observers at the same time,

> Modern industrial societies are marked by contradictory trends: increased political participation and civil liberties versus political repression and reduction of freedom.

> The movement of different age cohorts through the social structure brings changes to a society.

because the evidence was so compelling. Similarly, the theory of relativity marks a major paradigm shift. And some would say that the idea of eternal progress that is so much a part of the Western mind must soon give way to a conception of the limits of social change.

Crescive change appears to develop inevitably, while **enacted** change is planned and directed.

These are examples of *crescive* ("growing") change that appears to develop through the inevitable unfolding of the logic of history. In contrast, *enacted* change is planned, directed by specific agents toward particular goals. Classifying changes as either crescive or enacted, unplanned or planned, random or directed, is not as simple as may appear. Almost any event can be shown to have roots in the past and is therefore to some degree incremental. But it is also likely that any given outcome can be linked to agents of change, if only as midwives to the future.

REVOLUTIONARY CHANGE

Revolutionary change brings basic alterations in the political and socioeconomic structure of a society.

Revolutionary change involves a "sudden, basic transformation of a society's political and socioeconomic (including class) structure," (Skocpol and Trimberger, 1977). But revolutions do not simply happen; they emerge out of revolutionary situations. Just what situations at which historical moments are ripe for revolution is a question that has long occupied theorists of revolutionary change.

The most influential modern theory of revolution has been that of Karl Marx. As described by Skocpol (1979), Marx's theory has three main elements: (1) each revolution is historically grounded in a certain type of society; therefore, there can be *no* general theory of revolution; (2) organized movements for social change can succeed only where a revolutionary situation exists by virtue of irreconcilable class conflicts within the society; and (3) since class conflict is the defining characteristic of the revolutionary situation, the revolution is completed only when the power of the dominant class(es) is destroyed.

Skocpol (1979) modified Marx's model in light of actual events. The major modern revolutions have not occurred, as Marx had predicted, in industrial capitalist countries but rather in agricultural societies under pressure from outside economic and military forces. Moreover, the internal problems that make revolution a possibility have been political (competing power blocs) rather than economic (productive class conflict). And it has not been the oppressed workers, or even peasants, but members of the educated elite who assume leadership and who typically establish the new state organizations, while the revolutionary mass has historically been composed of peasants rather than an urban working class. Lastly, it is not the class system that changes as much as the political structure. These changes in the distribution and functions of the state organization may in turn lead to transformation of the social class and economic systems.

From her study of the French, Russian, and Chinese Revolutions, Skocpol (1979) concluded that the state structure—the political system—should be viewed as something more autonomous than the governing arm of the economic ruling class. Further, to understand modern revolutions, one must take into account the international military rivalry among industrial states and between the industrialized and developing nations within a capitalist world economy.

Social Changes and World Systems. It is increasingly difficult today—and probably has been since the fifteenth century—to consider changes within any society without reference to broader trends in what Wallerstein (1974) calls the "world system." The world system refers to the economic and political relationships among societies, particularly between the industrial states and the less developed nations. Modern industrial societies can be considered the economic 'core' of the world system, while the less developed nations are the 'periphery,' providing raw materials for the core countries and then becoming a market for those manufactured goods. This was the logic of colonialism, but in a

The Great Leap Forward

In 1949 the Communist rulers of China proclaimed the People's Republic and began the process of modernizing the economic base of that vast nation. An ambitious Five-Year Plan inaugurated in 1953 sought to expand industrial and agricultural production. Factories, railroads, banks and communication facilities were all *nationalized;* that is, they became state-owned enterprises. Farm land was seized from large owners and redistributed to the peasants who were organized into *collectives,* operated by groups of farmers who jointly worked the land.

The first Five Year Plan was such a success that a second, more ambitious one, called "The Great Leap Forward" was initiated in 1958. The emphasis was on heavy industry, but existing plants were not able to increase at the previous rates, and locally produced material was of very poor quality. The collective farms were expanded into huge communes where private plots and property were forbidden; agricultural production not only failed to increase but actually declined.

The failure of the Great Leap caused internal political tensions that ultimately produced the Cultural Revolution of the early 1960s during which bands of students (the Red Guards) attempted to coerce and intimidate peasants and laborers to meet the new production goals. Civil disorder followed until the army finally restored order in the late 1960s.

In an attempt to create an egalitarian society in accordance with Marxist ideology, the People's Republic of China has abolished the inheritance of private property, legalized the rights of females, and sent urban professional people to the farms to work with their hands for a year or two. Traditional religious practices have been discouraged, and the role of the eldest male in the family considerably reduced, so that citizens could direct their primary loyalties to the state rather than to the kinship group.

Here is planned change in every institutional sphere! The long-term incremental transformation of Chinese society is, however, accompanied by short-term dislocations and difficult decisions for the people involved, even those who agree with the long-term goals.

The current regime appears to be more sensitive to these pockets of resistance, as well as to the importance of traditional patterns of work, property ownership, and family life. Rather than leaping forward, the pace today is a brisk but steady walk into the future.

decolonized world the raw materials must now be paid for rather than taken, and markets must be won in competition with other exporters.

Third World countries that possess essential raw materials are now in a position of unaccustomed strength in their dealings with the industrial societies. This is what has happened with the oil-producing nations; their monopoly over a scarce resource has permitted them to raise prices on the world market, leading to a heavy outflow of money from core nations as well as to major changes in life styles and industrial growth within both the core and oil exporting societies.

But most peripheral societies do not have such a necessary raw material; most are extremely poor, overpopulated, and politically unstable. The distribution of the world's wealth has become increasingly more imbalanced; the poor nations grow poorer and the wealthy ones wealthier. This is a major source of political instability in the underdeveloped nations of Asia, Africa, and Central America, making these areas of the globe potential trouble spots in the rivalry between the United States and the Soviet Union for world influence.

Revolution may not always be deliberately planned but results from strains in the society.

In this new view, revolutions may not be deliberately planned but emerge from strains in the social structure as when a totalitarian regime in an agricultural society is threatened from outside and can no longer suppress peasant revolts. But each specific revolt will have its unique history within this general pattern, and if revolutions were to come in modern industrial societies, these would probably be very different in nature from the past or from those in developing nations. The outcome, however, is likely to be the same everywhere: increased centralization of power and bureaucratization when the new order is stabilized, and mobilization of the masses in support of the revolution. And one authoritarian state is succeeded by another with only the faces changed.

Revolutionary Events. Revolutionary situations must be distinguished from revolutionary outcomes. According to Tilly (1978), a revolutionary outcome occurs when one set of powerholders is displaced by another. A revolutionary situation exists when (1) two or more political units claim control over the state; (2) these interests cannot be reconciled; and (3) the opposition party receives support (money, loyalty, soldiers) from a sizeable segment of the population. The revolution ends when only one claimant remains. When these two variables—revolutionary situations and outcomes—are ranged along continua, Tilly identifies a range of revolutionary events, from a coup where one segment of the elite displaces another, to a silent revolution where a revolutionary outcome takes place with very little overt hostility (as in Quebec during the 1960s), to the great revolution where both the situation and outcome are at the extreme end of the continua (as in the American or French Revolutions).

A **coup** involves the displacement of one elite by another.

In this figure (20-1), the vertical line represents the degree to which a ruling *class* is displaced, from "no displacement" to "complete displacement." The horizontal line represents the extent of division in the society between rival groups claiming power, from "no internal split" to "one that cannot be reconciled."

As for the long term effects of the revolutionary event, these also vary by time and place. Tilly notes that there are very few examples of moral rebirth as a result of the revolutionary experience; people soon return to their usual round of activities. Some short term gains may be erased over the long run (for exam-

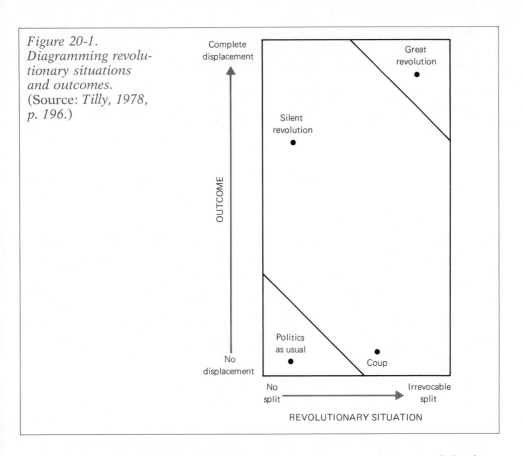

*Figure 20-1.
Diagramming revolu-
tionary situations
and outcomes.
(Source: Tilly, 1978,
p. 196.)*

ple, women's rights in the early days of the Russian Revolution), while short term setbacks are ultimately followed by broad scale transformation (the French Revolution). The general conclusion, then, appears to be that revolutions are much more complex than Marxian theory suggests, and that outcomes have positive and negative elements. And the costs may be very high indeed.

Theories of Change

Does change take place along a single path *(unidirectional)* leading to some predestined goal, the Kingdom of Heaven, for example? Or has the direction been a progressive decline from some Golden Age? Or does change occur in a circular fashion as civilizations rise and fall? You have probably heard popular versions of each of these theories of social change.

Unidirectional theories assume that social change occurs along one path only.

EVOLUTIONARY THEORIES OF CHANGE

In late nineteenth century England, unidirectional theories of evolutionary progress were very popular. From savagery, represented by the simple societies discovered by British colonizers, to high civilization, represented of course by Victorian England, was the major thrust (Spencer, 1876). Some Americans might make the same claim for the United States today as a nation divinely chosen to lead the free world against godless enemies. For colonial nations, the belief that one's social system is superior to that of other people provides a rationale for the economic exploitation of less developed societies.

CYCLICAL THEORIES OF CHANGE

Similarly, the thesis that cultures are like organisms, going through phases of development from birth to ultimate decline, fit into the intellectual currents of early twentieth century Western culture with its emphasis on biological functioning in various disciplines, and a feeling that European civilization was decadent and corrupt. The German philosopher Oswald Spengler summed up this perception in his masterwork, *The Decline and Fall of the West* (1928). His deep pessimism was justified by the rise of Hitler and Mussolini and a decade of war, but European civilization has proven far more resilient than his theory predicted. Cultures do flourish and decline in power over long periods of time, but there is little evidence that *cyclical* theories of social change have much predictive value. A more sociological theory of cyclical change has been proposed by Sorokin (1941) who suggested that world history has alternated between periods of rationality and order, on the one hand, and letting go, on the other.

Although cyclical views of change have enjoyed a brief vogue, the two theories of social change that stimulate most interest among contemporary social scientists are related to the two macrosocial perspectives of functionalism and conflict. A convergence of these two positions has been a connecting thread throughout this volume, and nowhere is this more apparent than in the analysis of change.

CLASSIC MODELS

Many of sociology's classical theorists have proposed two-part schemes to describe the cumulative thrust of social structural change. Durkheim, remember, contrasted *mechanical solidarity* in simple societies, where every member was interchangeable with others, to the *organic solidarity* of modern societies brought on by increasing division of labor so that members play complementary roles and are bound together by ties of interdependence.

Töennies' concepts of *Gemeinschaft* and *Gesellschaft* reflect a similar model of change: a trend from close primary relationships as the basis of social life to a more varied, fragmented, temporary, and role-specific mode of modern life. The same general process was described by the anthropologist Redfield (1941) as a drift from *folk communities* toward *urban society*. In all these schemes, structural complexity is associated with population density and specialization of tasks.

The model that we have used in this text is a more sophisticated version of these developmental schemes. *Neoevolutionary* theory makes no assumptions about the superiority of one form or another; nor is the term "progress" used to describe differentiation. It would be very difficult, as we noted at the outset, to claim that modern North Americans are any more happy, fulfilled, or intelligent than any other people (being a Tasaday might not appeal to many of us, but then few Tasaday might wish to be one of us).

The neoevolutionary model of cumulative change described by Service (1963) and others (see Lenski, 1960) is based on four simple propositions: (1) the mode of subsistence is basic; (2) changes in technology lead to new adaptations

---

Cyclical theories of change are based on the view that society is similar to an organism, going through phases of growth and decline.

Many social theorists have developed two-stage models of social change: from **gemeinschaft** to **gesellschaft,** or from folk communities to urban society.

Neoevolutionary theory traces changes in cultural and societal complexity without making value judgements about the superiority of one type of society over another.

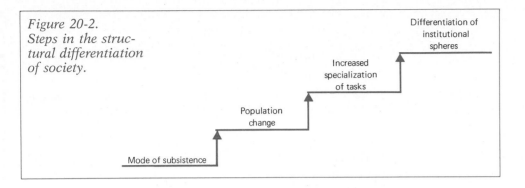

Figure 20-2. Steps in the structural differentiation of society.

that typically support larger populations; (3) increased density leads to specialization and coordination of tasks; (4) the need to create order among different kinds of workers leads to more complex organizations and the emergence of differentiated institutional spheres (illustrated in Figure 20-2).

Critics of the neoevolutionary model do not object to its assumptions of cumulative change and increasing structural complexity. It is the additional assumption made by functional theorists, that institutional arrangements tend toward balance and internal adjustment, that is severely questioned (Sherman and Wood, 1979). If, as functional theory suggests, social systems change in the direction of increased equilibrium or the smooth working of system parts, whatever disturbs a system is considered a dysfunctional intrusion from outside. In other words, functional theory minimizes the possibility of strain arising from *within* the system, generated precisely from the ongoing institutional arrangements.

Conflict Model.   The conflict perspective focuses on the recurrent and enduring sources of tension and struggle among individuals and groups within any society. The chapters in Unit III, Social Differences and Inequality, detailed the many ways in which power, prestige, and property are unequally distributed in contemporary North America. When inequality is perceived as inequity (unfairness), disadvantaged groups may organize to increase their share of scarce resources. Individuals and groups that benefit from the rules of allocation will struggle to maintain their dominance. At any given moment, social systems are composed of competing interest groups and conflict is a built-in attribute of social organization.

It seems to us that the conflict perspective does *not* invalidate the model of social and cultural change we have developed from functional and neo-evolutionary sources. Rather, conflict theory *completes* the model by specifying the sources and processes of change in the social system. It is only by examining the specific circumstances that give rise to discontent and change in any society that the observer can understand why some social systems endure and others disintegrate, why some undergo gradual and relatively peaceful change while others experience violent upheaval.

Conflict Theory and the Dialectic Process.   For Karl Marx, the competing groups within industrial society were social classes defined by their relation-

The **conflict perspective** stresses the recurrent and enduring sources of strain among groups within a society.

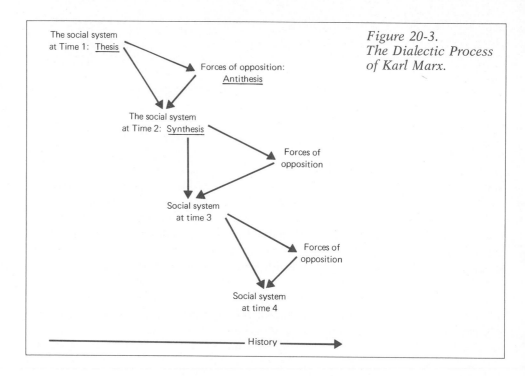

The social system
at Time 1: Thesis

Forces of opposition:
Antithesis

The social system
at Time 2: Synthesis

Forces of
opposition

Social system
at time 3

Forces of
opposition

Social system
at time 4

History

Figure 20-3.
*The Dialectic Process
of Karl Marx.*

ship to the means of production, namely, owners and those who sell their labor.
Marx thought that eventually the conditions of modern work would be so alien-
ating that workers would rise up in revolution against the owners of capital.
Yet, as we saw in the section on revolution, the working classes of the world
have not become revolutionary; quite the opposite, in fact. Ronald Reagan, a
candidate closely linked to capitalist interests, received almost half of all working class votes in the United States in 1980, an outcome that Marxists would
claim to be the result of "false consciousness" among the workers. Ironically,
perhaps, the workers of Communist Poland are more militantly class conscious
than those in North America, pressing their interests against the current con-
trollers of the means of production, who happen to be representatives of the
Communist Party.

But Marx's theory of social change does not rest on the necessity of violent
revolution. Viewing human history in its totality, Marx perceived a *dialectic*
process of change. At any given moment, the social system of interdependent
parts composes a status quo or *thesis*, out of which competing, or antagonistic,
elements emerge to challenge the given order of things. These forces of opposition are called *antithesis*. Since inequality is a feature of all past and present
social systems, antithetical movements are an ever-present fact of social life.
Out of the conflict between thesis and antithesis—the power of vested interest
and the forces of protest—comes a new social order: *synthesis* (see Figure 20-3).

One era's synthesis is, of course, another's thesis, and the process continues
through history. Sometimes change will be incremental and at other times sudden, but it is everywhere induced by class conflict, as new economic orders
emerge, become frozen, and are replaced. For Marx, the end of the dialectic, and

The **dialectic model**
specifies the pattern of
class conflict in historical change.

of history, was to come with the final synthesis—the communist society, in which owners and workers are one and the same.

A Unified Model of Change. To synthesize the neoevolutionary and conflict models, we propose that general change can be best explained in terms of transformations of the economic base of society. Groups that do not experience shifts in modes of subsistence are not likely to undergo changes in other institutional spheres—unless, of course, they are invaded. But where subsistence shifts do take place, other social patterns will ultimately be affected. Some changes, as in the case of the Ik, will be disastrous. Other societies will be more fortunate, adapting to the new conditions at a more complex level of organization. Such has been the cumulative pattern of history.

Change within a given society, however, can be analyzed in terms of class-based interests. The outcome of any conflict situation will depend on the power of those with vested interests to subvert, coopt, or suppress movements for change. Since the established elites are typically stronger than protestors, rapid and radical change is generally successfully resisted. However, incremental change within a society may occur so that over a long period of time major transformations in the social and cultural fabric of a group will become apparent.

Class-based interests compete to control the outcome and pace of social change.

The Future: What Next?

What can we expect in the future? Both social change and the problems of the future will be, in part, consequences and reactions to current technology and to institutionalized patterns of social relationships. One factor that has influenced our thinking about social change and our anticipation for the future is what has been called the *revolution of rising expectations;* that is, a rapid, continuous increase in individuals' aspirations or goals. In simpler societies, no such revolution takes place, and standards of living do not change quickly. In more complex and differentiated industrial and postindustrial society, where social change is rapid and constant, severe frustration or depression is likely to befall individuals and groups when opportunities for advancement do not keep pace with their levels of aspiration. In other words, where there is a discrepancy between level of aspiration and available opportunities to achieve this, feelings of relative deprivation and consequent *anomie* are likely. Possible responses to the gap between opportunity and aspiration include retreat from the society, ritualistic adherence to norms, rebellion, and criminal behavior. Of course, in actual practice, there is almost always a gap between our aspirations and our opportunities. However, it is only when this interval is perceived as unfairly large that people become discontent. Otherwise, small differences can spur individuals to greater efforts to realize their dreams.

Bell (1973) has suggested that the contemporary universal desire for a life of plenty has become a farce. While more and more societies compete in the revolution of rising expectations, very little good appears to have come out of this

The **revolution of rising expectations** refers to a continual upgrading of the aspirations and goals of members of modern societies.

A revolution of rising entitlements leads to pressures on the government to meet individual needs for goods and services.

race. At the same time, there has been a *"revolution of rising entitlements."* That is, dissatisfied individuals have placed greater pressure upon the government to meet a growing array of demands.

While there is a danger where competing groups are likely to come into conflict with one another, the revolution of rising entitlements has also produced positive social change. Anti-poverty programs have had limited success, civil rights have been extended, and job opportunities for minority groups and women are somewhat improved. Rising expectations create problems—but so do lack of expectations which tend to maintain the *status quo.*

In the past, the major industrialized nations of the world have relied upon cheap raw materials from preindustrial nations, and as a result have developed social and economic institutions largely based on the wasteful use of the world's resources (Chirot, 1977). We have grown accustomed to the idea of disposables—one car, toaster, dress, shoe, cup, or whatever, quickly replaced by another. There is mounting evidence that scarcity can be anticipated in a number of areas—scarcity caused by the demands of technology and by the widespread modification of the environment. For example, there are limits of water supply and fossil fuels, both of which could have profound implications for almost every mode of subsistence. These potential shortages could be delayed by reducing our consumption of water and fossil fuels, by manufacturing longer-lasting goods, and by planned recycling.

But this solution, too, has its costs. For example, if better goods were manufactured and built-in obsolescence reduced as much as possible, within a relatively short period of time, unemployment would probably increase. After all, fewer workers would be required to turn out fewer but longer-lasting products. Likewise, there is a trade-off between our need for imported sources of energy, such as oil, and balance of trade payments. The point here is that many social analysts claim that there is no single one-time solution to problems that we can expect to face within the forseeable future. Rather, what is needed are gradual changes in our institutional spheres that will allow a balance between growth and no growth, or between stability and change. These are choices that you will have to make in the years and decades ahead. It is our hope that the sociological perspective will guide you in shaping a social order that reflects your highest ideals of justice and fairness.

Suggested Readings

BASKIN, LAWRENCE, and WILLIAM A. STRAUSS. *Chance and Circumstance: The Draft, the War and the Vietnam Generation* (New York: Vintage, 1978). The authors examine how the impact of the war in Vietnam varied by social class for twenty-seven million American youths—those who were drafted, those who enlisted, the avoiders, evaders, deserters, and the exiles.

ETZKOWITZ, HENRY (ed.). *Is America Possible? Social Problems from Conservative, Liberal and Socialist Perspectives* (St. Paul, Minnesota: West, 1980), 2nd Edition. A well-balanced analysis of the major issues facing American society—the quality of life, life in the cities, crime, the environment, drugs, mental and physical health, taxes, the mass media, and inequality.

LIPSET, SEYMOUR MARTIN (Ed.). *The Third Century: America as a Post-Industrial Society* (Chicago, Ill.: University of Chicago Press, 1979). These sixteen essays, primarily from a functionalist perspective, examine the nature and implications of postindustrial society.

MARSDEN, LORNA, and EDWARD HARVEY. *Fragile Federation: Social Change in Canada* (Toronto: McGraw-Hill Reyerson Ltd., 1978). In this theoretical and empirical analysis of social change in Canada, Marsden and Harvey discuss the problems of ethnicity and language, as well as the effects of regional imbalance in resources and population distribution.

MEAD, MARGARET. *Culture and Commitment: A Study of the Generation Gap* (Garden City, N.Y.: Doubleday, 1970). A well-known anthropologist traces the effects of technological change in industrial societies on relations between generations.

SERVICE, ELMAN R. *Origins of the State and Civilization: The Process of Cultural Evolution* (New York: Norton, 1975). The neoevolutionary perspective is clearly illustrated in this examination of a number of traditional societies and ancient civilizations, including those of Central America, Peru, Mesopotamia, Egypt, the Indus River Valley, and China.

SLATER, PHILIP. *Earthwalk* (Garden City, N.Y.: Doubleday 1974). Always provocative, Slater turns his sights on the environment, our ideas of progress and belief in science, social change, and the human condition. The result is a stimulating essay in the sociology of knowledge.

Glossary

Absolute Deprivation—A state in which one is without the basic material necessities for survival.

Absolute Numbers—Actual counts of people, births, marriages, deaths, and so forth.

Achieved Statuses—Positions occupied as a result of choice, merit, or effort.

Accomodation—A phase in which members of a minority become aware of majority norms and values without internalizing them.

Acculturation—A process that occurs when members of a minority group internalize the norms, values, and behavioral patterns of the majority society but are not admitted to more intimate groupings.

Affinity Groups—Persons with a special bond, making the group strongly supportive.

Age Structure of Roles—The available role opportunities for people of different ages in a society.

Agents of Change—Individuals who occupy positions through which they can influence the direction of change.

Agents of Socialization—Individuals and organizations responsible for the transmission of culture, such as parents, teachers, and peers.

Agribusiness—Large landholdings owned by national corporations.

Aid to Families with Dependent Children—A federally financed welfare program that aids unemployed or underemployed single parents (almost totally mothers) and their dependent children (under 18).

Alienation—A feeling on the part of workers of powerlessness, meaninglessness, and estrangement due to their inability to control their work conditions and the results of their work.

Amalgamation—The mixing of cultures or races to form new cultural and racial types.

The American Ethos—A set of core values that informs the beliefs and behaviors of North Americans.

Androgyny—The combination of feminine and masculine traits that are found in individuals.

Age Structure—The distribution of different age categories in a population.

Anomie—Situations in which norms are absent, unclear, or confusing.

Anthropology—The study of prehistoric or preliterate societies.

Anticipatory Socialization—A form of role rehearsal in which a person practices in advance of occupying a status.

Apartheid—The practice of separation of the races.

Ascribed Status—Positions occupied based on those attributes over which the individual has no control, such as age, sex, and race.

Assembly Line—A mode of organization in which each step in a complex task is isolated and one worker does just that one set of activities.

Atheists—Individuals who actively profess no faith in a Supreme Being.

Authority—The legitimate exercise of power.

"Back to Basics"—A trend in education that focuses on discipline, respect for authority, and an emphasis on traditional subject matter.

Barrios—Distinctively "Mexican" neighborhoods in the United States.

Barter—The method of distribution in simple societies whereby one set of goods is directly exchanged for another.

Behavior Modification—A process of operant conditioning involving the withholding of rewards in exchange for desired behavior.

Biography—The life events of an individual.

Biological Determinism—A theory of behavior that rationalizes social outcomes as being inevitable because of innate differences between types of people.

"Born Again"—A concept in which an individual has an experience that changes his or her life through an acceptance of faith.

Birth Cohort—A category of people born within a certain time period.

Birth Rate—The number of births within a specified time period divided by the total population within that time period, multiplied by 1000.

Bourgeoisie—The group in an industrial society that owns a major controlling share of the means of production, such as factories and manufacturing plants.

Block Busting—A process by which real estate agents and developers succeed in buying property at low prices, redeveloping an area, and selling property at a high profit.

Boundary Setting—The process by which norms and values are established, setting limits on acceptable behavior.

Bureaucracy—One type of formal organization, characterized by rules and regulations, rationality, efficiency, merit, hierarchy, and a precise division of labor.

Capital Punishment—The application of the death penalty.

Capitalism—An economic system in which a small segment of the population owns and controls the basic means and resources of production.

Career Contingencies—A complex set of social factors that determine outcomes for individuals by opening up or closing off certain options.

Caste—A term used to describe separate and unequal status systems based on race.

Caste Systems—Societies in which most movement is within a narrow range of categories and which depend primarily upon ascription, so that family status at birth determines much of the future life of the individual.

Casual Crowd—An accidental assemblage of people who happen to be pursuing individual goals in the same place at the same time who share a common focus for a moment or so.

Cells—Numbers in the body of a table.

Censorship—The practice of forbidding the disclosure of certain information.

Census Metropolitan Area—A term used by the Canadian Census to denote a continuous built-up area of 100,000 or more persons.

Censuses—Inventories of an entire population in a specific area.

Charismatic Authority—Authority based on unusual qualities attributed by followers to a leader.

Church—An association of believers that has a clear structure of offices and places of worship and members.

Circuits of Agents—Individuals who are needed to finalize the definition of someone as a mental patient.

Civil Disobedience—Nonviolent but generally illegal actions such as sit-ins and peaceful demonstrations.

Civil Law—Law which punishes conduct against the interests of private individuals.

Civil Liberties—Rights held by individuals even against the state.

Class—Those at a common economic level who can become aware of their common interests.

Class Awareness—The recognition of differences based on income, occupation, prestige, and power.

Class Conflict—Struggle between social classes based primarily on relations to the means of production; the capitalists who own versus the workers who do not.

Class Consciousness—Making class awareness central to one's self-definition and to social action of the members of a class based on the awareness of their common situation and interests.

Class Systems—Societies based on achieved as well as ascribed characteristics, in which individuals can move through the stratification system in their lifetimes.

Coercion—The use of force to ensure compliance.

Cognition—The mental process of knowing.

Cognitive Dissonance—The mental discomfort associated with holding mutually-exclusive perceptions and ideas.

Cohabitation—The sharing of a residence by an unmarried couple.

Collective Behavior—A category of activities including crazes, panics, fads, mobs, and riots, all of which involve individuals who influence each other.

Commune—An intentional community usually separated from the larger society.

Compromise—A cooperative effort to minimize the all-or-nothing implications of competition.

Conflict—A response to the failure of groups or individuals to agree on rules for the distribution of resources.

The Conflict Model—A sociological model that examines dissensus and friction in society and interprets social structure as the outcome of competition for scarce resources.

Confrontation—A process of testing through which limits of acceptable behavior are identified.

Conjugal Relationships—Relationships linked by the bonds of marriage.

Consanguine Relationships—Relationships based on blood ties.

Consciousness Raising—The process of making people aware of the lower status of women and the possibility of raising it.

Consensus—A process which requires discussion of an issue until all present agree on a given course of action.

Conspicuous Consumption—A life style calling for the open and wasteful display of wealth.

Constants—Characteristics that do not vary from one person to another or from one time to another.

Consumption—The way goods and services are used by members of a society.

Contest Mobility—The type of social mobility resulting from a more open and meritocratic school situation in which students are not totally segregated on the basis of intellectual ability and in which there is the possibility of movement in and out of particular programs.

Contagion Theories—Theories which focus on the individual's sense of reality in a crowd situation.

Content Analysis—A careful counting of the number of references to certain items in a sample of publications.

Contraculture—An opposition to existing social patterns which strives to overthrow and replace these patterns.

Control Group—The sample in an experiment from which the independent variable is withheld.

Conventional Crowd—Those gathered as spectators or audiences at events governed by established norms, such as religious services or theatrical performances.

Conversion—An experience which transforms confusion and anxiety into inner calm and certainty.

Cooptation—The process of bringing individuals or groups into the mainstream power structure.

Coping Styles—How one interprets and reacts to stressful events.

Correlation—The effect of change in one variable upon another variable.

Corruption—Acts contrary to public expectation that involve deliberate engagement in or support of illegal activity by public officials.

Counter Movement—A set of opinions and beliefs in a population that is opposed to a social movement.

Counterculture—An alternative lifestyle for those who do not conform to the dominant norms.

Countervailing Forces—Competing power blocs that limit the power of any one group.

Coup—A transference of power which involves the displacement of one elite by another.

Crescive Change—Change that appears to develop inevitably through the unfolding of the trend of history.

Crimes—Those deviant acts which arouse such strong feelings that they are prohibited.

Crimes Without Victims—Crimes which are not directed against a person or property but are believed to endanger or offend the moral fiber of a society.

Cross-Cultural Comparisons—Studies that test the relationships among variables in a variety of societies.

Cross-Section Studies—Studies that take place at one time and are slices of an ongoing social life.

Crowd—A temporary gathering of individuals brought together around a common activity or concern.

Cult—The term used to describe religious groups which have separated from denominations and are even smaller in number and less organized than sects.

Cultural Integration—The consistency among cultural complexes and themes and institutional arrangements.

Cultural Lag—A term used to refer to the gap between a change in technology and a corresponding change in values, norms, and social relationships.

Cultural Pluralism—A model for the integration of minority groups which emphasizes the contribution of various immigrant cultures and the resulting cultural diversity of America.

Cultural Relativism—An attitude of objectivity assumed by social scientists toward other cultures, which involves the attempt to understand each culture in terms of its own values, norms, and standards.

Cultural Universals—Elements found in all cultures.

Cultural Variability—One culture's specific set of cultural items, rules, and behaviors.

Culture—The design for living of a group whose members share a common location, feel responsible for one another, and call themselves by the same name.

Culture Complex—A network of patterns encompassing each individual trait of culture.

Culture Contact—Contact with people from other societies—the most prevalent source of change within a society.

Culture of Poverty—A set of beliefs and behaviors for coping with poverty that are assumed to be transmitted from parent to child, thus reinforcing the cycle of poverty.

Death Rate—The number of deaths within a specified time period divided by the total population within that time period, multiplied by 1000.

De Facto Segregation—Segregation that occurs in fact, though not necessarily by law.

Deferred Gratification—A middle-class norm that encourages one to put off immediate pleasure in return for future success.

Definition of the Situation—The process whereby individuals interpret and evaluate a set of circumstances in order to select the appropriate responses and behavior for that situation.

Deinstitutionalization—A trend in treating mental illness that involves treating the severely mentally ill within their own communities.

De Jure Segregation—Segregation supported by law.

Demand Mobility—Societal determinants of the rates of movement up or down the stratification system.

Demographic Transition—The change from populations characterized by high birth, high death rates; to high birth, low death rates; to low birth, low death rates; to population stability (zero population growth).

Demography—The statistical study of human populations, shifts in the population, and the social meaning of population statistics.

Denomination—An organized religious group *within* a church.

Dependency Ratio—The proportion of the population earning an income compared to those not earning an income.

Dependent Variables—Those variables assumed to be influenced by changes in the independent variables.

Desocialization—Learning to give up a role.

Deviance—Variations from the rules for usual, approved behavior.

Deviants—People who violate certain kinds of group norms.

Dialectic—A conflict of opposites that ultimately creates a new reality which, in turn, creates new contradictions and challenges, and so forth through time.

Differential Association Theory—A sociological explanation for deviant behavior which assumes that criminal behavior is learned behavior.

Diffusion—The process by which items of culture spread from one society to another through culture contact.

Discovery—A creative achievement which involves the awareness of some aspect of nature that already exists but had not been perceived before.

Discrimination—The practice of unequal treatment of people.

Disinvestment—A practice of lending institutions—sometimes called redlining—under which they refuse to invest in neighborhoods that are perceived as deteriorating or likely to deteriorate in the foreseeable future.

Dissensus—Lack of agreement.

Distributive Justice—The belief that one should receive fair returns based on skill and effort.

Dominance—Control over central sectors of social life, including the power to define norms and standards of beauty and worth.

Dual Economy—The use of two distinct sectors of workers for different types of employment: core industries and peripheral industries.

Dyad—A two-person group.

Ecclesia—The situation of a "state" or "established" church in which the religious body is coterminous with the political state.

Economics—The study of the production, distribution, and consumption of goods and services.

Ectomorph—A body type with a thin, small-boned appearance.

Ego—The conscious part of the self that links the psyche to reality.

Emergent Norm Theory—A theory which emphasizes the interaction of participants in developing norms of conduct and meanings through an emergent construction of realities.

Emigration—The movement of people out of a given geographic area.

Empirical Referents—Observable acts used as evidence of the abstract concept.

The Empty Nest Phase—A phase of life for parents that begins when the last child leaves home.

Endomorph—A body type with a soft, fat appearance.

The Enlightenment—An intellectual movement in eighteenth century Europe characterized by its emphasis on the ideas of progress, order, political and economic liberalism, the scientific method, skepticism, and a profound belief in the ability of human beings to solve human problems.

The Equal Rights Amendment (ERA)—A proposed amendment to the United States Constitution which would outlaw the denial of equal rights on the basis of sex.

Ethnicity—National origin or cultural distinctiveness.

Ethnocentrism—The belief that one's culture represents the only true and good way, and the subsequent tendency to judge other cultures by these standards.

Ethnomethodology—The study of the meanings that people give to their words and behaviors.

Eugenics—The belief that humans can be improved through selective breeding.

Eumenopolis—A continuous series of cities interconnected nationally and worldwide.

Evangelical—A term that connotes an emphasis on salvation and dramatic witness to the presence of a divine spirit.

Experimental Group—The sample in an experiment introduced to the independent variable.

Exploratory (Pilot) Research—Research designed to find out what information is available before designing a larger study.

Exchange Theory—Based on the assumption that individuals make rational calculations of the costs and benefits of particular actions and relationships, a theory developed primarily by George Homens and Peter Blau.

Extended Family—A family unit that consists of two or

more nuclear families (married couples with their dependent children) that share economic and social responsibilities.

False Consciousness—Individuals fail to recognize their objective class status.

The Family—A set of norms and behaviors developed to ensure orderly reproduction, intimacy, and care.

Family Income—The income of a household with at least two related individuals.

Family of Orientation—The original nuclear family in which we are born and reared.

Family of Procreation—The new nuclear family we start through marriage and the raising of children.

Fertility Rate—The number of live births within a specified time period divided by the population of women between the ages of 15 and 49, multiplied by 1000.

Field Experiments—Experiments conducted in the everyday world.

Field Independence—The ability to pick out one detail from among many.

Field Work—The method by which anthropologists study the culture and social organization of human groups.

Folkways—Customs and habits passed from one generation to another.

Food Stamps—A federally financed welfare program that subsidizes food expenses for people with no income or below poverty level.

Forced Migration—Migration that occurs when people seek to escape political pressures.

Formal Organizations—Complex organizations characterized by hierarchy, large size, relative complexity, and duration longer than the members comprising it.

Free Market—A state of economic affairs in which the forces of supply and demand, under conditions of perfect competition, would by some natural mechanism determine true prices.

Free Migration—Migration which occurs when individuals make a free choice to move.

Full Disclosure—The scientific duty to make one's results available to colleagues.

Function—A consequence of any specific element in a social system for the entire system or some other elements within it. Function usually contributed to the continuing stability of a system.

Functional alternatives—Ways that different means can achieve the same goal.

Functional Requisites—Tasks necessary to individual and group survival over time.

Gatekeepers—Formal agents who regulate entry into treatment agencies.

Gemeinschaft—Toënnies' term for small, traditional communities characterized by primary-group relationships and intergenerational stability.

Gender Roles—The culturally defined attitudes, behaviors, and social positions of each sex.

Gender Stratification—Differences in the positions of the sexes caused by the higher evaluation of male contributions to the group or society.

Generalized Other—George Herbert Mead's term for generally-held expectations for any person in a given status; the community's standard of performance.

Genocide—The systematic slaughter of an entire race or category of people.

Gentrification—The migration of more affluent families back to the central city.

Gesellschaft—Toënnies' term for societies characterized by business-like contractual relationships, where social bonds are voluntary and based on rational self-interest.

Gestures—Verbal and nonverbal symbols shared by individuals.

Goal Displacement—A problem which occurs when the requirements of formal structures displace the original goals.

Group—Any collection of people bound together by a distinctive set of shared social relationships.

"Hard Core" Unemployed—Individuals who are unemployed because there are few appropriate jobs in their geographical area or because they lack the education, skills, experience, or motivation to secure and maintain employment.

Heterogamy—The crossing of religious, racial, ethnic, and social class lines in the choice of a mate.

Heterogeneity—The existence of many different subgroups in a culture.

Heterogeneous Society—A society in which members differ from one another in race, religion, nationality, beliefs, values, and culture.

Heterosexuality—Sexual attraction, feelings, and acts directed toward members of the opposite sex.

Hispanic Americans—A category comprised of various cultural and racial subgroups sharing the common language of Spanish.

History—The study of broad trends over time.

Homogamy—The selection of a mate from the same religion, race, ethnic group, and social class.

Homogeneous Society—A society in which members are similar in race, religion, and nationality.

Homophobia—The strong fear of homosexuality.

Homosexuality—Sexual attraction, feelings, and acts directed toward members of the same sex.

Horizontal Mobility—A change slightly up or down within the same social stratum.

Horticulture—Simple farming.

Household Income—An income statistic that includes the wages of all household members in the labor force.

Human Capital Theory—A theory that explains employability and earnings in terms of the training and skills an individual brings to the labor market.

Human Ecology—A term used to define the physical relationship between people and land use.

Hypotheses—Specific propositions derived from a general theory about the relationships among variables.

Id—The instinctual desires, drives, and urges of the individual.

Ideal Culture—Reflects the highest virtues, standards, and values of a society.

Ideological Hegemony—A concept, borrowed from the twentieth century Italian theorist Antonio Gramsci, that refers to the control of cultural objects and symbols by those in power.

Ideology—A set of beliefs that serves to explain the past; justify support and organize the present and offer a view of the future. In any given society the dominant ideology serves to legitimize the existing social order.

Immigration—The movement of people into a given geographic area.

"Impression Management"—The way in which individuals manipulate information about themselves to protect their self-esteem.

Imperialism—The political and economic control of one society or country by another.

Incest Taboos—Rules that forbid sexual relations between specified family members.

Incremental Change—A long, gradual process in which one modification is followed by another.

Indentured Servants—Workers who sign contracts for specific periods of time to perform services for employers.

Independent Variables—Those variables thought to come first, to be most important, or to be relatively unchangeable.

Indigenous—Native to a society.

Industrial Society—A society in which machines for the manufacturing of goods are predominant.

Infant Mortality Rate—The proportion of deaths to live births of children below one year of age to live births in the population.

Inflation—A state of economic affairs that occurs when too much money is in circulation relative to the goods and services being produced.

In-Group—A primary or secondary group with which one feels a strong identity.

Inner-Directed—A person whose behavior is governed by an internal set of values.

Innovation—In the area of conformity and deviance, a form of behavior involving new and perhaps socially disapproved means of achieving socially approved goals.

Innovation—In the area of social and cultural change, innovation refers to the introduction of both discovery and invention.

Institutional Spheres—Patterns of rules and behaviors developed to meet a crucial functional need.

Interaction Processes—The manner in which role partners agree on the goals of the interaction, negotiate behaviors, and distribute resources.

Intergenerational Mobility—Status change from one generation to another.

Intragenerational Mobility—Status change within an individual's lifetime.

Invention—A creative achievement which involves the combination of existing elements of culture in a novel fashion.

The "Iron Law of Oligarchy"—A generalization proposed by political theorist Robert Michels, that holds that even organizations dominated by the general membership will, over time, tend toward hierarchy.

Issei—The first generation of Japanese-born immigrants to North America.

Jargons—Special language adapted by subcultures to protect themselves from outsiders.

"Jim Crow" Laws—Laws passed in the South after Reconstruction that effectively segregated the races and denied voting rights to blacks.

Kinesics—The study of nonverbal communication.

Language—The means by which symbols are created and translated.

Latent Functions—Unanticipated, unintended functions.

Laws—Universal rules that set limits on the behavior of all members of the group and are enforced by formal sanctions.

Legal Authority—Authority based on impersonal norms established by law.

Life chances—All those goods and services, such as education, medical care, housing, transportation, vacations, and so on, that make life easier, longer, healthier, and more enjoyable, that are desired, but not afforded, by all.

Life Expectancy—The average length of life remaining to a person at a given age, typically at birth.

Lifestyle—Attitudes, values, and behavior that are typical of specific social groups and social classes.

Longitudinal Studies—Studies that follow one group of people over periods of time.

The Looking-Glass Self—A concept described by Charles Horton Cooley which states that we see ourselves reflected back in the impressions of others.

Machismo—The demonstration by males of their physical and sexual prowess.

Macrosystems—Social systems at a higher level of abstraction encompassing microsystems.

Magnet Schools—Schools that attract high-ability students by offering specialized educational programs.

Mainstreaming—The integration of handicapped children into the regular school program.

Manifest Functions—Open, stated, intended functions.

Marriage—A socially approved union between members of the opposite sex.

Mass Migration—Migration which occurs when large numbers of people relocate.

Matriarchal family—A family system wherein the wife has greater authority.

Matrifocal—Centered on the woman.

Matrilineal Descent—A family system in which inheritance and descent occurs through the female side of the family.

Matrilocal Residence—A family system wherein married couples are expected to live with the family of the wife.

Mean—The arithmetic average of a set of numbers.

Mechanical Solidarity—A form of social organization in which people are bound together by their alikeness on a variety of characteristics.

Median—The mid-point of a distribution of cases.

Mediation—The use of a third party to resolve conflict.

Medicaid—A federally financed welfare program that pays hospital bills and other medical benefits to all Americans with incomes below the poverty line.

Megalopolis—A spatial area with many social, economic, and transportation links between adjacent metropolitan areas overlapping with each other.

The Melting Pot Model—A model for the integration of minority groups which assumes that immigrants should lose their cultural uniqueness and become assimilated into the dominant American model.

Mentors—Guides and sponsors.

Meritocracy—A ranked order of talent produced by the educational system.

Mesomorph—A body type with muscular, big-boned appearance.

Microsystems—Very simple and elementary forms of social interaction.

Migration—The movement of people into or out of a given geographic area.

Military-Industrial Complex—A system of influence and contact between these in high positions in the Pentagon and in major United States corporations.

Mode—The single most common category of cases.

Mode of Subsistence—The way in which a culture adapts to its environment.

Monogamy—The marriage of one man and one woman.

Monopoly—A state of economic affairs in which either only one or very few producers of a good exist.

Monotheism—The belief in one God.

Moral Entrepeneur—A crusader with a heavy investment in the social control of certain types of behavior defined as morally reprehensible.

Moral Reasoning—The complex cognitive capacity to handle abstract ideas such as justice and fairness.

Mores—Customs and rules of conduct that have acquired a sense of necessity over time.

Multinational Corporations—Enterprises whose directors and holdings cross national boundaries.

Mutual-Aid Society—An organization in which resources are pooled to support small businesses and help those in trouble.

Mystification—The sending of contradictory messages that inhibit understanding.

Nationalism—A consciousness of shared identity among members of a politically distinct territory.

Nativistic Revivals—Social movements which arise when a group's traditional culture is disrupted, dramatically changed, or destroyed.

Natural Experiments—Experiments measuring the same population before and after a natural phenomenon.

Natural Increase—The birth rate subtracted from the death rate.

Negative Reinforcers—Reponses that do not encourage repetition of certain behaviors.

Negative Sanctions—Either the withholding of approval for the role performance or the transmission of information that criticizes the performance.

Neolocal residence—A family system wherein married couples are expected to set up a new residence away from both the wife's and the husband's families.

Net Migration—The difference between immigration and emigration within a specified time period.

Neuroses—Less serious forms of mental illness, generally characterized by anxiety.

The New Breed Ethic—A recent ethic, challenging the work ethic, stressing self-fulfillment, and enjoying the good life.

Nisei—The children of the Issei born in the United States or Canada.

Norms—Rules of conduct that define acceptable behavior in given situations.

Nuclear Family—A married couple and their children.

Objective Measurement—Standards of measurement that are not based on personal feelings, such as income, occupation, and education.

Objectivity—The ability to view the world from outside one's own immediate experience.

Oligarchy—The rule of the few.

Oligopoly—Situation in which a few firms exercise dominant control over an industry.

The "Open Classroom" Movement—A movement of educational reform encouraging the development of the creative talents of school children in an unconstrained, supportive setting.

Operant Conditioning—The shaping of behavior through the manipulation of rewards.

Operationalizing the Variables—Translating the abstract into something observable.

Organic Disorders—Biologically- or physically-based disorders.

Organic Solidarity—The unity of interdependent parts.

Organizational Crime—Illegal actions pursued by legitimate corporations for corporate advantage.

Organized (or Syndicated) Crime—Continued endeavors to accumulate wealth in defiance of the law by groups.

Origin Myth—An account of how the group originated.

Other-Directed—A person whose behavior is governed by cues from his or her external environment, including role partners.

Parochial Schools—Schools that are operated by religious groups.

Participant Observation—A type of research in which the researcher becomes part of the interaction under study.

Parties—Political groups with particular concerns that may or may not reflect class interest.

Patriarchy—The rule of fathers, husbands, elders, masters of the household, princes and all forms of nobles, and especially the sovereign.

Patrilineal Descent—A family system in which inheritance and descent occurs through the male side of the family.

Patrilocal Family—A family system wherein the husband has greater authority.

Patrilocal Residence—A family system wherein married couples are expected to live with the family of the husband.

Payoff Matrix—The perceived costs and benefits received from different courses of action.

Peers—Persons of similar age and social standing who are important sources of information and socialization.

Percentage—A statistic measuring the exact number in every hundred. Also known as the proportion.

Personality—A relatively stable pattern of feelings, thoughts, and behavior that characterize an individual.

Peter Principle—Coined by Lawrence Peter. In a given organization every employee rises to her or his level of incompetence.

Phenotype—Physical appearance.

Phrenology—The study of character and mental capacity from the general configuration of the human skull.

Plea Bargaining—An agreement between the prosecution and the accused to reduce the charges in exchange for an admission of guilt.

The Pluralist Model—A theory that assumes that power in a society is distributed among a number of groups and subsystems.

Pogroms—Religious wars against Jews.

Political Institutions—Patterned statuses and roles developed for order and defense.

Political Participation—Involvement in the process of selecting and electing who rules.

Political Polarization—Separations and tensions that occur when characteristics such as religion or ethnicity consistently divide the population into the same interest groups.

Political Science—The study of governments, politics, and power.

Political Socialization—The influences and experiences through which involvement with the political system and party affiliation are formed.

Political Action Committees (PACs)—Special interest groups formed by citizens, unions, business associations and other organizations aimed at influencing political outcomes.

Polyandry—A type of marriage in which a wife may have more than one husband at a time.

Polygamy—Multiple marriage partners.

Polygyny—A type of marriage in which a husband may have more than one wife at a time.

Population Growth—Condition of a society in which births exceed deaths.

Population Projections—Estimates of future growth of nations, states, and geographic areas.

Population Pyramids—Graphic summaries of the age and sex composition of a nation.

Positive Reinforcers—Reactions from others or the environment that encourage repeat performances.

Positive Sanctions—Those reactions that convey the message that the role performance is being well received.

Post-Industrial Society—A society in which the production and delivery of services—including finance, trade, transport, recreation, health, education, and government—become dominant economic activities.

Primitive Migration—The result of the inability of a people to cope with the natural conditions of their environment.

Power—The ability of an individual or group to realize its goals and impose its will despite the opposition of others.

Power Elite—A small network of influential and powerful persons who, according to C. Wright Mills, are in command of the top economic, governmental, and military positions in American Society.

Preindustrial Society—A society in which fishing, agriculture and mining predominate as the mode of subsistence.

Prejudice—Prejudgement (usually unfavorable) toward members of ethnic, religious, or racial groups.

Preliterate—Without a written language.

Preparatory Schools—Private schools that typically attract children from affluent families.

Prescriptions—Details of acceptable acts.

Prescriptive Norms—Norms about what should be done.

Prestige—Status stemming from possession of socially admired and respected attributes.

Primary Groups—Small groups in which members have warm, intimate, personal ties with one another.

Primary Production—Extraction of resources directly from the ground or water.

"The Principle of Legitimacy"—A societal principle that identifies one man as responsible for the protection of a woman and her children and the children's placement in the social system.

Profane Behaviors—Behaviors that are unholy, everyday, and understandable in their own terms.

Progressive Taxes—Those taxes that impose a higher rate on higher incomes.

Proletariat—All persons who work for wages and have little or no control over the enterprises for which they work.

Propaganda—The dissemination of information favorable to actions taken by the governing authorities.

Proscriptions—Lists of unacceptable actions.

Proscriptive Norms—Norms about what should not be done.

Pseudo-Primary Groups—Similar to primary groups in size, informality and structure, of limited duration and may not be characterized by shared norms, values and goals.

Psychology—The study of individuals' mental and emotional states, needs, motivations, and behavior.

Public—A substantial number of people who, though not necessarily aware of each other, share common interests in one or several issues on which opinions differ.

Public Opinion—The common interests, attitudes, concerns and opinions shared by a group of people representing a substantial segment of society.

The "Public Temper"—A feeling shared by members of the group and belonging to no one individual in particular.

Punishment—The infliction of pain or penalty.

Race—The distribution of biological traits in the population.

Random Sampling—A type of sampling in which all possible respondents have an equal chance of being selected.

Racism—The exploitation of and the discrimination against one racial group by another based on perceived inferiority.

Rate—The number of times a given event occurs in a specified population.

Ratio—A statistical comparison of one group to another.

Real Culture—The actual behavior of society's members.

Reciprocities—An intricate network of favors owed and unpaid debts that links people or groups in a society.

Redistribution—The collection of surplus goods and distribution on the basis of need.

Redlining—An illegal practice that occurs when banks do not make mortgage money available for home buying in certain neighborhoods.

Reductionism—The attempt to reduce social behavior to individual psychology or biology.

Reference Group—A group that exhibits a strong influence on one's identity, placement, norms, and values, whether or not one actually belongs to that group.

Reform Movements—Movements which work for change within the system that can be accomodated without radical restructuring of institutions.

Regionalization—A method to contend with the problem of imbalance between the more impoverished central city and the more affluent suburbs by creating area-wide governing bodies.

Regressive Taxes—Taxes that take proportionally more from individuals and families at the lower income levels than from individuals and families at higher income levels.

Rehabilitation—Restoration to a former state of health.

Reification—The logical fallacy of making a *thing* of an abstract concept.

Relations of Production—Legal property relations governing the forces of production. In capitalist societies they are privately owned; under communism collectively owned.

Relative Deprivation—What is felt by those who compare their existing situation with those who are better off or with a previous or expected state of wellbeing.

Relative Numbers—Proportions of certain types of people in the total population.

Reliability—The ability of an instrument to measure something consistently.

Religion—A set of beliefs and rituals associated with the sacred which serve to explain the past, organize the present, and give a view of the future.

Replacement Level—In a population, a situation which occurs when parents replace themselves.

Repression—For an individual, the process of placing anger, anxiety, guilt, and other emotions into the subconscious; that is, below the level of consciousness.

Repression—In a society, the use of arrest, imprisonment, and execution to control dissidents.

Repressive Control Systems—Systems characterized by unrestrained power to suppress deviance.

The Reputational Technique—A technique for deriving

status which involves questioning others about who is honored and respected in the community.

Resocialization—Learning new and often dramatically different ways to deal with new role partners and new norms and values.

Resistance Movements—Those movements which emerge to forestall significant social change.

Resource Mobilization Theory—A theory which stresses the supports available to protestors and the tactics used by social control agents.

Retreatism—A form of deviant behavior in which persons reject both socially approved means and goals.

Restrained Control Systems—Systems that are relatively more accountable and have less power to suppress deviance.

Retribution—A theory of punishment under which various forms of punishment (including executions) are seen as a visible means of redressing social wrongs.

Revolution of Rising Expectations—A continual upgrading of aspirations and goals among members of a society.

Revolutionary Change—Change which brings basic alterations in the political and socioeconomic structure of a society.

Revolutionary Movements—Movements based on the belief that only fundamental changes in values and social structure can accomplish desired goals.

Riot—Violent, destructive collective behavior.

Rites of Passage—Public ceremonies that mark an important change in an individual's societal position.

Ritualism—A form of deviant behavior in which the person overconforms to societies rules of good conduct.

Ritualized Releases of Hostility—The ceremonial occasions developed for the continued expression of conflict.

Rituals—Culturally patterned ways of dealing with biological drives and anxiety-producing life events.

Role—A code of conduct defining how a status incumbent is expected to act.

Role Conflict—A situation in which an individual occupies two or more roles with resulting contradictory or conflicting demands.

Role Creating—A process that occurs in new and ambiguous situations where the status incumbent must develop new roles.

Role Distance—The space that a role player places between the self and the self-in-the-role.

Role Modeling—The act of assuming the characteristics of admired and respected persons one wishes to resemble.

Role Partners—Those who convey expectations and judgments concerning role performance and thus influence each other.

Role Performance—Behavior that approximates the prescribed ideal.

Role Slack—A time in which one's capacities are underdemanded.

Role Strain—A time in which too many demands are made on a role player, or conflicting demands are built into the same role.

Role Taking—A reflexive process by which the individual projects himself or herself into the role of another person.

The Romantic Love Syndrome—A rationale for choice of husband or wife in which love is the major reason for selecting and keeping a mate.

The Ruling Class Thesis—The theory that a national upper class owns and controls a disproportionate amount of wealth and power.

Rules of Conduct—Proscriptions and prescriptions that guide behavior.

Rumor—A piece of information passed from one person to another without being verified.

Sacred Behavior—Behavior imbued with holy, divine, mystical, or supernatural forces.

Safety Valve—Limited deviance used as a means of ventilating frustration and anger.

Sample—A group of people representing a larger population.

Sample Surveys—Mini-censuses built on a small but representative sample of the nation or of a region.

Sanctions—The reactions of role partners that convey approval or disapproval of one's actions.

Scapegoating—Finding a person or group to blame for one's problems.

Science—The logical and systematic method through which facts are observed and classified with the aim of establishing verifiable theories that can be tested.

Scientific Method—A research process based on objective observation, precise measurements, and full disclosure.

Secondary Analysis—Research involving the use of data collected by others.

Secondary Groups—Groups characterized by few emotional ties among members and limited interaction.

Secular Mind—A way of thinking in a rational, scientific, this-wordly manner that may conflict with religious beliefs.

Secondary Production—Activity that transforms primary resources into some other commodity through the process of manufacturing.

Sect—A group that separates from a denomination, usually over a matter of theological interpretation and practice.

Sectarian Conflict—Interreligious strife.

Secularization—The transition from traditional societies to modern societies guided by science, rationality, technology, and belief in the efficacy of the individual.

Segmented Labor Force—A type of labor market that develops when women and nonwhites have lower status jobs and incomes than white men, although their skills and education may be the same.

Segregation—The practice of separating minorities from the majority.

The Self—A learned organization of perceptions about who one is.

Self-fulfilling Prophecy—An expectation about social behavior that influences actual behavior so that the results obtained reinforce the prophecy.

Sexism—The belief and practice of discrimination against women on the basis of assumed biological and psychological inferiority.

Sex Roles—See gender roles.

Sexual Scripts—Ways of interpreting events so that certain responses are either called for or repressed.

Significant Other—A specific person in the individual's environment whose approval and affection are desired.

Single Issue Interest Groups—Organizations with one goal to the exclusion of all others.

Single-Parent Families—Families headed by either the mother or the father, with little or no help from the parent of the opposite sex.

Small Group—A group with few members who relate to each other on face-to-face basis as complete individuals.

Social Change—The processes whereby values, norms, institutionalized relationships, and stratification hierarchies undergo transformation.

Social Control—Processes by which normative behavior is enforced.

Social Facts—Patterned regularities that form the special subject matter of sociology.

Social Father—Any individual who assumes responsibility for a child through marriage.

Social Integration—The extent to which a person is part of a larger group or community of believers whose members support and watch out for one another.

Social Injury Theory—A model of how norms are translated into law which assumes that laws are passed to protect members of society from harm.

Socialism—The theory and practice of using political planning in order to ensure equitable distribution of goods and services and wherein basic means and resources of production are commonly owned.

Socialization—The process involving the transmission of language, gestures and culture through which one learns to behave as a human being.

Social Mobility—Movement from one status to another within a stratified society.

Social Movement—A set of opinions and beliefs in a population organized to bring about or resist social or cultural change.

Social Movement Industries—Institutions which arise when a number of organizations unite around a single issue.

Social Movement Organizations—The formal organizations designed to achieve the goals of a movement or counter-movement.

Social Norms—Rules regarding behavior that are both prescriptions and proscriptions.

Social Science—A group of related fields that study different aspects of human behavior.

Social System—A set of linked statuses composing the whole.

The Social Self—A concept introduced by William James which states that there are as many social selves as there are others who recognize that person and carry an image of him or her in their minds.

Social Stratification or Inequality—The differential distribution of power, prestige, and property.

Social Structure—The ordering of behavior and social relationships in a predictable way.

Socioeconomic Status (SES)—An index that combines education, occupation, and income in a single measure.

Social Supports—Networks of friends, relatives, or teachers that assist and sanction successful role enactment.

Sociobiology—The study of the evolution of social behaviors.

The Sociological Perspective—A way of looking at human experience characterized by concern for the totality of social life, the content of social action, and the individual as a part of a social group.

Sociology—The study of human behavior, of group life, and of the societies created by individuals.

The Sociology of Knowledge—The study of how the production of knowledge is shaped by the social context of thinkers and ideas.

Sociopathy—A concept often used by mental-health professionals to describe those who violate moral or institutional norms.

"Special Education" Classes—Classes in which children with the same type of handicap are taught by specially-trained personnel.

Sponsored Mobility—The type of social mobility that results from the separation of some students from others early in their school careers in order to prepare them for eventual success.

Sports—Competitive activities guided by agreed upon rules.

Standard Metropolitan Statistical Area—A term used by

the U.S. Census Bureau to denote a continuous non-agricultural area containing a city of 50,000 or more persons.

The State—The political organization of modern societies.

State Capitalism—An economic system characterized by a private sector, limited by government regulations and planning.

Statistics—Numerical techniques for the classification and description of data.

Status—Position in a social system.

Status Cues—Signals of social rank conveyed through clothing, speech, friends, and other attributes.

Status Groups—Communities based on similar degrees of honor or esteem.

Status Inconsistency—The extent to which an individual occupies different statuses in different hierarchies.

Status Incumbents—Individuals who occupy certain positions in a social system at a given time.

Status Symbols—The outward signs of social rank.

Stereotypical Thinking—The process of attributing a single set of characteristics, favorable or unfavorable, to all members of a social group.

Stigma—A characteristic that differs from the normal or normative in a society.

Street Crimes—Acts that directly threaten one's person or property.

Structural Anomie—A lack of fit between acceptance of culturally-valued goals and legitimate access to the means of achieving those goals.

Structural Assimilation—The entry of minority-group members into intimate groupings and major social institutions of the majority society.

Structural Conduciveness—The way in which social institutions are organized that either permits or inhibits the expression of collective behavior.

The Structural-Functional Model—A sociological theory that explains the relationship between the parts and the whole of society.

Structural Mobility—Changes in the economic system that affect the distribution of occupational openings.

Subcultures—Subgroups within a society that display differences in values, beliefs, norms, and behaviors.

Subjective Measurement—How people rank others.

Subsocieties—Smaller societies or cultures within larger ones that protect and nurture minority group members.

Suburb—A part of a metropolitan area beyond the political boundaries of a city but connected with the central city by economic and social links.

Supplemental Security Income—A federally financed welfare program that pays benefits to the blind, disabled, and aged who have no other source of income or whose Social Security benefits are still below poverty.

Superego—The socialized self composed of prohibitions controlling the id.

Surplus Value—Key source of profit for capitalists, based on the difference between wages paid workers and the market value that their work yields.

Symbol—That to which arbitrary meaning is attached by members of a group. Language, signs, and gestures are examples of symbols.

Symbolic Interaction Theory—The study of the micro-system and how individuals relate to one another, think about themselves, and define and explain situations.

System—An entity with mutually-dependent parts joined in a patterned way so that change in one part will affect the other parts.

Table—A set of columns and rows of figures arranged in a way that clarifies relationships among variables.

Taboo—A strong social belief regarding acts that are prohibited and perceived to be disgusting by members of a group.

Technology—Knowledge directed to practical solutions of the material problems of social life.

Tertiary Production—The provision of services rather than goods is emphasized.

Themes—Core values and assumptions that shape beliefs and behaviors.

Theocracy—A society in which religious leaders also control the political apparatus.

Theory—A set of logically related statements that attempts to explain an entire class of events.

Therapeutic Community—A community in which each person contributes something to the system, and patients are encouraged to take more responsibility for their daily lives.

Tongs—Secret societies in Chinese immigrant communities that functioned, in part, to organize and regulate illegal activities.

Total Institutions—Institutions such as prisons, jails, and mental hospitals which control and monitor all aspects of life in a single bureaucratic setting.

Totalitarian—A single party government with unlimited political authority.

Traditional Authority—Authority based on habitual routine.

Tradition-Directed—A person whose behavior is governed by customs.

Trait—The simplest unit of culture that can be isolated for analysis.

Triad—A three-person group.

Two-Income Families—Families in which both spouses are employed outside the home.

Undirectional Theories—Theories that assume that social change occurs along one path only.

Urban Homesteading—A practice under which rundown

housing units are placed on the real estate market for very low prices, with the understanding that the buyer will rebuild the dwelling for his or her own use.

Urbanism—A way of life, including anonymity and sophistication, associated with cities.

Urbanization—The process in which the proportion of the total population, concentrated in metropolitan areas rises.

Utopian Movements—Movements which seek the creation of an ideal society among a group of believers.

Validity—The ability of an instrument to measure what the researcher claims it measures.

Value Conflict—Basic disagreement between groups regarding goals, policies, and values.

Value Consensus—General agreement among group members regarding goals, values, and achievement.

Value Neutrality—The premise that sociologists exclude personal judgements and biases from their research and conclusions.

Values—The central principles of a culture that provide a standard for the evaluation of concrete rules of conduct.

Variables—Factors that display differences among individuals or change from one measurement to another.

Vernacular—Everyday speech.

Vertical Mobility—A change upward or downward in social status.

Verstehen—A German word meaning the ability to imagine the world as others might experience it.

Vital Statistics—Records of important events such as births, marriages, and deaths.

Voluntary Association—Groups or organizations joined out of personal interest such as the student government, the alumni association or the League of Women Voters.

The Voucher System—An educational plan under which school tax monies would be redistributed to families as tickets, entitling each child to a certain number of dollars toward an education in any type of school available in that area.

A "Welfare State"—A less complete form of socialism in which the state provides health care, higher education, income, housing, and social services to the needy in order to minimize status and class differences.

"Wet-Backs"—A derogatory term used to refer to undocumented persons entering the United States from Mexico.

White Collar Crime—Illegal activities committed by persons of high status, usually by nonviolent means.

Zero Population Growth—A situation of no natural increase in the population over time.

Zero-Sum Conditions—Conditions under which one group's gains must come at the expense of another group.

Bibliography

ABELLA, IRVING, and DAVID MILLAR (eds). *The Canadian Worker in the Twentieth Century.* New York: Oxford University Press, 1978.

ABBOTT, JACK HENRY. "In Prison." *New York Review of Books,* XXVII(11) (June 26, 1980).

ADLER, FREDA. "Changing Patterns." In Freda Adler and Rita James Simon (eds.), *The Criminology of Deviant Women.* Boston: Houghton-Mifflin, 1979.

ALLPORT, GORDON, and L. POSTMAN. *The Psychology of Rumor.* New York: Holt, 1947.

ANDERSON, CHARLES H., and JEFFREY R. GIBSON. *Toward a New Sociology.* Homewood, Ill.: Dorsey, 1978, 3rd ed.

ARDREY, ROBERT. *The Territorial Imperative.* New York: Atheneum, 1966.

ARIÉS, PHILIPPE. *Centuries of Childhood: A Social History of Family Life.* Robert Boldick (trans.). New York: Knopf, 1962.

ARONOWITZ, STANLEY. *False Promises: The Shaping of American Working Class Consciousness.* New York: McGraw-Hill, 1973.

ARTHURS, R., and E. CAHOON. "A Clinical and Electroencephalographic Survey of Psychopathic Personality." *American Journal of Psychiatry,* 120 (1964): 875–877.

ASHLEY, M. C. "Outcome of One Thousand Cases Paroled from Middletown State Homeopathic Hospital." *State Hospital Quarterly* (New York), 8(1922):64–70.

ASHTON, PATRICK J. "The Political Economy of Suburban Development." In William K. Tabb and Larry Sawers (eds.), *Marxism and the Metropolis: New Perspectives in Urban Political Economy.* New York: Oxford University Press, 1978.

AVERITT, ROBERT T. *The Dual Economy: The Dynamics of American Industry Structure.* New York: Horton, 1968.

BAGDIKIAN, BEN. *In the Midst of Plenty: The Poor in America.* New York: Signet, 1964.

BAILEY, WILLIAM C. "Deterrence and the Celerity of the Death Penalty: A Neglected Question in Deterrence Research." *Social Forces,* 58(4) (June 1980): 1308–1332.

BALTES, PAUL and ORVILLE G. BRIM, JR. (eds.). *Life Span Development,* Vol. 3. New York: Academic Press, 1980.

BANDURA, ALBERT. *Aggression: A Social Learning Analysis.* Englewood Cliffs, N.J.: Prentice-Hall, 1973.

BANFIELD, EDWARD C. *The Unheavenly City Revisited.* Boston: Little Brown & Co., 1974.

BARASH, D. P. *Sociobiology and Behavior.* New York: Elsevier-North Holland, 1977.

BARKAN, STEVEN E. "Strategic, Tactical and Organizational Dilemmas of the Protest Movement Against Nuclear Power." *Social Problems,* 27(1) (October 1979):19–37.

BARNET, RICHARD J. "The World's Resources." *The New Yorker,* (April 7, 1980).

BARRY, H., M. K. BACON, and I. L. CHILD. "A Cross-Cultural Survey of Some Sex Differences in Socialization." *Journal of Abnormal and Social Psychology,* 55 (1957):327–332.

BART, PAULINE, and LINDA FRANKEL. *The Student Sociologist's Handbook.* Evanston, Ill.: Scott, Foresman, 1981, 3rd ed.

BAUGH, CONSTANCE M. "Her Scars and Her Strength." *Journal of Current Social Issues,* 16(2) (1979).

BECK, E. M. "Labor Unionism and Racial Income Inequality: A Time-Series Analysis of the Post-World War II Period." *American Journal of Sociology,* 85(4) (January 1980):791–814.

BECK, E. M., PATRICK HORAN, and CHARLES M. TOLBERT II. "Stratification in a Dual Economy: A Sectoral Model of Earnings Determination." *American Sociological Review,* 43(5) (1978):704–720.

BECKER, GARY S. "Human Capital and the Personal Distribution of Income: An Analytic Approach." Ann Arbor: University of Michigan, Institute of Public Information, 1967.

BECKER, HOWARD S. *Outsiders: Studies in the Sociology of Deviance.* New York: Free Press, 1963.

BELL, DANIEL. *The Coming of Post-Industrial Society.* New York: Basic Books, 1973.

BELLAH, ROBERT N. "Civil Religion in America." In Robert N. Bellah, *Beyond Belief: Essays on Religion in a Post-Traditional World.* New York: Harper & Row, 1970.

BEM, SANDRA. "Sex Role Adaptability: One Consequence of Psychological Androgyny." *Journal of Personality and Social Psychology,* 31 (1975):634–43.

BENEDICT, RUTH. *Patterns of Culture.* Boston: Houghton-Mifflin Co., 1934.

BENEDICT, RUTH. "Continuities and Discontinuities in Cultural Conditioning." *Psychiatry,* 1/(2) (1938): 161–167.

BENGTSON, VERN L., and LILLIAN TROLL. "Youth and Their Parents: Feedback and Intergenerational Influence on Socialization." In Richard M. Lerner and Graham B. Spanier (eds.), *Child Influences on Marital and Family Interaction.* New York: Academic Press, 1978.

BENSMAN, JOSEPH, and ISRAEL GERVER. "Crime and Punishment in the Factory." *American Sociological Review,* 28 (1963):588–98.

BERELSON, BERNARD, and GARY A. STEINER. *Human Behavior: An Inventory of Scientific Findings.* New York: Harcourt, Brace & World, Inc., 1964.

BERGER, PETER. *A Rumor of Angels.* New York: Doubleday, 1969.

BERGER, PETER, and THOMAS LUCKMAN. *The Social Construction of Reality.* New York: Doubleday, 1966.

BERGER, PETER. *The Sacred Canopy.* New York: Doubleday, 1969.

BERGER, PETER. *Invitation to Sociology.* New York: Doubleday, 1963.

BERK, RICHARD A., and HOWARD E. ALDRICH. "Patterns of Vandalism During Civil Disorders as an Indicator of Selection of Targets." *American Sociological Review,* 37 (October 1972):533–547.

BERKMAN, LISA F., and S. LEONARD SYME. "Social Networks, Host Resistance, and Mortality: A Nine-Year Follow-up Study of Alameda County Residents." *American Journal of Epidemiology,* 109/(2) (1979): 186–204.

BERNARD, JESSIE. *The Female World.* New York: Free Press, 1981.

BERNARD, JESSIE. *The Future of Marriage.* New York: Bantam, 1973.

BERRY, BRIAN J. R. *The Human Consequences of Urbanization: Divergent Paths in the Urban Experience of the 20th Century.* New York: St. Martin's Press, 1973.

BIGGAR, JEANNE C. "The Sunning of America: Migration to the Sunbelt." *Population Bulletin,* 34, 1, 1979. Washington, D.C.: Population Reference Bureau, Inc., 1979.

BILLINGS, DWIGHT, and ROBERT GOLDMAN. "Comment on The Kanawha County Textbook Controversy." *Social Forces,* 57(4) (June 1979):1393–98.

BING, ELIZABETH. "Effect of Childrearing Practices on Development of Differential Cognitive Abilities." *Child Development,* 34 (1963): 631–648.

BIRDWHISTLE, RAY. *Kinesics and Context.* Philadelphia, Pa.: Univ. of Pennsylvania Press, 1970.

BLAU, PETER M. *Exchange and Power in Social Life.* New York: Wiley, 1964.

BLAU, PETER M. and OTIS DUDLEY DUNCAN. *The American Occupational Structure.* New York: Wiley, 1967.

BLAU, PETER M., and MARSHALL MEYER. *Bureaucracy in Modern Society.* New York: Random House, 1971.

BLAU, PETER M., and W. RICHARD SCOTT. *Formal Organizations.* San Francisco: Chandler Publishing Co., 1962.

BLAUNER, ROBERT. *Alienation and Freedom.* Chicago: University of Chicago Press, 1964.

BLUMBERG, RAE LESSER. *Stratification: Socioeconomic and Sexual Inequality.* Dubuque, Iowa: Wm. C. Brown Co. Publishers, 1978.

BLUMENFELD, HANS. "The Urban Pattern." *The Annals of the American Academy of Political and Social Science,* 352 (March 1964):74–83.

BLUMER, HERBERT. "Social Movements." In R. Serge Denisoff (ed.), *The Sociology of Dissent.* New York: Harcourt Brace Jovanovich, 1974.

BLUMER, HERBERT. "Collective Behavior." In Alfred McLung Lee (ed.), *New Outlines of the Principles of Sociology.* New York: Barnes & Noble, 1951.

BOGARDUS, EMORY. *Imigration and Race Attitudes.* New York: Ozer, 1971.

BOILEAU, R., F. LANDRY, and Y. TREMPE. "Les Canadiens Français, et Les Grands Jeux Internationaux (1908–1974). *In* R. Gruneau and J. Albinson (eds), *Canadian Sport: Sociological Perspective,* pp. 141–169. Don Mills, Ontario: Addison Wesley, 1970.

BONACICH, EDNA. "Advanced Capitalism and Black/White Relations in the U.S.: A Split Labor Market Interpretation." *American Sociological Review,* 41(1) (1975):34–51.

Book of Criminal Justice Statistics 1973. Washington, D.C.: United States Government Printing Office, 1973.

BOSKOFF, ALVIN L. *The Sociology of Urban Regions.* New York: Appleton-Century-Crofts, 1970.

BOUVIER, LEON F. "America's Baby Boom Generation: The Fateful Bulge." *Population Bulletin,* 35(1) (Population Reference Bureau, Washington, D.C.) 1980.

BOWLES, SAMUEL, and HERBERT GINTIS. *Schooling in Capitalist America.* New York: Basic Books, 1976.

BOYER, PAUL, and STEPHEN NISSENBAUM. *Salem Possessed: The Social Origins of Witchcraft.* Cambridge: Harvard University Press, 1974.

BRIM, ORVILLE G., JR. "Male Mid-Life Crisis: A Comparative Analysis." In Beth B. Hess (ed.), *Growing Old in America.* New Brunswick, N.J.: Transaction Books, 1979. 2nd ed.

BRIM, ORVILLE G., JR. "Personality Development as Role-Learning." In W. Richard Scott (ed.), *Social Processes and Social Structures.* New York: Holt, Rinehart & Winston, 1970.

BRIM, ORVILLE G., JR. "Remarks on Life Span Development." Presented to the American Institute of Research. Mimeo. 1977.

BRONFENBRENNER, URIE. *Two Worlds of Childhood.* New York: Russell Sage, 1970.

BROVERMAN, I. K., et al. "Sex Role Stereotypes and Clinical Judgments of Mental Health." *Journal of Consulting and Clinical Psychology,* 34 (1979): 1–7.

BROWN, GEORGE W., and TERRIL HARRIS. *Social Origins of Depression: A Study of Psychiatric Disorder in Women.* New York: Free Press, 1978.

BROWN, MICHAEL, and AMY GOLDIN. *Collective Behavior: A Review and Interpretation of the Literature.* Pacific Palisades, Calif.: Goodyear, 1973.

BROWN, ROGER. *Social Psychology.* New York: The Free Press, 1965.

BURAWOY, MICHAEL. "Social Structure, Homogenization, and 'The Process of Status Attainment in lthe United States and Great Britain.'" *American Journal of Sociology,* 82(1977): 1031–1041.

BURGESS, ERNEST W. "The Growth of the City." In Robert E. Park, Ernest W. Burgess, and R. D. McKenzie (eds.), *The City.* Chicago: University of Chicago Press, 1925.

BUTLER, EDGAR W. *Urban Sociology: A Systematic Approach.* New York: Harper & Row, 1976.

BUTTON, JAMES W. *Black Violence: Political Impact of the 1960's Riots.* Princeton, N.J.: Princeton University Press, 1980.

CAMERON, WILLIAM. *Informal Sociology.* Philadelphia, Pa.: Philadelphia Book, 1963.

CAMPBELL, ANGUS, et al. *The American Voter.* Chicago: University of Chicago, 1980.

CAMPBELL, ANGUS, et al. *The Quality of American Life: Perceptions, Evaluations and Satisfactions.* New York: Russell Sage, 1946.

Canada's Families. Statistics Canada, October 1979, Ottawa, Canada.

Canada Year Book, 1978–79. Ottawa, Canada 1979.

CANTOR, MURIEL. "Women and Public Broadcasting." *Journal of Communication,* 27(1) (Winter 1977).

CAPLOVITZ, DAVID. *And the Poor Pay More.* New York: Free Press, 1963.

CARLTON, RICHARD A., LOUISE A. COLLEY, and NEIL J. MACKINNON (eds). *Education, Change, and Society: A Sociology of Canadian Education.* Toronto: Gage, 1977.

CARMICHAEL, STOKELY, and CHARLES V. HAMILTON. *Black Power: The Politics of Liberation in America.* New York: Random House, 1967.

CARTER, HUGH, and PAUL C. GLICK. *Marriage and Divorce: A Social and Economic Study* (rev. ed.). Cambridge: Harvard University Press, 1976.

CASSELL, JOAN. *A Group Called Women: Sisterhood and Symbolism in the Feminist Movement.* New York: MacKay, 1977.

CASTELLS, MANUEL. "The Wild City." *Kapital State,* 4–5 (Summer 1976):2–30.

CENTERS, RICHARD. *The Psychology of Social Class.* Princeton, N.J.: Princeton University Press, 1949.

CHEVALIER-SKOLNIKOFF, SUZANNE. "Infant and Ape Behavior." *Animal Kingdom,* (June 1979).

CHINITZ, B. "New York: A Metropolitan Region." *Scientific American,* 213 (1965):134–148.

CHIROT, DANIEL. *Social Change in the Twentieth Century.* New York: Harcourt, Brace Jovanovich, 1977.

CLARK, HENRY. "The National Council of Churches' Commission on Religion and Race: A Case Study of Religion in Social Change." In Phillip E. Hammond and Benton Johnson (eds.), *American Mosaic: Social Patterns of Religion in the United States.* New York: Random House, 1970.

CLARK, S. D. *Movements of Political Protest in Canada.* Toronto: University of Toronto Press, 1959.

CLARK, SAM, J. PAUL GRAYSON, and L. M. GRAYSON (eds). *Prophecy and Protest: Social Movements in Twentieth Century Canada.* Toronto: Gage, 1975.

CLAUSEN, JOHN. "The Life Course of Individuals." In Matilda White Riley, Marilyn Johnson, and Anne Foner (eds.), *Aging and Society.* New York: Russell Sage Foundation, 1972.

CLEMENT, WALLACE. "A Political Economy of Regionalism in Canada." In Daniel Glenday, Hubert Guindon, and Allan Turowetz (eds.), Toronto: Macmillan, 1978.

CLEMENT, WALLACE. *The Canadian Corporate Elite: An Analysis of Economic Power.* Toronto: McClelland and Stewart, 1975.

CLOWARD, RICHARD A., and LLOYD E. OHLIN. *Delinquency and Opportunity.* New York: Free Press, 1960.

CLYMER, ADAM. "Poll Links Economic Slide and Social Antagonism." *The New York Times,* June 27, 1980, pp. 1, D11.

COBB, SIDNEY. "Social Support and Health Throughout the Life Course." In Matilda White Riley (ed.), *Aging from Birth to Death.* Boulder, Colo.: Westview Press, 1979.

COCOZZA, JOSEPH J., and HENRY STEADMAN. "Prediction in Psychiatry: An Example of Misplaced Confidence in Experts." *Social Problems,* 25(3) (February 1978):265–277.

COHEN, ALBERT K. *Delinquent Boys.* New York: Free Press, 1955.

COHEN, JERE. "Rational Capitalism in Renaissance Italy." *American Journal of Sociology,* 85(6) (May 1980):1340–55.

COHEN, L. H., and H. FREEMAN. "How Dangerous to the Community are State Hospital Patients?" *Connecticut State Medical Journal,* 9 (1945):697–700.

COLE, CHARLES LEE. "Cohabitation in Social Context." In Roger Libby and Robert Whitehurst (eds.), *Marriage and Alternatives: Exploring Intimate Relations.* Glenview, Ill.: Scott, Foresman, 1977.

COLE, ROBERT E. *Work, Mobility, and Participation.* Berkeley, Ca.: University of California Press, 1979.

COLE, STEPHEN. *The Sociological Method* (3d ed.). Chicago: Rand McNally, 1980.

COLEMAN, JAMES S. *The Adolescent Society.* New York: Free Press, 1961.

COLEMAN, JAMES, ELIHU KATZ, and HERBERT MENZEL. "The Diffusion of Innovation Among Physicians." *Sociometry,* 20 (1957):253–69.

COLEMAN, JAMES. "Population Stability and Equal Rights." *Society,* 14 (May 1977):34–6.

COLEMAN, JAMES. "Recent Trends in School Integration." *Educational Researcher,* 4 (July/August, 1975):3–12.

COLEMAN, RICHARD P., and LEE RAINWATER, with KENT A. MCCLELLAND. *Social Standing in America: New Dimensions of Class.* New York: Basic Books, 1978.

COLLINS, RANDALL. *Conflict Sociology: Toward an Explanatory Science.* New York: Academic Press, 1975.

COLLINS, RANDALL. *The Credential Society: An Historical Sociology of Education and Stratification.* New York: Academic Press, 1979.

COLLINS, RANDALL, and MICHAEL MAKOWSKY. *The Discovery of Society* (2nd ed.). New York: Random House, 1978.

CONKLIN, JOHN E. *The Crime Establishment: Organized Crime and American Society.* Englewood Cliffs, N.J.: Prentice-Hall, 1973.

CONRAD, JOHN P. "Corrections and Simple Justice." *The Journal of Criminal Law and Criminology,* 64(2) (1973):208–217.

CONVERSE, PHILIP E., JEAN D. DOTSON, WENDY J. HOAG, and WILLIAM H. MCGEE III. *American Social Attitudes Data Sourcebook, 1947–1978.* Cambridge, MA: Harvard University Press, 1980.

COOLEY, CHARLES HORTON. *Human Nature and the Social Order.* New York: Scribner, 1902.

COOLEY, CHARLES HORTON. *Social Organization: A Study of the Larger Mind.* New York: Scribner, 1909.

COSER, ROSE LAUB, and LEWIS COSER. "Jonestown as a Perverse Utopia." *Dissent,* (Spring 1979):158–163.

COWARD, BARBARA E., JOE R. FEAGIN, and J. ALLEN WILLIAMS JR. "The Culture of Poverty Debate: Some Additional Data." *Social Problems,* 21(5) (June 1974):621–633.

COX, HENRY. *Turning East.* New York: Simon & Schuster, 1977.

CRYSDALE, STEWART, AND LES WHEATCROFT (eds). *Religion in Canadian Society.* Toronto: Macmillan, 1976.

CULLEN, JOHN B., and SHELLEY M. NOVICK. "The Davis-Moore Theory of Stratification: A Further Examination and Extension." *American Journal of Sociology,* 84(6) (1979):1425–1437.

CUMMINGS, JUDITH. "Proposal for U.S. Aid to Expand Key West Hotel Draws Criticism." *The New York Times,* October 22, 1979, p. A18.

CUMMINGS, SCOTT. "White Ethnics, Racial Prejudice and Labor Market Segmentation." *American Journal of Sociology,* 85(4) (Jan. 1980):938–950.

CUMMINGS, SCOTT, and DEL TAEBEL. "The Economic Socialization of Children: A Neo Marxist Analysis." *Social Problems,* 26(2) (Dec. 1978):198–210.

CUNEO, CARL J. "A Class Perspective on Regionalism." In Daniel Glenday, Hubert Guindon, and Allan Turowetz (eds), *Modernization and the Canadian State.* Toronto: Macmillan, 1978, pp. 132–156.

CURRIE, ELLIOT P. "Crimes Without Criminals: Witchcraft and Its Control in Renaissance Europe." *Law and Society Review,* 3(I) (August, 1968):7–32.

DAHL, ROBERT A. *Who Governs? Democracy and Power in an American City.* New Haven, Conn.: Yale University Press, 1961.

DAHRENDORF, RALF. *Class and Class Conflict in Industrial Society.* Stanford, Calif.: Stanford University Press, 1959.

DANIGELIS, NICK, and WHITNEY POPE. "Durkheim's Theory

of Suicide as Applied to Family: An Empirical Test." *Social Forces*, 57(4) (June 1979): 1081–1103.

DAVID, LEO. "Family Change in Canada: 1971–1976." *Journal of Marriage and the Family*, 24(1) (Feb. 1980):177–183.

DAVIDSON, LAURIE, and LAURA KRAMER GORDON. *The Sociology of Gender*. Chicago: Rand, McNally, 1979.

DAVIE, MAURICE R. *World Immigration*. New York: Macmillan, 1939.

DAVIES, JAMES C. "Toward a Theory of Revolution." *American Sociological Review*, 27(1) (Feb. 1962): 5–19.

DAVIS, JAMES A. "Conservative Weather in a Liberalizing Climate." *Social Forces*, 58(4) (June 1980):1129–1156.

DAVIS, KINGSLEY. "Final Note on a Case of Extreme Isolation." *American Journal of Sociology*, 45 (Jan. 1940):554–65.

DAVIS, KINGSLEY. *Human Society*. New York: Macmillan, 1949.

DAVIS, KINGSLEY. "Mental Hygiene and the Class Structure." *Psychiatry*, 1 (Feb. 1938):55–65.

DAVIS, KINGSLEY. "The Origin and Growth of Urbanization in the World." *American Journal of Sociology*, 60 (1955).

DAVIS, KINGSLEY, and WILBERT E. MOORE. "Some Principles of Stratification." *American Sociological Review*, 10 (April 1945):242–247.

DE LONE, RICHARD H. *Small Futures: Future, Inequality and the Limits of Liberal Reform*. Report for the Carnegie Council on Children. New York: Harcourt, Brace, Jovanovich, 1979.

DEMOS, JOHN. "Old Age in Early New England." In John Demos and Spence Boocock (eds), *Turning Points: Historical and Sociological Essays on the Family*. Chicago: University of Chicago Press, 1978, Vol. 84 pp. 248–287.

DERSHOWITZ, ALAN M. "Increasing Community Control Over Corporate Crime: A Problem in the Law of Sanctions." *Yale Law Journal*, 71 (1961):289–306.

DEUTERONOMY (The 10 Commandments). 5:7–18, Old Testament, Bible.

DEUTSCH, ANTAL. "Quebec 1980." *Dissent*, (Winter 1980):65–72.

DEUTSCH, MORTON. "An Experimental Study of the Effects of Cooperation and Competition Upon Group Process." *Human Relations*, 2 (1949):199–232.

DEUTSCHER, I. *What We Say, What We Do: Sentiments and Acts*. Glenview, Ill.: Scott, Foresman, 1973.

DEWEY, RICHARD. "The Rural-Urban Continuum: Real But Relatively Unimportant." *American Journal of Sociology*, 66 (July 1960):60–66.

DOHRENWEND, BARBARA S., and BRUCE DOHRENWEND. *Stressful Life Events: Their Nature and Effects*. New York: Wiley, 1974.

DOMHOFF, G. WILLIAM (ed). *Power Structure Research*. Beverly Hills, Calif.: Sage, 1980.

DOMHOFF, G. WILLIAM. *Who Rules America?* Englewood Cliffs, N.J.: Prentice-Hall, 1967.

DOOB, ANTHONY. "Deviance: Society's Side Show." *Psychology Today*, 5 (Oct. 1971):47–51, 113.

DORESS, IRVIN, and JACK NUSAN PORTER. "Kids in Cults." *Society*, (May/June 1978):69–71.

DOWNS, ANTHONY. "Urban Policy." In Joseph A. Pechman (ed), *Setting National Priorities: The 1979 Budget*. Washington, D.C.: The Brookings Institute, 1979.

DOXIADIS, C. A. *Urban Renewal and the Future of the American City*. New York: Oxford University Press, 1968.

DURKHEIM, EMILE. *The Division of Labor in Societies*. New York: Free Press, 1893/1960.

DURKHEIM, EMILE. *The Elementary Forms of the Religious Life*. New York: Collier Books, 1912/1961.

DURKHEIM, EMILE. *Suicide*. New York: Free Press, 1897/1966.

EDMONDS, RONALD R. "Some Schools Work and More Can." *Social Policy*, (March/April 1979):28–32.

EDWARDS, HARRY. *Sociology of Sport*. Homewood, Ill.: Dorsey, 1973.

EISENSTADT, S. N. *From Generation to Generation*. Glencoe, Ill.: Free Press, 1956.

ELLIOTT, DELBERT S., and SUZANNE S. AGETON. "Reconciling Race and Class Differences in Self-Reported and Official Estimates of Delinquency." *American Sociological Review*, 45(1) (Feb. 1980):95–110.

ENGLAND, PAULA. "Women and Occupational Prestige: A Case of Vacuous Sex Equality." *Signs*, 5(2) (Winter 1979):252–265.

ERIKSON, ERIK H. *Childhood and Society*. New York: Norton, re. ed., 1964.

ERIKSON, ERIK H. "Youth, Fidelity and Diversity." In Erik H. Erikson (ed.), *Youth: Change and Challenge*. New York: Basic Books, 1963.

ERIKSON, KAI. *Everything in its Path: Destruction of Community in the Buffalo Creek Flood*. New York: Simon & Schuster, 1976.

ERIKSON, KAI. *The Wayward Puritans*. New York: John Wiley, 1966.

ERMANN, DAVID M., and RICHARD J. LUNDMAN. "Overview." In *Corporate and Governmental Deviance: Problems in Organizational Behavior in Contemporary Society*. New York: Oxford University Press, 1978, pp. 3–10.

Espenshade, Thomas J. "The Economic Consequences of Divorce." *Journal of Marriage and the Family*, 41(3) (Aug. 1979):615–625.

Etzkowitz, Henry, and Peter Stein. "Life Spiral: Human Needs and Adult Roles." *Alternative Life Styles 1* (November 1978): 434–446.

Fallding, Harold. "Mainline Protestantism in Canada and the United States: An Overview." *Canadian Journal of Sociology*, 3(2) (1978).

Fallding, Harold. *The Sociology of Religion*. New York: McGraw-Hill, 1974, Chapter 15.

Farley, Reynolds. "Residential Segregation in Urbanized Areas of the United States in 1970: An Analysis of Social Class and Racial Differences." *Demography*, 14 (1977):497–518.

Feagin, Joe R. "We Still Believe That God Helps Those Who Help Themselves." *Psychology Today*, November 1972.

Featherman, David L., and Robert M. Hauser. *Opportunity and Change*. New York: Academic Press, 1978.

Ferber, Marianne, Joan Huber, and Glenna Spitze. "Preference for Men as Bosses and Professionals." *Social Forces*, 58(2) (Dec. 1979):466–476.

Festinger, Leon, Henry W. Riecken, and Stanley Schacter. *When Prophecy Fails*. New York: Harper & Row, 1966.

Feuer, Lewis S. *Marx and Engels: Basic Writings on Politics and Philosophy*. New York: Doubleday Anchor, 1959.

Firey, Walter, Charles J. Loomis, and J. Allan Beegle. "The Fusion of Urban and Rural." In Jean Labutut and Wheaton J. Lane (eds.), *Highways in our National Life*. Princeton, N.J.: Princeton University Press, 1950.

Fischer, Claude S. "Toward a Subcultural Theory of Urbanism." *American Journal of Sociology*, 80(6) (1975):1319–1341.

Fischer, Claude. *The Urban Experience*. New York: Harcourt, Brace, Jovanovich, 1976.

Fischer, Edward H., and Amerigo Farina. "Attitude-Relevant Overt Behavior." *Social Forces*, 57(2) (Dec. 1978):585–599.

Fishman, Pamela. "Interaction: The Work Women Do." *Social Problems*, 25(4) (1978):397–406.

Fitzgerald, Frances. *America Revisited*. New York: Little, Brown, 1979.

Foner, Anne, and David Kertzer. "Transitions Over the Life Course." *American Journal of Sociology*, 85(5) (1978):1081–1104.

Franklin, Benjamin. *Poor Richard's Almanac*. New York: McKay, 1784/1970.

Freeman, Jo. *The Politics of Women's Liberation*. New York: McKay, 1975.

Freeman, Jo. "The Social Construction of the Second Sex." In Sue Cox (ed.), *Female Psychology: The Emergent Self*. Chicago: Science Research Associates, 1976.

Freeman, Jo. "Woman and Urban Policy." *Signs*, 5(3) (1980): 4–21 (Special Supplement on Women and the City).

Freidson, Eliot. *Profession of Medicine*. New York: Dodd-Mead, 1970.

Freud, Sigmund. *Civilization and Its Discontents*. James Strachey (trans.). New York: W. W. Norton & Co., 1962.

Friedan, Betty. *The Feminine Mystique*. New York: Norton, 1963.

Fromm, Erich. *Escape From Freedom*. New York: Rinehart & Co., 1941.

Gagnon, John, and William Simon. *Sexual Conduct: The Social Sources of Human Sexuality*. Chicago: Aldine, 1973.

Gagnon, John. *Human Sexualities*. Glenview, Ill.: Scott, Foresman, 1977.

Gagnon, John, and Cathy S. Greenblat. *Life Designs: Individuals, Marriages and Families*. Glenview, Ill.: Scott, Foresman, 1978.

Galbraith, John Kenneth. "Economics and the Quality of Life." *Science*, 145 (1964):117–123.

Gamson, William A. *The Strategy of Social Protest*. Homewood, Ill.: Dorsey, 1975.

Gamson, William A. "Understanding the Careers of Challenging Groups: A Commentary on Goldstone." *American Journal of Sociology*, 85(5) (March 1980): 1043–1060.

Gans, Herbert J. *The Levittowners*. New York: Vintage, 1967.

Gans, Herbert J. "The Positive Functions of Poverty." *American Journal of Sociology*, 78(2) (Sept. 1972): 275–289.

Gardner, Hugh. *The Children of Prosperity: Thirteen Modern American Communities*. New York: St. Martin's Press, 1978.

Garfinkle, Harold. *Studies in Ethnomethodology*. Englewood Cliffs, N.J.: Prentice-Hall, 1967.

Geertz, Clifford. "Religion as a Cultural System." In Patrick H. McNamara (ed.), *Religion American Style*. New York: Harper & Row, 1974.

Gerbner, George, Larry Gross, Michael Morgan, and Nancy Signorielli. "Violence Profile No. 11." Mimeo, Annenberg School of Communications, University of Pennsylvania, April 1980.

Gerth, Hans H., and C. Wright Mills. *From Max Weber: Essays in Sociology*. New York: Oxford University Press, Galaxy Book, 1958.

Gertler, Len, and Ron Crawley. *Changing Canadian Cities: The Next Twenty-five Years*. Toronto: McClelland and Stewart, 1978.

GILES, MICHAEL W. "White Enrollment Stability and School Desegregation: A Two-Level Analysis." *American Sociological Review*, 43(6) (1978):848–864.

GILLESPIE, DAIR. "Who Has the Power? The Marital Struggle." *Journal of Marriage and Family*, 33 (1971): 445–459.

GINIGER, HENRY. "Canada Says Gap Persists Between Indians and Whites." *The New York Times*, June 29, 1980, p. 8.

GITLIN, TODD. "Prime Time Ideology: The Hegemonic Process in Television Entertainment." *Social Problems*, 26(3) (Feb. 1979):251–266.

GLENN, NORVAL D. "Psychological Well Being in the Postparental Stage." *Journal of Marriage and the Family*, 37 (Feb. 1975):105–110.

GLICK, PAUL C., and ARTHUR J. NORTON. "Marrying, Divorcing, and Living Together in U.S. Today." *Population Bulletin*, 32:5, Washington, D.C.: Population Reference Bureau, Inc., 1979.

GLUECK, SHELDON, and ELEANOR GLUECK. *Delinquents in the Making*. New York: Harper & Row, 1952.

GMELCH, GEORGE. "Baseball Magic." *Transaction*, 8 (June 1971).

GOFFMAN, ERVING. *The Presentation of Self in Everyday Life*. Garden City, N.Y.: Doubleday, 1959.

GOFFMAN, ERVING. *Asylums*. Garden City, N.Y.: Doubleday, 1961A.

GOFFMAN, ERVING. *Encounters*. Indianapolis: Bobbs Merrill, 1961B.

GOFFMAN, ERVING. "On Cooling the Mark Out." In Arnold M. Rose (ed.), *Human Behavior and Social Processes*. Boston: Houghton-Mifflin, 1962.

GOFFMAN, ERVING. *Stigma: Notes on the Management of Spoiled Identity*. Englewood Cliffs, N.J.: Prentice-Hall, 1963.

GOFFMAN, ERVING. *Relations in Public*. New York: Basic Books, 1971.

GOFFMAN, ERVING. *Frame Analysis: An Essay on the Organization of Experience*. New York: Harper & Row, 1974.

GOFFMAN, ERVING. *Gender Advertising*. New York: Harper & Row, 1977.

GOLDBERG, PHILIP. "Are Women Prejudiced Against Women?" *Trans-Action Society*, 5 (1968).

GOLDBERG, STEPHEN. *The Inevitability of Patriarchy*. New York: Morrow, 1973.

GOLDSTEIN, ROBERT JUSTIN. *Political Repression in Modern America: From 1870 to the Present*. Cambridge, Mass.: Schenkman, 1978.

GOLDSTONE, JACK A. "The Weakness of Organization: A New Look at Gamson's *The Strategy of Social Protest*." *American Journal of Sociology*, 85(5) (March 1980):1017–42.

GOODE, WILLIAM J. "The Theoretical Importance of Love." *American Sociological Review*, 24(1) (Feb. 1959):38–47.

GOODE, WILLIAM J. "A Theory of Role Strain." *American Sociological Review*, 25 (1960):483–496.

GOODE, WILLIAM J. "The Protection of the Inept." *American Sociological Review*, 32(1) (Feb. 1967):5–19.

GOODE, WILLIAM J. *The Celebration of Heroes: Prestige as a Social System*. Berkeley, Ca.: University of California Press, 1977.

GORDON, DAVID M. "Capitalist Development and the History of American Cities." In William K. Tabb and Larry Sawers (eds.), *Marxism and the Metropolis: New Perspectives in Urban Political Economy*. New York: Oxford University Press, 1978.

GORDON, MILTON. *Human Nature, Class and Ethnicity*. New York: Oxford University Press, 1978.

GOTTMAN, JEAN. *Megalopolis*. Cambridge: MIT Press, 1961.

GOUGH, KATHLEEN. "The Origin of the Family." *Journal of Marriage and the Family*, 33(4) (Nov. 1971):260–70.

GOVE, WALTER R., and JEANETTE TUDOR. "Adult Sex Roles and Mental Illness." *American Journal of Sociology*, 78(4) (Jan. 1973):812–35.

GOVE, WALTER R., MICHAEL HUGHES, and OMER R. GALLE. "Overcrowding in the Home." *American Sociological Review*, 44 (February 1979):59–80.

GRACEY, HARRY L. "Learning the Student Role: Kindergarten as Academic Boot Camp." In Dennis Wreng and Harry Gracey (eds), *Readings in Introductory Sociology*. New York: Macmillan, 1977, pp. 243–253.

GRADY, KATHLEEN E. "Androgyny Reconsidered." In Juanita H. Williams (ed.), *Psychology of Women*. New York: W. W. Norton, 1979.

GRAMSCI, ANTONIO. *Selections from the Prison Notebook*. Quintin Hoare and Geoffry Nowell Smith (eds.). New York: International Publishers, 1971.

GREELEY, ANDREW M. *The American Catholic*. New York: Basic Books, 1977.

GREELEY, ANDREW M. "Religious Musical Chairs." *Society*, (May/June 1978):53–9.

GREENBERG, DAVID F., and FAY STENDER. "The Prison as a Lawless Agency." *Buffalo Law Review*, 1972.

GREENE, MARK. *The Monopoly Makers*. New York: Grossman, 1973.

GREENWALD, ERNEST. "Attributes of a Profession." *Social Work*, 2(3) (1957):44–55.

GREENWOOD, E. "Attributes of a Profession." In S. Nosow and W. H. Form (eds), *Man, Work and Society*. New York: Basic Books, 1962.

GREER, COLIN. *The Great School Legend*. New York: Viking Press, 1973.

GRUENBERG, BARRY. "The Happy Worker: An Analysis of

Educational and Occupational Differences in Determinants of Job Satisfaction." *American Journal of Sociology*, 86(2) (1980):247–271.

GRUNEAU, R. S. "Sport, Social Differentiation and Social Inequality." In D. W. Ball and J. W. Loy (eds.), *Sports and Social Order: Contributions to the Sociology of Sport*. Reading, Mass.: Addison-Wesley Publ. Co. Inc., 1972.

GUBRIUM, JABAR F. *Living and Dying in Murray Manor*. New York: St. Martin's, 1975.

GUILLEMIN, JEANNE. "Federal Policies and Indian Politics." *Society*, 17(4) (May/June 1980):29–34.

GUINDON, HUBERT. "Modernization of Quebec and the Legitimacy of the Canadian State." In Daniel Glenday, Hubert Guindon, and Allan Turowetz (eds), *Modernization and the Canadian State*. Toronto: Macmillan, 1978, pp. 212–246.

HADAWAY, C. KIRK. "Changing Brands: Denominational Switching and Membership Change." In Constant H. Jacquet, Jr., *Yearbook of American and Canadian Churches, 1980*. Nashville, Tenn.: Abingdon, 1980.

HADDEN, JEFFREY K. *The Gathering Storm in the Churches*. New York: Doubleday, 1969.

HALL, EDWARD. *The Silent Language*. Garden City, N.Y.: Doubleday, 1959.

HALL, JOHN R. *The Ways Out: Utopian Communal Groups in an Age of Babylon*. Boston: Routledge & Kegan Paul, 1978.

HALLORAN, JAMES D. "Studying Violence and the Media." In Charles Winnick (ed.), *Deviance and Mass Media*. Beverly Hills, Calif.: Sage Publishers, 1979.

HAMILTON, CHARLES V. "Blacks and Electoral Politics." *Social Policy*, (May/June, 1978):21–27.

HAMILTON, RICHARD F. *Restraining Myths: Critical Studies of U.S. Social Structure and Politics*. New York: Halsted Press, 1975.

HAMILTON, RICHARD F., and JAMES WRIGHT. *New Directions in Political Sociology*. New York: Bobbs-Merrill, 1975

HANEY, CRAIG, and PHILIP G. ZIMBARDO. "It's Tough to Tell a High School From a Prison." *Psychology Today*, (June 1975):26ff.

HANNON, MICHAEL T., NANCY BRANDON TUMA, and LYLE P. GROENVELD. "Income and Independence Effects on Marital Dissolution: Results from the Seattle and Denver Income-Maintenance Experiments." *American Journal of Sociology*, 84(3) (1978):611–633.

HARRINGTON, MICHAEL. "Hiding the Other America." *The New Republic*, 176 (1977):15–17.

HARRINGTON, MICHAEL. *The Other America*. New York: The Macmillan Publ. Co., 1962.

HARRIS, CHAUNCY, and EDWARD ULLMAN. "The Nature of Cities." *Annals of the American Academy of Political and Social Science*, 242(3) (1945):7–17.

HARRIS, MARVIN. *Cannibals and Kings: The Origins of Culture*. New York: Random House, 1977.

HARTMAN, MOSHE. "On the Definition of Status Inconsistency." *American Journal of Sociology*, 80 (November 1974):706–721.

HARVEY, EDWARD B. *Educational Systems and the Labour Market*. Toronto: Longman, 1974.

HAUSER, PHILIP, and LEO F. SCHNORE. *The Study of Urbanization*. New York: Wiley, 1965.

HAUSER, ROBERT M., and DAVID L. FEATHERMAN. *The Process of Stratification: Trends and Analysis*. New York: Academic Press, 1977.

HEILBRONER, ROBERT L., and P. LONDON. *Corporate Social Policy*. Reading, MA: Addison-Wesley, 1975.

HENLEY, NANCY M. *Body Politics: Power, Sex and Nonverbal Communication*. Englewood Cliffs, N. J.: Prentice-Hall, 1977.

HENSLEY, THOMAS R., and JERRY M. LEWIS. *Kent State and May 4th: A Social Science Perspective*. New York: Kendall-Hunt, 1978.

HERBERG, WILL. *Protestant, Catholic, Jew*. New York: Doubleday, 1960.

HERNDON, JAMES. *The Way It Spozed to Be*. New York: Simon & Schuster, Inc., 1965.

HESS, BETH B. (ed). *Growing Old in America*, 2nd ed. New Brunswick, N. J.: Transaction, 1980.

HESS, BETH B., and ELIZABETH W. MARKSON. *Aging and Old Age: An Introduction to Social Gerontology*. New York: Macmillan Publishing Co., 1980.

HESS, BETH, and JOAN WARING. "Changing Patterns of Aging and Family in Later Life." *The Family Coordinator*, 27(4) (Oct. 1978).

HESSE, SHARLENE J., INA B. BURSTEIN, and GERI E. ATKINS. "Sex Roles in Public Opinion Questionnaires." *Social Policy*, (Nov./Dec. 1979):51–56.

HEWITT, CHRISTOPHER. "The Effect of Political Democracy and Social Democracy on Equality in Industrial Societies: A Cross-National Comparison." *American Sociological Review*, 42(5) (1977):450–464.

HEWITT, JOHN P. *Self and Society*. Boston: Allyn, 1976.

HEYL, BARBARA S. *The Madame as Entrepreneur: The Political Economy of a House of Prostitution*. New Brunswick, N.J.: Transaction Books, 1977.

HIGGINBOTHAM, ELIZABETH. "Is Marriage a Priority? Class Differences in Marital Options of Educated Black Women." In Peter Stein (ed), *Single Life*. New York: St. Martin's Press, 1981, pp. 259–267.

HIGHTOWER, JIM. "Hard Tomatoes, Hard Times: Failure of the Land Grant College Complex." *Transaction*, 10(1) (Nov./Dec. 1972):10–22.

HILL, ROBERT. "The Illusion of Black Progress." *Social Policy* (Nov./Dec. 1978): 14–25.

HILL, ROBERT. *The Strength of Black Families.* New York: Emerson Hall, 1972.

HINDELANG, MICHAEL J. "Sex Differences in Criminal Activity." *Social Problems,* 27(2) (1979):143–156.

HINDELANG, MICHAEL J., TRAVIS HIRSCHI, and JOSEPH G. WEIS. "Correlates of Delinquency: The Illusion of Discrepancy Between Self-Report and Official Measures." *American Sociological Review,* 44(6) (1979):995–1014.

HOLLINGSHEAD, AUGUST B., and FREDERICK REDLICH. *Social Class and Mental Illness.* New York: John Wiley, 1958.

HOLT, JOHN. *How Children Fail.* New York: Pitman Publishing Corp., 1964.

HOMANS, GEORGE C. *The Human Group.* New York: Harcourt Brace Jovanovich, 1950.

HOMANS, GEORGE C. *Social Behavior: Its Elementary Forms.* New York: Harcourt Brace Jovanovich, 1961.

HOOK, E. B. "Behavioral Implications of the Human XYY Genotype." *Science,* 179 (1973):139–150.

HOOTON, ERNEST ALBERT. *Crime and the Man.* Cambridge, Mass.: Harvard University Press, 1939.

HOPPER, REX D. "The Revolutionary Process." *Social Forces,* 28 (March 1950):207–279.

HOROWITZ, IRVING LOUIS. "The Life and Death of Project Camelot." *Transaction,* 3(1) (Nov.–Dec. 1965):3ff.

HOUSEMAN, JOHN. "The Men from Mars." *Harper's Magazine,* 197 (December 1948): 78–82.

HOWARD, EBENEZER. *Garden Cities of Tomorrow.* Cambridge: M.I.T. Press, 1965.

HOYT, HOMER. *The Structure and Growth of Residential Neighborhoods in American Cities.* Washington, D.C.: U.S.G.P.O., 1939.

HUMPHREYS, LAUD. *Out of the Closets: The Sociology of Homosexual Liberation.* Englewood Cliffs, N. J.: Prentice-Hall 1972.

HUMPHREYS, LAUD. *Tearoom Trade: Impersonal Sex in Public Places.* New York: Aldine, 1975.

HUNT, J. McVICKER. "Psychological Development: Early Experience." *Annual Review of Psychology,* 30 (1979):103–149.

HUNTER, FLOYD. *Community Power Structure.* Chapel Hill, N.C.: University of North Carolina Press, 1953.

HYMAN, HERBERT H. "The Psychology of Status." *Archives of Psychology,* 37 (1942):15.

IANNI, FRANCIS A. J. *Black Mafia: Ethnic Succession in Organized Crime.* New York: Simon & Schuster, 1974.

IANNIELLO, LYNNE. "The 'Missing Women' of Orleans." *Bulletin* of the Anti-Defamation League of B'nai B'rith, 26(6) (June 1969):3–4.

JACOBS, DAVID, and DAVID BRITT. "Inequality and Police Use of Deadly Force: An Empirical Assessment of a Conflict Hypothesis." *Social Problems,* 26(4) (April 1979):403–412.

JACOBS, JANE. *Death and Life of Great American Cities.* New York: Random House, 1961.

JACQUET, CONSTANT H., JR. *Yearbook of American and Canadian Churches, 1980.* Nashville Tenn.: Abington, 1980.

JAFFEE, JEROME. "Jaffee Defends Disorder Label for Habitual Smokers." *Psychiatric News* (American Psychiatric Association), (Oct. 6, 1975):35, 39.

JASTROW, ROBERT. "Have Astronomers Found God?" *The New York Times Magazine,* June 25, 1978, pp. 19–29.

JAY, KARLA, and ALLEN YOUNG. *The Gay Report.* New York: Summit Books, 1979.

JENCKS, CHRISTOPHER. "What's Behind the Drop in Test Scores." *Working Papers,* (July/Aug. 1978):29–41.

JENCKS, CHRISTOPHER, ET AL. *Who Gets Ahead? The Determinants of Economic Success in America.* New York: Basic Books, 1979.

JENSEN, ARTHUR. *Educability and Group Differences.* New York: Harper & Row, 1973.

JENSEN, ARTHUR. "How Much Can We Boost I.Q. and Scholastic Achievement?" *Harvard Educational Review,* 39 (Winter 1969): 1–23.

JOHNSON, CHARLES E., JR. *Non-Voting Americans.* Current Population Reports, Special Studies, series P-23, No. 102, April, 1980. U.S. Dept. of Commerce, Bureau of the Census.

JOHNSON, MARILYN. "Women and Elective Office." *Society,* 17(4) (May/June 1980):63–69.

KANDEL, DENISE, and GERALD S. LESSER. "Marital Decision-Making in American and Danish Urban Families." *Journal of Marriage and the Family,* 30 (Feb. 1969):134–138.

KANDEL, DENISE. "Inter- and Intragenerational Influences on Adolescent Marijuana Use." *Journal of Social Issues,* 30(2) (1974):107–136.

KANTER, ROSABETH MOSS. *Commitment and Community.* Cambridge, Mass.: Harvard University Press, 1972.

KANTER, ROSABETH MOSS. "Why Bosses Turn Bitchy." *Psychology Today,* 9(1) (May 1976):56–59.

KANTER, ROSABETH MOSS. *Men and Women of the Corporation.* New York: Basic Books, 1977.

KESSLER, RONALD C., and PAUL D. CLEARY. "Social Class and Psychological Distress." *American Sociological Review,* 45(3) (June 1980):463–78.

KING, DAVID R. "The Brutalization Effect: Executive Publicity and the Incidence of Homicide in South Carolina." *Social Forces,* 57(2) (1978):683–687.

KINSEY, ALFRED, WARDELL B. POMEROY, and CLYDE E. MARTIN. *Sexual Behavior in the Human Male*. Philadelphia: Saunders, 1948.

KIPNIS, DAVID. *The Powerholders*. Chicago: University of Chicago Press, 1976.

KITANO, HARRY. *Japanese Americans*. Englewood Cliffs, N.J.: Prentice-Hall, 1976.

KLUCKHOHN, CLYDE, and ALFRED L. KROEBER (eds). *Culture*. New York: Random House, 1951.

KLUCKHOHN, CLYDE, and HENRY MURRAY (eds.). *Personality in Nature, Society and Culture* (1st ed.). New York: A. A. Knopf, 1948.

KOCHAN, THOMAS A. "How American Workers View Labor Unions." *Monthly Labor Review*, 102(4) (April 1979): 23–31.

KOHN, MELVIN L. "Occupational Structures and Alienation." *American Journal of Sociology*, 82(1) (1976):111–130.

KOHN, MELVIN L. "Bureaucratic Men: A Portrait and an Interpretation." *American Sociological Review*, 36 (June 1971):461–474.

KOHN, MELVIN L. *Class and Conformity: A Study in Values* (2nd ed.). Chicago: University of Chicago Press, 1977.

KOMAROVSKY, MIRRA. *Dilemmas of Masculinity*. New York: W. W. Norton, 1976.

KORNHAUSER, WILLIAM. "'Power Elite' or 'Veto Groups'?" In Seymour Martin Lipset and Leo Lowenthal (eds.), *Culture and Social Character*. Glencoe, Ill.: The Free Press, 1961.

Kozol, Jonathan. *Death at an Early Age*. Boston: Houghton-Mifflin Co., 1967.

KRISTOL, IRVING. *Two Cheers for Capitalism*. New York: Basic Books, 1978.

KROEBER, A. L., and CLYDE KLUCKHOHN. *Culture*. New York: Vintage, 1952.

KUHN, THOMAS S. *The Structure of Scientific Revolutions*. Chicago: University of Chicago Press, 1962.

LACZKO, LESLIE. "Feelings of Threat Among English-speaking Quebecers." In Daniel Glenday, Hubert Guindon, and Allan Turowetz (eds), Modernization and the Canadian State. Toronto: Macmillan, 1978, pp. 280–296.

LAING, R. D. "Mystification and the Family." In Peter J. Stein, Judith Richman, and Natalie Hannon (eds.), *The Family*. Reading, Mass.: Addison-Wesley, 1977.

LAMB, MICHAEL. "Influence of the Child and Marital Equality and Family Interaction During the Prenatal, Perinatal and Infancy Periods." In Richard M. Lerner and Graham Spanier (eds), *Child Influences on Marital and Family Interaction*. New York: Academic Press, 1978, pp. 137–163.

LANER, MARY RIEGE. "Prostitution as an Illegal Vocation: A Sociological Overview." In Clifton D. Bryant (ed.), *Deviant Behavior: Occupational and Organizational Bases*. Chicago: Rand McNally, 1974.

LANG, ANTHONY. *Synanon Foundation: The People's Business*. Cottonwood, Ark.: Wayside Press, 1978.

LAPIDUS, GAIL W. *Women in Soviet Society: Equality, Development and Social Change*. Berkeley: University of California Press, 1978.

LARKIN, RALPH W. Suburban Youth in Cultural Crisis. New York: Oxford University Press, 1979.

LE BON, GUSTAVE. *The Crowd: A Study of the Popular Mind*. London: Ernest Benn, Ltd., 1896.

LE MASTERS, E. E. *Blue Collar Aristocrats: Life Styles at a Working Class Tavern*. Madison, Wisc.: University of Wisconsin Press, 1975.

LENSKI, GERHARD, and JEAN LENSKI. *Human Societies*. New York: McGraw-Hill, 3rd ed., 1978.

LENSKI, GERHARD. "Status Crystallization: A Non-Verticle Dimension of Social Status." *American Sociological Review*, 19 (1954):405–513.

LENSKI, GERHARD. "Marxist Experiments in Destratification: An Appraisal." *Social Forces*, 57(2) (Dec. 1978):364–383.

LENSKI, GERHARD. *Power and Privilege: A Theory of Social Stratification*. New York: McGraw Hill, 1966.

LEON, CAROL. "Employment and Unemployment in the First Half of 1979." *Monthly Review*, 102(8) (August 1979).

LEVINE, DANIEL U., and JEANIE KENNY MYER. "Level and Rate of Desegregation and White Enrollment Decline in a Big City School District." *Social Problems*, 24(4) (1977):451–462.

LEVINE, MARTIN P. (ed). *Gay Men: The Sociology of Male Homosexuality*. New York: Harper & Row, 1979.

LEVINSON, DANIEL. *Seasons of a Man's Life*. New York: Knopf, 1978.

LEVI-STRAUSS, CLAUDE. *Elementary Structures of Kinship*. Boston: Beacon, 1969.

LEVI-STRAUSS, CLAUDE. "The Principle of Reciprocity." In Rose Laub Coser (ed.), *The Family: Its Structures and Functions*. New York: St. Martins Press, 1964.

LEVITAN, SAR, and BENJAMIN H. JOHNSON. *The Job Crops: A Social Experiment that Works*. Baltimore: Johns Hopkins University Press, 1976.

LEVY, MARION J. *The Structure of Society*. Princeton, N.J.: Princeton University Press, 1952.

LEVY-BRUHL, LUCIEN. *How Natives Think*. (Authorized translation by Lilian A. Claire) London: G. Allen & Unwin Ltd., 1926.

LEWIS, MICHAEL. *The Culture of Inequality*. Amherst, Mass.: The University of Massachusetts Press, 1978.

LEWIS, OSCAR. *Four Families: Mexican Case Studies in the Culture of Poverty*. New York: Basic Books, 1959.

LEWIS, ROBERT (ed.) *Men in Troubled Times*. Englewood Cliffs, N. J.: Prentice-Hall, 1981.

LIEBOW, ELLIOT. *Tally's Corner: A Study of Negro Street-corner Men*. Boston: Little, Brown, 1967.

LIPETZ, MARCIA J., and CATHERINE WHITE BERHEIDE. "The Women's Movement." In Robert L. Ellis and Marcia J. Lipetz (eds.), *Essential Sociology*. Glenview, Ill.: Scott, Foresman, 1979.

LIPSET, SEYMOUR MARTIN, and REINHARD BENDIX. *Social Mobility in Industrial Society*. Berkeley, Los Angeles: University of California Press, 1959.

LIVSON, FLORINE. "Sex Differences in Personality Development in the Middle Adult Years: A Longitudinal Study." Paper presented at Annual Meetings of the Gerontological Society, Louisville, KY, 1973.

LOPATA, HELENE ZNANIECKI. *Widowhood in an American City*. Cambridge, Mass.: Schenckman, 1973.

LORENCE, JON, and JEYLAN T. MORTIMER. "Work Experience and Political Orientation: A Panel Study." *Social Forces*, 58(2) (Dec. 1979):651–676.

LOUV, RICHARD. "The Appalachia Syndrome." *Human Behavior*, (1977).

LUKES, STEVEN. *Power: A Radical View*. Atlantic Highlands, N.J.: Humanities Press, 1974.

LUNDBERG, FERDINAND. *The Rich and the Super Rich*. New York: Bantam, 1968.

LYMAN, STANFORD M. *Chinese Americans*. New York: Random House, 1974.

LYNCH, JAMES. *The Broken Heart: The Medical Consequences of Loneliness*. New York: Basic Books, 1977.

LYNDEN, PATRICIA. "Where the Donald Trumps Rent." *The New York Times*, Aug. 30, 1979, pp. C1, C8.

MACCOBY, ELEANOR EMMONS, and CARL NAGY JACKLIN. *The Psychology of Sex Differences*. Palo Alto, Calif: Stanford University Press, 1974.

MACKENZIE, R. D. "The Scope of Human Ecology." *Publications of the American Sociological Society*, 20 (1926).

MACKLIN, ELEANOR. "Nonmarital Heterosexual Cohabitation." *Marriage and Family Review*, 1(2) (March/April 1978).

MAIR, LUCY. *Marriage*. Middlesex, England: Penguin Books, 1971.

MALCOM, ANDREW H. "New Family Trends Reported in Canada." *The New York Times*, Jan.2, 1980, p. A7.

MALINOWSKI, BRONISLAW. "The Principle of Legitimacy: Parenthood, The Basis of Social Structure." In Rose Laub Coser (ed), *The Family: Its Structure and Functions*. New York: St. Martin's Press, 1964.

MALINOWSKI, BRONISLAW. *Sexual Life of Savages in Northwestern Melanesia*. New York: Harcourt, Brace, Jovanovich, 1962.

MALINOWSKI, BRONISLAW. *Argonauts of the Western Pacific* (1922). New York: E. P. Dutton & Co., Inc., 1961.

MALINOWSKI, BRONISLAW. *Magic, Science and Religion* (1948). Garden City, N.Y.: Doubleday Anchor, 1955.

MALONE, KAREN. *HMOS As an Alternate Mode of Care for the Elderly*. Washington, D.C.: Urban Institute, August 1979.

MANN, JOHN. *Learning to Be: The Education of Human Potential*. New York: Free Press, 1972.

MANNING, PETER, and LAURENCE REDLINGER. "The Invitational Edges of Corruption." In Paul Rock (ed.), *Politics and Drugs*. New York: Dutton/Society Books, 1976.

MARGOLIS, JON. "Revisiting the Watergate Cast." *Boston Globe*, Aug. 5, 1979, p. A-1.

MARJORIBANKS, KEVIN. "Ethnic and Environmental Influences on Mental Abilities." *American Journal of Sociology*, 78(2) (1972):323–337.

MARKUSEN, ANN R. "City Spatial Structure, Women's Household Work, and National Urban Policy." SIGNS, 5(3) (1980) (Special Supplement on Women and the American City): 523–544.

MARSDEN, LORNA, and EDWARD B. HARVEY. *Fragile Federation: Social Change in Canada*. Toronto: McGraw-Hill Ryerson Ltd., 1979.

MARSHALL, ELIOT. "Unemployment Comp is Middle-Class Welfare." *The New Republic*, (Feb. 19, 1977).

MARSHALL, VICTOR (ed.). *Aging in Canada*. Pickering, Ontario: Fitzhenry & Whiteside, 1980.

MARTIN, WALTER T. "The Structure of Social Relationships Engendered by Suburban Relationships." *American Sociological Review*, 21 (Aug. 1956):446–453.

MARX, KARL. *Selected Writings in Sociology and Social Philosophy*. London: McGraw-Hill, 1865/1965.

MARX, KARL, and FREDERICK ENGELS. *The Communist Manifesto*. London: Allen & Unwin, 1847/1948.

MARX, GARY T. "Issueless Riots." *Annals of the American Academy of Political and Social Science*, 391 (Sept. 1970):21–33.

MCCARTHY, JOHN D., and MAYER N. ZALD. "Resource Mobilization and Social Movements: A Partial Theory." *American Journal of Sociology*, 82(6) (May 1977):1212–1241.

MCGEE, REESE. "The Economics of Conglomerate Organization." *Society* (November/December 1979).

MCKINLEY, JOHN B., and SONYA M. MCKINLEY. "The Questionable Contribution of Medical Measures to the Decline of Mortality in the United States in the 20th Century." *Millbank Memorial Quarterly* (Health & Society Issue), 55(3) (1977): 405–428.

MEADOWS, DONNELLA H., ET AL. *The Limits to Growth*. New York: New American Library, 1972.

MERCER, JANE. *Labeling the Mentally Retarded*. Berkeley, Calif.: University of California Press, 1973.

MERCER, JAN. *The Other Half: Women in Australian Society*. Ringwood (Victoria), Australia: Penguin, 1977.

MERCER, JAN (ed.). *The Other Half: Women in Australian Society.* Ringwood, Australia: Penguin, 1977.

MERTON, ROBERT K. *On the Shoulders of Giants: A Shandean Postscript.* New York: Harcourt Brace Jovanovich, 1967.

MERTON, ROBERT K. *Social Theory and Social Structure.* New York: Free Press, 1957.

MERTON ROBERT K. "Manifest and Latent Functions." In *Social Theory and Social Structure.* New York: Free Press, rev. ed. 1968.

MERTON, ROBERT K. "The Matthew Effect in Science." In Norman W. Storer (ed.), *The Sociology of Science: Theoretical and Empirical Investigations.* Chicago: University of Chicago Press, 1973.

MERTON, ROBERT K. "Patterns of Influence: A Study of Interpersonal Influence and of Communications Behavior in a Local Community." In Paul F. Lazarsfeld and Frank N. Stanton (eds.), *Communications Research 1948–1949.* New York: Harper & Row, 1949.

MERTON, ROBERT K. *Social Structure and Anomie.* New York: Free Press, 1957.

MICHELSON, WILLIAM. *Environmental Choice, Human Behavior and Residential Satisfaction.* New York: Oxford University Press, 1977.

MILGRAM, STANLEY. "The Experience of Living in Cities." *Science,* 167 (March 1970):1461–1468.

MILGRAM, STANLEY. *Obedience to Authority.* New York: Harper, 1973.

MILGRAM, STANLEY. "Some Conditions of Obedience and Disobedience to Authority." *Human Relations,* 18 (1965):57–75.

MILLS, C. W. *The Power Elite.* New York: Oxford University Press, 1956.

MILLS, C. WRIGHT. *The Sociological Imagination.* New York: Oxford University Press, 1959.

MIRANDÉ, ALFREDO. "The Chicano Family: A Reanalysis of Conflicting Views." *Journal of Marriage and the Family,* 39(4) (Nov. 1977):747–756.

MOFFET, SAMUEL E. *The Americanization of Canada.* Toronto: University of Toronto Press, 1972.

MOINET, SHERYL M. "Black Ghetto Residents and Rioters." *Journal of Social Issues,* 28 (1972):28–45.

MOLLENKOPF, JOHN H. "The Postwar Politics of Urban Development." In William Tabb and Larry Sawers (eds.), *Marxism and the Metropolis: New Perspectives in Urban Political Economy.* New York: Oxford University Press, 1978.

MOORE, GWEN. "The Structure of a National Elite Network." *American Sociological Review,* 44(5) (1979):673–692.

MOORE, JOAN. *Mexican Americans.* Englewood Cliffs, N. J.: Prentice-Hall, 1976.

MORGAN, ROBIN. *Sisterhood Is Powerful.* New York: Random House, 1970.

MORGAN, WILLIAM R., DUANE L. ALWIN, and LARRY J. GRIFFIN. "Social Origins, Parental Values, and the Transmission of Inequality." *American Journal of Sociology,* 85(1) (July 1979):156.

MOROWITZ, HAROLD T. *Foundations of Bioenergetics.* New York: Academic Press, 1978.

MORRIS, DESMOND, et al. *Gestures.* New York: Stein & Day, 1979.

MOTTL, TAHI L. "The Analysis of Countermovements." *Social Problems,* 27(5) (June 1978):620–635.

MUELLER, CHARLES W., and HALLOWELL POPE. "Marital Instability: A Study of Its Transmission Between Generations." *Journal of Marriage and the Family,* 39(1) (Feb. 1977):83–94.

MUMFORD, LEWIS. *The Transformations of Man.* Peter Smith, 1956.

NAGEL, WILLIAM. "Stream of Consciousness: A View of Prisonia." *Psychology Today,* 14(3) (1980):78.

NELSON, RANDLE W., and DAVID NOCK (eds). *Reading, Writing and Riches: Education and the Socio-Economic Order in North America.* Kitchener, Ontario: Dumont Press, 1978.

NEWCOMB, PAUL R. "Cohabitation in America." *Journal of Marriage and the Family,* 41(3) (August 1979).

NEWCOMB, THEODORE. *Personality and Social Change: Attitude Formation in a Student Community.* New York: Dryden, 1943.

NEWCOMB, THEODORE. "Attitude Development as a Function of Reference Group: The Bennington Study." In Eleanor Maccoby, Theodore Newcomb and Eugene Hartley (eds.), *Readings in Social Psychology.* New York: Holt, 1958.

NEWFIELD, JACK, and PAUL DU BRUL. *The Abuse of Power: The Permanent Government and the Fall of New York.* New York: Penguin Books, 1978.

NEWMAN, O. *Defensible Space.* New York: Macmillan, 1972.

NEWMAN, PAULINE. "The Way It Was." *New York Times,* 9-1-1980.

NIEDERHOFFER, ARTHUR, and ELAINE NIEDERHOFFER. *The Police Family.* Lexington, MA: Lexington Books, 1978.

NIEMI, RICHARD G., and B. I. SOBIESZEK. "Political Socialization." *Annual Review of Sociology,* 3 (1977): 209–233.

NOCK, STEVEN L., and PETER H. ROSSI. "Household Types and Social Standing." *Social Forces,* 57(4) (June 1979):1325–1345.

NORRIS, VERA. *Mental Illness in London.* New York: Oxford University Press, 1959.

NORWOOD, JANET L., and ELIZABETH WALDMAN. "Women in the Labor Force." U. S. Department of Labor, Bureau of Labor Statistics, Report 575, October 1979.

OGBURN, WILLIAM T. *Social Change: With Respect to Cul-*

ture and Original Nature. New York: B. W. Huebsch, 1922.

ORUM, ANTHONY M. "Individual Autonomy and Social Constraints in the Political Arena: Signs and Designs in the United States." Paper presented at the annual meetings of the Society for the Study of Social Problems, New York City, 1976.

OTTO, LUTHER B., and ARCHIBALD O. HALLER. "Evidence for a Social Psychological View of the Status Attainment Process: Four Studies Compared." *Social Forces*, 57(3) (March 1979);887–914.

OUCHI, WILLIAM. *Theory Z Corporations: How American Business Can Meet the Japanese Challenge*. Reading, MA: Addison-Wesley, 1981.

OVERBEEK, JOHANNES. *Population and Canadian Society*. Toronto (Canada): Butterworth & Co., 1980.

PAGE, ANN L., and DONALD CLELLAND. "The Kanawha County Textbook Controversy: A Study of Politics of Lifestyle Concerns." *Social Forces*, 57(1) (1978).

PARENTI, MICHAEL. *Power and Powerlessness*. New York: St. Martin's Press, 1978.

PARRILLO, VINCENT N. *Strangers to These Shores: Race and Ethnic Relations in the United States*. Boston: Houghton-Mifflin, 1980.

PARSONS, TALCOTT, and ROBERT F. BALES. *Family, Socialization, and Interaction Process*. Glencoe, Ill.: Free Press, 1955.

PARSONS, TALCOTT. *The Social System*. New York, Free Press, 1951.

PEARCE, DIANE M. "Gatekeepers and Homeseekers: Institutional Factors in Racial Steering." *Social Problems* 26(3) (Feb. 1979):325–342.

PERSELL, CAROLINE HODGES. *Education and Inequality*. New York: Free Press, 1977.

Perspectives Canada III. Ottawa, Canada. Statistics Canada 1980.

PETER, LAURENCE J., and RAYMOND HULL. *The Peter Principle: Why Things Always Go Wrong*. New York: Morrow, 1969.

PETERSON, WILLIAM. *Population*. New York: Macmillan, 1975.

PHILLIPS, DAVID P., and KENNETH A. FELDMAN. "A Dip in Deaths Before Ceremonial Occasions: Some New Relationships Between Social Integration and Mortality." *American Sociological Review*, 38(6) (1973): 678–696.

PHILLIPS, DAVID P. "The Influence of Suggestion on Suicide: Substantive and Theoretical Implications of the Werther Effect." *American Sociological Review*, 39(3) (1974):340–354.

PHILLIPS, DAVID P. "Suicide, Motor Vehicle Fatalities, and the Mass Media: Evidence Toward a Theory of Suggestion." *American Journal of Sociology*, 84(5) (1979): 1150–1174.

PILIAVIN, J. A., and I. M. PILIAVIN. "Effect of Blood on Reactions to a Victim." *Journal of Personality and Social Personality*, 23 (1972):353–361.

PINCUS, FRED L. "The False Promises of Community Colleges: Class Conflict and Vocational Education." *Harvard Education Review*, 50 (August 1980):332–361.

PINCUS, FRED L. "On the Higher Voc-Ed in America." *Social Policy*, (May/June 1979): 34–42.

PINKNEY, ALPHONSO. *Black Americans*. Englewood Cliffs, N. J.: Prentice-Hall, 1975.

PINKNEY, ALPHONSO. *Red, Black and Green: Black Nationalism in the United States*. New York: Cambridge University Press, 1976.

PIVEN, FRANCES FOX, and RICHARD A. CLOWARD. *Poor People's Movements*. New York: Pantheon, 1977.

PIVEN, FRANCES FOX, and RICHARD A. CLOWARD. *Regulating the Poor*. New York: Vintage, 1971.

PLACEK, PAUL J., and GERRY E. HENDERSHOT. "Public Welfare and Family Planning: An Empirical Study of the 'Brood Sow' Myth." *Social Problems*, 21(5) (June 1974):658–673.

PLECK, ELIZABETH H., and JOSEPH H. PLECK. *The American Man*. Englewood Cliffs, N.J.: Prentice-Hall, 1980.

POPENOE, DAVID. *The Suburban Environment*. Chicago: University of Chicago Press, 1977.

POPULATION REFERENCE BUREAU. *Intercom*, 8(2) (Feb. 1980).

POPULATION REFERENCE BUREAU. *World Population Data Sheet, 1981*. Washington, D.C.

PORTER, JOHN. *The Vertical Mosaic*. Toronto: University of Toronto Press, 1965.

PRESIDENTS COMMISSION ON LAW ENFORCEMENT AND THE ADMINISTRATION OF JUSTICE. *The Challenge of Crime in a Free Society*. Washington, D.C.: U.S. Government Printing Office, 1967.

QUINNEY, RICHARD. *Critique of Legal Order: Crime Control in Capitalist Society*. Boston: Little, Brown, 1974.

QUINNEY, RICHARD, and JOHN WILDEMAN. *The Problem of Crime* (2nd ed.). New York: Harcourt, Brace, Jovanovich, 1977.

RADCLIFFE-BROWN, ALFRED REGINALD. *The Andaman Islanders*. New York: Free Press 1964.

RAGAN, PAULINE, and WILLIAM J. DAVIS. "The Diversity of Older Voters." *Society*, 15(5) (July/August 1978): 50–53.

RAINWATER, LEE. "Crucible of Identity: The Negro Lower Class Family." *Daedalus*, 95(1) (Winter 1966).

RAINWATER, LEE, and WILLIAM L. YANCEY (eds.). *The Moynihan Report and the Politics of Controversy*. Cambridge, Mass.: Massachusetts Institute of Technology Press, 1967.

RATCLIFF, RICHARD E. "Capitalist Class Impact on the Lending Behaviors of Banks." *American Sociological Review*, 45(4) (August 1980):553–570.

RAVITCH, DIANE. *The Great School Wars*. New York: Basic Books, 1974.

RAY, MICHAEL D., et al. *Canadian Urban Trends*. Toronto: Copp Clark, 1977.

REDFIELD, ROBERT. *The Folk Culture of Yucatan*. Chicago: University of Chicago Press, 1941.

RICHARDS, PAMELA. "Middle-Class Vandalism and Age-Status Conflict." *Social Problems*, 26(4) (April 1979).

RICHMOND, ANTHONY H. "Immigration, Population and the Canadian Future." In Daniel Glenday, Hubert Guindon, and Allan Turowetz (eds). *Modernization and the Canadian State*. Toronto: Macmillan, 1978, pp. 301–316.

RIDGEWAY, SALLY. "Suburban Women: Myths and Realities." Paper presented at the annual meetings of the Society for the Study of Social Problems, August 1981.

RIESMAN, DAVID. *The Lonely Crowd*. New Haven, Conn.: Yale University Press, 1950.

RILEY, MATILDA WHITE. *Sociological Research: A Case Approach*. New York: Harcourt, Brace and World, 1963.

RILEY, MATILDA WHITE, ANNE FONER, BETH HESS, and MARCIA TOBY. "Socialization to the Middle and Later Years." In David A. Goslin (ed.), *Handbook of Socialization Theory and Research*. New York: Rand McNally, 1968.

RILEY, MATILDA WHITE, MARILYN JOHNSON, and ANNE FONER. *Aging and Society, Vol. 3: A Sociology of Age Stratification*. New York: Russell Sage Foundation, 1972.

RILEY, MATILDA WHITE, and JOAN M. WARING. "Age and Aging." In Robert K. Merton and Robert Nisbet (eds), *Contemporary Social Problems*, 4th ed. New York: Harcourt Brace Jovanovich, 1976.

RIST, RAY C. *The Invisible Children: School Integration in American Society*. Cambridge, Mass.: Harvard University Press, 1978.

ROACH, JACK L., and JANET K. ROACH. "Mobilizing the Poor: Road to a Dead End." *Social Problems* 26(2) (Dec. 1978):160–171.

ROBBINS, THOMAS, and DICK ANTHONY. "New Religions, Families and Brain Washing." *Society*, 15(4) (May/June 1978):77–83.

ROOF, WADE CLARK. "Alienation and Apostasy." *Society*, (May/June 1978):41–45.

ROOF, WADE CLARK. *Community and Commitment: Religious Plausibility in a Liberal Protestant Church*. New York: Elsevier-North Holland, 1978.

ROOF, WADE CLARK. "Socioeconomic Differentials Among White Socio-Religious Groups in the United States." *Social Forces*, 58(1) (1979).

ROPER, ELMO, ET AL. *Virginia Slims Poll*. 1980.

ROSE, STEPHEN J. *Social Stratification in the United States*. Baltimore, MD.: Social Graphics Co., 1979.

ROSENBAUM, JAMES E. "The Structure of Opportunity in School." *Social Forces*, 57(1) (Sept. 1978):236–256.

ROSENBERG, MORRIS, and LEONARD I. PEARLIN. "Social Class and Self-Esteem Among Children and Adults." *American Journal of Sociology*, 84(1) (1978):53–77.

ROSENTHAL, ROBERT, and LENORE JACOBSON. *Pygmalion in the Classroom*. New York: Holt, Rinehart & Winston, 1968.

ROSOW, IRVING. "And Then We Were Old." *Transaction/Society*, 2(2) (1965):20–26.

ROSS, H. LAURENCE, DONALD T. CAMPBELL, and GENE V. GLASS. "Determining the Social Effects of a Legal Reform: The British 'Breathalyzer' Crackdown of 1967." *American Behavioral Scientist*, 13(4) (1970):493–509.

ROSSELL, CHRISTINE H. "School Desegregation and Community Social Change." *Law and Contemporary Problems*. 42 (Spring 1978).

ROSSI, ALICE. "Equality Between the Sexes: An Immodest Proposal." *Daedalus*, 93(2)(1964):607–652.

ROSZAK, THEODORE. *Making of a Counter-Culture*. New York: Doubleday, 1969.

ROTHMAN, DAVID. *The Discovery of the Asylum*. Boston: Little, Brown, 1971.

ROTHSCHILD-WHITT, JOYCE. "Private Ownership and Worker Control in Holland." *Working Papers*, 8(2) (March-April, 1981):22–25.

ROY, DONALD. "Banana Time: Job Satisfaction and Informal Interaction." *Human Organization*, 18 (Winter 1959):158–168.

ROY, GILLES. "Centrality and Mobility: The Case of the National Hockey League." M. Sc. Thesis, University of Waterloo, Canada, 1974.

RUBIN, JEFFREY Z., FRANK J. PROVENZANO, and ZELLA LURIA. "The Eye of the Beholder: Parents' Views on Sex of Newborns." In Juanita H. Williams (ed.), *Psychology of Women*. New York: W. W. Norton and Co., 1979.

RUBIN, LILIAN. *Women of a Certain Age*. New York: Harper & Row, 1979.

RUBIN, LILIAN. *Worlds of Pain*. New York: Harper & Row, 1975.

RUESCH, JURGEN, and GREGORY BATESON. *Communication: The Social Matrix of Psychiatry*. New York: W. W. Norton & Co., 1951.

RYAN, WILLIAM. *Blaming the Victim*. New York: Vintage, 1972.

SABINE, GEORGE H. *A History of Political Theory*. New York: Holt, 1947.

SAEGART, SUSAN. "Masculine Cities and Feminine Suburbs: Polarized Ideas, Contradictory Realities." In Catherine R. Stimpson, et al. (eds), *Women and the American City*. Chicago: University of Chicago Press, 1981.

SANDAY, PEGGY R. "Female Status in the Public Domain."

In Michelle Zimbalist Rosaldo and Louise Lamphere (eds.), *Women, Culture and Society*. Stanford, Calif.: Stanford University Press, 1974.

SAPIR, EDWARD. *Selected Writings of Edward Sapir*. In David G. Mandelbaum (ed.), *Language, Culture and Personality*. Berkeley, CA: University of California Press, 1949.

SATOW, ROBERTA. "Pop Narcissism." *Psychology Today*, (October 1979):14–17.

SATTERFIELD, J. H., D. P. CANTWELL, and B. T. SATTERFIELD. "Pathophysiology of the Hyperactive Child Syndrome." *Archives of General Psychiatry*, 31 (1974):839–844.

SCHACHTER, STANLEY. "Obesity and Eating." In Darrell J. Steffensmeier and Robert M. Terry (eds.), *Examining Deviance Experimentally*. Port Washington, N.Y.: Alfred Publ. Co., 1975. pp. 137–153.

SCHEFF, TOMAS. *Being Mentally Ill: A Sociological Theory*. Chicago: Aldine Publishing Co., 1966.

SCHEFF, THOMAS. "The Societal Reaction to Deviance: Ascriptive Elements in the Psychiatric Screening in Mental Patients in a Midwestern State." *Social Problems*, 11 (Spring 1964):401–413.

SCHOEN, KENNETH F. "The Strong Box." *Journal of Current Social Issues*, 16(2) (1979):68–70.

SCHOEN, ROBERT. "California Divorce Rates by Age at First Marriage and Duration of First Marriage." *Journal of Marriage and the Family*, 37(3) (August 1975).

SCHUMPETER, JOSEPH A. *Capitalism, Socialism, and Democracy*. New York: Harper, 1942.

SCHUR, EDWIN. *The Awareness Trap: Self Absorption Instead of Social Change*. New York: McGraw-Hill, 1976.

SCHWARTZ, BARRY. "The Effect in Philadelphia of Pennsylvania's increasing penalties for rape and attempted rape." *J. Crim. Law, Criminology, and Police Science* 59:509–515, 1968.

SCHWARTZ, BARRY. "The Effect of Increased Penalties for Rape and Attempted Rape", *Journal of Criminal Law, Criminology and Police Science*, 59:509–515, 1968.

SCHWARTZ, BARRY. In Steffensmeier, Darrell and Robert Terry (eds), *Examining Deviance Experimentally*. New York: Alfred, 1975.

SEARS, DAVID O. "Political Socialization." In Fred I. Greenstein and Nelson W. Polsby (eds.), *Handbook of Political Science, Vol. II*. Reading, Mass: Addison-Wesley, 1975.

SEEMAN, MELVIN. "The Signals of '68: Alienation in Pre-Crisis France." *American Sociological Review*, 37(3) (1972):385–402.

SERVICE, ELMAN R. *Profiles in Ethnology*. New York: Harper & Row, 1963.

SHARP, LAURISTON. "Steel Axes for Stone Age Australians." In Edward Sapir (ed), *Human Problems in Technological Change*. New York: Wiley, 1952.

SHEEHAN, SUSAN. *A Welfare Mother*. Boston: Houghton-Mifflin, 1976.

SHEEHY, GAIL. *Passages: Predictable Crises of Adult Life*. New York: E. P. Dutton & Co., Inc., 1976.

SHELDON, WILLIAM H. *Varieties of Delinquent Youth*. New York: Harper & Row, 1949.

SHELLOW, ROBERT, and DEREK V. ROEMER. "No Heaven for 'Hell's Angels,'" *Transaction*, (July-August 1966): 12–19.

SHEPARD, JON, and HARLAN VOSS. *Social Problems*. New York: Macmillan, 1978.

SHERIF, MUZAFER. "A Study of Some Social Factors in Perception." *Archives of Psychology*, 187 (1935).

SHERMAN, HOWARD J., and JAMES L. WOOD. *Sociology: Traditional and Radical Perspectives*. New York: Harper & Row, 1979.

SHIBUTANI, TAMOTSU. *Society and Personality: An Interactionist Approach to Social Psychology*. Englewood Cliffs, N.J.: Prentice-Hall, 1961.

SHIBUTANI, TAMOTSU. *Improvised News: A Sociological Study of Rumor*. Indianapolis: The Bobbs-Merrill Co., Inc., 1966.

SHIBUTANI, TAMOTSU. "Reference Groups as Perspectives." *American Journal of Sociology*, 60 (1955):562–569.

SHILS, EDWARD A. "Primary Groups in the American Army." In Robert K. Merton and Paul Lazarsfeld (eds.), *Continuities in Social Research*. Glencoe, Ill.: Free Press, 1950.

SHORE, ARNOLD, and ROBERT SCOTT. *Why Sociology Does Not Apply: A Study of the Use of Sociology in Public Policy*. New York: Elsevier, 1979.

SHOSTAK, ARTHUR. *Our Sociological Eye: Personal Essays on Society and Culture*. Sherman Oaks, Calif.: Alfred, 1977.

SILBERMAN, CHARLES E. *Crisis in the Classroom: The Remaking of American Education*. New York: Random House, 1970.

SIMMEL, GEORG. *The Sociology of Georg Simmel*. Kurt H. Wolff (trans.). New York: Free Press, 1950.

SIMMONS, J. L. *Deviants*. Berkeley, Calif.: Glendessary Press, 1969.

SIMON, RITA JAMES. "Arrest Statistics." In Freda Adler and Rita James Simon (eds), *The Criminology of Deviant Women*. Boston: Houston Mifflin, 1979, pp. 107–113.

SIMON, WILLIAM, and JOHN H. GAGNON. "Homosexuality: Formulation of a Sociological Perspective." *Journal of Health and Social Behavior*, 8 (1967):176–181.

SKOCPOL, THEDA, and KAY TRIMBERGER. "Revolutions and the World-Historical Development of Capitalism." Paper presented at 72nd Annual Meeting of the American Sociological Association, Chicago, 1977.

SKOCPOL, THEDA. *States and Social Revolutions: A Comparative Analysis of France, Russia, and China.* Cambridge: Cambridge University Press, 1979.

SKOGAN, WESLEY G. (ed.). *Sample Surveys of the Victims of Crime.* Cambridge, Mass.: Ballinger, 1976.

SKOLNICK, ARLENE. *The Intimate Environment: Exploring Marriage and the Family* (2nd ed.). Boston: Little, Brown & Co., 1978.

SKOLNICK, ARLENE. "The Myth of the Vulnerable Child." *Psychology Today,* (Feb. 1978):56–65.

SMELSER, NEIL J. *Theory of Collective Behavior.* New York: Free Press, 1962.

SMELSER, NEIL J. "Toward a General Theory of Social Change." In *Essays in Sociological Explanation.* Englewood Cliffs, N.J.: Prentice-Hall, 1968.

SMITH, WILLIAM CARLSON. *Americans in the Making.* New York: Appleton-Century, Co., Inc., 1939.

SNOW, DAVID A., LOUIS A. ZURCHER, JR., and SHELDON EKLAND-OLSON. "Social Networks and Social Movements: A Microstructural Approach to Differential Recruitment." *American Sociological Review,* 45(5) (1980):787–801.

SOCIETY. Special Issue on the Politics of Aging. Vol. 15, No. 5 (July/August 1978).

SOKOLOFF, NATALIE J. *Between Money and Love: The Dialectics of Women's Home and Market Work.* New York: Praeger, 1981.

SOLARI, P. *Arcology.* Cambridge; M.I.T. Press, 1969.

SORENSEN, ROBERT. *Adolescent Sexuality in Contemporary America.* New York: World Publishing, 1973.

SOROKIN, PITIRIM A. *The Crisis of Our Age.* New York: E. P. Dutton, 1941.

SPENCE, JANET T., and ROBERT L. HELMREICH. *Masculinity and Femininity.* Austin: University of Texas Press, 1978.

SPENCER, HERBERT. *The Principles of Sociology* (3 volumes). London: Greenwood, 1896/1975.

SPENGLER, OSWALD. *The Decline and Fall of the West.* New York: Knopf, 1928.

SQUIRES, GREGORY D. "Education, Jobs, and Inequality: Functional and Conflict Models of Social Stratification in the United States." *Social Problems,* 24(4) (1977):436–450.

SROLE, LEO. "Urbanization and Mental Health: Some Reformulations." *American Scientist,* 60, (September/October 1972):576–583.

SROLE, LEO, and ANITA K. FISHER (eds.). *Mental Health in the Metropolis: The Mid-Town Manhattan Study.* New York: New York University Press, 1978.

STAHURA, JOHN. "Structural Determinants of Suburban Socio-Economic Compositions." *Sociology and Social Research,* 63, (1979):328–345.

STACK, STEVEN. "The Effect of Direct Government Involvement in the Economy on the Degree of Income Inequality: A Cross-National Study." *American Sociological Review,* 43(6), (1978):880–888.

STARK, RODNEY, and WILLIAM SIMS BAINBRIDGE. "Networks of Faith: Interpersonal Bonds and Recruitment to Cults and Sects." *American Journal of Sociology,* 85(6), (May, 1980):1376.

STARR, PAUL, and GOSTA ESPING-ANDERSEN. "Passive Intervention." *Working Papers,* (July/August 1979):15–25.

STATISTICS CANADA. *Canada's Population: Demographic Perspectives.* Minister of Supply and Services, Ottawa, Canada, 1979.

STATISTICAL ABSTRACT OF LATIN AMERICA. Los Angeles, California: University of California at Los Angeles. Latin American Center Publications, 1978(Table 627):81.

STEADMAN, HARRY J., and JOSEPH J. COCOZZA. *Careers of the Criminally Insane.* Lexington, MA: Lexington Books, 1974.

STEFFENSMEIER, DARRELL J. "Sex Differences in Patterns of Adult Crime, 1965–77: A Review Assessment." *Social Forces,* 58(4) (June 1980):1080–1108.

STEIBER, STEVEN R. "The Influence of the Religious Factor on Civil and Sacred Tolerance 1958–1971." *Social Forces,* 58(3) (March 1980).

STEIN, PETER J. (ed.) *Single Life: Unmarried Adults in Social Context.* New York: St. Martin's Press, 1981.

STEIN, PETER J., and STEVEN HOFFMAN. "Sports and Male Role Strain." In Donald Sabo and Ross Runfola (eds), *Jock: Sports and Male Identity.* Englewood Cliffs, N. J.: Prentice-Hall, 1980, pp. 53–74.

STERNLIEB, GEORGE, and JAMES W. HUGHES (eds.). *America's Housing: Prospects and Problems.* Center for Urban Policy Research, 1980.

STIVERS, RICHARD. *A Hair of the Dog: Irish Drinking in America.* University Park, Pennsylvania: Pennsylvania State University Press, 1976.

STONE, DONALD. "The Human Potential Movement." *Society* (May/June, 1978):66–68.

STOUFFER, SAMUEL. *Social Research to Test Ideas.* New York: Free Press, 1962.

STOUFFER, SAMUEL ET AL. *The American Soldier: Combat and its Aftermath. Social Studies in Social Psychology in World War II.* Vol. II. Princeton, New Jersey: Princeton University Press, 1949.

STRAUSS, ANSELM. *Negotiations: Varieties, Contexts, Processes and Social Order.* San Francisco: Jossey-Bass, 1978.

STURGES, GERALD D. "1000 + 1000 = 5000: Estimating Crowd Size," *Transaction/Society,* 9(6), April 1972.

STRAUS, MURRAY, A., RICHARD J. GELLES, and SUZANNE K. STEINMETZ. *Behind Closed Doors: Violence in the American Family.* Garden City, New York: Doubleday/Anchor, 1979.

STRODTBECK, FRED, RITA JAMES and CHARLES HAWKINS. "Social Status in Jury Deliberations," in Eleanor

Maccoby, Theodore M. Newcomb and Eugene L. Hartley (eds.) *Readings in Social Psychology,* New York: Holt, 1958, 379–388.

SUMNER, WILLIAM GRAHAM. *Folkways.* Boston: Ginn, 1909/1940.

SUTHERLAND, EDWIN, H. "White Collar Criminology," *American Sociological Review* 5, pp. 1–12., 1940.

SWAFFORD, MICHAEL. "Sex Differences in Soviet Earnings," *American Sociological Review,* 43(5) (1978):657–673.

SWARTZ, JOEL. "Silent Killers at Work," *Crime and Social Justice,* 3 (Spring-Summer 1975):15–20.

SZYMANSKI, ALBERT J. *The Capitalist State and the Politics of Class.* Cambridge, Massachusetts: Winthrop Publishers, 1978.

SZYMANSKI, ALBERT J. and GOERTZEL, TED GEORGE. *Sociology: Class, Consciousness and Contradictions.* New York: D. Van Nostrand Company, 1978.

TABB, WILLIAM K. "The New York City Fiscal Crisis" in William K. Tabb and Larry Sawers (eds.), *Marxism and the Metropolis: New Perspectives in Urban Political Economy.* New York: Oxford University Press, 1978.

TAYLOR, LEE. *Urbanized Society.* Santa Monica, California: Goodyear Publishing Company, Inc., 1980.

TERKEL, STUDS. *Working.* New York: Random House, 1972.

THOMAS, WILLIAM I. and FLORIAN ZNANIECKI. *The Polish Peasant in Europe and America.* Chicago, Illinois: University of Chicago Press, 1918.

THORNE, BARRIE and NANCY HENLEY. *Language and Sex: Difference and Dominance.* Rowley, Massachusetts: Newbury House, 1975.

THUROW, LESTER. *The Zero Sum Society: Distribution and the Possibilities of Economic Change.* New York: Basic Books, 1980.

TIGER, LIONEL. *Men in Groups.* New York: Random, 1969.

TIGER, LIONEL and ROBIN FOX, *The Imperial Animal.* New York: Dell, 1978.

TILLY, CHARLES. *From Mobilization to Revolution.* Reading Massachusetts: Addison, Wesley, 1978.

TITMUSS, RICHARD M. *Social Policy: An Introduction.* Edited by Brian Abelsmith and Kay Titmuss. New York: Pantheon Books, 1974.

TITTLE, CHARLES R., WAYNE J. VILLEMEZ and DOUGLAS A. SMITH, "The Myth of Social Class and Criminality: An Empirical Assessment of the Empirical Evidence." *American Sociological Review,* 43 (October): 1978, 643–656.

TOENNIES, FERDINAND. *Community and Society.* (translated by Charles Loomis). East Lansing, Michigan: Michigan State University Press, 1957.

TOLBERT, CHARLES II, PATRICK M. HORAN and E. M. BECK. "The Structure of Economic Segmentation: A Dual Economy Approach," *American Journal of Sociology,* 85(5) (March 1980):1095–1116.

TREIMAN, DONALD J. *Occupational Prestige in Perspective.* New York: Academic Press, 1977.

TROLL, LILLIAN, and VERN L. BENGTSON. "Generations in the Family." In Wesley R. Burr, Rueben Hill, F. Ivan Nye, and Ira L. Reiss (eds.), *Contemporary Theories About the Family.* New York: The Free Press, 1979.

TUCHMAN, GAYE, ARLENE KAPLEN DANIELS, and JAMES BENET. *Hearth and Home: Images of Women in the Mass Media.* New York: Oxford University Press, 1978.

TUMIN, MELVIN. "Some Principles of Stratification: A Critical Analysis." *American Sociological Review,* 18 (August, 1953):387–393.

TURNBULL, COLIN M. *The Mountain People.* New York: Simon and Schuster, 1972.

TURNER, JONATHAN H. and CHARLES E. STARNES. *Inequality: Privilege and Poverty in America.* Santa Monica, California: Goodyear Publishing Co., 1976.

TURNER, RALPH N. "Sponsored and Contest Mobility and the School System." *American Sociological Review,* 25 (1960):855–867.

TURNER, RALPH N. and LEWIS KILLIAN. *Collective Behavior.* Second Edition. Englewood Cliffs, New Jersey: Prentice-Hall, 1972.

TUSSING, DALE. "The Dual Welfare System." *Society,* 11(2) (January/February 1974).

URBAN LEAGUE. *The Myth of Income Cushions for Blacks.* August, 1980.

USEEM, BERT. "Solidarity Model, Breakdown Model, and the Boston Anti-Busing Movement." *American Sociological Review,* 45(3) (June 1980):357–369.

USEEM, MICHAEL and S. M. MILLER. "The Upper Class in Higher Education." *Social Policy,* (January/February 1977):28–31.

USEEM, MICHAEL. "The Inner Group of the American Capitalist Class." *Social Policy,* 25(3) (February 1978):225–240.

U.S. BUREAU OF THE CENSUS. *Current Population Reports,* Series P-20, No. 360, "School Enrollment—Social and Economic Characteristics of Students: October, 1979." Washington, D.C.: U.S. Government Printing Office, April 1981.

U.S. Commission on Civil Rights. *Social Indicators of Equality for Minorities and Women.* Washington, D.C., 1978.

U.S. DEPT. OF COMMERCE, BUREAU OF THE CENSUS. "American Families and Living Arrangements." *Current Population Reports,* Special Studies, Series P-23, No. 104, May, 1980.

U.S. DEPT. OF COMMERCE. "Money Income of Families and Persons in the United States, 1978." *Current Population Reports,* Series P-60, No.123, June, 1980.

VAN DER TAK, JEAN, CARL HAUB, and ELAINE MURPHY. "Our Population Predicament: A New Look." *Population Bulletin*, 34(5), Population Reference Bureau, Inc., Washington, D. C., 1979.

VAN GELDER, LINDSY. "The Great Person-Hole Cover Debate." *MS*, (April 1980):120.

VAN DE WALLE, ETIENNE, and JOHN KNODEL. "Europe's Fertility Transition: New Evidence and Lessons for Today's Developing World." *Population Bulletin*, 34(6), Population Reference Bureau, Inc., Washington, D. C., 1980.

VAN GENNEP, ARNOLD. *The Rites of Passage*. Chicago: University of Chicago Press, 1908/1960.

VANNEMAN, REEVE D. "U.S. and British Perceptions of Class." *American Journal of Sociology* 85(4) (January 1980):769–790.

VEBLEN, THORSTEIN. *The Theory of the Leisure Class*. New York: Macmillan Company, 1899.

WALLERSTEIN, IMMANUEL. *The Modern World System*. New York: Academic Press, 1974.

WALL STREET JOURNAL. "Unemployment Rises in Sun Belt as Immunity to Recession Fades." By Liz Roman Gallese. (September 3, 1980):29.

WALUM, LAUREL RICHARDSON. *The Dynamics of Sex and Gender*. Skokie, Ill.: Rand McNally, 1977.

WASHBURN, SHERWOOD L. "The Evolution of Man." *Scientific American*, 239(1) (September 1978): 194–211.

WARING, JOAN M. "Social Replenishment and Social Change." *American Behavioral Scientist*, 19(2) (1975).

WEBER, MAX. *The Theory of Social and Economic Organization*. New York: Oxford University Press, 1947(1925). Translated by A. Henderson and Talcott Parsons.

WEBER, MAX. *The Protestant Ethic and the Spirit of Capitalism*. New York: Scribner, 1904/1958.

WEINBERG, MARTIN S. "Sexual Modesty and the Nudist Camp", in Earl Rubington and Martin S. Weinberg (eds.) *Deviance: The Interactionist Perspective*. New York: Macmillan & Company, 1968, pp. 271–279.

WEINBERG, MARTIN S. and COLIN J. WILLIAMS. "Sexual Embourgeoisment?" *American Sociological Review*, 45(1) (February 1980):33–48.

WERNER, FRANCES E., WILLIAM M. FREIJ, and DAVID M. MADWAY. "Redlining and Disinvestment: Causes, Consequences, and Proposed Remedies." *Clearinghouse Review*, 10(7) (1976):501–506.

WERTHMAN, CARL and IRVING PILIAVAN. "Gang Members and the Police". In David Bordua (ed.) *The Police: Six Sociological Essays*. New York: John Wiley and Sons, 1967.

WHYTE, WILLIAM FOOTE. *Street Corner Society: The Social Structure of an Italian Slum*. Chicago: University of Chicago Press, 1943.

WILENSKY, HAROLD L. "Life Cycle, Work Situation and Social Participation." In Clark Tibbitts and Wilma Donahue (eds), *Social and Psychological Aspects of Aging*. New York: Columbia University Press, 1962.

WILENSKY, HAROLD L., and CHARLES N. LEBAUX. *Industrial Society and Social Welfare*. New York: Press, 1965.

WILLCOX, PAUL. "Canadian Labour and the Capital Crisis: The Dynamics of Conflict." In Richard J. Ossenberg (ed.), *Power and Change in Canada*. Toronto: McClelland and Steward, 1980, pp. 65–99.

WILLIAMS, JAY R. and MARTIN GOLD. "From Delinquent Behavior to Official Delinquency." *Social Problems*, 20, (1972):209–229.

WILLIAMS, ROBIN. *American Society: A Sociological Interpretation* (3rd ed.). New York: Knopf, 1970.

WILLIE, CHARLES V. *A New Look at Black Families*. 2nd. ed. New York: General Hall, 1981.

WILSON, E. O. *Sociobiology: The New Synthesis*. Cambridge, Massachusetts: Harvard University Press, 1975.

WINKS, ROBIN. "Black Tile in the Mossaic." In Daniel Glenday, Hubert Guindon, and Allan Turowetz (eds), *Modernization and the Canadian State*. Toronto: Macmillan, 1978, pp. 356–371.

WIRTH, LOUIS. "Urbanism as a Way of Life." *American Journal of Sociology*, 44, (July 1938):8–20.

WITKIN, HERMAN A., ET AL. "Criminality in XYY and XXY Men." *Science*, (August 13, 1976):547–555.

WOLF, DEBORAH GOLEMAN. *The Lesbian Community*. Berkeley, Calif.: University of California Press, 1979

WOLFE, ALAN. *The Limits of Legitimacy: Political Contradictions of Contemporary Capitalism*. New York: Free Press, 1977.

WOLFE, ALAN. *The Seamy Side of Democracy*. Second Edition. New York: Longman, 1978.

WOLFF, KURT H. *The Sociology of Georg Simmel*. Glencoe, Illinois: The Free Press, 1950.

WOLFGANG, MARVIN. *Patterns in Criminal Homicide*. Philadelphia: University of Philadelphia Press, 1958.

WOLFGANG, MARVIN, and FRANCO FERRECUTI. *The Subculture of Violence: Towards an Integrated Theory*. London: Tavistock, 1967.

WOOD, R. C. *1400 Governments*. Cambridge, Massachusetts: Harvard University Press, 1961.

WORSLEY, PETER. *The Trumpet Shall Sound*. Second Edition. New York: Schocken Books, 1968.

WRIGHT, SAM. *Crowds and Riots: A Study in Social Organization*. Beverly Hills, California: Sage, 1978.

WRONG, DENNIS. "The Oversocialized Conception of Man in Modern Sociology." *American Sociological Review*, 26, (1961):183–193.

WYNNE, EDWARD A. *Growing Up Suburban.* Austin, Texas: University of Texas Press, 1972.

YANKELOVICH, DANIEL. *New Rules: Searching for Self-Fulfillment in a World Turned Upside Down.* New York: Random House, 1981.

YANKELOVICH, DANIEL and LARRY KAAGAN. "Proposition 13 One Year Later: What It Is and What It Isn't." *Social Policy,* (May/June 1979):19–23.

YEATES, MAURICE and BARRY GARNER. *The North American City.* New York: Harper and Row, 1976.

YINGER, J. MILTON. "A Structural Examination of Religion." *Journal for the Scientific Study of Religion,* 8(Spring, 1969):88–99.

ZALD, MAYER N. and ROBERTA ASH. "Social Movement Organizations" in Barry McLaughlin (ed.) *Studies in Social Movements.* New York: The Free Press, 1969, pp. 461–485.

ZELDITCH, MORRIS. "Role Differentiation in the Nuclear Family." In Talcott Parsons and Robert F. Bales, *Family Socialization and Interaction Process.* Glencoe: Free Press, 1955.

ZIMBARDO, PHILLIP, CURTIS W. BANKS, CRAIG HANEY, and DAVID JAFFE. "The Mind is a Formidable Jailor." *New York Times,* April 8, 1973.

ZIPP, JOHN F. and JOEL SMITH. "The Structure of Electoral Political Participation." *American Journal of Sociology,* 85(1) (July 1979):167–177.

Name Index

Subject Index